THE
PENGUIN HISTORY
OF CANADA

ALSO BY ROBERT BOTHWELL

Lester Pearson

C.D. Howe (co-author)

Canada Since 1945 (co-author)

Canada 1900–1945 (co-author)

Eldorado

Loring Christie

Nucleus

Pirouette (co-author)

Canada and Quebec

The Big Chill

A Traveller's History of Canada

ROBERT BOTHWELL

THE
PENGUIN HISTORY
OF CANADA

PENGUIN
CANADA

PENGUIN CANADA

Published by the Penguin Group

Penguin Group (Canada), 90 Eglinton Avenue East, Suite 700, Toronto, Ontario, Canada
M4P 2Y3 (a division of Pearson Canada Inc.)

Penguin Group (USA) Inc., 375 Hudson Street, New York, New York 10014, U.S.A.
Penguin Books Ltd, 80 Strand, London WC2R 0RL, England
Penguin Ireland, 25 St Stephen's Green, Dublin 2, Ireland (a division of Penguin Books Ltd)
Penguin Group (Australia), 250 Camberwell Road, Camberwell, Victoria 3124, Australia
(a division of Pearson Australia Group Pty Ltd)
Penguin Books India Pvt Ltd, 11 Community Centre, Panchsheel Park, New Delhi – 110 017,
India
Penguin Group (NZ), cnr Airborne and Rosedale Roads, Albany, Auckland 1310, New Zealand
(a division of Pearson New Zealand Ltd)
Penguin Books (South Africa) (Pty) Ltd, 24 Sturdee Avenue, Rosebank, Johannesburg 2196,
South Africa

Penguin Books Ltd, Registered Offices: 80 Strand, London WC2R 0RL, England

First published 2006

1 2 3 4 5 6 7 8 9 10   (RRD)

LIBRARY AND ARCHIVES CANADA CATALOGUING IN PUBLICATION

Bothwell, Robert, 1944–
The Penguin history of Canada / Robert Bothwell.

Includes bibliographical references and index.
ISBN-13: 978-0-670-06553-0
ISBN-10: 0-670-06553-6

1. Canada—History. I. Title.

FC165.B68 2006   971   C2006-905106-2

Visit the Penguin Group (Canada) website at **www.penguin.ca**

Special and corporate bulk purchase rates available; please see
www.penguin.ca/corporatesales or call 1-800-399-6858, ext. 477 or 474

To the memory of my teacher and friend, Kenneth McNaught

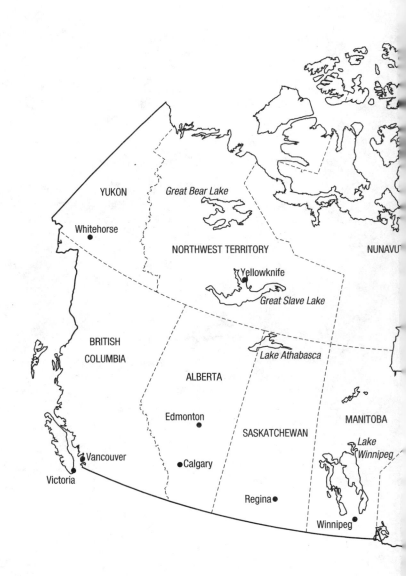

Hudson

Bay

ONTARIO

Lake Nipigon

Superior

L. Michigan

L. Huron

Toronto

L. Ontario

L. Erie

Iqaluit

NEWFOUNDLAND

AND LABRADOR

St. John's

QUEBEC

Charlottetown

PEI

Quebec

Fredericton

NEW

BRUNSWICK

NOVA SCOTIA

Halifax

Montreal

Ottawa

Contents

NATIVE LAND

Montagnais family, early 1600s, as represented
by Samuel de Champlain, 1612.

Canada, it's been said, has been the victim of too much geography. The second largest country on earth, it stretches from the rainforest of Vancouver Island to the pebbled desert of the Arctic, from the Atlantic to the Pacific, from the latitude of northern California (though barely) to the Arctic Ocean. Canada's extent, from sea (east) to sea (west) to sea (north), is a rhetorician's dream and an administrator's nightmare. Its prosperity, compared with most of the rest of the world, has saved many a politician the trouble of saying something original on occasions of public ceremony. Yet that prosperity, like the population, is unevenly distributed and heavily concentrated in certain favoured pockets. Fortunately, there aren't too many people and there's enough prosperity to go around. Perhaps only its sparse population has saved Canada from becoming a political impossibility.

Geography has certainly helped limit Canada's population, but accidents of geology also played a part. The continents of North and South America took their current form millions of years ago, separated from Eurasia and Africa by thousands of kilometres of ocean except for a tiny stretch of shallow water, the Bering Strait, between Alaska and Siberia. Crucially, the Strait wouldn't always be covered in water, for as the climate cooled the northernmost regions of Eurasia and North America became forbiddingly cold. During the Pleistocene ice age most of the northern part of North America was covered in successive glaciations, further isolating the remaining habitable areas of the continent—south of what is now the latitude of Washington, D.C.—from the rest of the world. As water was absorbed into the huge glaciers, the sea level fell and the Bering land bridge grew very large.

The Americas in pre-glacial times boasted an impressive array of fauna, similar to those found in Eurasia and including horses, mastodons, and tigers. Many of these survived the ice age, the more so because no predators existed with the capacity to drive them to extinction. Yet there were differences from Eurasia too, in plant phyla and in the range of animals inhabiting the continent. One such difference was the absence of human ancestors.

The oldest traces of human ancestors have been found in Africa, dating back to long before the Pleistocene era. The first variety of modern humans, *Homo sapiens*, seems to have evolved around 150,000 years ago, also in Africa. Superseding other human varieties, *Homo sapiens* spread from Africa into Eurasia, reaching the northeastern corner of that vast land mass, eastern Siberia, about twenty thousand years ago. The climate was cold and the terrain icy, covered with an immense glacier just over three kilometres thick and spreading down from the North Pole. The seacoast was, however, considerably farther out than at present.

Not everything was covered with ice. In particular, the area between Siberia and Alaska (which scholars have dubbed "Beringia") was dry, though cold and unpleasant. And even after crossing Beringia, early humans didn't find ice everywhere. Between fifteen thousand and thirteen thousand years ago the ice cap began to retract, opening an ice-free north–south corridor along what is roughly the line of the Rocky Mountains. Scholars dispute how soon and how much this corridor opened, but certainly by about eleven thousand years ago it was possible to move from Alaska through the interior of northwestern North America, down to the grasslands of the Great Plains and beyond to the temperate climate of northern Mexico.[1]

People did move, but their movements (which may have included movement by sea as well as land) have been difficult to trace and even more difficult for archaeologists to agree upon. Using the most cautious and conservative interpretation, humans reached Alaska around twelve thousand years ago and the southwestern United States eleven thousand years ago. At that time an ice sheet still covered most of modern Canada, east and west, though it was beginning to melt along its southern edges. As the ice retreated, the land exposed became first tundra, then spruce scrub, and finally woodland. Animals followed the advancing forest, and humans followed the animals.

The earliest humans to inhabit North America lived by hunting and fishing. They appear to have hunted some of North America's animals to extinction: mammoths, camels, mastodons, giant sloths, and horses, for example, disappeared. The two-metre giant beaver also passed out of existence. There was plenty of other game, deer, moose, bear, and beaver, enough to support a limited population.

The North American peoples of eleven thousand years ago, like other human groupings on other continents, used implements of stone and wood. But unlike the peoples of Asia and Europe they continued to do so right up to the era of "discovery," or contact with European explorers, in the fifteenth century. And that wasn't the only feature of human existence in the Americas that deviated from experience overseas.

In southwest Asia, in Mesopotamia, local societies domesticated both plants and animals. Practising agriculture, they were able to break away from hunting and gathering as the basis for existence. Agriculture required organization, but it would also support larger numbers of people. Villages arose, and then towns and then cities, and finally organized states, which appeared around 3700 BCE in Mesopotamia and slightly later in Egypt. Metal tools also appeared, first copper and bronze, and then, around 1000 BCE, iron. The invention of the wheel facilitated transport—transport based on the mastery of the horse. All these aspects of culture spread, making possible larger and larger states, culminating in the empires of Alexander the Great and then Rome, both of which were about five thousand kilometres wide at their greatest extent.[2] At the other end of Eurasia, China produced a state structure by 2000 BCE and emerged as a unified empire around 200 BCE. (Unlike the realms of Alexander and Rome, the Chinese Empire lasted into the twentieth century.)

Why did the Americas not follow the same path? They had, to begin with, an unfavourable geography, divided by mountains and deserts, making communication difficult. Another part of the answer lies in the available plants and animals. Far fewer plants were suitable for cultivation, and diffusion of agriculture was slow. Without the horse and the wheel, and without boats above a certain size, large-scale movements, whether of people or of goods, were seriously inhibited. Domestic animals consisted of the dog and the llama, and the llama was confined to the peoples of the South American cordillera. True, there were canoes, either dugouts or wood frame, but they couldn't compare to the larger ships of Eurasia.

Settlement of what is now Canada proceeded slowly, paced by the gradual disappearance of the ice sheet. Even as late as nine thousand years ago most of eastern Canada was covered by an ice cap centred in Ungava; it would take another thousand years to melt completely. Around the fringes of the ice cap were ice-fed lakes like Agassiz, in (or rather on) Manitoba, and Iroquois, more or less where the Great Lakes now sit. Fringing the ice cap was the advancing boreal forest, consisting of pine to the south, spruce to the west, and birch to the northwest and east. Behind the forest was the prairie, contracting in the west and shifting gradually to the east and north. Behind, or in, the forest were the people and the animals they hunted.

The geography changed. The melting of the ice cap raised the levels of the oceans. Beringia, the land bridge to Siberia, disappeared. The islands on the east coast—Newfoundland and the islands in the Gulf of St. Lawrence—took on their present-day dimensions. With the weight of the ice cap removed, the land rose. Finally, with the melting ice cap finished as a source of water, the great lakes in the interior of North America—Great Slave, Great Bear, Athabasca, Manitoba, and Winnipeg as well as the five "Great" lakes of eastern Canada—also assumed their present limits.

FIRST PEOPLES

Archaeologists have labelled the first inhabitants of North America the Paleo-Indians. The Paleo-Indians were simultaneously moving north and south, eventually to reach Tierra del Fuego in South America and the treeline along the edge of the tundra to the north. These people hunted in bands of fifteen to fifty, equipped with spears tipped with a flaked stone point—called Clovis points after their point of discovery, near Clovis, New Mexico.

As the climate improved, the Clovis culture evolved into a more elaborate and more densely populated form, called Archaic by archaeologists. This time is regarded as a period of adaptation during which the peoples of North America became differentiated by locale and in which many languages and local cultures appeared. Populations now numbered in the hundreds, supported by a more sustained and more predictable hunt for food. Though diet remained basically meat or fish, in the eastern woodlands native plants like the Canada onion were eaten and apparently cultivated and sunflowers were exploited for their seeds and oil. Farther west, on the Great Plains, the climate fluctuated between extreme dryness and rainfall close to what now prevails; this had its effect on the big game (such as bison) and thus the food supply. Consequently, the population of the plains also rose and fell considerably. There appear to have been population migrations during this period, linking the Dene of northwest Canada to the Navajos and Apaches of the American southwest—all belong to the Athapascan language group. The Dene themselves may well have arrived later in North America than other language groups.

Finally, there was the northwest coast—the coast stretching from northern California up through the Alaska panhandle. Heavily forested, with a mild climate, abundant rainfall, and a never-ending supply of fish, the region has been called a "paradise for hunter-gatherers."[3] A reliable food supply and freedom from the climatic extremes of most of the rest of North America allowed the development of a rich and socially complex culture in coastal British Columbia. The key was salmon, abounding salmon. Access to salmon and control over the best fishing grounds became the basis of wealth. One archaeologist characterizes the northwest coast culture as comprising "social stratification with hereditary slavery," while another points to "hereditary social inequality" and "semi-sedentary settlement with permanent winter villages."[4] These characteristics were in place by roughly two thousand years ago.

There remained the High Arctic, the frigid semi-desert found north of the treeline on the North American mainland and in the Arctic archipelago. In this region there was never any question of agriculture: food had to be hunted on the ice floes or in the barren lands. The Paleo-Eskimos spread from Alaska to Greenland and down the coast of Labrador as far as Newfoundland. (Use of the term *Eskimo* differs by location and date. In Canada and Greenland since about 1970 *Inuit* has superseded the older term *Eskimo*. In Alaska, however, *Eskimo* is still used.) The Dorset culture, which predominated from about two thousand to one thousand years ago, had most of the characteristics of the later Inuit; it was probably the Dorset people who made the first contact with Europeans along the Atlantic coast.

The Native peoples of the Americas had moved across the continent, north to south, south to north, west to east, mostly on foot to begin with, although small watercraft, canoes and kayaks, had come into existence by at least two thousand years ago. In Eurasia, however, larger ships were developed to sail the coastal waters of the Atlantic, Pacific, and Indian oceans, and intrepid mariners sometimes ventured into the unknown.

There seemed to be no point and certainly no profit in travelling far from the sight of land, especially into the cold Atlantic Ocean, and the chaos and impoverishment of European society after about CE 500 made adventuring west more a matter of chance than deliberate design. Nevertheless, there was a way to cross the Atlantic without getting too far from land: by hopping from Scandinavia via various groups of small islands to the larger islands of Iceland and Greenland. And in the ninth and tenth centuries small bands of Norse seafarers did just that, landing in Iceland in 874 and in Greenland a century later, in 986. (The Norse are better known under the name Vikings.) Having established permanent settlements on both islands, around 1000 the Norse ventured farther, to "Vinland" on the coast of northeastern North America, under the leadership of the first historically named individual in Canadian history, Leif

Ericsson. In 1960 the probable site of the settlement was uncovered on the north coast of Newfoundland, at L'Anse-aux-Meadows. It was certainly a Norse site; whether it was also Vinland is still disputed by some.

The Norse discovered that Vinland, or the land about it, was not uninhabited. They had several fierce encounters with Natives, whom they called Skraelings, and when the Norse sailed away the Skraelings held the field.

The Skraelings are generally assumed to have been Dorset Eskimos, who lived by hunting whales, seals, and other marine mammals along the coast of Labrador and Newfoundland. (The Dorset were the only Eskimo people to live south of the treeline, as their sites in Newfoundland attest.) The Dorset people gave way to the more technologically advanced Thule culture, with better weapons and better boats. It was the Inuit of the Thule culture who would occupy all the coastal Arctic into historic times.

To the south, the character of the woodland societies of the eastern seaboard and the Great Lakes regions had also been changing. Farther south, in Mexico, agriculture developed to the point that city states became possible, creating large urban centres of wealth and power. This wealth and power derived from corn, or maize, domesticated and culti-vated in Mexico, from which it spread very gradually northward to the southern United States by about CE 200. It continued to move northward, encouraged by the favourable climate of the period—the Medieval Maximum, as it's known, that also drew the Norse across the Atlantic. Corn became a major crop in what is now southern Canada only hundreds of years later, around CE 900, and even then it was much smaller and presumably less easy to cultivate than corn of the present day. It could only be grown at all because of the development of a variety that took less time to plant and harvest in the shorter growing seasons.

Agriculture altered the culture of the peoples of the Great Lakes and Atlantic regions, creating, in parallel to British Columbia, the basis for a larger population, a more permanent settlement, and a more hierarchical society. It drew in the ancestors of the Iroquois, who moved north up the Susquehanna, driving out the ancestors of the Algonquins, who moved farther east and north to the Atlantic coast, Ungava, and the Canadian Shield, and who remained predominantly hunter-gatherers. These were the societies that the Europeans found, and described, in the sixteenth and seventeenth centuries. South of the Great Lakes, though extending at a few points into modern Ontario, were the Mound Builders, whose largest centre, at Cahokia in Indiana, probably housed a population as large as many contemporary European cities. Cahokia also demonstrated the limitations of North American horticulture, for the crops its inhabitants cultivated depleted the soil. As food dwindled, so did the town. Cahokia was abandoned before 1500, and by 1600 the Mound Builders and their towns weren't much more than a memory.

The absence of any large towns or cities in northern and central North America didn't mean that the population of the continent was insignificant, merely that it was widely dispersed. It was subject, too, to disease and to the misfortunes of war. Though North Americans of the fifteenth century lived free of the scourges of Eurasian diseases, such as smallpox, their lives lasted no longer than those of contemporary Europeans. (The existence of some diseases such as malaria or syphilis in pre-contact America is also the subject of dispute among scholars.) The average life expectancy for men in North America has been estimated at twenty-five to thirty years—roughly what it had been in Europe. As to the total population, as a recent survey put it, "controversies abound." At the low end, the population of North America above the Rio Grande has been placed at 900,000, and at the high end, at 200,000,000. Both figures seem unlikely, and scholarly speculation has tended to cluster around figures ranging from two million to seven million.[5]

What these large figures meant in detail may be seen from the example of the Iroquois. The Iroquoian language group is divided into two— southern (Cherokee) and northern (Iroquois, Huron, Petun, Neutral, Susquehannock, and Wenro). The northern Iroquois lived north and south of the lower Great Lakes; another group of Iroquois, who lived in the St. Lawrence Valley, disappeared at some point in the sixteenth century. According to the archaeologist Dean Snow, the northern Iroquois

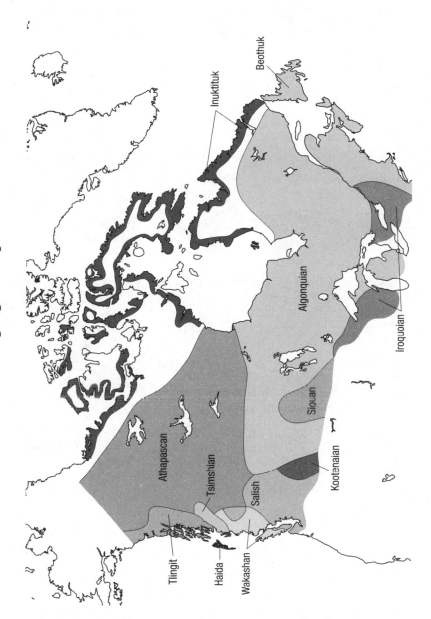

Native Language Groups, 1600

Inuktituk

Beothuk

Algonquian

Iroquoian

Siouan

Kootenaian

Athapascan

Tsimshian

Salish

Tlingit

Haida

Wakashan

collectively numbered ninety-five thousand at the beginning of the seventeenth century, before the Europeans made any substantial impact on
them. The figure was a historic high. The omens of catastrophe were all
around the Iroquois, but no one could read them.[6]

First Encounters

The catastrophe that befell the peoples of the Americas came from
Europe. With the exception of the brief Norse settlements in Greenland
and Newfoundland, the peoples of Europe were generally unaware of the
existence of the Americas until the very end of the fifteenth century.
Suddenly, in 1492, news circulated from the Spanish court that a Spanish
expedition led by a Genoese mariner, Christopher Columbus, had found
land far to the west. Columbus believed he had found Asia, and with it
the sea route to the riches of China and India.

In fact Columbus, in October 1492, had landed in the Bahamas. The
Spanish dubbed the inhabitants Indians, believing them to be natives of
India. This classic misnomer endured, though of course the Native inhabitants of the Americas had nothing to do with the inhabitants of India,
ethnically or culturally or linguistically.

If the Natives of the Americas were a surprise to the Europeans, the
Europeans were a wonder to the newly dubbed Indians. The Stone Age
was meeting the Iron Age, juxtaposing two cultures so different that in
some places the Europeans were thought to be supernatural. The impression did not last.

Initially, the Europeans were few. The resources required to project a
ship and its crew across the Atlantic were at first considerable, and so was
the mental stamina required for a voyage into the utterly unknown. At
least, that was the case for official voyages like those of Columbus and his
Spanish successors. Unofficially, there is ample evidence that some
Europeans—mariners from the Basque provinces of Spain and fishermen
from the west of England—had been crossing the Atlantic for quite a
while. They were seeking the cod, at first around Norway, then off Iceland

(greatly to the irritation of the kings of Denmark), and finally to the west of Iceland. Fishing was an established industry, with an established market in the towns and cities of Western Europe. That industry now extended itself across the Atlantic in search of a reliable supply.

The great port of the English West Country was Bristol, and out of Bristol, in May 1497, sailed another Genoese, Giovanni Caboto, known to his English hosts as John Cabot. Cabot was sponsored by the English king, Henry VII. Henry was a prudent monarch and did not risk much. By that time Columbus had made not one but two voyages to the New World, and it was clear that a sailor with a good compass and a certain amount of skill could sail west and encounter land—possibly China or India, which Columbus had so far failed to locate.

Cabot didn't find China, but he did find land, probably Nova Scotia and Newfoundland, and he claimed it for his patron, King Henry. Yet Cabot's discovery of land had far less immediate significance than his discoveries at sea. As the ambassador of the Duke of Milan reported home, Cabot's English companions described an ocean alive with fish, the northern cod, and claimed that "they took so many fish that this kingdom will no longer have need of Iceland, from which country there is an immense trade in the fish they call stock-fish."

Still, it was the hope of finding India or China, not fish, that stimulated monarchs like Henry VII. He outfitted a second expedition for Cabot in 1498, but thereafter Cabot passed into oblivion, and out of history, and with him any possibility that Henry VII might imitate his rivals in Spain and Portugal and found an empire beyond the seas.

Indeed, the next expedition to pass by was Portuguese, captained by Gaspar Corte Real, a native of the Azores. Corte Real skirted Newfoundland and Labrador in 1500 and 1501, though exactly where is unclear. Unclear too is Corte Real's fate: like Cabot, he vanishes from history at this point. With Corte Real, however, Portugal abandoned any official interest in an area beset with cold and fog—and of course fish.

The fish remained, and fleets of fishermen to harvest them. Conditions in the continental shelf off Newfoundland were almost perfect for the northern cod and many other fish species, either close to shore or on the Grand Banks: a large, shallow oceanic plateau—often less than a hundred metres deep—south and southeast of Newfoundland, dominated by the cold waters of the Labrador Current. Nowhere was it easier to harvest fish, especially such a useful fish as cod. The cod could easily be dried or cured in salt, and once cured it was comparatively light and thus easily transported.

Once its location was known the Newfoundland cod fishery proved an irresistible magnet for Western European fishermen, at first mainly from Portugal and the Basque provinces of northern Spain but later also from the west coast of France, especially Brittany. The English, curiously, mainly seem to have stuck closer to home, continuing to fish off Iceland until a decree from Iceland's overlord, the king of Denmark, raised the cost of fishing licences to the point where Newfoundland seemed a desirable substitute.

That would be many years later. In the meantime, the exploration of the east coast of North America was the province of others. By then the continent had a name, "America," after yet another Italian sailor, Amerigo Vespucci, whose descriptions of his voyages proved so popular in Europe that his name and not that of Columbus entered common usage. In 1523 the French monarch, François I, hired a Florentine navigator, Giovanni da Verrazzano, to find the route to Asia. Verrazzano didn't find the route, but he did discover New York and its deep protected harbour, and explored the coast as far north as Newfoundland. The route to Asia was evidently not easily found: Verrazzano's explorations seemed to point to a location farther north. He liked what he saw, comparing the land to the pleasant ancient Greek region of Arcadia. Suitably adapted, and moved north from Delaware where he had located it, "Acadia" became the common name for what later became the Maritime provinces of Canada.

Possibly along on the voyage with Verrazzano was a French sailor from the Breton port of St. Malo, Jacques Cartier. St. Malo was home to many of the French fishermen sailing to Newfoundland, and so it's possible that Cartier had already sailed west when he proposed to François I that he lead another expedition in search of the passage to Asia. The proposition was enticing, not merely because of the possibilities of trade with China but because the Spanish had by then conquered and looted the fabulously wealthy Aztec and Inca realms in Mexico and Peru. A Spanish explorer had discovered that another ocean, the Pacific, did indeed lie beyond America; in 1520 a Spanish expedition succeeded in crossing the Pacific and circumnavigating the globe, passing by the rich and culturally advanced markets of Asia en route. It was therefore natural for François to instruct Cartier to search for and bring back a "great quantity of gold, and other precious things."

Cartier made three voyages to the New World, in 1534, 1535–36, and 1541–42. As a result he helped define the map of eastern North America, identifying Newfoundland as an island and discovering the great St. Lawrence River, which he followed as far as his ships could go, to the rapids around Montreal. He named the large mountain in the middle of the island of Montreal "Mont Royal," and the name stuck—and gave rise to the name of the eventual French settlement there.

Cartier also made the first extensive contact by any European with the inhabitants of the continent, those who lived along the St. Lawrence from Gaspé in the east to Montreal in the west. Accounts from Spain made it clear that the Natives of America differed radically, not only from Europeans but among themselves. The accounts made another, crucial point: the peoples of the New World weren't Christians.

Roman Catholic Europeans had dealt with non-Christians before. In ancient times pagans had persecuted Christians, and when Christians came to power they returned the favour. Non-Christians were assumed to be hostile, though their fate varied according to the degree of power Christians possessed. Some pagans they converted, like Cartier's own Roman or German ancestors, the Norse in Scandinavia and Iceland, and the Slavs of Poland and Bohemia. Others they conquered and then converted, like the pagan tribes in eastern Germany and the Baltic. Some they enslaved, like the unfortunate inhabitants of the Canary Islands in the Atlantic. And some they fought, like the Muslim powers of Asia and

North Africa—a desperate fight, in which the most aggressive Muslim power, Turkey, was conquering and converting the Christian peoples of southeast Europe and advancing to the gates of Vienna. There was no such formidable opposition in the Americas—and so the Spanish tended to apply their experience in the Canaries, first in the West Indies and then in Mexico and South America.

The first assumption made by Christian Europeans (but not alone by Europeans, or by Christians) was that their own religion and practices took precedence over (or even negated) those of non-Christians. Theologians and politicians differed as to the proper treatment of non-Christians—but philosophy and statesmanlike restraint were in short supply among explorers and their sponsors, the profit-seeking speculators on the future of the New World. Resistance to European encroachment allowed Europeans to go to war—of course in self-defence—and, having defeated their enemies, to enslave them.

Christianity had developed in a world of menace, from pagans, from Jews, from Muslims. It continued so. In the sixteenth century Christianity was beset from without—by the Turks—and divided from within. As Cartier sailed to America, Christianity was dividing into Roman Catholic and Protestant parts, and the princes of Europe were taking sides for one or the other. Wars among Protestants and Catholics were already breaking out in the 1530s, and they would continue, almost unabated, for over a hundred years. It was, as the historian J.R. Miller puts it, "a historically important coincidence that much of the early period of European exploration and penetration of North America was a period of intense religious feeling."[7]

The sense of a religion under threat added a new urgency to the notion of conversion and to a disregard for the abstract rights of those who ignored Christian doctrine, wilfully or not. To that must be added the perception that the village-based societies of northern North America weren't political entities as the Europeans understood them. They had no real monarchs, and very little in the way of formal governing bodies. It was easy (and profitable) to argue that America was "terra nullius," a land belonging to no one. It could therefore be claimed by the explorers on the basis of discovery, and claimed, naturally, in the interest of the monarch who had authorized and likely paid for the explorer's trip to America. When Cartier raised a cross to mark his first landfall on the American mainland, in Gaspé in 1534, he was claiming the territory for Christ, but also for King François. The land itself he dubbed New France, as Mexico had been labelled New Spain by its conquerors. This didn't mean that the Natives either understood or accepted what Cartier was doing, though its implications, as the Spaniards showed farther south, could be quite drastic.

Of course, the Spaniards in Mexico in 1520 and Peru in 1532 had a predominance of power, and Cartier did not. This may seem strange, for the French expeditions to the St. Lawrence were not less numerous than those of some successful Spanish adventurers. (Indeed, on his third voyage, in 1541, Cartier had fifteen hundred men, far more than the Spanish armies that conquered Mexico or Peru.) Moreover, the Spanish faced rich and highly organized societies, which the French did not. But Cartier was essentially a sailor, however ruthless and greedy, and his company had a background similar to his own. His weapons were few, and his sailors were not a disciplined force. The Spanish leadership, on the other hand, was military, and its members were soldiers, and used to discipline. They brought with them horses and steel armour and guns, even cannon, and thus had marked superiority in technology over their Native opponents. Their leaders had the right stimulus—gold—and, seeing an opportunity, took it. The rewards were great, and not difficult to imagine.

The St. Lawrence Valley in 1534 and 1535 was an entirely different matter. Cartier met Natives on his first voyage and kidnapped two of them, taking them back to France as visible proof of his achievement. He had little else to show. There were furs, but these excited little interest compared with gold. Still, furs were better than nothing. There were rocks, but they were worthless. The Holy Roman Emperor, Charles V, who was also king of Spain, was at one point urged to block French colonization of the St. Lawrence. Certainly not, Charles replied, for the land was "of no value, and if the French take it, necessity will compel them to abandon it."

From that point of view, Cartier's second and third expeditions represented the triumph of hope over experience. He had at least managed to survive, and return to France, and that said something. Granted, he could not have survived without help. He had fortunately encountered two Iroquois villages: Stadacona, where Quebec City now stands, and Hochelaga, on the site of modern Montreal. Cartier and his men were visitors and, importantly, guests. Wintering in 1535–36, they were dependent on their Iroquois hosts. The alternative, in the Canadian climate, was misery and likely death. Deprived of fresh produce and suffering from scurvy, the French had to be instructed in boiling bark to provide the necessary anti-scorbutics to restore their health. Even so, twenty-five (out of 110) of Cartier's men died.

Cartier assumed he'd found a stable and permanent—if barbaric—society at Hochelaga and Stadacona, but that was not so. At some point before 1580 the Iroquois settlements disappeared, probably in war with another Iroquois people farther west, and their inhabitants were dispersed and absorbed by their conquerors. Those conquerors, the Hurons, would greet Cartier's eventual successors. They would be a long time coming. From what Cartier had shown, the St. Lawrence held little promise, merely bad weather, uncooperative Natives, and fool's gold in place of the real article.

The fishery, on the other hand, was big business. At least, it was big business in the aggregate, for its participants represented only themselves and needed to invest only enough capital to build and crew a boat. Yet by the late sixteenth century there were four hundred boats and an estimated twelve thousand fishermen, mostly French and English.

The English fished close to the coast, and dried their catch—cod—on racks on the shore. The French, with better access to salt at home, fished on the Grand Banks, hauled in their catch, and cured it on board, packing it in barrels. The English thus had an advantage as far as land was concerned, for their method of fishing made them at least seasonal settlers along the shore, from May to September every year.

Fish weren't the only desirable commodity to be found in North American waters. The fishermen discovered the walrus, plentiful along the shores of the Gulf of St. Lawrence. From the walrus they could get ivory from its tusks, oil from its blubber, and leather from its skin. The fruits of walrus-hunting could be supplemented by furs brought to the shores by the local Algonquin tribes and exchanged for desirable European goods. There proved to be enough walrus to withstand almost three centuries of exploitation, but exploitation eventually proved to be extermination: the last walrus in the Gulf was reported around 1800.

If there was a pattern to sixteenth-century exploration of the east coast of North America, it was its steady displacement toward the north. This was testament to the magnetic effect of the presumptive route to China. Verrazzano and Cartier showed that if there was such a route it probably lay north of the St. Lawrence, somewhere beyond Labrador. This route, variously called the Straits of Anian and the Northwest Passage, attracted explorers well into the twentieth century and was a major factor in raising funds and official support for exploration.

Ignorance was the other precondition for northern expeditions. Europeans knew very little about the north. What their maps told them was often if not usually fanciful—imaginary lands scattered almost as decoration around seas filled with conjectural but fearsome monsters. Experience was no guide either, for the lands of even northern Europe were relatively temperate compared with the continent of ice and snow that lurked beyond Labrador.

The result was a virtually open field for savants and speculators, a lethal combination for gullible investors, of whom there seems to have been a considerable supply. The centre of the resulting ferment was England, whose merchants were anxious to establish a stable and profitable connection with the usual target, the riches of Asia. Basing themselves on inaccurate maps and dubious texts, learned scholars "proved" that there was indeed such a thing as a Northwest Passage. Speculators then took the bit in their teeth, raising hopes and money in about equal proportions.

England in the later sixteenth century was ruled by an intelligent and reasonably cautious queen. Elizabeth I was a Protestant, and thus doomed to enter into conflict with the various Catholic powers and principalities that surrounded her island kingdom. She also had a surplus of adventurous gentlemen who were only too willing to go to sea in search of profit—Spanish treasure by way of piracy, or the gold of America and, after America, China, by way of exploration and discovery.

In the 1570s and 1580s a series of Englishmen mounted expeditions to assert England's interest across the northern Atlantic. (There was also a spectacular voyage to the Pacific led by the intrepid Sir Francis Drake; Drake came close to, though he probably didn't reach, Canada's western shores.) There were two attempts at colonization, in Newfoundland and Virginia, which received its name in honour of England's "virgin queen." There were, as well, voyages directly in search of the Northwest Passage (though even the Virginian expedition was fraught with fantasies about it).

These projects came to naught, and left behind little more than an aggregation of place names—Frobisher Bay, Davis Strait, and so forth. There was, it turned out, such a thing as too far north, because the severe climate of the Arctic and the short navigation season proved insuperable obstacles to a passage to the Pacific. This was discouraging news, though the discouragement wouldn't last forever.

Preoccupation in the religious wars of Europe did the rest. England and Spain fought for almost twenty years, on land and sea. Ireland was in a perpetual state of rebellion. France and the Netherlands were convulsed by rebellions and civil wars. European energies were concentrated at home, and what little remained focused on the well-known and well-understood North Atlantic fishery, and on minor exchanges in trade with the Algonquin peoples surrounding the Gulf of St. Lawrence.

Objectively, the Native peoples of Canada were little touched by the peripheral activities of explorers and speculators in the sixteenth century. They didn't know that in the minds of the kings of England and France they had become "subjects"—inhabitants of land claimed by one kingdom or the other. Neither country could in the sixteenth century make good on its claims to the North American wilderness, which had the beneficial side effect that neither was as yet ready to go to war over them. And North America was still viewed as too uncomfortable, too undesirable, too lacking in profit for a sustained and expensive effort at possession and settlement. That fate was, for the time being, reserved for Ireland, where Elizabeth I and her successors aimed to "plant" colonists. The grim experience of Ireland was an unlucky model for the New World.

LAND FOR
THE TAKING

Battle between the Iroquois and the Algonquins with their French allies, 1609.
This copper plate engraving is based on a drawing by Samuel Champlain.

T he explorers of the sixteenth century traced the outline of the Americas, and the cartographers followed. The resulting maps showed a more or less firm coastline along the Atlantic and Pacific, with indentations for the Caribbean and the Gulf of St. Lawrence. To the north and west, the lines faded into imprecision and then fancy. The sea route to China, the Northwest Passage, still beckoned to the hopeful as the seventeenth century dawned.

The land was vast, and the possibility of error was high. Perhaps the first explorers had left something out, or hadn't gone far enough. Could there not be a gap in the seacoast of Labrador? Might not the northern continent be little more than an isthmus, like Panama, with the Pacific just on the other side?

There was also the possibility that the land itself might actually be worth having. The Spaniards had found gold in Mexico and Peru. Couldn't the French and the English do so as well? If the Northwest Passage lurked beyond the next bend of the coast, gold was just over the next hill. They would have to be; otherwise, what was the point? The northeastern shores of the continent were cold, rocky, and windswept— "the land God gave to Cain," in Jacques Cartier's memorable phrase. That land "is of no value," a Spaniard advised King Carlos I in 1541. Let the French have it.

The advice was both sensible and short-sighted. The northern continent was indeed difficult and barren, and, worst of all, cold. Yet, as we have seen, some parts of North America were already turning a profit— especially the Newfoundland cod fishery. Sometimes the fishermen came ashore and fanned out in search of wood for fire or meat to vary their diet. Finding meat, they also found fur, and brought it home to Europe. At first North American fur was a curiosity, but it didn't take long to become a profitable curiosity. Fur was a luxury commodity in Western Europe, trimming the robes of the rich. Transformed into felt, it supplied the hatters' trade. Especially useful and especially prized was the fur of the North American beaver. It would be this unprepossessing rodent, with its orange teeth and scaly tail, that finally gave Europeans reason to come and trade in the territory that would become Canada, and then to stay there.

Had they relied on their own efforts, seasonal and sporadic, the Europeans would have made little of the fur trade. Trade required Native suppliers, and there began a partnership between European (mainly French) traders and indigenous hunters, who were happy to convert the apparently inexhaustible beaver into iron implements, steel knives, and guns. Natives living along the coast had the advantage, for they controlled access to the Europeans, who for their part did not venture into the interior.

It was an exchange that was profitable to both parties, if we exclude the cost of European diseases that the traders brought with them and communicated to the Natives. As far as the traders were concerned, most of the hard work was done by the Natives, universally called Indians because of the early mistaken belief that the Americas were outliers of the spice islands of Asia. Trade goods were relatively cheap, iron or brass or cloth or, increasingly, alcohol, for which many Natives discovered a fondness. Metal—copper—was not unknown to the Natives of eastern North America, but it was scarce and, in any case, soft. Brass, iron, and steel were much preferred, and those only the Europeans could supply.

In the valley of the St. Lawrence it was the French who predominated. Their interest in the lands explored and claimed for France by Jacques Cartier hadn't ceased, but there was little they could do about it as long as France was riven by wars between Catholic and Protestant. Finally, in 1598, the wars came to an end, leaving a Catholic convert from Protestantism, Henri IV, on the throne, with toleration between Catholic and Protestant as his policy. French attention to America promptly increased.

European governments of the early seventeenth century had few resources and little capacity for colonization. Lacking large standing armies and navies and consistent administrative competence, they relied on private entrepreneurs equipped with royal charters and driven by the hope of profit. The charters conferred varying degrees of monopoly power on individuals, usually nobles, who were then free to make what they could of the vast territories of North America. In return, they were to respect the rights of other Christians while subduing and converting to Christianity anyone else.

Under the leadership of Pierre du Gua, Sieur de Monts, an expedition was mounted to North America in 1604. It fixed on the Bay of Fundy, between what would later become Nova Scotia and New Brunswick, as the place to establish a post where for the first time the French would winter. But the French chose unwisely, settling on an offshore island, Ste. Croix, where they built a scattering of huts and endured a bitter winter. They had no choice but to rely on such stores as they had brought from Europe, but this meant they had no fresh food and, consequently, succumbed to scurvy, a disease caused by vitamin C deficiency.

Remarkably, some Frenchmen (for they were all male) survived the winter. Knowing that if they stayed at Ste. Croix another winter they would surely perish, they sought another and more salubrious location— and found it on the south shore of the Bay of Fundy, in a place they named Port Royal.

Port Royal was better designed and built than Ste. Croix, a quadrangle rather than a scattering of huts. It was also better run, for the leadership of the little colony devolved onto a mapmaker and navigator named Samuel de Champlain.

Champlain may well have been born a Protestant, around 1570, but like many others of his faith he probably converted to Catholicism at some point in the 1590s. He came from a seafaring family, and was later a captain in the royal service. He became, in effect, a member of the lowest rank of the nobility, and added the noble "de" to his name, a frequent occurrence at the time. What distinguished Champlain, however, was a fierce singleness of purpose: to establish a permanent French settlement in northern North America.

He originally favoured Acadia, the Fundy basin, for his project. But Acadia was unfruitful, and first Ste. Croix and then Port Royal were abandoned. In 1608 Champlain tried again. Acting as de Monts's lieutenant (a formal appointment), he sailed for the St. Lawrence in April 1608, arriving at the narrows of the river at Quebec on 3 July. There he built a fortified trading post, a *habitation,* surrounded by palisades and wide moats. He also planted wheat and rye, not that those crops could rescue his *habitation* from the inevitable scurvy that killed sixteen out of twenty-five in the party.

Life in the colony was dominated by the rhythm of its communications with France. The St. Lawrence was icebound between November and May, and the colony consequently isolated. Sea voyages were long, typically two to three months, meaning that orders placed in one year would be acted upon only in the next. Patience was more than a virtue under the circumstances, and morale a crucial consideration. Champlain acted ruthlessly when required to maintain discipline: in his first year at Quebec he uncovered a plot against his authority and promptly hanged its ringleader.

Champlain survived the weather, time, and conspiracy, and, resupplied from France, he set out for the interior in the summer of 1609. He proved an intrepid traveller, the first of hundreds of French *voyageurs* to explore the interior of the continent. Champlain did not travel unaided. He had two Frenchmen with him, but the bulk of his party was made up of Algonquins and Hurons, the latter an Iroquoian-speaking people who had worked out an alliance with the Algonquins and the French in pursuit of the fur trade. Encountering the rival Five-Nations Iroquois on the shores of what is now Lake Champlain, the Algonquins and Hurons prevailed in a brief battle. In that battle Champlain used a firearm, his clumsy arquebus, to intimidate the enemy, and it seems to have served its purpose.

After a trip to France in the winter of 1609–10 to report to King Henri IV as well as his superior, de Monts, Champlain returned for another expedition and another battle, in which he was wounded by the Iroquois. He again returned to France over the winter, this time to secure the economic and political backing that would preserve his little colony. In this he was successful, acquiring a variety of noble and politically powerful sponsors who could help him with the new king, Louis XIII. Just as important, in 1613 he published a narrative of his expeditions from 1604 to 1612, his *Voyages*, which established his reputation as a heroic explorer and helped shore up the fortunes of his colony as an emanation of France.

Champlain continued his interior explorations in the years that followed, mapping the Ottawa River and much of the Great Lakes basin. He also survived the vagaries of French politics. As one sponsor fell in royal favour, another rose; but always Champlain remained the "lieutenant" in charge of the Quebec colony, or New France. (The term "New France" dates back to 1529, as a mapmaker's label for the territory discovered and claimed in the name of the king of France.)

New France was in many ways fortunate. Its location in the frigid north was admittedly an invitation to scurvy, but the severe winter preserved its inhabitants from other diseases, such as yellow fever.[1] Although the number of actual settlers was low, the colony was buffered by its Native allies and so didn't suffer the devastating Native wars that nearly destroyed the English Virginia colony.

European politics were a constant danger, however. Champlain proved remarkably adept at manoeuvring his colony through the perils of the royal court. He secured the favour of the king's chief minister, Cardinal de Richelieu, who in 1627 organized the Compagnie des Cent Associés (Company of the Hundred Associates) to manage and, most important, to finance New France. Champlain became the cardinal's personal representative, a fact that did not save him or the colony when a hostile English fleet sailed up the St. Lawrence in 1629. (England and France had gone to war in 1627.) Champlain was bundled off into captivity in England, and returned to Quebec only in 1633. Peace had actually been made before the

English captured Quebec, though no one on the scene could have known it. The English found the fur trade profitable, and stayed on as long as they could.

The English interlude did not advance the colony's fortunes, but it didn't entirely kill them, and Champlain was able to rebuild what the English had destroyed. He didn't live to see his colony flourish, however, dying at Quebec in December 1635.

Champlain's achievement was nevertheless considerable. Following where Cartier had pointed, he obtained for France the St. Lawrence River, the only practicable water route into the heart of the continent, from the rocks of Gaspé to the prairies beyond the Great Lakes. Champlain's place as a geographer and explorer is incontestable; equally important, he was a notable publicist and indefatigable promoter, qualities that helped him navigate the shoals of the French court and a succession of rich and powerful patrons. His colony, as he predicted, was suitable for agriculture; by the time of his death there were the feeble beginnings of farms, growing such crops as a cold climate would permit.

Yet Champlain's colony remained utterly dependent on regular drafts of cash and favour from the French government. That government, in the 1620s and 1630s, was firmly Catholic and, as far as a powerful and rebellious nobility would allow, authoritarian. The only clergy permitted on the soil of New France after 1608 were Catholic, and indeed part of the attraction of the colony was that it afforded a field for the missionary efforts of the Catholic Church.

Trade and salvation were what the French consciously offered the Natives of North America, under both Champlain and his successors. To France the colony offered furs, profit, and souls, hoping in return for investors, soldiers, and settlers.

The government of France had other priorities, however. There was war between France and Spain, consuming money and soldiers. French politics were uncertain after the death of Cardinal Richelieu in 1642 and of Louis XIII in 1643, leaving the five-year-old Louis XIV an uneasy regency and restless nobility as his heritage.

And so the government was content to leave New France to the Company of a Hundred Associates, to nurture as best it could. The Company appointed a minor noble, Charles Huault de Montmagny, as governor—a title denied to Champlain—with the mandate to finance, populate, expand, and defend the colony. A new post, Trois-Rivières, had been founded upriver in 1634. Religion, as much as defence or trade, was the occasion for the foundation of Montreal in 1642 by the Sieur de Maisonneuve. And as an outer defence against Iroquois incursions, Montmagny established a fort at the confluence of the Richelieu and St. Lawrence rivers in 1641.

Finance was the least successful of Montmagny's efforts. The Hundred Associates never saw a profit from their colony, and in 1645 effectively threw in the towel, conceding a monopoly over the fur trade to a group of local merchants, the Communauté des Habitants, in return for an annual rent. In other areas, however, the company was more successful. A small but steady stream of immigrants came to New France under its administration, pushing the population to three thousand—all Catholics, as the French government required—by 1663. Such a number wasn't easy to displace or exterminate, and certainly to that extent the company must be rated a modest success.[2]

HURONIA AND THE IROQUOIS WARS

New France was more than a projection of Europe or France in America. It was also a factor in the balance of power, or force, in northern North America. Champlain's appearance on a battlefield in 1609, in a conflict between Algonquins and Iroquois that he barely understood, showed clearly enough that having the French as an ally could make a real difference in war. Better yet, having the French as a trading partner conferred great material and also political advantage. The key was location: straddling the lake and river routes to Quebec, the Huron and Algonquins could be the intermediaries between the French and the beaver-rich lands to the north and west of the Great Lakes. Others would do the hunting, and receive what prices the Huron chose; the Hurons themselves would deal with the French.

The French weren't the only Europeans in northern North America, however. The Dutch weren't far behind; as Champlain approached from the north they were exploring from the south, up the Hudson River. They would found New Amsterdam (present-day New York) and then Fort Orange (Albany). Fort Orange lay close to the eastern gate of the Iroquois confederacy, the Five Nations, and soon enough the Iroquois too were armed with European weaponry.

The French did not aim to become enemies of the Five Nations, but inadvertently they fell into an arrangement with another Iroquoian-speaking people, the Huron. Champlain travelled with the Huron and wintered with them as he explored the Great Lakes in 1615–16. The Huron saw plainly the advantage of dealing with the French; and the French saw the advantage of keeping the Huron apart from the neighbouring Iroquois, for together they would present a serious, and possibly fatal, military challenge to New France. To these mundane considerations was added the calculus of souls, for the Jesuits saw in the Huron ideal subjects for conversion. So the French attached a spiritual condition to their trade: the Huron must receive the Jesuits, in their characteristic black robes, and the Jesuits must be free to proselytize.

The Jesuits (properly, the Society of Jesus) weren't the first Catholic order to arrive in New France. That distinction belonged to the Récollets, who had come in 1615 and who by active vocation and austere inclination were rivals of the more worldly Jesuits, who landed only in 1625. It didn't help relations between the two orders that the Jesuits took over a former Récollet mission among the Huron in 1634.

Clerical rivalry was a minor, though sour, note in the Jesuit mission in Canada. The Jesuit enterprise was carefully planned and thoughtfully executed. They were essentially a missionary order, and by the 1620s had seventy years' experience in missions in Asia. The Jesuits naturally applied their experience to America. First learning the Native languages and studying the local culture, they lived among their prospective converts.

There was no thought of conversion by force—the nearest French soldier was eight hundred kilometres away, at Quebec—but rather conversion by example, a painstaking and time-consuming enterprise.

Many Hurons resisted conversion. They had a well-established religious culture, and preferred their own shamans to the French priests. The French, however, had another argument, though a dangerous one: the diseases they (among others) had brought from Europe and which in the 1630s swept through the Iroquois peoples of the Great Lakes region. If the shamans were effective, the Jesuits argued, they surely could prevent the epidemics. Of course they could not—but then neither could the Jesuits.

Conversion, not universal but substantial, followed among the Huron as the Jesuit enterprise took shape. At one point fifteen priests worked in Huronia, while Ste. Marie Among the Hurons, the principal mission, was a palisaded fort enclosing church, houses, and longhouses for Huron converts.

The Jesuit approach to conversion was effective, as far as it went. Because they adapted to Native customs and spoke Native languages, the Jesuits set aside much of the sense of superiority that marred European attitudes toward Native Americans. Yet there were limits that, given the brief duration of the Huron mission, were not fully overcome. Converts, individually or as groups, became in a sense wards of the priests, to be cared for, certainly, and treated humanely, but expected to settle into Jesuit-directed agricultural communities. And except in Japan, the Jesuits did not advance their converts to the priesthood, tacitly demonstrating that they considered them to be less than equals of the priests.[3]

The palisades, meanwhile, weren't enough to keep out the Iroquois. Ravaged by the same epidemics that decimated the Huron, the Iroquois population fell by at least half, disrupting society, emptying villages, and threatening the future of the Five Nations. It was an established practice among the Iroquois—Hurons included—that population could be replenished from captives taken in war, and the Iroquois set out to do just that. If the Huron wouldn't join the Five Nations as a group, and voluntarily, they would join by force.

Clashes had already occurred between Huron and Iroquois, sometimes over furs, sometimes in the form of raids. What followed, however, was more than conflict over trade or captives. Between 1648 and 1650 the Iroquois systematically destroyed the Huron nation, killing Jesuits they could capture, along with many of their converts, by customary and gruesome tortures. But destroying the nation didn't mean destroying its members, who as captives were marched back to the Iroquois homeland south of Lake Ontario and very often adopted or absorbed among their captors. Other Huron, accompanied by Jesuits, sought refuge near the French settlements on the St. Lawrence, while still others fled west, across Lake Michigan. There they were joined by the remnants of the Neutral, Petun, and other nations, also defeated and dispersed—or absorbed—by the Iroquois.

What would the future have been had the Iroquois not come and had Huronia survived under Jesuit tutelage? An answer may be found in the relatively more successful Jesuit colony among the Guarani in Spanish America—a sedentary, agricultural enclave, shielded by the priests as best they could from the depredations of the Spanish Empire and its subjects. But the colony was essentially static, with priests on top, converts below. Both priests and Guarani were eventually destroyed by the secular forces that had grown up outside, and almost as cruelly as the Iroquois had destroyed Huronia.

The French actually did set up refuges for Hurons and other Natives displaced by the Iroquois, one outside Quebec at Ancienne Lorette and another at Caughnawaga, across the St. Lawrence from Montreal. The Natives there were necessarily all converts to Catholicism, and lived under a loose form of religious tutelage. But these "praying Indians" were neither sedentary nor pacifist, and their style of life reflected a compromise between tradition and religion. It drew from both European and Native sources, and was neither European nor Native, but a dynamic blend of the two.

As the historian J.R. Miller has noted, the French did not cause the wars that destroyed Huronia, though they contributed to them in a variety of ways. There had been trade and there had been wars before the coming of the Europeans, and there would be after. The mere adoption of firearms or other trade goods did not fundamentally reshape Native society.[4]

THE SURVIVAL OF NEW FRANCE

The destruction of Huronia was only the first act in a sixty-year Iroquois war that raged along the frontiers of New France and in the fur-trading hinterland that supplied the colony. For a time in the early 1650s the Iroquois succeeded in blockading New France from the west, halting altogether the flow of furs from the upper lakes (called by the colonists *le pays d'en haut*), but over time the effort proved too much for the Iroquois to sustain.

Eventually Native traders got through to the French, and by the mid-1650s the fur trade was again flourishing. This time it was Algonquin tribes, especially the Ottawas, who conveyed the furs, but the French did more than wait passively for their delivery. Young men from the settlement travelled west with the Indians, choosing life in the woods and adaptation to Native ways as the best means to profit and, of course, adventure too. Such men were called *coureurs de bois*, runners of the woods. The authorities did not look kindly on their periodic departures, which no doubt deprived the colony of scarce labour and, worse, set a bad example for restless youth; perhaps in return the absence of the *coureurs de bois* made New France a more peaceful and orderly place, more suitable for the subjects of an authoritarian monarch.

Seventeenth-century authoritarianism could be—was—cruel and capricious, and derived much of its force from that fact. On the other hand, authority was distant, the Atlantic was wide, and travel even within New France was tedious and difficult. The king's writ ended at the edge of the woods, as generations of Canadians would learn, and beyond was a very different world. Who actually had authority in New France? There was a governor, it was true, but the governor was appointed by the Company of a Hundred Associates, which wielded a shadowy jurisdiction over the colony. The colony was more than a fur company; there were the fur traders themselves, and some farmers. There was also the Church.

New France was intended to be a monument to exclusive Catholicism. There was some sense in the notion, given the religious wars that tore France apart in the sixteenth century and Germany in the seventeenth. Why look for trouble in religious difference when a simple restriction would keep the colony spiritually homogeneous?

But keeping New France strictly Catholic did not prevent religious dispute; it merely redefined it. There were rivalries between Catholic missionary orders—the Récollets, Sulpicians, and Jesuits. There were "secular" clergy—that is, ordinary priests living outside an order. There were the female religious, who contrived to live autonomously in a society otherwise dominated by males. And there were the questions of how the Church was to be governed, and how it would affect government.

French Catholicism was by no means subservient to the Pope in Rome, as Protestant legend had it. The French monarchy kept a jealous eye on the Church in France and had appropriated authority over it. Cardinals, bishops, priests, monks, and nuns were all subjects of the monarchy, and conformed to a greater or lesser degree to the royal will. Rome did not find the situation congenial, nor did all the French clergy.

Louis XIV, the grandson of a Protestant, was particularly insistent on having his way with the Catholic clergy, and yet he was in most respects an extravagantly devout Catholic anxious to secure and expand the Church in France and abroad. Louis's expulsion of many (but not all) French Protestants supplied the English colonies and England itself with industrious workers, while his support of Catholic claimants to the throne of England would help embroil France in wars that would directly affect the future of New France.

The most direct representative of Catholicism in New France was François de Laval. Laval represented the part of Catholicism that preferred to keep the king at arm's length or beyond, and that preferred a Church as independent of secular authority as possible. Laval's appointment to Quebec in 1658 was not as a regular bishop, chosen by the king and subject to his authority, but as a vicar-general, appointed by the Pope, with the rank and status of bishop.[5]

To symbolize his authority, and his status, Laval insisted that in religious ceremonies he march ahead of the governor, greatly to the latter's displeasure. The two eminences set to quarrelling and scheming; henceforth in colonial politics there were two poles, one religious and one secular, with the religious one looking beyond the monarch in Paris to a world across the Alps in Italy—and from this trans-mountain conception derives the term "ultramontane" to signify a relationship with the Pope. It was a notion that would prove handy when Quebec was no longer ruled by a king of France.

Laval did not stop at questions of precedence. As vicar-general and later as bishop (he got the title in 1674) he set about creating a seminary to train priests (the séminaire de Québec, the nucleus of the future Laval university) as well as new churches and hospitals (staffed by nuns). Laval placed the Church at the heart of colonial society, and he and his successors exercised an unusual degree of control over what was publicly and morally permissible. For instance, even private theatrics were subject to close scrutiny. In a tiny colony there could be no professional theatre, and so theatrics were confined to the educated elite; indeed there was no public theatre at all until after the fall of New France and the arrival of the British. In one famous case, in 1693–94, the Church intervened to prevent the performance of Molière's play *Tartuffe*, whose target was censorious religious hypocrisy.[6]

ROYAL GOVERNMENT

Had the Company of a Hundred Associates performed according to its design, New France by 1660 would have had thirty thousand inhabitants, would have been a flourishing agricultural community capable of supplying its own food, and would have returned a steady stream of money to its owners and investors back in France. Instead, the colony had barely three thousand inhabitants, some scattered around the Bay of Fundy or in

Newfoundland, but most in enclaves along the St. Lawrence. This total compared very badly with the fifty thousand English settlers in New England, or the thirty thousand in Virginia, or the ten thousand Dutch in New Netherlands.

The colony was abundant in one thing: politics. There were disputes between merchants and the authorities, the Church and merchants, the Church and governor, and within the Church. The religious authorities objected to the liquor trade with the Natives and convinced the governor to ban it, to the rage and distress of the merchants. But the next governor removed the ban, and the liquor trade flourished as never before.

All this took place against the background of the endless war with the Iroquois, which resumed after 1658, not only blockading New France but afflicting it with raiding parties who killed or kidnapped the inhabitants within sight of the three fortified posts of Quebec, Trois-Rivières, and Montreal. Not even the Island of Orleans, off Quebec, was safe from Iroquois raids. The Iroquois roamed far to the north, toward Hudson Bay, and to the west, battling the distant Sioux to the west of the Great Lakes. As for Acadia, an expedition from New England had annexed it in 1654 and the English had no intention of giving it back—and would indeed only give it back in 1670.[7] Beleaguered and diminished, New France needed help. There was only one possible source.

Back in France, the royal government was bestirring itself. Louis XIV, aged twenty-three, finally assumed control of his own administration in 1661. This was in the short term a good thing, for Louis understood that he had to bring order to and revenues from his government if he was to find the glory he craved for himself and his country. The benefits would spread as far as his commands would carry, and thus to New France, and there, too, Louis would bring order. In the longer term, however, Louis's quest for glory contained the seeds of its own demise, for his ambitions entailed endless wars that would also involve New France and would, in their effects, long outlast his lifetime.

Louis decided to make New France a royal province, ruled, like all other French provinces, directly from Paris. At the king's demand, the

Hundred Associates gave up their rights to the colony in 1663 in return for unspecified and doubtless inadequate compensation. A governor was appointed. An advisory Sovereign Council was established. The bishop was, at least temporarily, appeased. Louis ordered a regiment of regular troops to the colony under an experienced and noble commander. And this, Louis promised, was just the beginning.

It was the end of the beginning. The first colonies in North America—French, English, and Dutch—were the fruit of public purpose and private enterprise. Weak European states relied on individuals and companies to claim, explore, and settle lands across the ocean. Lured by the prospect of immense wealth, first the treasures of the Orient and then the fortunes of fur, entrepreneurs risked and mostly lost their money in the attempt.

But New France was fortunate that its founder, Champlain, was more than a visionary. His careful choice of Quebec as the base and capital of New France afforded the colony a defensible fortress, a healthy if rugged climate, and isolation from the English colonies to the south. These facts would serve New France well for the next century.

EXPANSION AND CONSOLIDATION

The cod fishery in Newfoundland in the eighteenth century,
with French drying racks on the shore.

Between 1663 and 1713 the balance of power in North America shifted. In the 1660s the European colonies along the eastern seaboard clung to the shoreline, dependent on the neighbouring Indian nations for their security and prosperity. Their survival was no longer in question, but their future development was tenuous and uncertain.

Events in the 1660s changed the shape and the future of the European settlements in North America, transforming them from poor but permanent dependencies, caught between the next Indian attack and the arrival of the next supply ship, to provincial emanations of the great Western European powers, France and England. Because events in Western Europe in the late seventeenth century determined what happened next in North America, we shall turn to consider circumstances that were entirely outside the control of the settlements in America but that would prove crucial for their development.

Europe in the Making of America

War and the absence of war shaped what the colonies became. By the 1660s Europe had been in an almost constant state of turmoil for 150 years, with wars inspired by religion and ambition devastating the centre of the continent. In France a king was assassinated—Henri IV in 1610— and in England a king, Charles I, was beheaded in 1649 and a republic established. Civil disturbances preoccupied France and the British Isles throughout the 1640s and 1650s.

Under the circumstances, then, governments had other things to do than worry about colonies. Yet as the wars continued governments learned that it was possible to organize themselves better so as to make war more efficiently. And later, the more or less simultaneous abatement of domestic disturbances in France and England after 1660 afforded an opportunity for governments to strengthen themselves for any further wars. Also simultaneously, governments began to imagine a use for their colonies.

Stability at home came first. England's republican government, having reached its wits' end in 1659–60, negotiated the return of the monarchy as represented by the son of the executed Charles I. Charles II left his French exile, and the court of his cousin, Louis XIV, and arrived back in London in May 1660. He had no desire, as he put it, to go on his travels again, and governed England as prudently as difficult circumstances allowed. For though the fires of religious controversy were banked, they were not out: rivalry between Protestants and Catholics, and among various sects of Protestants, dominated English politics throughout Charles's lifetime and beyond.

Charles wasn't merely king of England, but king of Scotland and Ireland too. (He also claimed the French throne, though it had been centuries since an English monarch had allowed that to interfere with normal and generally peaceful relations with France.) The Scots were mostly Protestant, but with an active Catholic minority, and the Irish were mostly Catholic, but with a recently settled Protestant minority. In all three kingdoms Catholicism was officially suppressed, with Catholics suffering various degrees of persecution or disability at the hands of the state. The state was represented by Protestant parliaments that required— demanded—appeasement by their anxious monarch. Charles governed, but he did not, absolutely, rule. It was an uneasy compromise, even illogical, but it was what the situation demanded.

Many families were mixed in religion, and that included the Stuarts, Charles II's family. His grandmother and mother had been Catholic and his brother, the Duke of York, was too. Charles had leanings toward Catholicism but wisely kept them to himself; he was, he knew, a Protestant monarch at the head of a fiercely Protestant people. To act otherwise would be to risk his throne, if not his head.

Louis XIV viewed Charles's religious-political predicament with sympathy but also a certain amount of disdain. He too had seen civil disorder as a child and was determined not to repeat it. Louis set out to become an absolute monarch, and did. There would be no nonsense of parliaments, or elections, or subjects standing against their king. The Estates-General, the assembly of the orders of the realm, last met under Louis's father, in 1614. It would not meet again until 1789.

Louis cast a jaundiced eye on French Protestantism too. His grandfather had once been a Protestant, or Huguenot, and had granted a protected status to the sect. The grandson, however, believed in "One king, one law and one faith" (*roi, loi,* and *foi*) and revoked the protection in 1685, driving hundreds of thousands of Huguenots into exile in friendlier Protestant countries, including the English colonies in America. The number of Huguenot exiles, in any case, far outnumbered the thin stream of faithful Catholics induced to settle in the king's overseas colonies, especially New France.

Louis's system of government precluded a chief minister; the king had suffered too many overmighty advisers in his youth and was determined not to repeat the experience. But he wasn't averse to employing talented ministers, especially in the area of finance. Finance fed war, and war was the staple of the king's policy. Industry produced the implements of battle, as well as taxes. French economic policy was rearranged to encourage domestic industry while discouraging purchases abroad. And what couldn't be made in France might, perhaps, be found in the colonies—furs in the case of New France, sugar in the case of the French islands in the West Indies.

To run the economy and produce taxes, Louis employed Jean-Baptiste Colbert as controller general of finance (1662–83). Colbert managed well, repaying the national debt, reorganizing taxes, and encouraging industry—especially those industries that would support the country's expansion. He especially encouraged shipbuilding, for overseas trade and for the navy, to protect the shipping and to enhance national strength.

France had a natural advantage in terms of the European balance of power. It had the largest population of any state in Western or Central Europe, coherent and largely defensible frontiers, and, thanks to Louis's firm government, domestic peace. The population sustained a large army, numbering in the hundreds of thousands, the largest in Western Europe since the Roman Empire. Abundant finance—and as time went on, abundant taxation—meant that the king could pay, feed, and clothe his troops in uniforms, with consequent beneficial effects on obedience and discipline.

The frontiers of France expanded quickly, and French influence more quickly still. There was even a minor war with cousin Charles II of England, admittedly a half-hearted affair in support of Louis's ally of the day, the Netherlands, in 1665–67. Louis, fortunately, was in no position to attack the British Isles: his ambitions lay elsewhere, and his increasingly effective and professional armies marched where ambition and glory dictated. As far as the colonies were concerned, the war was half over before the colonial authorities, English or French, even learned it was on.

That war therefore produced no serious hostilities between France and England in America, but it did rearrange the political geography of coastal North America, and not to the benefit of New France. An English expedition sailed into the harbour of New Amsterdam, forced its surrender, and appropriated the Dutch colony to the English crown. Renamed New York, the city and its surrounding colony became an English province, linking New England to New Jersey (another acquisition). Nor was New York the last expansion of England into America: under Charles II new colonies were established in Pennsylvania and North and South Carolina—named, of course, after the king.

The Carolinas and Virginia were distant names, but New York was close by and geographically significant because the Hudson River brought ships and supplies near the frontier of New France. And along that frontier lived the Iroquois, who kept the colony in a constant state of fear.

Indian Diplomacy

Louis and his minister Colbert had a three-pronged strategy for New France. The first item was to make it a regular part of the French state. So in 1663 New France became a royal province, similar to the provinces of European France, and a royal governor was dispatched to represent the king. But true to Louis's conception of absolutism, the authority even of very important officials was strictly limited. This was especially the case with provincial governors, who were chosen from the nobility, men of dignity and honour, to be sure, but not to be trusted with unlimited power. The real power rested with a second royal official, the intendant, who managed finance, economic policy, and civil affairs generally, including justice and the courts. Finally, and rivalling the governor, there was the spiritual power, the bishop, with authority over such things as morals and education. Officials who offended the bishop risked excommunication from the Church, a state that under the pious Louis XIV wasn't likely to lead to promotion and might easily lead to something much worse. The bishop was also a link in government: because the basic unit of organization in New France was the parish, the parish priest accordingly took on a certain importance as a link to the bishop and the capital by acting as a source of information or a conduit for communication.

At its best, the administration of New France might be described as being in a state of creative tension. At its worst, the bifurcated powers of the colony produced stalemate and dissonance. From the point of view of the French monarchy, however, even an ineffective government was to be preferred to an autonomous province. An ineffective government, after all, was a dependent government, relying on France, months away by sea, to solve its problems.

The governor, the intendant, and the bishop were periodically reunited in a Sovereign Council. Part court, part cabinet, the Council acted by consensus and, where that was lacking, deferred to its presiding officer, the intendant.[1] The Council decided the more important legal issues (smaller ones were left to the intendant alone), but the Council's judgments could be and frequently were appealed to France, at least at first. The volume of appeals eventually became so great that in 1677 Colbert sent them all back. After that the Council was effectively New France's court of last resort.[2]

The Sovereign Council sat in Quebec. For purposes of local administration, lesser courts sat in Trois-Rivières and Montreal (where there were also local governors and sub-intendants); their decisions could be appealed to the Council in Quebec.

That didn't mean, however, that government was fixed in the capital. The governor's duties varied with the seasons, and summer was the season for trade and diplomacy with New France's trading partners in the interior, the Indian nations of the Great Lakes and the north. They came to Montreal every summer, the Iroquois permitting, and engaged in a round of feasting and, often enough, drinking. (Threats by the bishop to excommunicate anyone engaged in selling liquor to the Indians were ineffective.) There were ceremonies and exchanges of gifts, and for proper solemnity, the presence of the governor was frequently desirable. And so the governor moved to Montreal every summer, either to stay and feast or as a base for expeditions into the interior, for most of the governors of New France also led their troops in the field, as circumstances dictated.[3] (One governor, the comte de Frontenac, was well into his seventies when he led an expedition against the Iroquois—in his case the last of many.)

After the imposition of royal government there were troops to command. As a sign of the new order of things, troops were shipped from France with a new intendant, Jean Talon, who met Colbert's demanding standards for the post; Talon's first task was to ensure that the soldiers were fed, housed, and paid. The regiment of Carignan-Salières comprised about a thousand men, including no fewer than 117 officers, five of whom were over seventy and thirty over sixty years of age. The troops rioted when they learned where they were going, but willing or not they were shovelled aboard ship at La Rochelle, and arrived at Quebec in the summer of 1665.

Their mission was to overawe or if necessary defeat the Iroquois. Some of the Iroquois were willing enough to be overawed, and sent peaceful representations to Montreal. As for the most hostile, the Mohawks, the French tried a march into their territory in January 1666. Luckily the expedition avoided disaster, and the troops were able to reprovision themselves from the Dutch merchants at Albany. (The French learned, for the first time, that the English had conquered the Dutch colony; neither side knew that England and France were also at war.) A second, summer campaign followed, which achieved the desired effect: peace was made with the weakened Iroquois, who'd been undermined by renewed epidemics more than by the French.

The respite wasn't permanent. There would be more expeditions, and more Iroquois raids on New France, most notably in the 1680s, but there was enough abatement to allow for immigration and settlement. This was part of Colbert's plan.

THE SETTLEMENT OF NEW FRANCE

Over the 150 years of New France's existence, approximately ten thousand immigrants came to the colony. Almost all were French, direct from France; and almost all were, as Louis XIV desired, Catholic. They were not, most of them, a hardy race of peasants of Norman stock. The largest group came from Poitou, the region east of La Rochelle, but few of the western provinces of France were unrepresented, from Aquitaine in the south to Picardy in the north. A substantial number came from Paris, and some from other cities. Some came by compulsion, via the army, or as punishment for some minor illegality at home. Soldiers could obtain early release by staying in New France, and many found the offer too attractive to refuse. Others were indentured servants, trading their labour for a passage to New France. As the geographers Cole Harris and John Warkentin observe, "most [immigrants] came to Canada because they were sent."[4]

New France wasn't exactly a tempting prospect. By the mid-seventeenth century two things were known about the colony: it was the haunt of marauding Indians, and it was bitterly cold. Cold it certainly was.

Temperatures were much lower than in virtually any part of France. The growing season was shorter. French crops did not take easily to the Canadian climate, and some could not be grown at all. And before anything could be grown a forest had to be cut down, a hardship not faced by the French of France since Roman times. Finally, although the valley of the St. Lawrence was fertile, the lowlands did not extend very far either north or south of the river—eight kilometres at Quebec, forty-eight at Montreal. Beyond lay the Canadian Shield to the north and the Appalachians to the south. New France stretched in the middle, a ribbon following the St. Lawrence.

To organize the settlement, the government, like the Hundred Associates before it, relied on seigneurs, petty nobles to whom land was granted (seigneuries) in return for attracting farmers to till it. The farmers didn't own the land, but rented it from the seigneur. In theory the seigneur was lord of the manor, like his European counterparts, but in New France reality and theory frequently clashed. Seigneurs seldom had the capital to develop their land, to build a proper manor house and a mill where their tenants would grind their wheat. Nor could they hope to make up the difference from rents, which were low, or calculated in terms of labour rather than cash. Frequently, to survive, seigneurs either worked in the fields like their purported inferiors or moved to town in search of government jobs that alone could keep them in the state to which they would have wished to be accustomed. Many of the gentry of New France found employment in the military, either in local levies or in the army or navy of old France. They would uphold the French state, but as its employees rather than as semi-feudal grandees. In theory, the seigneurial system provided for authority and stability. In fact, it did nothing of the kind.

The pattern of settlement depended on the river, which until the middle of the eighteenth century was the only reliable means of transportation. Seigneurs and farmers sought river frontage, effectively for road access, and the result was narrow farms stretching away from the water. As roads developed near the only three settlements of any size, farmers did move away from the St. Lawrence, but this was a late development.

Ironically, although the government sponsored and maintained the gentry of New France, it also undermined their authority through another local institution, the militia. This was first organized in Montreal and then extended to the rest of the colony. Every able-bodied male between sixteen and sixty belonged to the militia, and the force was organized in each parish under a *capitaine de milice*—militia captain—who usually wasn't the local seigneur. Nobles were, however, exempt from militia service. (The post of *capitaine de milice* survived the French regime, and endured even into the twentieth century in rural areas of Quebec.)[5]

Others besides nobles avoided militia service. Compulsory service depended on whether one was around to be compelled, and many, males in the prime of life engaged in the fur trade, were not. It was a cause for resentment, but until the very end of New France, that resentment did not extend to refusing the military service on which the defence of the colony notionally depended.

Jean Talon, when he agreed to go to New France as intendant, did so on condition that it be a limited-term appointment. He also went on condition that he could trade privately in furs, which he also did, using some of the privileges of his position.[6] It is generally agreed that he was active and intelligent, and he instituted what may be called Canada's first "industrial policy." It was a mercantilist policy, founded on the theory that a successful state must maximize its own economic activity in competition with other, similar states. (And indeed other states, especially England, did have similar policies.) Manufacturing was encouraged by subsidies direct and indirect, and imports discouraged. Making New France self-supporting, encouraging it to earn its way, and directing it to contribute to the economy of France were logical objectives for Talon and Colbert.

Farming required manpower, however, and manpower was in short supply. In part this was because of underpopulation and in part it was because the fur trade lured young men in the prime of their working life. But over time the demands and profits of the fur trade levelled off, so that by the early eighteenth century farm labour was sufficient to provide not merely subsistence but a modest surplus in wheat, which was then sold in the French West Indies once domestic needs had been met.

Attempts to establish industry in New France were less successful. Gristmills were an aspect of seigneurial tenure, and grain had to be ground. Since high shipping costs inhibited competitive imports, effectively there was no competition—but the same high shipping costs made New French products uncompetitive back in France. Talon established a brewery and a tannery, and encouraged the production of iron and hemp. The results were almost uniformly disappointing, but even repeated disappointment didn't discourage the French government from a policy of industrial creation.

The key to the economy of New France was twofold. On the one hand was the fur trade, which to the end of the French regime and beyond enriched its participants, Indian or white. On the other was land, and plenty of it. The availability of land for farming meant crops for feeding the towns as well as the farmers and their families. The inhabitants of New France married young—earlier than in Europe. Absent contraception or any overpowering reason for limiting their families, they produced a child every two years. The resultant birth rate was higher than in France, though comparable to that of colonial New England. At the same time the death rate was lower, or slower, than in Europe, perhaps because society, once the Iroquois wars were over, was more tranquil and dangers to life and limb fewer.[7] The population therefore expanded, from three thousand in the 1660s to ten thousand in the 1680s, and eventually to seventy-five thousand.

The nature of French government, and French government policy, also produced an unusual distribution of population in the colony. We shall consider the policy below; for the time being we should note that the official establishment was large, certainly by comparison with the English colonies to the south. Troops and officials had to be supported, and the governor's miniature court maintained. Committed to a model of society in which nobility was to be recognized and rewarded, the government obliged with jobs, pensions, and gifts.[8]

In some respects, and certainly in times of war, New France was more or less a large garrison. During the Iroquois wars of the 1660s the king's professional soldiers numbered a quarter of the colony's total population. But these soldiers weren't replaced, though many chose to stay on in New France as settlers. In the 1680s the French government sent *troupes de la marine* under the authority of the minister of marine who was responsible for the colonies. These professional soldiers remained at the governor's disposal until the collapse of New France. At first they were recruited and officered by natives of France, but after 1690 the inhabitants of New France—the noble inhabitants of New France, that is—were eligible for officers' commissions in the service. By the 1750s the majority of the officers of the *troupes de la marine* had been born in Canada, but their soldiers, as before, were recruited in France.

At the end of the French regime, in 1760, there were only three settlements of any size, Quebec, Montreal, and Trois-Rivières. Quebec alone had eight thousand people, and Montreal five thousand. As Harris and Warkentin point out, this meant that a quarter of New France's population was urban, a higher ratio than in any of the British colonies to the south.[9] On the other hand, three-quarters of the population (estimated at around seventy to seventy-five thousand in 1760) lived in the countryside, and, for the most part, contentedly.

ACADIA

New France was more than the valley of the St. Lawrence. The fisheries had brought the French to North America, to the waters off Newfoundland and then up the St. Lawrence to harvest fur as well as fish. The first temporary French settlements had been along the Atlantic coast, in Acadia. These had been abandoned, but very slowly, and during the seventeenth century French settlers returned.

The centre of settlement was a tiny French fort at Port Royal on the east side of the Bay of Fundy. The settlers diked the marshlands for their farms, a practice still in use. Small it may have been, but insignificance did not protect it against English freebooters, and the settlement changed hands several times in the mid-seventeenth century. Nevertheless, when Acadia was finally returned to France in 1670, it had 350 French inhabitants, and by 1700, twelve hundred.

The return to French control seems to have been a signal for the colony to expand: new settlements were founded on the Isthmus of Chignecto, linking what is now Nova Scotia to New Brunswick, and along the Minas Basin. Interestingly, though England and France were frequently at war, the Acadians had no objection to trading with the enemy, actual or potential, and at times proved reluctant indeed to cooperate with the French authorities in turning away New English ships, even in time of war.

Acadia's best protection was peaceful relations between England and France. The long coastline couldn't be defended, and relative proximity to New England meant that English ships were a constant opportunity for trade but a constant threat in times of war.

Expansion and the Fur Trade

The real advantage of New France's position on the St. Lawrence became clear only after the temporary end of the Iroquois wars in the 1660s. The means to travel were at hand—light, portable birchbark canoes, easy to make and easy to replace, capable of navigating shallow waters, and easy to carry around rapids or from one river system to another. The *coureurs de bois* would drop into their canoes at Montreal and travel up the Ottawa River on their way to the *pays d'en haut*, the rich fur lands north of Lake Superior.

The fur traders' enterprise did not always please the colonial authorities, and a clash between the rulers of the colony and two particularly adventurous traders, Pierre Radisson and Médard Chouart de Groseilliers, provoked the two to take their business, and their knowledge of the fur trade, to England and the court of King Charles II.

The result was the foundation of yet another trading syndicate, chartered by the king in May 1670—the Hudson's Bay Company. Its purpose was to seek its shareholders' fortune in the northern interior of North America, not via the St. Lawrence or the Hudson but through the discovery by the explorer Henry Hudson in 1610 of an interior sea, Hudson Bay. Hudson had perished, but his bay lingered on in the fringes of cartography. Was Hudson Bay, forbidding as it was, really the opening of the fabled Straits of Anian, leading to the Pacific, China, and wealth? And what of the fur trade? True, the Bay was blocked by ice from November until June every year, and had a shoreline of swamp, rock, and muskeg, but what was discouraging to humans was delightful to beavers. If Radisson and Groseilliers were to be believed, the Indians beyond the Bay would jump at the chance of trading with the English.

Charles II obligingly claimed for England the lands of the Hudson Bay watershed, an unknown quantity then, but a vast piece of real estate stretching as far as the Rockies in the west and covering most of what would become the Canadian prairies. He then assigned the territory to the Hudson's Bay Company, which in turn dispatched ships loaded with trade goods to the Bay. The Company proposed to establish permanent trading posts along the shores of Hudson Bay and its southern extension, James Bay. (The reasoning was that only a fixed establishment could reliably attract Indians with furs on a regular basis.) It took several tries, since those who were unlucky enough to winter in the Bay, and lucky enough to survive it, did not wish to repeat the experience.[10] Endless winters and the experience of scurvy were serious deterrents, but not so serious as to prevent, finally, the establishment of a series of English posts by the mid-1670s.

It didn't take long for the authorities in New France to notice. Louis XIV had sent out a new governor, the comte de Frontenac. Frontenac quickly concluded that the only sure source of wealth in New France was the fur trade, and in order to secure it he was anxious to expand his colony into the interior and establish trading posts of his own. It was for the good of the colony, to be sure, but in an age when public and private interests were often one and the same, Frontenac hoped to reap personal gain as well. He attempted to lure Radisson and Groseilliers back into the French service, and sent emissaries to visit the English posts on Hudson Bay. He

The Exploration of Canada

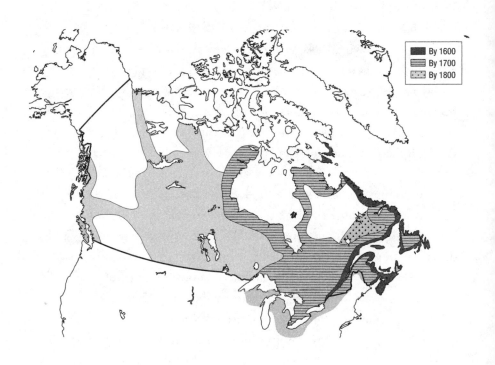

By 1600
By 1700
By 1800

had good reason to do so: his agents reported that the Indians of the interior, members of the Cree nation, were diverting furs to the Bay that otherwise would have gone to the French.

Commercial rivalry between the English and French continued through the 1670s and into the 1680s. The competition couldn't be taken to extremes, however, for England and France were at peace. Louis XIV and his Stuart cousins, Charles II and his brother and successor, James II, were on amiable terms. Louis was especially anxious to encourage James, a Catholic, in his attempts to promote Catholicism in a stubbornly Protestant country. James for his part was well aware that he needed French help, and was accordingly inclined not to offend his cousin. And so an unlikely link emerged between religious politics in Europe and the competitive international slaughter of the beaver in the lands beyond Hudson Bay.

A new governor in New France, the marquis de Denonville, became convinced that the survival of his colony demanded action against the English, and not merely in Hudson Bay but in New York too. He could do little directly about New York, where the Iroquois were in the way and once again at war with the French. As for Hudson Bay, in 1686 Denonville sent a small expedition with ambiguous instructions. The French, led by a young officer, the chevalier de Troyes, and a young Montrealer, Pierre le Moyne, Sieur d'Iberville, seized Fort Albany, on James Bay, from the English.

The English of the Bay and "the French of Canada" were thus already at war when fate removed James II from the English throne in November 1688. The Protestant country rejected its Catholic monarch and placed another cousin, the Dutch William of Orange, on the English throne. James's attempts to regain his crown were unavailing, and he lived out his life as a pensioner of Louis XIV. William of Orange became William III of England, and went to war with France.

The war between England and France was part of a larger conflict, formally called the War of the League of Augsburg, and in North America, more simply, King William's War. It lasted until 1697. In its North

American phase it merged with the existing French war against the Iroquois. That war in turn was part of an even larger confrontation between the Iroquois and the Algonquin peoples of the interior, and though the war is mostly remembered and recorded for such events as the bloody Iroquois raid on Lachine outside Montreal in 1689, it was really the Algonquins who fought the Iroquois to a standstill and finally defeated them. The French did their bit by organizing the various tribes into a single alliance with a common purpose and then supplying the allies. Frontenac, who enjoyed a second term as governor from 1690 to 1698, led his own expeditions into Iroquois territory. So while the French role was crucial, it was the allies who had the main task of, finally, rolling the Iroquois back into their heartland south of Lake Ontario.[11]

Frontenac also had the task of defending Quebec against a seaborne expedition from New England in 1690, and he faced down the English with his customary bravado. On the island of Newfoundland, where fishing berths were gradually developing into permanent settlements, the French led by d'Iberville did their best to drive the English off. But they were successful only in part, which meant, in effect, that they weren't successful at all. War raged in the north as well, as French and English leapfrogged around Hudson Bay in pursuit of victory and profit. In Europe and in North America, however, neither side achieved a decisive advantage, and the war ended inconclusively with New York still in English hands, New France still French, and Hudson Bay and Newfoundland still divided between them.

The peace of 1697 was probably of less significance for New France than was another peace, concluded in Montreal in 1701 under Frontenac's successor, Hector-Louis de Callière. This "great peace" put an end to the French and Algonquin war with the Iroquois. It was a peace the Iroquois had to have. Having it, they could continue as an important factor in the balance of power in North America between English and French, but in a larger sense the Iroquois were no longer decisive.

Nor were the French confined any longer to the St. Lawrence Valley. They had gone north, as we have seen, to Hudson Bay, and west to the head of Lake Superior. French posts were established at Fort Frontenac (now Kingston, Ontario) and Detroit. One of Frontenac's protégés, René-Robert Cavelier de la Salle, found a route from the Great Lakes basin to the Mississippi River, and then descended the Mississippi, reaching the Gulf of Mexico in 1682. He claimed the Mississippi Valley, naturally, for his master, Louis XIV.

THE SCENT OF EMPIRE

With hindsight, we can see that Louis XIV and his empire were past their apogee in the 1690s. Louis had taken the French state and organized it for war. Until the 1690s his wars were generally successful, with French prestige growing along with his conquests. Even Louis's distant Canadian colony was stabilized through a mixture of warlike policy and prudent economic development.

What should be done next? Caution dictated consolidation; France had an opportunity to recover from Louis's wars. And New France finally had an opportunity to escape from the shadow of the Iroquois wars and to develop in peace. The fur trade had reached a balance apparently favourable to France and French interests, even if the English had never been chased completely from Hudson Bay.

Louis did not make these choices. Instead he pursued fortune, as he saw it, in the expansion of French influence and prestige. He placed his grandson on the throne of Spain in defiance of the powers of Europe. In North America he determined to create an empire out of his explorers' discoveries. France wouldn't attempt to invade or destroy the existing English colonies along the Atlantic coast; rather, it would surround them by dominating the Mississippi Valley—named Louisiana after its guiding spirit.

By these policies Louis sought to expand his power and perpetuate his strategic advantage—the advantage that his wars up to that point had gained for him. Instead, he set in motion a new cycle of wars that would end in the destruction of the French Empire in North America.

4

THE WARS
FOR AMERICA (1)

Major-General James Wolfe explains collateral damage to a young Quebec couple
in misogynist fashion. "Mercy, general," they beg. "My orders are firm," he replies.
"For every man captured, a bullet. For every woman—two." The drawing
is by Wolfe's irreverent subordinate, Brigadier-General George Townshend.

For over a hundred years, from 1689 to 1815, North America was the seat of war. The wars were at first extensions of other and sometimes older conflicts—between the Iroquois and the French, or the Iroquois and the Algonquins, for example—but they fitted into the rivalry between the French and the English, and between the Spanish and the English, and were fought on a global scale.

The wars resulted in the destruction of the military capacity and hence the independence of the Indian nations of North America. They marked the rise of Great Britain and the relative decline of France's ability to sustain an overseas empire. And they brought about the division of North America along unanticipated lines, with the French settlers of Canada as part of a British Empire and most of the British colonists no longer British but American.

The French government set the scene. Unable to match the flood of immigration into the English colonies, the French decided to build posts in the interior. The peace of 1701 among the Indians and the French allowed the latter to travel freely along the Great Lakes. To secure their position, the French minister of marine, the official responsible for the colonies, established a fort at Detroit. Detroit would sustain the fur trade, to be sure, but its real purpose was to assist France's Indian allies in blocking the expansion of the English.

Detroit fitted into a strategy that connected Quebec to newly founded Louisiana on the Gulf of Mexico. Theoretically connected by the Mississippi River and the Great Lakes–St. Lawrence system, the French Empire in North America now extended, at least in maps, from

Newfoundland to the Gulf of Mexico and on to the tropics, to the French island colonies in the West Indies.

As the mapmakers depicted it, New France was vast, dwarfing the English colonies on the coast and overshadowing French islands like Guadeloupe, Martinique, and Saint Domingue, the modern Haiti. Over half the population of French America was Indian—indeed well over half. France directly ruled very little of North America, and very little of New France, Acadia, and Louisiana. It controlled only the valley of the St. Lawrence, a few pockets of settlement in Acadia, and a couple of posts in the interior. In effect, size and authority cancelled each other out.

Economically, New France was tiny compared with any one of the French islands, Guadeloupe, Martinique, or Saint Domingue, with their lucrative sugar exports. Despite the best efforts of the intendants and the encouragement of the home government, whatever profit accrued in New France came from the fur trade. Even there profits fluctuated wildly. In the 1690s the government even attempted, briefly, to close the west to traders, because too many furs had swamped the French market.

Nor were the interior forts simply little outposts of France. The western fur factories were intended to be rented out to entrepreneurs, who bore the costs and took the profits. This should have meant that the cost of government, which was really the cost of asserting French sovereignty in the wilderness, was borne by the market. Unfortunately, theory and reality only occasionally coincided. In times of too little profit, or none at all, the posts were handed back to the government and the entrepreneur became a civil servant until things looked up on the capricious Parisian fur market. For the government proposed to maintain its posts, and the empire they represented, at all costs.

QUEEN ANNE'S WAR

The war of 1689–97 between England and France was inconclusive. In North America it changed little; it might even be said to have preserved a French advantage through the seizure of the English Hudson Bay forts and aggression against the English fishery in Newfoundland. There were no large armies, few professional soldiers, and certainly no great fleets on the western side of the Atlantic: the outcome of the war was decided in Europe, and for European reasons.

Louis XIV did not abandon his dreams of empire. The decisions to found a post at Detroit, to establish a colony in Louisiana, and to construct a series of alliances among the Indians of the interior were a minor and local aspect of a larger French policy.

In 1700, Louis did two things. On the death of his cousin, the exiled James II of England, he recognized James's son as king of England. The aggressively Catholic king of France gave credence to a Catholic claimant (or "pretender") to the English throne. Second, Louis secured the Spanish throne for his grandson, who became Philip V of Spain. Philip had a claim to that throne, but so did the Austrian royal family. The Pyrenees notwithstanding, France and Spain united in a family alliance; perhaps on Louis's death they would be united in fact. It would certainly be a formidable combination, all the more so when France and Spain's American empires were added to the equation.

The war that resulted occurred mostly during the reign of Anne, Protestant daughter of James II and half-sister of his son the pretender, the so-called James III. In Europe the war was known as the War of the Spanish Succession, for obvious reasons. In English America it was remembered as "Queen Anne's War," for equally obvious reasons.

The war was mostly fought in Europe, and the details of the battles on that continent need not detain us. The strategy of the war was nevertheless important, as it affected not only the war underway but the wars to come in North America. The English enjoyed what might be called an economic advantage—that is, English finances were soundly based, allowing the government in London to build and maintain a large navy that gradually overshadowed that of France. The French might have been able to match the English at sea, but they were tied down in endless battles in Germany against the Austrian and English armies. In these battles Louis's generals were generally unsuccessful, and as the war progressed it moved from Germany and Belgium into France. The lesson, imperfectly realized and sometimes forgotten, was that the American empire, English or French, was best defended in Europe.

In America New France was bolstered by two main factors. First, there were hundreds of kilometres of trackless wilderness between the French colony and the nearest English settlements in New England and New York. Second, there were the Indians.

The Iroquois did not take a major role in Queen Anne's War. Their interest lay in keeping both sides out of their territory and their affairs, and taking whatever advantage they could from battles fought by others. Some of the English colonists considered this an entirely sensible attitude, especially after Indian raids demonstrated how vulnerable their frontier settlements really were. In the middle of the war, emissaries from Massachusetts visited Quebec and negotiated with the French authorities in the hope of securing some kind of modus vivendi between their colonies and New France.[1] No agreement was reached, perhaps because the French authorities did not take the possibility of a threat from the scattered and disunited English colonies very seriously.

In fact, not all the English colonies were equally at risk during the war. New York largely escaped French incursions, but New England was a different matter. The European colonists had no great military advantage over the Indians along their border: the militia was ill-trained and prone to panic, and the Indians preyed on the fears of the English. As settlement pushed out from the coast in New England it became extremely vulnerable.

The settlers naturally feared violence and massacre. They also feared captivity. In the wars between 1689 and 1760 roughly sixteen hundred New Englanders were captured by Indian raiders and became, as a Boston minister put it, "Captives, that are every minute looking when they shall be roasted alive, to make a sport and a feast, for the most execrable cannibals. Captives, that must endure the most bitter frost and cold, without rags enough to cover their nakedness. Captives, that have scarce a bit of meat allow'd them to put into their mouths, but what a dog would hardly meddle with; captives, that must see their nearest relations butchered before their eyes, yet be afraid of letting those eyes drop a tear."[2]

Sometimes the English were massacred, or killed after torture. The torture was spectacularly gruesome, of a kind that by the eighteenth century in Europe was performed behind the walls of fortresses or prisons. There was also cannibalism, which in Europe was regarded with the utmost horror and aversion. Many prisoners, probably most, were more kindly treated, and were marched away to Indian settlements and adopted into Indian families.[3] Many were later ransomed, but many others remained with their captors, absorbed into the culture and society that had kidnapped them. Despite a requirement in the eventual peace treaty to secure the return of captives, some never came back.

The New England colonies hadn't the means to reply against the Indians or their sponsors, the distant French in Quebec. They did have the means to harass the nearest and most accessible French colony, Acadia. Seaborne raids distressed some of the outlying French settlements in 1704, but did not attempt the tiny capital, Port Royal. Two further raids on Port Royal in 1707 had no effect. Projects to invade New France overland aroused some interest in the colonies, but the home government in London eventually vetoed them.

Finally, in 1710, the colonists had their way. Reinforced with ships and men provided by the home government, they appeared before Port Royal in September, besieged it for a week, and received the surrender of its garrison, outnumbered ten to one. A combined Acadian and Indian attempt to retake the fort in 1711 failed.[4]

In Europe the war was going badly for the French. Louis XIV sued for peace but refused the terms he was offered. The British government then decided that it would strike the French overseas, and in 1711 mounted a large and expensive sea expedition with the objective of taking Quebec. Sixty-four ships carrying five thousand troops—more than the population of Quebec—sailed from Britain. Poor charts, bad weather, and indifferent navigation defeated the fleet in the lower St. Lawrence: eight ships were wrecked, and the British turned back.[5]

The political balance in Britain was shifting. The war party, the Whigs, lost the support of the queen and then lost power, and their Tory successors were anxious to make peace as quickly as possible. Peace still took some years, but eventually, in 1713 at Utrecht, Holland, a treaty was signed.

The Treaty of Utrecht gave France a better peace than Louis XIV might have expected. Bankrupt, the French government needed peace badly, and some of the terms at Utrecht reflected that need. As far as America was concerned, the French gave up the Hudson Bay posts, "all Nova Scotia or Acadia," and Newfoundland. They managed to keep the islands of the Gulf of St. Lawrence, including the two largest, Isle St. Jean (now Prince Edward Island) and Cape Breton. (They had been ready to give up Cape Breton, even though its loss would have bottled up New France behind a screen of British islands and bases.) They did not give up Louisiana, or the interior forts, and as a result the imperial strategy of 1701 survived.

There were ambiguities in the treaty. There was no map showing the boundaries of Acadia, and the French interpreted them as narrowly as possible, meaning the Nova Scotian mainland only. The French inhabitants of ancient Acadia, now Nova Scotia, could stay and remain Catholic, "as far as the laws of Great Britain do allow." It was the British turn to be ambiguous, for British law was discouraging, to say the least, where Catholics were concerned.

Catholic or not, the British wanted the Acadians to remain in Nova Scotia, for without their farms the position of the few British troops there was doubtful indeed. The French authorities, meanwhile, urged the Acadians to leave for the remaining French territories, particularly Cape Breton Island. In the event, most of the Acadians stayed, unwilling to abandon their property for the hazard of a new colony. Yet they informed the British authorities that their allegiance to the British crown had strict limits—they would not fight against the French in any future war. Dismayed, the British accepted these conditions—conditionally, as it were, for as long as they had to.[6]

AN INTERVAL OF PEACE

France and Great Britain remained at peace for thirty years, though the British fought practically everyone else in that period. The French government recognized that it had lost the war, and that Louis XIV's bellicose policy had been fruitless. France needed time to recover under his successor, Louis XV, who came to the throne, aged five, on his great-grandfather's death in 1715.

New France needed the peace as well. The strategic advantages that had given Britain the victory in 1713 hadn't changed. The British had a larger economy, more disposable revenue, and a larger fleet than the French. If war came again, New France could be cut off by sea, by an enemy who could choose the time and place of attack, as long as it was in range of the ocean. Needing constant supply from France, and dependent on the transport of furs to Europe, New France had little choice but to appreciate the benefits of peace and pray that they continue.

The benefits of peace were apparent. With little immigration, New France doubled its population every thirty years. Settlement spread back from the riverbanks, with long, narrow farms reaching back in regular *rangs* or concessions. Parallel to the river, roads linked the farmhouses.

The houses resembled those of western France, particularly Normandy. Sometimes settlers constructed dwellings of large vertical timbers, with clay or rubble as infill, a common French technique. They may well have been the first in North America to build log cabins—horizontal logs with clay infill, the classic log cabin found everywhere in English-speaking North America, but not actually introduced in the English colonies until the eighteenth century.[7] The log house was and remained the dominant rural dwelling in New France and Quebec.

The towns of New France were more likely to be built of stone by the eighteenth century. Frequent fires disposed of most of their wooden predecessors, and the authorities mandated stone replacements. It was, however, the prosperity of the towns, with their steady diet of government contracts and military pay, that made the inhabitants prosperous enough to afford building in stone. In Quebec, crowded on a stubby peninsula, the houses were high and narrow in the Lower Town, beneath the cliffs; in the more fashionable Upper Town, seat of the governor and the bishop, houses were lower but more spacious.

The governor and the bishop lived ceremoniously and, as far as colonial circumstances permitted, comfortably. The governor had his own guard, presenting arms and beating drums when he passed, even if only to the neighbouring church. But it was the Church that had pride of place in Quebec, with numerous churches, convents, and a Jesuit college that a Swedish visitor described, in 1749, as four times larger than the governor's "palace," and "the finest building in town."[8]

From Quebec the governor—properly the "governor general"—presided over an empire millions of hectares in extent. Most of his "subjects" weren't French, nor white, but rather Indians whose relationship to the French crown would certainly have puzzled the authorities in Paris. To the Indians, the governor general was Onontio—a Mohawk version of the name of an early governor, Montmagny, subsequently applied to all his successors. Onontio was father, protector, and gift-giver, for as an intendant put it, referring to France's Indian allies, "These tribes never transact any business without making presents to illustrate and confirm their words."[9]

But which tribes? They were mostly the Algonquian-speaking nations of the Great Lakes region—the Ottawas, for example—but they also included a sizeable number of Iroquois (especially Mohawks) as well as the remnants of the Hurons and other tribes dispersed during the wars of the seventeenth century. The Mohawks were divided, some favouring the English, some the French. Some had come to the French as refugees, others as Catholic converts, and they were given land on the fringes of New France, outside Montreal (for the Mohawks) and at Ancienne Lorette outside Quebec City. These settlements were the direct ancestors of the later Indian reserve system adopted by the British and Canadian governments.

In council the governor was addressed as "father," and he replied to his "children," but it was not a relationship that allowed the French to command and force the Indians to obey. As in typical families, relationships weren't always harmonious, and were spiced by the existence of a British rival for the Indians' attention and custom. British traders to the north and south of New France, around Hudson Bay and in the Ohio River Valley, challenged French domination of the fur trade; and without this domination the French claims to the interior would shrivel and die, for the economics of fur were indissolubly linked to the pretensions of empire.

Yet in many, indeed most, respects the French succeeded in sustaining and expanding their fur empire. Operating from a very few posts, principally Detroit and Michilimackinac on the Great Lakes, the French scooped up most of the furs exported from North America. Confronted with the establishment of Hudson's Bay Company posts, in the 1720s and 1730s French traders and explorers pressed onward, penetrating the Great Plains and arriving in sight of the Rockies. As usual they were looking for a route to the Pacific, which as always eluded them, but they were also seeking to attract the Plains Indians to the French fur market, and in this they were successful. The Bay traders noticed their supplies drying up and their profits falling, but it wasn't enough to stimulate them to explore the interior themselves.

The French interior posts were lightly staffed and sparsely garrisoned. Aside from their economic function and residual symbolic value, they also served as way stations on an interior communications line that linked Quebec with New Orleans—a thin thread of reality that bound the parts of the French Empire together.

Most of the fur-trading enterprise depended not on permanent traders but on annual fur brigades setting forth from Montreal, year after year, for the interior. These men were born in the colony—and were increasingly known as *Canadiens* to distinguish them from their increasingly distant French cousins. They had to be relatively young, healthy, and vigorous to survive the rigours of the voyage, and they had to be adventurous and adaptable too, for they would be living in societies whose customs and expectations were far removed from those of France, or even New France.

Naturally they came mostly off the farm, and to the farm most of them would eventually return. In the meantime they would experience life without governors, priests, or military officers, once they had passed Michilimackinac.

Only traders bound for Detroit and Michilimackinac could hope to see their homes again in the same year. The others, most of the fur traders, were bound to be away for two or three years, without serious hope of news from home. They took society as they found it, living in Indian villages, eating as the Indians did, and finding consolation with Indian women. Such unions weren't always based on physical need or desire, but conferred advantage on both parties—affording Frenchmen an entrée into Native society and valuable links to the Native political systems.[10] Some formed strong attachments and stayed with their women and their mixed-race children, generally called the mixed ones, or the Métis. At one point in the early eighteenth century, a witness called the French of the interior and their Indian neighbours, allies, and hosts "one people," and certainly so many Frenchmen adapted to Indian ways that there is some justification in the comment.[11]

The Métis often became traders on their own, symbolizing what the historian Richard White has called "the Middle Ground" between the European colonies on the coast and the Native societies to the west. In the eighteenth century the Middle Ground was always expanding—a new society neither purely European nor purely Indian, reflecting the conflicting pressures and demands of each side. The Middle Ground would not, however, determine which empire would prevail in the contest for North America.

The French strategy of alliance with the Indians was as much the product of necessity as of an enlightened refusal to subjugate the Native population of New France. The number of people in New France wasn't sufficient to support the colonization of the interior. The French had moved into the largely empty lands of the St. Lawrence in the seventeenth century, and there they stayed, with more than enough land for the immigrants and their descendants until the end of the eighteenth century. The

French frequently pointed out to their Indian allies and clients the contrast between the benign French incursions, characterized by presents and protection, and the British colonization that displaced the Indians and gobbled up the land along the frontier.

Actual French settlements in the interior were few—a few farms to supply the needs of trading posts, and forts like Detroit or St. Louis on the Mississippi. Detroit was the largest, and relations there between the French and the Indians weren't always peaceful. Farther south in Louisiana were larger French colonies, for example around Natchez on the Mississippi. There, French brutality and arrogance produced a full-scale Indian rebellion, with the massacre of 227 French settlers and the capture of fifty French women and children in 1729. Given the meagre numbers of the French in Louisiana, this was a notable setback for the colony.

Retaliation followed. The French enlisted other tribes, enemies of the Natchez Indians, and killed and enslaved as many as they could find. "When it served their purpose," the historian Alan Taylor writes, "the French massacred and enslaved natives as vigorously as did the British." A French priest drew the moral of the experience: "God wishes that they [the Indians] yield their places to new peoples," as they certainly did.[12]

THE BRITISH CHALLENGE

The British Empire had emerged as the prime challenger to French supremacy in North America. It was no longer English, but British. Dynastic marriages, the merger of the English and Scottish royal families, and the Reformation, which converted most of the English and Scots into Protestants, created the foundation of a common state that was constitutionally united in 1707 into the kingdom of Great Britain. Its inhabitants became British, an invented identity that nevertheless took hold. It would be British armies, not English, that invaded New France, and the Scots became the most enthusiastic proponents of "Britishness."

The British monarchy was a Protestant monarchy. The kings and queens must be Protestants, and only Protestants could be elected to the

House of Commons or hold office. Good Britons held the Catholic, "Popish," practices of France to be abhorrent. The French were dreadful not only because they were French—witness the long history of medieval wars between England and France—but because they were slavish followers of the Pope in Rome. In an age of enlightenment and increasing tolerance, not every Briton held these views, but they ignored them at their peril.[13] As late as 1780 London was convulsed by anti-Catholic rioting, and religion (at least the Catholic–Protestant variant of it) remained a lively and often determining issue in the politics of Great Britain and all English-speaking peoples well into the twentieth century—and beyond.

Great Britain was smaller in population and size than rival France. It was, however, increasingly rich, and by the mid-eighteenth century had outstripped France in wealth, industry—and tax revenues.[14] The taxes went to support wars with France and the construction of a fleet that was second to none in Europe. All this, it should be emphasized, had little to do with North America; the wars of 1689–97 and 1702–13 were overwhelmingly European conflicts that projected into the colonies and not the other way around. The colonies contributed little to British finances, and those on the mainland of North America were economically insignificant in terms of trade with Great Britain until the middle of the eighteenth century.

France nevertheless remained rich—rich enough to try to compensate for the disadvantages conferred on it by the Treaty of Utrecht of 1713. The cession of Acadia and Newfoundland to Great Britain imperilled sea communications from France to New France. There remained only the islands of the Gulf of St. Lawrence, especially the easternmost, Cape Breton Island. Investigation revealed a large harbour on the eastern shore, and the site, named Louisbourg after the French king, Louis XV, became a French fortress.

Louisbourg was designed as a naval base and a commercial harbour, a point of refuge for French ships pursued by the British in time of war. Its elaborate and expensive defences, supposedly the best that military science could design, guarded the harbour with fortifications and plentiful artillery. (The French led the world in fortress design, thanks to Louis XIV's military architect, Marshal Vauban.) The French government sent endless money and supplies to build Louisbourg, but in the event there was less there than met the eye. Government agents complained of inadequate workmanship and poor construction materials. There was also a design flaw, for defences on the landward side were added only as an afterthought, in the 1730s and early 1740s. Maintaining the fort was another problem, and there were problems of morale in the garrison. Alarmed, officials at the fortress reported that Louisbourg could not be defended without substantial reinforcements, especially ships.

But when war—called in America King George's War after George II, the British monarch—broke out, finally, in 1744, the ships weren't there, nor could they be sent. (The war was actually a continental European war between Austria and Prussia about the right of a female, Maria Theresa, to inherit the throne of Austria, or at any rate those parts of it that Prussia wanted—and hence was known in Europe as the War of the Austrian Succession.) France had other commitments, mainly on land, and relative to the British the French navy was weak. The British, as a result, commanded the western Atlantic, and after a slight delay confined the French fleet in its ports on the Atlantic and in the Mediterranean. As a further ominous portent, the troops at Louisbourg mutinied; only abject concessions from Louisbourg's authorities brought them back to their duty.

The outbreak of war caused alarm in the British colonies as well. Massachusetts had suffered heavily from French and Indian raids forty years before, and the years of peace had only solidified the attachment of the Indian nations between the British and French frontiers—to the French. The situation in Acadia was unclear. The boundaries were imprecise, the Indians (mostly Mi'kmaq) were unfriendly, and the French had a strong point of attraction in nearby Louisbourg. True, the inhabitants, nearly ten thousand by the 1740s, had remained after the colony was ceded to Britain and renamed Nova Scotia, but that was a doubtful advantage, for they were at best neutral and might welcome the return of the French. Finally, Massachusetts was a fishing colony, and took a strong interest in the fisheries off Nova Scotia. Anything that could make the fishery more certain, exclude rivals, and attach it more firmly to Massachusetts was bound to find support there.

Governor Shirley of Massachusetts, assisted by the Royal Navy, mounted a land and sea attack on Louisbourg in the spring of 1745. His expedition proved the gloomy reports on Louisbourg's defences to be correct. The fortress's only hope was the appearance of the French navy, and the navy did not come. Marshal Vauban had established not merely the way to defend a fort but the way to take it. Using his prescribed methods of converging trenches and artillery bombardment, the Anglo-American force obliged the French garrison to surrender.

The siege of Louisbourg was the only great battle to be fought in North America in a war that lasted from 1744 to 1748. The main events of the war were in Europe, with an edge to the French, and in India, where the French had better luck than in America, capturing the important British trading fort of Madras. British predominance at sea was a crucial factor, but the British were assisted by the weather when a French fleet was wrecked by storms on its way to recapture Louisbourg in 1746.

In the interior of the continent, the French alliances with the Indian nations held. The Iroquois remained neutral, and the peoples of the Ohio Valley generally stood by the French, while trading with the British. The French alliance wobbled, but did not collapse under the pressure of scarce trading goods held back at their source across the Atlantic by British sea power.

The Treaty of Aix-la-Chapelle ended the war in 1748. The British exchanged Louisbourg for Madras, to the fury of the New Englanders who had captured it. Louisbourg had its importance, however, for it was British possession of the fortress that induced the French to accept a stalemated end to the war, with each side returning to the prewar status quo.[15] The treaty did not, however, resolve the exact boundaries of Nova Scotia, and, of course, it did not remove the counter-attraction of Louisbourg for the Acadian French.

Neither War nor Peace

King George's War made plain to the French authorities in Quebec that their American empire was precariously balanced between the British navy and the uncertain alliances that bound the Indians along the French frontier to King Louis rather than King George. New France depended on money, supplies, and troops from the mother country, and to get them across the ocean in time of war required a reinforced navy as well as the maintenance of French defences that stretched, thinly, from Louisbourg to New Orleans. As for the alliances, they demanded cheap and plentiful trade goods—in other words, constant subsidy—in order to compete with British traders from Virginia and Pennsylvania. These were fundamentally financial questions—unwelcome to a French government that didn't want to contemplate new and heavy expenditures. So the French prescribed what most governments do under the circumstances—half measures mixed with hope and fronted with a show of determination. Determination took the form of an aggressive promotion of French interests against the British traders in the Ohio country and the feeble British establishment in Nova Scotia. Before long troops were on the move, building forts and enforcing French territorial claims.

It was a dangerous game. King George's chief minister, the Duke of Newcastle, was soon complaining about "the wild French governors in America." The French couldn't justify their aggressive policies, and as for the British, Newcastle stated, "We can't bear [it]."

The first consequences of the aggressive French policy fell on the Acadian inhabitants of Nova Scotia. In the 1720s and 1730s, with an indefinite peace at hand, the French settlers had lived peaceably with the tiny British garrison of Port Royal. The British made no attempt to settle in Nova Scotia, and French missionaries maintained their influence over the local Indians, the Abenaki, Mi'kmaq, and Malecite. These nations were also under no direct threat from British settlement or the direct extension of British government.

The war changed all this. French missionaries took the lead in intimidating the Acadians and in encouraging the Indians to harass the British. War flared in the Acadian borderlands, though the French were unsuccessful in their attempts to capture the British capital at Annapolis Royal, the former Port Royal. The Acadians resented French demands for aid and furnished supplies only under coercion. But they wouldn't fight for the British either, and while that was better than nothing, it irritated some of the British authorities.

Peace in Nova Scotia was therefore little more than an armed truce. To reinforce their authority and to balance Louisbourg, the British poured three thousand settlers and £700,000 into a new base around the splendid natural harbour at Halifax, named in honour of the relevant British minister, the Earl of Halifax. The settlement did not flourish. The French and their Indian allies harassed the settlers, making the colony dangerous as well as primitive, and soon its reputation deterred most potential settlers. But not all: New Englanders were attracted to a maritime colony much like their own.

The Acadians had shown how to carve a respectable and comfortable living out of the marshlands around the Bay of Fundy. Economically, at least, their practice was exemplary. Politically, however, the Acadians were vulnerable. They regarded themselves as only conditional British subjects, and the reach of the king of France extended into their villages through the hands of his missionaries. The British did not, in the 1730s and early 1740s, press the issue: the local authorities even conceded that the Acadians did not have to bear arms in defence of their British monarch, George II. But the governors of the 1750s were less comfortable with that notion than their predecessors had been. To them, if the Acadians weren't wholly or reliably British, then they must be something else—and if they weren't subjects of the British king, then they must belong to the king of France. In a country with an uncertain frontier and an inconclusive war just over, the Acadians were a temptation to the French and a burden to the British. It wouldn't take much to get the Acadians to return to their old allegiance; could the British take that chance?

The French now began to back up their territorial claims with military force. They sent an army detachment to the isthmus of Chignecto, between modern New Brunswick and Nova Scotia, and built a fort, Beauséjour. The British too sent troops, mostly from Massachusetts, and built their own fort, Lawrence, named after the governor of Nova Scotia. There, through the early 1750s, the garrisons glowered at each other across a narrow river, waiting for a war they knew must come.

The French authorities were also setting matters in motion in the Ohio country. Their actions highlighted the differences between the British colonies, scattered, disunited, and unmilitary in their outlook, and New France, where large numbers of militia could easily be raised and dispatched long distances along the colony's river-highways.

Until the late 1740s the French could rely on the power of the Iroquois to hold the balance along the frontier and to act as a barrier between the British colonies and the lands claimed—but not occupied—by France. The Iroquois—first Five Nations and then, in the 1720s, Six—pursued their own interest, accepting gifts from both the British and the French but refusing to intervene on either side. In the 1720s and 1730s the Iroquois, their dependants, and their allies dominated the Ohio country. The nations of the Ohio and beyond contributed to Iroquois power, inflating to more than ten thousand the number of warriors the Iroquois could put in the field. (The Iroquois themselves could muster barely eleven hundred.)[16]

The Iroquois grip on the interior was, however, loosening, just at the point when pressure was building in Pennsylvania and Virginia for expansion. The Iroquois made what they thought were nominal concessions to the colonists, but in fact they gave, or seemed to give, far more than they understood—the right to occupy the whole of the Ohio Valley.

British settlers and land speculators followed British traders across the Appalachian Mountains, to the dismay of the existing inhabitants who were no longer protected by the Iroquois. The settlers made clear that they wanted the Indians off their land claims. The settlers' pretensions, as well as their behaviour toward the Indians, were a political bonanza for the French. The French told the Indians that it was the British who would dispossess them and drive them from their homes, and that the French themselves posed no such threat. The British, on the other hand, told the Indians that the French were blocking competition and the freedom to trade.

The fragile Iroquois empire could not support the contradiction between British and French interests and those of its subjects. In the 1740s Iroquois dominance frayed and then broke. The French began to intervene in Native affairs more forcefully, at first staking territorial claims. Then, in 1753, one of the "wild governors" in Quebec sent an army, the largest ever raised in New France up to that point.

Three hundred regular troops (the *troupes de la marine*), seventeen hundred Canadian militia, and two hundred Indians left Montreal for the Ohio country. The numbers weren't large by European standards, but for a colony with a total population of fifty-five thousand this was a major effort. They were to build a road the short distance from Lake Erie to the headwaters of the Ohio River and to establish forts along the route. The purpose was to keep out the British, whether traders or settlers, and thereby to reinforce the French alliances with the Indian nations of the interior.

The expedition was successful, in a manner of speaking. The troops built the road and forts and reinforced French prestige in the area. On the other hand, by the time the expedition reached the portage from Lake Erie to the Ohio, only eight hundred troops were still able to do the work; finally, four hundred of the two thousand died of disease, a tremendous loss for a small colony.[17] There was a legacy of bitterness among the survivors, for it was common knowledge that the authorities in Quebec, especially the intendant, François Bigot, had profited greatly by cheating the king and the king's troops. As the army in Quebec grew, with regular reinforcements from Europe, so did the opportunity for profit for the intendant and his associates by keeping and reselling supplies destined for the army. The soldiers certainly bolstered the defences of the colony, but local geography—expressed in distance and in roadless wilderness and disease—was still the principal defence of New France.

THE SEVEN YEARS' WAR

The wild governors had set the scene for an outbreak of hostilities along their fortified frontiers in Acadia and the Ohio country. The British responded with bluster, and then with force. Virginia sent the young officer George Washington—aged twenty-two—on a series of journeys across the Appalachians and into the Ohio Valley, and it was Washington's troops who fired the first shots at the French. Washington, captured by the French in 1754, was lucky to escape with his life.

The next British expedition, in 1755, wouldn't be so lucky. The British government raised £1 million and sent reinforcements to Nova Scotia and Virginia. The army in Virginia was commanded by General Edward Braddock; Washington would be his aide-de-camp. Braddock's army marched through the wilderness toward a French fort, Duquesne, on the site of modern Pittsburgh. They never reached the fort, having been ambushed and decimated by a small French and Indian force. Braddock was killed.

Another pitched battle occurred at the bottom end of Lake Champlain, the frontier between New France and New York. Despite a British attempt to intercept them, the French successfully sent twenty-six hundred regular troops to New France. (The British captured about four hundred of the original number.) The French sent the troops south, up the Richelieu River and Lake Champlain, to what is now Crown Point on Lake George. There the British defeated the French, regular troops and militia, and captured the French commander, Baron Dieskau, creating a vacancy in the military command in New France.

Finally, British troops—provincial troops from Massachusetts actually—captured Fort Beauséjour on the Acadian–Nova Scotian frontier. The Nova Scotian government, backed by the Massachusetts troops, now turned its attention to the Acadians. They were summoned, one last time, to swear unconditional allegiance to the British, and to agree to bear arms for King George if required. The Acadians, one more time, refused.

It was a fatal error. As many Acadians as the British could catch were rounded up, interned, and in the fall of 1755 placed aboard ships bound for other British possessions and, in some cases, Great Britain itself. In the process, families were broken up and farms burned. The precious dikes that protected the farmland were abandoned; the New Englanders certainly didn't know how to maintain them. The deportation of the Acadians did not account for all the French settlers—some fled into the wilderness or to French territory—but it changed forever the balance of population and thus of power in Nova Scotia. The Acadians were swiftly replaced by settlers from New England, and Nova Scotia became a British colony in fact as well as in name.

All this occurred in time of peace, when the British and French governments maintained diplomatic relations in Europe. But the pressure of events in America helped precipitate first a diplomatic rupture and then an actual declaration of war, in May 1756. (Later it would become known as the Seven Years' War.) In Europe the war was fought, mainly in Germany, between France, Austria, Spain, and Russia on one side and Great Britain and Prussia on the other.

The actual date of the declaration of war was almost irrelevant, because war in America and in the seas surrounding America was well underway. The French sent reinforcements to Quebec while they still could, under a new general, the marquis de Montcalm. There was a new governor general, too, the marquis de Vaudreuil, who was, incidentally, Canadian born.

Montcalm acted swiftly. In August 1756 he captured the only British post on the Great Lakes, Fort Oswego. The British authorities meanwhile dithered, while the various colonial governments varied wildly in their reaction to a crisis that promised to inflame their frontiers.

The next year, 1757, was no better. The British poured troops and generals into North America, and succeeded at very little. At sea, the French again managed to land reinforcements in Quebec, which Montcalm used in another audacious campaign, this time taking the British Fort William Henry near Lake Champlain.

The capture of that fort is best known for the subsequent massacre by

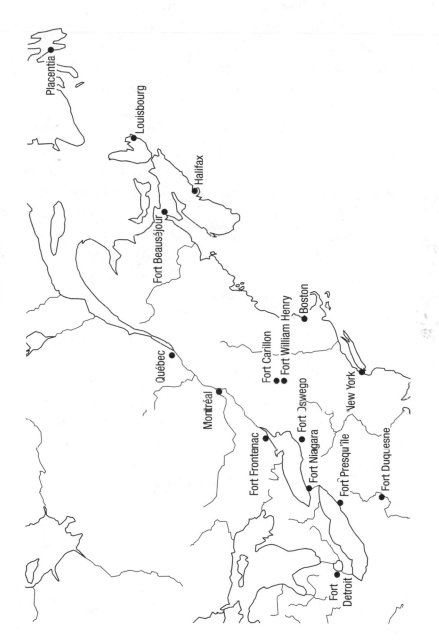

The Seven Years' War

Placentia

Louisbourg

Halifax

Fort Beauséjour

Québec

Montréal

Boston

Fort Carillon

Fort William Henry

Fort Oswego

New York

Fort Frontenac

Fort Niagara

Fort Presqu'île

Fort Duquesne

Fort Detroit

Montcalm's Indian allies of some of the surrendered garrison, immortalized in James Fenimore Cooper's later novel, *The Last of the Mohicans*. The events that followed the surrender of the fort were not precisely as advertised. Certainly some of the British prisoners were murdered by the Indians, while others were captured by them, for a captive Briton was a rare source of profit from ransom—a regular practice in the colonial wars.[18] Montcalm did rescue some of the captives from the Indians, almost certainly condemning others to death when their captors saw the hope of profit vanishing.

It was a clash of cultures. For the French and British, surrendered prisoners were sacrosanct. For the Indians, they were not. Indeed, Montcalm's Indian allies felt betrayed by the French general's interference in their normal practice of war. Many would not serve again with the French, a serious loss to French arms in this war. Montcalm certainly grew to loathe his Indian allies, not to mention the undisciplined colonial militia, and the events at William Henry were a stage in the disintegration of France's colonial military power.

Finally the British, both in the colonies and in the mother country, were appalled by the tales of robbery and murder that survivors of the massacre—and there were many—brought home with them. It marked a stage in British perceptions of the Indians, who were sometimes seen as romantic beings, "noble savages" unsullied by civilization. After William Henry, some opinions hardened. Indians weren't a better version of humanity than the civilized European, but much worse. There wasn't unanimity on the subject, and in this difference of opinion British Indian policy would be created.[19]

After two dismal years, British luck turned in 1758. A stronger government at home, headed by William Pitt the elder, along with better generals and stronger finances, began to count. Pitt lavishly subsidized the colonies to induce them to provide crucial assistance, in troops and supplies, for the army and fleet he sent across the ocean. The British fleet, the Royal Navy, kept the French navy tied up at the docks in port in France.

Montcalm and the other colonial commanders would have to rely on their own resources, or at most on whatever their colony could supply. Unluckily for the French, the harvest in Canada was bad and supplies began to run short—and to rise in price, to the great delight of the intendant, Bigot, and his cronies. General Montcalm and Governor Vaudreuil disagreed on strategy and tactics. But even their quarrelling could do little to alter the general picture, which was governed by British predominance at sea. The British could cut most of the links that bound New and old France together—and they did.

Sea power brought a British army unopposed to Louisbourg in 1758. Once the British had landed, nothing could prevent their victory, since they outnumbered and outgunned the French. Louisbourg surrendered in July 1758. Remembering Fort William Henry, the British commander, General Jeffrey Amherst, refused to grant the French the usual honours of war.

At the same time, the British were also victorious in the interior. One expedition captured Fort Frontenac (modern Kingston) on Lake Ontario, while another took Fort Duquesne in the Ohio country. Only on Lake Champlain did Montcalm prevail, defeating the British at Ticonderoga. But in the face of the other French defeats Montcalm took a very bleak view of his prospects in the campaign that must come the next year.

Montcalm anticipated a British attack on the colonial capital, Quebec, and he was right. In June 1759 a British fleet brought an army of eighty-five hundred under the command of General James Wolfe. Wolfe might have seemed an improbable choice—he was only thirty-two, sickly, unafflicted by charm, and jealously watched by his older, more experienced subordinates. Wolfe was, however, ambitious and politically well connected—well enough to get the command of the Quebec expedition.

Montcalm had prepared as best he could, establishing a long line of fortifications along the north shore of the St. Lawrence. Quebec, on its promontory, was protected by high cliffs and a narrow shore. Anyone wishing to take the city would either have to go around it or climb those cliffs.

Wolfe, it seemed, would do neither. He bombarded Quebec with his artillery and reduced much of the city to ruins without reducing Montcalm's defences in any significant respect. Wolfe then ordered the burning and devastation of farms and dwellings up and down the St. Lawrence, an act of notable savagery that did little to assist in the immediate task of defeating Montcalm. (It may have contributed in the medium term to a healthy respect for British power, or at least what the British would do with it, if provoked.)

It seems clear that by early September Wolfe had despaired of his task, just as Montcalm on his side despaired of his. As a last desperate gamble Wolfe decided to land his army under cover of darkness on a lightly defended shore, scale the cliffs above Quebec, and confront the French in the fields outside the walls of the city—the Plains of Abraham.[20]

Wolfe may well have been seeking a heroic death that would atone for his anticipated failure. Instead, he found a heroic death unencumbered by failure—a fortuitous victory handed him by the thoughtless and irrational response of his adversary, Montcalm. Descriptions of the battle have focused on the difficult climb up the cliffs to the Plains of Abraham on the morning of 13 September 1759. The problem was that if there was any serious resistance, or if the French were victorious, there was no way of getting down those cliffs.

The French were not victorious. Montcalm might have sheltered behind the walls of Quebec; he might have waited for reinforcements or circled around Wolfe's army. Fully assembled, the French outnumbered the British, and they had competent officers to lead them into a well-organized battle. Montcalm, however, did not wait. Relying too heavily on the Canadian militia—brave but disorganized—he sent his troops toward the British lines. Eighteenth-century armies were trained for the moment in which they stood in line and fired, calmly and regularly, at an approaching enemy. The British fired; the French lines crumpled and then fled. Montcalm was mortally wounded and was carried inside the city.

Quebec surrendered a few days later. The bulk of the French army was still intact and circled around the city, en route to Montreal, which remained in French hands. The British now had the unenviable task of occupying a city that had been largely ruined by their own artillery, with scanty supplies to keep them going, until relieved the following spring. The bulk of the British troops and fleet then departed, and Quebec entered its long winter's isolation.

Montcalm's successor, the very capable Chevalier de Lévis, brought the French army back to Quebec the following spring. They duly defeated the ill-considered response of Wolfe's successor, General James Murray, who imitated Montcalm by marching his army outside Quebec's walls. A chastened Murray hung on inside the walls, hoping that the first ship up the St. Lawrence would be British, not French. As it was.

The French had tried their best to reach Canada and extricate their fleet from the British blockade. Alert and talented British admirals frustrated them—in particular Admiral Hawke at Quiberon Bay on the west coast of France in November 1759. Hawke's victory was at least as significant as Wolfe's, and probably more so—but Hawke had the good fortune not to be killed, and so escaped the combination of romantic death and military triumph that immortalized Wolfe and the battle of the Plains of Abraham.[21]

The final episode in the conquest of Canada occurred in the summer of 1760. Under the overall command of General Jeffrey Amherst, three British armies converged on Montreal—from Lake Ontario, down Lake Champlain and the Richelieu, and up the St. Lawrence. They met in front of Montreal in September 1760—a highly unusual feat of organization for eighteenth-century armies. Outnumbered and outgunned, Lévis sought terms, which Amherst granted in the same manner as at Louisbourg. The French would not get the honours of war, and would not be allowed to march away with their flags and banners, towing a (symbolic) cannon. Lévis burned his flags, and the French duly surrendered on 9 September 1760. Lévis and his troops would be shipped back to Europe and eventually to France.

The military terms of the surrender were the ones remarked on at the time. The civilian terms were the more important. They dictated the departure of the senior civilian administrators and commanded the obedience of the remaining population to the British king. Existing laws and customs continued. The inhabitants of New France were guaranteed their property and the exercise of their Roman Catholic religion, though the British state was officially and determinedly Protestant. It was a provisional settlement, to be sure, an armistice, pending the conclusion of an official treaty of peace.

MAKING PEACE

The string of British victories in America was mirrored by British victories at sea, in Europe and in India. The British followed up, in 1762, with the siege and capture of Havana, property of France's luckless Spanish ally. Most of France's Caribbean islands also fell to British arms—the richest prizes of all.

There was one last Canadian episode—a French invasion of Newfoundland in 1762. The French were too few, and they duly surrendered—the last incursion of French military power on what is now Canada.

The British government was strongly inclined to make peace. The reasons were largely domestic and political. There was a new king, George III, new ministers, and new policies. Peace was highly desirable, and the British made some concessions to get it. The French of course were the principal losers. They gave up Canada, formerly New France, and Louisiana, partly to Great Britain and partly to compensate their ally Spain. Spain lost Florida, but regained Cuba. The French kept a toehold on two islands off Newfoundland, and kept the right to dry fish on the north coast of the island—the so-called French Shore.

The British gained the most, and especially in America. The entire continent east of Mississippi became British. New France was no more, and, with the direct French peril removed, the formerly French subjects of North America were leniently treated. The inhabitants of New France could go or stay, as they chose—to France if they preferred, or they could opt to stay in the valley of the St. Lawrence. Much remained to be decided, but it was clear that the British intended to rule peaceably as far as possible. That the Canadian part of Britain's new possessions would have a French character, a different character from the existing older colonies, was also indicated. Yet the French, too, would be changed by what had happened, and what was to come.

5

THE WARS
FOR AMERICA (2)

The harbour and defences of the British base
at Halifax, 1780, during the Revolutionary War.

T he Anglo–French wars of the eighteenth century supplanted one North American empire, the French, with another, the British. Contemporaries perceived the importance of the event and predicted, rightly, that great things would come of it. As often with such predictions, the details of the future foreseen proved to be quite wrong.

One consequence of the war was definitive. The political links between the French of North America and the French of France were severed. No French army would ever again march through Canadian forests. Louis XV and his successors in royal, republican, and imperial France never thought it worthwhile to reclaim North America with money or ships or soldiers— although, in one notable aberration, they would try it with words. But that is a much later story. (See Chapter 15.)

The economic links that bound New France to old France were also broken, to the relief of the French taxpayer. Military expenditures were gone, as were the subsidies that kept the fur trade afloat and the Indian allies friendly.

Culturally, the break wasn't nearly as clear. Law and religion had taken a distinctly French form. The Canadian Church was bound not just to Rome but to the French crown, which appointed the bishops and thus had a strong influence over how the Church on French territory conducted itself. As for justice, the law in New France was naturally French law: it was the "custom of Paris" (*coutume de Paris*) that regulated contracts and obligations and protected property. Secular culture must also come from Paris, for there were almost no alternative publications in the French language. In terms of material culture, matters weren't as serious. What could be made in France could be made in Great Britain, sometimes better and usually cheaper. What could be made, or grown or caught, in Canada could still be exported to Europe, although to Great Britain rather than France. Nor did traditional enmity preclude admiration or imitation—British styles, British goods, and British culture were admired, envied, and increasingly aped in Europe—and, of course, in Europe overseas.[1]

How to make permanent the break with France was the main question facing the new masters of Quebec, but it was only one issue among many for the imperial authorities in London. How to manage an empire that had more than doubled in size on the North American continent alone, how to pay for the war just past, and how to pay for the administration of the empire in the future were some of the issues that confronted George III and his ministers in 1763. Even more intractable than finance (and its accompanying nightmare, taxation) was a cultural question: How to absorb a substantial number of Catholics into a kingdom and an empire that were, by legislative definition, Protestant?

The British government tried to act responsibly, but in acting they disturbed the sleeping dragons of taxation and religion. They intended to put the empire on a firmer footing, but by their actions they undermined it, losing most of their American colonies in the process. If the fifty years before 1763 guaranteed that Canada would be British, the fifty years after 1763 ensured that it would not, at the same time, be American.

ACCOUNTING FOR EMPIRE, 1763–1774

Northern North America in 1763 had about 300,000 people—200,000 Natives and 100,000 whites, Europeans or the descendants of Europeans. It was divided into two colonies with one fishery, Newfoundland, and one commercial domain, the Hudson's Bay Company territories. The colonies were Quebec and Nova Scotia. Thanks to the defeat of the French, Nova Scotia expanded to include all of the former Acadia, including Cape Breton, Isle St. Jean, and what would later be New Brunswick. It was governed from Halifax, where the governor resided and where an elected assembly periodically met. In the structure of its government, its laws (English common law), and its language (English) it was the same as the other British colonies to the south. Its low population, partly caused by the Acadian deportation of 1755, was being remedied through the steady immigration of New Englanders and the arrival of shiploads of immigrants from Scotland and other parts of Europe, such as Germany. They joined the remnant of the Acadians, both those who had evaded deportation and those who had returned after the war. Nova Scotia was less a continuous colony—land communication was difficult and much of the province a howling wilderness—than a series of coastal pockets inhabited by Europeans and imposed on an undeveloped interior that was still occupied by the local Indian nations, especially the Mi'kmaqs and the Malecites.

The Newfoundland fishery was the part of North America most familiar to generations of Europeans. It attracted annual swarms of fishing boats to the Grand Banks from Western Europe to harvest the apparently inexhaustible cod. The French and the British both attempted to settle; thanks to the imperial wars only the British had the actual right to stay, though the French had a right of temporary residence on the north shore to dry and cure their catch. British fishing interests opposed the dilution of their fishery by a local population that might soon develop its own interests and divide the catch. Settlement was therefore officially discouraged, but it was hard to prevent a hardy few from taking root. As to the value of the fishery, there was no doubt: it was worth an estimated £600,000 in 1768, employing twenty thousand fishermen, twelve thousand of whom were from the British Isles.

Until the 1760s Newfoundland had no governor, no assembly, no elections, and no organized government. When a governor was appointed, he made it his business to deport as many of the inhabitants as he could. Nevertheless, officials estimated the permanent population at sixteen thousand, dispersed over many kilometres of coastline—a number and a space that defied the government's best efforts at depopulation.[2]

The settlers were partly responsible for depopulation of a different kind: the disappearance of the Native population of the island, the Beothuks. As elsewhere, disease played a major role; but on Newfoundland there was no interaction through the fur trade, no sense of mutual advantage or tolerance. Never numerous (their population at the time of first contact with Europeans is estimated to have been about a thousand), by the end of the eighteenth century the Beothuks were a handful. And despite efforts by the government to establish friendly contact, with an eye to preserving the race, the last known member of the tribe died in 1829. By that time, all the Natives of the Atlantic region of what would become Canada probably numbered no more than ten thousand.

Farther north and west, in the commercial domain of the Hudson's Bay Company, Indians were still economically and militarily significant in their interaction with white settlers and traders. The nations of the interior had long since adapted to European ways of warfare and commerce, equipping themselves with muskets and other trade goods. Farther west, on the prairies, another import from Europe, horses, had been adopted by the Plains Indians. The farther west and north, of course, the less likely were the Indians to be decimated by disease. Indeed, as late as the 1760s many had never even seen whites.[3]

Cultural differences mattered little compared with the attractions of trade with the Europeans. Even the Inuit of the far north weren't immune: those living along shipping or trading routes, like Hudson Strait, both benefited from trade goods and suffered from disease and alcohol, the mixed consequence of contact with Hudson's Bay Company ships.

The British government was uneasy about the Native populations of North America. The assistance or alliance of some Natives, and the neutrality of others, had been crucial in the war just past. In a sense, the Natives had become wards of the British crown, entitled to consideration and protection; as important, the occupation of the interior of the continent without their cooperation or at least their acquiescence would be a difficult and expensive proposition. It followed that British policies should be calculated to allay the fears of the Indians and gain their trust; unfortunately, the senior British general, Jeffrey Amherst, was inclined to do just the opposite.

As if to underline the point, war broke out around the western Great Lakes in the spring of 1763. One British post, Michilimackinac, fell to an Indian alliance led by the Ottawa chief Pontiac; another, Detroit, survived largely by luck. Pontiac's "rebellion" wasn't finally ended until 1765, and Pontiac himself submitted to the British only the following year.

The British government attempted to buy time by issuing a royal proclamation on 7 October 1763. The proclamation drew a line roughly along the Appalachians, reserving the lands to the west for the Indians and strictly regulating commerce there, to the irritation and frustration of land speculators, settlers, and merchants in the existing colonies to the east. The proclamation also constituted "the province of Quebec," in a rectangle that covered roughly the St Lawrence Valley. Quebec would be a province, unlike the colonies to the south, or Nova Scotia: it would not have an assembly for the time being. It would, instead, be ruled by a governor and an appointed council.

The most notable feature of the proclamation was its futility. By the time it was issued, thousands of settlers were already pouring across the Appalachians. Thousands more arrived in the years that followed until, in 1768, the British government conceded the point by concluding with the Iroquois, as nominal suzerains of the interior tribes, a treaty that ceded lands in the Ohio Valley belonging to other Indian nations.

The proclamation was only one facet of British colonial policy. What consumed the government's attention was revenue. Searching for money, the government found something else—colonial rebellion against imperial taxes imposed by a Parliament that did not represent the colonists.

The province of Quebec played little part in the drift to war and revolution. From the outset, British authorities were conscious that Quebec posed a problem because of its Catholicism, its French language, and its fresh loyalty to the French crown. To address these problems the local governors, James Murray and Guy Carleton, urged accommodation. Their choices were few. They hadn't enough troops to garrison a large province, and not enough money to pay for a domineering administration. The government of Quebec must depend on the consent of the governed, tacit or overt, and the best way to secure such consent was to employ what was left of the officials and officers of the previous French regime.

An important factor in governance was the Catholic Church, which in the early 1760s was headless in Quebec after the death of the previous bishop in 1760. Without a bishop, priests couldn't be consecrated, and without priests, parishes—the basic social and political unit of the countryside—would eventually lose their pastors. The problem was that the rulers of Great Britain, Protestants to a man, believed that Catholicism was the enemy of liberty, especially Protestant liberty, and the bulwark of tyranny. Expediency dictated a temporary compromise with Catholicism, involving the toleration of Catholic religious practice, but as a long-term measure such a policy was most undesirable, if not actually subversive. The superiority of Protestant liberty was surely demonstrated in the triumph of British arms, sustained by British (and colonial) prosperity, in the late war.

Despite these anti-Catholic sentiments, Catholics resident on British territory, even in the British Isles, weren't actually persecuted for their faith, and Catholic priests were winked at, provided they weren't too obtrusive. Political power rested securely with the Protestants, even when, as in Ireland, they constituted only a small fraction of the island's population. The Catholics submitted politically, and in return the Protestants ignored the small matter of their religious practice. It was natural enough to extend the same official oblivion to the colonies, even if many of the colonists also fervently believed that Catholicism was inimical to their country's well-being.

It was mainly because of religion that the British government hesitated over the form of governance for Quebec. Even a colony like Maryland (which had a Catholic lord proprietor) had removed the vote from Catholics in 1718. With the population at seventy thousand and rising in the 1760s, Quebec was larger than Georgia, Delaware, and Nova Scotia, and arguably as deserving as they to elect an assembly. The real problem was that all but a few hundred of Quebec's inhabitants were Catholics.

The few hundred Protestants saw nothing wrong with the notion that they alone should vote, monopolize a future assembly, and occupy all public offices. The successive governors, Murray (1760–66) and Carleton (1768–78), took a different point of view. How could they maintain order, enforce laws, and raise revenue in a system that discriminated against almost all the inhabitants of the province?

James Murray, younger son of a Scottish noble family, found the immigrant British merchants, whether from the American colonies or from Great Britain direct, objectionable: a bunch of "licentious pedlars," he grumbled. Their interests were not his, nor those of the whole colony, he was sure. Objections to his style of government reached London and offered his political opponents there a chance to unseat him. The merchants hoped for better from his successor, the lieutenant governor Guy Carleton, but Carleton, too, eventually disappointed them.

From the point of view of later centuries, the real issue in Quebec after 1760 was the fate of the French Canadians, the *Canadiens:* their place in politics, in society, and in the economy. Many of the economic actors of the period were also political actors, and attempted to influence the British government to serve their own interests.

But in fact there wasn't much to be said or done about the economy. New France had been propped up by French subsidies, its social structure reinforced by infusions of French gold and French honour and the prospect of warlike employment for its gentry. Not surprisingly, many of the latter departed for France in search of a familiar paymaster. As for the merchants of New France, some left and some stayed, but the commercial links on which they depended changed inevitably as New France passed from one empire to another and, accordingly, from one source of capital and markets to another. In a mercantile world—that is, a world ruled by theories of mercantilism—this was simply assumed to be natural.

The governors plied London with their views on Quebec, its inhabitants, its economy, and its prospects. The dispatches from Quebec were scrutinized by ministers who had to fit them into their own frame of reference and adjust them to the political realities of Great Britain, which in the 1760s and 1770s endured unstable politics, with the king, George III, hovering uneasily—presiding over, interfering in, but not controlling his governments.

The question of Quebec occupied a considerable amount of official and ministerial time in the British capital in the early 1770s as the government gradually and hesitantly reached a consensus on what to do. Finally, in 1773, the government, headed by Lord North, nerved itself to draft an act that did four things: it lifted restrictions on Catholics in Quebec, allowing them to assume public office; it extended the boundaries of the province to include all British territory south of Hudson Bay, east of the Mississippi, and north of the Ohio; it authorized French civil (but not criminal) law; and it established rule by governor and appointed council, without an elected assembly.

Of these by far the most important political item was the first, not because of anything it did in Quebec, but because it created a precedent that might eventually be used at home, in Great Britain and Ireland.[4]

THE PROGRESS OF THE REBELLION

The British government, meanwhile, had other things to preoccupy it. The late war with France had to be paid for. Arguably the chief beneficiaries of the war were the American colonies, through the removal of the French threat to their borders, their commerce, and their territorial expansion. It followed that the colonies should assist in paying debts incurred on their behalf.

The colonists did not see the matter that way. They resisted attempts to tax them by staging boycotts and riots. Eventually the government sent troops to Boston, the most obstreperous centre of colonial resistance, only to find that there were never troops enough to overawe the Americans.

Not all Americans were rebellious. One leader of the resistance to the British, John Adams, later estimated that a third of the colonists favoured resistance, a third were loyal to the crown, and a third were neutral or undecided. It was the resisters, or patriots, as they called themselves, who proved better organized and more politically skilful, playing on colonial fears of ministerial conspiracies against their property and their liberty. The protection of property and preservation of liberty were among the chief ends of government, and it followed that a government that subverted them must be illegitimate.

The timing of the Quebec Act, in 1774, was accidental, but it didn't seem that way to the fearful and resentful colonists. The Quebec Act had almost nothing to do with the larger colonial problem facing Great Britain—nothing but an unhappy coincidence. But the coincidence was enough to reawaken colonial fears of Catholic aggression, to remind colonists of the arbitrary nature of a French power propped up by a compliant Church.

Catching the spirit of the moment, General Gage, the king's governor in Massachusetts, advised ministers to raise troops and money, a million pounds or more. Loyal Americans from outlying areas began to arrive in Boston, fearing for their safety. Those who stayed faced ostracism, vandalism, and occasionally violence. Gage understood that authority was slipping from his control and into that of the "congresses," provincial and "continental," the latter meeting in Philadelphia in 1774 and 1775.

Ministers in London did not believe Gage until it was too late. They sent troops, but not enough, until Gage found himself besieged in his capital of Boston, surrounded by a growing colonial army. He appealed to his fellow governors to send reinforcements, and Carleton in Quebec sent most of what was already a small garrison to assist. Meanwhile the "Continental Congress," in Philadelphia, invited Quebec and Nova Scotia to send delegates and join in a united front against the government.

Nova Scotia took no action. Quebec had no mechanism to appoint delegates, having no assembly; even the Council provided in the Quebec Act couldn't come into being until the Act took effect on 1 May 1775. Carleton reasoned that he had little to fear from direct subversion in his province, and he was right. But subversion was just across the border, in New York and New England, where rebels seized the forts along Lake

Champlain, opening an avenue for invasion.

The Congress prohibited trade with any colony that hadn't sent delegates to its sessions, and then authorized privateers to prey on British shipping and other property, including that of the fishermen of Nova Scotia and Newfoundland. The economic weapon was powerful, but it cut both ways: it harmed even as it impressed, and it created an opportunity for Nova Scotians to fill the gap in the imperial economy left by the rebels. It was also possible that Nova Scotia itself could outfit privateers and return with interest the harm done by its neighbours.

In Nova Scotia there was some sympathy for the rebel cause among the recently arrived New England immigrants. (But recent arrivals from Great Britain or other parts of the empire were not immune to revolutionary sentiments.) It was a backwoods movement, far from the capital, Halifax, where the assembly, compared with those in the other colonies, remained respectful if not entirely deferential to imperial authority. It was also remote from the nearest New England towns, separated by hundreds of kilometres of trackless wilderness, and by Indian nations who were at best neutral to the rebel cause.

The rebel commander, George Washington, authorized the invasion of Quebec, which along with Nova Scotia would, he hoped, become the fourteenth or fifteenth colony to join the rebellion. In the fall of 1775 two rebel forces converged on Quebec, one directed at Montreal, where Carleton was trying to direct his province's resistance, and one overland through the Appalachian wilderness toward Quebec City.

Carleton hoped in vain for assistance from the nine thousand *Canadien* veterans of the Seven Years' War or from their numerous children. Some seigneurs rallied to his cause, but far too few. Most of the *Canadien* farmers—the *habitants*—felt no ties of loyalty to George III. They had suffered severely at the hands of the French authorities during the Seven Years' War, with high casualties and sizeable economic losses, and the British had capped the war by burning and looting up and down the St. Lawrence. It was enough to encourage caution in the face of the seigneurs' enthusiasm for a war that would justify their social status (as

The American Revolution

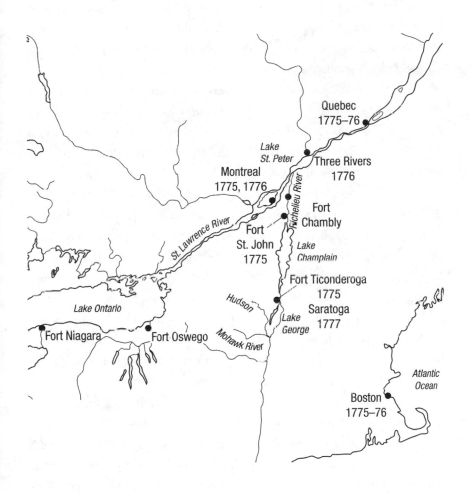

Quebec
1775–76

Lake
St. Peter

Three Rivers
1776

Montreal
1775, 1776

Richelieu River

Fort
Chambly

St. Lawrence River

Fort
St. John
1775

Lake
Champlain

Fort Ticonderoga
1775

Hudson

Saratoga
1777

Lake
George

Lake Ontario

Fort Niagara

Fort Oswego

Mohawk River

Atlantic
Ocean

Boston
1775–76

officers) and give them glory and rewards.

Beginning in 1775 Carleton received support from an unexpected quarter. The English-speaking immigrants to Quebec, whether they came from the British Isles or from the colonies, rallied to the government. Their main interest was the fur trade, and their markets were in Great Britain, not America. The war relieved them of American competition and returned Montreal to its former status as North America's fur-trading capital. Better still, those *Canadiens* engaged in the fur trade were also likely to see the advantage of the British connection. This was a growing sentiment over the years of war that followed, but initially it didn't do Carleton much good.

Finally, in mid-November, the governor abandoned Montreal to the Americans and fled down the icy St. Lawrence to Quebec, where another American army awaited him. Luckily for Carleton, he was able to form a defensive force from his few troops and from volunteers in the city; they were enough to resist an American army that fortunately lacked siege artillery and therefore had to rely on blockade or assault to take Quebec. Because many of the American troops hadn't enlisted past the end of the year, their commander, Richard Montgomery, attacked the city in a snowstorm on New Year's Eve, 1775. The British repulsed his assault, and Montgomery died in the fighting. The besiegers held on under Montgomery's successor, Benedict Arnold, until spring.

Spring brought British ships, troops, and supplies. The Americans fled to Montreal and then up the Richelieu. Carleton slowly followed, perhaps hoping that the less the bloodshed, the greater the chance of winning the Americans back to loyalty to the crown.

It was a vain hope, and Carleton has been justly criticized for failing to take the opportunity to destroy the American army in Quebec. The Americans retreated to fight another day, which they did under Benedict Arnold's command at Lake Champlain. As a result, a sizeable British army did not sail up Lake Champlain toward Albany and ultimately New York City in 1776, but awaited events in camps around Montreal. It seemed a poor return to ministers who had raised taxes and hired an army to crush the rebellion; Carleton would not again command an offensive army.

In March 1776 the British evacuated Boston and sailed away to Halifax, where a new British general, Sir William Howe, concentrated a large army, the biggest ever seen in North America. He sailed his army to New York, and hovered offshore while the rebels in the city celebrated the declaration of American independence from Great Britain on 4 July. From that point on, attempts at reconciliation were futile: the British alternatives were war or surrender to American independence.

With such a great army to hand they naturally chose war, and initially fortune favoured the crown. Reconquering such a large territory as America was a daunting task; strategically it made sense not because of the size of the British army, but because the British government could rely, or believed they could rely, on large numbers of Americans to support them, "on helping the good Americans to overcome the bad." As the historian Piers Mackesy puts it, "The British army would break the power of the rebels, and organise and support the loyalists who would police the country."[5] They also believed that in a straight fight the British could best the Americans. This appeared to be borne out when General Howe defeated Washington on Long Island in August, took New York City in September, and advanced through New Jersey on the rebel capital of Philadelphia. Howe hoped that the appearance of a great British power would rally loyal subjects previously intimidated by the rebels, and for a brief time it looked as if he might be right. And if the British continued to sweep the rebels before them, if the British army continued to seem irresistible, then the rebels might despair of their cause and the "loyalists" might finally assume control in the various colonies.

To demonstrate power, however, Howe had to occupy land, and occupation meant he had to scatter his troops in smaller garrisons across New Jersey, leaving them vulnerable to rebel counterattack. George Washington, the commander of the rebel army, did just that, rolling up several British outposts in New Jersey, driving the British back toward New York City, and, more important, negating Howe's political gains among the American population. It was a serious setback for the British and for the American loyalists. On the American side, the rebels had gained time, politically and militarily, to organize themselves, consolidate their rebellion, and seek allies in the struggle. In Europe, Britain's rivals, especially France and Spain, were taking notice, and while prudence dictated that the French government move cautiously, there was considerable enthusiasm for the rebel cause in intellectual and what would later be called "progressive" circles. But moderate and liberal Britons also found it hard to be truly indignant at their transatlantic cousins. As the American historian David Hackett Fischer observes, the English Whigs "could not crush American resistance without betraying the values which [they] believed that government to represent."[6]

The British government had one more year, 1777, to end the rebellion before French interest evolved into French interference. Difficulties in communication—the fact that it took weeks for information to travel across the Atlantic or even from Quebec to New York—challenged attempts at a coherent strategy. But the memory of the previous war against the French—when three armies had converged on Montreal and forced the surrender of the French army—was fresh. This time the British government planned to use its bases in Montreal, New York City, and the Great Lakes forts to launch a three-pronged attack on Albany and the Hudson Valley. If it succeeded, the colonies would be cut in two with the centre of rebellion, New England, isolated from the other colonies.

But it all had to work simultaneously; the orders, once sent, had to stand, and be obeyed. But they were not obeyed, and the plan failed. The northern army, under General John Burgoyne, had to make up the lost opportunities of the previous year. It moved slowly and methodically south toward Albany, affording the rebels time to assemble a large army of their own. The southern army, under General Howe, didn't move at all, and when it did went in the wrong direction, sailing around New Jersey to Philadelphia, the rebel capital. Howe took Philadelphia in September 1777 without much trouble, but having got there he wasn't sure what to do with it. Its capture was in any case perfectly useless as far as helping his colleague Burgoyne was concerned. Burgoyne, harassed and surrounded by the rebels, was forced to surrender at Saratoga in October. A third British force, consisting of regular troops and Indian allies, was also defeated well short of Albany.

A useless victory and two serious defeats were disastrous for the British cause. Diplomatically, the news of Saratoga encouraged the French government to sign an alliance with the American rebels early in 1778. War followed, in which a greatly improved French fleet contested Great Britain's mastery of the seas and forced the British government to divert naval resources from North America to home waters. The British evacuated Philadelphia in 1778 and retreated to New York. When in 1779 the Spanish declared war as well, Great Britain's strategic position worsened again.

The British government did attempt, too late, to reconcile the colonies to the empire. In 1778 a Declaratory Act agreed to what had been the colonies' main demand: Parliament solemnly conceded the right of taxation of the colonies. Henceforth, revenues raised in the colonies were to be spent in the colonies, not appropriated for imperial purposes. The Act wasn't quite a dead letter, for it could be applied immediately to those colonies where the British government's writ still ran, namely Nova Scotia and Quebec. The Declaratory Act would later be a founding principle for a renovated empire, but it was of no use in retrieving the lost colonies of America.

In North America the rebels were unable to assault the British in New York, did not have the sea power to threaten Nova Scotia, and could not spare the troops to attack Quebec. A guerrilla war along the Appalachians pitted Loyalist units with some Iroquois allies against frontier farmers in New York and Pennsylvania. Losses were considerable on both sides, and Iroquois who favoured the British were driven from their homes, ending up as refugees under the guns of Fort Niagara. Fort Niagara then became a base for bloody Loyalist and Mohawk raids on the colonial frontier.[7]

General Howe lost his job, but his successor, General Sir Henry Clinton, had no better idea than to keep trying to rally Loyalists to the British cause and finally re-establish British rule. His hopes weren't entirely unfounded, though the odds, after Saratoga and French intervention, were not good. There were, or had been, plenty of Loyalists in the south. Stalemated by the American army in front of New York, Clinton went south in 1779, taking Savannah and reoccupying Georgia, and then South Carolina, where Loyalists were numerous and active. For a brief moment it seemed the British might succeed in slicing up the rebellion colony by colony and rely on war weariness in the northern colonies to undermine the American cause.

Opportunity was fleeting. As in New Jersey in 1776, the British once again had to disperse their troops to protect their loyal supporters, and thus became exposed to a strategy of pinpricks from rebel guerrillas. The Loyalists reciprocated, and the result, as in most civil wars, was bloody and futile. The British were forced to retreat to the seaside towns of Savannah and Charleston, while the main British southern army was trapped by a Franco-American force at Yorktown in Virginia and forced to surrender in October 1781.

Charleston, Savannah, and New York were thereafter mainly useful as collection points for refugees fleeing the rebels' retaliation. Some escaped down Lake Champlain to Quebec, where the authorities established a camp at Sorel. Many Loyalists moved on to Great Britain, while others fled to Bermuda or the West Indies.

It was clear by the end of 1781 that their prospects of returning home in triumph were lost. They had bet on British power and against rebellion, against a disruption of the natural order of things, against disorder and violence, and disorder and violence had prevailed. Their future now lay in the hands of British diplomats sent to Paris to make whatever peace they could with the Americans, the French, and the Spanish.

PEACE, THE AMERICANS, AND THE LOYALISTS

The British had suffered a great defeat in their attempt to suppress the American rebellion, which, having been successful, became known as the American Revolution. They hadn't lost completely, however. At sea, the Americans could do little beyond raids or plundering British merchant ships. The British fleet maintained a sometimes precarious control over the Atlantic, enough to keep Nova Scotia, Newfoundland, and Quebec safe from invasion. The wilderness protected the approaches to Quebec and the Great Lakes, and the guerrilla war did not menace the main areas of settlement.

By the time the representatives of Britain, France, Spain, and the new United States of America sat down to discuss terms of peace, Nova Scotia and Quebec had already become a Loyalist refuge, and it was natural for the British government to view them in that light. The war hadn't shaken British notions of the value of colonies, though it had had an impact on the government's assumptions of how they could or should be treated. There was therefore not much disposition to give up the colonies: the French didn't want them, the Americans couldn't take them, and the British knew that under most foreseeable circumstances they could defend them against American attack. The French also knew this. North America might in the future be a steady drain on British resources as it dealt with a hostile American republic.

Crucial to the peace treaty was British recognition of American independence. Next in importance was the Americans' acceptance that they could not drive the British entirely from North America. There would be two English-speaking nations occupying the continent, the United States and Great Britain, and eventually Canada. The treaty laid down a boundary from the Bay of Fundy to the headwaters of the Mississippi. It provided for American fishermen off the coasts of Nova Scotia and Newfoundland, and allowed them to land and provision themselves in uninhabited bays. It "recommended" through Congress, the only common American institution, that the various states return property to Loyalists; but given the shadowy nature of Congress's authority, this was doubtful at best. The Loyalists were net losers in the civil war of the American Revolution.

The Indians were not present in Paris to negotiate their future. Their sovereignty wasn't recognized by any of the participants, and their territory was parcelled out like any other land.[8] The Iroquois of New York

State had already been disturbed and some of them dispossessed. Now the same fate awaited the Indians of the Ohio Valley in the new United States.

Who were the Loyalists? They came from every colony, but more came from the middle colonies, New York and Pennsylvania, than from New England. They were distributed across virtually all segments of society. In the northern colonies, Anglicans were more likely to support the British, as, naturally, were royal officials. Religious and ethnic minorities, and recent immigrants from the British Isles, were also more likely to be for the crown. Religious sects like the Quakers and the Amish in particular frowned on war and violence, and their members were unable to live up to the demands for conformity and support made by the revolutionaries.

Many Loyalists took up arms to fight for King George. Especially in the South black slaves escaped to British lines, and freedom.[9] Some battles, particularly in the south, were fought entirely between Americans, nor were the rebels always victorious. When the Loyalists left many departed by units, which gave their new settlements a definite character.

In many, perhaps most, cases, the Loyalists did not differ greatly from their republican neighbours, even in terms of politics. They accepted the assumptions of British political practice, believed in representative government, prized liberty and the protection of private property. They took a more optimistic view of British institutions than did the rebels, of course, believing that redress and security of property were more likely to come from the crown than from the mob rule that some rebel Americans used against their opponents.[10]

The British agreed to withdraw their troops from American soil. The British commander, Sir Guy Carleton, was sent to New York to supervise the dismantling of the British garrison and the evacuation of the Loyalists. (Savannah and Charleston had already been vacated by British troops.) Carleton frostily refused to return to his opposite number, George Washington, the escaped slaves who had trusted in British promises of freedom. They were transported to Nova Scotia, and then, most of them, to the new free colony of Sierra Leone in West Africa.[11] In November 1783 the British flag was hauled down and the last ships sailed.

CONSEQUENCES OF THE WAR

The Revolutionary War created two jurisdictions in eastern and northern North America instead of one. As a result of the war, a large number of Americans, perhaps eighty thousand, were dispossessed and became internal refugees. Of these, about half moved to Nova Scotia and Quebec, and were compensated by the British government with land and money. The size of the Loyalist migration, to largely uninhabited lands, meant that in some areas—backwoods Nova Scotia and western Quebec upriver from Montreal—the refugees became the majority. Their identity as loyal British subjects, but, equally important, as loyal *Americans*, with attitudes and identities formed on the west side of the Atlantic, would shape the politics and development of the colonies to which they moved.[12]

The Revolution divided Americans from each other, as it divided Great Britain and the United States. The experience of the war left many embittered. For some in the revolutionary generation on both sides the war never quite ended, and as long as that generation endured, the result of the war seemed accidental and impermanent.

It was by no means certain that the United States itself would endure and, if it did, what form the new republic would take. To many Americans a republic was a strange idea. Others had trouble adjusting to a federal form of government when the American constitution was adopted in 1787. The ex-Americans living in Canada took comfort from the teething troubles of the United States. Surely, they hoped, it would not, it could not, last.

Communication across the newly established border did not cease. The frontier stretched for well over fifteen hundred kilometres, and much of it was water and couldn't be seen, let alone policed. Across the border travelled Indians who did not wish to recognize it and settlers searching for land and security to whom it was a matter of relative indifference. To the south, Americans continued to read British publications, buy English products, and trade with Scottish merchants. British goods did not cease to flow across the ocean, nor did British immigrants to the new United

States. The English-speaking world around the Atlantic was not completely sundered, nor was all sentiment in one country hostile to the other. British radicals admired the American experiment, while American conservatives and American anglophiles continued to sympathize with many aspects of British life.[13]

The remaining British colonies became part of a larger Anglo–American relationship, but they were never the dominant part. Had the British government or the ruling elite been thirsting for revenge, obsessed with the shame of the loss of most of America, the future of Nova Scotia and Quebec, the nucleus of the future Canada, might have been different. But at no point was the notion of the reconquest of America ever seriously entertained in Great Britain. Nor would the remaining colonies have quite the importance of the old ones.

6

THE WARS
FOR AMERICA (3)

A colonial townscape: King Street, Toronto, Upper Canada, 1830s.

The Revolutionary War altered the political shape of eastern North America. And yet, as of 1783, the physical appearance of the continent was much as it had been. The forests and mountains of Appalachia, largely unbreached, separated the Atlantic coast from the Great Lakes and the Mississippi Valley. The most obvious, and certainly the most numerous, animal residents of America were the beaver in the Canadian Shield and the bison on the Great Plains. As for people, the Native inhabitants of northern (British) North America outnumbered the Europeans and their descendants.

The land in the northwest was still unknown, shading off into white on maps. The question of who owned the continent had been theoretically settled, but was practically unresolved. The Great Lakes, the St. Lawrence, and the heights of land dividing watersheds formed the boundaries between British and American sovereignty—but nobody was quite sure where the heights of land were, and in any case the British continued to occupy forts south of the Great Lakes. Their occupation of American territory suggested that the treaty of 1783 was unfinished or at least incomplete, and that peace might be little more than an interval of a few years until the next war.

To the west, beyond the Mississippi, Louisiana belonged to Spain, which did not have the strength to occupy most of it. Its white inhabitants were French, left behind in forts along the great river when Louis XV withdrew. Fur traders roamed the Great Plains, but no white explorers had ever crossed the Rockies. Had they done so they would have found on the habitable coast prosperous Native villages devoid of European occupation, as the British explorer Captain James Cook did at Nootka Sound on Vancouver Island in 1778. To the south, there were a few Spanish missions and small garrisons in California; to the north, there were a couple of Russian trading posts in Alaska.

In the thirty years after 1783 much of this changed. Explorers filled in the gaps on the maps as fur traders from Montreal followed the great rivers of the west to the Arctic (1789) and then the Pacific (1793). The Spanish advanced north up the coast from California, to Nootka Sound, and then retreated in the face of British pressure. The United States doubled its territory by purchasing Louisiana in 1803 from the French, who had briefly reclaimed it from the Spanish. This tipped the political balance on the continent, but the demographic balance tipped even more. The American population doubled between 1790 and 1810; of that country's 7.2 million inhabitants, almost 300,000 lived across the Appalachians in the new territories south of the Great Lakes. There was a continent-wide flow of immigration to the west, past and through the Appalachians, up the St. Lawrence, and on to the western end of the Great Lakes.

The population of rocky, swampy, icy British North America was much smaller, and the figures are less reliable. As best we can tell, there were roughly 166,000 white inhabitants in the land covered by the provinces of Nova Scotia and Quebec in 1784, and 392,000 in 1806.[1]

Travelling meant scows and barges along the navigable rivers, and portages around the many rapids or over the heights of land that divided the Atlantic from the interior. Some incomers were politically inspired, the prime example being the migration of loyal Americans—Loyalists—to British territory north of the new frontier. But when disloyal Americans reached the limits of British territory, coming later from the south and east, there was nothing to stop them—and much to entice them, for the inhabitants were sparse and the land plentiful. The logic of settlement dictated development, and development demanded population. Population there was, but it came from the United States.

Once settlers arrived, settlement was painful. Farms would provide subsistence, but they had to be cleared, chopping trees and hauling and burning stumps at the rate of a few hectares a year. It took time and money and luck before a farm, or a range of farms, could produce crops to sell in local markets that, thanks to the state of the roads, might be days if not weeks away. The best transport was by water, but in British North America (which was coming to be called Canada) transport was a seasonal thing, regulated by thaw and freeze-up and of course by the fall of snow on the roads. There were small sailing ships on the lakes, and canoes and barges on the rivers, but the supplies they could bring were limited.

To the inhabitants of British North America, Europe seemed a formidable distance in space and in time. News at best took weeks to arrive on the Atlantic coast, and far longer in the interior. Yet news, goods, ideas, and fashions did arrive, and were all the more prized because they came from faraway Europe. The colonists' identity, their self-image, was bound up with Europe, and with the mother country, Britain. British North America made no sense except as a projection of Great Britain, and decisions made in Great Britain profoundly affected the colonial societies on the other side of the ocean.

And not just the colonies; beyond them were the nations of Native America. By the 1780s, most North American Indians had direct or indirect contact with Europe and Europeans. Those close to the line of settlement were profoundly influenced and in many respects dependent on European commodities—cloth and metal, most obviously.[2] The Plains Indians had captured stray horses brought to Mexico by the Spanish: by the eighteenth century, hunting and warfare on the plains were conducted on horseback, and with guns.

The traders sought fur, especially beaver, and the farther west and the farther north they travelled, the better the fur became. Northern beaver grew thicker pelts, desirable and lucrative in the markets of London, and the best beaver were to be found in the Athabasca country at the northwest end of the Great Plains, in the lakes and rivers that flowed north, away from the Mississippi and Hudson Bay. Traders from Montreal had reached that far by the beginning of the 1780s. Nothing in the peace treaty would prevent them from going farther.

THE POLITICS OF EMPIRE

Quebec was the largest territory remaining to the British Empire after 1783, and in terms of population, the largest colony of settlement. It was neither the richest nor the most economically important British possession, but because of its history and location it was, for the time being, politically significant.

The North American colonies were costly. In a belated attempt to appease American opinion, Parliament had in 1778 passed a Declaratory Act that renounced its power to tax the colonies. That Act remained on the books and governed all future British relations with the colonies. In practice, it meant that taxes raised in a colony must be spent there. But there was another principle at work: the inhabitants of Quebec had no means of giving their consent to taxes, which must either be imposed by fiat or not levied. Giving consent involved constituting an assembly, and assemblies had to be elected. Something would have to be done, but what that would be no one could imagine.

The revolution did not change the British conception of empire as an enclosed political space, regulated if no longer directly taxed by the metropolitan government. The home country would produce goods for the colonies, which the colonies would exchange for their raw materials. Nova Scotian or Newfoundland fish would supply the British slave colonies in the West Indies, while Quebec wheat or New Brunswick timber would supply British needs. The colonies were assumed to be politically stable, and if they were not, it was the business of government to make them so.

The Loyalists thus formed part of a larger political equation. They were deeply disappointed by the outcome of the Revolution, for which they blamed their former neighbours, the rebels, and the incompetence of British generals in about equal measure. They were loyal but also sceptical, not automatically enthralled by each and every action of the British government; rather, they looked to that government to make amends.

Some forty thousand Loyalists arrived on Canadian shores. Many had fought for the king in the Revolution, and found themselves and their units in Canada when the war ended. They also found themselves largely without property, which the rebels back home had confiscated. In the short term they had to be housed and fed; eventually, they would have to be compensated for what they had left behind.

Rank-and-file Loyalists received land grants of two hundred acres (just over eighty hectares). Officers got up to five thousand acres (two thousand hectares), depending on rank. Because it would take time and effort to render the grants habitable and profitable, the government provided tools, housing, and food. Towns rose out of what one Loyalist described as a "howling wilderness." In the single year 1783, fifteen hundred houses were built in the new town of Saint John, New Brunswick. More were built at Shelburne, across the Bay of Fundy.

Saint John, as it happened, was well sited, with a good harbour and a fertile river valley behind it. Shelburne was not, and eventually the Loyalists there drifted away, some to go elsewhere in Nova Scotia, some to go back to the United States, and some to go as far away as Upper Canada.

Strictly speaking, neither New Brunswick nor Upper Canada existed in 1783. The government created them in 1784 and 1791 respectively, largely in response to Loyalist demands for an accountable local authority equipped with familiar and compatible institutions. Loyalty, it appeared, was not unconditional—these were loyal *Americans* who happened to differ with their American cousins about certain aspects of politics, or rather, politics as a later age would define them. On other issues, such as elected, representative assemblies, they did not disagree at all.

Politics in the late eighteenth century, in Britain as in North America, was barely differentiated from factionalism, and political parties were a very uncertain thing. The national interest, embodied by the monarch or, in the new United States, the president, stood above politics. The British governors of Quebec and Nova Scotia would not have differed from George Washington on this point. The problem, as always, was discovering the national interest, and getting the various politicians to agree to it.

Across the border, George Washington, a general, became president under the new American constitution, just adopted. In Canada, General

Sir Guy Carleton became governor of Quebec for the second time in 1786, replacing Frederick Haldimand, another general, in the post. Carleton's younger brother, Colonel Thomas Carleton, was already presiding over New Brunswick.

Government, Land, and the Indian Question

Government in the 1780s was a relatively simple affair. There was the central administration, governors, councillors, and clerks. There were the courts, using English criminal law, and, except in Quebec, English common law as well. There was the military, army and navy, and a militia, in which every able-bodied man between sixteen and sixty was expected to serve. There were revenue collectors, exacting customs and other fees. There was a post office, and an Indian Department.

The courts weren't a free-standing estate, but rather a part of government: judges were often councillors as well and intimately linked to the various governors and their policies. Governors controlled public offices, with their highly prized salaries and fees (officeholders sat in the executive council), and they distributed land. Land was the basis of wealth in Great Britain, as it was in the colonies. Aristocrats and gentry in the British Isles inherited, accumulated, and exploited great estates, often driving off their inhabitants who could then be used to populate the distant colonies.

It wasn't unusual for the friends of government to be rewarded with thousands of hectares of land. In one case, Colonel Thomas Talbot, an Anglo-Irish gentleman, and secretary to the lieutenant governor of Upper Canada, received a grant of five thousand acres (just over two thousand hectares). Talbot soon left the province to carry on soldiering, but during a brief truce in the wars with France in 1803 he returned to Upper Canada and struck a deal with the government. He became a land agent and speculator. Talbot was to settle immigrants on fifty- or hundred-acre (forty-hectare) plots and in return would receive 150 acres for each. A tract of land was set aside on the north shore of Lake Erie for his operations. It was an unequal bargain, but it worked: Talbot's settlers eventually cleared twenty-seven townships from the Detroit River to Long Point.

The colonel ruled his domain (his "principality" as he called it) eccentrically but not unfairly. He gave his settlers his personal supervision—not always appreciated because Talbot insisted that the settlers clear and farm ten acres (four hectares) of land forthwith and clear the road fronting their grant. Only then could they have security of tenure, and if they didn't comply they were summarily dispossessed. By the end of the 1820s Talbot had secured the construction of a road almost five hundred kilometres long from the head of Lake Ontario to the Detroit frontier.[3] When the government needed his help—during the War of 1812 or the Upper Canadian rebellion of 1837—it was given. Talbot, despite his gentrified ancestry and his military rank and connections, lived much like the settlers around him. He operated from a window cut into the side of a log cabin, dispensing land and favours or retaliating against those who had displeased him. Unlike other speculators, Talbot poured his own money into developing his lands, and at the end of a long life—he lived until 1853—he may well not have been much better off than when he arrived in Upper Canada. He granted his lands to anyone who came along—to people differing in religion, and with different ideas on how best to order society. Talbot wasn't a feudal aristocrat in the Canadian forests, nor did he found a backwoods dynasty. His habits were those of an unreformed British officer—indifferent where religion was concerned, hard-drinking, and bawdy in his conversation, to the horror of his later Victorian biographer.[4] When he died, unmarried and childless, he left his property to his servants.

What was truly different from the experience of earlier generations was the absence of hostile Indians. Essentially, the pre-revolutionary regime still applied on British land—and was governed by older agreements between the British and Indian nations (the Treaty of Halifax of 1752 with the Mi'kmaqs is an example) but above all by the Proclamation of 1763. The proclamations laid down principles governing white settlement of the interior and the peaceful acquisition of Indian land through purchase.

The Indian nations occupying the territory still deemed to be British weren't inclined to take up arms against the new settlers. In part, this was because some nations were almost entirely dependent on the British—the Six Nations refugees in the western part of Quebec were a good example. And in part it was because the Indians were too few in number to put up serious resistance, and were linked to British traders from Montreal through the fur trade. Finally, many of the Indians perceived the Americans as a much greater threat than the British. Against the Americans, they still hoped, experience to the contrary, that the British would assist them.

In the meantime, British administrators in Quebec negotiated with local Indians—the Ojibwa north of the Great Lakes—to buy land for the Loyalists and for the Iroquois along the Bay of Quinte and in the "Haldimand Tract" along the Grand River beside their white Loyalist counterparts. The Ojibwa were hardly in a position to resist, for their numbers were few: according to one estimate, barely two hundred lived in the territory north of Lake Ontario. They found British offers of trade goods desirable, certainly; and it's unclear whether the Ojibwa who ceded lands to the crown entirely understood that the land, once ceded, was gone for good. As they saw it, they were ceding use of the land, or trading land for security and support for the indefinite future. This latter confusion would later spawn political debate and legal argument two centuries on, but for the time being it allowed the free and peaceful settlement of thousands of crown-sponsored immigrants.

The history of the Grand River Iroquois, under their leader Joseph Brant, was unhappy. Brant hoped for a parallel destiny for his people, leasing land for income and thereby improving the land and securing a regular cash income. But Brant was frustrated in his design, as were the Iroquois who had remained on American territory.

Had it been up to the Loyalists, or to local British administrators, the Indians south of the new border might have been in luck. The decision, however, lay in London, and the main concern of the British government was to re-establish the national finances and recover from the war. That policy dictated peace with the United States and limited armaments.

Fortunately for Great Britain, the war had left France and its European allies even worse off financially, and the 1780s passed without any serious foreign entanglements.

Government could hardly be complete without a source of revenue, and this was the weakness of the post-revolutionary colonial system. The problem began with the best of intentions. The British government had tried to learn from the experience of the American Revolution. First, it accepted that it could no longer hope to tax the colonies for imperial purposes.[5] British garrisons in what was left of America had to be maintained by the British taxpayer, and colonists would not be asked to contribute to paying off the British debt, even if it was incurred in defence of the colonies. The colonies could levy local taxes for their own purposes, but those taxes would stay where they were raised. It was an important limiting condition on imperial dreams. Second, taxation of any kind presupposed the consent of the governed, that is, of the remaining British subjects in the colonies.

But how to secure the consent of the governed?

LAND AND LOYALTY

The peace of 1783 lasted not quite ten years. In 1789 a revolution began in France that by 1792 had toppled the French monarchy and established a republic whose leaders ruled through a reign of terror. The monarchs of Europe combined against the revolutionaries and invaded France. When the French in response executed their dethroned king, Louis XVI, the British reluctantly joined the war, in January 1793.

The revolutionaries should have been able to count on their fellow revolutionaries in America, out of republican solidarity and to fulfill the American alliance with France, which had helped win the revolution against the British. The British were at war with France; could the Americans be far behind? If the Americans joined in, surely the French of Canada would take up the cause of revolutionary France. A larger, stronger United States could swiftly topple the British army in Canada while Britain was preoccupied in Europe. The future of the British Empire in America seemed very dim.

But the events of the 1790s and 1800s did not follow this logical scenario. The Americans didn't join in the war in 1793. Instead, the alliance with France was quietly allowed to expire and, if anything, American relations with France worsened in the course of the decade. Though the French war continued with only a slight interval in 1802–03 until 1815, and though the United States did finally join in, in 1812, the Americans did not succeed in conquering Canada. And, finally, the French of Canada did not join the French of France to overthrow British rule. Despite British forebodings, the Canadian French—the *Canadiens*— cultivated their gardens and prospered as never before. They enjoyed the protection of their own laws, the security of their elected assembly, their own Catholic religion, and the autonomy of a province, Lower Canada, in which they were, for the indefinite future, a majority.

The creation of Lower Canada was the culmination of a complicated rearrangement of boundaries that reflected the economic and demographic developments of the 1780s. The problem was that the Loyalists were living in a province designed as a French-speaking and Catholic reserve, with no elected assembly to represent them. The contradictions mounted. Many of the new settlers were Catholics, either Loyalists or soldiers in disbanded British Highland regiments. Half a century before, they had rebelled back in Scotland against the Protestant English (actually German) king, George II; by the 1780s they had become one of the mainstays of the British military for his successor, George III. After the Revolutionary War, many settled north of the St. Lawrence in what they later named Glengarry, after their original home in Scotland.[6]

By the end of the 1780s, ribbons of settlement stretched along the east side of the Bay of Fundy, up the St. John River, and along the St. Lawrence west of Montreal as far as King's Town, the former Fort Frontenac, at the east end of Lake Ontario. (King's Town was soon contracted into Kingston.) Farther west there were pockets of settlement along the north shore of Lakes Ontario and Erie, the Bay of Quinte (where a group of

Iroquois had been granted lands), the Grand River (another Iroquois tract), and the Thames River.[7]

The presence of the settlers expanded direct British control as far as the Detroit River. The greatest expansion of British influence, however, occurred farther west, beyond the Great Lakes. There, fur traders based in Montreal competed with traders from the Hudson's Bay Company posts along the shore of Hudson Bay. The Montreal traders had a commercial advantage: they brought their goods directly to their customers, while the Bay traders hung back; when the Bay Company penetrated the interior it took years to overtake the Montrealers.

Not all the Native–white contacts were a happy convergence of market forces. Traders sometimes used force on unfaithful clients, or relied on addiction—to alcohol or tobacco—as a means of attracting customers. And there was always debt, binding a luckless Native consumer to a rapacious trading system.

In 1789 a Montreal fur trader, Alexander Mackenzie, travelled downstream more than two thousand kilometres from Fort Chipewyan (established the year before) on Lake Athabasca to the Arctic Ocean; the great river he followed was named the Mackenzie, after him. Mackenzie was disappointed: he had hoped to reach the Pacific, not the Arctic. In 1793 he repeated his performance, crossing the Rockies and finally reaching the Pacific at the mouth of the Bella Coola River, the first white man to travel overland across the continent.

Mackenzie represented a new coalition of Montreal interests, the North West Company, dominated by Simon McTavish and the Frobisher brothers but including a variety of British-born and American traders. They used a traditional technology, the birchbark canoe, inherited from the French and before them from the Indians, but expanded into the great *canot du maître*, with crews of six to twelve men and carrying up to 1360 kilograms of cargo. They travelled from Montreal up the Ottawa River and across the Great Lakes to the Grand Portage that linked the St. Lawrence system to the rivers of the west, supplying a series of posts that stretched from Lake Superior to the Rockies. The effort was huge, but the profits were very gratifying. The Montreal partners bought seigneuries, married aristocratic heiresses, socialized in their "Beaver Club," and built mansions—"Beaver Hall" for one of the Frobishers—that displayed their wealth.

Mackenzie's discoveries added to the gratification, for it was from the Athabasca region—up from 55 degrees north latitude, between 110 and 120 degrees west longitude—that the best, the thickest, the most luxuriant furs came.[8] The furs were transported by the *canots du maître* to Montreal and traded for the cloth, firearms, and firewater shipped up by the merchants there. Those merchants were, by the 1780s, almost entirely English-speaking, for it was they who had the connections, the capital, and the access to the fur markets of London—which, under the mercantile system, was effectively the only market.[9]

The emergence of a mercantile elite in Montreal, closely connected to trade and finance in London, added weight to the argument, bypassed at the time of the Quebec Act of 1774, that Quebec was too big and too important to be deprived of representative political institutions. A London Committee representing Montreal interests was established to press the British government to reform the government of Quebec. The influx of Loyalists into the distant western half of the province reinforced the argument that changed circumstances demanded new measures. The British government had to nerve itself and make Quebec a colony like the others.

CONSTITUTING BRITISH NORTH AMERICA

The old colonies of North America, those lost in 1783, had been entirely separate entities, each with its own governor and with a variety of governmental systems. The early British governors of Quebec and Nova Scotia had the same status as the governors of New Hampshire or Georgia, no more, no less. This changed after 1783: Cape Breton, St. John's Island, and New Brunswick all received lieutenant governors, a first step toward the consolidation of British North America under a single government.[10] It was only a first step: the governor in Quebec City received the titles, but not the authority, of "governor" in each of the British North American colonies, a toothless formula that gave little but formal pre-eminence.[11] In each of the colonies, except Lower Canada, it was the lieutenant governor who dealt with affairs, communicated with London, and managed the colonists as best he could.[12]

Sir Guy Carleton received the title in 1786—less than he had wanted, but he harvested another, Baron Dorchester, to speed his passage to Quebec. The appointment was a sign of favour, and an indication that the government—a Tory administration, headed by William Pitt the younger—would heed Dorchester's advice on the matter of governing and keeping the colonies that were left. The government also believed that Dorchester, as the principal author of the Quebec Act of 1774, would not be in a hurry to change it for another system.[13] Their hopes were justified: Dorchester temporized and dithered, and failed to produce any conclusive advice on what to do. Naturally, this only stimulated demands for change, demands that reached the ears of the opposition in Parliament, in London.

A Canada Bill was introduced, debated, and passed in Parliament in the spring of 1791. It appeared under Pitt's authority, of course, and the prime minister took a vigorous part in the debate, but its main sponsor was William Grenville (later Lord Grenville), secretary of state in the cabinet. Interestingly, the debate of 1791 lasted longer, and was more significant in British politics, than any subsequent parliamentary consideration of Canada—indicating that, in the opinion of the leading British politicians, more than the government or even the possession of Canada was at stake.

First, as a result of the proposed Canada Act, Canada was to receive the blessings of the British constitution and to serve as beacon for British political principles. The intended audience was the United States, but in the spring of 1791, with a revolution in France and the scent of violence wafting across the English Channel, the British principles of the Canada Act applied closer to home.

The approximation to the British model—Lords, Commons, and

King—was closer in the Act than was later realized. Parliamentarians spent much time debating what was in effect a Canadian House of Lords—an appointed legislative council. There was even provision for hereditary councillors, but in any case the members of the council were appointed for life. There would be an elected assembly, elected every four years (Pitt had proposed seven, like the British Parliament). There was to be an executive council, similar to the British cabinet, to advise the governors or lieutenant governors of Canada. The similarity went only so far. The members of the Canadian executive council held office at the pleasure of the governor, not by heredity or for life, or by election. They were accordingly entirely dependent on and advisory to the governor—very like the members of the American cabinet, then just being constituted under the first president, George Washington. No one in the 1790s could have predicted how the American system of government would actually function, but the principle of checks and balances among the estates of the American constitution was already explicit. In the Canadian colonies, Pitt and Grenville had supplied the checks without the balance, for beyond the abstract motivations of patriotism or the notion of the public good, there was little incentive for the revenue-producing element, the assembly, to work with the revenue-spending machine, the governor and the executive council.

The Quebec Act of 1774 accepted that the Roman Catholic Church was better than no church at all and accordingly lent the force of law to the support of that Church, through tithes, by its sometimes unwilling members. The Act of 1791 could hardly repudiate what had been granted not very long before, but it laid out at great length the true object of the British government, namely the establishment of a Protestant Church— the Church of England—in the colonies. The Canada Act endowed the Anglicans with what was virtually the only negotiable asset in the colonies: land—a seventh part of the value of land in each township. The land could be kept or sold, but the revenues were to go to the local clergy of the Church of England, independent of anything a local assembly might wish to do. As far as the British government could manage it, the established Church was made independent of local politics and politicians.

In Quebec, that also meant that the Church of England was independent of the Catholic majority—90 percent of the population in 1790. There would be two provinces in place of one, both called Canada. (It was already the common term for most of British North America; the Canada Act made it official.) The western province would be Upper Canada, underpopulated and underdeveloped, but overwhelmingly English-speaking and, for the time being, overwhelmingly Loyalist. The eastern province, down the St. Lawrence, would be Lower Canada, very largely French-speaking, with a considerably better developed economy. Economically, however, the language of Lower Canada was English, not French, and it's not surprising that the fur barons of Montreal opposed the division of Quebec, leaving them a small linguistic island in a French-speaking sea.

In some respects the Canada Act was the last appearance of the old British Empire, dominated by colonies of settlement that reproduced as far as they could the characteristics and institutions of the mother country. Such colonies were, and were expected to remain, dependent, framed by a restrictive trading system, mercantilism, in which Great Britain prescribed the pattern of colonial government, society, and trade for the benefit of the mother country. There was room for local variation in this system, but not for any radical departures. Its faithfulness to the original British model was its strength and its inspiration. It was what the Loyalists had fought for.

WAR AND THE HEALTH OF THE COLONIES

The debate of 1791 was the last time for more than three decades in which Canada got the attention of Great Britain. There were new crises to preoccupy the British government—for example, tension with Spain over the Pacific northwest, where imperial claims overlapped in Nootka Sound on Vancouver Island. (This crisis, once resolved, consigned what is now the coast of British Columbia to British suzerainty and limited the Spaniards to California.)

The troubles with Spain paled compared with the danger the British government perceived from France. The French monarchy collapsed in 1792, replaced by a revolutionary, republican government. The powers of continental Europe attempted to replace the French king on his throne, only to have the revolutionaries march the ex-king to the guillotine in January 1793. Great Britain now declared war on France, a war that would last for a generation, until 1815.

The war, or wars, of 1793–1815 were more than the usual dynastic squabble. France had experienced a social and political revolution that appeared to threaten the foundations of government, order, and society. The legitimacy of monarchical rule seemed to be at stake even in Great Britain, where revolution in the seventeenth century had produced a compromise between monarch, unelected noble grandees in the House of Lords, and an elected House of Commons—the balanced system of the eighteenth century, mediated by politicians like Pitt who tended to their governments by securing parliamentary majorities while keeping an eye posted for signs of royal favour or disfavour. Attention if not devotion to the position of the monarch, George III, was a crucial aspect of the British political system and of the British political class.

The rulers of Great Britain were alarmed by the French Revolution. Revolutionary sentiments were thought to be contagious, and Pitt's government kept a wary and repressive eye on presumed revolutionaries. The liberal gestures of 1791—the Canada Act—were forgotten in the rush to shore up authority at home and in the colonies—at any cost. The year 1792, when the new Upper Canadian and Lower Canadian legislatures met for the first time, was also the year of revolutionary violence, the storming of the king's palace in Paris, and the beginning of a bloody reign of terror in France. As the colonists held celebratory banquets and toasted British liberty in honour of their new legislatures—"May liberty extend to Hudson's Bay" was one toast—British ministers began to see the idea of "liberty" as a dangerous French import.[14]

Events in Europe were distant but not foreign to the colonials of British North America. Even though weeks, or more usually months,

passed before word of European events could reach the colonies—
frequently via New York—they were not less exciting or moving because
of the lapse of time. It occurred to some in the colonial government that
what had happened in France could happen in French-speaking Quebec.
Those with a vivid imagination looked south with dread, to the republican United States, and envisioned the spread of the democratic contagion
from the republic north to the British colonies. In that case, the danger
wasn't so much in Lower Canada as in Upper Canada—English-speaking,
British, but also, through the Loyalists, American.

The war did not go well. Revolutionary France repelled its enemies,
and then conquered most of the adjacent parts of Europe—the
Rhineland, Belgium, the Netherlands, and most of Italy. The Royal Navy
cruised the coasts of France and the Mediterranean, safeguarding the
British Isles and overseas commerce, but it could do nothing to impede
the victorious French on land. Meanwhile, France became first a dictatorship and then an empire under the brilliant leadership of Napoleon
Bonaparte. Painfully aware that he could not defeat the British at sea,
Bonaparte reached for the economic weapon, forbidding trade with the
British. Cut off from many of its (closer and cheaper) European sources of
supply, of food and, especially, timber to build ships for the navy, the
British looked to their colonies. The North American colonies produced
what Britain most needed, grain and timber. The British adjusted tariffs
and subsidies so as to discourage unreliable European imports and encourage colonial production, with gratifying results. The British traded subsidy
for security, and got an assured supply; the colonies acquired a predictable
and newly lucrative market. The mercantile system that linked the
colonies' trade to Britain now enjoyed an Indian summer, and the colonies
experienced unprecedented prosperity.

The colonies also exported to the empire. They sent food, wheat and
fish, to the West Indies, a trade formerly supplied by the Americans. The
Americans objected to this, ultimately successfully, but for over forty years
it was a rich source of dispute between Britain and the United States, and
of incidental profit to the British North American colonies.

The two colonies most affected by the changes brought about by war were Lower Canada and New Brunswick. Their lands were heavily forested, especially with white pine, tall and straight and suitable for masts, and both had broad rivers reaching deep into the hinterland. The technology of the timber trade was simple: using a broad axe, lumbermen cut down trees and then "squared" them into rectangles. The resultant square timber was then rolled into nearby rivers and floated in booms or rafts toward the nearest seaport, usually Saint John or Quebec, and loaded onto timber ships—the square shape made it easier to pile, and it wouldn't roll in Atlantic storms—for transport to Great Britain. Where there were no great rivers, but merely forests, as in Nova Scotia, the industry languished. Once the forests accessible by sea were cut down, the business moved on.

The timber trade brought immigrants and reshaped settlement patterns. In 1800 Philemon Wright led a party of Massachusetts settlers up the Ottawa River; by 1806 he was sending timber rafts downriver to the St. Lawrence and on to Quebec. Wright started his own firm, but sometimes timber merchants were employees of British companies— William Price, who arrived in Quebec in 1809, was one such. Price's company, Price Brothers, dominated the timber and lumber business in the Quebec region well into the twentieth century.

The quantities of timber exported were impressive: nine thousand loads in the early 1800s, twenty-seven thousand by 1807, and ninety thousand by 1809. In Lower Canada agriculture and timber displaced fur as the "staple" export of the colony: while fur continued to feed the fortunes of the merchants of Montreal, only a small and diminishing proportion of the province's population was employed in the trade.

Prosperity attracted immigrants and encouraged families: the population of New Brunswick rose from an estimated thirty-five thousand in 1806 to seventy-four thousand in 1824. The increase in population in Lower Canada was truly remarkable: from 165,000 in 1790 to 300,000 by 1815—more than four times what it had been in 1760. In New Brunswick, settlements spread along the rivers, while in Lower Canada the population spread north and south, away from the St. Lawrence to the limits of the Canadian Shield and the Appalachians. The numbers of English speakers grew too, to roughly 15 percent of the province's population by 1815, assisted by immigration from Vermont into what would become the Eastern Townships, south and east of Montreal. Lower Canada's cities also increased, but not as fast as the countryside.

UPPER CANADA

The opening of the Upper Canadian legislature took place in Newark, later Niagara-on-the-Lake, in September 1792, in the presence of the new lieutenant governor, Colonel John Graves Simcoe. Simcoe had commanded a Loyalist regiment in the Revolution; his experiences and those of his men made him bitterly anti-American or, as he saw it, anti-revolutionary. He relied on Loyalist veterans to staff his tiny administration, and on British troops to build the necessary infrastructure for his small—population twenty thousand—colony. Simcoe, finding his capital, Newark, too close to the American border, moved it across Lake Ontario to the shores of a spacious harbour framed by islands. He named the site York, and laid out roads, north from Lake Ontario (Yonge Street) and west (Dundas Street), naming them after British ministers. He dubbed another settlement to the west London, which was naturally placed on the Thames, a muddy stream snaking west to Lake St. Clair. (The capital actually moved to York in 1796, and the legislature first met there in 1797.)

Simcoe organized land surveys and settlement patterns, establishing a checkerboard pattern of farms alongside concession roads, interspersed with the clergy reserves mandated by the Canada Act. The British government had given very large land grants to senior Loyalist officers, which certainly served to differentiate them from the lower ranks, but it didn't work quite as planned. Without the necessary capital to clear the land and turn it into productive farms, the grantees often left it as they found it— a private forest awaiting the efforts of its neighbours to develop the land around it. Land-owning gentry became speculators, a drag on the development of the province. Leaders, as often as not, became scavengers.

Simcoe's reforms, providing transportation, defence, regular communication, and an orderly land settlement, were essential to retaining and attracting population. In that regard Simcoe and his policies were spectacularly successful. The population of Upper Canada soared from the twenty thousand he found in 1792 to an estimated seventy thousand in 1806. Some of that was natural increase, but most of the growth reflected a steady immigration from the adjacent United States. Simcoe had made land available, and on reasonable terms. It was good land, accessible by water and increasingly by road, but those who came to occupy it were, inevitably, Americans.

Simcoe had hoped that his province, and British North America in general, would be insulated by the bitter experience of its founders from the contagion of republicanism and rebellion. He wanted "the utmost attention ... paid to British Customs, Manners, & Principles in the most trivial as well as serious matters [and] ... inculcated to obtain their due Ascendancy to assimilate the Colony with the parent state."[15] But geography got the better of him, just as, in a different sense, it had prevailed over the British generals in the Revolutionary War. There was not time, nor were there resources, to deal with trivialities, and as for serious matters, what mattered most was to put the colony on a sound economic footing and eventually to relieve the British taxpayer of the burden of North American loyalty.

Simcoe did the best he could, but it was never enough. By coincidence, about the time of Simcoe's departure American settlers, who might or might not once have been Loyalists, began to flow into Upper Canada. They got two hundred acres (eighty hectares) each, on condition of occupying and improving the land—attractive enough terms, especially because Upper Canada's fertile lands lay athwart the most direct land connection between upstate New York and Michigan. Simcoe's successors would preside over a province that in its natural endowment was a reproduction of the states south of the lakes—similar in terrain, climate, and fertility, and ultimately in society and economy.

Similar, in fact, in all but politics, and even there, were things truly different? There was, it was true, a Loyalist tradition, and a requirement of loyalty as well as a dread of the creeping republicanism of the United States. Yet by 1812 one reliable observer estimated the later-arriving "American" portion of the population at not less than 60 percent.[16] Simcoe, through rational settlement policies, helped ensure that Upper Canada was a competitive destination for immigrants; in this as in many other ways he was the true founder of the province of Upper Canada. It's ironic that he would not have found its later development very much to his liking.

LOWER CANADA

The establishment of a Lower Canadian legislature was a calculated risk, and its British sponsors regarded it uneasily. The voting franchise was widely distributed—indeed some women were able to vote in early Lower Canadian elections before male privilege prevailed and closed any gender loopholes. But it wasn't so much democracy that worried the British as the certainty of a French-speaking political majority. Their misgivings seemed to be justified when, in the first elections in June 1792, there was disorder along ethnic lines. Yet the ethnic differences can be exaggerated—as they were at the time, for largely partisan purposes. In the first Lower Canadian assembly of fifty members, sixteen were English speakers, although the English minority could not have been larger than ten thousand out of a total population of 156,000.[17]

The legislature did what might have been expected. It elected a speaker from the ranks of the French majority, and it resolved that its debates and legislation should be bilingual. It also passed the necessary financial legislation to keep the province's government afloat (1795) and established a system of courts. Not everyone was pleased: one British merchant darkly wrote in 1792 that he feared many of the Canadian members were "infested with the detestable principles now prevalent in France."[18] He was probably wrong on that point: although there is no precise way of gauging the attraction of French revolutionary ideas in Lower Canada, there wasn't much public sympathy for France or the French cause in the war just beginning.

There was much suspicion, to which French diplomacy contributed. The French minister to the United States summoned French Canadians to rise against their British oppressors and join the cause of liberty. It's not clear how many French Canadians heard the call. For those who did, mainly the clergy and the seigneurs, it was an unpleasant reminder that the French Revolution had overturned order, authority, privilege, and the Catholic religion. They assured the government of their loyalty, and swore to protect the lower orders, the *habitants*, from revolutionary thoughts. The Bishop of Quebec instructed his clergy in November 1793 that "all the loyalty and obedience which they formerly owed to the King of France, they now owed to His Britannic Majesty," and he periodically renewed his exhortations in the years that followed.[19]

The Lower Canadian elite, French- and English-speaking, was frightened. Members of the lower orders—the *habitants*, for the most part—were insufficiently deferential and even insubordinate. An attempt by Dorchester to raise the Lower Canadian militia was resisted. *Habitants* refused to work on repairing the roads. The red "liberty cap" made an appearance—more than one, it was reported. The French revolutionary anthem, "La Marseillaise," wafted into frightened ears. Was revolution in the air? Would the loyal, Catholic inhabitants put their priests to the sword or into exile as their cousins did in old France? The clergy, the seigneurs, and the government hoped not, but they weren't sure. In November 1793 the legislature accordingly suspended the right of habeas corpus—and kept it suspended. The government could now imprison without trial, and without showing cause.

Perhaps those who weren't tried were the lucky ones. This was effectively demonstrated when a real revolutionary conspiracy occurred, the better for the government and all loyal subjects to take fright. The conspiracy centred in Vermont, where a group of politicians plotted with the

French to invade Canada and arouse the French Canadians, and to that end the French government contributed twenty thousand muskets for the arming of the *habitant* population. What the *habitants* would have done with the muskets we shall never know, since they were intercepted in the English Channel by the Royal Navy. One conspirator, David McLane, was convicted and hanged for treason in Quebec in July 1797. His head was then cut off and his body disembowelled. His judge was hailed as "the Queller of Riots and Seditions in the New World."[20]

The Quebec assembly, dominated in this period by seigneurial representatives in combination with the wealthy English-speaking merchants of Montreal, was effusively loyal. In 1799 it voted £20,000 to the British government for the prosecution of the war. Admiral Nelson's victory over the French fleet in the Battle of the Nile in 1798 was the occasion of public rejoicing and celebratory masses. After Nelson's death at Trafalgar in 1805, the merchants of Montreal erected a column to his memory. By then the war had resolved into a straightforward battle against French aggression and tyranny, for the revolution had given way to dictatorship and then to the empire of Napoleon Bonaparte. Bonaparte fought to dominate the world, and the British resisted, often alone.

It is less the Napoleonic period than the earlier, extreme or Jacobin, phase of the French Revolution that is of interest in Canadian political and cultural history. The possibility of revolution, the idea that the people of Lower Canada—and the inhabitants of the other provinces, for that matter—were not deeply attached to religion and monarchical authority, was eventually forgotten. The fact that there hadn't been a rebellion, or a revolution, was what mattered. As the Bishop of Quebec put it, there was now a clear break between French Canada and its French past. The conquest of 1760 had been a blessing in disguise, saving Quebec from the horrors of revolution and atheism. The message was reinforced by royalist and Catholic refugees, including fifty priests, from old France. Highly educated and fervently persuasive, they had a strong influence on the literary and religious culture of French Canada.[21] They brought the message that old France had abandoned true religion and that the conquest of

1760 had not been a deplorable historical accident, but the workings of Providence.[22] British Protestantism was preferable to French atheism, and fortunately the *Canadiens* had the liberty—British liberty—to choose.

True liberty was regularly contrasted with revolutionary enthusiasm, and the tyranny that revolution brought in its wake. For this line of argument, France was a handier example than the United States, and "Jacobin" conspiracies an easier target than plots with the American government. The problem with Jacobin conspiracies was that after 1797 there were none, except in the fevered minds of the authorities.

There was, however, an active political life in the province, which centred, naturally enough, on money—how to raise it and how to spend it. The Montreal merchants favoured a tax on land, while the rural majority favoured anything but. The appointed councils differed with the elected assembly, and English speakers with French speakers. A local party, loosely organized, emerged—the *parti canadien*, which by 1810 was urging, on the best British principles, a government responsible to the legislature and dependent on the consent, and votes, of the elected majority.

This brought the *parti canadien* into a clash with the appointed government, and the governor. The governor of the day was General Sir James Craig, who held the office from 1807 to 1811. Craig freely interpreted dissent as disloyalty, imprisoned the *parti canadien*'s leader, and dissolved the assembly in the hope of securing a better result with new elections. He did not, and the consequent uproar moved London to replace Craig with a less belligerent general, Sir George Prevost, previously lieutenant governor of Nova Scotia.

Prevost succeeded where Craig had failed—politically, that is. That was what London needed, for relations with the United States were deteriorating and, by 1811, pointing to war.

THE WAR OF 1812

War began in North America long before it was officially declared. In a manner of speaking it had never stopped, because the American occupation of the land beyond the Appalachians, the territory conceded in the treaty of 1783 and confirmed by Jay's Treaty in 1794, conflicted with the desires of the existing inhabitants, the Indian nations of the Ohio Valley. Through a combination of military force and shrewd diplomacy, the United States government sliced off successive strips of territory, forcing the Indians farther and farther back. The Indian nations were depleted by hardship and disease as well as war: they couldn't compete with the incoming Americans, who by 1800 heavily outnumbered them.

The American government did not seek conflict: it attempted, as best it could, to place its relations with the Indian nations on a secure and steady basis, concluding the first in a long series of treaties (eventually over four hundred) with the Natives. The Americans tried, with some success, to break the economic links that tied the Indians to the British and Montreal, but that process was slow and, by 1812, incomplete.

The Iroquois no longer dominated the other Indian nations. The Revolutionary War had broken their military power and permanently fragmented the Iroquois confederacy. Many Iroquois had followed the British north, to Upper Canada, and those who remained were scattered in small reservations in northern New York, surrounded by American immigrants. There was, however, a spiritual revival among the Iroquois that paralleled in some respects religious revivals among their neighbours. Its leader, Handsome Lake, preached a religion that stressed Iroquois traditions while urging adaptation to some, at least, of the Americans' ways—enough to guarantee Iroquois survival in what would otherwise have been an alien and destructive environment.[23]

Two brothers, Tenskwatawa and Tecumseh, from another nation, the Shawnee, took up the theme of Native survival, but where Handsome Lake had tacitly accepted that their future lay in a world dominated by whites, the Shawnee brothers had not. Tenskwatawa (known as "the Prophet") proclaimed visions that urged "personal and social repentance" as a means of not only recovering spiritual integrity but victory over the whites. Both brothers condemned accommodation with the whites and urged the various Indian nations to combine against the Americans.

The Americans, however, struck first, moving against Tenskwatawa's camp in November 1811 while Tecumseh, the more militarily gifted of the two, was away. In the skirmish that followed, Tenskwatawa's spells failed to protect his warriors and as a consequence his message was discredited.

War between the United States and Great Britain was by then imminent. There had always been contact between British Indian agents and the Natives of the American northwest. With war looming, the flow of presents and encouragement increased. The British commander in Upper Canada, Isaac Brock, encouraged Tecumseh to rebuild a coalition of the Indian nations. Brock, who felt he could rely on only a small and, he believed, inadequate force of regular British troops, needed all the help he could get.

The actual outbreak of the war was complex. American diplomacy had failed to protect the right of American ships to trade freely with the European combatants, Britain and France. The British, who had naval dominance off the French coast, blockaded French ports and confiscated the cargos of ships trading with the enemy. As the navy searched American ships for contraband goods, it also combed them for contraband sailors— British sailors who had left their country and its ships for more lucrative employment on American vessels. At the same time, the French asserted the same rights over neutral shipping, though without the same kind of power to enforce their claims as the British.

Two American presidents, Thomas Jefferson (1801–09) and his successor James Madison (1809–17), had tried to deal with the problem of "neutral rights" but failed in the face of the realities of economic warfare. The British, weak on land, ruled the sea. Napoleon, powerless at sea, forbade his subjects, and any other country he could occupy or overawe, to traffic with the British.

The British handled the Americans badly, resisting American pressure even as it became apparent that war was a possible outcome. The French, with nothing to lose, appeared to concede to American demands. Meanwhile, domestic American politics were increasingly dominated by demands for war. To the American "war hawks" it was all too easy. The

British were the enemy of 1776. They had been beaten then, and could be, would be, again. The British were preoccupied by war in Europe, and could not respond effectively. The British army in Canada was weak, but British influence over the warlike Indians of the northwest was strong. The recent American immigrants to Upper Canada would rise to support an American invasion, which would therefore be less a war than a triumphal progress. All North America would be united in a single republic, and the work of the Revolution finally completed.

On the other hand, the American army was weak too, with under four thousand men scattered over half a continent. Though the Republican party of President Madison had a majority in Congress, it faced a strong Federalist party opposition. The Republicans drew their strength from the south, far from the border, and from the west, where the population was as yet small and dispersed, and for the most part far from the frontier. In New England and New York there was no enthusiasm for the war, and yet effective attacks on Canada would have to be based in those two regions. Though the British army in Canada was small, it was being reinforced. The Royal Navy ruled the seas, including the waters off North America, and the American navy, while competent to fight single engagements, was too small to defeat the number of ships the British could bring to bear. The disruption of American shipping was certain, once war was declared. Finally, the war in Europe wasn't going badly. A British army under the marquis of Wellington had tied down a large French army in Spain, and in 1812 Wellington was advancing. Napoleon was at the other end of Europe, preparing to invade Russia with the greatest army yet seen, which meant that his army in Spain was weaker than ever before, and hence prey for Wellington.

The Americans nevertheless declared war, on 18 June 1812. The news travelled fast, testament to far better communications than in 1776. The governor in Quebec, Prevost, heard the news within a week, and Brock, the commander and acting lieutenant governor in Upper Canada, soon after. So did British fur traders in the northwest, who promptly put themselves and their Indian clients at the disposal of the British army.

Using fur traders and the threat of the horrors of Indian warfare, a local British commander secured the surrender of the American fort at Michilimackinac.

Michilimackinac was a small post, far away. Fort Detroit was closer to the action, and had a large American garrison—large, that is, by the standards of the war that was beginning, in which a force of five thousand would be very large indeed. (By comparison, Napoleon's army invading Russia in June 1812 numbered 691,000, while the largest single British army assembled during the war was 10,351 strong, for an attack on Plattsburgh, New York, in 1814.) The American commander at Detroit, William Hull, inspired by memories of the Revolution (he was a veteran) and encouraged by the belief that the inhabitants of Upper Canada would rise to join him, crossed the Detroit River to begin his march on the provincial capital at York (Toronto). He issued a proclamation that informed the inhabitants of Upper Canada that he was coming to liberate them. Consequently, all well-disposed Upper Canadians should take up arms against the king and join Hull's army. Should they resist, and be so misguided as to be captured fighting alongside their Indian allies, they would be hanged—"murdered without mercy" for keeping their oaths to the king and resisting their invaders, in the words of an American Baptist minister living in Upper Canada.[24]

Hull was not entirely mistaken in believing that many of the inhabitants of Upper Canada, being Americans, did not want to fight him. General Brock, his opponent, agreed, and despaired of being able to raise an army. But Hull's proclamation offended many, and his inertia gave those who favoured the United States no encouragement. Brock had a chance, and seized it. With a tiny regular force, and enlisting Tecumseh's warriors, he moved against Hull. Hull, dreading an Indian massacre, fled with his small army—albeit larger than Brock's—to Detroit. There he succumbed to psychological pressure, the terrors of the forest and the Indians, and surrendered the fort. Hull had defeated himself.

Hull's defeat was decisive. His invasion represented the best opportunity the Americans had of first neutralizing and then absorbing the

American inhabitants of Upper Canada. His defeat reversed the demoral-ization of the colonial government and its supporters, and inspired the local regular forces to resist long enough for reinforcements to reach them from Montreal.

The next invasion occurred at Niagara on 13 October 1812. Part of an American army crossed the Niagara River in small boats, to be met on the other side, on Queenston Heights, by a British force commanded by Brock. Brock was killed, but British resistance continued. Then American reinforcements, New York state militia, refused to cross the river. The failure of reinforcements to arrive doomed the Americans on the other side, who had to escape or surrender.

Worse than the defeat at Queenston was the failure of the Americans to cut the St. Lawrence supply route. The border ran down the middle of the river, the only serious connection between Upper and Lower Canada, but the Americans were unable to cut British river traffic bringing supplies and reinforcements from Montreal to Kingston. Montreal itself, less than fifty kilometres from the border, also remained untouched by American action. Better still, from the British point of view, Vermont farmers and merchants were happy to supply the British garrison in Lower Canada, while from the French-Canadian perspective British purchases of supplies and services for the troops were a shot in the arm for the local economy. (The colonial government enjoyed the enthusiastic support of the Catholic bishop and his clergy, who denounced the wickedness of the American invasion and the duty of every subject to rise to the colony's defence.)[25] In Nova Scotia the lieutenant governor, Sir John Sherbrooke, another general, offered to leave the inhabitants of New England and especially Maine undisturbed—provided they did the same for Nova Scotia and New Brunswick.[26] The Maritime provinces did, however, fit out privateers (private vessels licensed to attack enemy vessels and their cargo) to prey on American shipping, to their considerable profit.

Supply and transport proved critical for the next two years of the war. Supplies flowed easily across the Atlantic, as far as Quebec and Montreal. The St. Lawrence was safeguarded by a passive American policy—no U.S.

troops were even stationed at Ogdensburg, the principal border town, after early 1813.[27] The British and American navies ran a construction contest on Lake Ontario, as each side strove to build more and bigger ships. In April 1813 the Americans raided the provincial capital, York, where they burned public buildings and stole the speaker's mace from the legislature. The York raid was an isolated incident. Neither side achieved dominance, which meant that the British could maintain an army in Upper Canada, even though 1813 saw the loss of naval control of Lake Erie and consequently of the western part of the province (and Detroit) and the defeat and death of Tecumseh in the Battle of the Thames. An American invasion across the Niagara achieved partial success, but on the St. Lawrence and on the Lower Canadian border the Americans failed to break the British supply lines. By not losing to locally superior forces, and by keeping their Upper Canadian army intact, the British had in effect won again.

The naval war was, from the British point of view, even more satisfactory. There were individual losses in engagements with American ships, but the British had far more ships than the Americans, and succeeded in bottling up the ports of Boston and New York. Most humiliating of all, the Royal Navy established a base in Chesapeake Bay and levied "contributions" on the bayside towns in return for not burning them to the ground.

The same kind of depredations characterized the fighting in Upper Canada. After the British army withdrew from Detroit to Niagara in 1813 there was no authority and no force for order all along the northern shore of Lake Erie. There, guerrillas—partly made up of those few Upper Canadians who had cast their lot with the United States—roamed at will, plundering their former neighbours and burning their farms, mills, and houses. Even the presence of regular armies was no safeguard: when the Americans burned Queenston on a cold night in December 1813, leaving its inhabitants to fend for themselves, the British and Canadians retaliated by burning Buffalo and Black Rock. As much as anything else, the nature of the war in Upper Canada confirmed the formerly American inhabitants in their hostility toward the American army. By permitting the guerrilla war, American commanders abandoned any chance of securing their earlier objective in the war, namely the acquisition of Canada.

Meanwhile, the American government had difficulty recruiting, training, and keeping in the field any kind of sizeable force. The engagements fought along the Upper Canadian frontier were important strategically, but tactically they didn't compare to the great bodies of troops simultaneously manoeuvring in Europe. What is generally overlooked is that by 1813 the British had succeeded in assembling a very considerable army in Lower and Upper Canada, fifteen thousand all told, which compared very favourably with what the Americans could field on the Canadian frontier. (The fifteen thousand, though, were spread over thirteen hundred kilometres, and were never assembled in a single force.)

All this had the effect of depleting American enthusiasm for the war. It was also clear by the end of 1813 that the odds against American victory were increasing. Napoleon was foiled in his invasion of Russia, and lost most of his army in the process. The countries of central Europe threw off French rule, and combined to chase the French army and its emperor across Germany. The British invaded France from the south, where Wellington, now a duke, had liberated Spain from the French and restored the Spanish royal family. It was only a matter of time until the victorious British army under its great general could be redeployed across the Atlantic, if the American war continued.

The European war ended with the abdication of Napoleon Bonaparte in April 1814. The British government informed Governor Prevost that reinforcements were indeed on the way, fifteen thousand of Wellington's best troops, appropriately commanded. Hopes were high for a favourable end to the conflict, including the retention of Forts Niagara and Detroit, with Michigan to become Indian territory. There was no thought of conquering the United States, or reversing the outcome of the American Revolution: Wellington doubted the practicability of large-scale war on the European model in North America, and in any case emphatically told the government that he had no wish to go to America.

But 1814 proved to be another stalemated year. Heavy fighting—especially the battles of Chippewa and Lundy's Lane—continued along the Niagara frontier, with the British gradually improving their position but with no decisive change of fortune for either side. On the east coast, Sherbrooke occupied eastern Maine and diverted the revenues from taxes and tariffs there to Halifax, where they ultimately served to endow Dalhousie University. The British government dithered, balancing the possibility of renewed war in Europe against the possibility of using its new preponderance of force in North America to seek a decisive military victory and an advantageous peace. Wellington advised making peace, arguing that a decisive victory was unlikely and that enough had already been done to prove the defensibility of Canada. "[It] is my opinion," he wrote, "that the war has been a most successful one, and highly honourable to the British arms." It was true that the Americans still held some Upper Canadian territory, but that could be exchanged for American territory—eastern Maine and Fort Niagara—held by the British.[28]

And so it was. British and American representatives gathered in the neutral town of Ghent, in Belgium, and on Christmas Day 1814 signed a treaty of peace that returned to the status quo ante bellum, with borders and other arrangements to be just as they had been before the declaration of war in June 1812. The peace of 1814 concluded years of hostilities that had begun with the Revolutionary War. It was in many respects an affair of a generation—those who had fought in the Revolutionary War as youths were still in authority during the War of 1812, like President Madison or his secretary of state, James Monroe. Others, like the future secretary of state and president, John Quincy Adams, or his rival Andrew Jackson, remembered the war from childhood.

The war was now over. British power had not won against a revolutionary movement with strong popular support, outstandingly led. They had beaten back a feeble American invasion, indifferently led and doubtfully supported by American public opinion. As for the British provincials, in the Canadas or in the Maritimes, they had not rallied to the American cause at the outset, and afterward were sufficiently provoked by American actions to lend their support to their own, colonial, government. The provinces of British North America, American by geography, cultural affinity, and—except in Lower Canada—language and style, remained British. The British Empire, as of 1814, offered great and obvious benefits, in trade and defence, to its colonies. The empire would, reasonable colonists hoped, offer the same kind of substantial advantage in the future.

7

TRANSFORMATIONS AND CONNECTIONS, 1815–1840

Rural settlement: A recently cleared farm on the Rideau River, Upper Canada, 1830.

British North America at the end of the War of 1812 appeared externally and internally stable. The colonies had weathered the war. They were part of a triumphant empire, with its victorious army and a navy that faced no discernible rivals. There was no significant disloyalty or rebellion in any of the North American provinces, and Nova Scotia, New Brunswick, and Lower Canada had profited greatly from the war. The mercantile system guaranteed the colonies special economic benefits—favourable duties and a protected market—in the home country. Meanwhile, the business of economic development kept the local politicians happy, or at any rate preoccupied.

The world, or at least the colonies' place in it, was more uncertain than it appeared. The Treaty of Ghent had established peace in North America, but a very doubtful peace. To get peace, the British sacrificed their Indian allies, who were left to the mercy of the Americans, to be absorbed into the republic. Boundary questions remained unresolved; the American republic was in an expansive, aggressive mood; and in the middle distance the Spanish empire in America was convulsed by revolution. Fear of revolution at home obsessed the British government just as fear of revolution abroad obsessed its allies. There was no guarantee, no certainty that the United States might not try again to annex Canada and fulfill the dream of the American Revolution.

Things turned out very differently. Relations between British North America and the United States were never easy, but the War of 1812 proved to be the last officially sanctioned war along the border. Gradually the Americans turned their attention elsewhere and onto other matters in the years after 1815—to their western frontier, rather than to the north, to immigration and its problems, to war with Mexico rather than Great Britain, and to slavery and the internal contradictions of their own country. Canada and the United States did not grow apart, but they nevertheless became more distant.

The maintenance of the British connection had much to do with that, but so did the flow of British immigration to Canada, which eventually totalled in the hundred thousands—meaning that Canada was actually more British by 1840, in terms of its population, than it had been in 1800 or 1815. One estimate showed emigration from the British Isles to British North America rising from 3370 in 1816 to 23,534 in 1819 to 66,000 in 1832. The numbers continued to grow through the 1840s until, in 1847, British migrants to British North America numbered almost 110,000.[1] Of these numbers, well over half came from Ireland, and of the Irish total, Protestants outnumbered Catholics by roughly two to one.[2]

The immigrants came because British North America had entered a phase of chaotic growth and change. Timber and lumber brought development to New Brunswick and the Canadas. One driver of change was technology: the generation after 1815 saw the implementation of steam power—steam engines in lumber mills and factories, and on steamboats and in railways. Canals, elaborate and expensive, brought the ocean into direct contact with the Great Lakes. The invention and perfection of the railway transformed distance, and the steamship brought Europe and North America closer together. Communication no longer required travel—the telegraph replaced the dispatch rider and the railway replaced the stagecoach and the teamster's wagon.

Politicians tried to respond to the miracles of the age. Development was its own reward, since a more developed economy produced more affluent workers. Life was still hard, but not quite as hard. Timber flowed to Great Britain, and timber ships sailed back crammed with immigrants—slowly at first, but in huge numbers after the middle 1820s. Increasingly the ships sailed faster, as steam began to take hold. Sailing times and transoceanic fares dropped, and more immigrants signed on for the voyage. Governments were encouraged to invest in transport—in canals, first, and then in railways. They raised the money partly through taxes, but also through loans and hence debt. Taxes and taxpayers fed the appetites of developers and mercantile speculators; taxpayers, meanwhile, could meet the charge because of growth in immigration and population.

As the population grew it became more difficult for the British government to respond to the needs of the colonies. Increasingly, however, the British government didn't want to. There were two main reasons for this. The focus of empire was shifting, economically, politically, and militarily, toward the east, especially to India, but also to China and Australia. Lower Canada's importance, so apparently great in the 1790s, dwindled by comparison with India's, and the British garrisons in North America seemed minuscule in comparison with military cantonments in India. The army of twenty-nine thousand in North America in 1815 shrank to a mere three thousand by the 1850s. At the same time, larger populations in a more developed colony meant that the urgency of imperial subsidy diminished.

The rearrangement of the British army mirrored a rearrangement of the empire. The provinces of British North America were no longer the only colonies of settlement: Australia, starting in 1788, South Africa (from 1806), and New Zealand rivalled Canada in British attention. Granted, it was easier to get to North America—as little as four weeks' sailing in 1820—compared with Australia, which took nine or ten months.[3] The relatively short shipping time and the familiarity of the run across the North Atlantic encouraged trade and emigration with and to the Atlantic provinces and the Canadas. The timber trade in particular stimulated the availability of shipping, as it was discovered that timber ships could be easily, albeit cheaply and shoddily, refitted to carry immigrants on the outward voyage to Canada. Accommodation didn't have to match the numbers carried, however, and some wretched emigrants found themselves spending part or all of the voyage on deck or sheltering under lifeboats. Authorities in the colonies complained, with reason, about "the confined, crowded and filthy state of the vessels"[4] and hence the condition of their immigrants. Nevertheless, while Canada was still an obvious aspect of the empire, it was no longer unique among colonies of settlement.

The ties between Britain and the colonies remained tight. There was, above all, the mercantilist colonial system. Colonial goods, especially timber and foodstuffs, had preferred entry to the British market, and the British market was expanding. With the Industrial Revolution in full swing, factories sprouted on the British landscape, and with factories came new houses, even new cities. Canadian timber, the mainstay for the construction of naval ships, was even more desirable for housing. Demand in Britain stimulated log booms down the Saint John, Miramichi, and Ottawa rivers, profits for colonial timber merchants, and immigration to the edges of the Canadian forest.

The British government contributed to the colonial economy by building and rebuilding fortifications along the border with the United States and at Halifax and Quebec City. New canals were dug to bypass rapids along the Ottawa and St. Lawrence, but, mindful of the exposed transport route along the international frontier on the St. Lawrence, British army engineers built what was at the time the single largest and most expensive public works project in the empire: the Rideau Canal, which stretched southwest from the Ottawa River to Lake Ontario at Kingston. At £800,000 the canal *was* costly, with its large stone locks and kilometres of connecting waterways; in its defence it could be said that it was built to a very high standard. (Including canal improvements on the Ottawa and St. Lawrence and contributions to the new Welland Canal bypassing Niagara Falls, British taxpayers contributed £1,069,026 to the improvement of Canada's waterways.)[5]

The locks still stand and the canals remain a monument to nineteenth-century engineering, although the Rideau Canal is now essentially a tourist attraction. That canal helped populate eastern Upper Canada and in a minor way stimulated the lumber industry. A new settlement on the Ottawa, at the junction of the Rideau river and canal, was named Bytown after Colonel John By, the officer in charge of the project. Bytown never was used as a staging area for troops and military supplies, but it proved extremely convenient in forwarding log booms, and later for lumber mills.

Canals were the great technological attraction of the early nineteenth century, and induced speculators and speculative governments to invest millions in their construction and upkeep, but it wasn't the St. Lawrence or Rideau canal that had the greatest impact on Canada. It was, rather, a project conceived by the governor of New York State, DeWitt Clinton, linking the Hudson River with the Great Lakes at Buffalo and points along Lake Ontario. The Erie Canal, completed in 1825, competed directly with the inadequate canals along the St. Lawrence and secured New York City's position as the dominant port of entry to the continent. New York, after all, was ice-free year-round, while Montreal, its most logical rival, was blocked by ice from December to April or May.

By the 1820s Montreal was losing its trademark business, the industry that had founded the fortunes of the great merchants of the city. For 150 years fur brigades had annually left the city in the spring in their great canoes, heading up the Ottawa for the *pays d'en haut*, returning in the fall with their lucrative cargoes destined for the fur markets of London and Paris. The North West Company of Montreal competed directly and mostly successfully with the London-based Hudson's Bay Company. The Bay Company had finally bestirred itself and begun to compete directly with the Montrealers, sending traders into the interior and founding posts across the west, until, in 1819, the fur-trade rivals began negotiations to end the misery of competition. Along the Red River in what is now Manitoba, where one of the Hudson's Bay Company directors, the Earl of Selkirk, a Scottish peer, had founded a colony of displaced Scots, there was actual violence, including the murder of some of the settlers, and this attracted unfavourable notice at home.[6] By 1817 the disputes between the earl and the North West Company had become entangled in the corrupt Canadian legal system, heavily influenced if not dominated by the North-Westers and their connections. (One of Selkirk's men stated, accurately, that "the judges, juries and crown officers of Canada are a set of damned rascals," and that consequently the earl would act independently of "the rascally Government of Canada.")[7]

Understandably, the earl was not anxious for a settlement of the differences between the North West Company and the Hudson's Bay Company, short of the surrender and prosecution of most of the North-West partners. But the earl died, virtually bankrupt, early in 1820, speeding negotiations to put an end to his quarrels and to the competition they had come to symbolize. Putting an end to inter-company rivalry wasn't the only impulse in play, however. There was dissension inside the North West Company between the "wintering partners"—those in the interior who did the actual trading—and the Montreal end of the business.

Under the circumstances, the North-Westers were disposed to compromise. In a settlement confirmed at a council of "wintering partners" at Fort William in 1821, most of the North West Company's active personnel moved over to the Hudson's Bay Company. Those trading for the Bay ("chief factors" or "chief traders") would receive a share in the company's profits, regulated by a document specifying the division called the "Deed Poll." Over the longer term, the most important change was that the base for the fur trade shifted from Montreal and Fort William to the HBC posts on Hudson Bay. Guided in its operations by an able and ambitious Scot, George (later Sir George) Simpson, and encouraged by a relieved British government, the HBC would henceforth control the fur trade from Labrador to the Pacific and from the Arctic to the American border. But where, exactly, was the border?

DEFINING AND DEFENDING THE BORDER

The War of 1812 did not miraculously remove or release tensions between Great Britain and the United States, or between the British provinces and their American neighbours. The American government had trading ambitions, asking the British to allow American ships to trade into British West Indian ports and retaliating when they were not. There was a brief naval race in the 1820s. There were constant complaints about fisheries regulations off the Atlantic provinces. There were reports in the American press of discontent, and eventually, in the

1830s, rebellion among the provincials. Many Americans remained convinced that the provincials would, given half a chance, join them. Many American politicians in the 1820s and 1830s could reasonably be described as anglophobic, and many of their British counterparts were condescending if not contemptuous where Americans were concerned.

The border continued to be fortified and garrisoned. The British took expensive defensive measures, like the Rideau Canal, and maintained or expanded their fortifications, like the Citadel at Quebec. The Americans too built forts, including one on the British side of the frontier, owing to a surveyor's mistake. That fort, at Rouse's Point on Lake Champlain, had to be abandoned, and with it the $100,000 the United States had spent. The British government deployed a succession of generals to run the North American colonies—Sherbrooke, Richmond, Dalhousie, Maitland, and Colborne. They would have been available in case of war with the Americans, but the war never came. Instead, they were called on to deal, usually unsuccessfully, with local politics, which they managed, as we shall see, very badly.

Both the British and American governments, fortunately, had to pay off their previous wars and repair their relations with their taxpaying voters. British generals, including the apparently eternal Duke of Wellington, gave their opinion that the military odds in favour of the Americans were increasing, though the superiority of the British navy would allow Great Britain to hang on to port cities and coastal areas as well as blockade the American coastline. Increasingly, the defence of British North America seemed to be something that wasn't worth spending money on, and there were naturally other priorities, political and economic.

The British government had its own political difficulties: with Catholic Emancipation (giving political rights, including the vote, to Catholics), political reform (adjusting a scandalously outdated parliamentary system), and the government of Ireland (imprudently absorbed into the United Kingdom in 1801). Then there was emancipation pure and simple, freeing the slaves across the empire and ending slavery as an institution.

There was also a large empire to manage, and not just Canada.

These considerations made British cabinets increasingly careful of spending money on the colonies and, after the 1830s, especially on Canada. As long as there was a balanced relationship with the colonies, mercantilism offset by colonial acceptance of overall British political and economic direction, there would be little cause to change the meandering course of British colonial policy. But, as is so often the case, economics did not dictate the course of politics.

The United States gradually forgot about the British colonies. There was obviously no threat from the reduced British garrisons of the postwar period, and the forts and canals, though costly, were obviously designed for defence, not aggression. The British stopped subsidizing the Indians of the American northwest: they were on their own in dealing with the American government.

The Great Lakes naval fleets became early casualties of a drive for disarmament, a situation ratified by the Rush-Bagot Agreement of 1817, which limited rather than abolished warships on the lakes. That was followed by a convention in 1818 that ran the British–American boundary from the Lake of the Woods west to the Rockies along the 49th parallel. There was a further agreement to treat the territory west of the Rockies, north of Spanish California and south of Russian Alaska, which was to be called Oregon, as a condominium, a jointly sovereign space. It wasn't a stable arrangement, but in 1818 there was no need for government in the territory, no need for garrisons, and no point in courts. The Hudson's Bay Company became the principal commercial operator in Oregon, as in all British territory north of the United States and south and east of Alaska. It was free, for the time being, to pursue profit. In the east, a boundary dispute lingered in the Aroostook country between New Brunswick and Maine; it wouldn't be resolved for another generation.

The imprecision of these arrangements eventually caused disagreements, accompanied by a great deal of heated rhetoric. Neither the United States nor Great Britain especially wanted war, but there were occasional demands to cut through the compromises and reach a conclusion by annexing British America, even if that had to be done through war. One such publicist, John J. O'Sullivan, coined the phrase "Manifest Destiny" to encapsulate the inevitable absorption by the United States of the entire continent of North America.

Eventually, in 1846, the condominium was ended by a compromise, dividing Oregon into a British zone north of the 49th parallel but including Vancouver Island and an American zone to the south. The boundary farther east was also completed, by treaty (the Webster-Ashburton treaty) and an arbitration in 1842 that divided disputed lands along the upper St. John River and fixed the border between New Brunswick and Lower Canada on the one side and Maine on the other.

All this was possible because Americans were looking elsewhere: at the settlement of the Mississippi Valley, at the absorption of large numbers of immigrants, and at the question of slavery, which began in the 1820s to disturb and then to define American politics. There were quarrels with the newly independent, but militarily weak, republic of Mexico, and eventually there was a war that resulted in the annexation of Texas and California and the lands in between to the United States. All this took time and energy, with little political will left over to bring the British colonies into the fold.

There was no cause to disturb the provincials who so closely resembled Americans on the English-speaking side. As for the French of Lower Canada, they came to be seen as increasingly exotic, clustered in their villages along the St. Lawrence under the church spires. They were no longer a threat, given their Catholic religion and their French language, but rather a kind of tourist attraction. "To a traveller from the Old World, Canada East [Lower Canada] may appear like a new country, and its inhabitants like colonists, but to me," Henry Thoreau wrote in 1850, "coming from New England, and being a very green traveller withal ... it appeared as old as Normandy itself, and realized much that I had heard of Europe and the Middle Ages."[8]

The view of the United States from the Canadian side was darker. During the war, most of the American-born inhabitants of the colonies had remained loyal to the British side, or at least hadn't aided the American armies. But some had, especially in western Upper Canada. Captured, tried, and condemned at Ancaster in May 1814, eight Upper Canadians fighting on the American side were hanged. Their property was confiscated.

The question of "American" loyalty lingered after the war. Provincial elites used the loyalty issue, or the American issue, to consolidate their own power. Officiously loyal to the crown, they sought to exclude ex-Americans from public office. Given the large proportion of American-born people in the provinces, there was the possibility that half the population of Upper Canada could be discriminated against, if not completely disenfranchised. "[The] very first elements out of which our social system was framed," a Toronto lady wrote in 1837, "were repugnance and contempt for the new institutions of the United States, and a dislike to the people of that country."[9]

Seen from London, and through the prism of two hundred years, the concept of "British North America" seems natural—British colonies of more or less similar origins, political systems, economic ties, and general culture, Lower Canada always excepted. In the 1820s or 1830s, however, British North America was little more than a name. The governor in Quebec City was merely the titular head. The lieutenant governors in the Atlantic provinces took their directions straight from London, and the lieutenant governor in Upper Canada was hardly more subordinate. Politicians in the various provinces had little to do with each other, nor was there much movement of people back and forth. The economies of Nova Scotia, New Brunswick, Prince Edward Island, and Newfoundland faced outward, toward the sea, and across the sea to the West Indies or Great Britain.

The Atlantic provinces had more to do with New England than with the Canadas: old connections died hard, and Boston was still the regional metropolis as far as Nova Scotians were concerned. Certainly people on both sides of the border still recognized each other. When the Nova Scotian lawyer and judge Thomas Chandler Haliburton serialized the adventures of an imaginary Yankee peddler travelling through Nova Scotia in the mid-1830s, it quickly became a hit in the United States as well. The first American edition pointed out that Nova Scotians came from the same origins as Americans, and prophesied that eventually North America would be reunited as "one compact empire of friendly and confederated states."[10]

Haliburton's Yankee character, Sam Slick, was presented as a sharp dealer, active and enterprising. The British provincials, though amiable, were not, or not so much. It was an impression that occurred to many travellers moving through the United States and the British provinces in the early nineteenth century. An official observer, Lord Dalhousie, governor general in the 1820s, took a negative view: "The conclusion must be," he wrote, "that there is no natural disposition to public improvement—they would go on to the end of time, indolent, unambitious, contented, & un-enterprising."[11]

A visiting French magistrate, Alexis de Tocqueville, observed of the *Canadiens,* "All in all this race of men seemed to us inferior to the Americans in knowledge, but superior in qualities of the heart. One had no sense here of that mercantile spirit which obtrudes in all the actions and sayings of an American."[12] Much the same was said of the English-speaking Canadians, though it might be cloaked in appreciative terms; they were considered superior in gentility, or at least lacking in the vulgarity that some British travellers and some of their Canadian hosts claimed to discover in the United States.[13]

It was, therefore, a case of political differences and cultural resemblance. But even the political differences weren't so deep: as a political crisis developed in the colonies in the 1820s and 1830s, there was even the possibility that the colonies would abandon monarchy and the British connection and opt for republicanism and, presumably, annexation to the United States.

What was important was that the British connection didn't necessarily mean Toryism, a devotion to feudal or traditional forms of society or behaviour.[14] There were, certainly, Tories in the provinces, powerful in government and the Anglican Church and anxious to preserve privileges that amounted to a monopoly on public office and lucrative official patronage. But there were many more who weren't Tories, who belonged to different Protestant sects, who wanted a share in government and the things that government could facilitate—roads, schools, canals, and progress. Not for the last time, the provincials looked across the border and glimpsed progress, enterprise, and prosperity. Their sense of rivalry, or even envy, gave a special edge to politics. As it would turn out, the constitutional systems of the various colonies were ill adapted to contain serious political differences.

THE POLITICAL ECONOMY OF STALEMATE

The constitutional framework devised for the colonies in the 1780s and 1790s broke down in the 1820s and 1830s. The particulars vary with the province: all politics are proverbially local, and there was no common cause among the Maritime provinces and the Canadas and certainly no common leadership. Newfoundland was, as always, a very special case.

Newfoundland was both the oldest and most backward British colony. The island was most valued as a piece of rocky real estate surrounded by fish, and it was the fishing enterprise that was most important. The government had only grudgingly accepted and recognized permanent settlements along the coast, and the wars of the seventeenth and eighteenth centuries had stunted such habitation as there was. Authority was a seasonal thing, embodied in a British naval officer appearing and vanishing with the fishing fleets; only in 1825 did a governor arrive and take up permanent residence in the capital, St. John's. Seven years later this oldest British colony finally acquired an elected assembly, which thereafter quarrelled with the governor over revenues and expenditures, and, of course, patronage, the filling of offices.

Prince Edward Island had a much older governmental structure, with a lieutenant governor and assembly since the 1770s, but its society and politics were almost as unusual as Newfoundland's, centring not so much on who was who within the colony, as who was not—the absentee proprietors who owned much of the province's fertile land but who definitely did not wish to be taxed for the privilege.

In New Brunswick the key question revolved around not who owned land, but who leased it. Outside the fertile St. John Valley and a few other arable enclaves, land was valuable for growing trees, but not for farming. Forests were leased, not granted or sold. Who, then, could or should cut the trees and sell the resulting timber or lumber, and how much should they pay the crown—the provincial government—for the privilege? Since trees were the passport to wealth in New Brunswick, and since politics and government determined the leases, these were questions of the utmost importance.

They were also the easiest to resolve. The British government gave way before provincial insistence and in 1831 transferred control over crown lands from an imperial official to the local government, which, though still appointed and elitist, kept its profits at home.

Nova Scotia was the most populous of the Atlantic colonies, especially after it was reunited with Cape Breton Island in 1820. Nova Scotia's problems began with geography, a difficult terrain that separated rather than united the various parts of the province. Halifax, the largest town and the provincial capital, the home of the legislature and the Anglican bishop, was also the seat of an army garrison and a Royal Navy base.[15] Looking outward, to Britain and the seven seas, Halifax was often seen as remote and aloof from the concerns of the hinterland—whose inhabitants were non-Anglican, and were engaged in farming or fishing, or, in Cape Breton, mining coal.

If Halifax had an English or Loyalist character, other parts of the province were the domain of the Scots. Until the 1770s Nova Scotia was "New Scotland" by title only. Then, in 1773, Scots landed and settled at Pictou. Over time, and interrupted by war, more filtered in, encouraged by the desire of Scottish landlords to replace their human population, unprofitable and frequently needy and demanding, with sheep, who had a better attitude to property and could be converted into profit. These were highland Scots, frequently Catholic and Gaelic-speaking, abandoned by their clan chieftains: "The coward who now rules us," an emigrant poet wrote, "Evicted his own, few remain. / He prefers sheep in the hills to a kilted retinue."[16]

The later immigrants headed not for Pictou but Cape Breton Island, which they dubbed "the land of freedom and food," where landlords were mercifully lacking.[17] It was mainly a rural society they founded, divided between majority Catholics and minority Presbyterians, and with little direct connection to the rest of Nova Scotia. What was unusual was that by the middle of the nineteenth century three-quarters of the island's population spoke Gaelic, in part because of the remoteness and isolation of Cape Breton and, within the island, the absence of a major, offsetting centre of population and the lack of alternative immigrant streams.

Cape Breton did not exert much influence on the politics of Nova Scotia in the nineteenth century. Politics were, and had to be, Halifax-based, and it was in Halifax that the first serious political dissent arose. It began softly, with disputes over revenue between the elected assembly and the appointed council—which became known in a rather sinister way as the "Council of Twelve." (Thomas Chandler Haliburton, the author of *Sam Slick*, called them "the twelve old ladies," but there were plenty of aspiring politicians, sitting outside the charmed circle, who wished to join them.) Then, in 1835, a journalist, Joseph Howe, the son of a Loyalist refugee from Boston, levelled charges of misconduct against members of the local elite. They answered with a libel suit. Howe vigorously defended himself, and after ten minutes' deliberation, a Halifax jury acquitted him.

Howe had a gift with words. "The government is like an ancient Egyptian mummy," he wrote, "wrapped up in narrow and antique preju-dices—dead and inanimate, but likely to last for ever."[18] Howe set out to unwrap the mummy. Elected to the assembly in 1836, he cobbled together a rather shaky majority in favour of reform and in 1837 passed Twelve Resolutions that demanded, in effect, that the government be responsible to the elected assembly, as was the case in Great Britain. One prominent feature in Howe's propositions was the disestablishment of the

Anglican Church, so that all religious denominations might be placed on the same level. No demand better expressed the non-Tory nature of colonial society; and it represented, too, the large majority of the non-Anglican inhabitants of the province. It was a demand guaranteed to enrage the very Anglican Halifax establishment, and it did.

The British government's response was feeble, contradictory, and prolonged. In London the Whigs were in power, and had gained it using the issue of parliamentary reform, expanding the right to vote to whole classes of people previously excluded. The government collectively and individually was therefore uneasy about denying or defying the wishes of an elected assembly. "You deceive yourself," a colonial governor wrote to a conservative friend in Upper Canada, "the spirit of real, downright, *old Style* Toryism [is] extinct, dead, defunct, defeated and no more capable of revisiting the Nations of the Earth than it is possible for the sparks to descend or the stream to flow upwards."[19] Slowly the British government retreated—conceding this or that point while attempting to maintain its right to control, through the lieutenant governor, what it considered essential powers. The process was confused and messy, and reached no sudden satisfactory conclusion.

It could hardly move faster, because the case of Nova Scotia or New Brunswick could not be considered in isolation. What was conceded to one colony would ultimately have to be conceded to all, and the rhythm of change was set not by the coastal colonies but the larger provinces in the interior.

THE CANADAS

The Atlantic provinces had always been smaller in terms of population than Lower Canada, but by the 1820s they had fallen behind Upper Canada as well. It was the two populous Canadian colonies that would cause the most trouble for the British government through the 1820s and 1830s, until, in 1837–38, they actually produced armed rebellions.

The basic problem was the same. Local majorities came to believe that government was not responding to their needs or wants. The constitutional system made it impossible to rectify the problem, because the appointed government was independent of the elected assembly. Delays in response, or refusals to respond, from the local governors or from the Colonial Office in London provoked exasperation and, eventually, radicalized local political leaders.

The local reform politicians did have one weapon in their arsenal. If they could command a majority in the assembly, they could refuse to fund the government through taxes. The government, in its turn, tried to find ways to raise funds without asking the assembly for money. The easiest way to raise money was through tariffs—divided on a prorated basis between Upper and Lower Canada—and through the sale of crown lands. If sales were plentiful, the governors and their officials and supporters could live off the proceeds. This fitted in any case with the main business of government in the Canadas after 1815: to populate and develop the provinces. There was some urgency in selling and populating the vacant lands, for there were signs by the mid-1820s that the imperial government would not forever subsidize the North American colonies.[20]

In Upper Canada settlement should have been a relatively straightforward affair. The government sought out settlers, either directly or through some intermediary, such as a colonization agent or a land company. Sometimes the imperial government encouraged emigration, by locating disbanded regiments in the colony after the Napoleonic Wars, or by encouraging surplus populations, especially in Ireland, to emigrate.

The most extraordinary settlement scheme was the Canada Company, the inspiration of a Scottish novelist, John Galt: it purchased from the Upper Canadian government vast tracts of land—2.5 million acres (1 million hectares) at three shillings and sixpence per acre, or the equivalent of $295,000, payable over sixteen years.[21] The British government, seeing an alternative source of funding for Upper Canada, was very pleased. Despite some early reverses—Galt at one point was imprisoned for debt—the company was profitable and, as it turned out, long-lived. It sold its last lot only in the 1950s, when it was finally wound up.[22]

There were other changes in land policy. Though veterans and Loyalists continued to get free land, all others paid cash. The frontier of settlement moved north and west, to the edge of the Canadian Shield by 1850 and to Lake Huron in the west. During the 1820s and 1830s the population of Upper and Lower Canada virtually exploded. In Upper Canada this was mainly the result of immigration, but in Lower Canada it was a combination of factors.

LOWER CANADA

Language, or rather the difference in language, made Lower Canada unique. There was immigration, certainly, mainly from the British Isles. As a result some areas in Lower Canada took an English-speaking tone, and Montreal for much of the nineteenth century was mainly an English-speaking city. Even Quebec City had a substantial English-speaking minority. There were Anglophone enclaves to the south and east of Montreal, between the old seigneuries and the American border—the Eastern Townships; and there were English speakers in pockets around the Gaspé Peninsula and along the north shore of the St. Lawrence—the Lower Labrador coast. The French-Canadian majority more or less held its own as a proportion of the population, and grew in numbers. While French Canadians had been concentrated in the valley of the St. Lawrence, they gradually expanded, in the 1830s, into regions that had until then been English.

At the same time, agriculture was changing in the colony. That much is certain: but why it was changing, and what the effects of the change were, remain matters of dispute among rival historians. At the turn of the nineteenth century, around 1800, Lower Canada was a major wheat producer with a substantial surplus for export. By the 1820s that was no longer the case, and farmers had turned away from wheat toward mixed farming.[23]

There was also considerable population pressure, causing the division of farms and the expansion of farming into marginal lands. Some older farms were also becoming marginal as the soil deteriorated from overproduction. There may also have been a problem with the kind of wheat sown—only later in the century did hardier strains of wheat, more suitable for the Canadian climate, develop. Nor is there conclusive evidence that farming practices in Lower Canada were much different from or much worse than those of competitors in Upper Canada, or New England. Put another way, there is no conclusive evidence that French-Canadian farmers were worse at the business than anglophones—nor is there likely to be.

Wheat production did not so much disappear as stagnate, but the consequence seems to have been a decline in living standards if not genuine hardship in some parts of the province. Some historians have argued that an economic crisis contributed to the radicalization of politics in Lower Canada in the 1830s, but the problem with that analysis is that not every impoverished farming region, and certainly not every impoverished farmer, became radical, or took up arms when politics turned to violence in 1837–38.

The cities of Lower Canada, especially Montreal, did not stagnate. As the economy of Lower Canada prospered during the Napoleonic Wars, and as Upper Canada grew in wealth and population, Montreal became the distribution, commercial, and financial centre for the St. Lawrence basin; its commercial elite easily transformed themselves from fur traders to merchants, bankers, and manufacturers. Quebec City was too isolated, with a small agricultural hinterland, while Montreal sat at or near the confluence of three great rivers, the Ottawa, the St. Lawrence, and the Richelieu. The city became the entrepot for supplying and servicing the upper province. Canals and steamships facilitated the task, so that by the end of the 1820s there was regular land and water communication up and down the rivers.[24]

Encouraged by the prosperity, syndicates of Montreal merchants founded the Bank of Montreal in 1817 and McGill University in 1821. The town was expanding to the northwest; its newer streets were widening; and its stone buildings were striking to visitors. Edward Silliman, a geologist at Yale College in Connecticut, visited the town in 1819 and wrote that he was "much gratified at entering, for the first time, an American city built of stone." The new merchants' houses, he enthused, were "handsomely hewn and very beautiful, and would be ornaments to the City of London." (Some of the early nineteenth-century streetscapes have survived along streets close to the harbour.) Silliman wrote too early to describe the impressive Notre Dame church, built between 1824 and 1829, and at the time the largest building, apart from fortresses, in British North America. The merchants' city became the largest in British North America, and as a sign of its new status acquired a mayor and city council in 1832.[25]

It was a turbulent city, divided by language, religion, economic interest, and ethnicity. There was of course the large gap between English and French, but within the anglophone community—if it can be called that—there were subgroupings—the Irish, who were both Protestant and Catholic, the Scots (called in the nineteenth century the Scotch), and the English—and the Americans, who maintained some of their own separate identity.

It was natural to expect that English and French would be at each other's throats—as Governor General Lord Dalhousie put it, Lower Canada was "a country where violent party feelings have long separated the two distinct Classes of the King's subjects—the English and the French."[26] Dalhousie exaggerated, though in his time as governor general, 1820 to 1828, he did a fair amount to promote partisan bitterness and ethnic ill feeling. Some years later another governor general, Lord Durham, "found two nations warring in the bosom of a single state."

Matters were never that simple. Lower Canada was a divided society, divided between merchants, usually anglophones, and usually from Montreal, and rural interests, generally francophones. It was divided between Protestant and Catholic, and divided regionally, especially between Montreal and Quebec. Finally, it was divided between an older elite—seigneurs, placeholders, officers, and clerical dignitaries—and a newer group of politicians who wished to displace them, and yet some of the would-be reformers were themselves seigneurs, or rich men, or officers. Most important, both languages were found on both sides of politics.

The 1820s and 1830s were a time of liberal ferment around the world. There were rebellions in Spain, Belgium, and Poland, demands that the rights of nations be vindicated against empires and distant monarchs. That was most obvious in Latin America, where almost all the colonies, Spanish and Portuguese, severed their links with Europe and became independent. (Most also became republics, except for Brazil, which became an empire.) In the United States, there was a revolution inside the republican system, as older elites gave way before the agitation of newer interests, epitomized in the election of Andrew Jackson, a democrat and a populist, to the presidency in 1828.

There had been periodic stirrings in Lower Canada since the early 1800s. A *"Patriote"* party had formed and by 1810 it dominated the elected assembly, but its program was of a mild, constitutional kind: its leaders saw salvation in the British constitution and the rights of British subjects. These rights included the notion that the government should be responsible to the legislature for the tax money it spent. Governors general did their best to resist any such idea, and the Patriotes didn't press the issue. But they didn't give up on it, and it remained a serious question when Lord Dalhousie became governor general in 1820.

Dalhousie, one of Wellington's generals, was an active and improving governor. He had been a constructive if somewhat quarrelsome lieutenant governor of Nova Scotia, where he left behind a college that would eventually become Dalhousie University. Dalhousie's imperiousness served him badly in Lower Canada, where he overestimated his own judgment and underestimated the political dangers he faced, as well as the very real limitations on his position.[27]

No governor could escape the fact that to govern he had to govern *through* someone or something, and in the case of the Canadas that meant the appointed councils, executive and legislative. In Lower Canada the councils were predominantly English-speaking, though with a sprinkling of *Canadien* seigneurs and officeholders. Collectively, they were sometimes known as "the English party" and sometimes as the "Chateau Clique," after the Quebec residence of the governor general. Dalhousie approved the "firm and steady" character of the legislative council, but from the beginning he had problems with the assembly.[28] The House of Assembly was the obstreperous element in the constitution, but its cooperation could, with a certain amount of conciliation, usually be obtained.

The assembly wasn't especially radical in tone; its politics could be described as moderately liberal, accepting the benefits of the constitution of 1791 with an inclination to expand those benefits as far as possible. The most prominent figure in the assembly was its speaker, Louis-Joseph Papineau, himself a seigneur (of Montebello, on the Ottawa River). A comparatively young man—thirty-four in 1820—Papineau was already an assembly veteran (since 1809). He had served as a militia officer during the War of 1812 and in the early 1820s believed and proclaimed himself a loyal subject and strong supporter of the British connection. He prized the liberties that British rule had brought, not least the ability of the French-Canadian majority in Lower Canada to preserve its language and traditions even under anglophone and Protestant rule.

Papineau was nevertheless a man of contradictions—logically inconsistent, unstable, and opportunistic, as his biographer, Fernand Ouellet, has shown.[29] He personally did not believe in the Catholic Church, yet saw it as a bulwark of the *Canadien* identity and thought that as seigneur he should set the example for his tenants by attending mass. (Still, on his deathbed he would refuse the Catholic sacraments.) Papineau became after 1815 the unchallenged leader of the Patriotes, the mildly liberal, mildly nationalist majority grouping in the assembly, and over the next twenty years saw off any and all possible rivals. It was clearly the case that the Patriotes were expected to serve Papineau's ends, whatever these might be; but like the man himself these were often confused and uncertain, rhetorically bold yet often timid in practice. As so often with bold orators, Papineau understood that words were weapons and exploited their impact; yet he didn't understand that words once spoken couldn't easily be withdrawn, nor replaced with other, more temporizing sentiments.

What would turn out to be a defining event in Lower Canadian politics occurred in 1822. The "English party" had it in mind to alter the constitution in order to improve its own position and diminish that of the Patriote-dominated assembly. This was to be achieved by reversing one of the key provisions of the Canada Act of 1791, which had divided Upper and Lower Canada. The Canadas were to be reunited, with the cooperation of the government in London but without the consent and, initially, even the knowledge of the assembly. Accordingly, in 1822 the under-secretary for the colonies introduced a Union bill to the British House of Commons.

When the terms of the bill became known in Lower Canada, they caused an explosion. The bill made English the only language of record for government in the province, and after a pause of fifteen years, it provided that only English could be used in the assembly. It extended government control over the Catholic clergy, who could collect tithes from their communicants only if the tithes had been approved by the governor. It raised the property qualification for voters, something that could be assumed to be directed against the majority of the population. And with Upper Canada rapidly expanding in population, there was the prospect that sooner or later the new province of united Canada would have an English-speaking majority.

The assembly, needless to say, disapproved of the project, and sent Papineau to London to influence opinion against it. The bill had already become the target of opposition MPs, who had the power to delay and prolong debate on the subject, and that was sufficient to derail it. Papineau spoke, therefore, to the converted in London where, not for the last time, colonial affairs were seen as an impediment to the passage of more important business.

The episode seemed to have been satisfactorily resolved, but it set affairs in motion, gradually moving Lower Canada from a position as a fractious but contented colony to a state of armed rebellion in 1837. At first the Patriotes directed their ire at the "English party" whose scheme this was correctly seen to be. That raised the question of the governor's choice of advisers and the near certainty that he could choose better men, less encumbered by personal interest and prejudice. The assembly's weapon was revenue, needed, obviously, to pay officials, including those to whom the assembly objected. Dalhousie resisted to the best of his considerable ability until events finally forced his departure in 1828.

The British government did its best, too. It made concessions on revenue. It appointed conciliatory governors, Lord Aylmer (1830–35), who at least spoke excellent French, and Lord Gosford (1835–37), who had a well-merited reputation at home in Ireland as a broad-minded and conciliatory politician. Neither could make headway. As Aylmer's biographer Phillip Buckner has observed, the Lower Canadian politicians, led by Papineau, were determined to prove that even the best governor must be seen to be a failure.[30] Papineau by the early 1830s had evolved from a liberal constitutionalist to a radical republican, an admirer of the French Revolution of 1830 and an enthusiast for American-style democracy— provided, of course, his privileges as a seigneur were respected after the revolution, along with a few similar trifles. By 1832 Papineau had discarded many of his earlier, moderate associates, and his language pointed toward a fundamental revision of Lower Canada's constitution.

He and his followers refused British attempts to compromise over the control of revenue. If public money were to be spent, especially on office-holders, they wanted to determine who those officeholders must be. It was the negative of the proposition that was important: if Papineau chose the governor's councillors, it would not be the governor or even the British government who ruled the province.

Political hysteria mounted through the 1830s. Some of the Patriotes suspected that the government was trying to overwhelm them through immigration. But when the immigration produced a cholera epidemic in 1832, killing seven thousand people out of a population of 500,000, some Patriotes speculated that the government was really trying to kill off the *Canadiens* in order to replace them with English-speaking immigrants. That same year, 1832, an election riot in Montreal called out the British army to maintain order. The troops fired on the rioters, killing three—

more proof, if proof were needed, of British tyranny.

In 1834 Papineau and his supporters passed "Ninety-two Resolutions" through the assembly, demanding popular control of the government through elections; and thanks to elections they gained an overwhelming majority there. They used their majority to block all legislation, including revenue, until their constitutional demands were met. It was all or nothing, though Papineau may not have understood it as such. The governors understood it very well, and so, eventually, did the British government.

In response, the government did three things: it retained Sir John Colborne, an experienced general, in Canada; it began to make connections to more moderate politicians; and it did its best to shore up such revenues as it could extract outside the assembly's control, so as to keep some semblance of government functioning. Colborne had been a controversial lieutenant governor in Upper Canada—too controversial for the Whig imperial government's taste (see below), and the Whigs had accordingly recalled him in 1836. But as a general, he proved to be the right man in the right place at the right time. Lord Gosford, the governor general, was very much a man of peace and compromise, and for a time in 1837 and 1838 it seemed that his policy of compromise, of building bridges to the opposition, had failed. Yet as events would show, it did not fail even though Gosford himself, who resigned his office in November 1837 and left the province early the next year, wasn't there to see it.[31] It remained for Colborne to set the stage, assembling troops and fortifying his positions.

Papineau and Colborne were converging, without realizing it. In the summer and fall of 1837 Papineau convened a series of monster meetings— "assamblées"—around the province. The language at the meetings became wilder and wilder. As the historian Allan Greer points out, this may have been necessary in order to dislodge the French Canadians from a profoundly monarchical and traditional way of looking at the world. If republican notions were to be inculcated, Papineau and company would first have to get rid of monarchical language as a prelude to abolishing the monarchy itself. The young queen, Victoria, who had just mounted the throne, became a particular target for personal abuse.[32] Then, in an action reminiscent of the rebels prior to the American Revolution, Papineau established "committees of correspondence."

Caught between words and reality, Papineau put his faith in words. Just in case, he had been in contact with the radical leader in Upper Canada, William Lyon Mackenzie, and hoped for simultaneous uprisings, thus overwhelming the overstretched British garrison. The words failed, and instead of terrifying the government and its supporters, it galvanized them into action: local British patriots mobilized to defend their constitutional notions as opposed to Papineau's. The popular leader was at a loss. The governor suspended the constitution, authorized paramilitary forces raised from loyal (anglophone) subjects, and issued warrants for the arrest of Papineau and his associates.

Fighting broke out in November 1837, north and south of Montreal. The other regions of the province—and this was crucial—did not join in. Colborne was ready, and after some initial setbacks, he crushed the rebels. His regular forces and their unofficial paramilitary allies looted and burned, making an object lesson to show what rebellion and resistance would bring.[33] Papineau and some of his followers fled to the nearby United States, while others remained, to die or to be arrested.

There were sporadic risings and incursions from rebel sympathizers in the United States for about a year, but they were repelled. Looking at the rebellions as a whole, and at their suppression, the historian Allan Greer concluded that "it was a painful and costly episode with decisive and lasting results."[34] The rebels had read too much about the Paris revolt of 1830, which had toppled the unpopular Bourbon king, Charles X, or about the revolutions in Latin America that had ended the Spanish empire. They conceived and followed a scenario in which the forces of order were unprepared for resistance and crumbled at their approach, and not a situation in which the government was able not only to muster an effective army but to retain enough authority to order and enforce the arrest of the various rebel leaders.

Papineau was not, of course, among those arrested. In years to come this fact would be a standing reproach against him. The circumstances of his flight in 1837 would be endlessly rehearsed by his opponents, who came to include many of those who had followed him to the brink of rebellion, and often beyond. In the 1840s and the 1850s—for Papineau eventually returned to Canada with an amnesty in hand—he had the capacity to be a nuisance, but he was no longer the leader of the French-Canadian population.

Those who stayed suffered the consequences. Some were executed, some were exiled,[35] and some were arrested. Their fate depended on timing, and on chance. The government suspended habeas corpus in 1837, and did not restore it until 1840, which meant that suspected rebels could be kept in jail indefinitely without having to face charges or trial. Denis-Benjamin Viger, the financier of the aborted revolution, a rich man and himself a very prominent politician, spent two years in jail, until 1840. While he was absent, politics in Lower Canada took a very different turn. In that turn, the politics of Upper Canada were decisive.

UPPER CANADA

In Upper Canada, as in the lower province, radical politics and defective leadership constituted a toxic brew. The issues of Upper Canadian politics were more than local, though it was local matters that first gave them force. Liberalism and radicalism were the spirit of the age, in Britain, the United States, and Europe, demanding an end to privilege and inequality. In Upper Canada privilege and inequality were embedded in the constitution and structure of the province. Hierarchy and deference in politics, society, and religion would, according to the Upper Canadian elite, preserve British rule and repel republicanism. As the historian Carol Wilton has pointed out, loyalty and conformity to the established system were to them axiomatic. Upper Canada had been attacked once and would, they were certain, be attacked again. Division and discord advertised the colonies' weakness to the Americans.[36]

The American menace wasn't only external—there were also many thousands of American-born settlers inside Upper Canada. Fear of domestic republicanism drove the government and its supporters to attempt to limit the Americans' political rights during the 1820s. The effect was to arouse, not suppress, opposition. In the event, the American-born Marshall Spring Bidwell wasn't only elected and re-elected to the Upper Canadian assembly, but became its speaker.

The American or "alien" question was one of many. Religious differences also played a part, owing to the privileged position of the Church of England under the Constitutional Act of 1791. Believing that sound religion made for sound politics, Pitt and Grenville had provided for an established Church, endowed with the only asset the province had—land set aside for the support of a Protestant clergy, or rather *the* Protestant clergy, the ministers of the Church of England. Amounting to one-seventh of Upper Canada's available land, the Clergy Reserves awaited development and sale. Development, however, depended on the work of other settlers on adjacent lots, to clear trees, build roads, and establish farms. This increased the value of the land, to the profit of an absent or distant clergy.

This might have been borne had the majority of settlers been Anglicans, members of the official Church. At no time was this the case. Even in England most professing Protestant Christians weren't Anglicans, but members of dissenting sects—Baptists, Congregationalists, and the recently established Methodists. In the eighteenth and early nineteenth centuries, waves of religious revivals swept across English-speaking America—in the 1740s, the 1770s, the 1800s, and the 1820s. Saddlebag preachers, the Methodist "circuit riders," usually Americans, brought the Bible and a message of personal salvation to the English-speaking backwoods of Nova Scotia, New Brunswick, and Lower and Upper Canada. As unofficial preachers, living by their wits and through charity, the Methodists filled a gap left by the established Church, overcoming even their inability to perform legal marriages, which were reserved for the provinces' few Anglican parsons. Language was an insurmountable barrier in French Canada, but elsewhere the message was enthusiastically received, even by families or individuals who had previously been Anglicans.

Such a family was the Ryersons, loyalists and Anglicans from New Jersey, living in Norfolk County on the north shore of Lake Erie. Joseph Ryerson, a justice of the peace and militia colonel, adhered to the Anglican Church, barring his door to his son Egerton when the latter converted to Methodism. Despite his father's fears, Egerton did not see his choice of religion as determining his political allegiance; he had as a child experienced American marauders during the War of 1812,[37] and had no cause to admire the republic or its institutions. When an opportunity occurred to detach Canadian Methodism from its American cousins and return to its British roots, Egerton Ryerson, by then the Church's most influential publicist and journalist, seized it. But until the authorities recognized that the Methodists and the other dissenting Protestants weren't disloyal merely because they chose not to worship in the state Church, the religious issue undermined the harmony of the province.

It was the Methodists' misfortune to confront the immovable object of John Strachan, the Anglican archdeacon of York, later the first Anglican bishop of Toronto. Strachan, a Scot and originally a Presbyterian, was Anglicanism's fiercest and strongest, though not its ablest, defender.[38] A later governor general, Lord Elgin, called him "the most dangerous and spiteful man in Upper Canada."[39] Strachan did his best to create a province founded on if not dominated by his Church. A former schoolmaster, he saw his former pupils into positions of power, which they in turn used to enhance the standing of the Church. Strachan himself sat on the executive council, where he offered sectarian advice to lieutenant governors who were exceedingly disposed to accept it. But Strachan wasn't alone in his position, for he had the support of his fellows on the close-knit executive council and beyond them the acquiescence if not enthusiasm of prominent men from one end of Upper Canada to the other.

The three lieutenant governors of Upper Canada in this period, Sir Peregrine Maitland (1818–28), Sir John Colborne (1828–35), and Sir Francis Bond Head (1835–38), were not devoid of talent, though Head was so eccentric that his critics plausibly argued that he must have been appointed by mistake. They were all devoted to the principles of the

British constitution, which included, as they saw it, the Church of England. They were also devoted to a strict interpretation of their function, and of the proper relationship of a colony to the empire. Governors governed, and colonists, if they were truly loyal, accepted the result. Consequently, the governors rebuffed any and all attempts to compromise—over the clergy reserves, over education, or over the conduct of appointed officials.

As in Lower Canada, obduracy led in a straight line to confrontation. Strachan and his friends squelched an early attempt by a Scottish-born radical, Robert Gourlay, to question their conduct. Gourlay was arrested, twice acquitted by juries, but eventually convicted and deported in 1818. His departure made way for another, more difficult, Scot.

William Lyon Mackenzie was born in Scotland in 1795 and, after a misspent youth, immigrated to Upper Canada in 1820, settling finally in the provincial capital, York, in 1824. He brought with him to York his newspaper, *The Colonial Advocate*, along with a restless temperament, a lively sense of victimization both personal and general, and an unmatched talent for vituperation. In York he found plenty of fodder for his pen, and soon enraged the members of the capital's tiny elite, so much so that some of their sons took revenge on Mackenzie by dumping his printing press into the town's harbour in 1826. It was the making of Mackenzie, who thereafter was not merely a notional victim of official persecution, but a real one. The victim sued his tormentors and won, and with the money he got in compensation built up both his newspaper and his reputation.

Mackenzie began his Upper Canadian career believing and arguing that the British constitution, properly applied, would suffice for the colony's political needs and future prosperity. In this he did not differ from other reformers, like William Warren Baldwin, or his son Robert, or even Marshall Spring Bidwell. But like Papineau in Lower Canada he turned away from the British model, which he argued would never allow the people's voice—which he equated with his own—to be heard.

In fact, there were many other voices besides Mackenzie's demanding reform—Methodists and other Protestants demanding equality of treatment from the government and an end to the privileges of John Strachan's established Church, and farmers demanding better roads for their farms and better schools for their children and better prices for their product—and lower taxes. All these were denied them by an entrenched oligarchy. Mackenzie freely borrowed from contemporary American radicals for his economic program; confused enough in its original American version, it was hopelessly muddled by the time Mackenzie had finished with it.

The details hardly mattered. It was the struggle between Mackenzie and the oligarchs that dominated the political stage, and the oligarchs— the Family Compact—unwittingly did everything they could to help Mackenzie, expelling him from the assembly, thereby ensuring his re-election. The resulting brouhaha distressed the British government, which was pressing its own political reform program at home, and was accordingly sensitive to the charge that it was acting arbitrarily and repressively in its Canadian colonies.

The government's response counted heavily on appealing to loyalty and the British connection. Steady British immigration, the settlement of disbanded regiments, and an inflow of half-pay officers improved the odds, in some areas outnumbering the older American-born or -connected inhabitants. The politics of demography are always slow and uncertain, however, and a quicker method was needed. The Methodists were sectarians, it was true, unseemly and enthusiastic in their religious practices in the eyes of the Anglican establishment, but their main grievance was one of status and subsidy—or rather subsidy's lack. If both were provided, if the Methodists were no longer excluded but brought into closer association with their British cousins, might not something be done?

The colonial administration chose to swallow some of its pride. British Wesleyan Methodists had proved to be anything but radical in their politics—were in fact a bulwark of the British constitution. They were invited to come to Canada, where they offered the Canadian Methodists, American in their origins, political respectability. Led by Egerton Ryerson, the Upper Canadian Methodists seized the opportunity and supported the government. As Ryerson explained, there was "a simple and sufficient reason, [which was that] the administration of government towards them has been essentially changed." Seemliness in religion was easily twinned with a commitment to order in politics, at least as long as the Anglican establishment wasn't allowed to provoke the evangelicals.

This was difficult. Sir John Colborne in particular was determined to do right by the Anglicans, and as his parting gift to the province—he was in the process of being dismissed by an enraged colonial secretary— endowed forty-four Anglican rectories with about nine thousand hectares of land. Colborne thereby partially undid some of the good the rapprochement with the Methodists had done, and contributed to the final confrontation between government and radicals.

That confrontation was brought on by his successor, Sir Francis Bond Head. Head at first tried to conciliate public opinion by appointing moderate reformers, including Robert Baldwin, to his executive council. He proceeded to ignore their advice, precipitating the resignation of not just the reformers but of his whole council. He then confronted the assembly, with predictable results. Facing deadlock with the assembly, Head dissolved it and called a general election in which the lieutenant governor personally stumped the province, denouncing his enemies as disloyal. He had the support of an unusual coalition: moderate Methodists, local landowners like Colonel Thomas Talbot, the anti-Catholic Orange Order (recently arrived from Ireland), and the Catholic clergy, which in Upper Canada as in the lower province stood firmly on the side of legitimate authority.[40] (The Orangemen were so impressed by the display of Catholic loyalty that they called off their annual anti-Catholic 12 July parade commemorating the Protestant victory in Ireland in 1690.) The 1836 election, not surprisingly, delivered a pro-government majority.

Head had his majority, but it did not bring political stability. Deprived of their one useful weapon, the power to obstruct the government by tying up the legislature, the radicals under Mackenzie veered toward rebellion. They established the usual revolutionary paraphernalia of committees of correspondence, secret councils, and the like, and marched their supporters up and down farmers' fields north of Toronto, to prepare them for the uprising to come. The government was fortunate that it was Mackenzie who directed the rebels, for when it came to concrete action he proved irresolute and incompetent.[41]

Head did his best to even the odds, sending off the province's small garrison of regular troops to help in the graver crisis in Lower Canada. The forces of order and the radical rebels were now commanded by their respective pamphleteers. Mackenzie prepared a "Declaration of Independence" to inspire his followers, and if that weren't enough he promised them land and unspecified spoils, to be confiscated from the government's Tory supporters. It was not enough. Mackenzie never had enough followers, and even if he had, he lacked the ability to command them. Early in December 1837 he marched on Toronto, paused, retreated, and marched again. His pause allowed the government's supporters to reinforce Toronto by steamboat. It was now the government's turn to march. Mackenzie fled, eventually reaching safety in the United States.

The rebellion would henceforth be based in the United States rather than in Canada. Assisted by American sympathizers and American money, Mackenzie and his followers tried several times to invade Upper Canada. The British authorities raised troops of their own and garrisoned the frontier, and reinforced their local levies with regular soldiers. The American government, alarmed at the disorder along its northern border, did its best to cut off the rebels' supplies and discouraged their American supporters. In this they were buttressed by most American opinion.[42] After about a year of desultory guerrilla activity, the rebellion subsided.

The government had won. In the aftermath of rebellion, hundreds and possibly thousands of rebels or rebel sympathizers left the province. Those who stayed could be and frequently were arrested. Two of the rebels of 1837 were hanged. (Some of the later invaders of 1838, including a misguided Swede named Nils von Schoultz, were also hanged. Schoultz was defended at his trial by a rising young Kingston lawyer, John A. Macdonald.)

The government's victory changed the political balance. Politics after

1838 differed only in shades of loyalty on the fundamental question of whether Upper Canada should be British. How best to keep it British was the question of the day.

Lord Durham and the Union of the Canadas

The news of the Canadian rebellions and their successful suppression forced the British government into a more active form of contemplation. Lord Gosford had already resigned as governor general, his mission of conciliation an obvious failure. To replace him the Whig government sent a much more prominent figure, John Lambton, Earl of Durham. Durham was a wealthy mine owner from the north of England who had figured in radical politics during the 1820s (from which he got his nickname, "Radical Jack"). He was briefly a minister in the early 1830s, but, after quarrelling with some of his colleagues, he was sidelined as British ambassador to Russia (1833–35). Back in England he was a disruptive force inside the Whig party, stimulating thoughts among ministers of whether another distant mission might not be timely and appropriate.

Durham accepted the mission to Canada in January 1838.[43] He had broad powers, or so he thought. He would be governor general, with an authority that included the Atlantic colonies as well as the Canadas, and within those colonies he would be significantly less encumbered than his predecessors by constitutional and political obstruction. Durham would do more than govern; he would investigate what had gone wrong and make recommendations to London, which would, presumably, act accordingly.

After reviewing the Canadian files at the Colonial Office, Durham set sail for the colonies with a large official suite, arriving in May 1838. As governor, he acted decisively on the most pressing question of the day: what to do with the rebels captured and still in captivity. Durham sent some into semi-tropical exile in Bermuda, sparing them from any more extreme penalty. Unfortunately, Bermuda was beyond his jurisdiction. His action was promptly disavowed by the home government; when the official news reached Canada, Durham resigned, and set sail in October, after one of the shortest terms on record.

If that had been all, Durham would be remembered as little more than a flash in the pan. But the governor had passed a diligent summer, travelling, inquiring, and researching the problems of British North America, and on his return to England he and his staff prepared and submitted a report on the colonies and their problems, and how to solve them.

The fundamental constitutional difficulty was the deadlock between a popular assembly and a colonial government. The government relied on the assembly to raise taxes, but refused to allow it to determine how the taxes might be spent. Colonies were colonies—by definition they couldn't govern themselves or they would cease to be colonies. Durham suggested that the problem was artificial: as long as the home government controlled external affairs and defence, the colonial link was intact.

As Durham wrote, "The system which I propose would, in fact, place the internal government of the colony in the hands of the colonists themselves.... The constitution of the form of government,—the regulation of foreign relations, and of trade with the mother country, the other British Colonies, and foreign nations,—and the disposal of the public lands, are the only points on which the mother country requires a control." It was a form of "responsible government," a government answerable to its citizen taxpayers rather than to a distant imperial authority. Joseph Howe in Nova Scotia would have agreed, as would the Baldwins in Upper Canada, but would the British government? While the British taxpayer was still responsible for army garrisons and naval bases in North America, and when even Durham assumed that the British government and not a colonial authority must regulate—i.e., tax—trade, a truly self-sufficient colonial authority was still some distance off.

Durham did not think that responsible government by itself would cure colonial discontent. If colonial discontents were merely political, then a political reform would suffice. But, as he wrote in the most famous phrase in his report, he had found "two nations warring in the bosom of a single state." There could be no peace until the two nations became one, and that one must be English-speaking: political harmony would be served thereby, but also economic development.

The "single state" was Lower Canada. Lower Canada had a French-speaking majority that Durham identified as the source of most of its problems. The solution was to modify the boundaries of that state, merging Upper and Lower Canada and granting each section equal representation. (This was actually Durham's second choice, behind a federal union of all the British North American provinces: continuing disorder in Lower Canada in the fall of 1838 persuaded him that more immediate and drastic action was necessary.)[44] In the future combined Canada, French Canadians would become an artificial minority, because the anglophones of Montreal and the Eastern Townships joined to the anglophones of Upper Canada would create a permanent majority in the legislature. In addition, French would lose its privileged status in government and the courts; for good measure, Durham proposed doing away with French civil law and the seigneurial system—in fact, with everything that differentiated French-speaking from English-speaking subjects.

Durham's proposals have caused controversy ever since. Was this liberal governor the prototype for Anglo-Saxon racism in Canada? Some, including many French Canadians, have argued this was the case, but others, like the historian Fernand Ouellet, have seen Durham as essentially a liberal modernizer. "[His] conclusions derived less from ethnic considerations than from his liberalism and his great sympathy for the historical role of the middle class," he writes. "On finding the institutions of the [French] *ancien régime* functioning among the French Canadians as they had formerly in France, he may have tended as a good liberal simply to heap upon these people the scorn he felt for absolutist and feudal France."[45]

Another student of the period, S.J.R. Noel, strongly disagrees. In his view Durham's understanding of Canada and especially French Canada was "superficial," with "a paucity of factual information" shot through with "lurid racism." As for Durham's recommendations, they were "naïve" and "jejune."[46] The truth is probably somewhere in between. Durham naturally applied the perspective of a liberal and progressive Englishman to his subject—and that probably included a negative view of France and French despotism. His views on French Canadians were far less sympathetic than Tocqueville's a few years earlier, but they were not in fact radically different. Unlike Tocqueville, Durham was in a position to do something about the situation—or at least to have his strictures taken seriously by legislators.

It was a drastic prescription, and there was little to prevent it. In Lower Canada there was no assembly, merely an appointed Special Council. French-Canadian opinion was confused and demoralized; with Papineau in exile in France, his former lieutenants—those who weren't too compromised by the rebellion—disputed over his legacy and his leadership. There was even a faction that urged the acceptance of Durham's prescription for assimilation as a means for getting on with life and finding prosperity. The Upper Canadian assembly cheerfully voted for union, understanding that their own debt-ridden province would be joining the comparatively debt-free Lower Canada.

All that remained was for the Whig government to take action. First they appointed a new governor general, Charles Poulett Thomson, another Whig politician; he arrived at Quebec in October 1839.[47] Then they turned to what they hoped would be a longer-term solution. This they did through the Act of Union of 1840, which enacted the form but not the spirit of Durham's report. Upper and Lower Canada were reunited, and endowed with the same system of government as they had before—appointed executive and legislative councils, and an elected assembly of eighty members, forty from the former Upper Canada and forty from the former Lower Canada. The Act, like its predecessors in 1778 and 1791, allowed the new "Province of Canada" to live off its own resources, but unlike them it provided that the province must first pay the salaries of an enumerated list of officials and judges. The colony also remained subject to the British government's overall authority over trade.

This was scarcely a new beginning. It was the product of fear rather than hope: it guarded against past dangers and left hope, if any remained, to a very uncertain future.

8

COLONIES
INTO PROVINCES

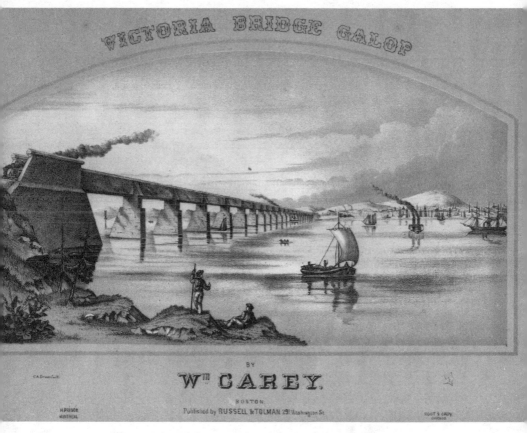

The wonder of the age: The Victoria Bridge across
the St. Lawrence at Montreal, celebrated in song, 1860.

T he years after the rebellion witnessed a revolution of a different kind. British North America did not cast off the British yoke, or repudiate its monarchical constitution. Quite the contrary—by the 1860s the colonies were more firmly connected to the mother country than they had ever been, through the voices of their inhabitants, expressed in a governmental system that developed autonomy as its defining characteristic. The old British Empire, classically conceived as a metropolis surrounded by economic and political dependencies, could never have tolerated such devolution of authority, but as British politics were reinvented in the 1830s, so the British Empire changed its shape and meaning in the 1840s.

The empire was literally closer together, because a revolution in transportation and communication slashed times of travel and transport through steamships and steam railways, and through the telegraph. By the 1860s British North Americans could learn of distant events almost instantly. No longer would soldiers die on remote battlefields, as at New Orleans in 1815, after the war they fought was over.

The empire was closer together for another reason—more of its subjects had moved from the British Isles to the colonial periphery, including the British possessions in America. The inhabitants of Newfoundland displayed an Irish accent, while the leading politicians of Canada—John A. Macdonald, for example, or his rival George Brown— spoke with a Scottish burr they had brought from their country of origin. By the 1860s there were enough of them to make it possible to speak of a new country, a federation of colonies within the empire—a viable, self-sufficient monarchy in the New World. Though such an event was not undreamt of in 1837 or 1840, it seemed wildly improbable, its feasibility at best doubtful.

The outward sign of the viability of the North American colonies lay in their population. In the 1810s the collective population of the British possessions in North America was roughly 700,000, including perhaps 100,000 Indian inhabitants. In the 1860s it was slightly more than 3.5 million, while its Native component was, perhaps, 150,000. Compared with the population of the United States, or Great Britain, or the British Empire, these were small numbers but, if compounded into a single entity, they were enough to form a country.

Reinventing the Empire

Until the 1830s, Europeans clung to the fringes of North America. The eastern coasts were fairly thickly settled, and although settlers had penetrated the interior, even around the Great Lakes the landscape had changed little. The forests still carpeted the land, and human settlement was merely occasional—clearings in the woods connected by atrocious roads. Sailing ships and steamboats alleviated the isolation in the summer, and there were sleighs in the winter to cross the ice and snow, but towns like Toronto in Upper Canada were weeks away from current news, and even more from fashions or inventions. True, travel was faster and more reliable than it had been in the 1730s or 1630s but, as in earlier centuries, the transmission of information depended on direct word of mouth, or the passage of pieces of paper from one point to another.

Disease travelled too, through immigration from Europe to ports like Halifax or Quebec or Montreal, where cholera appeared in June 1832. That year eighteen hundred victims died of it in Montreal and twenty-two hundred in Quebec City; it then moved along the waterways into the interior, to York and Detroit in the west and down the Hudson Valley to New York City. Cholera was especially dreaded, because its onset was quickly followed by a painful death, essentially from dehydration following diarrhea and vomiting. No one could say with actual certainty how it was spread (medical authorities blamed "miasmic vapours"), merely that it was transmitted by human contact, and so the authorities resorted to the age-old practice of quarantining affected populations and areas. At Grosse Isle, down the St. Lawrence from Quebec City, a special quarantine station was established, to which lower-class immigrants were directed; cabin passengers, paying higher fares, moved on directly to Quebec or Montreal.[1]

Quarantine could do little against another disease, typhus, also spread by contaminated water supplies. In Kingston alone, in 1847, fourteen hundred luckless Irish immigrants, fleeing famine at home, found only a Canadian grave thanks to typhus.[2] In the interior, the parade of European diseases continued to decimate the Native population as fur traders and then steamboats ascended the great rivers of the plains, and as contacts multiplied on the west coast, the same phenomenon occurred.

The towns and cities were tiny by later standards—Halifax roughly twenty thousand in 1850, Montreal almost fifty thousand, Toronto twenty-five thousand. It wasn't merely lack of population that limited their size. There were real restrictions on how large a place could grow until sewers were dug for waste, reliable water supplies replaced individual wells, and coal could replace wood as the principal means of heat. In Toronto the first sewers were dug in the 1830s, and gas (made from imported coal) for lighting appeared first in 1840. The touring British author Charles Dickens in 1842 complimented the city on its "bustle, business and improvement." There were, he told his readers, paved streets, gas lamps, and "excellent" shops.[3] Dickens was apparently not poisoned by the water, nor felled by disease during his stay in Canada, but in that he was fortunate. Toronto, like other colonial population centres—Saint John, New Brunswick, was the first to act—was still feeling its way, via private water mains, to a secure and healthy water supply.[4]

Getting the goods to the cities for their "excellent" shops was also a problem, for there were difficulties in transport too. The necessities of life had to be imported to cities, by cart over roads alternately muddy or dusty, or painfully unloaded on the mucky banks of the Bay of Fundy or the St. Lawrence or the Great Lakes. Wood for fuel was becoming harder to find in the areas of old settlement, and hauling it to town in wagons jammed the wretched colonial roads. Market gardens and other farms could supply local needs, of course, but getting to the market was a major enterprise for farmers.

Governments in the 1830s and 1840s experimented with road improvements. They used logs to make "corduroy roads" or investigated "macadamized" pavements (named after their British inventor). They chartered companies to build toll roads and canals, with landing stages and docks and wharves. In the Atlantic provinces there was not as far to go, for the difficult terrain of Nova Scotia posed problems all its own in terms of connecting one pocket of settlement to another over intervening rocks and bogs. And beyond Nova Scotia there were miles and miles of forests only sporadically punctuated by settlements that petered out entirely before they reached the height of land that divided the St. John River Valley from that of the St. Lawrence.

In the Atlantic provinces the limits of agricultural growth were soon reached, and even in Lower Canada the Eastern Townships, the last large tract of promising arable land, were filling up. The cash crop there, as almost everywhere in the North American provinces, was wood. There was wood for burning, and wood for building. Harvests of timber and lumber in New Brunswick and Upper Canada fed the urbanization of Great Britain where the Industrial Revolution was in full swing, its appetites for overseas supply apparently unlimited. In the process the population of Great Britain was rearranged, as farmers drifted into expanding cities and prosperity encouraged the birth rate. Families had to be housed and houses had to be built, requiring lumber, and people had to be fed, requiring wheat.

In distant North America, the forest frontier receded. Clearings grew in frequency and size until, by the 1840s, the land was transformed—the forest cover might have seemed to be on the way to disappearance.[5] (Paradoxically, reforestation began about the same time, as marginal lands along the Atlantic coast began to be abandoned for better, more fertile farms in the interior.) The deforestation of large parts of British North

America was a testament to the efficacy and efficiency of the colonial system, the by-product of a mercantile philosophy whereby the mother country and its colonies dwelt in a cocoon of mutual support. The local governors did no more than express a traditional understanding of the proper relationship of a colony to its imperial parent, and against that understanding Howe, Papineau, and Mackenzie battered in vain.

In the 1840s the relationship between the American colonies and the British Empire was transformed. The colonies became, for the first time, more or less self-sufficient—in any event capable of paying their way without constant infusions of cash from the home government. Colonial dependence on the empire moved from the physical realm—more immigrants, more soldiers, and ever more subsidies to develop the colonies—to the psychological.

At the same time British psychological dependence on the colonies as a secure source of supply in time of war—for food, or for timber—diminished as the memory of the Napoleonic wars receded. Old habits nevertheless died hard and late. Appeasing the colonies still had some appeal—and the British government early in the 1840s provided, for what turned out to be the last time, free entry into the British market for colonial grain (or "corn" as it was called in the British Isles). It was, however, a wasting game as colonial discontent, especially in North America, continued.

The traditional enemy, France, had been so thoroughly defeated in 1815 that it no longer had the military or economic power, or the political will, to threaten British interests. The Industrial Revolution and the increase in British wealth and power left Great Britain, by mid-century, without serious competition. British industry and British products need fear no rivals. They didn't need expensive tariffs or rigid protection, and there were cheaper sources of supply than the colonies, closer to home. There were riots against the high cost of living, and reducing tariffs on foodstuffs and building materials was one obvious way of responding to public discontent. Not surprisingly, British political leaders, and British opinion more generally, began to draw appropriate conclusions.

Unluckily for the colonists, tariffs and colonies were therefore combined into one supremely important political issue. Should Great Britain adopt free trade and abandon tariff protection, embodied in its "Corn Laws," and with it the system of controls and incentives that bound it to the colonies? Economists then and since plumped for an answer that was right in principle, but, as always in politics, the real question was somewhat different. More realistically, should Great Britain abandon a policy that brought costly food and expensive imports to a restive and riot-prone population? Should Britain maintain a policy of expensive food in the face of an impending famine in Ireland, caused by the failure of the potato crop? The Tory prime minister, Sir Robert Peel, decided in 1846 that it should not. He split his party, but on the great question of free trade, he won. Free trade became British policy for the next ninety years.

Peel's decision was deeply unpopular in the colonies. British policy had encouraged dependence, a profitable dependence that rewarded colonial allegiance with commercial advantages. Until 1846 grain exported from Canada to Great Britain enjoyed tariff preference, and on that basis Canadians invested in farms to grow wheat, canals to carry it, and mills to process it into flour. Under the existing colonial system, imports of American flour were transformed into Canadian products and could find their way down the St. Lawrence for export to Great Britain. A British traveller commented that he had seen a Canadian flour mill, "a new building of great size, and which must have cost many thousand pounds in its erection ... standing still" as a result of the latest British policy. The effect was to transfer trade to New York instead of Montreal.[6]

RESPONSIBLE GOVERNMENT IN AN IRRESPONSIBLE EMPIRE

The economic transformation of the British Empire thus helped to stimulate a political shift. If the empire was rethinking its relations to the colonies, so were the colonists with regard to the empire. The British governments of the early 1840s straddled the problem. They tried to maintain direct imperial control over the colonial governments in North

America, while simultaneously nodding in the direction of the principle that even colonial British subjects should consent to the policies by which they were governed. It was an uneasy compromise, workable only if the governor himself acted as a politician and exerted himself to secure a majority in the local legislature. Some governors tried politics—Lord Sydenham, governor general of Canada from 1839 to 1841, trounced his opponents at the polls and thereby obtained a usable though temporary majority. His successors tried first conciliation and then confrontation, dividing and combining the local politicians in the hope of establishing a stable government. It was a hopeless task, which in a system of more or less free elections was bound to produce a government led by opposition politicians.

This had already happened in Great Britain, where Peel's adoption of free trade led to the disruption of his Tory party and the victory of the opposition Whigs. The Whigs took a permissive attitude to the colonies. Lord Durham's son-in-law, Lord Grey, became colonial secretary, and not surprisingly he resurrected Durham's recommendation that governments should reflect public opinion as expressed in elections. The result was Responsible Government, as Durham had hoped and advised.

A new governor general, Lord Elgin, encouraged the process. The elections that followed weren't edifying, but they were decisive. Responsible Government was no longer an issue. Instead, Reformers denounced high salaries and elitist favouritism—the stuff of populism, and the staff of life to an alternating-party political system. In Nova Scotia they mobilized voters around sectarian allegiances, a feature that would characterize Canadian party politics for the next century. In New Brunswick the lieutenant governor simply harvested the results of a recent election, and after constructing a government left it to sink or swim as best it could.[7] In less-developed Newfoundland the reforming tendency expressed itself merely in the grant of representative government; fully responsible government would have to wait. In the province of Canada the outlines of a party system were already present, and an election in 1848 witnessed the triumph of the Reform party over their conservative opponents.

The Canadian party system had a special qualification absent in the other provinces. Politics in Lower Canada had always had a racial or linguistic tinge, and the rebellion of 1837–38, though not entirely fought along linguistic lines, nevertheless appealed to the French majority in the province. In its aftermath Durham had advised officially removing the French language from public life, and encouraging French speakers to adopt English, thereby promoting unity. The union of Lower and Upper Canada and the equal representation in the legislature of the two former provinces were but a first step in that direction.

The political realities of the 1840s reversed Durham's hopes for linguistic uniformity, but amply justified his ideas about colonial self-government. Upper Canadian Reformers led by Robert Baldwin and Francis Hincks, and Lower Canadian Reformers led by Louis-Hippolyte LaFontaine, combined in opposition to the various governors general and their conservative-minded supporters. In 1848 it was Baldwin and LaFontaine who were appointed to head a purely Reform government, following an election victory, and it was Baldwin and LaFontaine who had to face the crisis that followed the British government's adoption of free trade. That they were able to do so was a testament to the flexibility of responsible government, and the durability of the party system that animated it.

The imperial transformation was not quite complete. The Corn Laws and protective tariffs had been removed, but remnants of the Navigation Laws, which governed who might trade what in the colonies, limped on until 1849.[8] They were then abandoned, and with some alacrity. Some believed, and others feared, that it was a first step in the elimination of the North American provinces entirely. The sentiment that what was right for Britain was right for all, especially the colonies, had suffered a setback; but if Britain was no longer to govern the colonies directly, were they nothing more than an expensive and irritating encumbrance?

Great Britain was still committed to defend its overseas provinces, but not at any cost. In the face of belligerent American claims, the British government agreed to the division of Oregon along the 49th parallel in

1846; British authority and British commerce withdrew to Vancouver Island. The effect of the brief crisis over Oregon was to remind the government how expensive it would be to defend its American possessions, and how fortunate that diplomacy rather than the military had resolved the problem.[9] It was also fortunate that there was no great enthusiasm in the United States for war with Great Britain; instead, American energies were diverted into the annexation of Texas in 1845 and a subsequent war with Mexico. Indirectly these events were of great importance for Canada, for the United States gained in territory, wealth, and power—and for the first time the American population equalled that of Great Britain itself. The relative sizes and strategic capacities of British North America and the United States were already disproportionate; now they would remain so.

Discussing North America in "national" or "border" terms is to some extent misleading, for this period and for others. The boundary signified certain things, but there were limits to what it did. People crossed the frontier more or less freely, and ideas, fashions, and habits moved too.[10] Immigration to North America was a generalized phenomenon. Immigrants almost always came across the Atlantic from Europe and particularly from the British Isles. Thanks to the Navigation Acts and the timber trade, shipping was plentiful on the sea routes to British North America, and space on the westward voyage was cheap. As the historian Donald Akenson notes, "The cheapest way to get to the United States [from the British Isles] was by way of Canada."[11] Many immigrants therefore came to Montreal or Saint John with little intention of staying, but while they passed through they could well be a burden on the local authorities, sometimes because they were sick, and sometimes because they were indigent.

Local authorities did their best to cope with the phenomenon. Relatively few immigrants intended to stay in Lower Canada, but the cost of receiving them and passing them through fell on the local government. The provincial government therefore began levying a head tax to cover the cost, and increased it to cope with disease and hospitalization—and, indeed, burials.

The best remembered, or misremembered, group of immigrants came from Ireland.[12] It was the largest, and it had been the largest virtually every year after 1815. By numbers alone, but also in many other ways, the Irish transformed the colonies. It's generally assumed that "Irish" meant "Catholic Irish," but most of the time that wasn't the case. The majority of Irish immigrants to North America, north and south of the border, were Protestants. This gives rise to a further distortion, for Protestant is generally assumed to mean "Ulster Presbyterian," the so-called Scotch-Irish, the descendants of Cromwellian settlers who had shoved aside the native Gaelic and Catholic Irish. But the majority of the Protestant Irish who came to British North America were probably members of the Church of Ireland; that is, they were Anglicans, and not Presbyterians. Upper Canada, called Canada West after 1840, absorbed the greatest numbers, naturally enough because it had the largest amount of untenanted, available lands for farming, which was the occupation of most of the Irish immigrants. New Brunswick, however, also took in many Irish, not so much for farming as for lumbering; and many Irish also ended up in the lumber trade of the Ottawa Valley.

All immigrants bring with them customs and habits formed in their country of origin, and the Irish were no different. Protestants imported the Orange Order, a semi-secret society founded in 1795 to commemorate Protestant (and English) victory in the religious wars of the previous century, and taking as its symbol the Protestant monarch William III—"King Billy" to his followers and admirers. Such societies—the Masons were another example—gave needed relief and support in a society starved for diversion and fellowship. Along with church membership, they defined much of the society of Britain's backwoods American provinces.

Churches were of the essence back in Ireland, and it followed that they would be crucial in British North America. The main divide was between Roman Catholic and Protestant. There was some traffic across the divide, by conversion or absorption into the faith of the neighbourhood, but by and large Catholics remained Catholic and Protestants, Protestant. The line separating the various Protestant denominations was more fluid. As Akenson has pointed out, historians have tended to underestimate if not ignore the (Anglican) Church of Ireland, and indeed Anglicanism in its Irish, Scottish, and English branches was an important feature of colonial life. But denominational allegiance reflected not just deep sectarian conviction, but the availability of church services. Lacking a church or a minister, congregations could well wander into another sect.

By any standards, the attempt to establish a state church—the Church of England—failed. By the 1830s colonial administrators resignedly accepted the fact that their subjects would go their own way in matters of religion. With compulsion and favouritism removed from the religious equation, there was room for inter-sectarian cooperation, or more realistically neutrality, among the religious. The prospect of harmony, or at least the absence of bitter contention, made it possible to consider progress in such church-related issues as schooling.

Common education, compulsory and tax-supported, was popular in the abstract, but difficult to apply. All the colonies had school acts of some kind. A model existed, from Ireland, where a system of "National Schools" had been established with a common curriculum rigidly excluding anything that might offend any of Ireland's Christian sects, Catholic or Protestant. In Ireland the Catholics had the numbers to call the tune, but in British North America they were the majority only in Lower Canada. Elsewhere, Catholic rigidity met Protestant assertiveness, and it took all the genius that politicians could muster to camouflage the fact. The result was a series of compromises. In the province of Canada, legislation sponsored by a Catholic politician manufactured two parallel state-supported systems for Canada West. There was a public system, effectively Protestant, and a Catholic one, known as "separate" schools. In Nova Scotia and New Brunswick the arrangements were slightly different, but the result effectively the same: some schools were Catholic, and others Protestant.

THE USES OF GOVERNMENT

The schools were of course intended to inculcate religion, which was the concern of the various churches, but also to encourage proper civic values, from patriotism to orderly behaviour. Good order had always been an aspiration in the colonies—the early settlers set great store on the law and courts to regulate the unruly and to protect life, limb, and property. There was a small judicial apparatus at the top to handle the more serious cases, often badly, as we have seen (above, pp. 136–37), but most law and order was dispensed by local justices of the peace, prominent individuals who weren't afraid to take on the task of regulating their neighbours. Local magistrates also managed the affairs of townships, districts, and counties—roads and bridges, for example.

As the population grew, forests were cleared and crops spread, and the tax base also increased. Post offices were opened not merely in the larger towns but in remote villages. Canals spread along the St. Lawrence, and in 1829 the Welland Canal, the first of many, connected Lakes Erie and Ontario. Sometimes canals were government projects, publicly built and owned outright; sometimes they were private enterprise, heavily subsidized. Canals were swiftly overtaken by railways, the marvel of the age, and railways too were paid for, ultimately, by the public because for longer distances there was neither the traffic nor the freight to support them. Fortunately, thanks to responsible government, the taxes consumed by canals and railways were freely approved by citizen representatives in the legislatures, that is, the politicians, and it's not surprising that a flourishing, somewhat different, political class arose in the various colonies. The citizenry at large had no one to blame but themselves for the result; naturally, they scapegoated the politicians.

It was a system that suited alternating parties. These were ostensibly doctrinaire, originating in the ideological struggles of the 1830s. There were Reformers and Tories and eventually Conservatives and Liberals. The labels meant little on a left–right spectrum: the essence of the party system was caught by the eventual appearance in the 1860s of the "Liberal-Conservative" party. The parties were identified with personalities and the personalities with certain well-understood interests. The Liberals of Canada West, for example, tended to follow, or at least pay heed to, the brilliant but cantankerous editor of the Toronto *Globe*,

George Brown. Brown, born in Scotland, came to Canada via New York to take part in sectarian politics of the Presbyterian variety. He had a forceful if not domineering personality, and under his influence the Liberals shed successive layers of younger politicians, who wound up under the sheltering umbrella of John A. Macdonald's Liberal-Conservative party.

Macdonald, also a Scot by birth, was sinuous where Brown was forthright, accommodating where Brown was rigid. Where Brown was thought to be lacking in charm and consideration for others, Macdonald had those qualities in abundance. Brown considered Macdonald an unprincipled drunk, while Macdonald thought Brown a bigoted sectarian. Indeed, Macdonald frequently drank too much, while Brown wrote too frequently of the religious and racial failings of others, particularly Irish or French Catholics. But Brown understood that in an alternating-party system, compromise was necessary, and Macdonald accepted that there must be room in politics for larger ideas.

Macdonald was also fortunate in finding a French-Canadian partner, George-Etienne Cartier, a Montreal lawyer and, like many French-Canadian lawyers, a former would-be revolutionary.[13] Cartier had followed Papineau, learned from the experience, and switched to the Reformer LaFontaine. He was the inheritor of LaFontaine's formula of combination and conciliation, finding English-Canadian partners and constructing with them a new basis for politics. With their constitutional demands satisfied, Cartier's kind of French-Canadian Reformer found that their interests, and, so they thought, those of their constituents, pointed to a coalition with Upper Canadian Conservatives, and ultimately with John A. Macdonald. Macdonald and Cartier, or Cartier and Macdonald, dominated the politics of the later 1850s.

The great ideas of the 1850s were tariffs and railways. Tariffs came first, as they had to, for the crude administrative system of the day found them the best and surest means for raising revenue. It might be a slight exaggeration to say no tariff, no government, but it was close. Looking south, colonial politicians saw that the American states had put their revenues to good and creative use, and as a result were apparently abounding in prosperity. What was the secret of prosperity? The British had done away with tariffs as a matter of principle, and Britain had prospered. The British population as a result got cheap food and British industry cheap inputs from abroad. The result was contentment, especially among the politicians who directed the British state, its army, its navy, and its empire. Should the British colonies not do the same?

The colonials did not see things in quite the same way. It was all very well for Great Britain, already prosperous, to use free trade to enhance its wealth and dominate the markets of the world with its industrial production. Britain already had industries, it already had production, and it already had a superabundant population. The colonies did not have these things. Neither did other countries—Prussia, for example, or the United States. Before they could subscribe to the blessings of free trade, they would have to reach British levels of production and prosperity.

Both Prussian theorists and American practitioners had evolved explanations as to why free trade was unsuitable as a policy for a developing economy. Industries needed time to mature before they could hope to compete with the British, or with any other more advanced economy. Only then would free trade be possible (the "infant industry" theory). Another argument was founded in the recent and painful experience of the colonies, which had depended so much on exporting single, "staple" products, wheat and wood, to Great Britain. The colonies hadn't diversified their economies and as a result had nothing to fall back on when Great Britain removed their tariff preferences. Only the careful fostering of local manufactures through protective tariffs would safeguard the future livelihood of the colonial populations.

The immediate impulse in the colonies was to transfer dependence from one partner to another. If the British could undermine the economic basis of the old colonial system, then why should the colonials not abandon their political connection to Great Britain? A surge of annexationist sentiment passed through the colonies, affecting especially the moneyed classes. In Montreal, the Tories, enraged equally at the British government and at the provincial reform government of Baldwin and LaFontaine, drew up an "Annexation Manifesto" demanding union with the United States—American markets at the price of joining the American union.

It was a flash in the pan, momentarily dangerous, but doused with some skill by the governor general, Lord Elgin. With a return to prosperity in the early 1850s, the manifesto and the sentiment that inspired it were forgotten. Still, it was a sign that the colonial economies must be put on a more secure and reliable footing, and if trade with Britain couldn't be guaranteed, why not take the better half of the annexationist platform and seek a trading relationship with the United States?

Again, Lord Elgin played a crucial role. As early as 1849 he argued that secure and preferential trade with the United States would take the edge off the colonists' political grievances. Paradoxically, the closer the colonies were linked to the large and prosperous American market, the less likely they would be to seek annexation to the United States.[14] The United States, without intending to do so, could make the British Empire in North America more secure. As a bonus, the British government could safely reduce its expensive North American garrison, while the colonials could concentrate on the development and enrichment of their provinces.

As if to underline how expensive the colonies could be, the Royal Navy was called on to patrol Nova Scotian waters to fend off American fishing boats poaching and otherwise intruding inside the traditional three-mile (five-kilometre) limit of sovereignty along the coast. This induced New England fishing communities to think of compromise, making the Atlantic fisheries part of a grand trading compact between the United States and British North America.

Appeasing the fish interest of New England was only one component, though an important one, in negotiating a trade treaty with the United States. The American constitution had reserved power over tariffs and trade for Congress rather than the executive branch; yet it was the executive that dealt with foreign affairs. Tariffs were an explosive subject in American politics: in 1833 one state, South Carolina, had actually challenged the federal government's power to impose a higher tariff than the state's own politicians thought desirable.

But in the United States, tariffs had been overtaken as a subject of political controversy by the even more dangerous issue of slavery, permitted in fourteen southern states, where it was regarded as the basis of the economy and society. Slavery had over time been banned in the northern states, as it had been in the British provinces.[15] The American political system was finely balanced between north and south; the south demanded there be enough slave states to block northern, anti-slavery, influence.[16]

Naturally the first question about a trade deal with Canada was how it would affect the great question of slavery, and the American political balance. For many in the north, the attraction of a trade arrangement with the British provinces, apart from its economic consequences, was that it would serve to draw the colonials into the American orbit—that the American flag would follow American trade into the north. If that meant the admission of three or four new states, it would be enough to tip the balance.

For many southerners the argument was just the opposite. If the British Americans remained economically isolated and discontented, they would be tempted to throw off the British Empire and seek admission to the American union. If, on the other hand, they could find prosperity without admission to the union, they would remain separate and independent, thereby frustrating northern dreams of an anti-slavery majority.

Principles (even contradictory principles) were one thing. Tactics were something else again. The American executive was weak and almost indifferent, but that wasn't where the power over trade lay. The Canadians were forced to supplement the efforts of the executive and concentrate on persuading the legislature. Winning over Congress cost time and money, the Canadian government was told. Bravely the Canadians shouldered the burden, hiring "congressional agents" and sending cabinet ministers and even Lord Elgin down to Washington to reason with their fellow politicians over champagne, whisky, and cigars.[17] It was the first time, but certainly not the last, that Canadian negotiators engaged the American political system; and on this occasion they were successful.

It was a rare achievement. The Reciprocity Treaty of 1854 was one of only three trade treaties signed and ratified by the United States between 1789 and 1934. The treaty dealt with trade, navigation, and the fishery. An enumerated list of natural products could enter both countries free of duty—what would later be called sectoral free trade. Natural products included wheat, coal, timber, and "unmanufactured" lumber. The Americans secured access to the St. Lawrence canals and to the fishery off the Atlantic provinces.[18] In return, the colonials were allowed to fish in American waters north of the 36th parallel and to navigate Lake Michigan. The treaty would last for ten years, and thereafter could be terminated with one year's notice.

The Reciprocity Treaty coincided with an economic boom, and so its positive effects were enhanced by the effects of prosperity. A sharp depression in 1857 affected both the provinces and the United States, but thereafter the outbreak of the American Civil War ensured that the colonials had a market feeding the industries and armies of the Northern states in their war with the South.

POLITICS AND DEVELOPMENT

The current of development in the United States had swept past Canada after 1820. Highways, canals, and railways directed Americans west to the Mississippi Valley, and then across the prairies and mountains to Oregon and California, where there was a gold rush to entice immigrants. In place of settlers, there was commerce along the northern frontier, encouraged for the time being by the relative difficulty of communicating between the distant states of the growing union. It was easier and simpler for merchants along the northern border to derive their goods from Canada or New Brunswick, as opposed to Wisconsin or Missouri; and the same was true in reverse. Nevertheless, trade with Canada was relatively local and minor compared with trade with Great Britain, which remained until the 1920s the United States' principal trading partner.

Canada gradually became a backwater in the American mind. French Canada was exotic and quaint, though definitely inferior. English Canada, on the other hand, was closer to what Americans were used to. Travellers crossing the border commented that it was hard to tell which country they were in. What was familiar wasn't dangerous or even disturbing.

What was disturbing was slavery. The absence of slavery in the British provinces meant that escaping slaves directed themselves there, using a network of helpers collectively styled "the Underground Railroad." Once on British territory, they were free, and safe from legal extradition.[19] Perhaps thirty thousand ex-slaves arrived as a result, and most of them settled in the province of Canada.

They were not entirely welcome. On the one hand, there were numerous anti-slavery groups in the provinces, ready to support the refugees from the States. On the other hand, many Canadians feared what they didn't know or weren't used to—another skin colour.[20] The resulting racist prejudice kept blacks marginalized in much the same way as in the northern United States.

Meanwhile, many Canadians found themselves engaged, emotionally and intellectually, as the United States lurched toward disunion during the 1850s. Not for the last time, extreme American politics found a distant echo in the British provinces, although the provincials had issues of their own to concern them. As always, economics loomed large: the boom of the mid-1850s became the Crash of 1857. The boom had encouraged the politicians in Canada, New Brunswick, and Nova Scotia to plump for railways—in Canada's case, one of the longest in the world, the Grand Trunk, which eventually stretched from tidewater on the Gulf of St. Lawrence all the way to the Detroit River and beyond. Along with the railway mileage stretched government guarantees for railway investors—without which Canada's colonial railways would undoubtedly not have been built. The Grand Trunk occasioned one of the engineering marvels of the age, the Victoria Bridge across the St. Lawrence at Montreal, which was opened in 1859.

The Grand Trunk was, to be sure, an expensive feat. The only way to complete it was to rely heavily, and increasingly, on the Canadian provincial treasury.[21] The Canadian government could harvest the credit for getting the job done, but it also bore the brunt of criticism for the perceived deeds and misdeeds of what immediately became the province's largest and most visible corporation—one that wasn't owned in Canada, but in Britain. If Canadians complained about British investors, the investors complained about Canadians. "It was quite clear to me," one wrote, "that the colony was getting a good deal more out of the [railway] line than the shareholders were ever likely to get."[22]

The Grand Trunk and parallel lines like the Great Western were only partly designed to serve the needs of the British colonies. More importantly, they were designed to tap into the commerce of the American Midwest, and as such the colonial railways became part of a larger North American grid, integrating British America into the adjacent United States. And, of course, when an economic slump struck the United States, as it did in 1857, it affected the British colonies too.

The Crash of 1857 undermined provincial finances and ruined thousands of individual investors. Real estate values plummeted, and banks that had lent heavily in mortgages were compromised. (The Bank of Upper Canada, which was heavily into mortgages, never recovered and ultimately failed; the Bank of Montreal, which was not, survived and prospered.) But government had to be carried on: canals and railways had to be paid for. Governments reluctantly raised taxes, which in Canada's case meant the tariff.

The tariff rose high enough to come to the attention of British exporters, who complained that their goods were being excluded from the colonial market. What kind of an empire was it, they asked, when colonies could cripple imports from the mother country? Pressed by the British government, the Canadian government replied that unless British taxpayers were prepared to pay for the administration of Canada, they had better leave the Canadians to raise their own revenue as they saw fit. The British government subsided. Rather unexpectedly, Canada and ultimately all the other colonies had jumped a constitutional hurdle. (The self-governing colonies now included Newfoundland, which had gained responsible government in 1855.) Where taxes and trade were concerned, colonial autonomy was now virtually absolute.

The colonies continued to depend on Great Britain for several expensive items, most notably defence. The backbone of defence was the Royal Navy, based at Halifax on the Atlantic. (The Pacific base was in Valparaiso, Chile, and was moved to Esquimalt, on Vancouver Island, only in 1865.) There were no local disturbances during the 1850s to suppress, no call on Britain for reinforcements for North America. Canadians did, however, serve as individuals in Britain's imperial wars, for example in the Crimean War of 1854–56 against Russia and in the Indian Mutiny of 1857.[23]

The American Civil War

Neither Russians nor Indians were likely, or in fact able, to attack the British American colonies. Only the Americans could do that. As the United States teetered on the verge of civil war, some in the Northern states toyed with the idea of annexing the provinces, either to compensate for the loss of the seceding Southern states or as a last-ditch means of unifying the dis-United States against a convenient foreign enemy.[24]

The American Civil War broke out in April 1861, and lasted four long years. The North, under President Abraham Lincoln, fought at first to maintain the American union and prevent secession, while the South fought for independence and, with it, the preservation of slavery. Eventually, in 1863, the abolition of slavery became a Northern war aim, and Northern victory in 1865 therefore entailed the end of the South's "peculiar institution."

The South by itself could hardly hope to defeat the more populous and economically developed North; Southern strategy therefore sought to enlist foreign aid, especially that of Great Britain. The British government to some extent played into Southern hands by recognizing the South as a "belligerent"; the next logical step would have been to recognize the South as an independent country, making the Civil War an international conflict—rather like what had happened during the American Revolution.

The North resented the British attitude, and the resentment expressed itself in an incident in the fall of 1861, when a Northern ship intercepted a British vessel, the *Trent*, carrying Southern "diplomats" to Europe. This infringed British rights, though the British themselves had done the same thing during the Napoleonic Wars. The British government demanded that the Southerners be released, and there was a real danger that the North would refuse. Steamers left British ports carrying eleven thousand extra troops to reinforce the British North American garrison, and for a time it seemed that war was about to break out.

Cooler heads prevailed, the Southerners were released, and the war did not come. Meanwhile, the British provinces enjoyed the unaccustomed presence of the flower of the British army. Colonial society welcomed young and very eligible British officers, and the colonial economy welcomed their expenditures. The British treasury was not so pleased. Keeping the troops in North America was expensive, and, so it seemed, militarily futile. Strung out along a frontier twenty-four hundred kilometres long, from the Bay of Fundy to Lake Huron, the army could be cut off and gobbled up by any sizeable and competently led American army. Worse still, the colonies couldn't agree on their own defence, which might have left the British army largely unsupported in the event of war. Increasingly, it appeared that the colonies' best and cheapest defence was the maintenance of peaceful relations with the United States. The British certainly wanted it so. Exclaiming on the expense of defending Canada, the Conservative chancellor of the exchequer, Benjamin Disraeli, noted the "anomaly" of "an army maintained in a colony which does not permit us even to govern it!"[25]

As the Southern cause foundered after 1863, Southern agents in the colonies took desperate measures to provoke a war that was definitely not in the colonies' interest. They staged a couple of raids on American territory from the colonies, and with victory all but assured, the Northern response could afford to be more forceful than in 1861. Passport controls were slapped on travellers across the border, stranding unwary Americans visiting Toronto or Saint John or Halifax. The Reciprocity Treaty was denounced in March 1865; it would expire a year later, on 17 March 1866. It's tempting to ascribe the end of reciprocity to American irritation over border incidents, but it probably owed more to disgust at rising Canadian tariffs on American manufactured goods. Reciprocity did not lead to economic union, far less annexation. Absent political benefit, the economic gains of reciprocity could not outweigh American protectionism in Congress. There wouldn't be another such trade agreement for the next seventy years.

There was one more trans-border eruption. Many of the soldiers in the armies of the North were recently arrived immigrants from Ireland. Many of these longed for the independence of Ireland under the leadership of the revolutionary Fenian Brotherhood. The Fenians proposed to strike at Great Britain, not in distant Ireland, but in the adjacent British colonies. This definitely alarmed the colonial governments, which had to mobilize troops of their own to counter the Fenian threat.

The Fenians did invade from time to time, most notably on the New Brunswick frontier in April 1866 and then across the Niagara River in June. The American government didn't support them, and instead confiscated their arms and cut off their supplies. The Fenian menace eventually subsided, but it had been an expensive lesson for the colonists who had for the first time seriously to pay for their own defence. Money, as always, talked, in this case speaking to the colonists about what it meant, and what it cost, to remain British.

CONFEDERATION

Over the years British officials and colonial politicians had considered the feasibility of uniting the colonies—each colony was autonomous, and each had a political system that was discrete and self-contained. They had from time to time discussed the possibility, but until the 1860s the time was never ripe.

The driving force behind union was discontent in the western part of the province of Canada, the former Upper Canada, sometimes called Canada West. Overwhelmingly English-speaking, outnumbering the French of Lower Canada (also called Canada East) but condemned to equal representation in the legislature, the majority of Upper Canadians increasingly demanded "representation by population," or "rep by pop." The Lower Canadians naturally resisted any change that would diminish their political standing, or lessen their ability to control their own, largely French-speaking, society. The Canadian legislature was paralyzed, since no party or combination of parties—there were four, two for each section—could command a stable majority.

Finally, in June 1864, the leaders of three of the four parties, George Brown (Liberal), John A. Macdonald (Conservative), and George-Etienne Cartier (Conservative), agreed to form a coalition government with the object of seeking a federal union. The Lower Canadian Conservatives, who were interested in recovering the autonomy they had lost in 1840 with the union of the two Canadas, proved to have interests parallel to the Upper Canadian Liberals. Upper and Lower Canada would be divided, but they would also be united in a larger union that would include, if possible, the Atlantic colonies. As it happened, the three Maritime provinces, New Brunswick, Nova Scotia, and Prince Edward Island, were contemplating a conference to discuss Maritime union. Learning of this, the Canadian government let it be known that they would like to be invited.

In the event, delegates from all four colonies met in Charlottetown at the beginning of September 1864. The idea of a colonial union proved surprisingly attractive, and it was decided to meet again, in Quebec City, on 10 October. The Quebec conference included Newfoundland as well as the original four colonies at Charlottetown. Again, there was a large measure of agreement, so much so that the Quebec conference produced seventy-two resolutions that outlined how a colonial federation could be governed.

The process was not entirely smooth, but on the main issue of a federated combination of colonies there was little dispute. There was no serious disagreement on the distribution of powers that made the proposed central government considerably more powerful than the provinces. As for the provinces, there would be six: the four Atlantic colonies, and the redivided provinces of Upper and Lower Canada—Ontario and Quebec. There was further discussion, more prolonged, of the composition of the new federal Parliament, and the characteristics of its two chambers, the House of Commons and the Senate. But there would be a single entity with constituent federated parts, and it would be called Canada. Its capital would be the new Canadian capital of Ottawa, where grandiose Parliament Buildings were being constructed, in time to receive the new Canadian Parliament. The conference adjourned at the end of October, recommending its conclusions to the legislatures of the several colonies.

The course of the new "confederation" project did not run smooth. Newfoundland hesitated, and continued to hesitate, as opposition to confederation grew. Finally it stayed out altogether, and remained out until 1949. The government of New Brunswick, led by Samuel Leonard Tilley, went to the polls and was soundly beaten by an anti-confederate government. The government of Nova Scotia, led by Charles Tupper, had no need to risk an election, having been elected just the year before, in 1863; so Tupper pushed the project through his legislature, even though it was obvious that there was substantial opposition, later estimated at 65 percent of the population. All Tupper had to do was hold on until confederation could be made into reality, which meant getting it passed by the imperial Parliament in London. In Prince Edward Island, the forces of locality were too great. The island was too small; it would be swallowed up and ignored in a federation as large and populous as "Canada." As of 1865, confederation was in trouble in the Maritimes.

The greatest support for the confederation project came from the province of Canada, but even there it's debatable how much support there really was, especially in Lower Canada. There the local Liberals, called "Rouges" or "Reds," condemned confederation as a fraud. Cartier's Conservatives, or "Bleus" ("Blues"), argued that confederation was a victory for French Canadians, because it finally gave them a place of their own, the future province of Quebec, in which they would be the undisputed majority. True, the Rouges replied, but the main powers of government, over railways, telegraphs, the post office, trade, and taxation belonged to the new federal government.

To work as intended, "Canada" must include at least the mainland colonies, and there the key was New Brunswick. Fortunately the anti-confederate government of that province disintegrated in 1866, to be replaced by a pro-confederate administration under the durable Tilley. It helped that the Fenians were making fierce noises on the border, which encouraged feelings of solidarity with the empire and with other colonies that might contribute to New Brunswick's defence.

The action now moved to London, where with the assistance of colonial representatives the imperial government drafted an act to give effect to the Seventy-two Resolutions of the Quebec Conference of 1864, creating the Dominion of Canada. The resulting bill passed through Parliament on 29 March 1867 as the British North America Act, and took effect on the first of July of that year.

9

EXPANSION AND DISAPPOINTMENT, 1867–1896

The members of the Charlottetown Conference pause for photographic
immortalization: Charles Tupper, Nova Scotia (top row, third from left);
Thomas D'Arcy McGee (top row, seventh from left); George-Etienne Cartier
(in front of McGee); John A. Macdonald (sitting in centre); John Hamilton Gray, PEI
(second right from Macdonald); Samuel Leonard Tilley, New Brunswick
(in front of third pole); George Brown (far right).

T he Dominion of Canada established in 1867 disappointed some of the hopes of its founders. They predicted a great transcontinental country, abounding prosperity, and a population to rival the United States. They were not entirely wrong. The dominion was by 1896 the third largest political entity on earth, more than seventy-seven million hectares, behind only Russia and China. It had expanded to the prairies in 1870, buying out the lands of the Hudson's Bay Company, to the Pacific in 1871, with the addition of British Columbia, and filled out on the Atlantic in 1873, when Prince Edward Island finally joined. The British government transferred the largely empty Arctic Archipelago to Canada in 1880, extending the dominion's nominal jurisdiction all the way to the North Pole.

The land, however, lacked people. This fact occasioned first puzzlement, embarrassment, then resentment among patriotic Canadians. The acquisition of a transcontinental territory matching that of the United States, coupled with superior British institutions, seemed a logical formula for national greatness, with a population to match. As for the population—thirty, forty, a hundred million were plausible figures; plausible enough, at least, to float without serious contradiction in the oratory of the period.

Reality was somewhat different. The west had first to be acquired, and when it was it came with strings attached. There was a discontented local population on the prairies, made up of Indians and whites, and the Métis, who were a mixture of the two. They would have to be mollified and subsidized before they could be governed. Farther west there was British

Columbia, attached to Canada in 1871 by a Canadian promise of a transcontinental railway. But the railway cost money and took time. There was less money than expected, thanks to an international economic downturn in the 1870s. Nation-building turned out to be a heavier burden than expected, and it was hard to attract immigrants to a country with a disappointing economy and inferior prospects.

When Canada was judged inferior, it was always with reference to the United States, the giant next door. Canadians admired, envied, and resented their neighbour. Many Canadians measured their own status against that of the United States, and drew their own conclusions. American prosperity was its own advertisement, so much so that between 1867 and 1896 some two million Canadians left for points south and west.[1] Immigrants arrived to replace them in the lesser opportunities available in Canada—but never enough.

The departure of so many Canadians masked another trend in the population: Canadians were living longer, with life expectancy in urban areas rising, which mirrored improvements in medicine but also a rising standard of living. There were proportionately more females at the end of the century than at the beginning—due in large part to the development of safer practices regarding childbirth. Rising living standards beckoned people from farms to towns, or to Canada's few large cities.

If Canada was underpopulated, with a surplus of emigrants over immigrants, it was also divided. The divisions were racial, between Natives, or half-Natives like the Métis, and the majority whites; linguistic, again between Natives and whites, but also between English and French; religious, between Catholic and Protestant, and among the various Protestant sects; geographical, pitting region against region; and finally constitutional, between the layers of government in Canada's federal system, meaning the dominion against the provinces.

There were unifying factors too. Canada's British identity evoked varying degrees of enthusiasm, but few indeed railed against the empire and all it stood for. There was politics, especially the party system, which was organized on a pan-Canadian basis. Partisan loyalty subsumed some of the differences between religion and region and language. There was economic advantage, as local interests discovered that profit sometimes knew no boundaries. There were large corporations, especially the railways but also banks, manufacturers, and retailers, employing thousands from coast to coast in hierarchically organized companies. There was technology, linking east and west in Canada through the railway and the telegraph and then, in the 1880s and later, through the telephone and electricity.

Finally, there was government, which in the later nineteenth century was expanding. Sometimes government acted through agents—for example the government bankers, the Bank of Montreal, or the various railway companies that government patronized and subsidized. Governments sometimes competed on behalf of the interests they represented, or tried to monopolize rewards and other concessions.

At the head of government were the politicians, of whom the most successful, Sir John A. Macdonald, became prime minister on 1 July 1867 as leader of a Liberal-Conservative administration. So skilled was Macdonald that he occupied the post of prime minister for nineteen of the next twenty-four years; his was the mould from which most of Canada's successful political leaders were formed. Macdonald was fortunate in his associates, some of whom, like Sir Leonard Tilley, Sir George-Etienne Cartier, and Sir Charles Tupper, were former provincial premiers. Macdonald's particular skill was to bind his party to him in loyalty, for as he and his followers knew, in party politics loyalty is a precondition for success.

Canada was governed on three levels: provincial, for local matters; federal, with a government headquartered in Ottawa; and imperial, located, as always, in London. The London government spent little directly on Canada, but Canadians nevertheless relied on it for identity and support. The Union Jack flapped proudly over Canadian land. Portraits of Queen Victoria were universal, and in larger cities actual statues of the queen gave her a physical presence. But the main benefit of the queen and her monarchy for Canadians was psychological. Being part of Great Britain and the British Empire meant identity, tradition, and stability, at least for those Canadians who chose not to emigrate to the United States and harvest the fruits of republican prosperity.

Canada was fortunate in one respect: nobody wanted to attack it from the outside. The Americans were preoccupied with their own development, and had no time to spare for the colony to the north, so nearly identical, so inexplicably separate. Canadians shared with Americans the benefits of geographical isolation, protected by the Royal Navy from European intervention—the only direction from which an organized invasion could possibly come. Accordingly, the burden of defence was slight. Canada's defence establishment, such as it was, was primarily a social club, an occasion for Canadian males to wear bright uniforms and look fierce and gallant. Over the first thirty years of Canada's existence the military confronted an actual enemy only twice—both times in the distant west.

Riel and Railways

The largest aggregation of British territory in North America was, until 1869, Rupert's Land, the property of the Hudson's Bay Company. The company's rule sat lightly on the inhabitants of Rupert's Land, but light as it was, it was too much both for the company and for its western subjects. When the Canadian government came calling at the Bay Company headquarters in London with an imperial loan guarantee, it found a willing seller. In return for £300,000, some land around its western posts, and 5 percent of the estimated arable terrain of the west (about 2.8 million hectares), the company relinquished 390 million hectares of territory. The transfer of land was to be effective on 1 December 1869.

In Ottawa, Sir John A. Macdonald's government rejoiced. He appointed a lieutenant governor to manage Rupert's Land, and dispatched him via Minnesota (where there was the nearest rail line) to the territory's only large settlement, on the Red River.

The inhabitants of Red River had other ideas. Under the leadership of a youthful and charismatic figure, Louis Riel, some of the locals demanded promises and conditions before they would allow the foreign Canadians to assume control over themselves and their lands and properties. Riel's followers were both Métis and white—he himself was Métis—but the incident is usually called the Riel rebellion and chronicled as a predominantly Métis occasion.

There were numbers of Canadians at Red River, mostly from Ontario. Bold and irresponsible, their leaders tried to anticipate Canadian control and overthrow Riel, but were themselves overthrown. It was a foolish and pointless gesture, because by early 1870 negotiations were well underway to appease Red River's concerns. Riel followed with a foolish gesture of his own, appointing a firing squad to execute the most disruptive of the Canadian party, a young man named Thomas Scott. "We must make Canada respect us," Riel helpfully explained, but he had chosen the wrong gesture. An armed but bloodless rebellion was one thing; the quasi-judicial murder of Scott was something else.

Scott's untimely demise awakened demons in Ontario. English, Protestant, and an Orangeman, he could be fashioned into a symbol, a martyr no less, for Anglo-Protestant liberty against the French and Catholic Riel.[2] A military expedition composed of imperial and colonial troops was already being mounted under a British officer, Colonel Garnet Wolseley. Riel had furnished the Canadian part of the expedition with a war cry. But when Wolseley arrived at the old Hudson's Bay fort at Red River in August 1870, after a lengthy journey by steamer and canoe from central Canada—there was no railway north or west of Georgian Bay—Riel slipped out the rear gate, and escaped to the United States.

The Red River rebellion produced the province of Manitoba as part of Macdonald's hasty deal with Red River's inhabitants. (It was originally a tiny rectangle south of Lake Winnipeg.) Manitoba, like other Canadian provinces, had its own government and elected legislature, which was autonomous and representative of local politics and pride. Unlike the older provinces, it was totally dependent on subsidy from the dominion government, which gave it some utility as far as Macdonald was concerned. Manitoba thus became Canada's fifth province.

As prime minister, Macdonald had troubles enough. He had to create institutions to match Canada's transcontinental aspirations, and some of his early efforts stumbled. Two finance ministers resigned over banking policy; only the third, Sir Francis Hincks, succeeded in passing a Bank Act, which favoured, but not too obviously, the Bank of Montreal and the Montreal financial community over other regional banking centres such as Halifax and Toronto.

The government needed money. It taxed as best it could, within the limits of a revenue tariff, but to do what it needed to do it must borrow. Territorial expansion was expensive: there was the cost of buying Rupert's Land, and after that there was British Columbia, which was induced into joining Canada in 1871 by the promise of a transcontinental connection to the rest of the country. Macdonald promised a railway within ten years, to the British Columbians' initial surprise and pleasure. They knew, and he knew, that it would cost a great deal of money. British Columbia, vast in space and tiny in population, became Canada's sixth province.

Next came Prince Edward Island, which in the 1870s had many times the population of British Columbia, plus a fishery, and a railway. The Islanders couldn't afford their railway, and began to think of ways to pay for it. Canada might not have had much money, but it had more than the Island and, with the sun of imperial approbation beaming down, Prince Edward Island joined Canada in 1873, becoming Canada's seventh province.

Macdonald had the components for a country. Now he must join them together. He couldn't expect much help from outside: the British government, headed by the economically minded William Ewart Gladstone, did not wish to be reminded of what Canada had already cost. As part of his own program of economy, he withdrew the remaining British army garrisons from Canada, leaving only two residual naval bases at Halifax and Esquimalt, on Vancouver Island. It was an admission that Great Britain had little prospect of mounting a successful land defence of Canada.

Great Britain nevertheless retained responsibility for defence and foreign affairs. In token of the former, a British officer commanded the Canadian militia as well as a tiny permanent force. Canada didn't control its foreign relations, but Canadian concerns could still be heard within the empire. Thus the British government appointed Macdonald as one of three commissioners to visit Washington to resolve outstanding issues of Anglo–American diplomacy. Most of these related to American grievances over British conduct during the American Civil War.

The grievances were real enough. The British had allowed the Confederacy to build commerce raiders like the ship *Alabama* in British shipyards. There had been the St. Alban's raid in 1864, and other minor incidents of cross-border depredations. On the other hand, there were the costly Fenian incursions into Canada, which were arguably the product of American official negligence. The Americans complained about Canadian fisheries policy that restricted American fishing boats in Canadian waters, and the Canadians wanted to see the Reciprocity Treaty restored. Indeed, Macdonald hoped to use access to Canada's fisheries as bait to induce the Americans to return to reciprocity. Unofficially, the Republican senator from Massachusetts, Charles Sumner, suggested that the whole package of disputes could be wrapped up by the simple expedient of giving Canada to the United States in return for the cancellation of American claims on Great Britain.

That was never a prospect, but neither was reciprocity. Instead, the British paid handsomely for the *Alabama* and related claims, while the Americans rented access to the Canadian fishery for ten years, at a cost to be determined by arbitration. The Fenian losses were simply omitted. All this was embodied in a treaty signed in Washington.

The significance of the occasion was not lost on Macdonald. He resented the fact that the British had disposed of Canadian interests to meet their larger objective of re-establishing peace and harmony with the United States. Though in a sense three countries had been present at the negotiation, it was the two larger ones that decided the outcome. Canada's role was not to obstruct.

It was a lesson that the British Empire was not an equal opportunity association. A colony like Canada might no longer be subordinate, but it was definitely not equal to Great Britain. Colonial requirements might be considered or even indulged by British ministers, but they had not the same shape, urgency, or importance as strictly British interests. In any case, if relations between the United States and Great Britain did deteriorate, if negotiations failed to solve outstanding issues, Canadian interests in a larger sense would suffer.[3]

But would Canada have done any better negotiating on its own? The answer to that question, as Macdonald probably knew, was no, and as Sumner's half-serious suggestion that Canada be annexed indicated, there was more at stake than a discussion of limited issues. The Americans might not like what they saw in the British Empire, but the empire was a powerful entity, something that had to be considered.[4] Canada was not.

Macdonald, in any case, had to bear in mind that he needed British money to provide for Canada's future, if it was to have one. He needed it for the Intercolonial Railway connecting Quebec and Halifax, and he needed it for his railway to British Columbia, a huge undertaking. The United States, with its wealth and resources, had only just completed a rail link to California in 1868 over much more favourable geography.

The Intercolonial Railway, which was finally completed in 1876, by itself absorbed $21 million of borrowed money, and is estimated to have taken twice as long to build as it should have. Its chief engineer, Sandford Fleming, applied the experience to laying down a route for Macdonald's visionary Pacific railway.[5] Macdonald's friends and political allies seem to have benefited from the experience, which dispensed money in politically sensitive areas. The Intercolonial thus succeeded in knitting the scattered colonies together in a metaphysical as well as a physical sense.

The Pacific railway took longer, and of course required more money. The scent of money attracted railway promoters, such as the Montreal steamship magnate Sir Hugh Allan. Allan valued the prospect of heading up a railway syndicate (largely composed of American investors) so highly that he contributed freely to Sir John A. Macdonald's Conservative party during the 1872 federal election. Sir John, understanding Allan's interest, drew freely on him, at one point telegraphing "I must have another ten thousand."

The 1872 election returned Macdonald and his Conservatives to power, but Macdonald's ally, Sir George Cartier, was personally defeated in Montreal. Shortly afterward Cartier died. Macdonald was soon beset by rumours of scandal concerning Sir Hugh Allan's "Canada Pacific Railway." The rumours proved all too true. Some of Macdonald's MPs quailed in the face of public outrage, and his parliamentary majority melted away. Drunk and depressed in the face of so much adversity, Macdonald was unable to rally his troops. The government was defeated in the House of Commons on 5 November 1873.

Macdonald's collapse gave the opposition Liberals their chance. An ill-assorted collection of oppositionists, they had no natural leader, and settled on a parliamentary veteran, Alexander Mackenzie, originally a stonemason from Sarnia, Ontario. Mackenzie was at least hard-working and honest, though he was also unimaginative and vindictive—not the best recommendation for a party leader. An election swiftly followed, which even Mackenzie could not have lost. The Liberals were returned with a comfortable majority in the House of Commons, just in time for an international depression to take hold in Canada.

Mackenzie presided over a shrinking economy and an emigrating population. Less economic activity meant fewer imports, and therefore lower tariff revenue, the government's principal source of taxes. Mackenzie had little option but to raise taxes and spend frugally. His honesty and frugality did not benefit his party, since he had little in the way of patronage to hand out to his supporters.

What Mackenzie could do, he did. Construction began on a Canadian Pacific Railway along a route surveyed by Sandford Fleming. The government would build it, but given the government's limited financial resources, it proceeded very slowly, so that by 1878 it reached from Fort William on Lake Superior partway through Manitoba. Winnipeg, the new capital of the new province, was connected east to the Great Lakes and south to the American border. There was also a short stretch of railway east

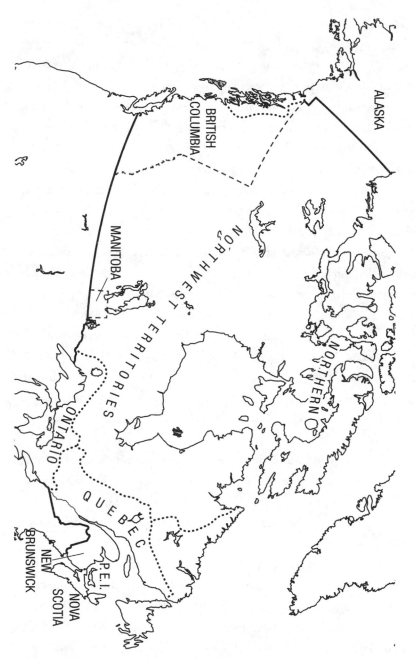

Canada, 1880

ALASKA

BRITISH
COLUMBIA

MANITOBA

NORTHWEST

TERRITORIES

N,

NORTHERN

ONTARIO

QUEBEC

NEW
BRUNSWICK

P.E.I.

NOVA
SCOTIA

from Fleming's chosen terminus on Burrard Inlet on the Pacific—the future Vancouver. In between, and from central Ontario to Fort William, there was nothing.

The Liberals also organized the West, beyond the postage-stamp province of Manitoba, into the Northwest Territories, with a capital first at Battleford, and later, after 1882, at Regina. All important questions were managed from Ottawa—especially land, settlement, and natural resources. As in the east, land was free to those who could afford to settle upon it, and then cultivate it. But few came—only fifty-six thousand lived in the Territories by the time of the 1881 census.

By 1878 the Liberals were out of power and Sir John A. Macdonald and the Conservatives were back. They returned to construction by private enterprise—heavily subsidized, to be sure. The railway must be seen to be Canadian, and government aid was justified by appeals to national sentiment. The line was built entirely in Canada, across the barren rocks of the Canadian Shield in northern Ontario. A syndicate of Montreal capitalists led by George Stephen and Donald Smith undertook to find the necessary finance, and under the direction of an American engineer, William Van Horne, the railway began to make progress. The government provided inducements on the American model—5 million acres (2.02 million hectares) of land, $25 million in subsidy, all the existing government-built portion of the railway (estimated at $38 million), and a monopoly on rail lines south to the United States. Prairie settlers would deal with the CPR—or nobody.

Generous as the government assistance was, it wasn't enough. The syndicate took its investment where it could find it—in Great Britain, but also in the United States, a fact that wasn't emphasized in government and company propaganda. Labourers were imported—many from central Canada, some from Europe, and many, an estimated fifteen thousand, from China, to work on the westernmost section. By early 1885 only a few gaps remained in the rail line between the Rockies and in northern Ontario.

SETTLING AND PACIFYING THE WEST

The railway was needed, for in that year Louis Riel led a new rebellion along the banks of the Saskatchewan River. Riel in 1885 was not the man he once had been. Older, sadder, scarred by experience and misfortune, Riel was convinced that he had a divine mission to secure justice for himself, for his people, the Métis, and more generally for the settlers of the West. Macdonald treated the West with distant unconcern, sending out governors and Indian agents and occupying it with a gendarmerie, the North-West Mounted Police (or NWMP, the ancestors of the later Royal Canadian Mounted Police or RCMP).

The government had signed treaties with the Plains Indians, to get them to surrender their lands in return for government-supported reserves. They could see easily enough from the Indian wars in the neighbouring United States what their fate would be if they tried to resist. Starvation helped the government's policy: those Natives who might have been disinclined to move onto reserves found they had little choice if they wished to feed their families.

A trickle of settlers moved in from the east, mostly from Ontario, with many stopping in Manitoba. The old Métis way of life was disappearing: the fur trade had shrunk and moved on, the buffalo were gone, and the settlers imported new ways of doing things and a government to enforce them. The Métis responded by moving farther west, to the Saskatchewan Valley; there, too, they had white neighbours. Many of the neighbours were disgruntled at what they took to be official neglect and eastern exploitation: the beginnings of regional feeling in western Canada can be reasonably said to date from this time.[6]

That settlers' grievances existed is certain. Were they justified? Most of their problems concerned land, land surveys, and land titles. Ottawa moved to respond, but for a variety of reasons—some beyond the government's control—the response was slow and too late. And so in the summer of 1884 the communities of the North Saskatchewan River, settlers and Métis, invited Louis Riel, in exile in the United States, to return to

Canada, and to advise if not represent them in their disputes with the dominion government. Riel accepted the invitation.

Riel's agenda was certainly different from that of the settlers. He was on the hunt for reparations and compensation, some for himself, and some for his people, the French-speaking Métis. He believed that the Métis were the inheritors of the land, along with the Indians; but unlike the Indians they hadn't conceded their patrimony by treaty to the Canadian government. There was no place in Riel's universe for the settlers, except as interlopers. The government did in fact negotiate with him, and it might have been possible to reach an agreement based on the land claims of the Métis in their river lots along the North Saskatchewan. But reality clashed with Riel's messianic fervour. He saw himself as a prophet and the organizer of a new church, in which the Bishop of Montreal, whom he admired, would be pope.

Macdonald saw greed and sharp practice in Riel while Riel saw delay and deceit in the government. When Riel turned to armed rebellion, Macdonald raised an army of eight thousand and sent the troops west over the new Canadian Pacific Railway. Transported by the CPR and supplied by the Hudson's Bay Company, the soldiers easily reached Riel's headquarters at Batoche, and defeated the insurgents in May 1885. Some of the rebel leaders fled, but Riel surrendered to Canadian troops. In his brief rebellion, some eighty people had lost their lives.

Riel was tried in Regina before a local jury and convicted of treason. His lawyers tried to persuade the court that their client was insane and, given his religious delusions, they had at the very least a plausible case. Riel, however, was anxious to establish his credibility as a prophet, and he was inspired by a genuine sense of personal grievance and injustice. He managed to convince the court that he was, indeed, sane enough to have committed treason. Convicted, he was sentenced to hang.

This was in August 1885. There followed a prolonged and very bitter political crisis. Riel was, after all, French Canadian and, in a sense, Catholic. His cause was widely adopted in Quebec, where he became a symbol of minority rights unjustly trampled by an unfeeling majority. The fact was that the majority too was aroused, and demanded that Riel hang, according to law. Sir John A. Macdonald was pressed to spare Riel's life from the side of Quebec, and to carry out the sentence from Ontario.

Macdonald was not inclined to sympathy, but he went through the motions of having Riel examined for proof of insanity. Two doctors, one English and one French, were sent to Regina to examine the prisoner, and they reported in precisely opposite ways. Then and later Macdonald played fast and loose with the medical opinions, misleading the House of Commons and effectively confusing the issue. In the words of a prominent Canadian historian, J.R. Miller, "Macdonald believed that no matter what his government did they would be damned by some group. If they were damned if they did and damned if they didn't, then he was damned well going to do what he personally believed was right."[7] Riel was hanged on 16 November 1885. He believed, until the end, that he would rise on the third day after his execution.

The rights and wrongs of Riel's life have remained controversial in Canadian history ever since. In Quebec there was considerable resentment. Some of Macdonald's French-Canadian supporters (including ministers) tried to defend the government, while others remained prudently silent, hoping the storm would pass.

The Liberal opposition, on the other hand, discovered both a vocation and a role in the storm over Riel. The Liberal leader, Edward Blake, questioned the policies and performance of Macdonald's government. A Quebec Liberal MP, Wilfrid Laurier, went further, telling a mass meeting in Montreal that if he had lived on the banks of the Saskatchewan, he too would have shouldered a rifle and marched beside Riel. It didn't help the Liberals in Ontario, but it would, eventually, have an impact in Quebec.

The Quebec Conservative party suffered considerable damage in the aftermath of Riel's execution. The provincial Conservatives lost an election in 1886 to the Liberals (travelling with a few ex-Conservatives under the label Parti National) under Honoré Mercier, and the federal party lost ground in the successive federal elections of 1887 and 1891. Nevertheless, the Conservatives did not entirely disappear in the province, and elsewhere Macdonald's western policies, and his stand on Riel, helped his party's fortunes.

Riel became the stuff of legend. He was a western symbol, a Métis hero, a French-Canadian martyr, and an Aboriginal champion. Historians of western Canada, and Canadian historians in general since about 1940, have reinterpreted Riel in a kindly light.[8] Politicians invoked his memory, usually favourably. An opera was written about him. In 1999 the Canadian House of Commons even debated and passed a bill asserting the justice of Riel's cause. (The "Louis Riel Act" never entered the statute books, expiring with the Parliament of the day when the 2000 election was called.) The governor general, flanked by an RCMP honour guard wearing Métis sashes, solemnly eulogized Riel, in effect admitting him into the pantheon of Canadian heroes. Insofar as Canadian history has produced a martyr, Riel is it.

The West, however, developed on very different lines from Riel's, lines that were already apparent when the Métis took up arms in 1885. The West of the buffalo hunt and unlimited prairies had vanished, and with it the basis of the hunting economy of the western Native tribes. More importantly, Indians were by the 1890s a small minority of the population of the Canadian West, an afterthought even in the minds of their neighbours, dependent on and powerless against a society that barely gave them a second thought.

What the settlers and their government were thinking about was wheat, and the settlement and development that accompanied it. Ontario had flourished because of wheat, but since 1860 there had been no new viable arable land in the province. The acquisition of the West gave Ontarians reason to hope: it meant land for their children and markets for their manufactures—"the promise of Eden." Government pamphlets extolled the richness of the West—its fertile soil, its mild climate, and its assured agricultural bounty. Even the semi-desert along the 49th parallel, named "Palliser's Triangle" after its first surveyor, was converted on paper into a bountiful garden.[9] But settlement was slow and sparse: by 1886 only 163,000 people lived on the Canadian prairie, including the older communities in Manitoba. The railway, completed the previous fall, would help change that, though slowly.

The dominion government did something practical to assist agriculture by establishing, in the 1870s, a system of experimental farms. Where wheat was concerned the main problem was the short growing season in the prairies, where frost came early and stayed late. The solution would not be found until 1903, when short-growing wheat, called Marquis, was developed. Marquis had as much to do with the subsequent wheat boom as any other factor.

And there were, of course, other factors. Agricultural machinery evolved considerably in the nineteenth century—steel plows first, then mechanical reapers and combine harvesters, which separated seeds or grain from hay. The combines made large-scale farming easier, much less labour intensive, and therefore cheaper. All this assisted settlement.

Most of the settlers were English-speaking, but not all. French speakers—some five thousand of them—came to the Red River Valley from New England. (Government encouragement to get more to come, from New England or Quebec, proved futile.) German-speaking and pacifist Mennonites arrived in Manitoba from Russia, happy to locate to a country where they wouldn't be conscripted into the army. The transformation was most obvious in Manitoba. The province's population grew from 25,000 in 1871 to 152,000 in 1891. But where the early population was evenly balanced between Protestant and Catholic, and English and French, by the 1890s Manitoba was overwhelmingly Protestant and English-speaking.

Farther west, in the foothills of the Rockies, a ranching industry grew up. Though similar in some respects to the cattle industry south of the border, the land tenure system was different, as was the social composition of the ranchers. (Land was leased from the government on a system adopted from Australia instead of pre-emption by squatters as in the United States.)[10] The ranchers used the new railway, the CPR, to ship their product: the first Alberta beef reached England in 1886.

RAILWAYS AND THE NATIONAL POLICY

Inbound, the railway brought supplies to the western farmers, many of them made in Canada. As part of the price of the CPR's construction, the government had guaranteed it a monopoly. At the time, facing an empty West, it seemed a good bargain. Later, as the West filled up with farmer-voters, it became clear that there was a political price to pay. The politics of Manitoba turned on the question of the CPR and its monopoly over rail traffic.

But the CPR was only a small part of the links that bound the citizens of the West to central and eastern Canada. It was paralleled by the railway connection between the centre and the east, the Intercolonial Railway. Owned and operated by the government, the Intercolonial provided rewards and employment to government supporters in the East, and helped shore up the structure of patronage and influence that character-ized party politics in the late nineteenth century.[11] The CPR and the Grand Trunk, more straightforwardly, gave money to the party in power, which could then dispense it in the form of favours or bribes as it saw fit.[12]

The railways did more than traverse the Canadian wilderness: they opened it for business, assisted by the simultaneous development of elec-tricity in the 1880s. The age of steam was supplemented, rather than replaced, by the age of electricity. Coal, distant and costly though abun-dant, was replaced as far as central Canada was concerned by hydroelec-tric power from the rapids and waterfalls of Ontario and Quebec's rivers. Niagara Falls, the most impressive of all, had functioned mostly as a tourist attraction since the eighteenth century. With the arrival of electric-ity, it became a destination of a different kind, boasting one of the world's largest hydroelectric generating stations.

In northern Ontario and Quebec, electricity and abundant water made possible lumber mills and then pulp and paper factories in the midst of the boreal forest. Crews blasting rock out of the railway lines discovered nickel near Sudbury; a huge nickel mine soon followed.

Governments actively meddled in the economy. Agriculture was

Canada's most important industry, and most Canadians depended directly or indirectly on farming. The federal government developed experimental farms to assist agricultural productivity and spread farming to areas previously considered too cold or too dry to attempt farming. The provinces dabbled in agricultural education. A federal geological survey, founded before Confederation, explored Canada's subterranean geography and published its findings. Governments subsidized railways to accomplish public purposes, built canals and docks, and dredged rivers and harbours.

There was nothing unusual in this—or different from what was happening at the same time in the United States. Technological developments were broadly similar in both places. Electricity, for example, made its appearance in Canada within a few years of its first American application. The telephone—another invention of the 1870s—was actually developed between the two countries as its inventor, Alexander Graham Bell, lived in both. The Americans too subsidized railways, dabbled in technical assistance to farmers and miners, and practised other forms of government intervention in the economy. This is a point worth stressing, given a later tendency among scholars and other ideologues to portray an inherent difference between Canada, a monarchical society, government-oriented and cultivating community, and the United States as a republic that was free-standing and individualistic. There is little in the nineteenth century to sustain such an analysis, and even less as time passed.

What was happening in both countries was that economic institutions were changing along with the economy. The new technological economy depended on time—the timely delivery of goods, the timely transport of people. That in turn meant that the companies that delivered goods and people, or assembled supplies into finished goods, must have reliable and precise standards of performance. The railways were the prototype, with their hierarchical organization, departmental subdivisions, and large workforces. Maintaining a roadbed, and ensuring supplies of water for engine boilers and of coal for furnaces, required organization.[13]

Other utilities followed, also organized from top to bottom to perform routine tasks predictably and reliably. In cities, department stores grew out of dry goods shops or general stores or fur trade posts: Eaton's and Simpsons in Toronto, Morgan's and Dupuis Frères in Montreal, and, eventually, the Hudson's Bay Company and Woodward's in Vancouver. Large, attractive, multi-storey retail palaces appeared in the downtowns of the larger cities, which customers could reach using horse-drawn streetcars, and later electric transit. But advances in merchandising weren't confined to the cities. As the railways made reliable supply and customer deliveries possible, some of the department stores established a catalogue sales business from large central warehouses, relying on the mail for delivery.

Electricity made many larger enterprises possible, and expanding markets made them desirable. Pulp and paper mills, chemical factories, carriage works, all grew in the late nineteenth century—up to a point. As late as 1910 the average Ontario factory employed fewer than thirty employees, certainly more than the blacksmith shops of mid-century, or the modest water-powered flour mills that still dotted the countryside at the century's end.[14] But except in the largest cities, "managers" were either clerks or foremen, not the basis for the sudden growth of a new, intermediate, class. In most Canadian towns, the local elite comprised the clergy, a lawyer or two, the doctor, and the local bank manager (himself part of a larger hierarchy) or, in Quebec, the notary, who often mixed (or mixed up) the law and banking.

Organization and hierarchy also expanded opportunities for the practice of tyranny, while removing most of the workforce from the direct scrutiny of a business's owners or even its topmost management. "Middle managers" made their appearance, supervising the departments or sectors into which a business was organized. And with large numbers of workers regulated and paid in common, it wasn't hard to discover common interests, which were expressed through the development of trade unions.

Workers and investors were mobile in late nineteenth-century Canada, and indeed neither labour nor capital was confined to the northern dominion. The same was true of their rudimentary trade unions, which in Canada dated back to the early nineteenth century. Workers travelled wherever there was work, moving freely across the frontier to the United

States. They arrived in distant cities anxious for their credentials to be accepted, especially in skilled trades, like printing. Communication between local Canadian unions and their American counterparts, and the common interests of their members, eventually led to absorption in larger American syndicates, like the National Typographical Union.[15]

The American character of Canadian unionism is worth noting. Many Canadian workers were British-born, coming from a country where trade unionism was very strong if not universally accepted, but although British trade unionism existed in Canada, Canadian workers mostly joined American unions that crossed the frontier. The National Typographical Union wasn't the only one. The Knights of Labor was another, more important, organization, and when it perished it was succeeded by others. There were Canadian unions too, but they were increasingly subordinated to the dominant American strain in trade unionism.[16]

Employers were not charmed by the emergence of unions, and none less so than George Brown, the imperious owner of the Toronto *Globe*. Brown's confrontations with labour dated back to the 1850s, and lasted all his life, which was terminated by a disgruntled ex-employee who shot him in 1880.

Sir John Macdonald, Brown's great political rival, further irritated the newspaperman by passing legislation regularizing and legalizing unions' status in 1872. Other regulations were much slower in coming. Employer resistance to the regulation of wages and working conditions kept the federal government from acting, at least under Macdonald; and it was left to the provinces to act, or not, as they saw fit. Ontario did act in 1884, hiring a single inspector to patrol all of the province's industries. Under the Ontario legislation, boys under twelve and girls under fourteen were forbidden to work. Once in the workforce they could work sixty hours a week or ten hours a day, though they could also work a maximum of six weeks at twelve hours a day. Things did eventually improve, but it was examples of this kind that gave Canada the reputation of being socially and economically very conservative, if not actually retrograde.

Local, national, and international unions faced an uphill battle in

Canada. They could organize, collect dues, and go on strike, but employers could respond by hiring replacements. Riots frequently resulted, which in turn gave employment to the local militia. Whether the militia gave satisfaction to those who called them out was another question. "[They] did not fire upon or bayonet the strikers," one labour newspaper happily observed. "They were workingmen themselves."[17]

The house of labour was, however, divided if not fragmented. "Workingmen" had an occupational identity and with it some kind of class solidarity, certainly. But they had religious, cultural, and regional loyalties as well. Self-interest didn't necessarily or even often mean left-wing or working-class politics, or translate into a working-class culture distinct from the bourgeois culture that surrounded it.[18] Even a large and occasionally militant union like the Knights of Labor organized itself with symbols and ceremonies and rituals that mimicked those of contemporary "secret" societies like the Masons. This was hardly accidental, since fraternal bonds—the "brothers and sisters" of the union movement—were at the core of union solidarity.

That kind of solidarity, in terms of the general culture of the time, was neither strange nor alarming. The workers weren't isolated from the world around them. That fact could, and did, mean that workers frequently listened to conservative politicians who promised them "protection," meaning a tariff so high as to keep out competition from lower-wage or lower-cost jurisdictions. As often they harkened to appeals from co-religionists, sometimes spiced with threats of celestial retaliation if they failed to vote their group loyalty on election day.

But, all things being equal, it was the question of the tariff as much as any other government policy that determined voting patterns down to 1896, mixing with other forms of devotion (ethnic, linguistic, and religious) to create an electorate willing to support national political parties. Tariffs are by definition a subsidy, transferring money from consumers to protected industries, but their special attraction to politicians was (and is) that most consumer-voters don't recognize this point.

Tariffs were the great theological question of nineteenth-century politics, and not just in Canada. Though the debate over free trade versus protection was stilled in Britain for most of the nineteenth century, it lurked in the background as one of the great taboos of British politics. In the United States tariffs remained a lively issue, especially among farmers who received little benefit from higher prices for farm machinery or textiles. The miracle was that in a predominantly agrarian country the tariff could be so powerfully sustained as to be practically untouchable.

Canadian governments would have preferred to return to lower tariffs with the United States, but that was an unrealizable ambition. There remained the domestic market, and the politics that surrounded it. Political advantage dictated a high-tariff policy, whose benefits were on display in the neighbouring United States, where tariffs were an invisible cement binding manufacturers to the high-tariff Republican party. The convergence of interests was veiled in nationalism, assuring voters that it was patriotic to support high tariffs. Macdonald saw no reason not to imitate the Republicans. He called his tariff regime the "National Policy." Inaugurated in 1879, it remained the basis of Canada's commercial policy for the next hundred years.

The technique was simple. The Canadian market, though small, was large enough to sustain local industry, if that industry was protected against competition from abroad. So the government asked interested industries to make representations, and then passed their ideas by a small group of advisers in Ottawa. Only occasionally did the consumers' interest play a part—if the consumer was another business interest able to make its influence felt in Ottawa. Politics certainly played a part: tariff exactions had to be weighed against resentment in the various regions of the country. For example, in British Columbia the tariff was a trade-off against the promised railway.[19] In rural areas the tariff was unpopular. In Ontario anti-tariff sentiment could be balanced by other interests and issues, while the Canadian West was still so underpopulated that its interests didn't count for much. The argument that industry was an essential component of nation-building was powerful, suggesting that present sacrifice in higher prices would be rewarded by future economic and political greatness. The result was a tariff that was certainly high enough, though less high than its American counterpart—which only showed that there was room for growth, in tariffs as in the economy.

The Americans Again—Trade and Reciprocity

Trade, in late nineteenth-century Canada, was the handmaiden of politics. It was the product not merely of Canadian politics but of American. (Because Great Britain maintained free trade with all comers, active British politicking wasn't a factor.) American protectionism ran high in the late nineteenth century; anti-protectionism or liberal trade views were restricted to academic economists, farmers, and other congenital complainers. It was a period of executive weakness and congressional dominance, and Congress harkened only to arguments that paid off in votes, or occasionally cash to buy the votes.

The prevailing idea was that trade with Canada should be considered product by product, as it came to Congress's attention; it depended on whether there were enough interests that could be mobilized to block a particular Canadian import. The fisheries were periodically a lively issue. New England senators responded with alacrity when their fishing constituents complained, which was bad news for the Canadian government, struggling to maintain primacy for fishermen from the Maritime provinces on Canadian fishing grounds.

The Treaty of Washington provided for the Americans' renting access to Canadian fishing areas and established an arbitral tribunal to determine the rent. The result, the Halifax Award of 1877, produced $5.5 million for Canada, more than the Americans had anticipated. The U.S. government paid the award with an ill grace as American politicians fulminated. In 1885 Congress instructed the American administration to denounce the fisheries arrangement, but as a result the fisheries question returned to its previous uncertain and confrontational state.[20] Congress offered no solution, leaving the hapless executive to manage as best it could.

Neither government particularly wanted a confrontation, and through a series of temporary expedients they staved off the worst. Fish formed the basis of a series of negotiations in the late 1880s that did little to resolve the problem, but had the effect of reviving, on the Canadian side, the whole issue of trade with the United States.

Many Canadians were troubled by their country's lagging economy. Canada's slow growth, the unremitting provincialism of its politics, and the relative lack of prosperity and opportunity compared with the United States persuaded some to seek a broader union with the republic. The most prominent proponent of this view was Goldwin Smith, a former professor at the universities of Oxford and Cornell, and in the 1880s Toronto's resident gadfly. Immune to local pressures thanks to his wife's money, Smith boldly wrote of the failure of the Canadian experiment and urged annexation to the United States.

It's not surprising that Smith's opinions irritated Sir John Macdonald and his government, but they were uneasily aware that many Canadians would plump for a return to the reciprocity agreement of the 1850s and the prosperity with which it was associated in the public memory. Macdonald knew he couldn't get it on any terms remotely acceptable to his party or to the country, for the only possibility of beguiling the Americans into any comprehensive or effective agreement was to combine economic agreement with political union.

Macdonald was lucky in his opponents. The Liberals hankered after free trade, but knew it wasn't enough to detach the various interests that Sir John's protectionist program—grandly styled the *National* Policy—had attracted to the Conservative party. Free trade plus access to the American market—there was the trick to confound the Tories and win the next election. Wilfrid Laurier, the Liberal leader since 1887, found the prospect irresistible. For the 1891 election the Liberals would stand for *Unrestricted Reciprocity* with the United States.

Once again, politics trumped economics in 1891. Sir John played the loyalty card, implying that the Liberals were at best a pack of fools—there was good evidence for that—and at worst villains and traitors. "A British subject I was born," Macdonald proclaimed. "A British subject I will die."

It was a promise that, at age seventy-six, he was in a good position to fulfill, and sure enough, after leading his party to victory in the March 1891 election, he died in June. All this left to one side the minor point that there was no very good reason to expect that the politicians in Washington considered Unrestricted Reciprocity without annexation a bargain they could not refuse.

A chastened Laurier was left to wonder why the reciprocity sword had wilted in his hand. He drew the right conclusion—tampering with Canada's British identity was political poison. Loyalty was the best policy, and high tariffs were indisputably a symbol of Canada's identity. Macdonald had grafted tariffs onto Canadian politics, and for the next century politics and protection were symbiotic in Canada.

A Liberal party convention in 1893 ratified a change in policy. The party still adored free trade in the abstract, but free trade counted as nothing compared with the prospect of electoral success. The Liberals therefore wouldn't tamper with the essence of the Canadian tariff. Tinkering at the margins of the tariff was permissible, for the sake of farmer-voters in Ontario and the West, but reciprocity with the United States was not to be contemplated. Not, at least, until memories of the 1891 election faded.

RELIGION AND PATRIOTISM

It was fitting that the nineteenth century should end in Canada as it began, on a note of religious difference. Religion counted for a great deal in Canada, as it did virtually everywhere in the Western world. In the United States, in Ireland, in Australia, as in Canada, political practice was rooted in sectarian differences, and religious persuasion was the single most reliable predictor of how a given individual would vote.

The main division was between Protestants and Catholics who, officially at least, regarded one another with fear and loathing. Protestant households still featured *Foxe's Book of Martyrs*, first published in 1563, detailing the bloody end of the Protestant saints at the hands of Catholic persecutors. The Orange Lodge kept green the memory of English liberty's narrow escape from Catholic tyranny in 1688, and the Orange Parade on 12 July was still a major event in a country that loved marching bands and processions as part of its meagre spectrum of free public entertainment. Like other patriotic festivals, 12 July in Canada was focused on a heritage and a world outside Canada—religion and empire were Canada's historical endowment.

The Irish Catholics had their St. Patrick's Day parades, and in Quebec no religious procession was complete without its marching contingent of Pontifical Zouaves—veterans or would-be veterans of the brief war to preserve the Papal States from incorporation into united Italy in 1870. As the historian Arthur Silver puts it, in Quebec there was a "marriage of religion and patriotism."[21] If English Canadians looked to Great Britain and by extension its Protestant monarch and political establishment, French Canadians contemplated the wider world of Catholicism. The reality of Catholicism was to be menaced by the forces of nationalism, Protestantism, modernism, and secularism, and these forces were at work in Canada too.

The Riel rebellions in 1870 and 1885 made their mark on French–English, and Catholic–Protestant, relations, but there were other frictions too. Religion and schooling were a volatile mixture. Schooling was highly prized, closely linked to progress and development but also to the moral formation of the future citizen. Education was a provincial matter, and all provinces supported schools through taxation. In Ontario and Quebec public (effectively Protestant) and Catholic systems coexisted, embedded in the constitution and beyond the ability of the local religious majorities to alter. Manitoba's constitution reflected the original balance between English and French speakers, and between Catholic and Protestant: French was officially sanctioned and there was a separate Catholic school system. Elsewhere the Catholic minority depended on the tolerance of the Protestant majority to fence off segments of the school system for Catholic education. Language practices were similarly a matter of grace and favour, for except in Quebec, Manitoba, and the federal Parliament and courts, there was no right to the use of French.

And yet there was an ambiguity in the relations of Catholic Canadians, English- and French-speaking, with other Canadians and the Canadian state. The Catholic Church cohabited with the Protestant state for over a hundred years, and in Quebec it absorbed it. In Ontario the state had accommodated the Catholic minority through a separate Catholic school system. Some Catholics were doubtful of the bona fides of Queen Victoria and her ministers, British and Canadian, but others were not. There was the sense that as a minority they couldn't go too far in provoking the majority; put another way, many Catholics were anxious to prove that they too were loyal—that their religion was as loyal and patriotic as any other.[22]

Catholic and French patience was tried by the actions of the Manitoba government. In the 1880s the province had filled up with Anglo-Ontarian settlers, while the proportion of French speakers steadily declined. The provincial election of 1888 ratified the demographic fact. The Liberals, under Thomas Greenway, took power and promptly moved to abolish both the official status of French and separate schools.

The British North America Act had provided for such an eventuality. The federal Parliament had the right to pass legislation to remedy the grievances of the minority in Manitoba and, eventually, the Conservative government in Ottawa nerved itself to do just that. By the time it did, in 1896, the Conservatives were on the brink of losing power. Four prime ministers passed in quick succession: Sir John Abbott, 1891–92; Sir John Thompson, 1892–94; Sir Mackenzie Bowell, 1894–96; and finally Sir Charles Tupper in 1896. It was Bowell, ironically an Orangeman, who acted on the Manitoba Schools Question, but Bowell was about to be deposed by his own party. It was therefore Tupper who confronted Wilfrid Laurier in the 1896 federal election, and Tupper who decisively lost it. Tupper was bound by the Conservative record on Manitoba Schools, while Laurier's position on the question was impossible to discern. Instead of confrontation with Manitoba, Laurier recommended "sunny ways" and conciliation as the key to an amicable solution. It should not have recommended itself to Quebec, but it did.

In the election it was Quebec that made the difference to Laurier's success or failure. In seeking an explanation as to why Quebec rejected the Conservatives, who were supporting the French language and Catholic rights in the West, it is well to bear in mind that there were other issues and other circumstances before the electorate. The Conservative party leadership was old and vulnerable. As with any long-entrenched government, the Conservatives had offended widely. Younger and brighter politicians had become discouraged, or, like the very able Israel Tarte in Quebec, deserted the party. Laurier at fifty-five was hardly youthful, but he was at any rate younger than the seventy-five-year-old Tupper. In an age that prized oratory, Laurier was a brilliant and eloquent speaker, and he proved to be a resourceful leader. In June 1896 he emerged from the federal election with a majority of thirty in the House of Commons. He would be prime minister for the next fifteen years.

10

BOOM AND BUST,
1896–1914

Nineteenth-century consumers: Women shoppers in the elegant
Morgan's department store in Montreal, 1880s.

I t was fitting that Canada should be led into the twentieth century by a man of the nineteenth. Wilfrid Laurier was perhaps the most perfect political leader Canada produced—tall (over six feet), slim, and good-looking, with chestnut hair gradually shading into white, eloquent and bilingual (with a Scots accent in English), intelligent and well-educated. Laurier was born into a Patriote family in the countryside north of Montreal, but unlike many ex-Patriotes, he remained "rouge." He was trained as a lawyer and was a gold medallist at McGill. At a time when parish curés instructed their flock that "Le ciel est bleu, l'enfer est rouge" (Heaven is [Conservative] blue, Hell is [Liberal] red"), Laurier stuck to the Liberal faith.[1] He took liberalism, into active politics, becoming first a member of the Quebec legislature, then a member of the federal Parliament, and finally, in 1877, a minister in the Liberal government of Alexander Mackenzie.

Youthful if not young, lively, imaginative, and active, Laurier embodied what many considered to be the archetypal Canadian virtues. Yet like the country he led, his values and attitudes were more those of the century just passing than those of the new century whose promise he claimed to understand. Unlike many Canadian partisans, who came by their politics by way of inheritance or self-interest, Laurier saw Liberalism as a set of clear principles. His definition of Liberalism shaped his party and transformed it into the dominant institution on the Canadian political scene. Laurier had to define where his party stood because of the opposition of the Catholic Church, inspired by the very conservative Pope, Pius IX, to political "liberalism," which Pius considered to be one of the great errors of the modern age.

Speaking to an audience of two thousand in Quebec City in June 1877, Laurier proclaimed that he was a reformer, not a revolutionary. "I am one of those who believe that in all human affairs there are abuses to reform, new horizons to discover and new forces to develop." England was the model that Canada should follow. Liberal reforms had "made the English the freest of peoples, the most prosperous and the happiest in Europe." He continued: "The policy of the Liberal party is to protect [our] institutions, to defend them and spread them, and, under the sway of those institutions, to develop the country's latent resources. That is the policy of the Liberal party and it has no other."

The affection for England, or Great Britain, was genuine. Laurier admired British institutions and revered the British Empire. Nor was he indifferent to British wealth and power. The wealth, he hoped, would fertilize the Canadian economy, and British power, unassailable because of the Royal Navy, protected Canada from harm—or at least from harm coming from overseas. There was always the United States, but it was better to deal with the United States as part of a powerful empire than as a small peripheral country huddled along the great republic's northern border.

Loving England did not mean loving the English, especially the *Anglais* of Canada. Laurier was well aware of the sectarian divisions in the country, and the national animosities. He hoped to transcend them, but realistically he settled for avoiding them as much as possible. In certain parts of the country, and to ultra-Protestants, he would always be suspect as a Frenchman and a Catholic. (French he certainly was, but it's doubtful that Laurier was a believing, as opposed to a practising, Catholic.) At home in Quebec, he was suspect to conservative Catholics and *nationalistes* who believed that accommodating the English and consorting with Protestants was the first step on the road to Hell.

Laurier took Canadian institutions pretty much as he found them. His Canada was not so much an insular country as an isolated colony. And while he talked the language of nation and nationalism—in two languages—he did not intend to rush events. Canada would become a nation, eventually, under its own steam and Laurier did not intend to be rushed. That was one of the great attractions of the British Empire, which to the end of his days Laurier believed to be almost all-powerful, unchallengeable outside North America, and unlikely to be challenged even there. His world was the world of the mid-nineteenth century, a world in which Britain would be, forever, Great. In such a world and such an empire, Canada could mind its own business.

Laurier prized local autonomy, for Canada inside the British Empire, and for the provinces inside Canada. He understood provincial power and prized provincial rights, and may, indeed, have been the most decentralist politician to hold the job of Canadian prime minister. His victory in the 1896 election was as much the result of provincial grievances against the federal government as it was a repudiation of a senile Conservative administration. As a sign of the times, Laurier brought three provincial premiers into his cabinet, from Ontario (Oliver Mowat), New Brunswick (Andrew Blair), and Nova Scotia (W.S. Fielding), and the attorney general of Manitoba, Clifford Sifton. With the exception of Mowat, who was past his prime, they were strong men and powerful politicians, but if they could serve under Laurier then Anglo-Saxon voters could surely trust him too.

Laurier in 1877 had stressed "development," and it is a term that needs some explanation. Laurier and his generation of politicians saw Canada as a "young" country. The image most often propagated at the time was either of a youthful but virtuous young woman—"Our lady of the snows," as the imperial bard Rudyard Kipling put it—or a strong young man, also virtuous, and promising but not fully developed. Canada, in Laurier's view, needed time and space to become mature and prosperous. "The prospects of Canada are truly great," in the words of an enthusiast of the time, but they were *prospects,* not yet realized, and Canada needed to be left alone to take advantage of them.

Developing Politics

When it came to economics, Laurier was an optimist, like most of his fellow citizens, and that was undoubtedly part of his electoral appeal.

Laurier was also lucky, for his arrival in power coincided with an economic upturn and prosperity. Transportation costs fell, giving better access to the European market. With better methods of cultivation, including Marquis wheat, the arid and frost-prone Canadian plains suddenly became attractive. It wasn't surprising that immigrants came to "the Last, Best West," the largely empty Canadian prairie, and that they chose this moment.

Laurier gave the task of peopling the prairie to his interior minister, Clifford Sifton. Sifton sought to attract immigrants through advertising, though under the circumstances of the time they would probably have come anyway. He extended the harvest of migrants to Eastern Europe, bringing Slavs, mostly Ukrainians, to Canada from the Russian and Austrian empires. This aroused atavistic animosities among conservative Canadians, which the Conservative party unwisely tried to exploit in various federal elections. It made Sifton's remaining task easy: he was the first, though not the last, Liberal politician to remind immigrants that they had come to Canada under a Liberal government.

The immigration statistics, and population statistics in general, are impressive. In 1891 the Canadian prairie had roughly 250,000 inhabitants, mostly in Manitoba. In 1911 there were no fewer than 1.3 million people. Immigration rose from 17,000 in 1896 to 42,000 in 1900 to 141,000 in 1905; it would peak at 400,000 arrivals in 1913.[2] There were so many people that in 1905 Laurier created two new provinces, Alberta and Saskatchewan, and by 1911 Saskatchewan ranked third in provincial population in Canada, behind Ontario and Quebec but ahead of Nova Scotia and the other Maritime provinces. The Maritimes during this period continued to be a source for out-migration, either to other provinces (Ontario and points west) or to New England.

Quebec was in some senses a special case. The province's fertility rate and the number of births were high—much higher than Ontario's or the Maritimes'. This was offset by high infant mortality and disease generally, and by the marked preference of immigrants for settlement in the prairies and Ontario. There was virtually no immigration from France, and the immigrants who did come to Quebec would, for the most part, adopt

English as their language. At the same time French Canadians continued to leave for New England.[3] Though the population of Quebec almost doubled between 1871 and 1911, it actually increased less (68 percent) than the population of the rest of the country (95 percent), thanks to disease and migration patterns, outbound and inbound.[4]

Acreage seeded to wheat is another index of growth. In 1890, wheat acreage was 2.7 million; in 1900, 4.2 million; and in 1911, 11 million. Wheat production, measured in bushels, was 42 million in 1890, and 231 million in 1911. (Other crops, such as oats and barley, rose in volume and value as well, though not so spectacularly.) Winnipeg suddenly became one of the world's major centres for trading in wheat.[5] Until 1900, Canada had lagged far behind other wheat producers, such as the United States, Argentina, and Australia, in the international wheat trade. Economically Canada was no longer a colonial backwater.

Though prairie settlement is the best known destination of immigrants in the Laurier period, it wasn't the only one. The industrial cities of Canada received hundreds of thousands of migrants: virtually all Canadian urban areas grew in population, with Winnipeg growing the fastest. Montreal, the largest city, received the most, and the most visible, immigrants, turning the St. Lawrence Boulevard area, "the Main," into what was effectively the city's Jewish quarter. In Toronto, it was "the Ward," just south of the university, and in Winnipeg "the North End."

The arrival of new varieties of immigrants strained Canadians' sense of tolerance, never strong. That tolerance did not extend to Asian immigrants, who were discouraged by a series of ingenious, and onerous, burdens: Chinese by a head tax, Japanese through a quota agreed to with the Japanese government, "East Indians" (from India) by impossible conditions on travel. To manifest local sentiment, troublemakers in Vancouver staged an anti-Japanese riot in 1907, and it had its effect, especially on nervous politicians thinking ahead to the next election. Blacks from the United States were also discouraged. Canada was, obviously but unofficially, to be white.

But if you could get to Canada, and be admitted, there were jobs to be had—presumably, well-paying jobs. Judging from the statistics, jobs of all kinds were expanding and, from what we can deduce, wages were rising.[6] It should not be forgotten that the American economy was open to immigrants from Canada and Europe. Those who came to Canada by error, or were disappointed, could move on. But most did not. Nationally, the number of "operatives," factory hands, rose from 543,000 in 1891 to 933,000 in 1911. Other employment categories rose as well—owners and managers, for example, which included contractors for a building boom that straddled the turn of the century and well beyond.

Electricity was the key to industrial development, and thanks to its many fast-flowing rivers and waterfalls, Canada was well positioned to take advantage of the new technology through hydraulic generation. For the country as a whole, hydroelectric installations rose from 72,000 horsepower in 1890 to 977,000 by 1910; that figure doubled during the next few years to almost two million horsepower in 1914. Electricity was especially important to Ontario, which had no coal and very little oil and gas to keep its factories running and its citizens warm. To Ontario, hydro-generated electricity meant personal security and industrial competitiveness. In the words of one hydro developer, it was a "genie out of the bottle," or, as the Toronto *Globe* put it, "magic merged in business."[7] So profoundly and so obviously did electricity transform the economy and daily life that it soon came to be seen as an absolute necessity, which soon enough created implications for the political agenda.

Electricity powered streetcars, previously horse-drawn. Electric "radials" connected cities around the Great Lakes, making it theoretically possible to travel from Toronto to Cleveland by transferring from streetcar to streetcar. Electric appliances began to appear—stoves, vacuum cleaners, even refrigerators—in the houses of the very well to do.

Mineral production also increased. Its most spectacular manifestation was the last of the great gold rushes, in the Canadian Klondike in the newly organized Yukon Territory. Gold was discovered near Dawson in 1896, and by 1898 an estimated hundred thousand miners, or would-be miners, were packing their bags and heading for the Yukon, either overland or, more usually, by sea through American-owned Alaska. Dawson City briefly became a real city, with thirty thousand residents in 1898. The Gold Rush climaxed in that year, and was essentially over by 1900, leaving behind a railway from the sea at Skagway to Whitehorse, and a variety of mining enterprises. It also helped stimulate a boundary dispute between Canada and the United States, as we shall see (below, p. 271).

Other mining enterprises were more lasting, and more professional. The Dominion Geological Survey plumbed Canada's rocks for promising formations, and private geologists and prospectors followed in its wake. Gold, silver, lead, zinc, and the uncommon nickel were all in production by 1914, in mines from the Rockies to Quebec. There were already coal mines in southern Alberta and British Columbia, as well as the long-lasting and productive mines in Cape Breton, where an iron and steel industry was taking root.

Some of these developments were, in a sense, deceptive. Mining, forestry, and agricultural homesteading were "frontier" activities, feeding the Canadian notion that Canada was still an adolescent country, even compared with the United States. The American frontier had "closed," according to the historian Frederick Jackson Turner; Canada's was still open, even though, by 1914, most of the feasible arable land had been taken up by farmer-settlers. But at the same time the big cities—Halifax, Montreal, Toronto, Winnipeg, Vancouver, and even Victoria—were sprouting mansions for the newly rich. Canada was still developing, and its politics, even its culture, remained by definition underdeveloped.

RAILWAYS AND OVERDEVELOPMENT

Luck led to optimism and optimism to confidence where Laurier was concerned. Laurier (Sir Wilfrid Laurier after 1897) met the new century with another election victory in November 1900 and a mandate to carry on with the development of the country. What the country needed, in the prime minister's opinion, was more settlers, and to entice them, he prescribed railways.

Laurier had already intervened in railway matters. The western farmers needed cheap access to markets, and the railways had an unquenchable thirst for subsidies. So in 1897 Laurier and his interior minister, Sifton, did a deal with the CPR that reduced the railway's rates for grain shipments in return for cash to build rail lines in southern British Columbia—the Crow's Nest Pass Agreement.

Andrew Blair, the railways minister, was in a minor way a reformer. He was neither enamoured of private railway companies nor afraid of public regulation. He extended the Intercolonial Railway, still government owned, to Montreal, and in major matters kept it free from party patronage. He also established a Board of Railway Commissioners to give the vexed question of railway charges an expert and impartial supervision—or so he hoped.[8]

The culmination of Laurier's railway policy was the issue, much discussed and much anticipated, of a second Canadian transcontinental railway line. Laurier had his own ideas about such a railway. It should start not in Montreal, but in Quebec City, which was Laurier's own political base. It should cut across central Quebec to northern Ontario, with the hope of opening up the territory to development and perhaps settlement, as had happened in the rest of Ontario. But its prospects were as economically discouraging as they were politically attractive, for the northern Quebec route was likely to be barren of revenue and a money-losing burden to whoever built it.

Blair, with a much greater sense of caution, and of responsibility for the public purse, preferred to cobble together a new system out of existing lines, building afresh only where necessary. The Quebec City route was, in his opinion, definitely not necessary. Laurier persisted, negotiating with the Grand Trunk, and in 1903 his project was nearly in place. Blair resigned, calling Laurier's scheme "wild, visionary, unbusiness-like and everything else."

Blair was right in the long run, but the spinoffs of railway construction in contracts and local development were overwhelmingly attractive in the shorter term. In the end, not one but two new transcontinental rail lines

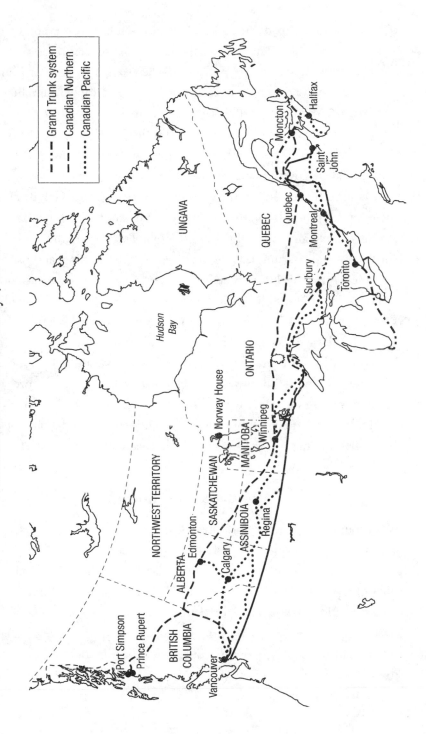

Transcendental Railways, 1915

Legend:
- ·—··— Grand Trunk system
- ——— Canadian Northern
- ········· Canadian Pacific

UNGAVA

QUEBEC

Hudson Bay

Moncton

Halifax

Saint John

Quebec

Montreal

Sudbury

Toronto

ONTARIO

NORTHWEST TERRITORY

Norway House

Winnipeg

MANITOBA

SASKATCHEWAN

ASSINIBOIA

Regina

ALBERTA

Edmonton

Calgary

BRITISH COLUMBIA

Port Simpson

Prince Rupert

Vancouver

were built across Canada, the Grand Trunk Pacific, an extension of the existing Grand Trunk Railway, and the Canadian Northern, the creation of two Toronto capitalists, Sir William Mackenzie and Sir Donald Mann.

The new railways were financed by largely British capital, supplied by the proverbial old ladies and retired colonels who populate the literature of investment. The money was, as far as profit or even security of investment was concerned, poured down a rat-hole with every sign of approval from Canadian governments, which themselves invested in Mackenzie and Mann's schemes, and in the ever-growing debts of the Grand Trunk. There was no profit, but rather depression and war, just as the lines were nearing completion. Both the Grand Trunk Pacific and the Canadian Northern went bankrupt, leaving the investors with nothing, and Canada with a network of steel that could never hope to repay the money, let alone the hopes, of those who had paid for it. (The Grand Trunk and Canadian Northern were combined in a single government system, the Canadian National Railways.) Many years later Canadian newspapers still carried the occasional letter from a bilked British investor, pleading for justice.

There was only one way out: nationalization. Long before the Canadian government reached for that particular solution, Laurier was out of office. He could console himself that he was not out because of his railway policy. That was too tangled a web for the voters to unravel.

THE ECONOMIC BOOM

As the railway experience indicated, Canada in the 1900s was still an outpost of British capital. Canada was also becoming a source of capital and investment in its own right. The colonies before 1867 had developed banks of their own, with varying success. Much of colonial politics turned on favours done by or for a particular bank, and the position of the government's bank was highly prized. Unlike the United States, Canada had a branch banking system, which encouraged concentration and stronger banks, albeit not strong enough to save some banks and their depositors from ruin.

There was no central bank, though banking was made the definite responsibility of the dominion government in the BNA Act. The governments, Macdonald's and Laurier's and those in between, relied on advice and funding from Canada's banks to keep the dollar steady and the economy ticking over. In a financial panic in 1907, for example, it was the Bank of Montreal that told Laurier what to do, and on whom Ottawa relied to see the country through without a run on its currency. (The currency was, however, only partly that of the dominion government: the banks issued their own notes as well.)

Canadian investors early began moving abroad, and the banks followed the investors, especially into the Caribbean and Latin America. A connection already existed between the Maritimes and the British and Spanish colonies of the Caribbean (Spain retained Cuba and Puerto Rico until 1898), not just through the fish trade but through sugar. Sugar-driven prosperity made Cuba a particularly good receptacle for investment, and even after politics, rebellion, and war took the shine off Cuban investments, there was still profit to be made. Canadian banks established utilities companies, railways, and mines, and extended the banking system. The Royal Bank of Canada and the Bank of Nova Scotia, both Halifax companies, became dominant features in the financial districts of Havana and other cities.[9] In some countries, such as Mexico, Canadian investment was an important and sometimes predominant part of "British" investment. Ordinarily, home governments kept an eye on their citizens' interests abroad, but not Canada's: it was British diplomats, not Canadian, who looked after Canadian overseas investors.[10]

British investment flowed into railways, utilities, mines, insurance, mortgage companies, banking,[11] land, and even buildings; along with American funds, it totalled $2.4 billion between 1900 and 1913. In 1913 British investment accounted for 75 percent of foreign capital in Canada, down from 85 percent in 1900. The United States accounted for 21 percent, up from 14 percent.

The difference between British and American outlays wasn't merely quantity. British money went largely into loans—via bonds—to governments or large corporations like the Grand Trunk Pacific or the Canadian Northern. British money financed Vancouver's new sewer system. British money also laid the tracks that took the Grand Trunk across the Rockies to Prince Rupert, that railway's hopeful alternative to Vancouver. Many Canadians put their money into the Bank of British North America or Barclay's Bank, both British-owned.

What the British did not do, by and large, was establish manufacturing branch plants—subsidiaries of foreign firms that vaulted the tariff wall so as to produce for the Canadian market. Their products were more expensive than the original, and variety was often lacking, because it didn't pay the foreign investor to make every possible line for the small Canadian market. Unquestionably, however, they produced Canadian jobs along with their Canadian-made goods.

Branch plants were usually American, and went back, in some cases, to the middle of the nineteenth century. Some Americans actually moved to Canada to be with their investment, and became naturalized along with their factories. Much of the lumber business in this way passed from "American" to "Canadian" hands, though the hands were usually the same; later this would apply to another firm, the Aluminum Company of Canada, Alcan. "Canadian General Electric" (CGE) was usually assumed to be a branch of General Electric in the United States, but it was in fact owned in Canada until the 1920s. Over time, in some industries, American investors did buy out Canadians who had originally been their partners. This was the case with the new automobile companies, such as Ford and General Motors, located in southern Ontario close to their American parents over the border in Detroit.

The Canadian government also borrowed for its railway adventures, but its ordinary revenue came from taxation, of which the tariff was the most important feature. The Laurier government, through its finance minister, W.S. Fielding, was most innovative on the tariff. First Laurier, anxious to make a gesture toward the British Empire, established a lower tariff (or "preference") for British goods. The British did not reciprocate at the time, but the Canadian gesture remained for most of a century; it could be said to have outlasted the empire itself. This gave the Canadian tariff three levels: British preference, the lowest charge; "most favoured nation" for countries with which Canada had trade treaties and consequently concessions on duties; and finally the "general" or highest level.

Fielding also introduced special punitive duties to combat "dumping," meaning goods that had been "dumped"—sold—in Canada at a price lower than in their place of origin. Dumping was held to be a predatory practice, designed to clear the market of competition, bankrupting domestic manufacturers. Once the market was depopulated, the importer could then raise prices to extortionate heights because his goods would monopolize the market. Under Fielding's anti-dumping legislation, duties could be used to raise the price of imports to a "fair" level, thus protecting local industry against "unfair" (very low-priced) competition. As Michael Hart, the historian of Canadian trade policy, has observed, this was a genuine Canadian innovation that soon affected international trade practice because it was quickly and universally adopted.[12] Trade negotiators, including Canadians, are still trying to get rid of it.

Despite government fiddlings, economic conditions remained generally favourable. The depression of the early 1890s passed away, and a brief stock market panic in 1907 was a mere hiccup. Only in 1913 did bad times return, with a sharp recession or depression. The many unemployed of 1913–14 would therefore be available for other work.

Organizing Reform

The dramatic changes in the economy, and the growth and dispersal of population, strained existing social forms and loosened the proprieties and other expectations that had bound Canada together. In managing change, government was less the leader than a reluctant follower, and none was more reluctant than Sir Wilfrid Laurier.

The heroes of the age were individual reformers—Florence Nightingale, who chivvied the British government into the systematic care of its wounded during the Crimean War of the 1850s; Louis Pasteur, the great French scientist, who revolutionized health care; Alexander Graham Bell, who invented the telephone—and in Canada too. The first obvious application of the principle of organizing government for direct human betterment was by Charles Saunders (later Sir Charles), the inventor of Marquis wheat.

Saunders was a civil servant, a reminder that individuals in government could make a difference. There were also things that only government could do. The organization of cities was the most obvious case in point. As cities grew, so did the substratum of sewers and water mains beneath their streets. Whereas the nineteenth century had left these to private enterprise, the twentieth increasingly preferred public ownership.

The standard for public enterprise was set first on the Prairies, where there weren't as many entrenched interests. Mistrust of monopoly, based on bitter experience, spurred on not merely "reformers" but the business classes, who saw their own economic welfare jeopardized by private utility owners. A case in point was Niagara Falls, where power generation was firmly in the hands of private interests. Very quickly an influential pressure group was organized in southern Ontario, demanding that this public resource be publicly owned. The proponents of public power were swept into office as part of a reforming Conservative government, which promptly created a government-owned utility, Ontario Hydro.[13] It would become the largest electric utility in North America, and a monument in its day to public enterprise.

The most obvious non-governmental organizations were the churches, old and new. Canada was a church-going country, and in all but a few cities the biggest, the most ornate public structures were the churches, dwarfing the usual symbols of secular authority, the post office or the courthouse or the school. The older churches, Catholic and Anglican, had been weaned with some difficulty from their position as the spiritual branch of government, though in Quebec church and state were still symbiotic, at least for the large Catholic majority. Protestants suspected that the Catholic Church would have preferred the state and church to be linked, with the state as junior partner if not willing servant of the church, and undoubtedly some Catholic clerics would have welcomed it. But most church leaders, Catholic or Protestant, weren't so unworldly as to believe that a church-state of the true medieval kind was really possible.[14]

The example of the Catholic countries of Europe, even those where Catholicism was still the state Church, was not promising. There the Church was as often as not the handmaiden of government, and not the other way around. Alternatively, the Church would become one political faction among many, with all the hazards of defeat and victory in party politics.[15] In such a case the Church might well be defeated. That was what was happening at the time in France, where the state secularized what had previously been a Catholic system of education, to the amazement and fury of conservative Catholics in Quebec as well as France.[16] There was, of course, another alternative, a reversion to authoritarian forms of rule in a separate Catholic state, but in the 1890s and 1900s that was not seriously considered.

The churches could have been satisfied with their influence in society, and could have argued that society was the better for their work—more orderly, less violent, and more concerned with the social and mental well-being of the citizenry. That was not enough for some. As two historians have observed, "Between 1900 and 1930 the Methodist and Presbyterian churches envisioned their mission as nothing less than the complete Christianization of Canadian life."[17] What that meant was rather complicated. Christianity, in the minds of activist clerics, stood for justice, not merely in the next world but in this one. As William Booth, the founder of the Salvation Army, put it, there was no point preaching salvation to hungry people.[18] A literate and educated clergy was a significant part of Canada's educated elite, and it shouldn't be surprising that they shared and contributed to the notion that society must be organized to combat the various aspects of social evils present—especially—in Canada's cities.

This certainly didn't mean that everyone in the churches contemplated returning to or preaching for a bucolic and godly version of the past—rather the opposite. They harkened to a vision of society united through a godly concern for the welfare of all its members, not torn apart by class warfare. Nostalgia for an older and undivided social order still existed—the rural society of an earlier age was one attraction, though not for all. In Quebec, some of the clergy recommended expansion of the farming frontier into the rocks and bogs of Abitibi to the north. In the face of emigration from an overcrowded countryside into New England, the Church was prepared to adapt to industrialization inside Quebec, and if the capital establishing a factory happened to be English and Protestant, it was nevertheless doing God's work by keeping French-speaking Catholics closer to home.[19] On the whole the churches hoped to establish agencies for social welfare that would respect and reflect their own values, and they knew that to do so they needed the help of the state.

Since the mid-nineteenth century groups or individuals with the various churches had preached the prohibition of alcohol, and by the turn of the twentieth century they were able to force Laurier to hold a plebiscite on the issue. The prohibitionists almost prevailed, and won a few more votes than their opponents. Laurier, however, noted that Quebec voted strongly the other way, and rather than risk division between French and English on the issue, he declined to act. He abandoned the field to local option, by which a municipality could vote to become "dry," and to the provinces.

The movement for prohibition had another effect. It mobilized and energized female reformers, and taught them the techniques of political struggle. If women's voices mattered on such an issue as this, why should women not be heard more generally? In a society dominated by men, in which women were legally excluded and subordinated, this was a revolutionary point of view. It was also one that could, potentially, organize women from all social classes into a demand for the vote, the suffrage. Why, suffragists asked, should respectable, hard-working women, educated or not, be denied the vote when any drunken male loafer could exercise the franchise?

Suffragists asked and kept asking, but for many years there was never incentive enough to give them a positive answer. Plainly the women's movement did not mobilize enough women to overcome the fixed view that women's place was in the home and that all that was required was a few marginal adjustments to home life to take care of the supposedly few cases of genuine injustice or misery—the example being the proverbial drunken husband. It was a peculiar position to argue: in some situations, such as farms, the home *was* the workplace, and directly dependent on female labour; and female labour in any case made up about 5 percent of the industrial workforce.

Nevertheless, when Laurier or the various opposition leaders made up their lists of issues suitable for elections, women's suffrage never appeared. There were always other issues to be debated and decided. There was, for example, the empire.

IMPERIAL POLITICS

The British Empire was an inescapable fact. Its symbolism pervaded Canadian life, from the universal lithographs of Queen Victoria stuck to kitchen walls to the Union Jack flapping proudly above public buildings from the Atlantic to the Pacific. Iron statues of the queen stood in parks and on the precincts of the Parliament Buildings in Ottawa. The royal family was an unending source of interest to Canadians, judging from their newspapers, which retailed everything from tales of royal bastardy to improving morality fables involving the queen's endless mourning for her late husband, Prince Albert.

The queen never visited Canada, though if she had she would have found Prince Albert, embodied as a town in central Saskatchewan, or seen him commemorated in the district (later province) of Alberta.[20] She herself gave her name to the capital of British Columbia, a town in Quebec (Victoriaville), and counties in New Brunswick and Ontario, to name only a few. If the United States was a country of Washingtons, Canada was a land of Victorias.

The queen's father, uncle, two sons, a daughter, and a couple of grandsons toured Canada or spent time there, but no reigning monarch actually set foot on Canadian soil until 1939.[21] The monarch was represented instead by a governor general in Ottawa. This personage was always a British aristocrat, usually with political connections, who saw no harm in residing most of the year in a smallish mansion in a tiny colonial backwater. The position of governor general seems to have increased in prestige as time went on, though it was seldom occupied by political figures of the first rank.[22]

Some of the governors were better at the job than others. Lord Dufferin, governor general in the 1870s, proved to be a skilled and sensitive diplomat—a harbinger of a later very successful diplomatic career. Lord Lansdowne, who succeeded him, commented shrewdly on Canadian issues but did not weigh very heavily in Canadian politics. The Liberal peer Lord Aberdeen, present for the transition from Conservative to Liberal rule in 1896, smoothed the process by insisting that the soundly defeated Tupper recognize the fact by resigning forthwith. Lord Aberdeen's wife had a more lasting impact by helping found the National Council of Women, a long-lasting female pressure group of a distinctly respectable kind.

It was Laurier's misfortune to coexist with two of the more active governors general, Lords Minto and Grey. Both were enthusiasts for the British Empire—"imperialists" in the terminology of the time. Minto was a soldier, determined to bring order to the partisan, patronage-ridden shambles that was the Canadian defence establishment.

Minto assumed that the Canadian military was intended for defence, even for combat. And since combat was scarce in a North American setting, that could only mean that it could or should be employed elsewhere, in imperial wars. But before that could happen, incompetent officers and feckless soldiers would have to be whipped into shape, or sent packing.

Laurier saw the military—which was almost entirely a voluntary militia—rather differently.[23] It was in his eyes a kind of uniformed fraternal organization like the Masons or the Elks or the Odd Fellows, but with guns and wearing the queen's uniform. These latter features made the militia especially desirable, conferring ratification of the militiaman's

social status. The government provided them with clubhouses—
armouries—in which they could gather and debate the important things
of life, run up mess bills, and buy gaudy uniforms. Building armouries was
useful patronage, reminding a community who its friends were in government. Conferring military commissions was even better, since it rewarded
the friends of the government with honour and prestige, and the status of
officers, at very little cost.

As long as soldiering was a matter of parades, parties, and balls, the
system worked very well for whatever party was in power, and for their
military clients. The defence of Canada—safeguarded by the empire, the
oceans, and an American disinclination to military expenditures—was a
matter of high return for low cost. As for Canada defending the empire,
that was in Laurier's opinion a contradiction in terms.

The empire depended in large part on the non-resistance of its
subjects, and the weakness of its enemies. Prestige as much as anything
defended the British Empire and British interests, assisted by a large fleet
that showed the flag around the globe. From time to time British public
opinion grew excited by perceived threats to the empire. One such occasion was in 1885, when a rash and adventurous general, Charles Gordon,
operating in the Sudan, managed to get himself besieged by Muslim insurgents in the city of Khartoum. Public opinion in Great Britain forced the
Liberal Gladstone government to send a relief expedition up the Nile to
rescue Gordon. Someone in the British War Office remembered that
Canada had large rivers and raftsmen—the very thing.

The British government forthwith appealed to Prime Minister Sir
John A. Macdonald. Macdonald did send raftsmen, non-combatants, but
as Gordon's situation worsened—he would be overwhelmed and killed by
the insurgents in February 1885—there was pressure for Canada to do
more.

Macdonald resisted the pressure. Gladstone was the economically
minded prime minister who had withdrawn the British garrison from
Canada in 1871, leaving local military defence to the Canadians.
Gladstone's was the government that had insisted on appeasing the

Americans in the Treaty of Washington that same year. Macdonald remembered. Why, he asked, should "our men and money" be "sacrificed to get Gladstone & Co. out of the hole they have plunged themselves into by their own imbecility[?]"[24] The Canadian army, such as it was, remained at home. Its only foreign activity was the departure of the graduates of Canada's newly founded (1876) Royal Military College for British army units abroad, since there was no use for their talents at home.[25]

Macdonald had set a standard for resisting imperial adventurism, but it was not a hard task. Gladstone abandoned his intervention in the Sudan and concentrated instead on the eternal problem of securing the government of Ireland. There too he was unsuccessful, driving off from his Liberal party a "unionist" faction led by one of the most promising of his ministers, Joseph (Joe) Chamberlain. Chamberlain eventually led the dissident ex-Liberals into coalition with the Conservative party. When the Conservatives won office in 1895, Chamberlain had his pick of cabinet positions. Oddly, in the minds of his contemporaries, he chose the previously obscure and somewhat downmarket Colonial Office.

Chamberlain was colonial secretary from 1895 to 1903. Under his direction, life in the colonies was certainly not dull. He wanted to draw the colonies closer to the mother country. A geopolitician, Chamberlain believed that, faced with American and German economic power, Great Britain would soon no longer be great. He assembled a Colonial Conference in London that was timed to coincide with Queen Victoria's Diamond Jubilee, her sixtieth year on the throne, in 1897.

The Colonial Conference was a gathering of the premiers of the self-governing colonies meeting under the presidency of the colonial secretary.[26] The idea of "Imperial Federation" was in the air, though no one had as yet produced a version with any appeal to the constituent parts of the empire. The British did not wish to give their colonies any significant say on such items as an imperial foreign policy, or a common imperial tariff policy. The colonies, meanwhile, feared returning to British tutelage because Great Britain in power, wealth, and population dwarfed the various self-governing colonies.

Chamberlain hoped to secure emanations of unity from the conference, but he procured, at best, only a superficial harmony. The colonial secretary had little to offer the premiers. As far as the British cabinet was concerned, there was no question of offering the colonies a return to preferential duties and a privileged position in the British market. British politics were founded on free trade, which was as close to a universal consensus as might be imagined; and it was a rash politician who would question it. Chamberlain privately questioned free trade, and would eventually oppose it—but not yet. British immigrants and British capital were flowing to the colonies in any case, and there was nothing the British government wanted or needed to do to spur them on.

Laurier gazed on the parades, attended banquets, was charmed by the requisite contingent of aristocratic hostesses, and travelled to Cheshire to meet his real hero, the retired Liberal leader Mr. Gladstone. After collecting a knighthood—he would say he didn't know how to refuse it—Sir Wilfrid Laurier returned to Canada.

Chamberlain had other matters to keep him busy. The colonial secretary was determined to solve the "problem" of South Africa, where two British colonies cohabited uneasily with two independent, Dutch-speaking republics, the Transvaal and the Orange Free State. (Their inhabitants were known to themselves as Afrikaners, but they were more commonly called Boers, Dutch for farmers.) To add spice to the mixture, gold and diamonds were present in large quantities in the Transvaal, attracting miners to South Africa. Inevitably, many of them were English-speaking and, indeed, British subjects. The Boers, fearing they would be overwhelmed by immigrants, limited their political rights. To resolve this and other issues of "persecution," Chamberlain opted for force.

A belief in force was one strain in British political thought in the nineteenth century. It derived from the sense of superiority acquired in the long French wars and ultimate victory over Napoleon in 1815, and was underlined by a hundred minor conflicts over the next eighty years. The choice of enemy varied, but on one occasion when war seemed to be impending against imperial Russia, a popular song proclaimed, "We don't want to fight, But by jingo if we do, We've got the ships, we've got the men, we've got the money too." The ditty gave rise to the term "jingoism," meaning fierce, aggressive patriotism.[27] As far as the Boers and the empire were concerned, Chamberlain was a jingo, and as a good politician he knew he could appeal to that sentiment not just in Britain, but in Canada, Australia, and elsewhere in the British settlements in the empire. In Laurier's political lexicon there were few terms more freighted with dread. Jingoism was an incalculable force, moving the public in potentially dangerous directions. It was all the more dangerous because in French Canada jingoism had few echoes and no effective political support.[28]

Chamberlain first tried an unofficial filibustering expedition in 1895, the so-called Jameson Raid, to overthrow the Boer governments and unite South Africa. But the raid failed, and British policy was revealed to be not only belligerent, but duplicitous. The Jameson Raid was a first-class diplomatic disaster for Great Britain. It appeared to be an attack by a great power on two much smaller countries, an action cloaked in hypocrisy, which many continental Europeans already believed was an essential part of the British character. Britain reaped only hostility and isolation in Europe.

Chamberlain was left with the option of outright military force. He began to assemble an army in South Africa, and in his own mind began to consider how best to involve the rest of the empire in a war that he knew could not be far off. The Boers bought arms, organized themselves as best they could, and struck first, in October 1899. The British army was unready, and incompetently led. In a series of small engagements the British were defeated and driven back. The loss of prestige was tremendous, and deeply wounding to British pride.

The South African question was closely followed in Canada. In English Canada, at least, there was almost no question that Chamberlain and Britain must be right, and the Boers, under their curious bearded president, Paul Kruger, deeply wrong. Laurier did not share this conviction, but he mixed his scepticism with insouciance, believing until the end that war wasn't likely.

When war broke out Laurier was in Chicago. Travelling home, he was told by his English-speaking advisers that he must of course send troops. Chamberlain had asked for troops, the British general in charge of the Canadian militia had publicized the call, and the governor general, Lord Minto, was in favour. Plans already existed, the press learned.[29] More pertinently, English-Canadian public opinion would stand for nothing less.

To his credit, Laurier did try to hold out against a contribution, giving in only when prominent English ministers told him they would quit and split the party. The character of English-Canadian public opinion was already apparent: "Canada disgraced," the *Montreal Star* proclaimed. More would follow, from Halifax, Toronto, and wherever else jingoes flourished.[30] Laurier was able to modify the British requirements for a contribution of troops. The British War Office wanted small, company-size units that could be integrated at will in existing British units. The Canadian government wanted Canadian troops to fight together, in larger formations, and on that point they prevailed. The British picked up the costs once the Canadians got to the theatre of war.

On another point Laurier was less plausible. The dispatch of Canadian troops, he proclaimed, was not to be considered a precedent. He embodied this assertion in an order-in-council at the insistence of his Quebec lieutenant, Israel Tarte. Not everyone believed him. For Henri Bourassa, a young and promising Liberal MP and Papineau's grandson, sending troops to South Africa was the last straw. He had gone along reluctantly with Laurier's compromise on Manitoba schools, even though he felt, correctly, that it left the French-speaking minority disadvantaged if not defenceless. He cherished the hope that Canada could indeed become a united country, shared between English and French, but he believed as well that a precondition for this was to persuade the English Canadians to put Canada first, not the British Empire. This was plainly not the case in 1899, and Bourassa took the occasion to resign from the House of Commons on the issue, and run for re-election opposing Laurier's South African policy. Bourassa was re-elected, but in a general election in

November 1900 Laurier carried the country, and actually increased his margin in Quebec, taking fifty-seven of the province's sixty-five seats.

Some six thousand Canadian troops served in South Africa. They arrived at the right time, after competent generals had taken command of the British army and reorganized it for a campaign to take the enemy capitals. The Canadians participated in the army's advance and accompanying battles which culminated in the capture of the Transvaal capital, Pretoria, in June 1900. The Boer army had been defeated but not, as it turned out, the Boers.

Canadians could follow the campaign in their newspapers. The *Montreal Star*, the most excitable jingo newspaper in the country, did its best to encourage confrontation at home as well as abroad. When McGill students paraded before the city's French-language newspapers as the seat of "suspected disloyalty," the *Star* contributed beer to the cause. Naturally there was a riot, the militia had to be called out, and the governor general sent worried dispatches home to say that there was "cause for anxiety." Carman Miller, the historian of these events, comments on the "verbal abuse and violence of the yellow press" in Montreal—precisely what Laurier feared.[31]

The anxiety dissipated, though the war dragged on. The Boers fought a guerrilla campaign against the imperial forces, who responded by rounding up Boer non-combatants and putting them in concentration camps, where many perished from disease. The intention was to cut off supplies and support to the guerrillas, and to assist the army in wearing them down. Eventually the Boers did have enough, and surrendered.

Queen Victoria did not outlive the war, and it was her successor, Edward VII, who presided over the proclamation of peace, just in time for his coronation in June 1902. Since all the colonial premiers were coming to London for the occasion, Chamberlain staged another colonial conference.[32]

Despite victory in South Africa, the situation was not as rosy as it had been in 1897. The British had been diplomatically isolated during the South African War, and British unpopularity in continental Europe was painfully obvious. At the colonial conference Laurier again resisted Chamberlain's blandishments for imperial unity, however it might be embodied; but even if he hadn't there is no reason to think that the British government itself would have accepted serious reforms in the empire's constitution. Things remained much as they had been, although Chamberlain was no longer in government to see it. In 1903 he quit the British cabinet on the issue of "tariff reform"; that is, the reconstruction of a British tariff wall to shield the British economy against foreign competition. Chamberlain's departure removed tariff reform from the empire's table for a generation; when it returned, in 1931, it would be in very different circumstances.

There were other reasons to be dissatisfied with the empire. The Treaty of Washington had left a bad taste, but it had not after all been a disaster for Canada. In the years that followed Anglo–American relations were generally pleasant, though punctuated by occasional eruptions from Washington. Those eruptions were symptomatic of a larger problem. As Oscar Wilde put it, the United States and Great Britain were separated by a common language—that is, they could express their disagreements, and be understood. There remained culture, and history. And there was race, very important in the race-conscious 1890s. Ancient attitudes and customs inherited from the British Isles persisted, dating back long before the American Revolution.[33]

The British government was dimly aware that, while the United States might not be precisely friendly, it was at any rate not hostile. With Britain isolated in Europe, and the balance of power uncertain, the British reasonably opted for prudence in dealing with the United States.[34] British and American interests did not clash strongly, and the British hastily cleared away as many irritations as they could find.[35] The British were therefore not especially pleased that Laurier had created another along the boundary of the Alaska panhandle.

The boundary had been established by a treaty between Great Britain and the Russian Empire, Alaska's owner, in 1825. Russia conceded the interior to Britain, and secured the coast for itself. When Russia sold

Alaska to the United States there was no change in the boundary, and no interest in changing it until the Klondike gold rush. At that point interest quickened. The Canadian government now claimed that the treaty really gave it access to the sea; the American government maintained the contrary. The matter festered for a number of years, into the administration of Theodore Roosevelt, when in 1903 it was put to arbitration by six "jurists of high repute."

It was an unusual arbitration. There were three Americans, all of them known partisans of the American case. There were two Canadians, equally partisan on the other side, and the unfortunate British lord chief justice, Lord Alverstone. On virtually all points, Alverstone ruled in the Americans' favour, as he was expected to do. Roosevelt had accepted arbitration only because he was assured he would win it, which gave the process the character of a slow-motion pantomime.[36]

Laurier was annoyed, perhaps more annoyed than the strength of his case allowed. Speaking in the House of Commons in October 1903, he let his feelings show. "I have often regretted, Mr. Speaker," he said, "and never more than on the present occasion. That we are living beside a great neighbour who, I believe I can say without being deemed unfriendly to them, are very grasping in their national acts, and who are determined upon every occasion to get the best in every agreement which they make."[37]

CLEANING THE SLATE

The Alaska boundary dispute might have been the harbinger of a century of trouble with the Americans, but it was not. Relations between the Laurier government and the Roosevelt administration sharply improved, and for the first time it was possible to speak of Canadian–American relations of an intergovernmental kind.

Roosevelt wished to be dominant and unchallenged, but he did not wish to be unfriendly. His secretary of state, Elihu Root, took the same attitude, and he met a very friendly response from the British ambassador to Washington, Lord Bryce. Bryce had his own agenda. Most of the business of the British embassy was, in fact, Canadian business, the thousand-and-one housekeeping problems associated with a forty-eight-hundred-kilometre border. Getting instructions from Laurier was a painfully complicated process, which sometimes produced nothing at all.

Bryce's first task was to persuade Laurier to answer his mail from Washington; his second was to ensure that the content of that mail was friendly and constructive, and not confrontational. Bryce persuaded a senior Canadian civil servant, Sir Joseph Pope, to organize an office in Ottawa that would handle correspondence to and from abroad.[38] It could not be a department of *foreign* affairs—that would concede too much to Canada, which was, legally speaking, just a very large and important colony. Instead it was labelled the department of *External* Affairs, which was self-explanatory and not especially assertive. It was located above a barber shop in downtown Ottawa, though it would later move to grander quarters. A junior minister was handed the job, but more importantly Sir Joseph Pope took charge of the office.

Bryce proceeded to "clean the slate" of pressing Canadian–American problems. They weren't for the most part matters of high policy and didn't require major negotiation. One item did stand out. Many rivers crossed the Canadian–American boundary, and the frontier ran through the middle of the Great Lakes. Some of the boundary lands had been settled for over a hundred years—settled increasingly thickly.

The inhabitants of the Great Lakes basin, the Saint John Valley, the Red River, and coastal British Columbia exploited the ground on which they lived. They built cities, which required water, and into the water they also poured sewage. The city of Chicago even proposed to divert Great Lakes water so that it could flush its sewage, eventually, down the Mississippi. The price of progress was industry, and industry produced pollution, chemical waste, coal dust, noxious effluents. Cities usually buried their problems, as once-sparkling streams became polluted ditches, but it was impossible to do it on a grand scale. Inevitably, Canadian and American economic habits impinged, and interests clashed along the border. Who was poisoning whom?

These were not questions that politicians preferred to solve. Pollution was taken for granted. The grime of cities and the smells of paper mills or mineral refineries were a condition of life, even a signal of prosperity-inducing activity. Reversing pollution was to shake the foundations of society—something best left to the churches.

Remarkably, then, the Canadian and American governments signed a Boundary Waters Treaty in 1909. It established an International Joint Commission (IJC) of three members from each country, and this time there was no provision for British membership. The IJC was to investigate, report on, and, if asked, arbitrate issues relating to boundary waters—which included the Great Lakes.[39] It could, if asked, do more, serving as a tribunal on any issue the Canadian and American governments cared to refer to it.

Roosevelt was in his last months in the White House by the time the treaty was signed. It was his successor, William Howard Taft, unlike Roosevelt an eminent lawyer, who undertook to implement it. Taft saw the IJC as a court, a kind of international version of the American Supreme Court. He was willing to accept such a court with Canada, it seemed, because he saw Canada with its common-law traditions and similar customs as an acceptable partner in an arrangement that assumed the limitation of American and Canadian sovereignty along the border. To put it another way, the two countries pooled their interests and saw no contradiction in doing so.

The IJC did not perform precisely as Taft hoped. Laurier did not assign it any great importance, and in fact he failed to appoint any Canadian members before his time in office came to an end. It was Laurier's successor, Robert Borden, who made the first Canadian appointments, and turned the IJC into a working organization, with a permanent staff and offices in Washington and Ottawa. In practice it established facts through detailed investigation and proceeded to conclusions dictated by the evidence and expert opinion. Its members functioned more as international civil servants than as representatives of their own governments.[40]

Our Lady of the Snows

When Laurier and W.S. Fielding invented the preferential tariff in 1897 they attracted favourable attention among the enthusiasts of the British Empire. A young Anglo-Indian poet and journalist, Rudyard Kipling, composed a poem to honour Canada, "Our Lady of the Snows." Perhaps because it wasn't one of his better efforts, it would be endlessly quoted: "Daughter am I in my mother's house / But mistress in my own."

Mother's house was considered to be in increasing need of repairs in the years after 1900. Diplomatically isolated at the time of the Boer War, Great Britain set about acquiring allies: first Japan, through a formal alliance in 1902, and then, rather more informally, France and Russia. (The French and Russian arrangements were so informal that some members of the British cabinet didn't know of them; but they existed nevertheless.) The combination with the French and Russians was more or less complete and functioning by 1908, to the deep irritation of the German government and its sovereign, the emperor Wilhelm II.

Wilhelm was Queen Victoria's grandson, an excitable, irascible, and inconsistent personality. As emperor he was the most important political figure in Germany, but his will was not absolute and he was very well aware that he needed the good opinion of important elements in German society. Wilhelm was therefore expressing not merely his personal desires but a strong political current in Germany when, beginning in 1898, he set about constructing a large German navy where there had been practically none before. His naval policy, to be successful, required that he be able to get his ships out of German ports through the North Sea and into the Atlantic Ocean, and to do that he had somehow to outface the British fleet. That in turn meant that he must have more and better ships than the British could float in the waters between Great Britain and Germany.

Wilhelm's desires must have seemed very odd in distant Canada, but more than any other foreign policy issue they resonated in the North American dominion. Wilhelm became a factor in ending Canada's colonial isolation. He would also, eventually, help bring the British Empire to an end by exposing its internal inconsistencies and the differences in interest between Great Britain and its colonies, including Canada; but that result lay in the distant future.

The machinations of European courts and the construction of distant alliances held no interest for Sir Wilfrid Laurier. If he ever seriously thought about the matter, he probably believed that British resources were nearly infinite and British power superior. He might have conceded that the British sometimes needed time to get up to speed, but they would get there in the end. Canada's role in terms of British foreign policy was to observe and applaud a spectacle designed and directed from London. Laurier had only once had the experience of being "daughter in my mother's house," during the Boer War. He had no wish to allow the experience to become a regular event.

Laurier did, however, see that British statesmen were politicians like himself. He did not hold them in awe because they were surrounded by vast fleets and marching armies. Fleets and armies had to be paid for, like any other governmental activity, and finding money for such activities was the most painful part of the political process. It was a fundamental tenet of the imperialist self-definition that Britain was weak, not strong, in peril, not secure, and inadequately funded, not infinitely rich. Laurier would have had trouble with any of these propositions.

He reluctantly countenanced some reform in the Canadian army. He paid little attention to expositions by British ministers at imperial conferences (renamed from colonial conferences), and, in fact, those ministers returned the compliment by failing to inform Laurier of what they were about in their European alliance commitments.

Laurier, like the rest of the country, spent much of 1908 contemplating the awesome fact that there had been permanent European settlement in Canada for three hundred years. Propelled by a coalition of local boosters from Quebec City in league with the governor general, Lord Grey, Laurier and the premier of Quebec, Lomer Gouin, financed a huge celebration of the event. The Prince of Wales came, and spoke good French, rather like the governor general. The Duke of Norfolk, an aristocrat of ancient and Catholic lineage, came and charmed the bishops. The vice-president of the United States came, and a French admiral, and the descendants of Wolfe, Montcalm, Lévis, Murray, and Carleton. It was a memorable occasion, and best of all it left a residue of permanent historical reconstruction of the ramparts of Quebec and in useful public works around the city.[41]

And so Laurier was not prepared in 1908–09 when a wave of hysteria swept the English-speaking part of the country. The Germans were planning to overtake the British fleet using the naval symbols of the day, dreadnought-class battleships, faster and heavily armoured. Britain must have immediate help, in the form of dreadnoughts. The Conservative opposition, led by Nova Scotia's Robert Borden, obliged with alarmist rhetoric. In the great battle of words that resulted, Borden prevailed, up to a point.

Laurier became convinced that something must be done to pacify public opinion, and he proposed to do it in the form of a *Canadian* navy. It would consist of smaller ships, not lumbering dreadnoughts, and the ships would be proportionate to what Canada itself might actually need on or near its own shores.[42] (The dreadnoughts could only be used overseas, as part of the British Grand Fleet consisting of similar ships.)

A Naval Service Act was duly passed in 1910, naval bases were established at Halifax and Esquimalt where the Royal Navy had formerly resided, and, while Canada's own ships were being built, two surplus British warships were acquired, one for each coast. In the opinion of the opposition, and imperially minded Canadians, this was not enough. A "tin-pot navy," the critics scoffed.

In the eyes of French-Canadian *nationalistes*, it was far too much. In a 1910 by-election in Drummond-Arthabaska, in the heart of rural Quebec, the opposition dressed up its agents in blue suits and sent them around posing as naval officers taking a census of young and militarily viable males. It would be for Monsieur Laurier's navy, they helpfully explained to voters. The Laurier candidate was accordingly beaten.

The opposition also reached for the elixir of scandal as a means to lever the Liberal ministers out of office with charges of "wine, women, and influence peddling," but their efforts, while exciting to the press, had no effect on Laurier's majority. The party, like its leader, was growing old, however, and the ministers were tired. "I carry my advancing years lightly, but I no longer have the same zest for battle. I undertake today from a sense of duty, because I must, what used to be 'the joy of strife,'" Laurier wrote in December 1909. The government made some minor advances in conservation policy and in labour laws, but it needed more to show that it was truly abreast of the times. Only one minister, Mackenzie King, aged thirty-six, could actually be said to be youthful, and Laurier himself was approaching seventy.

To assist the prime minister in concentrating his mind, the farmers of the West sent delegations to Ottawa in 1910, demanding action on a series of agricultural issues. Foremost among these were complaints about the tariffs, which benefited eastern manufacturers by forcing western farmer-consumers to buy expensive Canadian-made goods. At the same time farmers had to sell their product, grain, on the world market. Laurier was reminded that, thanks to immigration, there were many more farmers than there had been and many more westerners too. The political balance in Canada might tip, and tip against the government.

Luck and timing are important assets in politics, and Laurier, most of his career, was lucky. His luck appeared to hold when the Republican administration of William Howard Taft concluded that it also faced a problem with its western farmers. Like their Canadian cousins, western Americans resented high tariffs, and they made their displeasure known in Washington. Facing a revolt of western Republicans, Taft reached for reciprocity with Canada to demonstrate that his government actually had farmers' interests at heart. Canadian and American negotiators reached a speedy deal that restored free trade in natural products while limiting it for manufactured goods. Laurier had hit the jackpot: Canadian farm products got free entry into the American market, while Canadian manufacturers kept most of their beloved protective tariff. A triumphant finance minister announced the agreement to the House of Commons on 26 January 1911.

The Conservatives were plunged into despair. Trapped behind an uninspiring leader, Borden, and unsuccessful in their stratagems, they had been sandbagged by Canadian politics' ultimate weapon. Reciprocity had been the dream of a generation, always out of reach because of American refusal even to consider it. Caught in a desperate situation, the Conservatives grasped at the politician's last resort: an appeal to principle.

Fortunately, there was one available. Sir John A. Macdonald had opposed "unrestricted reciprocity" in 1891 with an appeal to British Empire patriotism. It might work again. Laurier had seriously underestimated Canadian manufacturers' attachment to tariff protection. Liberal businessmen, who had been pacified by the Liberals' 1893 conversion to protectionism, became unsettled by the prospect of reciprocity. Led by Sir Clifford Sifton, Laurier's former minister of the interior, they flocked to Borden. The Conservatives used delaying tactics in Parliament until finally, in exasperation, Laurier called an election for September 1911. He believed he had every prospect of winning.

Laurier miscalculated. In English Canada the Conservatives had a monopoly on the patriotic side of two issues: the naval scare and reciprocity. Reciprocity was inflated into much more than a commercial arrangement leading to prosperity. Instead it was a slippery slope leading to annexation. "We must decide," Robert Borden intoned, "whether the spirit of Canadianism or Continentalism shall prevail on the northern half of the continent." No less a political personage than the Speaker of the U.S. House of Representatives said so: he hoped to see the day when "the American flag will float over every square foot of the British North American possessions, clear to the North Pole."

That opened the floodgates. The American flag was booed in cinemas. Unlucky Americans visiting Canada were subjected to personal abuse. Sunday newspapers, crime, and divorce, well-known features of the American way of life, would become prevalent. Only Borden could stop it, and if proof were needed of his commitment to the British Empire, his firm policy on a "contribution" of dreadnoughts to the Royal Navy provided it. That was in English Canada.

French Canada featured a different campaign. There the spectre was the British Empire, not the United States, and the cause was Laurier's Naval Service Act. Leading Quebec Conservatives were aware of the contradiction between their platform and Borden's, but they reasoned that the main objective was the defeat of Laurier and the Liberals.

The opposition prevailed. In English Canada Laurier fell for being pro-American and anti-British and in Quebec he lost for being too pro-British. The Conservatives won 134 seats to the Liberals' 87. A pleasantly surprised Robert Borden became prime minister of Canada. At age sixty-nine, Laurier returned to being leader of the Opposition.

DEPRESSION AND WAR

Having achieved office, Borden had no idea what to do with it. The Reciprocity Agreement was dead, that much was certain. But what about the great naval issue? Taking two different stands had harvested twenty-six MPs (and only 0.5 percent less of the vote total than Laurier) in Quebec. What would happen to them if Borden proceeded to send money to London for dreadnoughts, as his English-Canadian supporters expected?

Like any sensible leader, Borden postponed the issue. He would go to London himself and ask the British what they really needed—an act of stunning naïveté. At least he wouldn't have to go for a number of months. In the meantime, Borden suspended the operation of Laurier's Naval Service Act and with it the construction of the "tin-pot navy."

The prime minister duly visited London in the summer of 1912, collecting a knighthood en route. He asked Winston Churchill, the First Lord of the Admiralty (navy minister), whether he needed money for dreadnoughts, and unsurprisingly Churchill said yes. Borden was also admitted to the inner councils of the empire, attending a meeting of the grandly named Committee of Imperial Defence. He was not told that the Committee was to all intents and purposes dysfunctional, being paralyzed by quarrels between the army and the navy. In any case the British ministers attending did not tell Borden the truth, that extra battleships were needed because they wanted to make a complicated switch of ships with their unofficial ally, the French.[43]

Happy but ignorant, Sir Robert Borden returned to Canada. The naval contribution would have to go through, he told his colleagues. Winston Churchill wanted it. One of his Quebec ministers resigned, but his other Quebec colleagues put party before promises. Borden's naval contribution passed the House of Commons, only to be stalled in Canada's appointed Senate. There it stayed, for the Liberals had a majority in the Senate, and on the naval issue they could reasonably argue that the legitimacy of Borden's action was questionable. Borden toyed with calling an election on the matter, but put it off.

It was by now 1914, and electoral prospects for the Conservatives were growing dimmer. A severe depression afflicted Canada in 1913–14, straining the country's limited social services. There were rumours of starvation, but no suggestion that the dominion government should fill the gap. In the spring, Borden was preoccupied with repelling a shipload of Sikhs who had got around Canada's immigration laws by chartering a Japanese ship, the *Komagata Maru*, to bring them to Vancouver. There they sat under the guns of Canada's museum-piece navy while Borden struggled with the law (but not his conscience) to find a way to send them back to India. Borden was in luck: the Sikhs gave up and agreed to go home, just in time for the prime minister to take a summer vacation in Muskoka. He hadn't been paying much attention to the newspapers, though he was aware that there was a crisis in the Balkans—the third in as many years. Doubtless it would be resolved. That was the British government's business, not Canada's.

On that point Borden and the British government were in full agreement. It mattered not at all what Borden thought of the assassination of the Austrian Archduke Franz Ferdinand in Sarajevo on 28 June 1914. Borden knew nothing of the precarious politics of the Austro-Hungarian Empire and how they meshed with the need to assert Austrian predominance over the empire's troublesome neighbour, Serbia. With German encouragement, Austria-Hungary confronted Serbia, which set in motion Russia, supporting Serbia, and France, supporting Russia. By the end of

July the two sides were lined up prepared for war, with only the lingering uncertainty of Great Britain standing in the way. In the end the British government could not betray its commitments to France, realizing that if Germany prevailed over France, the German position in Europe would be immensely strengthened, to Britain's peril.

The German general staff did the rest, laying down an invasion of France via neutral Belgium, which the British, the French, and everyone else had once agreed to leave alone and neutral in any conflict. Britain could therefore go to war in defence of neutral rights—Belgium's—and that was what the empire could be told. Britain declared war on Germany on 4 August 1914.

The news was well received in some quarters in Canada. As elsewhere in the Western world, politics and society seemed ill-matched. The spectacle of politicians scratching away on the surface of the world's problems irritated the earnest. There had been too many compromises, too many small corruptions; Canada, and the world, needed decisive action. Canada's minister of militia and defence, General Sir Sam Hughes, felt the need and heard the call. He had feared he might not, that this man and his hour of destiny would not after all be matched. When it seemed that peace might prevail, briefly, he had the Union Jack fluttering outside his headquarters hauled down. On the fourth of August, Hughes proudly returned it to the top of the flagpole. It was a grand thing to be British, after all.

11

BREAKING THE MOULD, 1914~1930

Art and patriotism: Miss Canada urges a farmer to contribute in this poster advertising the Canadian Patriotic Fund, 1919.

In 1914 and again in 1939 Canada went to war because Great Britain went to war. As the War of 1812 was in many ways the continuation and resolution of the American Revolution of 1776, so the Second World War of 1939–45 was an extension of the Great War of 1914–18.

On the surface, the Canada of 1939 was very different from the Canada of 1914. Shorter skirts, lighter clothes, and a faster pace to life were the most evident signs of change. Yet above the crowds, the streetscapes were much the same. The Victorians had built for the ages, and their monuments lined Canadian streets. Churches were still the most common, certainly the most obvious, public buildings. Gothic or gingerbread or neo-classical, government buildings were meant to impress. So were the temples of business, the banks and insurance companies, for example. The great Sun Life Building on Dominion Square in Montreal was the prime specimen, solid but tall, "reminiscent of imperial Rome," according to one critic.[1] Their monuments could be all the more impressive, and much taller, because behind the pillars, stone, and concrete they were supported by steel girders and accessed by electric elevators. The downtowns of Canadian cities accordingly pointed up, and urban areas as small as Regina acquired their ten-storey "skyscrapers" in the 1910s and 1920s.

Downtown was still downtown, the hub for offices, shopping, and finance. Canadian downtowns were curiously familiar, coast to coast, in styles of building or streetscapes but also in the names on the buildings. Canada was becoming a country of large companies. Its banking system had consolidated into relatively few banks, headquartered by the 1920s in Montreal and Toronto, each with many branches. (Only in Quebec did a co-operative savings movement, the *caisses populaires*, vary the formula, but even there the national, Canadian, banks predominated in the cities.) The department stores were familiar too, Eaton's and Simpsons, based in Toronto, being the main ones. Eaton's and Simpsons stores reached beyond the cities, with catalogue offices in towns of all sizes. Canada's oldest firm, the Hudson's Bay Company, prospered, with its network of trading posts across the north; it too had expanded into department stores in the west.

The rhythm of life was not very different from before the Great War. Sunday remained reserved for religion, and trying to get service of any kind other than religious in most of Canada was an impossibility. Meals outside the home were sparse, drinks except in Quebec were few, and secular entertainments, from libraries to movies, banned. None of this would have been surprising to a visitor from 1900, though the war had added extra restrictions under the guise of reform.

The technologies that served and defined daily life were developments of technologies that had existed twenty-five years before. Movie theatres were larger and more universal: every town of any size had at least one. Movies talked after 1927, telephones were more frequent, and there were more aircraft in the skies. There was radio, which in the 1920s was the province of private enterprise. For information, people still relied on newspapers. Yet most people still travelled on streamlined versions of the coal-fired locomotives that had carried people from place to place in 1914, and passenger planes were still exotic. There were more paved roads and more cars than in 1914, it was true, but most traffic moved, as it had in 1880, by rail. The railways had different names and ownership: the Borden government was compelled to nationalize the bankrupt Canadian Northern and Grand Trunk, and combined them into a single company, Canadian National Railways, which competed with the vigorously private Canadian Pacific. Telegraphs and the post office were still the usual means of communication between cities. The post office was the largest department in the federal government, in 1914 and throughout the 1920s, in terms of numbers of employees.[2]

Progress and reform weren't merely about technology and its uses. For half a century reformers had strained to limit society's abuses, especially alcohol, and with the generation of 1914 they largely succeeded. The war provided the opportunity, for in the context of heroism no sacrifice could be too great. Efficiency and morality combined to legislate prohibition, an end to alcohol sales. As a result it was more difficult to get an alcoholic drink in Canada in 1939 than it had been in 1914. What was different, by 1939, was a concern that laws prohibiting or limiting liquor went too far—although for many not far enough.

The various governments did what they could. Outside private clubs, which flourished during this period, consuming alcohol was made as uncomfortable as possible—limited for the most part to "beer parlours" where low-alcohol beer might be quaffed. Quebec, as always, was the exception. There, under the eye of a benign and corruptible police force, there were few limits, as generations of thirsty Ontarians came to learn. Naturally, Quebec was cited as a bad example by prohibitionists elsewhere.

Prohibition and the fight against drink were just one of the trends apparent in 1914 that continued through the 1930s. Urbanism was another. More Canadians lived in cities, and by the 1920s urban Canadians formed a clear majority of the population, which was already predictable in 1914. Urban life created new needs, as old neighbourhoods and rural connections were left behind. Social and educational services expanded to meet the need.

Professionalism—impersonal, fair, and expert—had been one of the hallmarks of the progressive era before 1914, and was even more apparent in 1939. Experts, from engineers to doctors, were more varied than in 1914 and probably better trained in universities in Canada and abroad; their presence grew in government and in large companies. Above all, there were more managers.

The prime minister in 1914, the lawyer Sir Robert Borden, hadn't gone to university, but as an eminent professional he had taught at one, Dalhousie in Halifax. Borden was half a generation on from his predecessor, Sir Wilfrid Laurier, born in 1841, and much more than Laurier he espoused the notion that the fruits of progress—especially in technology—were to be found in Canada in abundance and needed only proper channelling, which would be provided, if necessary, by the state. Borden sang the hymn of proper organization that was the progressives' signature tune.

The prime minister in 1939 was yet another generation on, born in 1874 compared with Borden's 1854 birthdate. William Lyon Mackenzie King was a university graduate, as Laurier had been, and a lawyer, like Borden and Laurier and most of Canada's prime ministers, then and since. He was also a trained economist, and a labour negotiator by profession. It was as an expert that the Laurier government hired him as Canada's first deputy minister of labour, and he took his skills with him into politics as a member of the Laurier cabinet and, after Laurier's death in 1919, leader of the Liberal party.

No Canadian prime minister has ever been a complete teetotaller, as far as personal conduct was concerned, and also in terms of public policy.[3] Prohibition was enacted under Borden, but as enforcement loomed, the prime minister was quick to order in supplies of Scotch by the case. Mackenzie King, outwardly sanctimonious, was not a man to refuse a sherry or a martini. On state occasions, he reminded himself that he was really drinking for two, himself and his country. Think of Canada, one can hear him murmuring. If state occasions required a banquet, it would likely be held across the Ottawa River from puritan and Protestant Ontario, in Catholic and—where alcohol was concerned—latitudinarian Quebec.

Neither Borden nor King would go very far in defying society's conventions. Indeed, both made their careers by implementing them, the Liberal King more than the Conservative Borden. King, as a result, seemed an even safer bet than Borden, reassuring to a generation that experienced more than the usual share of war and disruption.

WAR AND DIVISION

The first months of the First World War were optimistic in Canada, as they were everywhere else. Crowds cheered, bands played, and people and politicians exchanged vows full of purpose and unity. There was no question, for the time being, that the empire's cause was just, that right and wrong were in play, and that Canada must do all it could to make the right prevail. Sir Wilfrid Laurier proclaimed a political truce, and cancelled all his partisan meetings. When Parliament met in emergency session in August 1914 the Liberals cooperated fully; it was Laurier who guided Borden in shaping the government's emergency legislation, the War Measures Act.[4] Even Henri Bourassa, editor (and founder) of the "bon" newspaper *Le Devoir* in Montreal,[5] agreed that Germany's invasion of Belgium justified Britain and its allies in resisting aggression.[6]

The government pledged money, supplies, and troops for the war. Money was admittedly a problem. The country was in a depression; trade was down; and imports were sagging and with them the tariff revenues that were the government's mainstay. The government had few economic instruments at its command. There was no central bank, no income tax. Provinces had their own revenue needs. And so the government did what Canadian governments always did when faced with a shortage of funds: they went to the London money market for a loan. They got one, and with it a warning that they should not rely on London in the future, as the British government had little money to spare for the colonies. In the case of Canada, there was an obvious alternative: New York. It was a sign of changing times, and the times would change even more in the next few years.

As for supplies, Canada had plenty of wheat and the harvest was approaching. Canada offered wheat to Britain, and the gift was accepted. As for troops, from coast to coast militiamen were anxious to serve. There were few professional soldiers to dampen the enthusiasm of the recruits with the counsels of experience. The minister of defence, Sir Sam Hughes, was madly enthusiastic, fearing only that the war might be over before his troops could get to Europe.

Hughes was not unique in his keenness for the war effort. Recruits swamped military depots. In Edmonton alone, two thousand men marched from the United Services Club behind a band playing "Rule

Britannia" and the French and Russian national anthems.[7] A similar enthusiasm swept the country—except, apparently, in the French-speaking parts of Quebec. The politicians followed the crowd, publicly repudiating partisanship and calling for unity. Yet, as always, in a few months the need for political skills and the art of compromise would bring partisanship back.

Hughes swiftly assembled the components of an army at a camp outside Quebec City, and sent it overseas, unready and untrained, on the first available shipping. The Canadian Expeditionary Force (CEF), as it was called, became part of the British Expeditionary Force, but it was some time before any of the Canadians would reach France. They had to learn how to march, and shoot, and dig. The medical corps had to learn how to cope with sanitation and disease: the first casualties of the CEF occurred in camp, in England, far from the battlefield.

The CEF began as an amateur force under amateur commanders, enthusiastic but undisciplined.[8] (Ironically, the few permanent-force officers were most needed on the technical side—signals and artillery, for example—and many had to be retained in Canada to keep the military organization functioning.) On reaching Great Britain, it was stiffened with professional officers supplied by the British, especially in staff positions. The higher the rank, or the more technical the function, the more likely it was that the relevant officer would be British.

So were many of the troops. Canada enjoyed heavy British immigration before 1914. (More than 10 percent of Canada's 1911 population was British-born.)[9] Many of these immigrants had been disappointed by what they found: Canada was not quite what they had hoped for. Many were single men, and many of the single men were, in 1914, unemployed and, as a consequence, fairly mobile. Canada's reputation as a land of opportunity was rather strained, particularly in the face of reports of third-world conditions in city slums. In Montreal, the infant mortality rate was said to equal Calcutta's. Evidently, there wasn't much for many of Canada's soldiers to leave behind. Of the first contingent of 36,267—those who left by the end of March 1915—23,211 were British immigrants, 10,880 were born in Canada, and of them, 1245 were French Canadians.[10]

It was clear from the beginning that Canada did not enter the war a united country. True, there was no real opposition to going to war, but underneath the official enthusiasm were signs of disquiet. Perhaps French Canadians could enlist in units that would serve with the French army, the Montreal newspaper *La Presse* suggested. Perhaps they shouldn't enlist at all: Canada would best serve the empire by shipping wheat and other commodities. Reluctance on one side was matched by suspicion on the other. In Montreal, police even discouraged citizens from singing "O Canada" instead of the official anthem, "God Save the King."

There were issues dividing English from French. There was always prejudice: fear of the other language, or the Catholic religion, or, on the other side, of the Protestants. There was disputation over French as a language of education in the English-speaking provinces, suppressed in the West and under assault in Ontario, where the provincial government had banned the teaching of French in the school systems, public and separate. The government's action was supported by the English-speaking Catholic hierarchy of Ontario and enforced by squads of school inspectors.[11] How, then, could French-Canadian soldiers fight for justice abroad when they were denied it at home?

The federal government could do little about schools and language; the last time it had tried, in Manitoba in 1896, it had received a bloody nose. Borden wasn't much interested in the issue, and even less interested in what the weak French-Canadian contingent in his cabinet could tell him. The Ontario government—Conservative, like Borden, and with powerful sympathizers inside his cabinet—refused to budge. Accordingly, Borden did nothing.

The issue of "Ontario Schools" certainly embittered French–English relations in Canada during the Great War, and did nothing to encourage French-Canadian recruitment during that conflict. Yet French-Canadian antipathy to overseas military adventures was already well established—the precedents of the South African War and the naval controversy of 1909–13 show that clearly enough. There was a long history of disagreement over some of Canada's great public issues—language and schools in the West and the Riel rebellion being obvious examples.

There was also a strong tradition of reconciliation and compromise in the national political system, and especially in the two great political parties, Conservative and Liberal. Laurier was almost the perfect embodiment of the tradition, weaving among obstacles, balancing interests and prejudices, giving way where necessary, going along and getting along. Cities like Montreal and Quebec had their own, smaller versions of the national system, with political and business elites of both languages getting along because they had to. In Montreal, the mayoralty alternated between English and French Canadians before 1914, and even after 1914, when the mayoralty passed permanently into the hands of French Canadians, English speakers remained an important feature of the city's politics.

On the great issue of the empire, opinions differed. French Canadians weren't republicans. Prominent French Canadians accepted the knighthoods showered on prominent Canadians, and participated enthusiastically in the folklore of monarchy—the pomp and parades and ceremonies, and the adoration of visiting royalty. To this were added the parallel and equally vivid ceremonies of the Church, which were also more frequent and thus presumably more engaging on a daily basis. The Roman Catholic Church was anything but a subversive force, and its hierarchy never questioned, in public at least, the powers that were—of whom the Church and its bishops were definitely a part. The Church also offered an alternative for those discontented with the minority status of French, or the difficulties of being Catholic in a majoritarian Protestant country.

Nevertheless, a constant tension simmered between the English and French groups in Canada. English Canadians subscribed to the idea that there was one Canadian nationality, a construct of British-imperial and Canadian identities. Ethnic groups were subordinate to this national identity—at most, ethnic differences existed to enhance, not contradict, the larger nationality.[12] As the historian Arthur Silver has argued, this approach made the French not very different from the Welsh or perhaps the Irish.[13] And yet the Irish-Canadian bishops themselves spotted the difference made by language—which was why, before the war, they identified their interests with the English-speaking (though Protestant) majority of the country, and not their fellow Catholics.

French Canadians, then, were not moved by the same sentiments, nor subject to the same psychic temptations, as their fellow citizens. Politics in Canada on the national level usually took this distinction into account. Ordinarily, politicians fudged the distinction—the Laurier technique. Even Henri Bourassa, while admitting present and actual differences, predicted a day when French and English would coalesce into a single nationality— once English Canadians had abandoned the follies of empire and dropped their pretensions to racial superiority. Unlike Laurier, Bourassa did not try to escape or avoid the contradictions between the Canadian ideal and the Canadian reality. And unlike the relatively few extreme nationalists of his day, he did not escape into fantasies of separatism.[14]

Instead, Bourassa set out on his own course, explaining to English Canadians where and when he could that their commitment to empire as expressed in whole-hearted participation in the war was mistaken. The grievances of the French Canadians of Ontario should be the priority, not the wrongs of distant Europe and the excitement of empire. For his pains he was almost mobbed on a theatre stage in Ottawa in December 1914, and was saved only by the manager ringing down the curtain.[15] He said the same, even more emphatically, to French-Canadian audiences, where his arguments met with much greater resonance. "In the name of religion, liberty and faithfulness to the British flag," Bourassa wrote in *Le Devoir*, "the French Canadians are enjoined to go fight the Prussians of Europe. Shall we let the Prussians of Ontario impose their domination like masters ... under the shelter of the British flag and British institutions?"[16]

It's estimated that out of the 619,636 men who served in the CEF, 35,000 were French Canadians, 14,000 of whom had volunteered for the army before June 1917. These figures are not quite what they appear to be, since another 228,000 of the 619,000 were born in the United Kingdom, and overall just over half were born in Canada. Quebec had fewer immigrants from Great Britain than other provinces, and fewer unmarried men. (Recruitment in the Maritime provinces, where there were also fewer immigrants, was lower than in Ontario and the West, though not as low as in Quebec.) More French Canadians were farmers, compared with other ethnic groups, and across the country farmers were slow (if not impossible) to enlist. It is nevertheless indisputable that French Canadians did not serve in the armed forces in anything like the same numbers or proportions as English Canadians. That fact in itself was much commented upon at the time, especially in the English-language media, and may have contributed to the further erosion of recruitment in Quebec.

Recruitment of French Canadians wasn't a complete failure, and even some *nationalistes* joined up—the prominent politician Olivar Asselin, for example. Bourassa's cousin Talbot Papineau also joined the army, and engaged his relative in a well-publicized debate in the press over the rights and wrongs of participation in the war. And despite Hughes's reluctance to encourage purely French-Canadian units, several French-speaking battalions were formed, the most successful of which, the 22nd Battalion (now the Royal 22nd), is still in existence.

By 1916, with no end in sight to the fighting, Canadian politics had reached an impasse. Recruitment was slowing to a trickle, and increasingly fervent appeals to sacrifice, justice, and the common cause drew little response. With Laurier's agreement the Borden government secured a year's extension of the term of the Parliament, which would have expired in the fall of 1916. Borden was faltering by that point, and it was unlikely that Laurier would agree to another extension. War or no war, politics had returned to fever pitch by the beginning of 1917.

POLITICS, MONEY, AND MUNITIONS

Canada's problems seemed to be exacerbated by the uncertain leadership of the prime minister, Sir Robert Borden. Borden, a Nova Scotian and at one time one of Canada's leading lawyers, had been Conservative leader since 1900. He had survived two election defeats at Laurier's hands before winning in 1911; by 1915 all the signs pointed to yet another defeat whenever the next election took place.

Borden was slow and methodical in his approach to life and politics. His pronouncements and platforms suggested he was a reformer, and he showed few accomplishments for his first three years in office. In 1914 he did what the occasion warranted, but instead of bold initiatives he worked through the politicians—the ministers—his party provided. They were a doubtful and possibly wasting asset. The Conservative party was on the wane in 1915 and 1916. As Conservative governments tumbled in Manitoba and British Columbia, it seemed that more could be done. But what?

Borden was slightly less sluggish when it came to the political problems caused by his defence minister, Sir Sam Hughes. It didn't take Hughes long to become unpopular with his own troops. Stories circulated about the minister—how his cronies got supply contracts (true); how he favoured his son, who became a general like his father (indisputable); how his behaviour was capricious and erratic. A waiter who pleased the minister with prompt service was said to have been rewarded with an officer's commission. It hardly mattered whether the story was true or not; it was plausible, and it was believed.

The most notorious case was the Ross rifle, a marksman's gun made in Quebec City. Hughes preferred the Ross to the British standard rifle, the Lee-Enfield, even though the Canadian rifle was difficult to load, jammed frequently, and stopped functioning altogether in the mud. The troops responded by scrounging Lee-Enfields wherever they could, meanwhile cursing the minister for the Ross.

As a result Hughes weakened the government, even among its supporters. A scandal broke out over contractors for the manufacture of artillery shells, held to be both defective and insufficient, and the scandal was tracked back to Hughes.

Borden responded by gradually stripping the minister of his authority, in 1916 creating a new minister for the overseas army. Hughes resigned, to Borden's great relief. Hughes's mistake had been to assume that running an army in time of war demanded nothing more than the tried and true methods of the old politics—favouritism and patronage spiced with patriotism. Borden knew that this was no longer sufficient, and that his government wouldn't survive unless it demonstrated a greater capacity for professionalism and objectivity.

Borden was uncomfortable with many of the ordinary tasks of politics. He got on badly with his more political ministers; from their point of view, he failed to understand that his Conservative party needed stronger sustenance than the thin gruel of "good government." In the short run they were mistaken, but over the longer term it's hard to escape the conclusion that Borden wrecked the existing party structure without putting very much in its place. By the time that fact became apparent, the war was over and Borden was gone.

The prime minister suffered no great damage from the Hughes episode, but it hardly indicated that he was a confident and decisive leader. It took external circumstances to galvanize him to reshape his government and its objectives. As casualties mounted among the Canadian troops sent overseas, and the effort to sustain them became intolerable under the political system that then existed, Borden came to the conclusion that their sacrifices demanded a different response. The war broke Canada's political mould: it was up to Borden to do what he could to transform it.

STRATEGY AND CASUALTIES

Canada's volunteer soldiers, the CEF, were fed into Great Britain's volunteer army, the BEF. Great Britain was the only combatant not to rely on conscript forces in 1914; as a result, the British army was tiny compared with the German or Russian or French militaries. Those armies had been planning for war for years, with elaborate mobilization schemes based on railway routes and timetables. Moving and sustaining an army was an immense enterprise; once begun, it was difficult to stop.

The combatants of 1914 did not want to stop. They created a war on two fronts, along Germany's eastern and western frontiers. The Germans attempted to strike first in the west to dispose of the formidable French army before turning on the Russians. They did not succeed in defeating the French or capturing Paris. Though casualties were heavy, the French held off the Germans before their capital, and then outflanked them in a series of manoeuvres that extended the battle as far as the North Sea coast of Belgium, in front of the medieval city of Ypres. As the armies marched north, they entrenched along the route, until by December 1914 a line of trenches—"the Western Front"—ran from the Swiss border, for Switzerland was neutral, to Ypres.

The British and French armies met at Ypres, and there the first Canadian soldiers were sent, in the spring of 1915. The Germans selected Ypres for the trial of a new weapon. Their chemists had concocted a poison gas, and the German high command released it on the Allied soldiers. It was effective, up to a point. Some of the Allied troops melted away, but the Canadians held their line, and the Germans did not after all break through. Poison gas signalled that this war was more frightful than earlier conflicts, but it was only one of the mechanical devices that ensured that the "Great War" would be different from any other. Poison gas was used by both sides, more easily by the Allies, because the prevailing winds came from the west. Gas masks were soon evolved to cope, and gas did not prove to be the decisive weapon its inventors had hoped.

That was also true of a later development, the tank. Essentially a mobile artillery platform, tanks were first used on the Western Front in 1916. Developed by the British, they were imitated by the other major combatants. Heavily armoured but underpowered, the tanks were prone to breakdowns after only a few hours of use. Because of this defect, the tanks of the Great War were marginal weapons, sometimes useful but never decisive.

The Great War was a war of artillery and machine guns at the Front, and supplies—food and ammunition—at the rear. The artillery was supposed to clear a way for the infantry to attack by demolishing the enemy's trenches. The infantry would then "break through" and the

Major Engagements of the
Canadian Expeditionary Force, 1914–1918

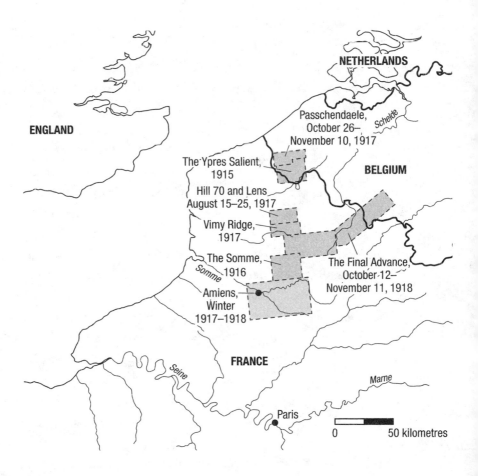

cavalry would pour through the gap the infantry had won. For nearly four years the cavalry waited, fortunately for them, because the infantry did not break through on either side. The reason they didn't succeed was the strength of the defences, again on both sides: the trenches, with machine guns and strong points made of concrete in which troops could shelter during artillery bombardments. Artillery shelling, used by the ton by all the attacking armies,[17] may even have advantaged the defence rather than the offence because it signalled in a fairly mechanical and predictable way that an attack was underway, and where the attack was intended to go.

The objective, the strategy, of the various armies wasn't really to gain territory—though that was useful—but to destroy the enemy's army. The enemy army must be defeated in the field, and killed or captured. In itself this strategy made sense. The problem was a mismatch between strategy and tactics. That was particularly the case from the Allied side, because the German trench systems were thicker, better fortified, and better designed. Behind the lines railways chugged along the Front and up from the rear, bringing reinforcements and supplies to the immense armies that confronted each other.

The armies didn't spend their entire time assaulting one another's trenches. Most of the war was spent in periods of boredom, punctuated by acute terror—the terror of going "over the top" of one's own trenches toward the enemy's, or the terror of an enemy sniper, or the crushing bombardment of the enemy's artillery. Most casualties were caused by artillery.[18]

The Great War was remarkable for another phenomenon. It was the first war in modern times, perhaps in human history, in which more soldiers died in battle than from disease. Advances in medicine, organization, transport, and supply meant that the wounded had a much greater chance of rescue and transport and better methods of treatment than ever before. (The death rate for Canadian soldiers in the Great War was 114 per thousand; it would be lower still in the Second World War.)[19] Once wounded, a soldier would be evacuated toward the rear, to dressing stations or field hospitals. For the severely wounded, it was a trip back to England ("Blighty" in contemporary slang—and such injuries were "Blighty" wounds) for proper care and recuperation.

The perfection of military technology and organization, the efficient staff work that moved 458,000 Canadian troops across the ocean, the men and women who fed, clothed, and trained them, then evacuated the casualties and cared for the wounded made the continuation of the war possible.

The war lasted for more than four years. The decisive battle imagined by the commanding generals never happened. Each year the generals presented their plans to the politicians. It was up to the politicians to find the men and supplies, and the money to pay for it all, only to discover that there was never enough, and that the generals' promises melted into the mud of the trenches.

The politicians blamed the generals for their failures, which were real, and the generals blamed the politicians for their deficiencies, which were partly imaginary. They did not blame the politicians for their real failure, which was to have set war aims that could not be negotiated, only imposed through victory or accepted through defeat. Sometimes the politicians nerved themselves to fire a general or two, but because the military commanders had become iconic figures, symbols of hope and skill and bravery, it was difficult to do so. There were only two commanders of the BEF, Sir John French and Sir Douglas Haig. Haig, who led the British Empire's armies in France from 1915 to 1919, oversaw the disastrous Battle of the Somme in 1916, the equally disastrous Flanders offensive in 1917, and the near-defeat of the British army at Amiens in 1918. His conduct of the war was measured in literally millions of British dead and wounded, including over 200,000 Canadians (56,000 dead, 150,000 wounded).

The politicians resented what the generals were doing, but they had nothing better to offer. The politicians, after all, were the men who decided on war aims, and the absolute incompatibility of the war aims of the belligerents was what determined the length of the war. The Allies—Great Britain, France, and the Russian Empire—agreed early on not to make a separate peace and, remarkably, stuck to it. They claimed to be fighting for justice and the rule of law; practically speaking, they were fighting to prevent German hegemony in Europe. Though the Allies didn't know the details, that was in fact the German objective.

Because the war proved much more costly in terms of treasure and lives than any of the combatants had reckoned, it became necessary to appeal to transcendental values of sacrifice among the civilian populations. The fruits of victory grew, while the perils of defeat grew too. The villainy of the enemy was not left to the imagination, but cultivated by propagandists. Canadians learned, from their newspapers and official propaganda, that the Germans (labelled Huns after the barbarians of old) looted, pillaged, and raped their way across Belgium and France. War posters depicted the bestial Hunnish soldiery; politicians and publicists declaimed the message from the platform; ministers and priests amplified it in the churches. As the months and years passed, the shrillness of the rhetoric made it more and more difficult to reach any kind of compromise peace, and in the event, there was none. The war would have to be won or lost on the battlefield, and on the home front, not in the chambers of diplomacy.

The home front could be a point of weakness. In Russia, a weak government and a chaotic political system combined with economic disruption and military defeat to sap the foundations of the imperial system. In March 1917 the Russian emperor was swept away and replaced by an uneasy alliance of bourgeois politicians and labour militants. They in turn were overthrown in November by the radical Bolshevik faction of the Russian Social Democratic Party under V.I. Lenin, who claimed to represent the workers and peasants. Lenin and the Bolsheviks took Russia out of the war, agreeing to whatever conditions the Germans pleased in March 1918. The Germans exacted harsh terms, and in so doing gave the rest of the world a sense of what a German-dictated peace would be like. The Russians and the Bolsheviks had, however, demonstrated that it was possible to end the war and survive, and their example was, in the climate of 1917–18, contagious.

ACCIDENT AND PRECEDENT:
CANADA AND THE BRITISH EMPIRE

Before 1914 Canada did not have, and could not have, a foreign policy. As a colony of the British Empire, Canada enjoyed internal autonomy, including the ability to legislate its own taxes, among them tariffs. It conducted its own commercial foreign policy as an extension of this tariff autonomy, negotiating and implementing trade treaties (though always with a British signature) with various countries, including France and the United States. But when it came to defence policy, and other aspects of political foreign policy, Canada accepted whatever the British chose to do. If the occasion was important enough, as in the South African War and the Great War, Canada was bound to participate. No Canadian representative was present when the British cabinet decided on war in August 1914, nor were there any Canadians in the room when British ministers received intelligence about the war, or decided on war policy.

To underline the obvious, British ministers were responsible to the British electorate, not the Canadian. Their decisions involved Canada, and legally they represented Canada in foreign affairs, but they did not have to manage Canadian politics or cope with the local consequences of imperial decisions. That was left to Borden and the Canadian cabinet. And Borden, sixty-four hundred kilometres away from the seat of empire and the war, had his own priorities, even if, in the summer and fall of 1914, they had been superseded by imperial obligations.

Until 1914 imperial obligations had never imposed much stress or cost on Canada. Now they had, and imperial–colonial relations took on much the same form as they had in the 1830s. If the colony was paying in cash and in kind, and its ministers were assuming the political risk of extracting men and money on a continuing and apparently indefinite basis, then there must be consultation, and responsibility, between the imperial government and its colonial associate.

The problem was that there was no institution, no organization where representation and responsibility could cohabit. There were the old problems of communication and distance. There was the force of habit, for British ministers were unused to sharing decisions with their colonial counterparts. Some members of the British government wondered aloud if the problem might not be best solved by giving independence to Canada and Australia as an alternative to sharing Britain's sovereign power.[20]

Borden visited Britain in the summer of 1915. Instead of determination and decision, he found hesitation, confusion, and disunity. Canada's contribution—by then several divisions of troops—was appreciated, but no one could tell the Canadian prime minister how or whether there would be a victorious end to the war. When he returned to Canada, Borden found that once again his main source of information was the newspapers. Irritated, he drafted a letter in January 1916 in which he compared the dominions' position in the empire to "toy automata." He went on to ask, "Is this war being waged by the United Kingdom alone or is it a war waged by the whole Empire?"[21]

There was no satisfactory answer. British politics were unsettled, and British politicians distracted. Borden, meanwhile, had problems of his own. In Canada, recruitment was faltering during 1916, controversy over the Ontario Schools question reached new levels of bitterness, and scandals over the distribution of war contracts plagued the government. Against this background, Borden was in no position to press his demand for greater dominion representation in the formulation of war policy.

The answer, when it came, was the result of political change in Great Britain, not Canada. David Lloyd George, a senior Liberal minister in the British government and most recently minister of munitions, deposed his predecessor, the Liberal H.H. Asquith, in December 1916. Lloyd George had for some time recognized the importance of the dominions militarily and economically to the British war effort. A very practical politician with the ability to think in new patterns, Lloyd George found it easy to conceive of the dominions as a factor in British politics. He promptly asked their leaders, including Borden, to come to London to confer on the strategy of the war. To manage the dominion representatives, Lloyd

George invented an Imperial War Cabinet—essentially the existing British war cabinet made up of the most senior ministers, plus dominion representatives.[22]

Borden arrived in London in February 1917, in time to witness the British reaction to the Russian Revolution and the entry of the United States into the war in April. (Borden knew little more about American politics or the American president, Woodrow Wilson, than his British colleagues, though he claimed to.) The main business before the empire's ministers was the authorization of a new offensive in France, led by Field Marshal Haig, as he had recently become. Haig was optimistic, and the Imperial War Cabinet gave him what he wanted. The ministers also discussed manpower, which in Britain and the colonies was beginning to run dry. This Borden knew from his own experience—efforts to recruit more volunteers for the army in France had been spectacularly unsuccessful, and the registration of men of military age had failed to stimulate a rush to the colours. There were not, therefore, enough replacements for the army.

Borden took the occasion of his trip to London to visit Canadian troops in France—now four divisions organized in the "Canadian Corps," efficiently led by a Canadian officer, General Arthur Currie, and recently victorious in a large though limited battle on Vimy Ridge. Borden was especially moved by his visits to military hospitals, and came away with the fixed conviction that in order to keep faith with the troops at the Front he must send reinforcements.

Returning home in May 1917, Borden told his cabinet that it must compel men to join the war through conscription. He knew such a measure must be controversial, not least because the recruitment figures showed that French Canadians hadn't volunteered for the army in anything like their proportion of the population. Accordingly, Borden tried to win over Sir Wilfrid Laurier, offering him and the Liberals half the places in the cabinet and any seat except the prime ministership.

Laurier refused, in what may have been his most important political decision. Partisan loyalties ran deep, as did an old Liberal aversion to conscription and compulsion that wasn't limited to Canada or Canadian Liberals. Laurier was conscious and fearful of the consequences in Quebec. If he joined a coalition or Union government, he would abandon Quebec to Henri Bourassa and the *nationalistes*. He would not do so, and appealed to his followers to follow his example.

Many of the English-speaking leaders of the Liberal party would have preferred to take Borden's offer, but they had a problem. The party rank and file, even in English Canada, were unwilling to break ranks with Laurier. In Ontario and the West many Liberals were recent immigrants, unmoved by appeals to British race and patriotism. Many were farmers, and farmers as a group resisted volunteering. Traditional Liberals in the Maritime provinces also hesitated.

Borden had to offer not merely a necessary policy but political safety. This he did through the Wartime Elections Act, which disenfranchised any citizen who had immigrated to Canada from an enemy country— meaning mostly Austria-Hungary—after 1902. Doukhobor and Mennonite conscientious objectors also lost the right to vote. The Act created new voters—the wives, sisters, and daughters of the military. Another act allowed military voters, who would presumably vote appropriately, to cast their ballots in whatever constituency they chose or had chosen for them. Then Borden rammed conscription through Parliament in August 1917. The government's electoral prospects immediately brightened, helped along by Borden's promise to exempt farmers from conscription. Farmers and other voters outside Quebec also got the impression that the necessary reinforcements would be found in that province.[23] The non-Quebec rural vote suddenly became much friendlier to the Conservatives and anyone else who chose to run under Borden's banner.

An election was scheduled for December 1917. As he had hoped, Borden collected his dissident Liberals, who added strength to the government in Ontario and the West. The issues were simplified for partisan purposes: "Do we want German rule?" a Saskatchewan newspaper demanded.[24] If so, then vote for Laurier; if not, Borden was the man. Laurier found himself leading a French-Canadian party with a few party faithful attached. Those English-Canadian candidates who did run under Laurier's banner knew they were mostly doomed—men like Mackenzie King, the former minister of labour. King hesitated, but in the end he made the right choice, or had the right choice forced on him. He would lose in 1917, but in losing he would establish a public record of fidelity to Laurier, and to the cause of English–French compromise in Canada.

Borden won a majority of seats, and he got conscription. His followers won in a campaign that came very close to preaching racial hatred, a fact that did not pass unnoticed in Quebec. As in 1911, Borden wasn't too choosy about the method by which he won—a classic case of the end justifying the means. In the short term, it did. But politics are run not merely for the present, but in memory. The election of 1917 would play again and again over the next twenty years in Quebec, with toxic results for the Conservative party.

A trickle of reinforcements reached the army in France, including some draftees from Quebec. Borden had partially achieved his object, but at considerable political cost. In a very real sense it was Laurier who won the struggle, if not the election, though it was certainly a contest he would rather not have conducted. As Liberal leader, he felt abandoned and betrayed by some of his oldest associates. But in Quebec it was Laurier, not Bourassa, who carried the day. Bourassa retreated to the sidelines. Opposition to Borden and his policies remained in the hands of the Liberals in Quebec, and the Liberals were quintessentially the party of the establishment. Even Bourassa then and later was not a separatist, and did not preach the departure of Quebec from the Canadian federation.[25]

Certainly there was evasion from the draft, and other forms of resistance. In Quebec City troops from Ontario fired on rioters, but instead of spreading, the riot subsided. By the spring of 1918 resistance in Quebec was the least of Borden's worries. In March the German army stormed the British lines in France, and almost broke through. Faced with the possibility of imminent military defeat, Borden broke his election promise and applied conscription to farmers' sons.[26]

Borden also travelled to London in the spring of 1918 for another round of the Imperial War Cabinet; he would stay until August. The mood among the assembled ministers was sceptical if not despairing. There was no question that the war must go on; the question was how. The answer, as always, was more of everything—more reinforcements, more supplies, more taxes to pay for it all. This was less depressing than it might have been, because on the economic front the Canadian government was doing far better than expected.

Although the results of Borden's conscription measure were disappointing, his industrial mobilization was not. Once responsibility for munitions was removed from Sam Hughes, war production boomed. Responsibility for the manufacture of armaments in Canada was transferred from the Canadian government to the British. Under the direction of a Toronto businessman, Sir Joseph Flavelle, production of all kinds soared in 1918: it was estimated that a full 25 percent of the shells fired on the Western Front that year came from Canada.

Even more surprising, the money to pay for war production came from Canada. Borden's government began the war borrowing in London, and then New York. Taxes were raised, and eventually a very modest income tax was imposed.[27] The federal government did this reluctantly, for it represented an incursion into areas of taxation previously reserved for the provinces and municipalities. Most of the money, however, came from selling bonds inside Canada—the Victory Loans of 1917, 1918, and 1919, which yielded in the billions of dollars and were purchased by over a million subscribers.[28]

As a result, Borden spoke for a stronger, less dependent Canada in 1918. It could even be argued—and it was—that it was the British who were now dependent, using Canadian funds for imperial armaments, firing Canadian-made weapons, eating Canadian-produced food, and relying on dominion soldiers (mostly Canadian and Australian) as the shock troops for the BEF. To the British prime minister, Lloyd George, Borden told tales of incompetent British generals, inefficient staffs, and misguided tactics. Together with Lloyd George and the other dominion prime ministers, he interviewed candidates to replace Field Marshal Haig as BEF commander in readiness for Haig's next failure.

Ironically, in August 1918 Haig succeeded. The German army had been worn down by four years of war, and even reinforcements from the former Eastern Front weren't enough. Canadian troops led the break-through in France, at Amiens, and led the British advance into Belgium. Canadian soldiers for the first time in three years passed beyond the hellish landscape of craters and trenches and into fields and forests not yet devas-tated by war. With American troops arriving by the hundred thousand, the German army collapsed. Their high command demanded an immedi-ate end to the fighting. As German envoys drove to meet the Allied commander in chief, the French Marshal Ferdinand Foch, Wilhelm II fled and the socialists took power in Berlin.

At 11 A.M. on the eleventh of November, 1918, the fighting stopped. Canadian troops at that point had reached the city of Mons in Belgium; in a small skirmish some Canadians were killed just as the fighting ended. (One Canadian, from Saskatchewan, was the last Allied soldier to be killed, at 10:58 A.M.) The Germans and the Allies signed an armistice, a ceasefire, not a treaty of peace. The peace would come some months later, after a conference in Paris.

THE RESULTS OF THE WAR

The Great War seemed to have strengthened the British Empire. The German naval menace was finished. British red encircled maps of the world: in 1919 British Empire forces occupied more than a quarter of the earth's land mass. British troops patrolled the Turkish capital, Constantinople; Baghdad and Jerusalem were under British occupation; there were Canadian troops in Vladivostok and Murmansk, as part of Britain's intervention against the Bolshevik government of Russia.

The leaders of the Allies and their "Associated Power," the United States, met in Paris to set the terms of peace, which the Germans would be obliged to accept. Sir Robert Borden attended the Paris Peace Conference as a member of the British Empire Delegation, but also as the

Canadian prime minister. Canada had a place of its own in Paris; Borden insisted upon it, and Lloyd George secured his allies' consent to the arrangement. Borden argued that Canada's sacrifices during the war demanded recognition, making the point that Canada was now a significant power in terms of both its military accomplishment and its economic importance.

Borden did not bring to Paris a fully evolved plan for the independence of Canada. The idea of independence would have horrified him; what he wanted was a British Empire condominium in which the dominions and the British government shared responsibilities. In 1917 Borden and the South African General Smuts had persuaded an Imperial Conference to recognize the autonomous governments of the empire, abandoning any claim to British superiority or supervision. They left until after the war a thorough revision of the empire's constitutional arrangements, and until that happened the legal position remained as it always had been, with the ultimate authority in the hands of the British Parliament, and the British government of the day.

Lloyd George didn't mind. Cooperation with the dominion prime ministers got him what he wanted and needed—an advantage over the Conservative politicians who otherwise dominated his government. If Lloyd George spoke for the empire beyond the seas, the prime ministers' imperial synapses could be counted on to fire appropriately. Realistically, he may simply have thought it made little sense to try to retard a constitutional development that couldn't be prevented.

Borden had misgivings about the conclusions of the Paris Peace Conference. Its principal fruit, a League of Nations, which was intended to enforce perpetual peace, offended his sense of the practical. If the definition of peace was the settlement of 1919, and the perpetuation of the international system as it existed at that point, Borden had his doubts. The League of Nations was, however, the particular project of the American president, Woodrow Wilson, and Borden was not the man to stand in Wilson's way. Canada needed Wilson's acquiescence in its new international standing, and got it. Canada, by virtue of its presence at the Peace

Conference and its signature on the final treaty (the Treaty of Versailles), became a founding member of the League of Nations in its own right and not merely as part of the British Empire.

Borden returned to Canada before the treaty was signed. There were problems at home. "Bolshevism invades Canada," the *New York Times* told its readers, and Borden's ministers tended to agree. The world had been swept by a wave of radicalism at the end of the war, and Canada was no exception. The Russian Revolution of 1917 inspired radicals and socialists everywhere, with Lenin's seizure of power as a model for the future—the near future. Only terror would keep the bourgeoisie at bay, Lenin believed, and terror became the signature of Communist power.

Radicals in Canada were ecstatic. The Canadian bourgeoisie, including Borden and his government, were apprehensive. Borden withdrew Canadian troops from Siberia,[29] but he and his colleagues were determined to suppress bolshevism at home. The government confronted romantic would-be revolutionaries in Winnipeg, where a general strike occurred in May 1919. The strike was a graphic demonstration of labour's power, and as such was intended to intimidate the opposition. It potentially superseded existing governments by allowing only such activity as was authorized by the strike committee. All this was backed up by gusts of revolutionary rhetoric.

There is good reason to believe that the strikers did not intend to overthrow constituted authority, and that their objectives were primarily economic and relatively modest. But much could happen by accident, and precedents were also important. No one forgot that hundreds of thousands of troops were coming home within months, and that in Russia demobilized soldiers had been a crucial factor in Lenin's revolution. The authorities acted firmly. They arrested the strike leaders, and confronted the strikers with the North-West Mounted Police. Shots were fired, two demonstrators fell dead, thirty were wounded, and the crowds scattered. Within days, if not hours, the strike was over.

The Winnipeg General Strike was one strike among many in the last years of the Great War. Without intending it, the Borden government had presided over a boom economy—full employment, full production, scarcity of supply, and rising wages and prices. Prices, however, rose faster than wages, so that after 1916 Canadian workers were falling steadily behind in terms of their purchasing power. Small wonder that unions grew and flourished and strikes multiplied.

The composition of the workforce was also changing. Female employment had been growing even before the war, and some professions, such as school teaching, and secretarial and stenographic services, were now dominated by women, and remained so. Labour shortages during the Great War had stimulated the hiring of female replacements for males gone to the war, but when the war ended almost all of these reverted to males and males only.

The greatest change was political. Women had been agitating for the vote for years, linking female suffrage with non-partisanship and reform. Manitoba and Saskatchewan gave in first, in 1916, and then it was Borden's turn. The Borden government first enlisted certain classes of women voters for the 1917 election, but the next year granted the federal suffrage to all women over the age of twenty-one, just like men. All the other provinces except Quebec followed suit. Quebec, like France and Switzerland, retained, for provincial purposes, a male-only franchise; this "peculiar institution" would prevail until the next great war swept it away.

There was another political change. Sir Wilfrid Laurier died in February 1919, and the Liberal party held a convention in August to replace him. In his last years Laurier had been a symbol of division for Liberals. Dead, he could be honoured as a symbol of past glory and a benchmark for Liberalism's future aspirations. His successor was Mackenzie King (aged forty-four), who was preferred over the party elders because he, unlike them, had been publicly loyal to Laurier in 1917. Many dissident Liberals returned to the fold in 1919, or, like Borden's minister of agriculture, T.A. Crerar, moved away from Borden's "Union Government" into opposition.

That was especially the case with farmers, or farming members of Parliament. Like labour radicals, farmers called for the recognition and implementation of their own class interests. There was an analogy, certainly, but there the resemblance ends. "United Farmers" governments were formed in Alberta, Manitoba, and Ontario, usually at the expense of the Liberals who until then were the usual harvesters of the agrarian vote. In Ottawa, farmers' representatives coalesced as "Progressives," determined to implement a platform that favoured themselves.[30] That meant lower tariffs, especially on farm equipment, and other concessions to the farming interest. It definitely did not mean labour-friendly policies or anything else that might inhibit the free practice of agriculture, such as the pasteurization of milk merely on the grounds that it might prevent the spread of bovine tuberculosis.

Borden retired before the full blast of the farmers' movement affected national politics. His successor, as of July 1920, was the talented and acerbic minister of the interior, Arthur Meighen. It was easy to admire Meighen's administrative capacity, easy to fear his wit and his ability, and difficult to love him. He wasn't a natural fit as a political leader, for he believed, in the teeth of all current political manifestations, that the old policies that had shaped and governed Canada since the 1870s were actually the best policies. Meighen was a high-tariff man and there was no room in his party for anyone who was even slightly wobbly on the issue. "I was impressed by his eloquence but repelled by his policies," a young Conservative wrote, just before becoming a Liberal.[31]

As often happens in politics, Meighen inherited the resentments generated by his predecessor. Borden had offended many by his efforts to reform traditional politics. Patronage, the elixir of life for Canadian political parties, had been practically abolished, and the politicians hadn't had time to find a substitute. The wartime marriage between Liberals and Conservatives was for many an unnatural union, and there was no time to generate loyalty to Meighen's hybrid government. Conscription was a fresh memory for French Canadians and farmers, dooming government candidates almost before they were heard. Finally, Meighen allowed his own prejudices to run away with his judgment. He had for many years disliked and despised Mackenzie King, whom he'd known at university.

He couldn't believe the electorate would take the shapeless, formless King seriously. And so the results of the election were all the more unbelievable for Meighen, who sat dumbfounded in his office for weeks on end, and had to be nudged by his staff to resign. He had won only 50 out of 235 seats in the House of Commons, while King had got 116. With the help of 64 Progressives, not to mention five independents, King was assured a functioning majority.

POLITICS AND THE ECONOMY IN THE TWENTIES

Mackenzie King had that most useful political attribute: luck. Canada had suffered a sharp economic downturn in 1920–21. Unemployment and economic misery had contributed to Meighen's defeat; a slow recovery would assist King's political prospects.

King was in many respects an American- or British-style Progressive, with all that implied in favouring state responsibility for economic and social policy. Yet one of the controlling factors in King's politics was a deep aversion to deficits and debt. Canada in 1921 had a debt of $3.018 billion, compared with $750 million in 1914. It was the conservative King, not the reforming King, who gnawed away at its fringes during the 1920s. As a percentage of gross national product, though not in absolute terms, the federal debt fell as King's early cabinets, composed largely of politicians senior to him in age and experience, approved a policy that rejected new and dangerous opportunities for expenditure and instead paid down the national debt. Naturally they understood that King must lower some taxes—tariffs on farm machinery for example—in order to buy off the Progressives and corral their support. As a result, most of the time, the Progressives backed the Liberals. As time passed, it became increasingly difficult to distinguish some Progressives from Liberals; never strong on party discipline, the Progressives quarrelled among themselves while their party fractured. In the background, King quietly assisted his most senior ministers to retire and recruited prominent provincial Liberals to take their places.[32]

King was later remembered as a political master, but that wasn't the impression he created in the 1920s. In 1925 his party came close to defeat at the hands of Arthur Meighen and the resurgent Conservatives, but in a Parliament of minorities, King could scrape by with the support of the Progressives and a few Labour members. He won the early votes of confidence in Parliament, watching from the sidelines because he'd gone down to personal defeat in his own constituency and had to wait for his Saskatchewan allies to open up a safe seat for him. At that precise moment a scandal broke out in the Customs department and the revelations proved too much for the minor parties to bear. They deserted King, who promptly went to the governor general, Lord Byng, and asked for a dissolution of Parliament.

Lord Byng, without entirely understanding what he was doing, refused. King resigned, and Byng sent for Meighen to form a government. The problem, politically, was that while the Progressive and Labour members might have been willing to vote against King, they were unwilling to vote for Meighen.[33] Meighen was therefore defeated in the House of Commons, then asked Byng for Parliament to be dissolved, and got his wish.

King did not hesitate to grasp the opportunity of a lifetime. The election issue was simplified to the fact that Byng had given Meighen the dissolution he'd refused to King. It was the People versus the Peer, and it proved a most unequal contest. King, representing the People, won and Meighen, carrying the can for the Peer, lost. Byng soon departed, and Meighen resigned as Conservative leader.

It was Mackenzie King who would preside over Canada's diamond anniversary, in 1927. (The half-century mark actually fell in 1917, which was not considered a good year to celebrate anything.) Everyone came, at least everyone who mattered. From Great Britain there was the glamorous Albert Edward, Prince of Wales, who could then proceed to his Alberta ranch. Prime Minister Stanley Baldwin came too, the first serving British prime minister to visit Canada, "the Britain of the West," in the words of an enthusiastic Canadian bard. Choirs sang, cannons boomed, bands played, and it was all broadcast over the radio, coast to coast. Mackenzie King budgeted $250,000, a very large sum, for the event and himself helped to prepare the ceremony, inserting his Presbyterian sensibilities. (The celebratory booklet was found to be offensive to Catholics, a point that had not occurred to King.)

DIPLOMACY, INTERNAL AND EXTERNAL

King was by profession a labour negotiator. Conciliation came naturally to him, as did compromise and half-measures. "Do nothing by halves that can be done by quarters," a Canadian poet wrote of the prime minister. It was a shrewd assessment, and one that King might even have agreed with. He would have seen quarter measures as contributing to his success, eking out the minimum level of satisfaction for the maximum number of interests across his very diverse country.

His most important task was to find means of conciliating French Canada, and especially the 90 percent of French Canadians who lived in Quebec, where they in turn formed 80 percent of the population. He was visited in his dreams by Sir Wilfrid Laurier, who would periodically reproach him for not learning French. But King did the next best thing: he early acquired a prominent and capable Quebec lieutenant, Ernest Lapointe. Lapointe bridged the gap between the Catholic allegiance of French Quebeckers and liberalism—Catholic enough to satisfy most of the clergy, liberal enough to keep abreast of contemporary political currents.

Certainly Lapointe was more liberal on most issues than the very conservative-minded Liberal premier of Quebec, Louis-Alexandre Taschereau. Lapointe had a better and more natural political touch than Taschereau, the latest representative of a provincial Liberal dynasty first elected in 1897, and who held office as premier from 1920 to 1936. It was to Lapointe and beyond him to Mackenzie King that younger and socially minded Liberals in Quebec looked. "Rouge à Québec, rouge à Ottawa" was the watchword. Strong in themselves, the Liberals had the added benefit of a Conservative opposition discredited by the memory of conscription. Conscription conferred an endless electoral advantage on the Liberals, who ran on the issue whenever they could—which was always. At the same time, the Liberals' exploitation of conscription weakened the old party system in Quebec by turning the Conservatives, the alternative party, into an unelectable rump. But for the time being the political sun shone on Mackenzie King, as it shone on Taschereau.

Ottawa and the provinces shared responsibility for development during the 1920s. It might have seemed that prosperity would mask if not solve jurisdictional quarrels between the federal and provincial levels, but such was not the case. Prosperity there was, if one looks at aggregate figures. Canada's gross national product increased steadily after 1921, spurred by an export boom, up from an estimated $3.5 billion in 1921 to $6.1 billion in 1929. Canadian governments, federal and provincial, applauded and did what they could. They didn't much care that the exports were going to the United States, for the most part, and that Britain's share of Canada's trade was declining. So was British investment in Canada, both because Britain had less available capital to export, and because British investors lost heavily in the crash of the Grand Trunk and Canadian Northern railways.

Pulp and paper, minerals, and wheat led the boom, encouraged by provincial trade restrictions that demanded processed rather than raw exports. As a result, pulp-and-paper production moved north of the border from the United States; American threats of retaliation did little to arrest the process. The federal government saw a golden opportunity to expand wheat acreage and accommodate veterans, who got very favourable terms for their acreage and easy loans to begin farming. Settlement spread into marginal areas on the prairies, to the parklands in the north and to the arid Palliser's Triangle in the south, which had been previously considered fit only for ranching. Wheat acreage and wheat production grew, until in 1928 Saskatchewan harvested a record 321 million bushels. Railways built branch lines to bring grains and minerals and paper to market. New power projects were constructed to bolster electricity supplies to mines and mills, and to Canada's expanding cities.

As far as Mackenzie King was concerned, prosperity encouraged trouble. The Prairie provinces gained confidence during the decade, and became more and more impatient with the fact that the federal government retained control over crown lands and settlement, and their revenues. They demanded that it surrender the lands, and the resources and revenues derived from them, and they were supported by the older provinces, especially Ontario and Quebec.

Ontario was in a state of jurisdictional war with the federal government, as it had been virtually since Confederation. Governed first by the Conservatives (1905–19), then the United Farmers (1919–23), and then by the Conservatives again (1923–34), its government had little in common with Mackenzie King, who couldn't even get elected in his native province. The Maritime provinces, more reliably Liberal, had their own discontents: they were stuck in an economic slump through the 1920s, and they wanted help from Ottawa.

All the provinces, except perhaps Quebec, faced a real revenue problem. They had highways and schools and hospitals to build, welfare obligations in times of recession or depression, and limited tax resources. Like other North American jurisdictions, they found a gasoline tax a new and lucrative well of money, but what they made on the gas tax would be spent on the highways. Morality, too, had a price, as far as the provinces were concerned. Prohibition might be well and good, but liquor taxes soothed most political consciences. Sin turned out to be profitable, and not only for the sinners. But even with gas and booze, the richest and most diversified province, Ontario, ran regular deficits and borrowed to pay its way.[34]

Conservative Ontario and Liberal Quebec wanted the same thing from Mackenzie King: money, an objective shared with all the other provinces. Ontario led the demand that Ottawa vacate the income tax field that it had invaded in 1917.[35] Ottawa refused. There was a billion-dollar debt from the war, and the federal government had to carry it alone. There followed endless, fractious negotiations. The federal government had hopes of its own, securing a means to amend the Canadian constitution, the British North America Act, inside Canada. That was the last thing on the provinces' mind, and ultimately neither King nor Lapointe, by then his justice minister, could devise an acceptable formula.

In the end King gave the provinces what they would settle for. The Prairies got their natural resources, like any other provinces, plus some additional subsidies. Ontario and Quebec were appeased with concessions over water power. The Maritimes got a royal commission, ventilation of their grievances, some fiddling with the Interprovincial Railway, and more subsidies.

Mackenzie King had more than the usual rhetorical reasons for desiring a formula to amend the constitution. He knew that changes were coming in Canada's external standing. The British in 1926 conceded effective independence to the dominions, and they promised to match the principle with formal legislation.

This was a major change from the situation as Borden had left it in 1920. Resolution IX of the Imperial War Conference of 1917 had provided for equality among the nations of the British Empire, but had also promised a great constitutional conference after the end of the war, with no commitment as to the outcome of that conference. Canada did, it's true, become a separate member of the League of Nations along with Australia, New Zealand, South Africa, and India (though India was hardly independent from Britain). In general terms, the Canadian delegation to the League cooperated with its British counterpart, but received its instructions not from London, but from Ottawa.

The Unionist Borden and Meighen governments nevertheless tried as best they could to place Canada within a common Imperial foreign policy. That suited their understanding of Canada's traditions, and they believed as well that Canada would have a greater voice internationally if it acted as part of a great imperial power rather than as an ex-colony isolated north of the United States in an unfamiliar hemisphere. Their policy was put to the test in an Imperial Conference in 1921. The British prime minister was still Lloyd George, and his government, like Meighen's, was an uneasy continuation of his wartime coalition. Lloyd George wanted the Imperial Conference to ratify his decision to continue Britain's alliance with Japan, which was due to expire. Such a decision meant much to Australia and New Zealand, which needed the protection the alliance could give, and it would relieve Britain of some of the expense of protecting the Pacific dominions. But in taking this decision, Lloyd George ignored signs of hostility in the United States, whose government asked, reasonably enough, against whom the Anglo-Japanese alliance could be directed, now that the German navy was at the bottom of the ocean. Canada was the part of the empire closest to the United States, and the most exposed to American wrath.

The Imperial Conference produced a clash between two imperial strategies—Canada's, promoting harmony with the United States above all else; and Lloyd George's (and Australia's), arguing that a rational appraisal of the empire's defence needs must take into account the danger of offending Japan. Meighen told the conference plainly that Canada could not and would not accept a policy that offended the United States. At first Lloyd George stuck to his guns. Let the Canadians go, if they must.

But Lloyd George's position was more the product of folly and misinformation than of principle. He did not believe that the Americans were actually irritated. When, very belatedly, he learned that they were (and that Meighen had been right all along), he executed a 180-degree turn. The Anglo-Japanese alliance was put on hold, and the British Empire agreed to a naval conference with the United States and other interested powers in Washington. After that conference, in 1922, the Anglo-Japanese alliance was no more, replaced by a multilateral naval disarmament pact and agreements for specific disarmament around the Pacific Ocean. Australia had to be content with the result; Canada certainly was.

By the end of the Washington conference there was a new government in Ottawa. Mackenzie King hadn't experienced imperial solidarity during the war; unlike Borden, he saw the war primarily as divisive at home, though he certainly had no intention of calling into question the sacrifices Canadians had made to win it. King inherited Laurier's distrust of imperial scheming, although—also like Laurier—he didn't doubt that Canada's identity was primarily British. But being British had limits, which King early on explored when Lloyd George attempted to drag the empire into an ill-conceived war with Turkey in October 1922—called the Chanak incident after its geographical focus. Chanak ruined Lloyd George, and destroyed his government. There was no war with Turkey, but if there had been, King made it clear, in public, that Canada would not be an automatic participant.

King explained his views to the new British prime minister, the Conservative Stanley Baldwin, at an Imperial Conference in 1923. If, he said, "a great and clear call of duty" came, then Canada would be at Britain's side, as in 1914. Chanak hadn't been such a call, and by extension no other minor imperial adventure qualified either.

He reinforced his position by appointing as his senior civil-service adviser the very nationalistic dean of arts of Queen's University, Dr. O.D. Skelton. Skelton shared King's tendencies toward Canadian isolation, which during the 1920s were in the ascendant. He hoped that in a peaceful decade the "great and clear call of duty" would not put King's Anglo-Victorian traditionalism to the test.

King and Skelton were lucky. The British foreign secretary, Lord Curzon, had no intention of conducting "an imperial foreign policy" if that meant he had to consult the dominions about British foreign plans. The dominions could put up or shut up. Since King chose to put up resistance, he could be written out of British policy, and under the guidance of Curzon and his successors, Canada and any other reluctant dominions were written out of British treaties. Canada could join if it wished, but it didn't have to. In the future as in the past, Britain would inform but not consult the empire; and in the meantime Britain, like Canada, would trust to luck.

The culmination of this process was reached in another Imperial Conference in 1926. That conference formally recognized, through a report presented by a respected ex–prime minister, Lord Balfour, the complete autonomy of the British dominions. Balfour's report also recognized that the dominions chose to continue as members of the British

Commonwealth, a term that was taking the place of "the Empire," and that they were bound together by a common allegiance to the crown.

Mackenzie King was quite satisfied. He invoked, as he frequently did, the memory of his grandfather, the rebel William Lyon Mackenzie, smiling down in King's vivid dreams on Canadian autonomy. King in fact loved the pageantry of monarchy, and remained British to the core. For the Canadian prime minister, the notion that Canada was "the Britain of the West" was no anachronism, but a deeply felt defining characteristic of Canada's identity.

There remained details to be wrapped up. Discussions among the members of the new Commonwealth in the late 1920s led to another Imperial Conference in 1930. That conference put the finishing touches on a new constitution for the self-governing empire—the Statute of Westminster passed by the British Parliament in 1931.

By the Statute of Westminster the British Parliament renounced forever its right to legislate for the empire. The self-governing dominions were henceforth completely self-sufficient, legally and constitutionally— with a couple of notable exceptions. First, the right of appeal to what was effectively the imperial supreme court, the Judicial Committee of the Privy Council, continued unless and until abolished. Second, the Statute recognized that the components of the Canadian federation, the federal government and those of the provinces, could not agree on how to amend the Canadian constitution. Yet the constitution did need to be amended from time to time, and against that eventuality the Statute continued the power of the British Parliament to amend the British North America Act.

Canada thus entered on its autonomous—its independent—existence a qualified country. It could take any necessary political decisions; it could exercise its own jurisdiction over whatever Canadian subject it chose—as long as it fell on the right side of the division of powers, federal and provincial, in the British North America Act. Perhaps it was fortunate that by the time the Statute of Westminster took effect, Canadians had something else to worry about. It was, after all, the second year of the Great Depression.

12

UNFRIENDLY WORLDS, 1930~1945

Mackenzie King (top) and Ernest Lapointe address the Canadian public.
These caricatures are by the pre-eminent cartoonist Robert La Palme.

In 1931, through the Statute of Westminster, Canada became sovereign to all intents and purposes. Not much changed as a result. Canada might be a sovereign state, but it was one among many. If Canada had a special identity, it was as a part of the British Commonwealth, linked to Great Britain by tradition and trade. All parts of Canada flew the Union Jack, although on festive religious holidays Quebec also flew the yellow and white papal banner.

One of Canada's most important identifiers, the Royal Canadian Mounted Police, the "Mounties," wore British red in their dress uniforms and, of course, in movies, for the American film industry was fond of the force. Canadians in turn appreciatively watched Hollywood's regurgitation of a version of a Canada composed mostly of ice, snow, and trees and populated on the criminal side by mad trappers and claim-jumpers instead of the standard movie-issue bootleggers and gangsters.[1]

The gangsters, of course, belonged in the United States as far as most Canadians were concerned. Canada did have its own bootleggers and gangsters, but they never achieved the level of notoriety of the American Al Capone or John Dillinger. No one knew what the RCMP would do if confronted by a Dillinger; the Mounties were too busy acting as provincial police, or keeping an eye on radicals and communists.

Radicals and communists were the other part of the iconography of the 1930s. They were often presented to the public as aliens, speaking with thick accents and displaying dubious standards of hygiene. They preyed on innocent citizens, deceiving them into disaffection or even disloyalty toward Canadian institutions. The cardboard radicals were at least a little closer to reality than the cinematic Mounties, though there was a connection to the national police force. The Mounties dealt with a world of primary products, furs and gold and sometimes timber—what economists then and later dubbed "staples." Their main task was to prevent people from stealing these valuable items, and on the grand scale they were doubtless right to do so. Furs, gold, and trees were major components of the Canadian economy, to which could be added wheat and other grains, and a sprinkling of base metals. Canada's exports—its staples—consisted largely of such commodities, dug up, chopped, and piled or baled.

There were other exports too, though, and different kinds of workers to produce them. In fact, compared with the populations in other Western countries—especially the United States—the Canadian workforce was regrettably prosaic. It lived for the most part in cities, worked in factories—or didn't work, for in the 1930s the economy took its most serious and prolonged downturn in living memory. It was the downturn that helped make the 1930s a decade of crisis—"the Dirty Thirties" of popular memory. The poet W.H. Auden called it "the low, dishonest decade," but Auden was referring to something besides unemployment, welfare, and discouragement. He meant the desperate efforts of democratic politicians to cope with a situation for which they had no training, no signposts, and no policies. Lacking real policies to deal with the crisis, they pretended to have them. The voters, for their part, had to believe them, for to do otherwise was to lose faith in society and the way in which society was organized. And so, in Canada and in many other countries, the 1930s was not a revolutionary spasm, but a rather conservative decade. In Canada this was symbolized by the politician of the *longue durée*, Mackenzie King, in office in 1930, and still (or rather again) in office in 1940.

Canadian politics are often taken to be a parochial affair, a collection of neighbourhood issues and minor personalities whose sum total demonstrates that, in the words of Tip O'Neill, "all politics is local," meaning that all politics is limited. That was sometimes true, but it was definitely not the case in the 1930s.

Canadians had an alternative politics, brought to them by the newspapers, by movies and especially movie newsreels, if they could afford to view them, and over the radio. They knew that the Depression extended far beyond Canada, that the Americans had it, and that it existed in Britain and Europe. In Britain there were hunger marches, political crises, and a "National Government," a coalition of patriotic politicians dominated, as during the Great War, by Conservatives. In Germany the Depression undermined democracy and spawned a dictator, Adolf Hitler. Hitler shrieked from the newsreels in front of ominously uniformed crowds, first carrying shovels and later rifles. It was meant to impress, and it did, but Germany was, after all, a very long way away.

Closer to home, and to reality as Canadians saw it, were Franklin Delano Roosevelt, president of the United States, and his New Deal. Roosevelt told Americans that they had "nothing to fear but fear itself" when he took office in March 1933. He spoke at the depth of the Depression, when American national income had shrunk by half since 1929 and a quarter of the workforce or more were unemployed. Canadians could empathize with that—for the same things were true in Canada. They listened attentively to Roosevelt's exhortations, and compared them with the barking speeches of Canada's own prime minister, Richard Bedford Bennett—"R.B."

OLD NOSTRUMS, NEW FAILURES

Bennett was a prisoner of his own limitations. An able lawyer, a masterful administrator, and a highly intelligent egotist, he liked to personalize his policies. "I will blast a way into the markets of the world," he told the electors during the 1930 federal election. That resonated with his audience. They, like Bennett, understood that Canada must export or die, that prosperity came from Canadians producing abundance at home and selling that abundance abroad. It was a call to the staples theory—though it's doubtful whether Bennett or his listeners or anybody other than a few academics had ever heard, much less used, the term. But the staples theory embodied what most Canadians understood about their country: that it was dependent on other people buying their exports. No exports, no money, no job—this they also understood.

So Bennett's promise of blasting a way into the markets of the world offered hope, and hope bought votes. In what was essentially a two-party contest, his Conservatives won 48.5 percent of the vote to the Liberals' 45.2 percent, and 137 seats in the House of Commons compared with the Liberals' 91.[2]

Mackenzie King hadn't expected to lose the election; he resentfully vacated his office and retired to his country home, Kingsmere, north of Ottawa, to await events. Bennett was the one, therefore, who had to confront a problem so far beyond his imagining that it would undermine his health, his government, and his career. Canadians' choice of political leadership in 1930 meant that it was the Conservatives who would offer the first solutions for the Depression.

Of course, in 1930 no one called it that. There was an economic slump, certainly. There was a decline in the market and price for wheat, and for pulp and paper. The gross national income for 1930 was markedly lower—7 percent down—than that for 1929. It was still higher than 1927 though, a good year. Surely there was cause for confidence, if not exactly abounding optimism.

Yet the downward trend continued. The year 1931 was worse than 1930, and 1932 worse than 1931. Bennett raised Canada's tariffs, the first step in his "blasting" program, with the idea that he could then bargain them away for concessions in other countries' tariff schedules. It was an unfortunate strategy, because every other country was trying the same thing. The result was slowly to strangle what was left of international trade. Bennett's blaster turned out to be a popgun.

The prime minister could argue that he needed the revenue increased tariffs produced—though on a diminished flow of goods—because he had to pay for the costs of unemployment. But technically, as Bennett knew, he didn't have to. A British judge had once compared the federal–provincial division of powers in Canada's constitution to watertight

compartments on an ocean liner. The purpose of watertight compartments, the judge didn't need to add, was to keep the ship afloat.

The 1920s had already shown that the provinces were struggling with
inadequate revenues. Their solution was to borrow, and to count on an
expanding economy to keep their finances buoyant. So when the economy
started to contract the provinces couldn't cope—at least not for very long.
Their problems were multiplied by those of their junior governments, the
municipalities. Towns and cities were exclusively a provincial responsibility, and the provinces allowed them to raise their own revenues through
property taxes, income taxes, and sales taxes. The municipalities found
that issuing bonds was a good way to bring in the money to build schools
and roads and sewers during the 1920s, and like the provinces they relied
on continuing prosperity.

Municipalities weren't the only institutions who gave hostages to
fortune. In the Prairies, farmers embittered by struggles with the railways
and private grain dealers had formed "pools" to manage their multi-
million-bushel harvest. The federal government had established a compulsory pool during the Great War—the Board of Grain Supervisors, later the
Canadian Wheat Board—but abandoned the experiment at war's end.
The later pools, one per province, were voluntary, but together they
controlled about 60 percent of the Canadian wheat crop.[3] The pools tried
to bring regularity and predictability to the uncertain craft of farming:
they advanced their farmer-members money based on the size of their
crops, then sold the grain to recoup, settling up later when it was sold and
the money was in. It all depended on the international market price,
which during most of the 1920s was rising.

In 1929 the price fell and the pools were caught short. Unnerved, the
three provincial governments bailed them out, but in 1930 the situation
didn't improve. Low prices now combined with the beginnings of drought
in Palliser's Triangle. It was Ottawa's turn, for a sum determined by the
flinty R.B. Bennett (ironically, a Calgary MP). Bennett paid, but at the
price of taking over wheat marketing. The pools were relegated to being
collectors of grain from the local elevators that dotted the prairies and fed

into larger ones at Canada's grain-shipping ports.[4] Prices continued to fall and the drought worsened. By the mid-1930s the land was taking flight as hot winds blew the soil across the prairie. Observers as far away as Winnipeg, on the eastern edge of the prairie, saw the sky darken to the west. Farms were abandoned and their families fled. Those who were left suffered poverty and deprivation of a kind not seen in the settled parts of Canada since the previous century. (Poverty and deprivation were all too frequent, though, on Canada's Indian reserves.)

The disaster overtaking the pools soon caught up with the provincial Prairie governments. They were already heavily indebted; now, to provide welfare for the unemployed and destitute, they had to borrow again. City finances, too, dried up. Taxpayers couldn't pay, and although cities could foreclose their properties, the defaults were so widespread that property sales couldn't hope to keep up with city debts. The banks became alarmed.

They were alarmed even in diversified and relatively more prosperous Ontario, where farmers were in desperate straits and where the pulp and paper industry was entering the long night of Depression. Idle factories exemplified the waste people perceived—trained workers, modern plants, and no money. Parts of the countryside in Ontario and elsewhere re-entered a barter economy, paying for services—medicine, for example—in chickens or milk, which the service providers—doctors, for example—were happy to receive. The Canadian Medical Association began to print articles on socialized medicine for its members to read and ponder. Some things might be better than the market.

Even Prime Minister Bennett had to admit concern. Bennett specialized in public unpleasantness—he had "the manners of a Chicago gangster," one British politician reported—but there was only so much humiliation he could dole out to his wretched provincial colleagues. Thanks to Mackenzie King's unimaginative fiscal management during the 1920s, the federal government was the most solvent in Canada. Bennett knew that if any other significant government failed—went bankrupt—it would affect Ottawa's own credit. He could not be indifferent to the plight of the provinces. Small cities might go bankrupt—and some did: Windsor and Saskatoon, to name only two—but not Toronto or Montreal. Some provincial governments were kept afloat, making payments to their bond-holders, only with money from Ottawa. If the subsidy tap were ever turned off, four or five of the nine provinces would face bankruptcy.

The struggle over subsidy consumed Bennett's domestic policy over his five years in office. His external policy was a distinctly secondary consideration, even though initially he'd made trade and trade policy the centre-piece of his election promises. Circumstances did allow the prime minister one accomplishment in trade. Fortuitously, Great Britain had reached the end of its tether with free trade. The pound had been forced off the gold standard and British trade was suffering from the high tariffs imposed by other, non-believing nations in defiance of the logic and dogma of free trade. The British government—the National Government—had to take action and, after crushing its opposition in an election in 1931, it did. It would impose tariffs. Temporarily, the dominions were exempt, since a system of imperial tariff preferences was anticipated. There would be an Imperial Economic Conference that would regulate the conditions of trade inside the Empire-Commonwealth. It would meet in Ottawa in July 1932.

The time and venue for the Ottawa conference were unfortunate. Only one room was large enough in the Canadian capital to accommodate the delegates from all over the empire—the House of Commons, in the recently restored Centre Block of the Parliament Buildings. The Commons chamber wasn't set up for cooperation: its forte was confrontation and its design matched its function. Worse, nobody seems to have taken Ottawa's climate into account; in July the capital is typically very hot and very steamy.

Tempers flared, especially between the British and Bennett, as the British delegation discovered that while Bennett believed in imperial economic unity, he thought it was somebody else's job to pay for it. Canada already gave Britain a reduced tariff; it was up to the British and the other delegations to find the means to match it. The result was a series of agreements, bilateral in form, in which the various parts of the empire favoured one another in terms of trade. Despite their unpleasant origin in Bennett's pressure cooker, the "Ottawa Agreements" were extensive and had a considerable effect. To take one example, automobiles, Canada could export on favourable terms all over the empire. The "Big Three" American automobile companies, Ford, General Motors, and Chrysler, already had plants in Canada, and now they expanded them. For years thereafter Canadian-made Fords and Chevrolets roamed the byways of the empire, testimony to the efficacy of the great (and last) Imperial tariff.

The Ottawa Agreements, like other Canadian tariffs, had the effect of encouraging American investment in Canada. They also impressed the American government—not by themselves, but in conjunction with the single greatest economic catastrophe to hit the United States as far back as anyone could remember. Seeking a reason for the severity and duration of the Depression, Americans found it in the United States itself—or rather in the U.S. Congress.

Congressional power over trade was a fact of life for all countries trading with the United States, none more so than Canada. Congressional tariffs in the 1890s, 1900s, and 1920s had regularly scythed Canadian exports. The most recent, called Smoot-Hawley after its sponsors, was more of the same. Canada had its own high-tariff policy, of course, though it allowed lower rates to countries who had signed trade agreements. There was no functioning agreement with the United States, to be sure, and hadn't been since the expiry of the Reciprocity Treaty of 1854–66. (Canada wasn't alone in this: in the 150 years of the United States' existence it had ratified only three trade agreements with other countries, so jealously did Congress guard American sovereignty.) So the United States faced not merely high but higher tariffs exporting to Canada. The Ottawa Agreements seemed to say to the United States that the countries of the empire would get along without them.

The American explanation for this was "We made them do it." There was some truth in this, though there were certainly other factors and other explanations to be considered. To undo the damage required an expression of American good faith, if not repentance, and this was formulated in an early enactment of the Roosevelt administration, the Trade Agreements Act of 1934. The Act stipulated, for the first time, that the executive might make trade agreements with other countries, trading reductions (reciprocity) in tariffs for up to half the existing level of U.S. duties.

R.B. Bennett leapt at the opportunity. His negotiators laboured through 1935 to reach an agreement, and it was at hand when the five-year term of the Canadian Parliament expired and Bennett very reluctantly had to face a general election. He knew that Canadians in 1934–35 viewed the United States very favourably indeed, not merely as a rich trading partner but as a model for what should be done more generally about resolving the Great Depression.

Franklin Roosevelt's "New Deal" had the great virtue of promising action. It spent public money, sometimes lavishly, on internal improvements. It sought to appeal to the "Forgotten Man." It mattered not at all that the New Deal's activities were sometimes contradictory, sometimes ineffective. The impression on the public—including especially the Canadian public—was of action and concern. The Depression disarmed and discredited Roosevelt's enemies, the erstwhile leaders of business and their political friends. Roosevelt regularly took to the air waves and gave the nation "Fireside Chats." The Chats reached Canada too.

Bennett got the message. To their amazement, in the winter of 1935 Canadians heard their prime minister rasping on the radio proclaiming a New Deal of his own. He would establish labour standards, he would legislate fair treatment for all, and he would use his government's power on behalf of the unfortunate. In the spring session of Parliament, he did so.

Mackenzie King's reaction is instructive. King believed, or so he told his diary, that Bennett had gone mad. If he hadn't gone mad, then he'd become a fascist, like Hitler or the Italian dictator Mussolini. They, too, promised forceful action on behalf of the downtrodden, and to a traditional liberal like King this was the stuff of tyranny. King didn't share Bennett's new-found enthusiasm for Roosevelt or the New Deal. He had no proposals of his own, but that made no difference. He sat back and watched Bennett cook his own goose, counting on the suddenness of Bennett's conversion to social action to undermine his established reputation for ruthless conservatism.

The Liberals ran in the general election of 1935 under the slogan "It's King or Chaos." It didn't take much imagination to establish who Chaos was—certainly not soft, pudgy, familiar Mackenzie King. King won the election handily, though with a lower percentage of the popular vote than he had got in 1930. It was the collapse of the Conservative vote, to an unheard-of 29 percent, that gave King the victory. Two new parties also picked up seats in 1935: Social Credit, centred in discontented and impoverished Alberta, and the Co-operative Commonwealth Federation (CCF hereafter), a socialist party that was strongest on the Prairies.[5]

King and Chaos

King was, as we have noted, a very lucky politician. By the time he came to power, economic conditions were improving. Things were desperate on the Prairies, but Ontario and Quebec, with their diversified economies, weren't doing too badly. There was still a crisis in provincial finance, meaning further bailouts of the provinces, which King managed in the same grudging and parsimonious spirit as his predecessor. But Bennett had already borne the burden of the Depression. Their resentment largely discharged, Canadians mostly didn't blame King. That was just as well, for King had absolutely no idea how to fix the Depression, and it may have made matters worse that he was a trained economist, for orthodox economics had no solution to offer.

King did, however, sign a Reciprocal Trade Agreement with President Roosevelt—the one Bennett had negotiated. He then defended Canada's position in triangular trade talks among the British, Canadians, and Americans in 1937–38. Believing that the British would look after their own interests first, and Canada's a long way after, he insisted on compensation for any British concessions to the United States.

In dealing with the British and the Americans King was on familiar ground. He had spent time in both countries, and had a Ph.D. from Harvard. He'd been at Harvard at roughly the same time as Roosevelt, and the two men immediately invented a past that would justify their present official friendship. In a curious way King and Roosevelt were actually friendly. King had a range of acceptable social acquaintances, and was cautious and discreet. Best of all, the prime minister was careful not to make too many demands of the president, but when he did Roosevelt listened. Roosevelt even favoured King with political advice. Noting King's difficulties in balancing French and English Canada, Roosevelt advised him to assimilate the French Canadians as quickly as possible. It was working in the United States, where there was a large French-Canadian population centred in New England; it should work in Canada too.[6] King made no recorded reply.

Roosevelt was right to grasp that King spent much time managing relations between English and French Canadians. During the 1920s King depended absolutely on Quebec to produce Liberal pluralities in Parliament. Ernest Lapointe, his Quebec lieutenant, led a strong Quebec Liberal delegation into Parliament and into the cabinet in 1935. King relied on Lapointe, and the evidence suggests that, even when he didn't sympathize with or even perhaps understand Lapointe's arguments, he would accept them, such was his faith in his lieutenant's judgment.

Lapointe knew that parts of Quebec were hard hit by the Depression, and that a great deal of social and political ferment was brewing in the province. The political direction signs in Quebec pointed right, not left, as on the Prairies. Lapointe, a man of somewhat liberal tastes, deplored the drift, but he concluded that, to keep Quebec relatively calm and cooperative inside Canada, he must work with Quebec as it was and not as he would like it to be. He sensed, and King knew, that the international situation was volatile and potentially very dangerous. A general war was a possibility, and if one occurred it would be hard to keep Canada out of it.

The Great War was an ever-present memory for Lapointe, and for King. It hadn't had good press in Quebec, and if possible conscription was a livelier issue in 1935 or 1936 than it had been in 1917 or 1918. It's plain that Lapointe feared, though he didn't explicitly say so, that if another war came Quebec might not cooperate—or worse.

The rightward drift in Quebec wasn't universal, but it's probably true to say that in the 1930s the French-speaking part of the province was very nearly self-enclosed, apart from the dealings of a small political and business elite at the top and plentiful but inconsequential contacts among ordinary English and French Canadians. In parts of the province the English created management garrisons in company towns, with their own clubs, schools, and even golf courses, plunked down in a world where French Canadians couldn't rise above the level of foreman in the plant.[7] Westmount, the city on the hill above Montreal, dreamed its own dreams and lived its own, almost entirely English life, whether one was a socialist or the deepest Tory.

Nationalists especially lived in a world of their own. François Hertel wrote in 1936 of "a federal government with Protestant inclinations; the supreme domination of a Protestant empire; the radio, which has become a broadcaster of Protestantism; the cinema, a carrier of immorality; our French press itself which, for the most part, is Catholic in name only."[8] When a young and well-connected French Canadian, André Laurendeau, wanted to investigate the English, their views and their habits, he realized he didn't know any of the hundreds of thousands of English speakers who lived within a few kilometres of his own house.

The stereotypical French Canadian of the period, the one to be found in representative fiction, is put upon when not downtrodden, and the English, though not generally malignant, were also stereotyped as insensitive and uncaring. This is not to say that there weren't wealthy or privileged French Canadians who were anything but downtrodden, or that some regions such as Quebec City were run without much need of reference to the English. The phenomenon speaks to self-image, and such a self-image was not the stuff of cooperation or fellow feeling with the English majority in Canada.

Not all the English speakers were *Anglais*. There were also *les Juifs*, the Jews. They were seen by the French as distinct from the English—English-

Canadian anti-Semitism made sure of that, with quotas for admission of Jews to McGill University among other disabling considerations. Jews were also seen as clever, able, and vulnerable, for many of them, as recent immigrants, were still humbly employed—shopkeepers, rag merchants, or ordinary workers alongside their French-Canadian counterparts. Against the Jews was directed the *achat chez nous* movement of the 1930s, urging French Canadians to patronize their own stores and not those of the alien. And yet, paradoxically, there was a sense that the Jewish merchant was a better businessman than the French Canadian.

The Liberal party was the great beneficiary of immigrant votes in Canada. The Liberals had supported immigration, or were thought to have supported it. The great influx of immigrants to Canada, and Montreal, came during Laurier's time, and it transformed the centre of Montreal. The immigrants supported Mackenzie King and Lapointe federally, and Taschereau provincially. One Jewish member of the Quebec legislature, naturally a Liberal, collected more than 100 percent of some polls in his riding, a fact that was duly noticed and denounced by the "bon" newspaper in Montreal, *Le Devoir*.

But the Taschereau government was old and corrupt and crumbling. In 1935 Taschereau lost most of the promising younger members of his Liberal party, and almost lost an election. The premier didn't know how to cope, and an atmosphere of *sauve qui peut* overcame his cabinet and his caucus. The government disintegrated under the prodding of an alert and pitiless leader of the official Conservative opposition, Maurice Duplessis. Taschereau resigned in May 1936, as crowds surged around the legislature. "La foule conspue Taschereau et les Juifs," *Le Devoir* reported.[9]

In August 1936 the Liberals were swept from power in Quebec. It's easy to concentrate on the Liberal defeat, but the Liberal party survived the election, though with a narrower, more urban political base than in the past. What was really important about the political events of that year was the disappearance of the provincial Conservative party, and its absorption into a new political formation, the Union Nationale. "Nationale" didn't really mean "national" in English, though that was the official translation;

it referred and was understood to refer to the French-Canadian nation.[10] It was that fact that worried Lapointe, for if the Union Nationale was allowed to consolidate its grasp on power it would rival not the provincial Liberals in Quebec City but the Mackenzie King Liberals in Ottawa, and by extension the whole system of political accommodation on which Ottawa's politics was founded.[11] Premier Duplessis understood the point well. An accomplished orator and an equally skilful demagogue, Duplessis was determined to stay in power come what may. The Ottawa Liberals accurately appraised his willingness to extend the bounds of what was permissible in politics. Should he do so, they were anxious that he should lose.

All this had political consequences. It meant that the Liberal government hesitated to make decisions that might aggravate the situation in Quebec. "National unity"—meaning, this time, Canadian unity—became King's watchword. It had a particular meaning for the Jews: frightened by the *nationalistes'* willingness to exploit the Liberals' links with the Jewish population of Quebec, King and Lapointe drew back from any action— admitting Jewish refugees—that could reinforce that connection in the minds of the electorate.[12]

What did "national unity" mean? How was it put into practice? King was as likely to act by omission as by commission—he created the illusion of calm waters by steering around storms, avoiding debate, and (his specialty) shrouding controversies in a fog of vague words.[13] His favourite formula was "Parliament will decide," a phrase mockingly echoed by his critics.[14] There was a paradox here: King prided himself on his democratic roots, as the grandson of William Lyon Mackenzie, that tribune of the people. But King had experienced the vagaries of public opinion, losing personally in the 1911 election and again in 1925, and watching Canada convulsed by ethnic and provincial hatred in 1917. These were lasting impressions.

King paid unusual attention to public opinion, as far as he could. It was the hallmark of the good politician to divine what people were thinking, since there were no opinion polls to shape the political art. The rash politician presumed that if he was right, the public would follow. That was Meighen's style, which King despised. Instead, the prime minister rightly feared what public opinion might say, the more so because he realized that several publics existed in Canada, whose views were, sadly, contradictory. That was a problem to be managed and shaped, cautiously and slowly— or as slowly as events outside King's control allowed.

THE COMPLICATED POLITICS OF APPEASEMENT

Time hadn't healed all wounds between English and French Canada. The situation in the late 1930s was more volatile than it had been before 1914 on the French-Canadian side, and somewhat less so on the English Canadian. The French side was a spectrum, from a minuscule leftist fringe, denounced by the Church and shunned by most of society, through moderate liberal, still small, through a large clerical-conservative majority, until finally there was another fringe on the right. Nationalism was superimposed on this spectrum, but while it was probably true that most on the right were nationalist in some sense, the very furthest right, the fascist followers of the Parti National Social Chrétien, were in fact pan-Canadian, joined to far-right-wing English Canadians by anti-Semitism.[15]

The English-Canadian counterpart to French-Canadian nationalism was imperialism. In the absence of public opinion sampling—the first "scientific" polls didn't appear in Canada until after 1939—we must rely on the guesswork of observers, including the politicians. The politicians and their associates, journalists and civil servants, certainly believed that imperialism was alive and well. Dr. O.D. Skelton, a political scientist by training before he became undersecretary for external affairs (1925–41), hoped that death would solve the problem, as the older generation passed away with its political beliefs. Dr. Skelton himself believed that Canada wouldn't survive another bout of imperial warfare along the lines of the Great War, but even he was obliged to admit the importance of Canadians' British attachment as a political factor.

Skelton wasn't opposed to imperialism alone, but to any kind of international activism. Some Canadians put their faith in "collective security" and the League of Nations, hoping and expecting that the nations that had signed the League's founding document, the Covenant, would honour their promises to join in the fight against international aggression, should any occur. There was a League of Nations Society with thousands of members which sought to pressure the Canadian government to do the right thing and support the League. Skelton regarded them as a nuisance, though not especially dangerous. League supporters were found among all the federal political parties, but they were never distributed or configured in a way to guarantee the allegiance of any party. Enthusiasts for foreign policy discovered that the Canadian electorate and the politicians who guided it thought in terms of a multiplicity of issues, and that foreign affairs as such were seldom crucial in the public mind.

What was crucial was the economy. There was too little money, too little work, too many jobless, too few employed. These considerations affected two foreign policy–related issues, trade and immigration. Politicians and economists were agreed that prosperity would revive only with trade; where they disagreed, or threw up their hands in despair, was how trade could be revived. As for immigration and immigrants, the country didn't want any more. The police scoured the backstreets for radical immigrants who could be deported, and were. No more need apply.

Anti-immigrant sentiment reinforced the views of Canada's director of immigration in the 1930s, Fred Blair. Blair was indeed an anti-Semite, and he held his office just as Hitler began his campaign to persecute the Jews of Germany. Jewish refugees could go somewhere else as far as Blair was concerned. He was certain that no politician would publicly advocate the admission of refugee Jews to Canada, and he was right.[16]

Mackenzie King had other reasons for hesitation about foreign policy issues. A generation of sceptical commentators had dissected the reasons for the outbreak of the Great War. The confidence that Britain's cause was just and right wasn't quite as firm as it once had been. In the United States a congressional committee was examining, with the fullest publicity,

whether the war hadn't been a conspiracy of bankers and munitions-
makers. King himself doesn't seem to have been influenced by these spec-
ulations, but Canadian opinion wasn't impervious to waftings from the
United States, and there was some support for the notion that North
America was qualitatively different from Europe, and ought to remain
aloof—isolated—from European machinations.

King did his best to avoid a crisis over foreign policy. He repudiated
his own envoy to the League of Nations when the latter tried to make the
League's regime of sanctions work to arrest and reverse Italy's invasion of
Ethiopia in 1935. Canadian opinion was divided on the issue, along
linguistic and religious lines, a clear signal to the prime minister that
Canada must avoid involvement. A similar division occurred the next
year, when right-wing, monarchist, and Catholic forces began a civil war
in Spain against a secular and socialist republican government. Canadians
disagreed on the rights and wrongs of the question, again along racial and
religious lines; and again King drew back, refusing to take a position
except to urge Canadians not to become overtly involved. Despite his
warnings, some did, fighting for the Spanish republic in the "Mackenzie-
Papineau battalion." There is no sign that King was moved by the invoca-
tion of his revolutionary grandfather's name.

King visited Europe several times in 1936 and 1937, and became a
regular caller at the White House, where in this period he was the most
frequent foreign visitor. King called on Roosevelt before attending an
Imperial Conference in London in 1937, but Roosevelt, trapped by his
own isolationist public opinion, was unable to offer any aid or promise of
aid to the British, who were increasingly worried by the rise of Nazi
Germany and the defection of fascist Italy from alliance with Britain after
the Ethiopian incident. Only France remained a steadfast ally to the British
and that, as the French might have said, was *faute de mieux.* The British
vainly sought promises of aid from King in 1937, but he refused to give
them explicitly. Yet during a visit to Berlin, King then told some of Hitler's
disbelieving ministers that, if Germany attacked Britain, Canadians would
swim the Atlantic to come to the aid of the mother country.[17]

The signs were there for the British to read: in an international crisis of the kind fast approaching, Canada would once again go to war for the British Empire. (King sent a memorandum of his Berlin conversations to the British government, including his remark that Canadians would wish to come to Britain's aid.) The British, however, didn't read the signs, and spent 1938 and 1939 in a fog about Canada's intentions.

In fact, King strongly approved of the policy of the latest British prime minister, Neville Chamberlain (1937–40). Neville was the son of Joe, Laurier's old *bête noire*, but in King's eyes that was a remediable defect. Though imperious, even arrogant, in his own government, Chamberlain strongly believed in the art of conciliation—appeasement—in foreign affairs. It was a familiar strategy for the British during the 1920s and 1930s. Anything seemed better than war and its horrendous casualties, costs, and disruptions. The Great War had undermined Britain's financial position, so that Britain would start any new war worse off than in 1914. (King and his colleagues had exactly similar fears about Canada's economic position.) No one could tell how Britain would survive another conflict, and it was entirely rational to avoid one.

Chamberlain proceeded to try. He avoided a confrontation when Hitler annexed Austria in March 1938, and actively sought a compromise when Hitler concocted a crisis with Czechoslovakia the following September. In a conference at Munich, conducted in the glare of extreme publicity, Chamberlain gave Hitler most of what he wanted, made what was left of Czechoslovakia indefensible, and ensured that Hitler could swallow the rest when he wanted. That bill came due in March 1939.

Seen from a purely diplomatic perspective, appeasement in 1938–39 is a sad story of naïveté, deception, and folly. There is, however, another perspective—that of the politicians at the time. Chamberlain and King were mindful that the British government of 1914 had been criticized for not doing all it could to avoid war, that the diplomacy of July and August 1914 was secretive, and that millions were subsequently sacrificed for a cause they couldn't have hoped to understand, much less resolve. The diplomacy of 1938–39 didn't do that. Hitler's perfidy, brutality, and recklessness were on display for all to see; even the blindest critic had to admit that the allies, Britain and France, did not seek war. When war came, and Hitler invaded Poland in September 1939, there was no argument that could claim the Germans were provoked, or the British too belligerent.

Before war came, there was one last imperial entr'acte. In May–June 1939 King George VI and his consort, Queen Elizabeth, arrived in Canada for a long-planned royal tour. George was the respectable younger brother of the raffish Prince of Wales, who had briefly served as king in 1936 (under the name Edward VIII) and then passed on the crown to his brother when his ministers (including Mackenzie King, who was asked his opinion) opposed his choice of an American divorcée as royal consort.

The visit was, in the view of a Saskatchewan historian, "the event of the decade" on the drought-stricken and impoverished Prairies. The reception of the royal couple speaks volumes about the attitudes and loyalties of Canadians in the 1930s. In Regina on 25 May 100,000 people waited in the rain for the king and queen. The crowd was larger than the city, but what was truly astonishing was their reception in Melville, Saskatchewan (population four thousand), on 3 June: 60,000 people drawn from as far away as Manitoba and North Dakota waited for hours under a sign painted on the local grain elevator—"Welcome to their majesties."[18]

In Quebec City, as in Vancouver and Halifax and every point in between, Canadians enthusiastically received the king and queen. It may have been merely a spectacular counterpoint to a drab decade, but it was surely much more. Canadians understood its significance, even Canadians like the diplomat Lester B. Pearson, who cynically observed that it was one way for the British to firm up Canadian support for the war that must come. Come it did, just two and a half months after the royal couple set sail back to England.

In 1914 Canadians went to war easily and reflexively; in 1939 they went reflectively. Their hesitations were behind them, part of the chronicle of miserable events of the spring and summer of 1939. If enthusiasm was muted, there was also a sense that no other course was possible. Mackenzie King matched up the residual imperialism of so much of the

Canadian population with a cause that anti-imperialists (including most of French Canada) could accept.

On the question of war and peace, the partnership of Lapointe and King worked smoothly. They seem to have drawn the conclusion early in 1939 that war was more likely than not, and within the year. Lapointe accordingly made a speech in Parliament outlining why the Canadian people would accept war, if it came, and King made one that emphasized that he would bar the door against any useless or frivolous adventure.

The signal that war was inevitable came at the end of August, when Hitler's Nazi Germany signed a public "non-aggression" pact with Stalin's Communist Soviet Union. The treaty actually opened the door to German aggression, and divided the spoils with the Russians. The Canadian government summoned Parliament, proclaimed the War Measures Act, and prepared to call for volunteers for the armed forces.

The Germans invaded Poland on 1 September 1939; Britain and France declared war on Germany on 3 September; and the Canadian Parliament met on 7 September. The government presented a resolution declaring war on Germany. Duly passed against minimal opposition, the declaration of war, Canada's first, was signed by George VI on 10 September.

THE SECOND WORLD WAR BEGINS

Canadians in 1914 were confident when they embarked on the Great War. It was of course a confidence born of ignorance; and the same could not be said of 1939. Aerial bombardments, poison gas, submarine warfare—developments of the Great War—were available for the Second World War. As if to underline the point, the Germans promptly sank an ocean liner, the *Athenia*, carrying British evacuees bound for Canada.

The Canadian government followed the course laid down in 1914, but it could study the mistakes made by Borden's government, and try not to repeat them. The government assumed control over Canada's foreign exchange reserves and imposed controls over international transactions.

Thanks to R.B. Bennett, there was a government-owned Bank of Canada to manage the currency and advise the government. The government promptly raised taxes, and thanks to Borden's income tax it had the means to do so. As in 1914 there was a burst of "national unity" sentiment, but it lasted an even shorter time than in 1914.

The problem came first with the provinces. Most of them were pensioners of the federal government: British Columbia, the three Prairie provinces, and the Maritimes. Two were not: Ontario and Quebec, although they too appreciated federal help when they could get it. Quebec, under the Union Nationale premier Maurice Duplessis, needed to borrow money, and it wanted to borrow it in New York. Thanks to the untimely outbreak of war, it could not. Duplessis had the option of telling his electors that he had mismanaged their finances (which was true) and that consequently he needed to raise taxes. That would have been political suicide, so the premier took another course. He called a provincial election. He blamed Ottawa, he attacked the war, and he told a public meeting that Quebec would not participate—whatever that meant. It was a dramatic gesture, however foolish, and once made it could not be retracted.[19]

Duplessis's threat could mean a great deal. To the Quebec delegation in King's cabinet it was a challenge, and under Lapointe's direction (and over King's objections) they decided to meet it. The federal ministers would intervene directly in the provincial campaign (the taboos against doing so weren't as strong in 1939 as they would later become, even though there is still no absolute rule or firm practice). They would go all out to beat Duplessis, and if they lost they would resign. That would mean that Mackenzie King and the English-speaking Liberals would govern Canada without any French-Canadian mediation—more or less what Borden had done in 1917. As long as they were in the cabinet, the Quebec ministers promised, there would be no conscription. If they were out, could Duplessis then protect his province against that possibility? It was an effective threat, and it was backed up by money raised by the federal Liberals. In the result, Duplessis lost. Quebec would have a Liberal government, friendly to Ottawa and supportive of the war effort, for most of the war.

Next there was a challenge from Ontario, where, paradoxically, there *was* a Liberal government. Unfortunately the Liberal premier, Mitchell Hepburn, hated Mackenzie King. Hepburn was prey to impulse, and prone to overestimate his own importance and that of his provincial government. He too challenged Mackenzie King's right to run the country, and demanded instead a business-dominated government of national unity, a proposition that was very well received on Bay Street, Toronto's financial district.

King promptly called a federal election, in which the Conservative opposition had little choice but to run as the cat's paw of Bay Street, as a future government of national unity. The electorate found their arguments unconvincing. The Liberals—and the Conservatives too—promised that there would be no conscription, which of course resonated in Quebec; but in 1940 it did no harm elsewhere either. King won a majority of the popular vote and three-quarters of the seats in the House of Commons in the election of March 1940. Not enough was left of the Conservatives to mount an effective opposition, and to make matters even worse, King and his ministers shortly and easily recruited some of Canadian business's hottest talents to help run the war effort. (The recruits, known as "dollar-a-year men," even included Sir Robert Borden's very able nephew Henry.)

It was a prescription for success, but success only as measured in domestic Canadian terms. Success in the war depended on the senior allies, Britain and France, and their prospects appeared cloudy. The British were short of cash, and tried to save money on orders to Canada, and indeed on any orders outside Britain's own currency zone (known as the "sterling area"). As a result, Canadian industry in 1939–40 did little. Recruitment for the armed forces soaked up many of the unemployed, and still there were workers to spare, especially if willing women workers are counted in the total available. A Canadian Expeditionary Force did sail for Britain in December 1939, and by the spring they were almost ready for deployment alongside the British army in France.

Events moved too swiftly for the British government, still headed by Neville Chamberlain. The Germans, after conquering Poland in September 1939, gobbled up Norway and Denmark in April 1940, driving the British back across the North Sea. Defeat in Norway caused Chamberlain to be replaced by Winston Churchill on 10 May 1940, the same day the Germans launched an invasion of France and the Low Countries. Five weeks later the British army was driven from France, and the French sued for peace. A remnant of the French government, headed by a junior minister, General Charles de Gaulle, fled to London, where they tried to inspire resistance in the French Empire under the title "Free France." For the time being, however, Britain stood alone against Germany, with only the empire to support it. Of the nations of the British Empire, Canada was the closest to Britain, and the most significant in terms of economic and short-term military support. It was a sobering thought, given the state of Canadian mobilization in June 1940.

In Canada the newly elected Parliament was meeting as catastrophe rained down upon it. It was fortunate that just at this point one of King's talents came to the fore. Unlike Borden during most of the Great War, King had an unusually strong cabinet, which he reinforced in 1940. In charge of war production—which the British had had to take over during the Great War—he placed C.D. Howe, who possessed an unmatched ability to make varied decisions quickly and a managerial competence so often lacking among politicians. The minister of finance, J.L. Ilsley, was similarly endowed and enjoyed the ability to explain and justify the government's decision to adopt a "pay-as-you-go" policy for the war, which enforced a program of high taxes and low inflation, backed up by a stringent wage and price control program. Wage and price controls became necessary toward the end of 1941, as war industries and military recruitment vacuumed up the unemployed[20] and material shortages developed because scarce supplies were diverted to the war effort. Lapointe, as minister of justice and senior minister, headed a strong contingent from Quebec, though in 1940–41 his health was beginning to fail; he would die in November 1941.

Howe and Ilsley, backed by King, decided to risk the government's credit by embarking on a full war-production program. Recruiting for the armed forces—army, navy, and air force—was voluntary until June 1940, but after that it was backed by a modified conscription law, passed after the fall of France, which provided for compulsory enlistment for home defence, with service limited to the North American continent. Volunteers continued to proceed overseas, until by 1942 an army of four divisions was assembled and waiting in Britain.

No amount of reinforcements or recruits from Canada would have made a sufficient difference to help the British win the war. Britain itself couldn't raise enough troops to do more than defend the periphery of the empire in North Africa, while keeping a watchful eye on what Japan, an ally of Germany since 1940, could do in the Far East. Fortunately, Hitler couldn't easily cross the English Channel; equally fortunately, his attentions were diverted, to the Balkans and then to confront Stalin and the Soviet Union. Hitler's invasion of Russia in June 1941 gave the British Empire an unwilling but extremely important ally, as long as Stalin and his commanders could avoid complete defeat at the hands of the German army.

The Russian army did manage to hang on against fierce German attacks until December 1941, but even the Soviet Union with its huge reserves of manpower wasn't necessarily enough to turn the war against Germany. Then, on 7 December, Japan attacked the Pacific possessions of Great Britain, the Netherlands, and the United States. The United States immediately declared war on Japan, to which Japan's ally, Hitler, riposted by declaring war on the United States. Canada, naturally, declared war on Japan. Canadian troops, who formed part of the imperial garrison of Hong Kong, had been among the first to be attacked; regrettably, there was no way of rescuing Hong Kong, deep behind enemy lines, or salvaging the soldiers, who passed into almost four years of captivity on Christmas Day.

The politicians and officials who administered the war effort were pleasantly surprised in 1941–42 to find that Canadians on the whole accepted their rules and regulations, paid their taxes, and endured shortages of everything from food and clothing to automobiles. This was in part because so many Canadians had experience with endless and intractable unemployment, and in part because jobs in war factories paid well, so that despite heavy taxation hundreds of thousands of Canadians were better off than they had been in the 1930s, and possibly ever. With unemployment down to 2 percent in the fall of 1941—effectively nil— there appeared to be jobs for anyone who wanted one.

The government attempted to use existing resources by subcontracting production in what was called a "bits and pieces" program. This meant that war production could be widely dispersed, and in a regionalized country of vast distances, such a program was politically as well as economically important. It's nevertheless true that the greatest concentration of war industry was in the large metropolitan areas, Montreal especially, then Toronto and its surrounding region ("the Golden Horseshoe" spanning the northwest shore of Lake Ontario), Winnipeg, and Vancouver.[21] Population flowed to Ontario, Quebec, and British Columbia, and also Nova Scotia, owing to the concentration of military bases in that province. It flowed out of the Prairies, especially Saskatchewan and Alberta, and out of New Brunswick and Prince Edward Island. It flowed from the country to the city.

In many cases, service in the military was considered preferable to life in existing jobs. Mining and forestry were especially unpopular, but because so many industries depended on them, the government made a special effort to keep miners and lumberjacks in their existing jobs. Recruiters were instructed not to accept miners and forestry workers, and those who had already enlisted were in some cases sent back to their civilian occupations.

The war wasn't supplied exclusively from forests, factories, or mines. Agriculture was one of Canada's great strengths, even if it had been devastated by low prices and drought in the 1930s. Canadian wheat had fed the Allies in the Great War, and it seemed reasonable to expect that it would do so again. But the customers, thanks to Hitler, weren't there. Occupied

Europe couldn't buy Canadian wheat, and that meant that a good wheat crop in 1940 went largely unsold and unexported. The answer was to diversify prairie agriculture—more coarse grains, which fed more meat production. Steak didn't need to be rationed in wartime Canada, which made the dominion an attractive destination for touring American and British officials. Money again flowed to the prairies, and the farmers bought machinery such as tractors and combines (not rationed because of their importance for production), and paid off their tax arrears.

The figures for gross national product tell much of the story. In 1939 Canada's GNP stood at $5.621 billion. In 1945 it was $11.863 billion. Put in terms of constant dollars, using 1971 as a base, gross national expenditure rose from $17.774 billion in 1939 to $29.071 billion in 1945, a 61 percent increase.[22] Household income rose steadily, from $731 in 1939 to $992 in 1945, although the gains in consumption were mainly in the first three years of the war. Shortages thereafter limited purchases, but benefited the nation's ability to save for a better day, whenever that might be.[23]

Because the government was proactive in regulating and controlling the economy, it was less surprised than the Borden government had been by incidents of labour unrest. There were fewer labour troubles, though they did occur. To supplement lower incomes, the government contemplated a "baby bonus," payable to mothers, not fathers, in families with children. The baby bonus (children's allowances) was enacted but didn't actually take effect until after the end of the war, when its origin as an income supplement that could get around wage controls had been forgotten.

The federal government did more: using the War Measures Act it regulated labour relations in all war industries, superseding the usual provincial jurisdiction. A federal labour code was implemented by order-in-council in 1944: it liberalized the rules governing trade unions, which were, in any case, expanding their appeal and signing up workers from coast to coast.

THE CURSE OF CONSCRIPTION

The Second World War was accepted as a fight against a real evil. It did not take much propaganda to present Hitler and his allies as monstrous, their governments as vicious, and the prospect of their victory as appalling. If anything, Allied propaganda, still reeling from the rhetorical exaggerations of the Great War, underestimated the atrocities of the Nazis and the villainy of their regime. It followed that against a great enemy great means should be employed. The phrase of the day was "total war," meaning total commitment from all segments of society. Newspapers and politicians preached sacrifice, but to justify it they had to promote *equality* of sacrifice.

To a much greater extent than in 1914–18 the government mobilized Canada's economic resources, with stringently high tax rates that in the upper income brackets approached 100 percent. Even in the middle tax ranges the government dug deep into taxpayers' pockets. Some Canadians did notably less well during the war, especially those on fixed incomes. Only those who earned little or nothing before the war did better—but, of course, there were many of those. Company profits were controlled, in a well-publicized effort to prevent war profiteering.

Conservative Canadians accepted the inevitable. Perhaps, in addition to the war experience, they had been shaken by the 1930s. Not only were they paying their taxes, but they were sending their children to war, or into war work. And it wasn't just conservative Canadians who began in 1941, that year of defeat and disaster, to bring up the subject of conscription—and not merely the limited conscription for home defence that the King government had introduced, but full compulsory service. Given the military situation as it existed at the end of 1941, the demand that Canada resort to compulsory service had a strong resonance.

The resurgence of conscriptionist sentiment was captured by opinion polls, some public, some conducted in secret for the government's eyes alone. Over Christmas 1941 the prime minister worried, but as he worried he began to make certain dispositions against the future.

First, Mackenzie King needed to replace Ernest Lapointe as minister of justice and Quebec lieutenant. After some hesitation, he selected a prominent Quebec City lawyer, a former president of the Canadian Bar Association, Louis St. Laurent. St. Laurent accepted the offer, and was duly elected to Parliament for Lapointe's old seat in February 1942. Given the Liberals' dominance in Quebec that was practically a foregone conclusion, but there was one feature of the by-election that was much commented upon in Quebec. St. Laurent did not repeat his predecessor's pledge against conscription. He wasn't bound by the same promises as Lapointe and the other Quebec ministers had been since 1939.

English Canadians were paying close attention to another contest, held in suburban Toronto at the same time. The Conservatives, leaderless since the 1940 election, asked Arthur Meighen, the former prime minister and King's bitter enemy, to return to lead them. Meighen accepted, and took his stand, as he had in 1917, on the issue of conscription. Conscription was meant for all, and there should be equal sacrifice in the great cause. He meant what he said, of course, but he also knew that his supporters understood that equality of sacrifice meant Quebec, and Quebec recruits. French Quebeckers, they believed, were enlisting at much lower rate than the national average; conscription would equalize matters. That was less true than during the Great War—19 percent of the armed forces were French-speaking, as opposed to 12 percent in 1914–18; and the King government had made a major effort to create and sustain French-speaking units.[24]

King was alarmed. His diary bears witness to his torment as he contemplated having to spend the rest of his political life—which might be brief—with Meighen. Fortunately, he didn't have to. Liberal party organizers refused to run a candidate against Meighen, and instead threw their support and money to the socialist CCF. The CCF beat Meighen, whose political career was abruptly terminated. King rejoiced, but as he gloated he was preparing the next step.

The government called a national plebiscite to release it from its election pledges of 1939 in Quebec, and of 1940 to all of Canada, not to enact conscription. In that plebiscite French Canadians voted "non," by and large, and English Canadians voted "yes." There were exceptions, naturally. In the little Quebec town of Shawinigan, one unilingual French Canadian, with the very unusual name of Wellie (for Wellington) Chrétien, voted "oui." Wellie Chrétien was a contrarian, and across Canada there were undoubtedly a fair number of Wellies, distributed on both sides of the question. Another very prominent French Canadian, the minister of justice, St. Laurent, also voted "oui," and St. Laurent proposed to take the consequences of his stand. He backed King when the prime minister introduced a bill that would legalize conscription for overseas service. One of the other Quebec ministers resigned, while the others shuffled uneasily. For them, King had an answer, which has entered Canadian political lore as a classic: there would be "not necessarily conscription but conscription if necessary." The law was on the books, but it wouldn't be applied—yet.

The reason was simple: there was as yet no need for reinforcements. The Royal Canadian Air Force suffered heavy casualties in certain categories, particularly in the bombing campaign over Germany, and the navy was also heavily engaged. The great fear was what would happen when the army was engaged—but until 1943, except for Hong Kong and a bloody failed raid on the French seaside town of Dieppe, the Canadian army wasn't directly fighting the enemy. Its main enemy was boredom, so much so that the Canadian government agitated to have the army take part in the Allied invasion of Sicily in July 1943. At the cost of dividing the army, leaving some in Britain and sending the rest to the Mediterranean, this was done.

There was another factor that deserves emphasis. The horrendous casualties of the Great War made the British generals of the next generation—men who had been mid-ranking officers in the earlier war—exceedingly cautious about expending the lives of their soldiers. Canadian generals, serving under overall British command, absorbed the lesson, and if they did not, they were removed, as happened with the general commanding the Canadian army in Britain at the end of 1943. The

British advised that continuing him in command would be dangerous, and the Canadian defence minister agreed.

The Italian campaign, in which the Canadians participated from the summer of 1943 to the winter of 1945, was bloody but in the largest sense indecisive. Italy was a sideshow. The Germans could mount an effective defence and manage a very gradual withdrawal to the north. They had plenty of difficult terrain to force the Allies to fight over. The Canadians distinguished themselves in this fighting, but they were far from the main action.

That was in France, in Normandy, where the Allies—the United States, Britain, and Canada—landed on 6 June 1944. The Allies enjoyed overwhelming air superiority, and as time drew on they could exploit their advantages in equipment. The Germans had an excellent army to fight them off, but not enough of it, and they had the handicap of Hitler's mad interference with the direction of combat. The Canadians and the neighbouring British held their own against the Germans, but little more, until an American offensive outflanked the Germans and opened the way to Paris in early August.

The Normandy battles lasted nine weeks, and for the Canadian army they were exceedingly costly in terms of casualties. Where there had been no reinforcement crisis before, there was one now, just as the army moved up for the next series of battles, opening the approaches to the great Belgian port of Antwerp so that supplies could easily flow to the Allied armies. The defence minister, J.L. Ralston, visited the troops at this point, and, shocked at what he found, returned to Canada to tell his colleagues that conscription must be applied, right away, for the army to be able to fight effectively. It wasn't just a matter of efficiency, but a matter of honour.

This was unwelcome news for Mackenzie King. The prime minister twisted and turned. He dismissed Ralston, and replaced him with the general whom Ralston had dismissed from the command of the army in Europe. The general, A.G.L. McNaughton, promised he'd secure the necessary reinforcements by appealing to the conscripts in their camps in

Canadian Army Engagements in Europe, World War II

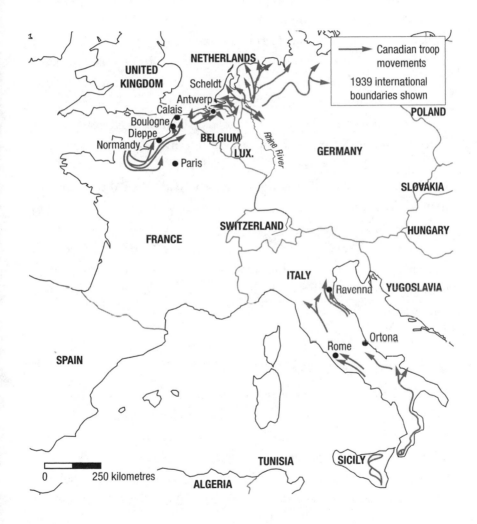

the rainy and frigid mountains of British Columbia and other unpleasant places across the country. But they refused. King had no alternative: after firming up St. Laurent's support and receiving the resignation of another Quebec minister, he told his cabinet that he would bring on conscription after all. It seemed undignified, but in King's desperate manoeuvring there lurked the germ of political survival.

King's sense of timing and his mastery of political infighting bought him and the government time. They were also in luck, for the war wouldn't last much longer. The Germans surrendered in May 1945. The Canadian army was then fighting in the Netherlands, and so it was the Canadians who had the satisfaction of accepting the surrender of the German army and liberating Holland.

By the time the Germans surrendered, Canada was engaged in a general election. King posed as a veteran international statesman whose experience and talents were indispensable for the peace sure to come. In Quebec, he was remembered as the man who had opposed conscription, until finally overwhelmed. King hadn't necessarily kept his promise not to have conscription, but for Quebec he was the man who was necessary. Quebec's votes kept King in office, with a narrow majority, but when all was said and done he hadn't done too badly in the rest of the country, even though—for the third time—he lost his seat. He now had a chance—a third political life, so to speak.

THE THIRD LARGEST ARMY

Canada's accomplishments in the Second World War were considerable. In the first place, the country survived, and survived to emerge richer and more stable at the end of the fighting than at the beginning. This was primarily a political achievement, owing to a combination of experience— the lessons of the Great War—circumstance, and personality. Political stability ensured that domestic political quarrels were limited in scope and importance.

Just as important, Canada fielded armed forces and produced munitions and other supplies in astonishing quantities given the population of the country. Canada's 11.5 million people, in the 1941 census, produced 1.1 million enlistments in the armed forces, though not all served at the same time. At its peak, the army numbered about 500,000, including 15,000 women; the air force just under 100,000; and the navy around 200,000. These were large numbers, and in 1944 they placed Canada third among the Western Allies in military personnel.

That said, it was a distant third. The United States and Great Britain had far more troops than Canada. If the economic contribution is measured, again Canada was third, and again it's a long way back, representing perhaps 5 percent of the Allied war production total. The Canadian government was conscious of these ratios, and in its favour it should be said that it seldom reached for exaggeration as a weapon. Canada's contribution was enough to get attention when needed. Credibility and influence were resources to be rationed, not dissipated, in Mackenzie King's Canada.

The prime minister was virtually the only significant minister in terms of political foreign policy. Other ministers, such as Howe, the munitions czar, or Ilsley, the finance minister, had contacts outside the country, enough to ensure the smooth functioning of their departments. They didn't try to go beyond them; indeed, Howe resisted attempts by Canada's political diplomats to use his munitions supply as a bargaining tool to pry greater recognition for Canada from the senior Allies, the British and the Americans. What the Allies did with the supplies after they got them was their affair; if Canada started dictating conditions, in Howe's opinion, it would not long remain an important source of supply.

Canada's greatest concern was with the United States. In the Great War American supply and, initially, American loans had been crucial in keeping the Canadian economy afloat. In 1939 Canada was largely dependent on the United States for coal and oil; and in 1940 Canadian war administrators discovered that Canadian industry couldn't tool up for production without American components, such as machine tools and aircraft engines. Canadian foreign exchange reserves were drained to pay for American supply, and no help was forthcoming from the British, who faced the same dilemma. It was at this point, in April 1941, that King cashed in on his good relations with Roosevelt, and supervised a deal (the Hyde Park Agreement, named after Roosevelt's country estate) in which the United States, tooling up for war, bought what it needed from Canada, on the same basis that it would have bought war materiel in the United States. Canada's foreign exchange problems were essentially solved for the duration of the war because of American purchases, and a precedent was set for integrating Canadian and American war production. At the same time Canada was able to draw on American aid to Britain for components in manufacturing supplies for the United Kingdom.

King and his ministers and other officials were gratified that the Canadian–American trade and foreign exchange imbalance was solved on the basis of trade, not aid. There was an exchange of goods, not a donation of money, nor the accumulation of debt to a large, powerful creditor next door. As a result, Canada did not end the war indebted to the United States, and Canada's sovereign equality in dealing with the Americans was not impaired. The disparity in population, wealth, and power remained, naturally, but as with the Boundary Waters Treaty of 1909 and the subsequent International Joint Commission, Canadian–American relations were conducted on a level playing field, according to agreed rules that were supposed to work impartially on both sides of the border.

As for the other great power ally, the Soviet Union, relations were materially significant, but politically important only in a particular sense. Canadians—that is, English Canadians—were by and large pro-British and pro-American, admiring both Allies and inspired by their leadership, Churchill and Roosevelt. The same wasn't generally true of the Soviet Union, but there was a faction of Canadians, the Communist Party of Canada, that deeply admired Stalin and saw the Soviet Union as the hope of the human race. Canadian communists were faithful foot soldiers of international communism, which meant accepting every twist and turn of Stalin's sometimes convoluted and frequently self-defeating policies. Between 1939 and 1941, when Stalin and Hitler were friendly, Canadian communists did what they could to obstruct the war effort. After 1941, with the Soviet Union under attack by the Germans, the communists evolved into hyper-patriots and enthusiasts for total war.

The Soviet Union opened an embassy in Ottawa, and used it to solicit Canadian supplies, which were provided under a program called Mutual Aid. The aid sent to Russia was dwarfed by the supplies sent to Britain, but it was nevertheless important. The Soviet embassy's other program was equally official, but was carefully concealed from the Canadian authorities. Using their sympathizers in Canada, the Soviets set up an espionage network to discover what the Canadians and the other Western Allies were up to. This network, Canada's first, was revealed only after the war, and its importance will be explored in the next chapter.

After Russia, there was France. France also had a domestic political importance not matched by any other ally, because of its significance in Quebec. Two versions of France contended for support in Quebec, and in Canada. There was the France of Marshal Pétain, whose government had ended the war with Germany, and which lived on German sufferance in an unoccupied district in southern France. Pétain promised to cleanse France of the decadent and impure elements that had—so he claimed— undermined and left it ripe for defeat. The Pétain government was underpinned by right-wing Catholicism, as well as outright fascism, but its official values, *"Travail, famille, patrie"* (Work, family, country), had a strong appeal in right-wing Catholic circles in Quebec.

On the other hand, there was Free France, run by General Charles de Gaulle out of London. It condemned the peace with Germany, and promised to restore France by helping the Allies defeat Germany. At first painfully weak, de Gaulle's movement grew in strength in 1941, as parts of the overseas French Empire rallied to his cause. Stern, visionary, and uncompromising, de Gaulle was a difficult partner for the British and Americans; President Roosevelt detested him, while Churchill, originally his patron, admitted that the general wasn't easy to live with. Mackenzie King did rather better, even though for a time Canada actually had relations with both Vichy France and Free France. English Canada proved a hospitable environment for the Free French, and bilingual Montreal was at least a base from which de Gaulle's emissaries could proselytize. The Canadian government favoured de Gaulle's capture of St. Pierre and Miquelon from Vichy in December 1941, and proved a remarkably reluctant partner when the U.S. government demanded the islands be restored to Pétain (they were not). In June 1944 de Gaulle paid a triumphal visit to Ottawa, and gave every sign of sincere friendship for Canada, which was preparing to assist him with material aid and credits when he returned to Paris later that summer.

Canada's wartime diplomacy was modest, proportionate, and effective. Canada was not a great power, and did not manifest great power pretensions. But its government was able to act effectively in the Canadian interest by not overstretching its reach and not abusing its credibility.

But what, after all, was Canada, and what was the Canadian interest? Just at the end of the war, King's subordinates decided that they would break with tradition. Canadian troops, sailors, and air personnel had fought in British uniforms but with a "Canada" shoulder patch. King's subordinates decided to try the equivalent, and flew the Canadian red ensign instead of the Union Jack from the Peace Tower of Canada's Parliament Buildings on the day of the German surrender. It was a timid gesture, but it gave Mackenzie King palpitations, both on his own behalf and because he feared the wrath of traditionally minded voters. Could Canada have a symbol distinctly its own? Had Canada become a country?

13

A TIME OF GIFTS,
1945–1963

The atomic age: The head shaft of the uranium mine
at Port Radium in Great Bear Lake, mid-1950s.

C anadians in 1945 were mildly apprehensive. There were reasons enough: the Allies had ended the war by dropping an atomic bomb on Japan, transforming the world of weaponry and creating a new kind of danger should the wonder weapon ever fall into the wrong hands. But that wasn't what mostly worried people. Canadians saw the world mostly in domestic terms. The war had been fought, it was won, and it was over. Life would go on, but not quite as it had been. The past foreshadowed the present, and the past was economic disappointment—the failed hopes and stalled society of the Great Depression. The past was also the organizational triumph of the war—the recent past of full employment and prosperity. Which past would now prevail?

In the nervous spring of 1945, a plurality of Canadians voted for the recent past, for Mackenzie King and the Liberals. Even a plurality of the military vote went Liberal, despite King's well-advertised reluctance to send conscripts overseas in the last stages of the war.[1] Canadians did not select the rebaptized Conservative party—*Progressive* Conservatives since 1942, under ex-Premier John Bracken of Manitoba. They did not opt for experimenting with socialism with the CCF party. They left the CCF mostly inside its Saskatchewan bastion, where it had won an election in 1944. The CCF still had enough support in Nova Scotia, Manitoba, Ontario, and British Columbia to act as a national party.

Canada was a complex, vast, and potentially divided land. Its federal system had bent but not buckled under the economic and political strains of the Depression and the war. The federal government, and the federal government virtually alone, had the financial resources to ride out the storm. Regional, and generally provincial, politicians rose and fell during the Depression, but the impoverishment of the provincial treasuries meant they could do little but hurl verbal thunderbolts at an impervious Ottawa.

Politics in Canada were complicated by the bifurcation of Canadian society between an English majority and a French minority. Yet during the 1930s both English and French Canadians had been remarkably conservative in their attitudes to society and government. Taxes had been low, matched by the government services they funded. Free enterprise of a relatively untrammelled sort predominated, surprising visiting Americans, who reported home that Canada was definitely a conservative if not backward country compared with the United States. In Catholic and French-speaking Quebec it was the Church that managed most social services. Even among the largely Protestant English, churches played an important if not decisive role in ordering society. Canada was, after all, a churchgoing nation, and a Christian country: what the clergy said and did mattered. Those who dissented, intellectually or socially or even sexually, from majority practice did so in isolation or quietly under the cover furnished by the larger cities.

Canada's self-image was raw, rural, and underdeveloped. The reality was urban and industrial. Canadians traditionally lagged behind other comparable countries in productivity and standard of living—behind the United States, the world's richest country, to be sure, but also, in the 1920s, behind Great Britain, Australia, and even Argentina.

That was no longer the case in 1945. Canada did well out of the war. GDP per capita finally passed that of wealthy Australia in 1944—for the first time in 150 years.[2] (It lagged substantially behind the United States, at about 60 percent of the U.S. figure.) Virtually immune to enemy attack, Canadians expanded old industries and built new ones. The federal government experimented with new forms of federalism, appropriating most of the country's tax revenue for the all-consuming needs of the war. The government paid as much as it could raise from very high taxes, and borrowed the rest; in terms of collective sacrifice Canada's war effort could stand comparison with the British and was probably greater, in per capita terms, than the American.

The cost could be seen in grimy transport, fraying clothes, and dilapidated housing. Though many were better off in 1945 than they'd been in the 1930s, they sustained themselves with deferred hopes rather than immediate consumption. (The government made sure that it was easier to save than spend, and enforced the policy through rigid and remarkably effective controls.)[3] The war's effects could also be seen in the "Vive Pétain" slogan painted on the cliffs at Quebec City to greet the returning troops as they disembarked.[4]

The government was ready: gasoline rationing was abandoned, freeing Canadians to take to the roads in their cars, if they had them. Left behind were the wartime savings plans and other restrictions. Government tax incentives encouraged manufacturers to convert their factories to civilian production, and none more readily than the automobile industry. With money in hand, Canadians wanted to consume. Automobile sales rebounded—78,000 new cars sold in 1946, 159,000 in 1947. The statisticians were amazed, not so much by the volume of car sales as by the fact that "ready cash in large amounts in the hands of the public allowed the outright buying of this commodity," without loans.[5]

This was a change, and there were others. Unemployment through the 1930s was a too familiar feature of life—an aspect of normalcy. Economists feared the worst, and politicians followed in their footsteps. Active government had ended unemployment by planning and spending; it followed that government must now plan the economy to provide "full employment," the favourite phrase of the 1945 election. In April the Liberal government produced a White Paper that laid down its policy for full employment—or almost.[6] The White Paper served its immediate purpose: getting the government re-elected. And, miracle of miracles, there was full employment. The government and its friends put it all down to good planning, and in the good times that prevailed forgot that there was little or no planning at all.[7]

The war ended, and employment did not fall, or fall very much. A new kind of normalcy took hold. Canadians married. The new families bought refrigerators, stoves, clothes. They wanted to buy houses, but it took time to organize the supply of that particular commodity. If they were veterans, they bought education—for some the university kind, but for others, vocational training. The government paid the costs through a generous benefit scheme.

What veterans would not postpone was marriage and families. The 1930s had been a bleak time for marriage. With economic prospects ranging from uncertain to dismal for most, marriages were put off. The age of marriage rose, and the birth rate fell. The war changed things. Men and women volunteered for the armed services, but, given the assumptions and gender roles of the day, men did so in much greater numbers. Women were challenged to replace men in civilian jobs, and many did. The challenges varied, from compulsory war "service" for female university students (at the University of Toronto knitting was preferred) to driving trucks for the Red Cross, and everything in between.[8] Females reached 30 percent of the non-agricultural work-force in 1944—a 33 percent participation rate overall. There was also a final challenge—the expectation that at the end of the war women filling soldiers' jobs would quietly and happily depart. Some did; some did not.

In reaction to disruption, young men and women sought security, and found it in a vision of family.[9] Hasty marriages, husbands departing for the war, and wives engaged in war work often made the experience anything but romantic. Nevertheless, throughout the war the number of marriages rose, both in Canada and overseas among the troops. (The latter event wasn't officially encouraged, but, with 500,000 young men overseas and in garrison in Great Britain for much of the war, it took place regardless.) When the Canadian military returned from Europe they brought 43,000 war brides and 21,000 children. (And they left behind 30,000 illegitimate children.)[10] They also brought the optimism that all those marriages implied.[11] They had the positive experience of victory, and appreciation of the organization that had made it all possi-ble. Expectations were great, and it was those expectations more than anything else that drove the agenda of the next twenty years.[12]

The Baby Boom

One of the most enduring images of the postwar years is children. More families meant more children, and as family formation crept up during the war years the term "baby boom" appeared.[13] There were more children, and healthier children, thanks to a sinking rate of infant mortality[14] and the discovery of "wonder drugs," like the Salk vaccine that protected against poliomyelitis, until then the annual scourge of Canadian summers.[15] More children meant more schools, with a million more students added to primary and secondary schools between 1945 and 1955, and 900,000 more between 1955 and 1960. The federal government, which distributed "children's allowances" after 1945, made them conditional on school attendance; and that, coupled with the enactment of compulsory schooling in Quebec under that province's wartime Liberal government, supplemented the birth rate as a source of enrolment.

The burden of child-rearing largely fell on women. Full employment in the 1940s and 1950s meant full employment for men. Patterns of work drew men out of the home and into the factory or office, from eight or nine in the morning until five at night. Most women, especially married women, stayed home, tending to children or other domestic chores. Female enrolment in universities grew absolutely, but as a proportion of the total remained remarkably stable, around 21 percent, from the 1930s to the 1950s. In the labour force, the proportion of women actually rose slightly from 1941 to 1951, to 22 percent. Female labour was concentrated in categories such as education (teaching in the primary and secondary schools) or health (nursing).[16] Virtually all cultural phenomena and media, from women's magazines to union halls, reinforced the pattern: where women worked, they did so in what were mostly traditionally female occupations.

Reconstruction and Reconversion

Families and children required housing, and housing was in short supply. Housing was a social need, but it was also an economic tool, and as such fell under the government's "reconstruction" policy. Reconstruction was a grand name for a smaller thing. It implied rebuilding, designing anew, making something different. Structurally, in terms of the economy, that didn't happen, though plenty of alternative ideas were on the table. The biggest was socialism, the appropriation by government of the means of finance and production. Less sweeping, but nevertheless impressive, was the notion that the government should "direct" the economy using the tools that "planners" put at its disposal—a continuation in many people's minds of what had been done so successfully during the war.

The King government rejected both alternatives. In the opinion of the minister responsible, Howe, micro-planning was beyond the ordinary capacity of government.[17] Macro-planning, the idea that government should generally supervise the economy and manage economic conditions through adjustments in the levels of taxation and spending, was something the ministers could accept, though for most it was a strange and difficult notion.

The federal government approached housing with a two-pronged policy: first, as far as possible, home ownership was to be promoted; second, housing should be left to the private sector to build. The government encouraged mortgages, and passed legislation making them easier to get. It also made money for housing available to veterans and decontrolled supplies as fast as it could. C.D. Howe, the minister responsible for reconstructing the civilian economy, was deaf to protests that as often as not came from business, which disliked the short-term chaos as the housing market established itself and regretted the absence of subsidies from government. As Howe wrote to a prominent businessman, in a slightly different context, the whole idea was to place business back in private enterprise.

If the federal government after five years of war found the notion of planning strange, if tempting, the provinces were much more backward. To begin with, they had little talent in their money-starved bureaucracies. During the 1930s and especially during the war Ottawa was a magnet for the young and talented. It was where the excitement was, and the excitement continued after 1945. The provinces had no such appeal. In 1941 the federal government used its predominant power, constitutionally but more importantly politically, to chivvy the provinces into agreeing to forgo most of their revenues for the duration of the war, receiving instead a pension from Ottawa that allowed them to carry on with their most important functions. Even obstreperous Ontario, but also Liberal Quebec, agreed.

These arrangements expired with the war. Nevertheless, to Ottawa's economists, proper economic planning demanded that the wartime structure of centralized taxation be retained for the proper macro-economic management of the country. More, the civil servants hoped to ride the wave of wartime success into a reformed governmental system, prescribing a complete welfare state, including pensions and government-sponsored health care—cradle-to-grave security. Indubitably, the constitution gave the provinces their own revenue sources to do with as they pleased, but surely that consideration could be transcended in the interests of the greater common good. Federal–provincial consultations began in 1945, and in 1946 a full-fledged dominion–provincial conference was held. The dominion government tabled a Green Paper (so-called from its cover) that invited the provinces to hand over to Ottawa the power to enact and finance a system of universal social security. It had the support of the cabinet, especially from the minister of finance, Ilsley, and the minister of justice, St. Laurent. Asked by a colleague whether Quebec would not object, St. Laurent said that it would, but Quebec could be expected to object to practically anything. He was, of course, quite right.

Mackenzie King viewed the whole enterprise as a risky business. He was no constitutional expert, though he was trained as a lawyer, and no economic theorist, though he had a Ph.D. in economics. King was, however, an expert politician, with an eye to the future as well as a wealth of past experience. He had a good sense of the strengths as well as weaknesses of the players in Canada's political game, and he knew that the end of the war would allow provincial politicians, if they chose, to reassert their constitutional rights, against which sweeping federal social welfare policies, however well conceived and intelligently argued, could not stand.

This meant that the provinces, if they chose, would recover their taxation powers, including the power to set their tax rates at whatever level they wanted. King knew he couldn't prevent them from legislating their own social welfare policies, and that without provincial consent Ottawa couldn't do it for them. He also understood that he would have facing him in the conference two very strong partisans of provincial power, Maurice Duplessis of Quebec and George Drew of Ontario. Duplessis was by far the more conservative of the two, being philosophically opposed to state intervention in such fields as social welfare—something best left to charity, or to the churches, in his opinion. He was an economic liberal of the old school: markets and private entrepreneurs were best equipped to sort out wages and working conditions, and trade unions were at best a distortion of nature. Duplessis could mix these convictions with the elixir of French-Canadian nationalism; by identifying "English" Ottawa with social theories he found obnoxious, he could hope to rally Quebec opinion against the rest of the country.

Drew was fuzzier on such issues. He disliked experts and theories, especially of the kind found in Ottawa. On the other hand, he was well aware that most Ontarians expected their governments, federal and provincial, to look out for personal security. Drew therefore had to offer his electorate the idea that he and his Progressive Conservative colleagues could do better than Ottawa could, deploying arguments that Ottawa was hobbling the provinces.

United against the federal government, Drew and Duplessis derailed the Green Paper proposals. It was what Mackenzie King had expected, and he wasted no time in mourning what was for him a too ambitious and dangerous attempt to rewrite the Canadian constitution.[18]

What King did do was eliminate war-related expenditures as fast as possible, demobilizing the armed forces and bringing the troops home. Wisely, the government put some of the money saved directly into veterans' benefits—into housing, education, and vocational training. Unlike the veterans of 1919, the returning soldiers of 1945 were tangibly and frequently thanked by the society they had defended. Consequently, the terrors of radicalism were avoided; a generous social program, rationally applied, made for a more conservative society as it spread security, or opportunity, very widely.

MONSTERS TO DESTROY

The Second World War was fought to ward off not so much dangers to Canada directly but dangers to Canada's allies and associates. Alone and isolated, Canada was nothing; and so Canadians fought abroad against an enemy whose chances of reaching and landing in North America by air, land, or even sea any time soon were negligible. The only neighbour, the United States, shared Canada's immunity from external attack, and from the platform of a perfectly safe home front both countries went abroad, in John Quincy Adams's phrase, "in search of monsters to destroy."

The science and technology that created atomic bombs, and the air fleets to deliver them across vast distances, destabilized the peace. Weapons of mass destruction were a twentieth-century novelty, and soon a whole industry was devoted to manufacturing fantasies about "the atomic age" and what nuclear weapons made possible. Admittedly, it was a matter of arithmetic—build enough bombs and explode them in anger and the end of civilization was nigh.

Canada was involved in atomics in two ways. During the war the Canadian government mined and refined uranium, the raw material for the bomb, and it hosted an atomic laboratory, British-run, on Canadian soil. Its purpose was military, to produce an atomic bomb, but it was overtaken by a faster American team that produced the bomb dropped on Japan in August 1945. Canada was a partner in "the atomic secret," and as a result Canada shared with the United States and Great Britain the burden of deciding what to do with the "secret." Should it be, could it be, truly secret? If not, should it be shared as the basis of a new era of trust and reciprocity among the nations of the world? Could other nations be trusted with the secret?

The answer to these questions was no. The person who mainly answered them was the dictator of the Soviet Union, Joseph Stalin, who in addition to being the national leader of his Communist empire was also pope to the international communist movement, which had its branch in Canada as in most other countries. The Canadian Communist Party had come a long way since its founding in 1921. Persecuted at home and craving support from abroad, it ended up in Stalin's menagerie of "fraternal" Communist parties, bought and sold by the great central Communist Party in the Soviet Union. The price of support was obedience, and the Canadian party gave that in abundance, following every twist and turn of Stalin's cynical and frequently incompetent political strategy.

Stalin certainly didn't trust the Western democracies, and fearing their wealth and ingenuity, he set out to discover what they were about. It didn't take long to penetrate the atomic mystery, using idealistic scientists to prise out capitalist "secrets." The secrecy was in large part illusory, because the science of atomic physics was well understood from Moscow to Montreal to Madras. The technology was admittedly more difficult and much more expensive, but once Stalin learned that atomic weaponry was theoretically possible, he put every available resource in a devastated Soviet Union to work.

Some of Stalin's information came from Canada. Officials in the Soviet embassy in Ottawa ran two spy networks seeking atomic secrets. They found some, and duly reported them back to Moscow. But their cover was blown by a defector from the embassy, Igor Gouzenko, who in September 1945 told all to Canada's astounded government. So unused was Mackenzie King to this kind of activity that he seriously considered giving Gouzenko back; in the end he shared him with his senior allies, American president Harry Truman and British prime minister Clement Attlee, the successors of Roosevelt and Churchill, respectively.

It was the beginning of what came to be called the Cold War, a forty-five-year confrontation between the Western powers, led by the United States, and the Soviet Union. There was never any question in anyone's mind, even Stalin's, as to where Canada would stand in the Cold War.

Canadian society was Western, capitalist, and liberal. It was relatively open, a "bourgeois democracy" in the contemptuous Soviet term. The Soviet Union, by way of contrast, was a "people's democracy," in which the Communist Party by definition spoke for "the people." Communism promised progress and prosperity, enlightenment and equality, and for that reason it attracted supporters outside the Soviet Union, even in the relatively prosperous countries of North America and Western Europe, where progress and prosperity were already in residence. The key was that the Communists did not disavow violence and revolution; they understood that to turn any society upside down while installing enlightenment would require coercion, and the idea of coercion as the real and best solution to bourgeois politics found its adherents in the West, and even in Canada. In the shaky postwar years, and with the memory of economic depression fresh in people's minds, there were many in Western Europe who were attracted by communism's brutal directness as well as its idealism.

If communism was a menace, there was only one country that could stand against it—the United States. The war had sapped the economies and societies of Western Europe. The British had sacrificed much of the treasure of their empire, and to keep going through the war they promised that when it ended they would liberate its most advanced part, the Indian subcontinent. In truth the British could no longer afford an empire, financially or politically, and in 1947–48 they hastily abandoned India, Pakistan, Burma, Ceylon, and Palestine. Ready or not, the British Empire was on the way to freedom, while the British concentrated on rebuilding their own society—as it happened, in a democratic-socialist Labour party model that was close cousin to Canada's own democratic-socialist party, the CCF.

The American government, and American politicians generally, were at first uncertain as to what they should do. Once it became clear that by 1947 Great Britain was a great power only in name, President Truman nerved himself and his country to act as leader of what came to be called "the Free World." The Canadian government did little to persuade him, though American diplomats had no doubt where Canada stood. The Canadian Liberal government, Mackenzie King's until November 1948 and Louis St. Laurent's after that, accepted and applauded American leadership. Its misgivings, if it had any, were that the Americans might tire or become impatient—more specifically, that the American system of government, with its balance of interests and institutions, might prove too complicated or too slow-moving to allow Truman and his successors to provide wise and timely leadership.

Some Canadians—Charles Ritchie, later a very senior and influential diplomat, was one example—lamented the decline of Great Britain. Canada was more important than ever in British terms, for a weakened Great Britain needed and relied upon Canadian assistance. The assistance was forthcoming—a $1.25-billion loan (one-tenth of Canada's gross national product) in 1946, a wheat contract that ensured cheap grains to Britain, and cooperation, understanding, and support as the British adjusted the empire into the more nebulous Commonwealth of Nations in the later 1940s. When Ireland finally cut its constitutional ties to the monarchy and the Commonwealth in 1948, it got no sympathy from Canada; Canadian eyes were fixed firmly on Great Britain, and on shared institutions like the monarchy. It was no accident that Mackenzie King's last overseas trip was to Great Britain, to attend the wedding of Princess Elizabeth; earlier that year he had decided to abort a project for a customs union with the United States while thumbing an old volume on the British Empire. A British subject King was born, and in a very real sense, a British subject he died, in July 1950, after a brief retirement.

King set little store in the new international institution he had helped to create in 1945, the United Nations. He had had a similarly low opinion of its predecessor, the League of Nations, and as he grew older—he was seventy when he won his last general election in 1945—some of his staff wondered if he had confused the two. The "UNO" ("O" for "Organization"), as it was mostly called then, was swiftly paralyzed by quarrels between the Western powers and the Soviet Union. All the great powers (the U.S., the USSR, the UK, France, and China) had vetoes, and the veto, or even the threat of the veto, was enough to halt UN action. King was aware that the less formal Conference of Foreign Ministers, or CFM, which brought together the ministers of Britain, France, the United States, and the Soviet Union, was also paralyzed by 1947.

The Americans understood that Europe had problems that must be solved, with Soviet cooperation if possible, without it if necessary. Germany had been thoroughly defeated, conquered and occupied, but the occupying armies couldn't just sit there, spending money on food and welfare while they waited for something more permanent. Something had to be done to render Germany self-supporting both economically and politically. And the German problem was combined with a perceived political crisis in some of the other countries of Western Europe, where the Communist Party was politically strong and inclined to exercise its influence by disrupting the local economies while creating the impression that it and it alone had the key to Europe's future.

The American response took the form of an $18-billion aid program, named the Marshall Plan after its sponsor, U.S. Secretary of State George Marshall. It is usually thought of as a reconstruction program, literally rebuilding shattered economies. In fact what it did was to solve a dollar shortage in Western Europe, including Great Britain, while turning the actual allocation over to the Europeans themselves, who had to devise and justify their own plans for spending the American money. Canada was involved in the Marshall Plan, not as a donor, but as a supplier of products bought by the Europeans with American dollars. Canada had a dollar shortage of its own, forcing the government to place emergency restrictions on imports in the fall of 1947 and triggering the Canadian–American trade talks that King terminated in early 1948.

King presided over the first stages of negotiating a permanent and formal alliance between the countries of North America and Western Europe. An informal alliance with the United States already existed, based on reciprocal and public promises of aid and support by Roosevelt and King in 1938, and a number of joint boards and cooperative arrangements embodied it. Though King saw himself as strongly pro-American and believed he'd suffered politically because that was his reputation among the voting public, he didn't want to see Canada absorbed in the United States, or so closely tied to the Americans that it had no independent or autonomous diplomatic wiggle room. When negotiations began with the British and West Europeans in Washington in the spring of 1948, King hoped that a new alliance would be able to solve Canada's economic or trade problems as well as its political and military security. He considered them as part of the same package, for without economic security Canada couldn't hope to solve its political problems as well.

King saw the negotiations for a North Atlantic treaty in, but he did not see them out. Old and tired, he knew it was time to move on, and at a Liberal party convention in August 1948 he stage-managed the selection of Louis St. Laurent as his successor.

St. Laurent retained most of the cabinet. King had already added Lester B. Pearson as external affairs minister. Pearson was known as "Mike"; with his cheery smile and characteristic bow tie he embodied a variation on the old theme of homburg hats and striped pants that still characterized the statesmen and diplomats of the day. He was a veteran of the Great War, and between the wars had served in London and Geneva, where he watched the failure of collective security first-hand. Reluctantly, he came to believe that, in the axiom of the day, "peace was indivisible," that Canada had an overwhelming interest in the maintenance of general peace, and that his country must therefore take an activist, interventionist part in foreign affairs.

Pearson signed the North Atlantic treaty, creating the North Atlantic Treaty Organization (NATO) in Washington on April Fools' Day, 1949, while the U.S. Marine Band played a selection of popular tunes, including "I've Got Plenty of Nothin'." NATO, as originally conceived, was a political organization whose members were pledged to mutual defence. Deterrence, not combat, was NATO's purpose, and its founders assumed that mobilization would not prove necessary.

Events belied the hopes of NATO's founders. In September 1949 the Soviet Union tested a nuclear bomb, breaking the American monopoly over the weapon. In October a Communist "People's Republic" was proclaimed in China, under Mao Zedong. In January Mao signed an alliance with Stalin. Mao and Stalin next gave their approval to Communist North Korea to invade anti-Communist South Korea (the former Soviet and American occupation zones, respectively). Stalin and Mao assumed that the United States wouldn't react, and that Communist victory would be a foregone conclusion.

Observers in Washington in the spring of 1950, including the Canadian ambassador, Hume Wrong, would not have disagreed. The United States, like Canada, had demobilized at the end of the war. The American armed forces were so reduced as to be largely ineffective—as were Canada's. But the calculation that the United States would do nothing reckoned without President Truman, and when the North Korean attack took place, on 26 June, Truman reacted. He sent planes and ships, followed by ground troops, to North Korea. He did more, going to the United Nations and denouncing North Korean aggression. Truman reasoned by analogy: Germany, Japan, and Italy in the 1930s had been encouraged by the passivity of the Western democracies in the face of their provocations. And so, assisted by Stalin's diplomatic stupidity—Stalin was boycotting the UN, thereby negating the Soviet veto—the United States secured a UN mandate to repel North Korea.

The Canadian government was surprised but pleased. This was what the UN was for, after all, even if ordinarily it was paralyzed. The UN afforded a platform for smaller countries like Canada to speak and bring influence to bear—in theory. The fact, however, was that the United States was overwhelmingly the largest contributor to the UN army in Korea, followed by South Korea, which was entirely dependent on the U.S. for support and supplies. Other countries gave only a fraction of the troops and, as it turned out, the size of one's participation was the barometer of one's influence.

In Canada there was a moderate divergence between the diplomacy and the politics of participation in the Korean War. Politically, the Canadian public wanted Canada to respond. The cabinet hesitated. Many of its members recalled the conscription crises of the Second World War, and what had happened in the Great War. But this was a war against aggression and, more important, against communism. The Roman Catholic Church, dominant in Quebec's public life, was strongly anti-communist, and the premier of Quebec, Duplessis, was himself a fulminating anti-communist and could hardly complain when the government of Canada sent troops against the common enemy. When St. Laurent called for volunteers to fight in Korea in August 1950 they were forthcoming in abundance, and in Quebec criticism was spotty and muted. Canada sent planes, ships, and troops to Korea; eventually 10,600 served there, and 403 were killed.[19] But that wasn't the entire, or even the most important, part of the response to the war.

The Korean War was unexpected, and upset most Western calculations of Soviet intentions. The Canadian government viewed Stalin and his regime as a very unpleasant but not directly dangerous phenomenon. Stalin's main interest, Canadian diplomats argued, was the preservation of Communist rule in Russia and after that the reconstruction of an economy and society devastated by war and the consequent loss of twenty million dead. If that wasn't the case, and Korea suggested it was not, then it became necessary to provide against Soviet aggression elsewhere. Korea was a sideshow, poor, underdeveloped, isolated—and dangerous, if the Americans allowed themselves to be sucked in too far, or became unduly panicked by the course of the war.[20] Europe was the prize in any East–West contest, and it was there that Western efforts should be concentrated.

Starting in the summer of 1950, the Canadian government began to mobilize. The armed forces were more than doubled in size, new equipment was bought, and $5 billion budgeted for rearmament. In cooperation with the United States, radar lines were built across the Canadian north to warn against incursions by Soviet bombers. A reinforced army brigade was sent to Europe to serve as the nucleus of a future Canadian overseas army. An air division was also sent, and during the 1950s would be a significant part of NATO's military establishment in Europe. The navy was strengthened to include an aircraft carrier and accompanying ships. All this required a great deal of money, which meant that the Canadian budget was militarized too: throughout the 1950s and into the 1960s, defence was always the main budgetary item.

Foreign affairs were in a kind of permanent crisis, and this had an effect at home. The consequences in terms of domestic public opinion were clear enough. Canadian anti-communism, present ever since the Bolshevik Revolution in Russia in 1917, was confirmed, even institutionalized. Communists were a tiny minority, but they were suspect, as potential agents of the Soviet Union. There was no need to worry about their political impact. The Canadian Communist Party was never outlawed, though it was kept under surveillance. There was no danger that Canadians would turn to communism, and indeed communism's political support dropped steadily during the 1950s. Resistance to communism, especially as embodied in NATO, proved enduringly popular.

NATO was different from what its founders had intended. It was militarized, and from its headquarters in Paris, under an American general, it planned the defence of Western Europe against Soviet attack. The Soviet attack did not come, and today there is some doubt that it would ever have materialized. Though there were moments of concern, even panic, over the next ten years—especially in 1961, when it appeared that the Soviets might move on the isolated Western occupation force in Berlin— the Soviet danger in Europe appeared to recede. But as it diminished in Europe, it seemed to grow elsewhere, in Asia. That proved to be a different kind of struggle, and it evoked a different kind of Canadian reaction.

CANADA AND THE END OF EMPIRE

The decline of British power transformed Canada's relations with the outside world, and eventually had an impact on Canada's own institutions and political balance. Canada had always been part of some empire, French or British or Roman Catholic, and Canadians' identities were bound up with the identity, real or assumed, of their empire.

At first there was some optimism that the "British Commonwealth of

Nations" could take the place of the British Empire. There was a new queen, Elizabeth II; Britain had begun to recover economically from the war; and some of the old reliable figures of British politics, especially the revered Winston Churchill, were still on the scene. Canada participated for the first time in development aid, through the Colombo Plan, devised at a Commonwealth conference in that city in 1950. From an early date Canada assigned real importance to influencing the newly independent states of the Commonwealth, especially India. From the standpoint of population alone, it was hard not to see the newly independent nations[21] as an important factor in the world balance; and if the West didn't help them and secure their interests, the Communists would.

Some Canadian diplomats were aware that the senior Western powers, Britain, France, and the United States, were widely disliked or at least mistrusted in many of the countries of independent Asia. As one of them put it in a memorandum of August 1947, "The Western powers may have the great majority of the colonial and coloured peoples hostile or unfriendly to them in the event of war with the Soviet Union.... [The] longer independence is delayed the greater are the chances that the colonial independence movements may come under Soviet influence or control."[22] Canada should do what it could to hasten the end of empire, and to tidy up the mess that empire left behind. This was admittedly a great change to the world that Canadians had grown up in, but the transition was eased by the re-invention of the British Commonwealth.

The Commonwealth was founded in part on the pretence that its members shared a common and valuable British inheritance, and indeed the antagonism between ex-colonials and ex-masters inside the organization was highly nuanced and often contradictory. The fact that Commonwealth prime ministers sat down in conference every few years on a basis of equality was not entirely displeasing to the recently ruled, to be sure, but there was a romance to the Western point of view that wasn't present in the Asian.

That said, some circles in Canada held the view that colonial rule, especially as applied in Asia and Africa, was inherently unjust.[23] The prime minister, Louis St. Laurent, had a strong anti-imperialist streak, which most of the time he kept to himself.[24] St. Laurent combined anti-imperialism with a much more traditional sense of missionary charity, which for him was a large part of the justification for giving modest amounts of Canadian aid to underdeveloped countries, although at first merely to those in the Commonwealth.

The British were remedying their imperial problem, for which anglophile Canadian public opinion gave them some credit. The Canadian public preferred to believe that Asian countries like India were evolving as Canada itself had done—or was believed to have done—and that consequently there was a natural affinity between Canada and, especially, India, "the world's largest democracy," in the journalistic cant of the time. There was also a sense that India, as a democracy with a similar British heritage, subscribed to the same "international norms" as Canada, and in this perception there was the kernel of what much later became a pronounced trend toward human rights in Canadian diplomacy.[25]

The core of Canadian foreign policy in the 1950s was resistance to the immediate danger of the Soviet Union, though Canadian attitudes on communism included a strong affinity for the human rights of East Europeans suffering under Soviet hegemony and Communist dictatorship. To that end, Canadians strongly backed NATO and the American alliance, and resisted situations that might have destabilized Western solidarity. Pearson and St. Laurent stoutly defended to the sceptical and neutralist Indians the good intentions of the United States, even when it meant that the Americans were arming India's neighbour Pakistan—in the interest of anti-communism.[26]

Canadian solidarity with the Western alliance continued even after relations with the Soviets began to thaw with the death of Stalin in March 1953 and the end of the Korean War soon after. St. Laurent and Pearson, supported by an exceptionally competent diplomatic service, remained firmly orthodox in their approach to the Cold War. But for Pearson it was by no means clear that "frozen now" in terms of Soviet policy meant "frozen forever."

The best example of St. Laurent's and Pearson's diplomacy occurred in the fall of 1956, when two simultaneous crises occurred. The greater, or at any rate the longer-lasting, was a dispute between Great Britain and France on the one side and Egypt on the other over the ownership and management of the Suez Canal. The second was the November invasion by the Soviet Union of its satellite Hungary to suppress a rebellion against Communist rule.

The Canal had been an imperial property for seventy-five years, linking Britain and Asia through a waterway owned by British and French investors and garrisoned by British troops. Yet the Canal had once belonged to Egypt, and traversed Egyptian territory populated by Egyptians. That was what necessitated the British garrison, whose purpose was to defend the Canal and themselves against local guerrillas. In 1956, however, the garrison was withdrawn—it was needed elsewhere, and it was expensive—and the Egyptian government of Gamal Abdel Nasser took over the defence of the Canal, promising to let the British back in if ever there was trouble.

In July 1956, after a British and American refusal to finance a major development project, Nasser nationalized the Suez Canal. He promised to pay off the investors, and otherwise to maintain the waterway just as it was. Britain and France, and especially the British prime minister, Anthony Eden, took the nationalization as a challenge to their hitherto undoubted supremacy as imperial powers in the Middle East. Eden and the French decided to invade Egypt and retake the Canal. For Eden it was a last chance to prove that Britain was still a great power, and he wouldn't listen to contrary advice from anyone.

That included Canada, whose government thought it high time that Britain got out and stayed out of Egypt, and the United States, whose president, Dwight D. Eisenhower, was doubtful of the justice and the practicality of Britain's reassertion of empire. The Canadians were sensitive to the damage a British invasion of Egypt would do to the image of the West in the underdeveloped world—"neo-imperialist" and "neo-colonial" were words to conjure with in the Third World, and Eden seemed determined to prove that they described a real phenomenon. The Canadians also began to worry that a quarrel between Britain and France on the one hand and the United States on the other would disrupt the Atlantic alliance, and possibly destroy NATO. For Canada this was unimaginable.

Eden responded to differences with his North American allies by attempting to deceive them, right up to the moment of his invasion of Egypt. His plans also featured a secret alliance with Israel, which invaded Egypt a few days before British and French troops were scheduled to land. No sooner had the Anglo-French invasion landed than things started to go wrong, not so much in the fighting as in the diplomatic context that surrounded it. The Americans ostentatiously stood apart, but more to the point they refused to assist the British and French with oil and money. The oil was needed to take the place of Middle East supply, cut off by Arab suppliers in sympathy with Egypt, and the money to prop up the British pound and French franc, threatened by panicky sell-offs in the world currency markets. The British and French didn't have the resources to save themselves, and from that moment their adventure was doomed.

The Third World now took centre stage. Led by India, whose prime minister, Nehru, had close ties to Nasser, the Third World countries proposed to condemn the British and French at the United Nations. This would be a tremendous propaganda defeat for the Western powers, the more so because it was occurring just at a point when the Soviet Union was making plain that its dominance of Eastern Europe did not depend on the consent of its allies, but on its own military force, ruthlessly deployed against Hungary. It proved impossible for Western diplomats to secure the Third World's support against this particular atrocity while the British and French were invading Egypt. The Canadian high commissioner to India, Escott Reid, was particularly frustrated, but he need not have been especially surprised. Pearson, his minister, had already decided that remonstrating with the Indians, or with any other Third World country, was pointless. The support wouldn't be forthcoming because the interests weren't the same.[27]

On the other hand, at the United Nations, Pearson proved skilful in representing the views of an improbable coalition that included both the United States and India. He masked a diplomatic defeat for the British and French by the creation of a UN "peacekeeping" force that would at first stand between the combatants around the Suez Canal and then take the place of the departing British, French, and Israelis. Canada contributed to the force, called UNEF (United Nations Emergency Force), which was initially commanded by a Canadian general. It was a diplomatic triumph for Pearson, who got the Nobel Peace Prize for his achievements. The Nobel committee recognized Pearson's unusual diplomatic skill, which had cobbled a coalition and a solution out of practically nothing. There probably wouldn't have been a major war had he not succeeded, but both the United Nations and the Western alliance, as well as relations between the West and the Third World, would have suffered.

The Soviet attack on Hungary in November 1956 also had consequences for Canada. The federal government admitted an influx of Hungarian refugees who were fleeing the Soviet invasion and the revenge of the Soviet-installed puppet government in Budapest. At the same time the Canadian Communist Party entered a state of terminal decline. Already weakened by its complete subservience to the Soviet Union, the Communists found their claim to moral authority undermined by the very public, and widely televised, Soviet invasion of Hungary. The Communists lost many of their most promising members over Hungary—some of whom later proved quite successful as capitalists, given the opportunity.

If political dissent was subsiding on the left, it rose on the right. The Progressive Conservative opposition had waged ineffective political warfare against the governing Liberals for decades, only to be deflected time and again—losing a record five elections in a row from 1935 to 1953, inclusive. But thanks to Suez, St. Laurent, and Pearson, the Conservatives' spirits revived in the fall of 1956. The imperial spirit rose once more in Canada, as Conservative orators condemned Pearson's betrayal of Britain. Canada's place in 1956, as in 1939, was at Britain's side, they argued, whether to fight against Hitler or "the Hitler of the Nile," as Nasser was called. English Canada was divided on the issue (French Canada was not), and Conservative speakers kept returning to the theme, a sure sign that they were having an impact. Canadians, it turned out, were uncertain about where their country stood, or where it should stand. The government's unexpected weakness in public opinion over foreign policy now combined with its weakness in another area—energy, or more properly, the secure supply of energy.

ENERGY POLICY

Heat and light are or should be close to the heart of Canadian politics. Canada could be settled because heat sources grew alongside the settlements, but as the population increased, heating by wood became impractical. Nineteenth-century Canada mined coal in Nova Scotia and later Alberta or imported it from Pennsylvania, and coal and steam power fuelled the growth of cities and the spread of railways. Electricity allowed the cities to grow up as well as out, as cheap urban transport spread and suburbs expanded. It also powered the factories and thus made possible the employment of a large urban workforce. Canadians liked to believe that electricity was the product of the nation's mighty rivers and waterfalls, and much of it was. But even at the best of times there wasn't enough water power to go around, and much of Canada used coal to heat the boilers that made the electricity, or converted coal into artificial gas. Canadian cities in the first half of the twentieth century were dirty from coal grime and industrial waste, but they always had been—pollution was a fact of life and a condition of progress and prosperity.

During the Great War power and fuel had to be rationed, and in the 1920s and 1930s provincial governments concerned themselves with the provision of power—electricity—for home and industry. The optimistic government of Ontario, for example, contracted to buy power from Quebec to feed its industry—just as the Depression was looming. The pessimistic government of Ontario then spent thousands of dollars in legal fees—fuelling at least one industry—to escape from the contracts, only to need the power once more as the Second World War pushed demand for electricity to new heights. The postwar government of Ontario had to cope with brown-outs as it struggled to match electricity supply with demand. The Ontario premier judged it useful to fire the head of Ontario Hydro, the provincial utility, as a scapegoat for the brown-outs. That seems to have had very little effect on the power supply, though it did improve the province's hot-air quotient. Slowly, Canada began to build thermal electric stations—2.6 million kilowatts in thermal production capacity in 1957, 9.3 million in 1967.[28]

The federal minister of trade and commerce in the 1950s, C.D. Howe,[29] was the same man who had presided over Canada's war production and, consequently, its power supply. Howe disliked finding his country at the far end of American natural gas supply, or dependent on Venezuelan oil piped through Maine to market in Montreal. The Americans were good neighbours and reliable suppliers, but in case of emergency, fuel and power supply became not an issue for the international energy market but for the American government. Howe preferred to find his energy in Canada, but there was a problem of geography and geology. Geography made the waterpower still untapped in the 1940s remote and expensive, while geology had left behind only two small oil fields, one near Edmonton and the other in southwestern Ontario.[30] While there should have been more oil in Alberta, no one could find it.

Until 1947, that is, when a gusher was tapped at Leduc, south of Edmonton. Howe rejoiced and so, with at least as much reason, did the provincial government of Alberta, which saw the province transformed from a have-not stretch of dry prairie to the Canadian equivalent of Texas. Once the oil and accompanying natural gas could be got to market, Canada would have a secure energy supply and, not coincidentally, a much improved balance of payments as purchases of American petroleum declined with the availability of Canadian resources.

Howe took the lead in getting Canadian oil and gas to Canada's largest domestic market, in the central provinces. He encouraged the construction of an oil pipeline, which ran partly through the northern United States and branched off to serve Midwestern American markets.

The pièce de résistance was a natural gas pipeline to Toronto and Montreal. That project, Trans-Canada Pipelines, took time and imagination and, above all, money. It also consumed much of the government's political capital, as it rammed a subsidy for part of the pipeline through the House of Commons in the summer of 1956. This "Pipeline Debate" gave the government a black eye politically because of the way in which Howe, the sponsoring minister, overrode opposition objections, believing them to be irrelevant and without merit (as, by and large, they were). Much of the noise centred on Canadian nationalists' anxieties about American investment and this pipeline's American ownership. Howe, the opposition argued, was giving away Canada's heritage to the Americans, and it was not forgotten that the powerful minister was himself of American birth. In reply Howe promised that American investment in the pipeline would be temporary, necessary only to reassure and secure New York capital for the project. The pipeline was completed in two years, and, as Howe had promised, it came to be owned mostly in Canada.

Howe encouraged another energy source. During the war Canada had one of the few uranium mines in the world, and the most accessible uranium refinery among the Allied powers. Canada therefore participated in the race to build an atomic bomb, and along the way acquired a functioning nuclear scientific establishment, which constructed the first primitive nuclear reactor outside the United States.

In 1947 a much better model, called NRX, was inaugurated at the federal atomic research establishment at Chalk River, Ontario.[31] Canada developed its own line of heavy-water, natural-uranium reactors, which were extended in the mid-1950s for power production. Howe and his advisers hoped that the Canadian model of reactor—eventually called the CANDU—would service both the domestic and export trade. Their hopes were frustrated, though not at first. Reactors became the focus for the expansion of the largest provincial power utility, Ontario Hydro, in the 1960s and 1970s; an experimental reactor was constructed in Quebec; and New Brunswick took a reactor for its own power needs. The export market remained limited: there were some sales, but never enough.[32] The reactor program also proved costly, even if, based on the first decade of operation, the CANDU design was considered the best in the world.

Canadian uranium sales were the most profitable feature of atomic energy. From a small and depleting mine off Great Bear Lake in the Northwest Territories, the industry grew to be the second-largest producer in the world in the 1950s, and eventually the largest in the 1980s and after. Until the 1960s virtually all Canadian production was sold to the United States and the United Kingdom for use in their nuclear weapons programs. Eventually, however, the United States developed a uranium mining industry of its own, and Canadian sales to that country ceased in the later 1960s. Canada's uranium mines struggled for the next couple of decades, until, in the 1990s, they came to dominate the world market.

Canada's energy policy cannot be seen in isolation from American economic needs and American politics. In some areas, such as the hydro-electric development of the St. Lawrence, the two countries cooperated closely. In petroleum, atomic reactors, and uranium, where there were competing American interests anxious to seal off the domestic market, they did not.

Petroleum exports moved between the two extremes of cooperation and exclusion, as the American executive branch sought a balance between its political needs—reaping votes and campaign finance in oil-producing states—and its strategic priorities—preserving domestic American oil supply and consequently security. The politics usually won, though for a time Canada was given preferred status among foreign oil suppliers, much to the irritation of the competing Venezuelans. Venezuela's irritation at its treatment contributed to the formation of an oil producers' association, the Organization of Petroleum Exporting Countries, better known as OPEC. Unimportant in the 1960s, its time would come soon enough.

NATIONALISM AND ANTI-AMERICANISM

Anti-Americanism is in some respects as old as Canada itself. Oscar Wilde's quip that the United States and Great Britain were divided by a common language could be expanded and applied to the Canadian–American experience—geography, history, politics, religion, and economics both unite and divide the two countries. (The existence for many years of a substantial Franco-American community that retained its language provides, up to a point, a parallel on the other side of the great linguistic divide.)

When Mackenzie King in 1948 drew back from the idea of a customs union with the United States, he had in mind the negative reaction that Canadian public opinion (or much of it) would have probably had—even after the shared experience of war and alliance, and the generally positive view that Canadians had of American policies and political leaders (especially of the late Franklin D. Roosevelt). The sentiment expressed itself in the 1950s—so much so that when one American diplomat left Canada (and, simultaneously, the diplomatic service) he published an article upbraiding Canadians for their anti-Americanism.[33] His readers were no doubt surprised, but there was an uncomfortable reality at the core of his critique.

The difficulty was all too often a clash of nationalisms. The U.S. embassy began to include a section in its reports to Washington entitled "Canadian Nationalism," while Canadian diplomats lamented (or fulminated about, according to taste) American pig-headedness and indifference to Canadian interests. One American ambassador ascribed Canadian anti-Americanism to a fear that Canadians were at bottom second-rate Americans.

There was nevertheless a fair degree of mutual confidence between the professional diplomats who managed Canadian–American relations. The confidence would be shaken by the next turn of events in Canadian politics.

THE DIEFENBAKER PHENOMENON

On 10 June 1957 Louis St. Laurent and his Liberal government were narrowly defeated in a general election. St. Laurent could have done what Mackenzie King once did, and waited for Parliament to assemble to see if the two minor parties, the CCF and Social Credit, could together lend the government enough votes to survive. Instead, he resigned and made way for the Progressive Conservatives under John Diefenbaker.

Diefenbaker was a new party leader, but an old parliamentarian and partisan. A prominent and successful lawyer from Saskatchewan, he had been in the House of Commons since 1940. He was three times a candidate for his party's leadership, and he succeeded on the third try, in 1956. Diefenbaker was a man who stimulated strong reactions. Some members of his party actively disliked the leader: they believed that he had a long and vindictive memory for slights real and imagined, and they were right. What they had to admit was that as an orator Diefenbaker was second to none and, properly prepared for a speech in Parliament or on the hustings, he was a veritable weapon of mass destruction. They had to admit, too, that after twenty-one years of electoral failure the Conservatives needed a boost, and Diefenbaker was definitely that.

Diefenbaker was of course a Westerner, which eventually proved to be an electoral advantage, but his real strength was that he did not hail from metropolitan Canada. Indeed, his strength lay more in what he was not than in what he was. Ideologically, there was little that divided the Progressive Conservatives, or Diefenbaker in particular, from the Liberals. Politically, at least in terms of political tactics, his hero was Mackenzie King, whom he had studied from the opposition benches in the 1940s. King had taken his time in making up his mind on controversial issues, and Diefenbaker followed his example. Socially, there was a difference, for the Conservatives traditionally drew their strength from English speakers, Protestants, and the upper-income brackets.

Despite Diefenbaker's own lack of identification with the large cities, the large cities voted for him and his party, especially in the snap election he called in March 1958. The Liberals in that election had a new leader, the Nobel Prize–winning Lester Pearson, who had replaced St. Laurent in January. The Nobel Prize did Pearson little good. An actual majority of the electorate adopted the Tory slogan to "Follow John" to an overwhelming victory: 208 out of 265 seats in the House of Commons. From coast to coast, Canadians voted for Diefenbaker, including Quebec, where the ex–Conservative premier Maurice Duplessis threw his support and his organization behind the Conservatives to crush the hated Liberals. It was the year of "Dief the Chief," as he was affectionately dubbed by his followers.

Yet little changed. The Diefenbaker government did not have or propose policies that were philosophically distinct from those of the Liberals. It tackled some overdue problems, such as small and uneconomic farms, encouraging farmers to leave the land if it couldn't support them. It increased pensions. It adjusted energy policy, ensuring a market for Alberta oil in Ontario at slightly more than the world price. It finished the St. Lawrence Seaway, a Howe project, and it promoted nuclear power, a Howe project. It tried to sell another Howe project, the Canadian-made Avro Arrow supersonic jet fighter, and failed. As a result, Diefenbaker shut down the Arrow project, for which Howe refused to condemn him. It was a lesson that not all the Liberals' ideas were good ones. As one of Diefenbaker's ministers ruefully reflected years later, the Conservatives had seen the Ottawa civil service make the Liberals look good all those years; now it was their turn.[34] They were surprised to discover that Diefenbaker proved to be less an alternative to the Liberals than an epilogue.

This fact was masked by several factors. Diefenbaker, more than St. Laurent, made himself the very visible head of the government, seeking publicity and credit for "his" policies. Publicity—of the favourable kind—therefore came to be the barometer by which success was measured, and as time passed, other considerations were increasingly sacrificed to it. Diefenbaker depended on the press, and the press came to depend on Diefenbaker. Unlike St. Laurent, "Dief's" personal foibles became the stuff

of contemporary legend. Diefenbaker, who had made the right choice on
the Avro Arrow, harvested such abuse and bad publicity, not to mention
political damage, that he hesitated to make another unpopular decision.
Cabinet meetings degenerated into festivals of delay as the ministers
endlessly debated the political consequences of their actions. Diefenbaker
proved to be an unskilful manager of his cabinet, and it did not take long
for old animosities to filter out. One perceptive analyst of the
Conservative party has suggested that the Conservatives had spent so
much time losing that they acquired habits and attitudes that were, in a
political context, pathological.[35] They fed on themselves rather than the
opposition.

That might not have mattered had the opposition, as so often
happens, been directionless and incompetent. Pearson himself was not a
born manager, nor was his personal judgment always good, but he was
blessed with colleagues who respected his leadership and subscribed to the
old adage, "If we don't hang together, we'll all hang separately." The
Liberals renovated their policy platform, brought themselves up to date
with the latest liberal fashions, and benefited from a resurgence of liberalism in the United States, manifested in the victory of the youthful and
very handsome Democrat John F. Kennedy in the presidential election of
1960. The works of the expatriate Canadian economist, John Kenneth
Galbraith, became required reading in advanced circles. Encouragingly for
the Liberals, public opinion polls moved in their direction in 1960 and
remained steady thereafter.

If Pearson, aged sixty-three in 1960, became identified with new ideas
and renovation, Diefenbaker failed to make the necessary leap in voters'
minds. His Canada was an older Canada—not necessarily a less liberal
Canada, but one that had missed the boat in adjusting to a new reality.
Diefenbaker looked painfully old-fashioned, even bucolic—a hayseed out
of place in a modern and shiny world. The charge was unjust: Diefenbaker
was anything but a hayseed, but it was true that his habits and his outlook
were ill suited to an era that was, demographically and in terms of style
and culture, increasingly youthful.

CULTURE AND SOCIETY AT THE END OF THE FIFTIES

The late 1950s was the age of the teenager. Teenagers had existed before, of course, but only in the 1950s was there the right combination of numbers, leisure, and prosperity to push them to the forefront of popular culture. The leading edge of the baby boom was creeping upwards. Children's programming became a major feature of the new television networks—the CBC in Canada, and the big three American systems, ABC, NBC, and CBS, from stations across the border. The outward sign that something was changing was the phenomenon of rock 'n' roll, symbolized by Elvis Presley—his guitar, his ducktail hair, and his pelvic gyrations on stage. Rock 'n' roll was strictly for teens, and parents and other authority figures fell all over themselves to condemn it.[36]

The new music crossed borders easily, and given television, radio, and the easy availability of 45-rpm records and cheap record players, rock 'n' roll didn't spread so much as flow into Canada. Some condemned rock 'n' roll because it was immoral, some because it was American (or both), but to be American was, in the late fifties, to be stylish, up to date, and cool. Diefenbaker, to use an obvious example, was not cool, nor was his elderly contemporary, American president Eisenhower. It was hard to imagine Diefenbaker waltzing, let alone gyrating Elvis-fashion.[37]

Diefenbaker presided over the slippage of some of Canada's national traits. Canadians were or had been pro-British, monarchical, and conservative. These characteristics had helped to get Diefenbaker elected in 1957, and they helped define a kind of conservative nationalism that still bore traces of the Canada of Sir John A. Macdonald, one of Diefenbaker's heroes.

Diefenbaker also presided over two royal visits by Elizabeth II, in 1957 and 1959; by the end of the second one, which was quite lengthy, complaints were beginning to be heard. The visits were strong on parades and pageantry, which had worked so well in 1939 for George VI. Perhaps in the age of mass entertainment and easily available images a royal progress, handshakes with notables, and flowers weren't enough. Perhaps too there was the sense that the pomp and circumstance were a charade, masking an absence of power rather than the real thing. Britain in 1939 had been one of the world's truly great powers; Britain in 1959 was, compared with Canada, down on its luck. The memory of the Second World War was beginning to fade; just possibly the Canadian veterans of the war were content to let the British side of it fade.[38] There was in any case the Cold War to fight, and pageants and heritage did not quite fit with its metallic sense of urgency. Still, it would take some time for the growing sense of disenchantment to take root, and it was easier to ignore the signs in English Canada than in the French section of the country.

AMBIVALENT QUEBEC

English Canadians in the 1950s generally believed that French Canada, especially French Quebec, lived in a kind of medieval, Catholic trance. It was hard not to believe it: Premier Duplessis embodied a view of the world that would have been old-fashioned in 1900, let alone 1950. The hand of the Church was visible everywhere in Quebec—in the big churches and high steeples that soared over town and village and city, in the classical colleges run by the clergy, in the monasteries and nunneries that dotted landscapes urban and rural. Quebec had come late and reluctantly to universal education, and the educational standard was lower there than in the rest of the country. There were fewer Quebec veterans than elsewhere, and consequently fewer French Quebeckers who had benefited from veterans' benefits. The country was in the throes of suburbanization and home-buying, but in Quebec home ownership was lower than elsewhere; it was still a province of renters. English Canadians, including English Montrealers, comforted themselves that Quebec was backward—perhaps forever, given the apparently immutable power of the Church and the prevalence of conservative politics.

Yet there were many changes in *la belle province*, the motto that appeared on Quebec licence plates. Some changes derived from Duplessis. The premier had inaugurated a Quebec flag, recalling the banners of pre-revolutionary France, and the flag caught on—a very visible symbol that Quebec was indeed different. Official nationalism was right-wing and repressive, but it should not be thought that it was unpopular or without effect on the younger generation. Many intellectuals drew back from Duplessis's political practices, but that didn't mean they had chosen Canada as the best alternative. Some did, to be sure, but others waited, using federal institutions or the provincial Liberal party—exempt from Duplessis's bullying, up to a point—without subscribing to a pan-Canadian ideology.

The latent quality of Quebec came to a head in 1959–60. Duplessis suddenly died, in September. His successor, Paul Sauvé (incidentally a Second World War hero), died on New Year's Day, 1960. His successor, Antonio Barrette, a parish-pump politician, led Duplessis's Union Nationale to defeat in June. The victor was Jean Lesage, formerly a federal Liberal MP (1945–58) and cabinet minister (1953–57). These events coincided with a resurgence in liberalism—along with optimism and a sense that reform and progress were possible, even after Duplessis and even after Diefenbaker—that was drifting across Canada and that was soon to be mirrored in Kennedy's victory in the United States.

Lesage stood for reform, not revolution, and his cabinet was a mixture of party warhorses and "modern" recruits. Lesage could rely on the former—after all, he came from their ranks. The latter included people like René Lévesque, a journalist and broadcaster for Radio-Canada, the French arm of the CBC, and Paul Gérin-Lajoie, a noted constitutional lawyer. Lesage may have had in mind that he was a logical successor to Lester B. Pearson, his erstwhile cabinet colleague, as national Liberal leader and prime minister (certainly Pearson thought of this). But Lesage proved not to be in control of his fate, and Pearson's later attempts to bring the two together again proved futile. For the time being, and eventually for the foreseeable future, Canada and Quebec were on different paths.

DIEFENBAKER'S DOWNFALL

Diefenbaker had the misfortune to lead a Canada divided by generation and by language. To these cleavages he added regional disharmony and a genuine foreign policy crisis. Diefenbaker had few policies of his own, and the attitudes he brought to government were the bromides of a forgotten era. Confronted by rumblings from French Quebec, he produced bilingual federal government cheques—something that had last been a live issue in the 1930s. Aware that French-speaking MPs and some of his own ministers dozed or fretted through parliamentary debates or the sessions of the cabinet, Diefenbaker produced simultaneous translation.

He was out of synch with English Canada too. His devotion to the monarchy and his references to the past—his past—began to seem quaint, and irrelevant. In a general election in June 1962 Diefenbaker saw his parliamentary delegation melt away from 208 MPs to 116, and with it his majority in the House of Commons. Politically vulnerable, "the Chief" watched the wolves circling—not all of them on the opposition side. His own followers blamed him for the evaporation of their comfortable majority and their prospects for indefinite power. Canadians had got used to indefinite governments under King and the Liberals; now Diefenbaker's seemed to have its future measured in months.

Even so, Diefenbaker might have survived. He still had some resources, including a diminished but still respectable contingent from Quebec, where the old forces were not yet totally vanquished. He held most of Canada's rural seats, and dominated the Prairie provinces, which had developed affection for a man who, whatever his faults, at least came from the West. There were two minor opposition parties, the New Democrats or NDP (successors of the CCF since 1961) and Social Credit, which through a bizarre turn of fate was now mainly francophone, and from Quebec. But neither the NDP nor the Social Credit wanted to replace the wounded Diefenbaker with Pearson, whose Liberal party was a more deadly foe to their own political prospects.

Diefenbaker's own nemesis didn't even live in Canada. John F. Kennedy, the president of the United States, had hoped for much from Canada when he was inaugurated in 1961. He immediately visited Diefenbaker to urge on him a kind of partnership in the Americas and elsewhere in the world. There was nothing wrong with the spirit of Kennedy's suggestion, but the devil was always in the details, and they included the usual disparity in wealth and population between the two countries at a ratio of ten to one. It wasn't hard to figure out where most of the decisions would be made, even if Kennedy fully intended to have Diefenbaker sitting in when they were taken. The more important the decision, the less the consultation.

A good example was the defence of North America against Soviet attack. In the fifties it was assumed, accurately, that such an attack would come from manned long-range bombers, which would rain nuclear bombs on the cities of the previously invulnerable continent. Soviet aircraft would have to cross Canada, which with the United States maintained radar lines and an air defence organization to detect and shoot down the Russians. The Americans took the lead, as they had to: they had the money and they had the technology. They were also determined to survive a nuclear attack, and with Diefenbaker's assistance conducted several air raid alerts to familiarize the civilian population with what would happen when and if a nuclear war occurred.

The alerts (one had the happy name of "Tocsin") did not have quite the desired effect. They alarmed the civilians they were meant to reassure—though how a projected casualty figure in the millions could have been reassuring was a mystery the planners did not reveal. The plans called for Diefenbaker and his chief ministers to head for a bombproof shelter outside Ottawa, a concrete-lined hole in the ground that wags dubbed "the Diefenbunker." Even pillars of the Tory establishment began to have doubts about the wisdom of a policy that seemed to take the prospect of worldwide incineration with aplomb.[39] For the first time since the inception of the Cold War, there was respectable pressure on the government to do something about a strategic impasse that offered devastation as the alternative to defeat.

The issue of nuclear weapons became more pressing when, in 1961–62, the Kennedy administration pressured the Diefenbaker government to honour Canadian commitments—some made to NATO as far back as 1954—to equip Canada's armed forces with American nuclear warheads. (These would continue to be owned and controlled by the Americans, and would become operational only by mutual consent between Canada and the United States.) In particular, Diefenbaker had bought an American missile system, the BOMARC,[40] to shoot down incoming Soviet bombers; the BOMARC would only work with nuclear weapons. Diefenbaker was caught between Canada's international commitments and his sense that a political storm was brewing at home on the issue. Worse still, his external affairs minister, Howard Green, and his defence minister, Douglas Harkness, held diametrically opposed positions on the issue, with Harkness urging the adoption of nuclear weapons and Green opposing them.

The nuclear issue was brought to a head in October 1962, during the Cuban Missile Crisis. Cuba had acquired, through a revolution in 1959, a Communist government headed by Fidel Castro. The presence of communism 150 kilometres across the Florida Straits from Key West dismayed the American government, which under both Eisenhower and Kennedy did what it could to overthrow the Cuban dictator. Kennedy backed a hare-brained invasion by Cuban exiles in 1961 (unsuccessful) and then sponsored various schemes to murder Castro—for example with an exploding cigar. Castro resented this, but his communist faith told him that this was what good communists should expect from capitalism. He appealed to the mother of all communists, the Soviet Union, and the Soviets were delighted to help. Cuba was a beachhead in the Americas, and it altered the strategic balance, especially if the USSR were able to place missiles (with nuclear warheads) in Cuba. The Americans discovered these when the launch pads were in the last stages of construction, in mid-October 1962, and the Cuban crisis was on.

Kennedy sought solidarity from his allies, sending a senior diplomat to Canada to brief Diefenbaker on what the Soviets were doing and what he proposed to do in response. He was surprised when he learned that Diefenbaker actually questioned his evidence—that Canada was the least cooperative of his major allies. Fortunately, the crisis was solved soon enough, and Diefenbaker's hesitations made no practical difference. But the news soon leaked, and it damaged the prime minister's standing in Canadian public opinion, which expected him to maintain unity with the allies and especially the United States.

A few months later, in February 1963, the nuclear weapons question came to a head. Kennedy issued a statement that blamed Canada for the failure, after years of negotiation, to reach an agreement on nuclear deployments. Diefenbaker's ministers immediately set to quarrelling, the defence minister resigned, and the government was defeated on a confidence motion in the House of Commons. Diefenbaker had accomplished the impossible, persuading the three opposition parties to vote together to defeat him when the support of only one would have been enough to preserve the government.

An election was called for 8 April 1963. Diefenbaker, his cabinet in chaos, was defeated. Pearson, the Liberal leader, didn't so much win as harvest the fruits of Diefenbaker's political ineptness. Diefenbaker himself seems to have found the outcome hard to grasp and harder to accept. That, combined with his natural vindictiveness, would make Canada's political history for the next few years very colourful.

14

AFFLUENCE AND ITS DISCONTENTS, 1960–1980

St. Mary's Roman Catholic Church, Red Deer, Alberta, designed by prominent Canadian architect Harold Cardinal. Cardinal's blend of the old and the new recalled Canada's past and traditions for an anxious and uncertain age.

W riting about the state of Canada in 1980, three historians termed the country's recent history "a success story." In many respects it was, but it was a qualified success. Materially there was almost no doubt. The years between 1960 and 1980 were a period of almost unbroken prosperity. Canada was rich. In terms of purchasing power, Canadians earned twice as much in 1985 as they had in 1960.[1] In the measurement Canadians always used, how much they earned relative to Americans, they reached an all-time high in the early 1980s—83 percent of American per capita income in 1981.[2]

There were other measures of success, and in these Canada hadn't done so well. Canadians reacted to prosperity in the 1960s not by coming together but by coming apart. The problem with affluence, it turned out, was there wasn't enough of it—or, paradoxically, too much. With so much new-found wealth, impatience mounted over what to do with it, leading to frustration among policy-makers trying to devise and impose rational solutions to what they assumed to be soluble problems.

Generationally, regionally, and linguistically the country struggled over what do with money and the things money could buy. Regions left behind in the 1940s and 1950s demanded the same opportunities as the rest of the country. Ethnic and racial minorities pointed to inequity and discrimination, historical and actual, and demanded that something be done, and quickly. Many of the young questioned why money was so important for a good life, a message that might once have come from the churches but which, in a secularizing age, came from lay prophets rather than religious pulpits. Discontent as much as affluence set the agenda for the 1960s and 1970s.

For most of these decades fortune smiled. Canada's GDP rose steadily through the 1960s, in fact until 1974, and then after a brief hiccup continued to grow until 1981. Unemployment fell to 3.4 percent in 1966, and then rose and fell in waves, with each successive trough higher than the last—4.4 percent in 1969, 5.3 percent in 1974, and 7.5 percent in 1980, before reaching double digits in 1982. Canadian unemployment rates paralleled those in the United States, but were significantly higher than those in Western Europe and Japan, until the early 1980s.[3] By the early 1960s Western Europe had already largely recovered from the war, which meant that incomes and purchasing power increasingly resembled Canada's. Not surprisingly, immigration to Canada from continental Europe tended to decline; so did that from the United Kingdom.

The prosperity was visible as you crossed the country. Being prosperous was something of a novelty, but even crossing the country by car was something that earlier, poorer generations could not have contemplated. Thanks to the Trans-Canada Highway, a federally funded road completed in 1965, it became possible to travel from Newfoundland to Vancouver Island.[4] The highway linked all the provinces, and just in time, as Canada's transcontinental railway system was beginning to contract: after 1969 it was no longer possible to cross Newfoundland by train.

Across Canada, growing cities sprawled. Farmland vanished into suburbs or industrial parks, linked by four-lane highways. Urban areas grew not only horizontally, but vertically. "Skyscrapers hide the heavens," a contemporary poet wrote.[5] It was literally true, but symbolically true as well, for the concrete office and apartment towers eclipsed the church spires that once dominated Canadian settlements, large and small.

Migration, from the countryside and from abroad, filled the cities. The number of immigrants fluctuated wildly, from a high of 223,000 in 1967 to 72,000 in 1971, and then remained over 100,000 for most of the 1970s. Until 1963 and for a few years after, Canada's birth rate also played a major role in population growth. Schools bulged and suburbs grew according to the rhythms of family formation, which in the years after 1945 was abundant. The baby boom was on, and in the early 1960s showed no sign of ending. It was in itself a sign of prosperity, the growth in human capital matching the capital investment in concrete and steel.

Urbanization implied a change in the way Canadians thought of themselves, or thought of their society, but cities were hardly the only influences on how society functioned. Canada's was a youthful society, where the balance of generations was migrating downward. Styles of life, of thought, and of politics shifted with the changing generations, producing a Canada in the early seventies that would have been unimaginable in 1963.

Some articulate Canadians found the country altogether too contented, too quiet, and even too smug, but in the popular imagination they were a minority, confined mostly to socialist-run Saskatchewan or to the larger cities; the latter variety might be expected to move to New York or Europe, where discontented Canadians with the means or the incentive to move on often went. "I had been a failure as a Canadian," one such wrote. "The patience, the mildness, the taste for conformity that seemed prerequisites for a tolerable life were beyond me."[6]

Those who didn't have the means to move on usually went unnoticed, but they existed in the nation's system of Indian reserves, or in the slums of Canada's larger cities, or in distant enclaves of rural poverty. The old or the sick were at risk—and worse still was the plight of the old *and* sick; the elderly had their health insurance cancelled when they turned sixty-five and became a greater actuarial risk for their insurance companies. Some parts of the country were less prosperous than others— Newfoundland, for instance, and the Maritime provinces, rural Quebec, and marginal farmers on the Prairies or in central Ontario. In Alberta the oil and gas industry had delivered prosperity, but not enough to make the province a northern Texas or Calgary the new Houston. Oil prices were low, and markets uncertain, and the memory of the impoverished 1930s very recent.

The crude population statistics catch the reality of a country of regions—the Atlantic provinces, Quebec, Ontario, Saskatchewan and Manitoba, Alberta and British Columbia. The Atlantic region grew slowly in the 1960s. Newfoundland's high birth rate had kept its population growing in the 1950s, but in the 1960s the rate of increase fell sharply until, in the early 1980s, it barely grew at all. Quebec's population grew, but failed to keep pace with Ontario's. Saskatchewan actually lost population in the 1960s and most of the 1970s, while Manitoba grew very slowly. Alberta, on the other hand, pulled in immigrants from abroad and from other provinces to share in its oil-based prosperity, rising from 1.3 million people in 1961 to 2.2 million in 1981.[7] British Columbia didn't do quite so well, but a steady flow of migrants gave the Pacific province a clear vote of confidence.

Political thought and economic capacity changed as well. The two were closely related, for prosperity fed, or at least coddled, ideology. The early sixties were a time of hope and expansiveness. The industrial economy that had matured in North America during the Second World War reached its apogee—large factories, huge workforces, and perpetual profitability characterized companies like Ford or Chrysler or General Motors ("the Big Three"), each with its Canadian branch plants. Canada in many ways was a smaller replica of American capitalism—including the "international" trade unions like the United Auto Workers that organized labour in Canadian car plants.

Economic life appeared to be dominated by great corporations based in the gleaming towers of Manhattan. (One of the most impressive, the Seagram Building, designed by Mies van der Rohe and erected in 1958, bore the name of a Canadian liquor company that was headquartered at the time in Montreal.) It was familiar and foreign, enviable and envied.

In terms of income, capitalism American-style was raising the American working class into the middle class. It was industrial workers who were leaving the cities and moving to the suburbs and sending their children to college. And with a certain time lag, it was happening in Canada as well. Prosperity dampened opposition and homogenized American politics and then Canadian politics, and to a remarkable degree. Socialism became a variety of welfarism, and welfarism characterized not merely the political left but also large businesses, which could afford to pay out not only higher wages but, increasingly, benefits for their workers.

There was some doubt whether the old categories of "left" and "right" applied any more. In the United States one academic, an ex-socialist, argued that society had reached "The End of Ideology."[8] The CCF party abandoned socialism as its political objective in 1956, and then in 1961 transmuted itself into a more centrist political formation, the New Democratic Party. New Democrats didn't demand the wholesale nationalization of large enterprises; instead, they concentrated on government organization and regulation of social welfare—for which, needless to say, prosperity would pay.

Government, too, enjoyed a good reputation. Government had organized the last war (meaning the Second World War), and the Cold War as well. The Cold War no longer seemed as urgent after the Cuban Missile Crisis of 1962, the Test Ban Treaty of 1963, and the gradual decompression of confrontation in Europe. Government could turn its attention elsewhere. Now it could reform health care and pensions for those too old or too sick to share fully in the good times and high incomes of the 1960s. It could look to the margins of society, and to problems that prosperity had ignored or by itself couldn't solve.

To these ideas, which weren't new or unique to Canada, there was also a tinge of nationalism. The Americans' tendency to blithely equate Canadian life with their own offended some, perhaps many, in Canada. Their country, they argued, was "taken for granted," its identity obscured, its concerns unheard. During the 1950s the United States embassy in Ottawa had maintained a regular file on Canadian nationalism in its routine reports to Washington, and kept a wary eye on the Canadian predilection for finding fault with the United States.

In the 1960s there was plenty to report. Nationalism had become effectively synonymous with anti-Americanism, though it differed from the views of older generations because it no longer had much of an "imperial" or British tinge. But what did anti-Americanism mean? In the largest sense, it was almost the same as a complaint against the homogenizing effects of modern life. The philosopher George Grant, in his 1965 book *Lament for a Nation*,[9] deplored the fact, as he saw it, that middle- and upper-class Canadians had abandoned their heritage for the glittering prizes offered by American (or American-style) business and technology.[10] Others, like the prominent Toronto businessman Walter Gordon, resented the fact that executive jobs, and with them the capacity for executive decision-making, were transferred out of Canada. Canada, in Gordon's view, couldn't be an independent country unless it also had an autonomous business sector.

These ideas, like Canada's prosperity, were distributed by region and by age. It was all very well for Canadians in prosperous, industrial Ontario to reject the fruits of American investment. (Ontario already had lots of American investment, which was unlikely to decamp any time soon.) The hinterland craved investment of any kind, and American money looked as good as any other. (In fact there were complaints that unadventurous Canadian money was hard to get, and that foreigners' funds were the only kind on offer.) Older Canadians, remembering depression and war, were less inclined to reject investment, industry, and jobs.

Younger Canadians proved to be different from their elders. It wasn't just a question of nationalism, though the generation of the 1960s was a nationalistic generation. They dressed differently—blue jeans first became universal in this decade. They followed different styles of music, of which their parents, like their parents before them, ritually disapproved. They called their lifestyle a "counterculture"—*the* counterculture—and attributed to it the usual romantic traits of authenticity and spontaneity and, of course, generational exclusiveness. "Don't trust anyone over thirty" was the watchword.[11]

The boomers (an American term, freely adapted) took job security and a prosperous economy for granted, never having experienced anything else. They were self-consciously Canadian, and immediately identified with the new Canadian flag that the Pearson government adopted in 1965. They were not, however, all that different from young Americans or Europeans or Australians, in culture, ideas, or general lifestyle.[12] Nationalist in politics, international in style, the baby boom set the tone for the last third of the twentieth century.

The Politics of Security

Lester Pearson was remembered, after his death, for his role in international security, but his government is best remembered for its provision of national security—personal security, meaning the expansion of the Canadian social safety net. Though a minority in two Parliaments, elected in 1963 and 1965, the Liberal government between 1963 and 1968 enacted and implemented fundamental reforms to Canada's old-age pension system and designed a comprehensive and universal health-care system. Because neither of these programs fell in federal jurisdiction, Pearson, his ministers, and officials negotiated ceaselessly with the provinces to secure their consent and cooperation and, miraculously, they usually got both.

Pensions, private and public, were a continuing irritant in Canadian politics. A federal-provincial pension scheme was put into place in 1927, very much at the insistence of two Labour members of Parliament.[13] It was reformed and considerably expanded by the St. Laurent government in 1951. Nevertheless, Canadians continued to look enviously across the border at the American Social Security program, which provided both contributory pensions and unemployment insurance.

Health care—its availability, affordability, and efficacy—had been an issue in most Western societies since the late nineteenth century. Public health—disease prevention, sanitation, and the quarantine of infectious diseases—had always been a responsibility of government, usually provincial or municipal. (The federal government had responsibilities in its own jurisdiction, such as the military forces and veterans, and immigration.) The phrase "catastrophic illness" had real meaning in Canada, beyond its effect on the body or mind. Some sicknesses, both acute and chronic, could undermine a family's finances. Although there was medical insurance, private and voluntary, it wasn't enough for most Canadians. The St. Laurent government, in its last year, did implement a hospital insurance scheme, with the support of the provinces: Canadians need no longer pay for basic hospital services (interpreted as ward care), though private health insurance continued to pay for "frills" such as semi-private or private rooms.

Doing something about pensions and health care was the program of the CCF/NDP, but Canada's socialist party (after 1956, semi-socialist) was never going to attract enough support to form a national government. The CCF did have power in Saskatchewan, however, and under Premier Tommy Douglas in 1961 it implemented a government health insurance scheme that was both compulsory and universal. After a vivid and much televised skirmish with the province's medical association and its supporters, Douglas successfully put health insurance on the agenda of national politics. The fact that a province could take the lead, could pioneer an important national initiative, was a point that should have been remembered. It was also a boost for the federal NDP, to which Douglas now moved as national leader.[14]

The national Liberal party platform promised to reform both pensions and health insurance. Party support for such reform was strong but not unanimous; as it happened, though, the reformers held most of the levers of power and policy. Walter Gordon as finance minister and Tom Kent as Pearson's main policy adviser were determined to proceed, and they carried a sometimes wavering prime minister with them. With Kent in particular, the ideas of the Canadian-born Harvard economist, John Kenneth Galbraith, may be said to have come home.[15]

Pensions came first. Pearson proposed a "Canada Pension Plan" (CPP), which would be portable but not universal. Its principles were negotiable and its financing at first cloudy. It encroached on provincial jurisdiction, and so depended on enough of the provinces coming on board. And as it turned out, the federal proposals weren't exactly what were adopted as the basis for the future CPP.

Quebec, rather to Ottawa's surprise, was first in the field, with a comprehensive and practicable contributory pension scheme. Pension reform was certainly attractive to Quebec, but what made it especially so was the prospect of harvesting contributions. The pension fund would accumulate hundreds of millions of dollars in a relatively short time, and that money could be available to the Quebec government to invest. Pensions, or rather pension contributions, were the key to the Quebec government's desire to build a "modern" economy—autonomously. So in order to get to its objective of a national pension plan, the federal government had first to negotiate with the provinces, and negotiate seriously.

As it finally emerged in 1964, the Canada Pension Plan was contributory, universal, and portable. But it was bifurcated, one plan for Quebec, the QPP, and one for the rest of the country. This was a hard pill for the Conservative government of Ontario to swallow, but eventually, and after appeals to national unity, it did.

Next came health care. There was considerable debate in the more conservative provinces like Ontario and Alberta as to whether a government plan was desirable, and whether viable private and voluntary schemes weren't sufficient. Nor was it forgotten that Saskatchewan's adoption of health insurance—medicare—had provoked a doctors' strike and much public ill feeling. On the other hand, the Saskatchewan doctors' tactics and extreme language had helped to discredit opposition to medicare, not just in the province but across the country.[16]

In the summer of 1965 officials in Ottawa under the overall supervision of Tom Kent devised a plan that was administratively simple and politically workable. Ottawa would pay half the cost of doctors' services[17] if the provinces would pay the other half, subject to provincial acceptance of four basic principles: universality of coverage; a comprehensive definition of what doctors' services were; transferability of benefits from province to province; and public administration. The ensemble was labelled "medicare."

Medicare's timing was directly related to the Liberal government's need for a platform in the 1965 election, which Pearson called in a desperate attempt to secure a majority in the House of Commons. He failed to get his majority, but that failure made no difference to medicare. The federal terms were so attractive that Quebec overcame its opposition to shared-cost programs with the federal government, Ontario its preference for private insurance, and Alberta its objections to universal coverage.[18] By the end of the 1960s, Canada had a universal, portable, and publicly funded and administered medicare system, which Tom Kent correctly identified as "the most important of all the social reforms introduced by the Pearson administration."[19]

The development of a social welfare system fundamentally changed the way "Canada" did business. During the 1940s and 1950s the business of "Canada" was, essentially, war and external security, and "Canada" meant the federal government. But government, especially in Canada, is a collective noun. Because defence was urgent, and because defence was expensive, the provinces and their priorities were shoved to one side. From the perspective of international affairs, Canada was a small actor, and so it needed to concentrate its resources if it was to make a contribution to the collective defence and have a corresponding weight in an alliance system. The needs of Canadian defence, as much as anything else, left little room for an expansive social welfare program.

After 1968, however, Canada had just such a program. Its size and cost were sufficiently large that Mitchell Sharp, Gordon's successor as minister of finance, got his colleagues to postpone implementing medicare for a whole year, until 1968. Meanwhile, defence and mutual aid descended from 23.45 percent of federal government expenditure in 1961 to 13.7 percent in 1969; by 1975 it was 7.1 percent. Social welfare, on the other hand, rose from 20 percent of federal government expenditure in 1961 to 23 percent in 1969 and to 33 percent in 1975. Ministers and most other politicians did not remind the electorate that government was about choices, and that what was spent in one area would not be spent in another. But so it was: Canadians might well be better off at home, and in their daily lives, because through their governments that was where they had chosen to spend their money. As a consequence, they would spend less on defence, and the industries and programs related to defence, and Canada was bound to play a lesser role in its alliances and to be more reticent in its international engagements.

THE TERMS OF TRADE

While the Pearson government was redefining Canadian society, it was also altering Canada's economic geography by reworking the country's trade policy. Pearson and his government might have seemed ill-equipped by both experience and ideology to do much about trade. Pearson was primarily a political diplomat, most comfortable in alliance negotiations or debates at the United Nations. Ideologically, the government's minister of finance, Walter Gordon, was a fervent Canadian nationalist who was anxious to enhance local control over the economy, a principle that was apparently at odds with a cooperative trade policy.

Principles had little to do with circumstances. The political environment of Canadian trade had changed considerably. Whereas before 1939 Canadian trade was balanced between Great Britain and the United States, after 1945 the trend shifted south. Under the General Agreement on Tariffs and Trade (GATT) Canada participated in periodic tariff-lowering exercises, but these GATT "rounds" did not fundamentally affect the high tariff wall that protected Canadian industry from competition. What the GATT did do, however, was to limit the ability of the nations of the British Commonwealth to create their own economic or trading zone. All nations belonging to the GATT must have the same rules and offer the same tariff levels—though existing arrangements, like British preference, were "grandfathered." The only exception allowed countries or groups of countries to form free trade zones.

In 1957 six continental European nations, France, West Germany, the three Low Countries, and Italy, formed a Common Market. Britain chose not to join, and was later excluded by France. The Common Market, led by France, proved to be highly protectionist, especially in the use of subsidies to encourage European agriculture. The results could be bizarre—a butter mountain, or a wine lake, could have been constructed out of subsidized European agricultural products. And of course Europe, a temperate continent, produced many of the same crops as Canada. Canadian agricultural exports—like wheat, apples, and cheese—to Europe were gradually strangled. Though these still had entry to Britain, a traditional market, it was clear in the 1960s that British accession to the Common Market was merely a matter of time. So when it came to trade and economics generally, Canada had increasingly little choice: the United States was the only game in town.

The Canadian government was unwilling to lower trade barriers to the larger and more productive American economy, but at the same time it was uneasily aware that the Canadian economy, with its limited domestic market, was insufficient. Canadians' prices were higher, and their choices more limited, than were the Americans'. This was especially true in automobiles, where Canada's American-owned car industry was notoriously inefficient. Canada ran a large deficit in its automotive trade with the United States, year after year, with depressing results for Canada's balance of payments.

From time to time the Canadian government toyed with the idea of adjusting the auto industry. Walter Gordon took up the issue, seeking more production and investment in Canada and offering incentives in return. His first attempts ran into American opposition, and threats of retaliation; but they weren't fruitless. The notion of fixing the auto industry in a way that would keep the Canadians happy stimulated thought inside the American government and in the Big Three car companies.[20]

The solution was a Canadian–American agreement (the Autopact of 1965) that created a system of managed trade in the industry. The auto companies got free trade for parts and cars in return for guaranteed levels of production and investment in Canada. They used their new-found freedom to rationalize the car industry. Instead of duplicating production in Canada to make small numbers of high-priced vehicles for the Canadian market, they could service all of North America from a single plant. In 1964, 7 percent of Canada's automobile production was exported; in 2002, the figure was 60 percent. On the other side, 40 percent of vehicles purchased in Canada were U.S.-made, another quite significant increase. In Canada, investment rose; employment rose too, from 75,000 in the mid-1960s to 491,000 by 2002; and prices dropped. Production rose so far that by 1970 Canada had, for the first time, a small surplus on the auto trade. Automobiles moved to first place in Canada's manufactures—12 percent of manufacturing GDP by 2002—and in its exports, displacing forest products.

Some Americans noticed. The Autopact became an item on a list of U.S. grievances centred on the increasing American imbalance of payments, and in the early 1970s it several times came close to being unilaterally cancelled. But it was not. As a result, Canadian–American trade increased, and Ontario's economy, in particular, was reoriented— north–south as well as east–west.

There was an irony in the Autopact. Its main progenitor, Walter Gordon, wished to recapture the Canadian economy. Yet he also wanted the country to prosper, by expanding, in this case, high-paying manufacturing jobs. In this he succeeded, but in terms of strict economic nationalism he did less well. Before 1965 the Canadian automobile companies were American subsidiaries, but because they dealt with a separate Canadian market they had a high degree of autonomy. That was no longer necessary under the Autopact, and effective decision-making—indeed a whole variety of executive functions—moved to head office in the United States.

The Autopact experience illustrated the workings of the Law of Unintended Consequences. It pulled the United States and Canada closer together, changing the balance of the economy in the process. (Multilateral trade negotiations under the GATT, the Kennedy Round of 1964–67, reinforced this tendency, reducing or abolishing tariffs on billions of dollars' worth of trade between Canada and the United States.) Most Canadians, however, would have been surprised to learn how successful, and how important, the Autopact was to the country, and, if they lived in Ontario, to their daily lives. As far as most Canadians were concerned, relations with the United States were actually entering a decline in the 1960s and, as far as political and cultural relations were concerned, they were right.

THE SHADOW OF VIETNAM

Situated beside the United States, Canadians had always been in an excellent position to absorb what was happening across the border, in the country's backyard, so to speak. Through exposure to the American media, especially television, American presidents and other prominent politicians became known in Canada too. Truman, Eisenhower, and John F. Kennedy were popular in Canada, the handsome and youthful Kennedy immensely so; and when Kennedy was assassinated in Dallas in November 1963, Canadians shared their neighbours' grief.

They weren't sure what to make of Lyndon Johnson, the veteran Texas politician who succeeded Kennedy. Handsome and photogenic he was not, but he was politically skilful—enough to override scattered opposition to the Autopact with Canada in 1964–65. That was a minor triumph for Johnson, and he celebrated by inviting Pearson and his external affairs minister, Paul Martin, down to his ranch for a signing ceremony. It was a rough and tumble occasion which Pearson did not greatly enjoy—his sense of informality tended more to a quiet glass of Canadian Club whisky in front of a cozy fire.

The Johnson ranch visit involved a terrifying car ride, piloted by Johnson himself; urinating by the side of the road at the president's insistence; and mounds of indigestible food. The noise and confusion that surrounded Johnson were not to Pearson's taste. It was, however, the pleasantest meeting the two men would have. They would soon clash, and when they did, it was over international affairs; in the broadest sense, it was a difference over where the United States and Canada stood in the world.

One thing that distinguished Pearson from Johnson was a sense of limitations—he saw American power and American resources, political and economic, as more limited and more fragile than did Johnson. Their contrasting visions clashed over South Vietnam, where a Communist insurgency and an invasion from its Communist twin, North Vietnam, threatened to overturn a pro-American government in the early 1960s.

South Vietnam became, for Johnson and his supporters, a symbol of American determination to resist Communist subversion. Should it fall to the Communists, Johnson decided, American credibility worldwide would be undermined. In 1965 he committed American troops to save South Vietnam; by 1968, Johnson's army in Southeast Asia was 500,000 strong, most of them conscripts.

Pearson did not question the administration's anti-communism, but its choice of time and place. He thought that waging distant wars with conscript armies was not a proven formula for success, as the Korean War and especially France's recent experience in Algeria showed. Through Canadian diplomats serving on a futile truce supervisory commission in Vietnam, he understood that the Communists would not compromise and were ready for virtually any sacrifice. He dreaded the effect on the United States, where his liberal friends begged him to say something that would deter Johnson from his disastrous course.

Pearson tried, in a speech in Philadelphia in April 1965. Today the speech makes curious reading. It went to great lengths to praise the United States, its motivation, and its policies. But it also suggested a pause in the American air offensive in Vietnam.

Since the suggestion of dissent, of an alternative policy, played to Johnson's opposition in the United States, Johnson saw Pearson's act as a betrayal. He suspected that Pearson was in cahoots with his domestic opposition, and he resented it. He knew that a pause was insufficient, unless it was followed by American withdrawal and the recognition that South Vietnam must be left to a Communist future. That was for Johnson political suicide, though he suspected that military action might be a costly mistake—also politically fatal. A sulphurous meeting at the president's rural retreat at Camp David followed. "You pissed on my rug," Johnson snarled, grasping the prime minister by the lapels of his suit. Back in Ottawa, Pearson wrote a cringing letter to Johnson, which didn't help. The American president went on his way.

Johnson's fireworks were mostly verbal. He had enough to cope with in Vietnam, and left the Europeans, and the Canadians, alone. The

Australians did join his war, and paid the price of political disruption at home, with no ability to influence American policy or military strategy. But Australia was distant and isolated, and couldn't count on American support if it were attacked by its Asian neighbours. Canada, right beside the United States, had no such strategic dilemma.

The Vietnam War divided American society. The young, who had to fight the war, were generally against it. Even the children of conservatives, like the future U.S. president George W. Bush, managed to stay out of Vietnam. Demonstrations and riots swept American campuses. Draftees into the U.S. military refused induction, and perhaps fifty thousand draft dodgers and their supporters fled to Canada. American opinion gradually turned against the war, followed by Canadian opinion. Assailed on all fronts, Johnson's Democratic administration crumbled; and in the presidential election of 1968 Americans elected the Republican political warhorse Richard Nixon. Nixon might not be exactly fresh, but he was different. He would still try to win in Vietnam, but, a more ruthless politician than Johnson, he was willing to make peace if he couldn't. As for Canada, all he asked was that it not make trouble.

TIMES OUT OF JOINT

In 1968 Lester Pearson, frustrated and tired by his turn as prime minister, announced his resignation. The Liberals' choice to replace him was unusual but not unexpected—Pierre Elliott Trudeau, the minister of justice. Trudeau promptly called an election for June, and the Liberals headed out on the campaign trail under a leader and prime minister who was, to say the least, untried.

In politics for only three years, Trudeau had been a public figure in his home province of Quebec for much longer. He'd been educated at the University of Montreal, Harvard, the London School of Economics, and the Sorbonne, and was also a world traveller, a public intellectual, and, most recently, a law professor. Unmarried, very fit, mysterious (as far as most English Canadians were concerned), and apparently romantic, he appealed to youth—though he was a mature forty-eight.

What Canadians saw was a man who defied convention—wearing turtlenecks and sandals, driving his own Mercedes convertible, sporting a rose in his buttonhole or between his teeth. "The state has no business in the bedrooms of the nation," he quipped, taking homosexual practices out of the Criminal Code. On television, his natural medium, Trudeau was alternately bold and defiant, or utterly charming, with the hint of a shy smile.

Trudeau's place on the ideological spectrum was equally a mystery. He was a liberal before he was a Liberal, but he was realistic enough to be willing to make the compromises that party leadership demanded. In his speeches Trudeau talked of a "Just Society," words that fitted broadly in the spectrum of late-sixties liberalism. That didn't really distinguish Trudeau or the Liberals from either the NDP or the Progressive Conservatives; in effect the three parties competed to show who was more caring, more just, and more competent to fit "the liberal moment" in Canadian history.

There was one point on which Trudeau's position was known and perfectly clear. He would have no truck with Quebec nationalists, and he had no regard for Quebec separatists. The one thing led to the other, as far as he was concerned. All nationalisms were to be regarded suspiciously. He may have drawn on his own experience, for in his youth Trudeau had flirted with extreme French-Canadian, Catholic nationalism, only to drop it in the mid-1940s as his experience broadened and his mind matured. Now he was the head of Canada's government, the executive in charge of the Canadian nation. Governments, even Trudeau's, were fuelled by nationalism, and by force of circumstance if not official ideological conversion, Trudeau became a promoter of Canadian nationalism.

It was a particular kind of nationalism—and in some respects it wasn't especially or uniquely Canadian. It can be seen, from a much later perspective, as the first instalment in the culture wars that in the 1990s and after dominated politics and society. Trudeau's "Just Society" reflected the urban and the progressive, and the self-consciously modern. It would be open and tolerant and, if someone could figure out how to manage it, caring. It was a philosophy that suited a country that was about to change, and change radically; its openness masked the fact that, in many ways, it didn't work.

Trudeau won a mandate from the Canadian electorate in June 1968. The Liberals won a majority in the House of Commons, and seats in every part of the country. The prime minister did particularly well in his home province, where the main opposition wasn't so much the Conservatives as the bucolic and nationalist-tinged Créditistes.[21] The night before the election, Canadians saw the prime minister stand his ground in front of a mob of rock-throwing separatist thugs in Montreal while the mayor of Montreal and the premier of Quebec scuttled for cover.

Trudeau then settled in to govern. There was a flurry of minor social programs suitable for a youth-oriented society—Opportunities for Youth, for example, which funded projects designed by and for young Canadians. There was the question of what to do about the West, where there were complaints that the prosperity of central Canada, especially Ontario, was not shared. There was the problem of the East and rural Canada, lagging behind the prosperous industrial cities of the centre. The Trudeau government did what it could, confident that it had the money, the time, and the expertise to manage society.

And it did have the money, for the economy was producing regular budgetary surpluses. All that was required was to redirect some of it into the new social programs established by the Pearson government and expanded under Trudeau. It promoted regional economic expansion, with a particular eye to Cape Breton Island. It fiddled with unemployment insurance and poverty. It mused about cities, and it contemplated the mysteries of research and development, lagging in Canada.

The obvious source of funds, apart from rising tax revenues, was defence. Fortune favoured the government. Vietnam was distant, and no significant group in Canada favoured going into the war. (That did not prevent thousands of young Canadians from enlisting in the U.S. military and fighting for Uncle Sam.) Europe was stable. The United States and its allies in NATO, including Canada, would defend their existing space if attacked, but accepted that that was unlikely. Western communists were disillusioned by the Soviet repression of rebellion in Hungary in 1956, and became still more disillusioned in 1968 when the Soviets did the same thing in Czechoslovakia.

Though there were still revolutionary festivities on the campuses and in the streets and squares of Western cities, with accompanying arson and looting, the self-proclaimed revolutionaries were either bought off or settled into a posture of principled irrelevance. They did not, in any case, take the Soviet Union for their model. It was corrupt, grey, and stodgy. More romantic were Mao Zedong's "cultural revolutionaries" in China; better still the Albanian communist tyrant Enver Hoxha. People knew little about China, and less about Albania, and so they became natural attractions for the science-fiction politics of the extreme left in Canada and elsewhere. In this, Canada was not especially different from other Western countries. There was one advantage about China, though not quite what its admirers touted. Mao Zedong's regime was so ruinous economically and so preoccupied with its internal revolutionary struggles that it posed no serious threat to anybody outside China's own borders.

The Soviet Union, though militarily formidable, was beginning to decay economically as well, and its leaders were inclined to seek stability over confrontation. (Its agents abroad, including a few spies in Canada, no longer worked for the revolution, but for cash.) NATO had already approved undertaking discussions with the Soviets in Europe, and in the early seventies this process resulted in a Conference on Security and Cooperation in Europe (CSCE) as well as discussions on various forms of arms limitation. The Americans, led by Nixon's foreign policy guru Henry Kissinger, pursued "détente" with the Soviet Union, while the Germans, who had emerged as the most economically powerful and politically stable of the European allies, tried out a formula for constructive engagement with the Eastern Bloc, and especially its evil twin, the German Democratic Republic, or East Germany. This policy, labelled "Ostpolitik," eventually accomplished its objective, buying off the East Germans with increasingly expensive gifts and subsidies while reassuring the Soviets that West Germany would not seek to overthrow the settlement of 1945.

Whatever was required in the Europe of the 1970s, it wasn't Canadian military power. The Canadian garrison in Europe was more symbolic than practical—a symbol of transatlantic connections more than a bulwark between the Communists and the Rhine. (A Canadian general who had commanded Canada's brigade group in Europe once observed to the author that in the event of a war he assumed his troops would get in their Volkswagens with their families and head for the nearest port.) The Trudeau government, after a lengthy and painful self-examination, announced in early 1969 that it would pull out half of Canada's European garrison, army and air force. The Europeans, especially the British, took the news badly, and there is no doubt that Canada's voice in NATO was as a result considerably reduced. Trudeau did not especially care. He viewed NATO as not much more than a forum for set speeches and frozen positions, and a place where the military voice was excessively loud.[22]

In fields other than the military, Canada played little role in the continent's consciousness, and none at all in terms of its priorities.[23] These facts applied as much if not more to Great Britain as to France and Germany.[24] The British could do little to protect Canada's trade, and Canadian exports sank steadily as Great Britain adjusted its tariffs to abolish Imperial Preference while opening its market to European goods.

Changing Canada

There was another reason to be sceptical of the Europeans. Canada was changing, and so was Europe—as Europe faced east toward the Soviet Union, and inward toward its own Common Market or Economic Community, Canada was finding alternatives to the Europeans. European links were dwindling, especially in immigration. The comparative statistics were telling. Between 1946 and 1966, out of 2.7 million immigrants to Canada, well over 80 percent came from Europe; immigration from China and India totalled around fifty thousand, while Korea wasn't even listed as a separate source of immigrants. Anyone looking at Canadian migration patterns or at Canadian ethnicity in the late 1960s might have been pardoned for concluding that Canada was likely to carry on as it had been for the previous 150 years—an overwhelmingly white country whose culture reflected its ethnicity.

In terms of North American migration, the principal event of 1966 wasn't Canadian, but American: the revision of American legislation that altered that country's traditional preference for immigrants from the Americas—including Canadians—while ending discrimination against immigrants from other parts of the world. After 1967, Canadians could no longer move freely across the border in search of greener pastures. But Canada was prosperous, and the standard of living was rising, and so the constriction of what had been a traditional Canadian option was little noticed.

Canadian discrimination against non-Europeans followed much the same pattern as American. As prejudices against non-white races abated in the 1950s and 1960s, immigration practice changed in Canada as elsewhere. For the first time non-whites outnumbered Europeans as immigrants to Canada in 1971. Non-European immigration was assisted by racial tensions in some of the Commonwealth countries of East Africa, where citizens of Indian origin were made unwelcome by local governments, especially the homicidal regime of Idi Amin in Uganda. This experience, coupled with earlier inflows of Hungarian (1956) and Czechoslovak (1968) refugees, influenced the revision of Canada's immigration legislation in 1978.

Changes also occurred in Canada's own ethnic pockets. The 1951 census recorded fewer than 10,000 Inuit and about 150,000 status (officially recognized) Indians. By 1981 their numbers had more than doubled, and by 2001 would double again, to 675,000; of these, 283,000 lived off reserves. In some parts of the country, notably the territories plus the northern parts of Quebec, Ontario, Manitoba, Saskatchewan, and British Columbia, Indians and Inuit were an increasingly important and increasingly noticed section of the population. Yet they were still governed according to the standards and practices of the eighteenth century, as wards of the crown, subsidized but subordinate and governed by civil servants out of the federal department of Indian affairs. Two hundred years of trusteeship had resulted in a constellation of (mostly) rural slums whose inhabitants enjoyed much less than the standard of living of their white compatriots.

This situation seemed at variance with the mood of the times—against discrimination, racial categorization, and second-class status. The solution seemed obvious: abolish the special status of the Indians, and integrate them into the larger Canadian community. A federal White Paper, sponsored by the Indian Affairs minister, Jean Chrétien, recommended as much in 1969.[25]

The White Paper ignored another trend of the times, and some of the results of federal policy. Inadequate though federal Indian policies may have been, they had produced a small, active, and better-educated group of Native leaders, far less willing than their predecessors to accept direction from Ottawa. To these leaders, the federal proposals were nothing more than a prescription for assimilation and absorption while letting the federal government off the hook for generations of neglect and abuse. They resisted Chrétien's policy, and aborted his proposed reforms. Whatever the fate of the Native peoples of Canada was to be, they demanded to control their own destinies.

The reaction to the White Paper sent Native–white relations into an entirely different direction. For the Indian leadership, it was no longer a question of poverty or equality in a larger society. Questions of autonomy, self-government, nationality, and even independence bubbled up. While the White Paper had discredited the old system of government control over Native bands, the government had nothing to put in its place. Instead, various Indian organizations grew up—some ad hoc, directed at a particular region or established for some special cause, others more general and more heavily institutionalized, like the National Indian Brotherhood, which in 1980 morphed into the Assembly of First Nations. The Assembly in turn was recognized by the federal government for some purposes and on some occasions, without conceding the Native sovereignty that some more radical Indian spokespeople were demanding. To complete the confusion, the federal department of Indian affairs continued to act as a funnel for subsidies to the various Indian bands.

FEDERAL–PROVINCIAL HORRORS

The partial devolution of authority to Indian bands mirrored a trend to decentralization in other parts of Canadian government. As the Depression and the Second World War receded in memory, so did some of the justification for constructing a powerful central government. As time passed, the provinces acquired larger and better civil services, ending Ottawa's near-monopoly of bureaucratic skills. It followed that the provinces could advance better arguments when they negotiated with Ottawa, either bilaterally or through the medium of formal federal–provincial conferences, meetings of the prime minister with the provincial premiers that increased markedly in frequency as the 1960s drew on.[26] At first commentators drew attention to the diplomatic quality of these meetings;[27] later, however, the impression grew that federal–provincial conclaves had become a third order of government. The impression was reinforced as the terminology used to describe these conferences inflated. "Federal–Provincial Conferences" became "Federal–Provincial Conferences of First Ministers" in 1974, and then "First Ministers' Conferences" in 1985. Where formerly they dealt with special subjects—unemployment insurance or pensions, for example—they became annualized and generalized in that same year, 1985.

The proliferation of high-level political meetings was an indication of the intricate overlapping of jurisdictions in Canadian government. The Pearson government recognized the complication, and contributed money so that the provinces could manage health care and pensions while maintaining the right of all Canadians to interchangeable services from province to province. Federal contributions to provincial needs also insulated Ottawa from the charge that it had too much money, thanks to its broad taxing powers, and avoided any kind of fundamental realignment of taxation. At the same time, Ottawa's abundant revenues gave it the advantage in dealing with the provinces—even the biggest. If the federal budget was growing, so was the economy, and so did federal surpluses. It was a happy coincidence, and like most coincidences, it did not last.

Freezing in the Dark

It began with an election. Four years into its mandate the Trudeau government headed to the polls, calling an election for 30 October 1972. "The Land Is Strong," the Liberals fatuously assured the voters. It was one of those occasions when more modesty and less hyperbole might have served the politicians better. Unemployment, after all, was low at 6.3 percent, though higher than in 1968 (4.8 percent). Economists would later blame higher interest rates and a more generous unemployment insurance system for a rise in Canada's unemployment levels. The baby boom and a more open immigration policy were having an effect too—more and younger workers were looking for work. Often enough, having found work, they went on strike, in numbers not seen since the inflationary days of 1946.[28] As for those who hadn't joined the labour force—for example, students at university—the early seventies were equally a time of disruption approaching chaos, as militants complained of grievances real or fancied and took "action" against complacent or repressive authority.

It wasn't surprising that Trudeau took the blame. The Liberals' majority in the House of Commons melted away and the government emerged a scant two seats ahead of the rival Progressive Conservatives. The government's fate depended on the two minority parties, the NDP and the Créditistes, and on its ability to manoeuvre past what seemed a hopeless political situation. To guide the government, Trudeau appointed a veteran politician from Nova Scotia, Allan MacEachen, as government leader in the House of Commons. To guide his policies, Trudeau turned not to academic experts or management theorists but to his professional political advisers. Not surprisingly, they advised him to do whatever was popular. With an eye to refurbishing his image, the prime minister abandoned philosophy and posed as a street fighter, defying and mocking the opposition by turns. It was an image that suited him, and it too proved popular.

The government was sustained in its first vote of confidence in the House of Commons. The issue was the American bombing of Hanoi and Haiphong over Christmas, 1972. Canadians disapproved. The left was vocal on the issue, and the NDP demanded that Canada take a stand. And so, via a resolution of the House of Commons, Canada did. The NDP had to vote for it. The Créditistes, who shared Quebec's isolationist traditions, also disapproved of war, and they voted for it too. Trudeau and his ministers, who knew that this was a simple-minded solution to a complex issue, voted for it to keep the government in office. President Nixon was enraged, but he needed Canada's help in camouflaging American defeat in Vietnam by creating an international peacekeeping force to supervise his troops' withdrawal. The issue was soon forgotten, and in any case Nixon would shortly be swallowed up by a great domestic scandal, becoming the only American president to resign his office, in 1974.

Nixon's troubles distracted the United States and a watching world—for it was the television drama of the century—for most of 1973 and 1974. Throughout, Nixon doggedly pursued détente with the Soviet Union and a rapprochement with China, and tried to keep the lid on a Middle East situation that threatened to drag in the Americans and the Russians, thus endangering the peace of the world. A brief Arab–Israeli war in October 1973 was patched up, but not before the Arab world joined forces against the United States and the West, embargoing the shipment of Middle East oil to "unfriendly" Western countries. This action set in motion an energy crisis that would last for most of a decade—that would never, in fact, entirely go away.

Mid-twentieth-century Canadians, like their American cousins, took energy for granted. North Americans sat on top of apparently unlimited supplies of coal, oil, and natural gas. There was waterpower, channelled and dammed by great engineers. There was nuclear power, fuelled by Canadian uranium and produced in the CANDU series of Canadian-designed and -manufactured reactors. Canada's energy policy, accordingly, was a policy of plenty and even surplus. Every year, geologists reported that they had discovered more oil and natural gas; and every year the government lobbied the United States to give Canada—secure, safe, and allied Canada—a part of the American energy market. The government did its best to encourage Alberta, reserving most of the Ontario market for more expensive domestic oil, but allowed politically volatile Quebec and the less prosperous Atlantic provinces to import cheaper fuel from the lower-cost international market.

That market was changing. Starting in 1960, American oil reserves began to deplete faster than geologists could find replacements. The Canadian government lobbied harder and faster, only to find that congressional obstruction was more than a match for any argument based on dwindling oil reserves. Eventually, in 1970, Canada also ran into the same problem as the United States: proven petroleum reserves peaked and began to decline. With that development Canadian enthusiasm for unlimited sales to the United States began to decline too.

The Arab oil embargo was only the most visible sign of the oil crisis. Economists and alarmists, represented by the fashionable Club of Rome, had been arguing for years that the world was facing a Malthusian emergency—there was too much demand chasing too few resources. It followed that prices ought to rise, and they did. For several years prior to 1973, the governments of petro-states had been demanding and getting better terms for their product, using their trade association (the Organization of Petroleum Exporting Countries, or OPEC) to organize an oil cartel. The great Western oil companies, known collectively as the Seven Sisters, found that their governments either would not (the Americans) or could not (the British) sustain their market dominance. The international price of oil rose and kept rising.

This was good news and bad news for Canada. It was definitely good news for Alberta, whose most lucrative product, oil, was buoyed by the international price. It almost seemed that Alberta's resource-based economy, which had so often been the victim of international markets beyond its control, had finally turned the corner; for the first time markets were working for, not against, the province. It was bad news for those parts of Canada that imported oil. Soon the media were promoting images of old ladies freezing in the dark as their energy supply was cut off either by boycott or by unaffordable price hikes. It was popularly believed that the oil companies were behind the oil crisis. And it followed that some good old-fashioned state regulation would bring an artificial emergency smartly under control.

The minority government was not the best instrument to handle a politically volatile situation that affected many if not most Canadians. In a series of ad hoc decisions, the Trudeau government secured Canada's own energy supply first, and made it available at an affordable price across Canada. The definition of affordable was debatable, but it was also and inevitably political. Americans didn't vote in Canadian elections, so it followed that Americans could pay the international price and bear the brunt of any reductions in Canadian petroleum output. But Maritimers and Quebeckers did vote, and, given the minority Parliament, would soon be voting again. It followed that they must be protected—and with them Ontario, the country's largest oil market.

The election came sooner rather than later, in July 1974, following a contrived parliamentary defeat. Trudeau returned with a majority, a majority with a difference. The Liberals had no seats west of Manitoba: the majority was based on a combination of Quebec, Ontario, and the Maritimes. Trudeau proceeded anyway—though fortunately there were no desperately contentious issues to bring to Parliament. (The most important issue of the day, the election of a separatist government in Quebec, will be dealt with in the next chapter.) This was odd, for the later 1970s were the heyday of a new and unexpected economic problem, stagflation, in which the economy defied accepted wisdom and produced both inflation and stagnation at the same time.

Stagflation would eventually prove extremely important in political terms. Unemployment rose, budgets (thanks in part to subsidies designed to prop up the two-price system for oil) went into deficit, and the federal government thrashed around for ways and means to make ends meet and found them, inevitably, in reducing its payments to the provinces for such items as post-secondary education and health care. Unionized Canadians expressed themselves by striking—in record numbers (10,908,810 working days were lost in 1975, more than triple the number lost in 1971, and over ten times the figure for 1963).[29] Because many of these strikes were in the public sector, where unions were newly permitted, the public was bound to notice, and it did. Confidence in the government's ability to manage the economy sagged. Though it wasn't apparent at the time, this was a fundamental change in public attitudes, and helped set the stage for the politics of the next two decades.

By 1979 it was clear that the prime minister was irritating the electorate, and there was some sense that the feeling might be mutual. Trudeau postponed the election until the last possible moment, in May 1979. Always a good campaigner, Trudeau did his confrontational best, but it failed to deliver. It was the Progressive Conservatives, under a young (thirty-nine) and untried leader, Joe Clark, who bested Trudeau and the Liberals, obtaining a plurality of seats in the House of Commons. After a few months of rest and reflection, Trudeau announced that he would retire from politics and devote himself to his young family. (Like many other Canadians, Trudeau was a divorced single parent.)

Clark lacked only a few seats for a majority, and determined to govern as if he had one. This would show determination and decisiveness and offset his image as an accident-prone political wimp. ("It's the Year of the Child," snorted his senior colleague, the unrepentant John Diefenbaker.)[30] Clark expected that, once he had established his bona fides with the public, he could go on to call and win another election, as Diefenbaker had in 1957. He presented a budget that raised taxes on gas at the pump. Administratively, it was the right thing to do; politically, it was a disaster.

Even though the Liberals weren't sure they even had a leader, they knew that Clark's Conservatives were behind—far behind—in the public opinion polls. Clark with his new gas tax was digging the hole deeper, while energetically thwacking himself on the head with the shovel. Dragging the hapless NDP and Créditistes after them, the Liberals defeated the government on 13 December 1979. A few days later it was announced that Trudeau would not, after all, be leaving.

An election was called for February 1980, which Clark duly lost. In a memorable scene, Trudeau faced the cameras from his headquarters at the Château Laurier hotel in Ottawa. "Well, welcome to the 1980s," he told Canadians. He did not need to tell them that it would be quite a ride.

15

TWO NATIONALISMS

Quebec separatism meets authority: An RCMP officer
is knocked down by a demonstrator in Montreal, 1967.

W hen writing of Canadian nationalism in history, it's prudent to specify that Canada enjoyed two nationalisms—the English- and French-speaking. *Canadiens français* carefully distinguished them- selves from the English, while English Canadians usually didn't think of French Canadians at all. French-Canadian nationalism was a force, cultur- ally and socially and sometimes politically. It was undeniable that French Canada and especially French Quebec were politically distinct, even as the French lived beside and often among the English. Montreal was known to be the second largest French-speaking city in the world, but it was also a bilingual city. If the French dominated politics, municipally and provin- cially, the English ran the economy. Until the 1940s it was a tradition that Quebec's treasurer, the provincial finance minister, was English, because, after all, English was the language of business.

The French population of Quebec was relatively secure. French, Catholic Quebec had a high birth rate. Everywhere but Montreal and a few scattered pockets in western Quebec, French was not only dominant, but practically universal. Though immigration fed the English-speaking community, the English often moved on to other parts of Canada, or to the United States. True, the French-speaking communities outside Quebec were tending to decline over time, but even in these communities there were advances, like the election of an Acadian premier, Louis Robichaud, in New Brunswick in 1960.[1] As well, older animosities and prejudices among the English seemed gradually to be subsiding. Meanwhile, fantasies like *"la révanche des berceaux"* (the revenge of the cradle)—the notion that French Canadians would outbreed the English, and by force of numbers come to dominate northern Ontario and New Brunswick—also subsided. How could they not, for the birth rate on which they were based was sagging; between the late 1950s and the early 1970s Quebec moved from the highest birth rate in Canada to the lowest.

By the 1970s the birth rate was declining across the country. Technology played a part, but also affluence and urbanization. Contraceptive devices, technically illegal in Canada until 1969, were more likely to be available in urban areas. Richer people had fewer children, on the whole, and Canadians were definitely richer. Educated women had careers, and remained unmarried longer. The appearance of the birth control pill, which became widely available by 1965, had an obvious impact, first in large cities but eventually across the country. Of course, birth rates in cities, including Quebec cities, were always lower than in the countryside, but by the 1970s birth rates in the countryside had declined to the same level.

By the time the anti-contraceptive law was repealed, resistance from traditionalists had crumbled. The Roman Catholic Church, doctrinally opposed to contraceptive devices, conceded that the law as it existed was unenforceable and ought to be removed. Good Catholics should eschew artificial birth control, but as a matter of conscience, not law. Even in Quebec, where the clerically inclined newspaper *Le Devoir* was one of the last to concede the point, contraception had long outpaced the Church's teachings. As for the government that finally repealed the law, it was headed by a devoutly Catholic French Canadian, Pierre Elliott Trudeau.

French Quebec, like English Canada, was changing in the 1950s— much more than the English, including those in Quebec, realized. The greatest change was occurring in the most traditional area of society, the Roman Catholic Church. For years it had run welfare and education, which meant that Quebec, unlike most other Canadian provinces, was administered in large part along denominational lines. The Church depended heavily on the support of the faithful, who contributed both human and financial capital to sustain their faith. But the support of the faithful was insufficient as time passed and problems grew. State aid, in the form of grants from the provincial government, became the staff of life for Catholic welfare organizations. There was a price for all this: "The bishops eat out of my hand," the Union Nationale premier Maurice Duplessis boasted. And Duplessis, in a hundred ingenious ways, reminded the bishops of this fact. Most notably, when the archbishop of Montreal, Joseph Charbonneau, got out of hand politically, he found himself translated forty-eight hundred kilometres to manage the finances of an old-age home in Victoria, British Columbia.

Duplessis's style of politics eventually became an embarrassment. To English Canadians, it was his pandering to French-Canadian nationalism that marked his regime as obnoxious and obsolete. To the French, however, it was his corrupt, patronage-ridden, and personal style of government, which starved education and other public functions of the money they needed to catch up to the modern world. Duplessis's death, in 1959, signalled an explosion of public activity. The "Révolution Tranquille" (Quiet Revolution) officially occurred under the succeeding Liberal government under Jean Lesage (1960–66). Lesage, a rather traditional politician from an elite family, sometimes seemed rather surprised at the policies that his government was enacting.

The times also helped define what now happened in Quebec. There were changes in the Catholic Church, coincident with the Second Vatican Council ("Vatican II") which liberalized the Church after decades of conservatism. There was a wave of secularism, which hit Quebec with particular force. What the government had previously subsidized, through the Church or churches, it now did for itself. For the first time in almost a hundred years Quebec had a department of education headed by a government minister. Eventually, by a constitutional amendment in 1997, the school system was secularized, ironically by a strongly federalist Canadian Parliament at the behest of the very separatist government of Quebec. Though still divided, Quebec education was now bisected officially along English–French lines rather than religious ones.

The 1997 amendment was in a real sense the logical end of the Quiet Revolution. It wasn't actually quiet at all; like any other part of Canada afflicted by the baby boom and the youth or counterculture, Quebec endured a lot of noise, mostly oratorical, during the 1960s and 1970s; but in Quebec, unlike the rest of Canada, there were also bombs.

The reappearance of discontent was no surprise to those who had cherished the nationalist flame for many years. Quebec history had always attracted those who felt a sense of grievance over the Conquest of 1760 and its consequences. Nationalism was certainly a force to be reckoned with, but as with Premier Duplessis, it had its limits. Nationalists in the 1940s and 1950s confined themselves to defending "provincial rights" against Ottawa's centralizing tendencies. From time to time separatists appeared who dreamt of an independent "Laurentie" on the banks of the St. Lawrence, but their ideas had no political purchase among mainstream politicians or in the Quebec electorate. Such separatist nationalists inhabited the extreme right wing of politics, and in the liberalizing climate of the times they were easily dismissed as cranks.

Suddenly, in the early 1960s, separatism acquired both force and respectability. In this it was responding to international currents—rather like the nationalism of the 1830s (see above, Chapter 7). Between 1945 and 1975 the European colonial empires collapsed almost completely. The nostrums of empire—which expressed racist ideas of white supremacy—lost their power in the face of colonial populations' unwillingness to be ruled from abroad and from above any longer. France fought a few fruitless colonial wars, in Indochina and Algeria, only to find that the metropolitan population was disinclined to support them. Great Britain had the same experience on a smaller scale, in Kenya and Cyprus, as did Portugal in Mozambique and Angola. Great Britain, the Netherlands, Belgium, France, and finally Portugal abandoned their overseas possessions, except for a few fragments. (And, of course, except for the Soviet Union, which believed, wrongly, that socialism transcended its imperial history.) Most of Asia and Africa suddenly achieved independence.

The logic of independence and independence struggles attracted attention in Quebec. (Algeria was of particular interest.) Resistance from the colonial establishment was to be expected, but it would be swept away by irresistible revolutionary force. It didn't matter that Quebec had representative and democratic institutions, the separatists argued: Quebec politicians really served the English establishment ensconced in its mansions in Westmount.[2] The Westmount mansions were impressive piles, certainly, though on a scale of international luxury they paled beside the constructions of the British, American, or French elites; and their stone walls and panelled dining rooms frequently hosted obnoxious opinions about the French population who surrounded them.[3] That most English-speaking Quebeckers didn't live that way could be ignored in theory—theory was what counted—if not in fact. And to get things moving, theory prescribed terror.

During the 1963 election campaign an unexploded bomb was found on the route of Prime Minister Diefenbaker's campaign train. More bombs followed in the spring, in mailboxes in Westmount, seriously injuring an army explosives expert. Opinion inside the province and out became alarmed. To discover what to do, Lester Pearson promised a royal commission if he were elected prime minister, and he kept his word, appointing the cumbersomely named Royal Commission on Bilingualism and Biculturalism in 1963. (Inevitably it was called the Bi-Bi Commission, or styled after its two chairs as the Laurendeau-Dunton Commission.)

Premier Lesage discovered that members of his cabinet were moving with the times, and that keeping up with them was, as he put it, "a struggle to control a bear."[4] Paul Gérin-Lajoie, the minister of the newly created department of education, wanted to expand provincial jurisdiction—legitimately, he believed—into fields hitherto occupied by the federal government. René Lévesque, his minister of natural resources, wanted to nationalize Quebec's private power companies and annex them to the government's existing Quebec Hydro system (which dated from 1944). Most provinces had government-owned utilities, so nationalizing Gatineau Power or Shawinigan Power caused little comment outside the province. Inside, however, the move was understood to be a blow to the English exclusivity that had for so long dominated Quebec's economy.

Lesage explained it to his cabinet as "economic liberation."[5]

Lesage called an election on the question, in the fall of 1962. Not surprisingly, he won. The private companies were nationalized, and folded into the new, very large, French-speaking Hydro-Québec. Hydro-Québec turned out to be a means to an end, only part of a much larger plan to reform Quebec's economy and society. It now became clear that Quebec was not to be "a province like the others" but a free-standing entity. It must be an expansionist, activist state—for the state was the only Quebec institution indisputably under the control of French Canadians, and run for their benefit.[6] And it must have its own industrial policy, financed after 1965, out of the Caisse de dépôt et placement du Québec.

Marc Lalonde, then a young lawyer in Montreal, remembered that René Lévesque "started making speeches in support of a steel industry in Quebec, and advanced the creation of Sidbec ["Sid" stands for *sidérurgie*, meaning steel industry], which was eventually created on the theory that somehow we had to have it: as he said, 'We owe it to ourselves to have a steel industry.'"[7] What Lévesque meant was that the "nation" of Quebec should have an industrial apparatus like other nations. Mentally, the minister had already segregated his province's destiny from the rest of Canada.

Quebec got a steel industry, like Ontario's, as it got an automobile plant, like Ontario's. They were a monument to government mercantilism, and a visible sign of Quebec's autonomy from the English-run Canadian economy. (One should, however, observe that a fascination with heavy industry was not unique to Quebec, as the simultaneous creation of a federal department of industry indicated.) Their actual history turned out to be not quite as Lévesque and his ideologues expected. Eventually Sidbec was sold—not to the English, but to the Chinese—and the General Motors plant at Ste. Thérèse was closed by its owner in 2001.[8] It was not the best of times to be putting your money into heavy industry, and it eventually turned out that national standing did not after all depend on having a steel plant or two.

Pearson, an experienced diplomat, applied his talents to the task of appeasing Quebec, leaving international affairs to Paul Martin, a veteran Liberal politician from Ontario. The Liberal party was strong in Quebec, where it was the establishment party, and Pearson was able to draw on an array of talent for his caucus and cabinet. Increasingly, however, Pearson found that he couldn't count on the support of the provincial Liberal party, which formally separated itself from its federal cousin. Some provincial Liberals supported the federal party, and some ostentatiously kept their distance. If they were too close to Ottawa, how could they safeguard Quebec's interests?

Indeed, how could Ottawa, an English-speaking government, properly represent Quebec's interests? To Paul Gérin-Lajoie, and to Quebec's senior civil servants, it was an impossibility. Gérin-Lajoie spoke as both minister and constitutional expert (which he was) when in April 1965 he told a gathering of the Montreal consular corps that Quebec should represent itself in areas of provincial jurisdiction.[9]

Gérin-Lajoie's assertion was promptly rejected by the federal government. Paul Martin, as minister of external affairs, issued a statement arguing that Canada's sovereignty was indivisible, and that Canada must speak abroad with only one voice, Ottawa's. That Ottawa must negotiate with the provinces was a fact of life, inside or outside its foreign policy power. The result could be messy and sometimes incoherent, but on the whole it worked, permitting Canada to be represented at UNESCO or to make commitments in regard to human rights.[10]

The Pearson government acted to limit the possibility of mischief-making by the government of Quebec. It was important to prevent the province from setting any precedents by getting a foreign government to make an agreement or even a treaty with it, thereby recognizing Gérin-Lajoie's doctrine of a bifurcated foreign policy jurisdiction. The only foreign government likely to do so was France, and its government was of several minds on the issue. The French president, Charles de Gaulle, was coming to the conclusion that the independence of Quebec was both inevitable and desirable. His diplomats, with a couple of exceptions, disagreed. So apparently did his foreign minister. Accordingly, the governments of Canada and France in 1965 concluded an umbrella agreement (*accord cadre*) that authorized agreements between Canadian provinces and France on cultural matters, but also recognized Canada's sovereign unity in foreign affairs.

Being treated as just another province was precisely what the government of Quebec did not want, and increasingly Quebec's political and intellectual class agreed with it. Quebec could not submit to minority status within Canada; and yet, with only 5.1 million French speakers in a population of eighteen million (in the 1961 census), that was inevitable. It was in a curious way a reprise of the arguments of the 1850s over representation by population (rep by pop). The politicians of the 1860s had devised a ramshackle (and short-lived) solution of a "double majority." The politicians of the 1960s, in Quebec, now surfaced with its twin— "two nations" (*deux nations*). Two nations could mean anything and everything. It could mean "special status," a cloudy phrase of the period. It might mean associate status, another undefined buzzword.[11] It could mean that the consent of both nations was necessary—for example, for amending the constitution, perhaps for important questions, perhaps for anything. Relations between English Canada and Quebec would no longer depend on rep by pop, but on mutual consent.

The Progressive Conservative party toyed with the two-nations idea at a conference at Montmorency outside Quebec City in the summer of 1967. It resolved that "Canada is composed of two founding peoples (*deux nations*), with historic rights, who have been joined by people from many lands; the constitution should be such as to permit and encourage their full and harmonious growth and development in equality throughout Canada." The doctrine was music to the ears of the Union Nationale premier of Quebec, Daniel Johnson, who had won a surprising election victory and replaced Jean Lesage in 1966. Johnson had written a book, *Egalité ou Indépendance*, which proposed that Quebec receive equal status with the rest of the country, which would allow it to stay within Canada, or what was left of it. Failing equality, as defined by Johnson, Quebec should choose independence.

Perhaps because English Canadians refused to believe that he could possibly mean that five million or so French-speaking Quebeckers could balance the thirteen or fourteen million non–French speakers in Canada, Johnson functioned more or less as Quebec premiers always had. An opportunist in practice if not by nature, he looked around for a means of bolstering his position vis-à-vis the English; and in Paris he found one.

Charles de Gaulle, the symbol of French resistance during the Second World War, had returned to political life in 1958 and had become French president in 1959. De Gaulle presided over what he saw as the necessary dismantling of the French colonial empire, ending the running sore of the Algerian war in 1962. He battled rebellious generals and disgruntled rivals, and emerged triumphant by 1963. Finally, through clever diplomacy he re-established France's pre-eminence in Europe. But it was not enough. There were, after all, only about sixty million French speakers around the world, compared with hundreds of millions of English speakers that the British Empire had left behind. Nor was France a first-class economic power, and its military power was strictly limited. Under the circumstances, de Gaulle decided to reclaim the French speakers of America and to recall them to their destiny, whatever that might be.

De Gaulle's aims were as cloudy as Johnson's, but for the time being, in 1966–67, they agreed that the status quo was unsatisfactory. De Gaulle, given Johnson's dichotomy of equality and independence, was definitely for independence. Johnson, on the other hand, would probably have preferred equality. For a while, however, they were travelling in the same direction, on a road that led to Montreal in the summer of 1967.

Expo 67 and After

In 1967 Canada would celebrate the centenary of its creation, and to mark the occasion it would host a world's fair in Montreal that summer. Planning began under the Diefenbaker government and was well advanced by the time Pearson came into office. Pearson and his colleagues organized Canada-wide celebrations, but the centrepiece was to be in

Montreal, where several islands in the middle of the St. Lawrence were linked together as the site for Expo 67, "Man and His World." The best of Canadian design was represented, and governments around the globe were happy to use Expo as their showcase. Canadians awaited the opening rather nervously, but when it did open, Expo proved to be a brilliant success.

Monarchs, presidents, and prime ministers were expected to make ceremonial visits. Even the president of the United States, Lyndon Johnson, who didn't want to come, came. Johnson had problems of his own, a war in Vietnam and an impending war in the Middle East, and he didn't like Lester Pearson, but he was willing to do the necessary minimum. Queen Elizabeth II, Canada's monarch as well as Great Britain's, came too. Surely Charles de Gaulle would come, as representing Canada's other mother country.

Very late in the day, for visits had to be carefully scheduled so as not to overlap, de Gaulle consented to visit. In July 1967 he arrived by French warship at Quebec City, straight into the hands of an enthusiastic Daniel Johnson. Over the next few days Johnson learned that he'd got more than he'd bargained for. He had hoped to impress the English; de Gaulle wanted to enrage them. "I am going to strike a strong blow," he told his son-in-law, General Alain Boissieu. "Things are going to get hot. But it is necessary."[12] The culmination of de Gaulle's visit was a cavalcade through rural Quebec en route to Montreal city hall, on 24 July. De Gaulle's language and demeanour were not reassuring to his Quebec hosts. Johnson was heard to mutter that, by the time de Gaulle's motorcade reached Montreal, "We'll have separated."[13]

That evening, from a balcony overlooking a square that featured a statute of the British naval hero Lord Nelson, de Gaulle spoke to an ecstatic crowd in Montreal and on radio and television to all of Canada. The speech was certainly exciting. His Quebec motorcade that day was like the liberation of France in 1944, he told his audience. The crowd cheered. They wanted liberation too. Encouraged, de Gaulle ended with a series of salutations. *"Vive Montréal! Vive le Québec!"* and, naturally, *"Vive le Québec libre!"* The crowd broke into the French national anthem, "La Marseillaise." His work done, de Gaulle went on to dinner and bed.

"Vive le Québec libre" was one of the main slogans of the separatists. Certainly the separatists understood its meaning. So did de Gaulle's foreign minister, who termed his master's performance *"une connerie."*[14] Perceptive English Canadians also got the message, and were, as expected, enraged. In Ottawa the cabinet met all the next day to decide what to do. Telegrams and telephone calls flooded Ottawa, expressing Canadians' fury at de Gaulle. Demonstrators paced outside French consulates, which prudently locked their doors.[15] Pearson eventually read a statement terming de Gaulle's remarks "unacceptable," which they were, and expressing the forlorn hope that the general would still visit Ottawa. Naturally de Gaulle did not. Whistling up an Air France Caravelle jet, he departed for Paris where his nervous ministers waited on the airport runway, scrutinizing their chief for signs of dementia.

De Gaulle left behind a legacy of discord. René Lévesque left the provincial Liberal party and established his own separatist movement, which eventually turned into the Parti Québécois (PQ). Pearson's common sense kept Ottawa's reactions on an even keel. Canada did not break diplomatic relations with France. Johnson too backed off. He wasn't ready to declare independence, and Pearson gave him no provocation. Quebec business leaders warned Johnson of the dire consequences to the province if independence went ahead. Instead, in a conference with Canada's other premiers in November, Johnson poured oil on troubled waters. Quebec and Canada would carry on beyond the centennial. Pearson obliged by opening a conference on the Canadian constitution in order to explore provincial grievances and their possible solutions.

The conference convened in February 1968. Proceedings were televised, and proved remarkably popular, if only because they exposed a new personality on the federal scene. Pierre Elliott Trudeau, Pearson's minister of justice, carried the ball for the federal government. Trudeau took pains to demonstrate that Johnson did not alone speak for Quebec, and his performance was so effective that by the end Johnson was barely speaking at all. Wounded and humiliated, and in ill health, Johnson passed from the scene; in September he died prematurely of a heart attack.

By September Pearson was no longer prime minister. He found the job increasingly burdensome, and, at seventy, he judged the time was right to depart. His main political adversary, John Diefenbaker, was retired by his Progressive Conservative party in September 1967 and Pearson would likely not have done as well against Diefenbaker's successor, the upright and reticent premier of Nova Scotia, Robert Stanfield.

At a Liberal party convention in April 1968 the glamorous Trudeau swept his rivals aside. The evening of Trudeau's victory, 6 April, the CBC reported events from a Plexiglas bubble high above the convention floor, using its Ottawa bureau chief, Norman DePoe, and the Quebec national-ist journalist, Claude Ryan, as commentators. When Trudeau's vote total was read out, and it became clear that he had prevailed, Ryan made a gesture of rage. He was convinced that Trudeau was absolutely the wrong man to succeed Pearson. Trudeau, unlike Pearson, was not a man of soft words, but of hard edges.

Few paid attention to Ryan's misgivings at the time. Trudeau was the man of the hour, as he would be for many hours, not to say months and years thereafter.

THE OCTOBER CRISIS AND AFTER

The rhythms of society rolled on much as before, with no discernible difference. Trudeau might talk of a "Just Society," but Canadians seemed to have very local, sometimes quite personal, definitions of justice. It was a time of strikes and unrest at home and abroad, as one group after another scrambled to get a larger piece of the national pie. Separatism refused to go away, though fear of separatism helped bring the provincial Liberal party under a new and untried leader, Robert Bourassa, to power in Quebec City in April 1970.[16] René Lévesque and his brand-new Parti Québécois managed to win 23 percent of the vote, but only seven seats in the legislature (which had been renamed the National Assembly in a gesture intended to affirm the standing of the Quebec nation). The Union Nationale got more seats than the PQ, but fewer votes; it began its passage to the political dustbin, and the PQ effectively became the alternative to the Liberals.

Quebec's place in Canada seemed to be secure, but things were not what they seemed. The extreme fringe of the separatist movement hadn't given up on bombs or other violent acts, and in October 1970 they were successful in kidnapping two victims: the British consul in Montreal, James Cross, and Bourassa's minister of labour, Pierre Laporte.[17] Because Cross had diplomatic status, his fate became the concern of the federal government, which had jurisdiction over foreign affairs.

Panic ensued. The Bourassa government had no idea what it was confronting, the police didn't know whom to arrest, and the media fed the notion of a hydra-headed conspiracy, unknown, unknowable, but of course infinitely dangerous. The terrorists appropriated the name Front de libération du Québec (FLQ). It sounded impressive—the analogy was to the successful Algerian liberation movement, the Front de libération nationale (FLN), and its struggle against colonial domination. In fact, the FLQ was a collection of scattered radical grouplets ("cells" as they called them), who communicated among themselves, in that pre-computer age, with great difficulty and uncertainty.

The FLQ solemnly presented a series of "demands," including the reading on television of their semi-literate manifesto, but not forgetting gold and transport out of the country, as well as the liberation of various separatist miscreants who had already been locked up for roughly 250 crimes committed between 1963 and 1970.

The Quebec political establishment was shaken. A public meeting— mostly of students—in Montreal culminated in chants of "FLQ, FLQ." A confrontation between the authorities and FLQ supporters was the formula prescribed by radical theorists for riots and revolution—a familiar scenario on North American campuses in the late 1960s. Some prominent nationalists and separatists demanded that the Bourassa government negotiate with the terrorists. There was loose talk that the government no longer had the capacity or the legitimacy to govern. (It had been elected only six months before.) But Bourassa finally did act decisively, calling on the federal government to put into effect the War Measures Act, which provided extensive emergency powers to the federal cabinet to use more or less as it saw fit.

In addition, Bourassa asked for and got the Canadian army, which was tasked to maintain order in Quebec, protect dignitaries against kidnapping, and generally help with the crisis. Soldiers marched up and down, carrying weapons and looking fierce; the only recorded casualty of military action was a self-inflicted wound. Using powers granted by the War Measures Act, the police rounded up nearly five hundred individuals who might (or might not) have had something to do with separatist agitation. The agitation probably counted for more, in the eyes of the authorities, than the separatism.

Though these actions reinforced the power of the state, they did nothing to save the unfortunate Laporte, who was murdered by his kidnappers, his body dumped in the trunk of a car parked at an air base. The murder had tremendous shock value, but the effect was not what the terrorists imagined. Support for the FLQ drained away—but not support for separatism, which was in any case neither outlawed nor suppressed.

Eventually the police found Cross's hiding place and negotiated an end to his kidnapping. His captors were flown to exile in Cuba. The remaining terrorists—those who had abducted and killed Laporte—were discovered in a rural cellar, arrested, and put on trial. They received sentences of varying severity, but eventually all would be released, to be occasionally feted by separatist militants.

That was the end of the October Crisis, which had lasted roughly three months. It was the culmination of seven years of sporadic violence, whose object had been to bring Quebec to a revolutionary condition that would shake off the forces of repression and colonialism. The terrorists had never managed to get beyond the fringe; although, since Quebec was a small place and its elite compact, many of the actors on all sides had met. One revolutionary theorist, Pierre Vallières, had even worked with Trudeau in an earlier manifestation. After a spell in jail, Vallières landed a federally funded job, which may have been Trudeau's way of showing that even revolutionaries have their price.

Trudeau's management of the crisis drew on the strong streak of theatricality in the prime minister's character. The press helped. On one occasion, a reporter in Ottawa demanded to know from the prime minister what all the soldiers bearing guns were doing. (The implication, if one can be discerned, was that Trudeau was displaying hitherto hidden militarist and possibly dictatorial tendencies, aimed at creating a police state.) Trudeau's response was still being replayed thirty years later: "You know, I think it is more important to get rid of those who are committing violence against the total society and those who are trying to run the government through a parallel power by establishing their authority by kidnapping and blackmail. And I think it is our duty as a government to protect government officials and important people in our society against being used as tools in this blackmail." The prime minister then continued: "There are a lot of bleeding hearts around who just don't like to see people with helmets and guns. All I can say is, go on and bleed, but it is more important to keep law and order in the society than to be worried about weak-kneed people who don't like the looks of ..."

Q: At any cost? How far would you go with that? How far would you extend that?

A: Well, just watch me.

Canadians watched, and approved: according to polls, support for Trudeau and his actions approached 90 percent, and was higher in Quebec than in the rest of Canada.

Not all the consequences of the October Crisis were positive. The crisis created the impression—not entirely unfounded—that Bourassa and his ministers had fumbled, and had to be rescued by the clear-thinking and decisive Trudeau. The use of police power turned out to be a blunt instrument, and those who were unjustifiably detained cherished an understandable resentment of Trudeau. Because some were journalists or other minor public figures with access to the media, they helped cultivate a legend of a kind of "Black October."[18] There was a predisposition to believe them—Canada was a liberal society, after all, and Trudeau's actions, not to mention those of the terrorists, were definitely illiberal. Whereas once Trudeau had been the darling of English-Canadian intellectuals, their admiration for him after 1970 fragmented.

The passage of the October Crisis reminded Canadians that Quebec was unfinished business. The Trudeau government was working on a constitutional reform package that it hoped would command Quebec's adherence while allowing all the provinces and the federal government to tie up loose ends on jurisdiction, create a process for constitutional amendment, and generally adapt the constitution to the needs of the late twentieth century. The federal government recognized what was already true, that the provinces had primacy in such fields as pensions and social policy. The provinces could participate in naming judges to the Supreme Court. There would be a limited charter of rights, applicable to all Canadians. There was an amending formula, which gave Ontario and Quebec, the two largest provinces, a veto over amendments. The use of French in the courts and provincial legislatures would be expanded. Bourassa agreed to all these points, and there was supposed to be a ceremonial agreement to a new Canadian Charter at a federal–provincial conference in Victoria in June 1971.

At the last moment, intimidated by protests at home in Quebec, Bourassa hesitated. He needed more time. With more time, his hesitations increased, and finally he refused to sign. It was not enough. What would have been enough? For the separatists, no agreement was the best agreement. For Quebec nationalists, an important component in Bourassa's cabinet and in the provincial civil service, there was the fascination of making Canada truly "deux nations," meaning that Quebec and the rest of Canada would negotiate *d'égal à égal*, equal to equal. There was also the desire to capture more and larger federal powers. As one separatist-leaning civil servant said to Jean Chrétien, then a junior minister in Trudeau's cabinet, "We'll separate from Canada the same way Canada separated from England: we'll cut the links one at a time, a concession here and a concession there, and eventually there'll be nothing left."[19] The Victoria Charter didn't do that, and so was incompatible with their vision of an autonomous and powerful Quebec. Such a Quebec, linked more by treaty than by a democratic constitution, was impossible, as far as English Canada was concerned, and so the Victoria Charter died. The most important factor in the rejection of Victoria wasn't constitutional at all, but fear—fear that Quebec's French-speaking identity would be swamped by a wave of English.

Fear of English provided a parallel agenda for Quebec politics for the rest of the 1970s. Quebec governments had traditionally been laissez-faire on language matters: let the English do one thing, French Canadians another. English was the language of roughly 20 percent of the province's population, or 888,000 people. It was true that, had English Quebeckers actually remained in the province, there would have been 700,000 more; but they did not. Thus the proportion of English speakers was actually maintained by immigrants from abroad. What was of more interest was the fact that the proportion of French speakers in Canada was declining, as well as Quebec's share of the Canadian population. The internal balance in Quebec was less alarming than the province's slowly diminishing weight in Canada—and it must not be forgotten that emigration did tend to reflect economic and other opportunities elsewhere.

The system worked well enough down to the 1960s—so well that when the political climate changed, many politicians and other public figures were caught by surprise. As late as 1969 the Union Nationale government of Jean-Jacques Bertrand, responding to language disturbances in a Montreal suburb, passed legislation reaffirming parents' right to freedom of choice in language of education. The Liberal Bourassa, Bertrand's successor, did not at first propose to change the habitual order of things, but under the pressure of linguistic fears, reinforced by the declining birth rate, the premier decided he must act.

The Liberals were uncomfortable about language. Removing freedom of choice, of use, in language was an illiberal act, and grated on some members of the cabinet. There was danger in irritating the party's hitherto solid political support in the English-speaking community. Some Liberals may have thought that the fears stoked by Quebec's linguistic nationalists were irrational if not chimerical. But if the government didn't act, legally and officially, there might be unofficial action, illegal and violent. Bourassa put forward Bill 22, which stipulated that only children with a sufficient knowledge of English could be admitted to English-language schools.[20] It also regulated the language of signs, encouraged the "francisation" of the workplace, and made French the only official language of Quebec. That was arguably its most important accomplishment, for it turned the English-speaking community from partners into a minority, psychologically. For a hundred years and more Quebec had been a bilingual province. Choice of language rested with the individual rather than the collectivity.[21] That was no longer the case, and English-speaking citizens of the province took note of the fact.[22]

Bill 22 was too much for the English, who made their disapproval manifest, and not enough for Quebec nationalists, who believed, as a separatist newspaper put it, that French speakers were being "dispossessed of their collective rights by a massively anglophone immigration." Trudeau was embarrassed, but could do little to protect the English minority.

Language discontent wasn't restricted to the provincial scene. Trudeau and his French-speaking colleagues from Quebec intended to demonstrate that the federal government and its institutions belonged to French speakers too. Something had to be done to counter the attraction of Quebec City as the "national" government of French Canadians (or as those inside the province increasingly called themselves, Québécois). Parliament therefore passed, in 1969, an Official Languages Act that greatly enhanced the position of French in government.[23] Many English-speaking civil servants found they must now learn French, both to communicate inside their departments and with the public at large, for the public now had a right to service in the two official languages. The Act also provided encouragement and funding to minority-language communities.[24]

With Trudeau and a few influential Quebec ministers behind it, the Official Languages Act changed much in Ottawa's official culture. It encouraged French-speaking civil servants and it had a positive political effect in Quebec during the 1970s. As events showed, language policy had a powerful influence over political attitudes inside Quebec, as federalists scrambled to put together a case for keeping the province inside Canada. They weren't always successful, as events would show.

Bourassa and the PQ

Politically, the 1970s were a time of missed opportunities. There was the opportunity afforded by the Liberal party holding power simultaneously in Quebec and Ottawa from 1970 to 1976. All federalists together, or so it seemed, it should have been easy for Ottawa and Quebec City, Pierre Trudeau and Robert Bourassa, to work out a deal or at least a strategy that would strengthen Canada and keep the separatists at bay. Instead, the Liberals lost power—or, perhaps better, power slipped from their grasp. Trudeau, as we have seen, gave way to Joe Clark and the Progressive Conservatives in Ottawa, part of the normal alternation of major parties that had characterized Canada since its foundation in 1867. Bourassa, however, lost to René Lévesque and the PQ in 1976, thereby plunging Canada into a prolonged political crisis that, thirty years later, had not ceased.

The times weren't easy for any government in power. There was the oil crisis and the ramping up of petroleum prices. There was inflation and there was unemployment: the stagflation that plagued the Western world. In Quebec, it was the heyday of radicalism, as the old Roman Catholic Church relaxed its grip and new forms of worship arose. Marxism remained a fringe sect, its power and influence exaggerated by its popularity among university academics. Quebec wasn't unique in this; what was unusual was the fervour with which Quebeckers embraced unions, radicalism, and labour all at the same time. Gone were the old practices that subordinated the largest union "central," the Quebec Federation of Labour (QFL), to its parent, the Canadian Labour Congress; gone were some of the old forms, like the Canadian and Catholic Confederation of

Labour of the 1950s, replaced by first the Confederation of National Trade Unions (CNTU) or Confédération des Syndicats Nationaux (CSN).

The union movement was inflated, as elsewhere in Canada, by an influx of previously unorganized workers from the public sector; and the public sector was in any case expanding. Given the emphasis placed by the Quiet Revolution on state action and state agencies, it wasn't unnatural for Quebec labour organizations to favour socialism as the ultimate and most desirable form of government. In the rising climate of Quebec nationalism it seemed to follow automatically that Quebec socialists would also be Quebec separatists, and by the early 1970s the trade union leadership was urging its members to vote for the separatist party, the PQ.

But voting was not Quebec labour's main concern. Like the radicals of 1919 they preached the gospel of confrontation, and the immediate target was the Quebec government, which was, after all, the employer of first or last resort for so many union members. In 1972 three union centrals, the QFL, the CSN, and the teachers' corporation, went on strike simultaneously as a "common front," defying the government to do its worst. For the first time in fifty years the words "general strike" were heard in the land.

The Bourassa government responded as governments usually do when confronted with an assertive parallel power: by demonstrating that legal authority still resided with the people duly elected to exercise it. The National Assembly legislated the workers back to work. When the unions defied the law, their three principal leaders went to jail. Dire consequences were threatened, and continued disruption. Disruption there certainly was: the common fronts reappeared in 1976, 1979, and 1982. Each time the response from government was the same. The difference was that in 1979 and 1982 the government wasn't the class-enemy Liberals, but the very party the unions had supported in elections good and bad: the PQ.

The PQ had taken advantage of the slipping fortunes of the Bourassa Liberals. At first it seemed they wouldn't slip very far, if at all. The government wasn't a bad one, times were good, and the province was benefiting from a mega-project of the most spectacular kind, the Olympics of 1976. It naturally recalled Expo 67, and was meant to be the boost that the city of Montreal hoped for, and needed, for the metropolis's economy was lagging, both absolutely and by comparison with rival Toronto. Part of the problem, economists told the federal government, was that Montreal didn't have a big enough hinterland. Also symptomatic was that, even for some of the companies that kept their headquarters in the city, like the Bank of Montreal or the Royal Bank of Canada, many functions had been transferred to Toronto.

The Olympics was intended to mask if not reverse these trends, but it did not do so. Instead, the construction of grandiose Olympic facilities (including and especially an Olympic stadium) on a strict timeline became a nightmare for the city and its ambitious mayor Jean Drapeau. Drapeau told the press that the Olympics could no more have a deficit than a man could have a baby. Cartoonists by 1976 were having a field day depicting a visibly pregnant mayor on his way to the Olympics.[25] A large part of the problem was the construction unions, which perceived that they could demand and get practically anything they wanted with the merest hint of a strike.[26] At one point even the mint making commemorative coins for the Olympics went on strike. Hinting at strikes in Canada in 1976 did not require much imagination;[27] the labour situation in Quebec in the mid-1970s was only a more extreme version of a trend across the country. "To hell with the public," one postal union leader told a reporter.[28] The public took note.[29]

Strikes—at the Olympics, in construction, in the Canadian Post Office—were endemic in the mid-1970s. And then the air traffic controllers struck too. Their issue was language. Until 1976 the language in the skies over Canada was English, as was the common practice internationally. The customary argument was that those using the crowded skies must use a common language, and of all languages English was the most widespread. In Canada, however, the use of language was political as well as practical, and a group of Quebec pilots and air traffic controllers demanded the right to use French at least some of the time over the province. The federal transport minister, Jean Marchand, agreed; the English-language pilots did not. The strike disrupted air traffic for a brief period, but it also quite successfully disrupted linguistic harmony in Canada.

Bourassa chose the moment to call a provincial election. He wasn't quite three years into his five-year mandate, but he seems to have thought that if he waited he would only do worse. The government was beset by troubles, including charges of scandal, as well as problems of language in the schools and in the air, labour disorder, and an economy that wasn't doing as well as people thought it should. Bourassa ran an ineffective campaign. As one of his ministers reflected years later, "Innuendoes and half-truths were used very skilfully; they played well in the media and thus created an image problem."[30] The Liberals were defeated in the election, with the lowest vote in their history, and the premier lost his own seat. Most notably, for the first time since 1939, the English-speaking community defected from the Liberals, in response to Bourassa's language legislation. Bourassa, not for the last time, had seriously underestimated his ability to offend English Canadians. The separatist PQ, headed by René Lévesque, took power.

Le Combat des Chefs: Trudeau and Lévesque

English Canadians hadn't been expecting a separatist government in Quebec, although for weeks before the election all reasonable signs had been pointing that way. Pierre Trudeau himself had recently reassured Canadians that separatism was dead, politically speaking. That was obviously not the case.

The immediate effect was to give the Trudeau government a new lease on life. Supporters urged the prime minister to call an election as soon as possible, but Trudeau hung back. He responded, instead, with a task force to investigate constitutional options and soundings of the provinces to see whether, collectively or singly, they would cooperate in a constitutional reform that might look well in Quebec without giving up any essential, as

Trudeau saw it, federal power. None of these efforts bore fruit, and in the end Trudeau's mandate expired before anything could be done. Defeated in the 1979 federal election, he prepared to retire from politics, only to be recalled to win the February 1980 election after Joe Clark's unexpected defeat in the House of Commons the previous December. Trudeau's Liberal majority in the House of Commons included, and depended upon, seventy-four out of seventy-five of the seats in Quebec—a fact that was not irrelevant to what would follow.

The separatists hadn't been idle. Premier René Lévesque appointed a more than competent cabinet, reflecting the fact that many of the intelligentsia or near-intelligentsia in the province had already passed over into the separatist camp. His first order of priority was to pass a Charter of the French Language, Bill 1 of the new legislative session in 1977. (For largely—but not entirely—procedural reasons, it was renamed Bill 101, and it has passed down into history with that title.)[31] The principal author of and driving force behind Bill 101 was Camille Laurin, whose sentiments it undoubtedly reflected. In terms of language, Laurin, a psychiatrist by profession, was a hardliner, believing that the province would not become "normal" until the abnormal notice given to English was removed.[32]

In a White Paper that preceded the Charter, the public appearance of English in Quebec was called "difficult and embarrassing," and Bill 101 did its best to expunge the embarrassment. English-language signs, with a few exceptions (for example, on churches), were banned. Bilingual signs, mandated under Bourassa's barely cold language law, were also banned, though given time to disappear. Attendance at English schools in the province was made, effectively, hereditary to the descendants of people who had already attended such schools—and only to them. English-speaking immigrants from abroad, or from the rest of Canada, would have to take their schooling in French. Language tests were imposed for professional qualification, for example in nursing, which all defined professionals had to take, and pass. A compulsory process of "francisation" was instituted, under a language commission, which was given substantial powers of enforcement.

In the evolution of PQ language policy little regard had to be given to the sentiments of the English, outside or inside Quebec.[33] Outside, there was the fact that French minorities had fewer opportunities in the matter of education than would remain to the English in Quebec, even after Bill 101. Inside Quebec, there was no realistic hope that the English would ever form part of the PQ majority.[34] (The first draft of the Charter of the French Language in fact defined "the Quebec people" as French-speaking.) It sufficed, in the minds of PQ militants, that the party represent a majority of the French-speaking citizens, and it was to that majority that Lévesque's government spoke. Laurin even overrode the soft objections of his own premier, Lévesque, who would have preferred a less draconian language code; but Laurin knew his man and understood that Lévesque would not insist.[35]

Bill 101 therefore went into effect pretty much as intended. The business community in Montreal took it badly, and one of Montreal's most prominent companies, Sun Life Assurance, whose massive headquarters dominated the downtown, announced that it was moving to Toronto.[36] Its most obvious effect was on the school system. English-language schools in Quebec shrank, and shrank drastically: between 1975 and 1983 their enrolment dropped by 53 percent.[37] According to Statistics Canada figures, the English-speaking community in Quebec suffered a net loss to interprovincial migration of 50,000 from 1971 to 1976, 106,300 from 1976 to 1981, and 41,600 from 1981 to 1986.[38]

The natural increase, as we have seen, was falling in Quebec and elsewhere in Canada—as it was across the Western world. Bill 101 solved one problem—it halted the spread of English in the province and answered the worries of Quebec nationalists. The English would adapt or depart. Many adapted—by the twenty-first century about 30 percent of the English-language community would be married to French speakers. The rate of bilingualism among English speakers soared. Only one thing was missing: a steady flow of immigrants to keep French-speaking Quebec topped up.

Demographers could now worry about something different. Quebec grew more slowly after 1970 than other parts of Canada. This did not greatly concern Quebec nationalists, fixated as they were on statistics that applied to the province only. Between 1971 and 2005, Quebec's population grew from 6.14 million to 7.6 million, according to provincial statistics. More of them spoke French, absolutely and proportionately, than in times past. That was the good news. But if one in forty inhabitants of North America regularly used French in 1977, when the French-language charter was passed, one in fifty used it in 2001. In effect, the Charter guaranteed French-speaking Quebeckers a larger piece of a shrinking pie.

The PQ had got itself elected in 1976 only by denaturing its raison d'être, the quest for sovereignty. Indeed, the sovereignty aspect of its platform had always been heavily qualified, because Lévesque insisted on "sovereignty-association," political independence combined with an economic union with the rest of Canada. For the 1976 election that was qualified some more: electing a PQ government wouldn't immediately bring independence, but rather an eventual referendum on whether the province should negotiate sovereignty-association with Canada. Only if the negotiations didn't happen or proved fruitless would the PQ government ask the ultimate question of whether the province should become independent. In the meantime, the PQ would show that it wasn't just a bunch of impractical nationalist fanatics, but a sober and responsible government, worthy of being entrusted with independence.

Eventually, of course, the PQ had to keep its promise and hold a referendum; not to have done so would have destroyed its electoral base. The referendum was set for 20 May 1980.

By that point the government in Ottawa had once again changed hands. The Conservatives' Joe Clark was gone, and Trudeau was back, and heading a powerful group of French-speaking ministers, especially Marc Lalonde in energy and Jean Chrétien in justice. Chrétien, with a deserved reputation as both an unqualified federalist and a powerful, folksy orator, became Trudeau's point man for handling the referendum. There was never any question that Ottawa politicians would participate in the referendum. Trudeau as prime minister could hardly stand aside as the legitimacy of the federal government was brought into question. By the same token, however, the federal government accepted the legitimacy of the referendum; should Lévesque's question pass, it would demonstrate that Ottawa could not command the allegiance of a majority of Quebeckers.

The nominal head of the federalist or "no" camp was the provincial Liberal leader Claude Ryan. Ryan was a Quebec nationalist as well as a Canadian—he believed he could and should be both. Trudeau, not a Quebec nationalist at all, was hardly Ryan's soulmate. He believed in a strong central government that would direct the affairs of a country continually beset by centrifugal forces. As he saw it, Canada must be more than the sum of its parts, and the national prime minister more than a headwaiter for the provinces. Ryan had worked through a thoughtful program for a decentralized Canada in which Quebec would play a part; Trudeau thought the balance of powers just as it was had weakened the federal government and could barely hold the country together. Nevertheless, the awkward and angular Ryan came to the painful realization that without the charismatic and confrontational Trudeau he might not be able to carry the day against Lévesque. Yet though Trudeau dominated the campaign, his actual interventions were carefully husbanded.

The two sides in the referendum debate, the *Non* for the federalists and the *Oui* for the sovereignists, as the separatists called themselves, struck predictable chords. The separatist camp promised great things for an independent Quebec, free at last from English tutelage, condescension, and assimilation.[39] The federalists painted Canada as a country that had stood the test of time, had protected the French language, and had become a secure economic haven. Quebeckers' political and economic security would be at risk if Canada were disrupted. English Canadians at the time tended to believe that the economic argument would do the trick; certainly the premiers of the other nine provinces talked as if the economy alone—and its attributes, like federal subsidies to Quebec, a have-not province—would be a winning argument. Little did they understand that separatist supporters believed that Quebec would be *better* off economically if it became independent. Quebec, in their opinion, was the goose that laid the golden eggs for Canadian federalism.[40]

Trudeau appealed, instead, to a sense of common purpose, to pride in Canada, and to confidence that Canada's constitution could and would be reformed. (He also appealed to the fact that his prestige in Quebec outweighed Lévesque's: according to a witticism at the time, Trudeau was what Quebeckers would like to be, while Lévesque was what they actually were.)[41] He promised as much in a speech in Montreal. To separatists and Quebec nationalists generally, constitutional reform should only mean devolution, giving the province more powers if not all powers. Trudeau meant no such thing, but he didn't clarify his meaning.[42] As a result, when the *Non* side won, as it did by a sixty–forty margin (and a majority of French speakers), Trudeau was expected to follow through on reforming the constitution—a promise he hadn't made. Since he didn't do so, he was ever after considered—by the nationalists—to be a trickster who had deceived the Quebec people. In his concession speech, Lévesque ungraciously claimed that the *Non* side hadn't played fair, which also bolstered the nationalist legend that separatism's defeat was somehow illegitimate.

Yet there was, for the time being, no question that the outcome was binding. Exhausted, Quebeckers looked to Ottawa for the next round in Canada's constitutional saga. "Lévesque was a political eunuch," a Western premier observed. "It was up to the rest of us to take on Trudeau."[43] What would follow was up to Trudeau, the victor.

TRUDEAU'S CONSTITUTION

Had Pierre Trudeau left office for the last time in 1979, he would be remembered as an interesting but unsuccessful prime minister, his time in office a bridge between the liberalism of the 1960s and the neo-conservativism of the 1980s. He would have been a disappointment, rather like John Diefenbaker in his failure to seize the moment and change the country for the better. Yet thanks to a series of political accidents—Joe Clark's failure to obtain a parliamentary majority in the 1979 election, and his subsequent political misfortunes—Trudeau got that rarest of commodities, a second chance in politics, like Sir John Macdonald in 1878 and Mackenzie King in 1935. Macdonald and King were remembered among Canada's great prime ministers; would Trudeau be the same?

This time, Trudeau determined, he would not become a prisoner of process. He would not make concessions to local or provincial interests—he'd tried that in the 1970s, and it had only stimulated an appetite for more.[44] He would leave his mark on the country by reshaping the constitution, and thereby solve the Quebec problem once and for all. He would also, incidentally, preserve Canada by entrenching the powers of the federal government.

Trudeau's constitutional ideas were well known. He wanted to bring the power to amend the constitution to Canada from Britain, where it had been becalmed since 1931. (This was called repatriation, which strictly speaking it was not, since the power to amend had never resided in Canada.)[45] He wanted a charter of rights, rather like the American bill of rights, empowering individuals by defining and defending their freedoms. He would achieve Henri Bourassa's dream of a new and better Canada by entrenching bilingualism from coast to coast—including Quebec.

Constitutional amendments in Canada involved the provinces, whose consent was traditionally sought for any change that might affect provincial powers. Once a package was agreed to, as with unemployment insurance in 1941, the federal government would forward the agreement to its British counterpart, which would then introduce to the British Parliament an amendment to the British North America Act.

In the summer of 1980 Trudeau followed the customary procedure, sending his justice minister, Chrétien, to the provincial capitals to secure unanimous consent to the repatriation of the constitution, plus a charter of rights. But, just as Trudeau had discovered in the 1970s, Chrétien found that an agreement wasn't possible without concessions to every province. This became obvious when the premiers gathered in Ottawa in September 1980 and, before the television cameras, made it clear that in no reasonable way could Trudeau get what he wanted.

There was another way, laid down in a federal strategy paper that had been leaked to the press during the summer. Assuming that the provinces were incapable of agreeing to a constitutional deal, it advised Trudeau to manoeuvre the premiers toward a spectacular failure, demonstrating that they were collectively unfit to manage the nation's business. Trudeau should simply disregard the premiers and proceed with his constitutional amendments, passing them through Parliament and forwarding them to London without provincial consent. It was a daring gamble. It assumed that most Canadians' primary allegiance was as individuals to Canada, and that their identity was not divided or mediated through the provinces.[46] Trudeau would thus directly challenge the notion that the Quebec "nation" found primary expression through the provincial government in Quebec City, but would challenge as well all the other regional and provincial claims to primacy.

Trudeau proceeded to do exactly that. He produced draft amendments for consideration by Parliament, and during committee hearings the legislation was substantially amended to reflect concerns from women's groups, civil libertarians, and minority groups.[47] He brought on side two out of the ten premiers, the politically astute Bill Davis of Ontario and the unusually intelligent Richard Hatfield of New Brunswick. Both were Progressive Conservatives, which wasn't surprising: there were no Liberal governments left in the provinces. The most obdurate in opposition were the governments of Newfoundland, Quebec, Manitoba, and Alberta; with the other four provinces they made up "the Gang of Eight." They immediately referred the constitutional amendments to three provincial courts of appeal. Eventually, the Supreme Court took up the case, and rendered its decision in September 1981.

The decision was confusing. Custom, the justices ruled, supported the provinces' contention that the constitution could not be amended without their consent. But legally, Trudeau was within his rights. He could proceed to take his amendments to London for final passage—if he dared. That he would dare seemed a safe bet until Bill Davis let Trudeau know that a compromise of some sort was necessary; failing that, Ontario and New

Brunswick would withdraw their support for the federal position, and that might well fatally affect the prospects of getting the amendments through the British Parliament. A federal–provincial conference was about to meet in Ottawa, in November 1981. It was time to see what federal–provincial diplomacy could do.

The Gang of Eight was less solid than it appeared. Several governments were wavering, especially Saskatchewan's, and there was a division between René Lévesque and the others. Lévesque had an interest in seeing negotiations fail; the other premiers, in the final analysis, did not. There was always the possibility that Trudeau was right, and that the citizens of the various provinces would support Ottawa's cause over that of the provinces. At the very least there would be a bruising fight.

Trudeau led in the formal conference, smoothly outmanoeuvring René Lévesque by openly putting the Quebec premier at odds with his colleagues; Chrétien handled negotiations behind the scenes.[48] Working with Roy McMurtry and Roy Romanow, the attorneys general of Ontario and Saskatchewan respectively, he secretly worked out a deal that satisfied seven members of the Gang of Eight. Only one member of the gang didn't know what was going on: René Lévesque. The next day, Lévesque was the conspicuous exception to the universal chorus of acclaim for the new constitutional package. In Quebec, many saw this fact as yet another betrayal—a "Night of the Long Knives," to use the common term.

The constitutional compromise of November 1981 gave everybody a bit of what they wanted. Trudeau got the most—there would be a Charter of Rights and Freedoms, largely along lines he had laid down, and the power to amend the constitution would be transferred to Canada. The Charter would allow Canadians everywhere in the country access to education in English or French—though the same stipulation did not apply to immigrants. Bill 101 was thereby modified.

On the one hand, the formula for amending the constitution was the one devised by the dissenting provinces, a complicated and layered series of consents that would make future amendments very difficult to achieve. On the other hand, no province, however large (like Ontario) or however unique (meaning Quebec), had a singular veto over future amendments. Lévesque had actually conceded the point when he signed on to the provincial amending formula. Finally, there was a unique clause designed to appease believers in the old British tradition of parliamentary supremacy, which had hitherto obtained in Canada. (The main advocate of parliamentary supremacy was the very Conservative premier of Manitoba, Sterling Lyon.) Parliaments and legislatures had always been free to legislate on whatever they chose. If in the future Parliament or a provincial legislature wished to pass a law that contradicted the Charter of Rights, they could still do so, using what was called the "notwithstanding" clause. Use of that clause had to be specific, and it had to be renewed every five years. There was some thought that a government wouldn't wish to suffer the embarrassment of admitting that it was violating a right or freedom ordinarily enjoyed by Canadians.

Agreement by and with the provinces—or nine of them—wasn't quite the end of the story. Trudeau had to get the constitution past the British Parliament, and in the end the British Parliament did what it was asked to do, and the constitution passed. It was formally signed by Elizabeth II in a ceremony on Parliament Hill in Ottawa, on a rainy 17 April 1982, with a very pleased Pierre Trudeau looking on.

WHAT DID TRUDEAU ACCOMPLISH?

The Canadian constitution with a Charter of Rights and an amending formula was Trudeau's main achievement as prime minister. From his point of view it was probably the Charter of Rights that made the exercise worthwhile. The amending formula was desirable, as signifying the completion of Canada's sovereignty, but it was hardly crucial. Writing back in the 1960s, Trudeau had argued that the constitution with its existing division of powers between Ottawa and the provinces was satisfactory as it stood. Quebec in particular had all the powers it needed.

Trudeau had no patience with the nostrums and "traditional demands" developed by Quebec governments between the 1960s and the 1980s.

Canada was not "deux nations," Quebec and the rest, with coequal status. He was equally allergic to "special status," which has also caused some confusion among commentators. It was true that Quebec had legal attributes that were different from other provinces, such as its civil code, or the official use of the French and English languages in its legislature and courts. But "special status," as it was understood in the 1960s and after, meant that Quebec should receive *more* powers than other provinces, a halfway house on the road to "deux nations" and Daniel Johnson senior's notion of "equality or independence." Trudeau understood the game very well, along with the special interpretation of Canada's history that went with "special status." It was a game he was not prepared to play.

Canada was not the sum of its provinces either. The federal government had to have the power and the ability to be a national government, by and for the Canadian nation. To that end, Trudeau tried to hold the line on devolution of power to the provinces; admittedly, as his critics have pointed out, during the 1970s he was prepared to consider concessions to provincial demands.

This doesn't suggest that Trudeau's thoughts on the constitution were contradictory or his behaviour necessarily opportunistic and unprincipled; if anything it was a barometer of his commitment to a process of negotiation and compromise. That process ended with the election of 1980. A transfer of significant power to the provinces, Trudeau had learned, only stimulated a provincial appetite for more power and more money, each successive settlement a platform for another, higher set of demands. Convinced that concessions to the provinces were a mug's game, Trudeau returned to the status quo in terms of the distribution of powers in the final constitutional negotiations of 1980–82.

Trudeau and the Liberals did not prosper after the constitutional triumph of 1982. In 1984 Trudeau retired, and his party was heavily defeated in the subsequent September 1984 election. Of the seventy-four Liberal seats in Quebec in the 1980 election, only seventeen survived. It was a judgment, of a kind, on Trudeau's performance in office, but in an election no single issue is usually dominant. The Liberals did even worse elsewhere in Canada than in Quebec—especially in Ontario, where their percentage of the popular vote was even lower. There had been inflation, sky-high interest rates, and the worst recession since the Second World War. The government had provoked Alberta, the business community, and the traditional right wing.

Trudeau would be remembered for many things. "He haunts us still," two of his biographers wrote in 1990.[49] Like his fictional hero, Cyrano de Bergerac, Trudeau's panache, his cold magnetism, defined him in people's memories. The Charter of Rights became part of Canadians' self-definition. A poll in 2003, three years after his death, called him "transformational"; in the opaque language of the social sciences, this is a high compliment.[50] He stuck in people's memory; his death and funeral stirred emotions, mostly positive.[51]

And yet, as James Marsh noted, when Trudeau died the headline in *La Presse,* Quebec's largest newspaper, read, "The Hero of English Canada."[52] Trudeau's reputation in his own province had always been fraught with contradiction. The longest-serving French-Canadian prime minister, the man who swept the province in 1980 and defeated its popular premier in a referendum, was at first judged unelectable in any French-Canadian constituency, and was exiled to the riding of Mount Royal, the safest English seat in Quebec, where he remained from 1965 until 1984.

Trudeau consciously—some would say self-consciously—swam against the current, and never more so than in Quebec. An intellectual, Trudeau was usually in the minority among intellectuals—in French as well as English Canada. As French-speaking intellectuals veered toward nationalism and then separatism in the 1960s, Trudeau proceeded in the opposite direction. It may be that fact that explains both the power and the fragility of his achievement. It may explain why the ultimately hapless René Lévesque remained a more popular and evocative figure in Quebec.

16

BUST AND BOOM IN THE EIGHTIES

The singing summit: Flanked by two entertainers, Brian Mulroney,
Mila Mulroney, Ronald Reagan, and Nancy Reagan sing
"When Irish Eyes Are Smiling," Quebec City, 17 March 1985.

T he 1980s began with the bang of Trudeau's re-election in February 1980. They continued with a whimper, as the economy sank into the worst recession since the Second World War. While Trudeau may be remembered for his confrontation with Quebec and his reform of the Canadian constitution, what was equally troubling at the time was rising unemployment and soaring interest rates.

Trudeau and his government didn't cause the recession. Canada's economy trailed other Western economies, and Canada's economic policies resembled those of larger countries, especially the United States. Suffering from the same problems, Canadians tried the same solutions. Canadian GDP fell between 1981 and 1982, and of course per capita income fell as well, not recovering to 1980 levels until 1984. Virtually every country in the Western world participated in the economic downturn, and in some countries, like France and Germany, unemployment rose to a permanent, and high, plateau. Governments helped to foster this development, raising interest rates to the point where inflation could be squeezed out of the economic system. So it was, but at a considerable cost in plant closures, collapsing retail sales, and unemployment.[1]

Monetary policy is seldom an issue in electoral politics, and it was natural that Trudeau and his ministers were fixated on other things. Oil prices were rising, thanks to a revolution in Iran, and heading, it was believed, for $60 a barrel. This posed problems for Canada's two-price system for oil, in which the domestic price for oil and natural gas was less than half the world price—the price at which petroleum could be exported to the United States.[2] But what was a problem was also an opportunity. The federal government was already running a deficit, in part to pay for the two-price system. Why then should the federal government not profit from the oil bonanza, help pay for its oil-related deficit, and also use the occasion to make the Canadian oil industry more Canadian-owned?

The Trudeau government proceeded to do just that. Failing to agree with Alberta on oil pricing (as the brief Progressive Conservative Clark government had also failed), it proclaimed a National Energy Program (NEP) in the federal budget of October 1980. Ottawa set the domestic price itself, anticipating a rise from $16.75 a barrel in 1980 to $66.75 a barrel in 1990. This calculation projected a much higher world price, and assumed that the oil producers' cartel, OPEC, would continue to dominate the world oil market. A combination of subsidies, special pricing, and tax incentives encouraged Canadian ownership of oil production. Ottawa gave itself the right to take a 25 percent interest (called a "back-in") on existing oil-lands leases in the "Canada Lands"—offshore and in the federally administered Territories. Ottawa had changed the rules, to the surprise and discomfiture of investors who had poured money into oil production with quite different expectations. Put another way, foreign-owned oil companies were discriminated against, and thus encouraged to sell to Canadian companies, including the federally owned Petro-Canada (established in 1975). The federal government had the power to impose its will because of its control over interprovincial and international trade, as well as its purported ability to legislate for "the peace, order and good government of Canada."

The objective was to give Canada greater control over its energy supply, let the federal government share in the oil-price bonanza, and keep profits at home through domestic ownership. The *Toronto Star*, Canada's leading liberal-nationalist organ, called the NEP a "comprehensive energy program that can pay enormous dividends for this nation in the years ahead. It deserves the support of all Canadians."[3]

The Alberta government, the oil industry, and the provinces generally took the NEP rather badly. The provinces owned their natural resources under the constitution, and consequently had the power to dispose of them as they saw fit. Albertans saw the NEP as the appropriation of the resources of what until very recently had been a have-not province, in the interest of richer and better-developed central Canada. The West had a deep-seated grievance over what it saw as the tendency of populous central Canada to rearrange the country's economic affairs to its own advantage. A hundred years of the National Policy convinced western Canadians that eastern Canadians preferred to sell their own products dear, under tariff protection, while buying Western resources cheap, at world prices. Now for the first time the world priced a Western product high, and the East was, typically, reacting in its own narrow economic best interest.

The Alberta government's policies also tended to reflect the attitudes of the oil industry, largely headquartered in Calgary, and the oil industry saw the back-in provision of the NEP as confiscation of its property. "The real gamble," claimed the *Edmonton Journal,* "is that given Ottawa's bent towards confiscation and nationalization, the industry and the investment community will still feel it is worthwhile to develop Canada's oil and gas."[4] Premier Peter Lougheed of Alberta certainly had the support of most people in his province when he reduced Alberta's oil production rather than pay money to Ottawa. "Let the Eastern bastards freeze in the dark" appeared on Alberta bumper stickers.

Despite the heated rhetoric, much of which he himself had stimulated, Lougheed was not ultimately averse to a compromise with Ottawa. Less production, after all, meant less revenue for Alberta, and if the federal projections were right, and the international price rose, there would be plenty of revenue for everyone. A complicated series of arrangements was negotiated that allowed "new oil" to get close to the world price and provided other fiscal concessions to the province. And so a deal was struck between Ottawa and Edmonton (as well as parallel arrangements with Saskatchewan and British Columbia).[5]

The 1981 arrangements did not last long. International oil prices proved to have peaked in 1980, and were already on their way down, below $20 a barrel by 1985, and on down to $11 by 1987. Revenue followed, to the dismay of both the federal and provincial governments. Investors who had harkened to Ottawa's alluring NEP incentives and borrowed to buy in the energy field found themselves with falling incomes and rising interest rates. Bankruptcy became the common theme of the Alberta oil patch, and it is the economic hardship of 1981–82 and its aftermath that would be remembered long after the NEP had vanished from the statute books. In fact, much of the misery would likely have occurred even if the NEP had never existed. Alberta prosperity followed the international oil price south after 1981, along with the oil rigs and exploration teams who departed the province as a direct consequence of the NEP regime. The direct, ascribable consequences of the NEP became muddled with the effects of other phenomena, over which Ottawa had no control. Nevertheless, it was the NEP that was remembered, and not the vagaries of the market. As an exercise in political theatre, the NEP had practically no equal, but whether it was tragedy or farce remains debatable.

By 1984 the NEP and the assumptions that lay behind it were in ruins. Trudeau had gambled and lost, not merely economically but politically, and the consequences were long-lasting. First, they contributed to the Liberal defeat in the 1984 federal election. Only two Liberals were elected west of Ontario, and one of these was the new party leader, John Turner. There was more. In the West, but especially in Alberta, the NEP became the equivalent of the conscription issue in Quebec in the thirty years after 1917. When Trudeau died, in 2000, Alberta newspapers ignored most of his accomplishments to zero in on the original sin of federal intervention in the oil patch.

That kind of intervention, the opposition Progressive Conservatives trumpeted, would vanish with the Liberals. "Canada is open for business," the victorious Tory leader, Brian Mulroney, proclaimed. His first order of priority was to dismantle the remnants of federal intervention and control over oil. This pleased Alberta greatly—and of course Mulroney had won every one of the province's seats in 1984 and would repeat the performance in 1988. It did not displease Ontario, even as the two-price system for oil came to an end. Oil prices were lower and getting lower still, and the pain of adjustment was consequently not acute. But what Mulroney could deliver to the oil patch he could not easily manage for the rest of the country.

MULRONEY, POLITICS, AND TRADE, 1984–1993

Brian Mulroney was the fifth prime minister to come from the province of Quebec; there had once been another anglophone Quebecker in the job, in 1891–92, Sir John Abbott, but except for the name of a junior college, he had been forgotten. Mulroney came from Quebec's distant hinterland, the north shore of the St. Lawrence east—far east—of Quebec City, in the town of Baie Comeau. Born of Irish-Canadian parents, Mulroney was educated locally and at St. Francis Xavier University in Nova Scotia, where he added conservatism to his native Catholicism. A former law partner observed that Mulroney was a "minority within a minority," the kind of person who never saw himself as a member of the establishment.[6] And yet Mulroney did have some establishment credentials. He was already fluent in French, and it was a natural choice to migrate, eventually, to Laval University law school, where he mixed easily with its overwhelmingly French-Canadian clientele. Upon graduation he moved to Montreal, where he became a prominent labour lawyer while continuing to be active in Conservative party circles.

Mulroney adapted easily to labour law. Reconciling labour demands with management concerns came naturally to him. He had charm, a certain ruthlessness, and obvious ambition. He also had a flair for publicity, and was well enough known to be a plausible candidate for the national Conservative leadership in 1976. Beaten by Joe Clark, he bided his time, while enhancing his reputation and his prosperity by becoming president of the Iron Ore Company of Canada, an American-owned firm dedicated to the extraction of iron ore from Ungava for transport to the steel mills of the American Midwest. He became something of a figure in Montreal society, and carefully cultivated his Conservative connections there and elsewhere. In 1983 he used these to assist Joe Clark out the door as Conservative leader; Mulroney was his natural replacement.

In Canada's system of alternating parties, the Conservatives were the inevitable replacement for the Liberals. A new Liberal leader, John Turner, did not impress the electorate—not enough for voters to forget twenty years of grievances against Trudeau and his party. Mulroney trounced the hapless Turner in a televised election debate—these events had by then become fixtures of federal election campaigns—and led his party to a majority of the popular vote and a seat total of 211 out of 282 in the House of Commons. Turner did manage to win his own seat, in Vancouver, and was condemned to soldier on at the head of his much depleted party, which had almost been overtaken by the third party, the NDP, in seats.

Mulroney's first order of business, as we have seen, was to get rid of the hated NEP. But what would he do next? The government's policy cupboard proved to be almost bare. Like most opposition parties, the Conservatives had campaigned against waste and extravagance, and Mulroney did set up a study group under his deputy prime minister, Erik Nielsen, to winkle it out. But waste and extravagance function as kind of cosmetic in politics, to rouge the corrupt face of power. Compared with the big-ticket items of government, like social spending, waste and extravagance dwindle in importance, and so it was with the Mulroney government. Mulroney had sought to reassure Canadians that he wouldn't touch their social welfare programs, like pensions and medicare, and he didn't. Accordingly, there would be no conservative revolution in public finance. Though the Conservatives benefited from better economic times, they found themselves stuck with a large deficit and a growing national debt.

Mulroney and his ministers were becalmed, while the first hints of scandal whispered around his government. Their accomplishments were few. The Canadian armed forces got new uniforms—on the old tri-service model that had been abolished in the 1960s. At the same time, Mulroney's defence minister was forced to resign after he left his briefcase, with its presumable cargo of state secrets, behind in a German nightclub. The prime minister began to look for a new policy, some striking initiative, that would lend purpose and positive character to his government.

There was one, and it was as old as the country: free trade with the United States. Canada had been partly founded on free trade's rejection by the United States, in the 1860s, and it remained a lively issue in Canadian politics—though not in American—for the next fifty years. Gradually, trade relations with the United States had improved to the point where, by the 1980s, more than 80 percent of Canadian exports to the Americans landed duty-free south of the border.

Federal officials concerned with Canada's trade worried. The United States economy was more vulnerable and less uniquely prosperous than it once had been. The Americans ran a perennial deficit on trade, while their nation's industrial heartland, south of the Great Lakes, withered, as jobs departed for the sunnier, union-free South or Southwest, or left the country altogether for Mexico. Mulroney didn't have to be told that: declining shipments of iron ore from Baie Comeau to Cleveland recorded the decline in American steel production and its substitution by imports from abroad. American legislators began to invent new ways of protecting U.S. producers against foreign competition, and some of those ways impinged on Canadian exports. Seen from this perspective, the 80 percent–plus of Canadian exports destined to the United States could be as much a liability as an asset, should the Americans move to choke off trade.

Canada was not without friends in the United States, and chief among them was the American president, the Republican Ronald Reagan (1981–89). Reagan didn't know a lot about Canada, but what he knew he liked. Some of his friends in his previous career as a Hollywood actor had been Canadians like Mary Pickford and Glenn Ford. Reagan knew that Canadians generally resembled Americans, that relations across the border were always peaceful and generally friendly, and that trade with Canada was important. As a Californian, Reagan was also conscious of the much closer neighbour, Mexico, and he linked Canada, Mexico, and the United States in a project he called "the North American Accord." Nobody, certainly not his staff, knew what that meant.

Reagan's main interest was strategy, the place of the United States in a world defined on communist/anti-communist lines through the Cold War with the Soviet Union. Canada fitted on the American side of that chasm, though with Pierre Trudeau as Canada's prime minister, Reagan's advisers sometimes wondered. Trudeau gave the impression that he saw the United States and the Soviet Union as "equivalent," and that it was only the hazard of geography that had put Canada on the American side.

There was no doubt where Mulroney stood. Raised in a town enriched by American investment, working in the iron ore business (though at head office, far from the ore mines), Mulroney had a strong notion of the importance of Canadian–American links and the beneficial nature of the connection with the United States. He wanted great relations with the United States, he told audiences in the 1984 election. And he needed something—an idea, a policy, an initiative—to shore up his sagging government. Suddenly, in 1985, his civil servants recommended such a policy—free trade. It was true that he'd explicitly repudiated any such idea in the course of the election campaign, but it was easy to convince himself that he'd really meant something else.[7]

A summit meeting with President Reagan was in the offing in Quebec City in March 1985. It would later be best remembered for a quartet of the prime minister, the president, and their wives singing "When Irish Eyes Are Smiling," a piece of unalloyed sentimentality that would for years afterward be considered a landmark of bad taste among Canadian intellectuals. (It seems not to have been noticed by American intellectuals.) That did it no harm with Mulroney, and indeed it wasn't exploited by the opposition parties in future elections, which suggests that the gesture was not unpopular among Canadians. Mulroney mentioned to Reagan that free trade was something that should be looked at, and Reagan agreed. After a summer of study and preparation, Mulroney and his cabinet finally agreed to risk a negotiation. In September 1985 the two countries formally agreed to negotiate free trade, and Congress very narrowly agreed to let the process begin. American law mandated two things for the future agreement: the negotiations must be concluded within two years, and when complete the agreement would be subject to a strict up- or down-vote in Congress, without Congress adding any last-minute unilateral amendments.

Mulroney had two objectives. First was free trade, meaning the abolition of tariffs along the border on products made in the two North American countries. As important or more important, Mulroney wanted the agreement to deal with non-tariff barriers, which by the 1980s were a fearsome obstruction to unfettered commerce across the border. As tariffs dwindled and the protection they afforded became more and more insignificant for domestic interest groups, producers in the United States and elsewhere came to rely on "anti-dumping" legislation, or in American parlance, "countervail." This was actually a Canadian idea, dating back to Laurier's finance minister, William Fielding. To prevent dumping, or subsidized imports, the Canadian Parliament enacted special anti-dumping duties. Other countries, especially the United States, admired Fielding's ingenuity and devised anti-dumping duties of their own, to be applied to any import that was unfairly priced (dumped), or unfairly subsidized in its country of origin.

No two countries agreed on what precisely constituted dumping, or what a subsidy really was. That was left to national laws, which could be changed from time to time in response to domestic pressures. It was all in the interest of establishing a "level playing field," and having not merely *free* trade but *fair* trade as well. Thus the United States could take the lead in pressuring other countries to lower tariffs and extend "national" treatment to foreign investors, while maintaining trade barriers if trade harmony, or an international liberal trading system, went too far.

Ideally, the United States and Canada would abolish their respective anti-dumping and countervail measures, but if that was too much to hope for, then to regularize them by applying a standard method of interpretation to what were, after all, extremely specialized and complicated regulations. Mulroney therefore plumped for a "dispute resolution mechanism" that would bind both countries in the future.

Mulroney and Canada did not get what they wanted. Mulroney had staked a large part of his political future on the achievement of a free trade agreement. He appointed Canada's most experienced, and highest profile, trade negotiator, Simon Reisman, to head the Canadian team. Reisman wanted a comprehensive agreement, and he wanted it badly. The American side, it appeared, did not. They may have been waiting for Canadian concessions, but those were not forthcoming. Negotiations dragged, to the point where, in September 1987, the Canadian negotiators abandoned them and flew home from Washington. This handed the game back to the politicians on both sides, who had to decide, with time pressing, whether anything could be salvaged. There wasn't much doubt that Reagan and his treasury secretary, James Baker, wanted something positive to emerge and, eventually, something did.

The Free Trade Agreement (FTA) of 1987 provided for the progressive abolition of all remaining tariffs on Canadian- and American-produced goods between the two countries. It provided a dispute-resolution mechanism as well, but with a restricted mandate—to determine whether each country was properly applying its laws regulating trade. The United States was free to change its statutes governing countervail whenever it chose, and there is every indication that Congress would agree to nothing less. Mulroney and his advisers considered the deal a triumph, and the government sought its immediate passage through Parliament.

What was opportunity, even salvation, for the government was also opportunity for the opposition Liberals, under their leader, former prime minister John Turner. Turner didn't like the deal, and knew that it wouldn't protect Canada or Canadian interests against future changes in U.S. law. Turner was politically weak: his party was divided and his leadership uncertain. He did have one advantage, however. The Liberals had a majority in the appointive Senate, and they used it to block the FTA's passage. Mulroney was forced into an election, in which free trade would be the dominant issue.

The election was called for 21 November 1988. At first it seemed that the Liberals were doing their best to defeat themselves. Some prominent

Liberals even suggested that Turner should resign as leader while the election was on in order to stimulate confidence in their party—surely the most incredible suggestion ever made by apparently serious people in Canada's political history. The Liberal government of Quebec approved of free trade, as indeed did Quebec separatists, for it reduced Ottawa's control over trade and provided a free-standing market for Quebec exports. Federal Liberal support in Quebec accordingly shrank.[8] The leader of the NDP proclaimed that the Liberals' hour was done, and that his party would take over the opposition and, in Canada's alternating political system, eventually the government. Much depended on Turner's performance during the campaign, and especially in the televised leaders' debate.

In a dramatic reversal of fortune, Turner rolled over Mulroney in the debate. Canada, he argued, represented the triumph of politics over geography, the conscious imposition of an east–west axis across the continent to offset the natural attractions of north–south trade. Mulroney proposed to end that, and to substitute a regime of political and economic dependence on the United States. The prime minister's spluttering protests were lost against the rhetorical force of Turner's argument.

The Liberals supplemented their debating victory by clever television advertising. The most effective ad depicted the negotiation of the free trade agreement through a conversation between two negotiators. Only one line needed changing, the "American" negotiator observed. Which one, the surprised "Canadian" replied. *This* one—showing the American erasing the border. Public opinion polls picked up an immediate reversal in the public mood. The Liberals surged, while Mulroney's Conservatives fell behind. "The allegations and fears promulgated about free trade became more outrageous by the hour," one of Mulroney's supporters later wrote.[9] Canadians' fears were plainly aroused. Free trade was now in danger of defeat.

The Conservative riposte showed what effective politics could be. Money flowed into the party's coffers from an alarmed business community, most of which fervently supported free trade. New Conservative party ads were run showing "typical Canadians" (actually party workers) denouncing Turner as a liar. In a hundred subtle (and unsubtle) ways Canadians were informed that their prosperity and even their jobs hung in the balance—no free trade, no job, because business X or factory Y could no longer afford to stay in Canada. Even if some industry or some area was disadvantaged by free trade, the Conservatives promised they would identify the problem and deal with it—after the election, of course. Now it was the Conservatives' turn to pull ahead, and the trend held all the way to election day.

On 21 November the Conservatives won a majority of seats (169 to 83 for the Liberals and 43 for the NDP) in the House of Commons, and a mandate to pass free trade as soon as Parliament could be convened.[10] Parliament duly passed the necessary legislation, and on 1 January 1989, Mulroney and Reagan signed the documents putting the FTA into effect.

Mulroney had got his legislation and a second majority, though with only 43 percent of the popular vote. He would carry on as prime minister for another four years. John Turner had lost the election, his second as Liberal leader. Custom and personal preference dictated his departure, and he duly resigned his post, to be replaced by a party convention in June 1990. Nevertheless, the Liberals had doubled their seat total, achieved a respectable share of the national vote, and remained the alternative government. The NDP were the real losers of the election. They had missed their chance to displace the Liberals, despite their highest-ever seat total in Parliament. If the Conservatives' star waned, it would be the Liberals who would have the advantage in the next election.

The FTA of 1987–89 wasn't the last of Mulroney's achievements in trade policy. The United States was also interested in a free trade pact with its other neighbour, Mexico, and under Reagan's successor, President George H.W. Bush, negotiations were begun. The Canadian government was at first disinclined to join in, but reversed itself and participated in what became a tripartite negotiation.[11] The reasoning behind its decision was straightforward—Canada preferred a three-way trading relationship to a hub-and-spoke affair in which the United States would be the hub and its trading partners the spokes. Nevertheless, as one observer put it, Canada was "a less than eager participant" in the trade talks.[12] To get into the talks at all, however, Canada relied on the very close personal relations between Prime Minister Mulroney and President Bush. "I found him easy to talk to," Bush later wrote, "gregarious, and possessed of a great sense of humor." Mulroney was, in Bush's opinion, "a strong leader for Canada and a true friend of the United States."[13] The decision to admit Canada or exclude it was Bush's to make, and he made it in favour of Canada and his friend, Mulroney.

The NAFTA negotiations weren't completed until late 1992, and ratification of the agreement took rather longer. NAFTA was an issue in both the American and Canadian general elections of 1992 and 1993; it may well have contributed to the defeat (among many other factors) of George H.W. Bush by Bill Clinton in 1992 and to the defeat of the Progressive Conservatives in Canada in 1993. The most important consideration was that Mexico had a much lower standard of living than either Canada or the United States; consequently, as one American politician argued, there would be a "great sucking sound" as jobs vanished from high-wage and highly regulated economies in the north to the low-wage culture of the south. It was also true that Mexico had a different political and institutional culture from Canada and the United States; democracy Mexican-style was a recent and feeble phenomenon, and there were doubts about the rule of law in Mexico.

These weren't the only concerns, either in the original Canada–U.S. treaty or the later NAFTA version. Besides lowering tariffs and establishing mechanisms for review and appeal of the application of trade laws, the agreements dealt with questions of energy and investment. In what could be termed the anti-NEP clause of the Canada–U.S. agreement, both sides promised not to cut off energy supply to the other, and, if reductions in supply had to be made, they would be pro-rated according to existing trade patterns.[14] Similarly, both countries guaranteed "national treatment" to each other's investors, once established—which meant that anything like the "back-in" provisions of the NEP would in future be prohibited.

On the other hand, given the fact that Canadian investment in the United States was larger, proportionately, than American investment in Canada, Canadian investors south of the border received some extra protection.

One clause, Chapter 11, of the NAFTA agreement has received considerable attention. This clause allows non-national investors (in Canada, meaning from the United States and Mexico) to sue for damages in case government regulation interferes with their probable profits. The clause has been used in all three countries by investors to squeeze compensation from governments over environmental regulations, or to force governments to rescind such regulations. Paradoxically, domestic companies couldn't access the provision—only investors from the other two NAFTA countries. This usage came as a surprise to at least some of the original negotiators of NAFTA. As the deputy chief negotiator for the United States later put it in an interview, "I can see how you can take that particular set of phrasing and say, oh, well, what business is saying is if I'm—if you regulate and make me less profitable, pay me off. I'm not sure whether that was the intent...."[15]

The effects of the original free trade agreement and of NAFTA were less economically disastrous for Canada than opponents feared, and probably less definitively favourable than fervent free traders would wish. Vintners in British Columbia and Ontario rejoiced, as their wines not only survived but flourished. Competition could also prove to be beneficial. "In 1989, I said publicly that free trade would really hurt our company," an Ontario furniture manufacturer told *The Washington Post*. "I would have said privately that it was necessary to get the industry on its feet—and it was. It's a pretty good industry now [1999]. Without free trade, that wouldn't have happened." Not every company was so fortunate; a third of Ontario's furniture manufacturers didn't survive. In some cases, American firms closed their Canadian warehouses, or their Canadian branch plants: the Canadian market could now be serviced from south of the border. But overall, trade and exports grew, so that by 1998 "an astounding 40% of [Ontario's] GDP" was exported to the United States, compared to 20 percent in 1989. The same was true of

Quebec, which experienced a "huge growth" in exports to the U.S. Yet employment in manufacturing declined by 10 percent.[16]

The FTA and NAFTA did bring order and predictability to Canadian–American trade, thanks in large part to the dispute-resolution mechanism. And thanks to Chapter 11 of NAFTA they brought uncertainty too, as governments and the political classes in all three countries debated how, or whether, they could still exercise the power necessary to enforce such things as pollution standards, or to run government enterprises like the post office—the subject of a Chapter 11 challenge in Canada.

Dispute-resolution panels could only do so much. They could interpret existing statutes, and definitely could not limit what sovereign legislatures or parliaments could pass into law. The most notorious, though not the only, case in point was Canadian softwood lumber. By the 1980s, the American construction industry relied heavily on Canadian softwood lumber exports, harvested off provincial lands in Canada and sent south to feed the American appetite for suburbs. (Softwood is usually pine and spruce.) Canadian provinces employed various systems to enable lumber companies to harvest wood; some of their arrangements, for example in the Maritimes, were similar to those typically used in the United States. Other provinces, especially Quebec, Ontario, and British Columbia, used what was called "stumpage," a fee charged to lumber companies for the right to harvest wood off public lands.

The problem was that Canadian softwood was very competitive with American softwood, and Canadian exports attracted the ire of U.S. lumber companies. In 1982, pre-FTA, American companies petitioned their government for a countervail on "subsidized" Canadian lumber. Their argument failed, but the issue didn't go away. Instead, the aggrieved Americans formed a more effective special-interest lobby and returned to the charge in 1986—very inconveniently for the FTA negotiations that were proceeding at just that point. This time they got their countervail, stringent duties on Canadian lumber exports (though not those from the Maritimes), and indeed had they not done so it might have meant more trouble for the future FTA in Congress. That meant trouble for Brian Mulroney, since the softwood lumber case underlined and highlighted what wouldn't be covered by the free trade agreement. Under pressure, Canada agreed to an export tax in 1986, let it expire in 1991, and then negotiated another export tax in 1996. When it lapsed in 2001, the war resumed, with no prospect for resolution until one side or the other surrenders. Even Jimmy Carter, the former American president—who on most issues had views entirely compatible with a majority of Canadians, but who was also the owner of a softwood lumber plantation—argued that Canadian stumpage practices were a disguised subsidy, designed to maintain full employment in the Canadian lumber industry.[17]

The power and political effectiveness of the American lumber lobby meant that it dictated U.S. trade policy on softwood. Canada could appeal to trade tribunals through first the FTA, then NAFTA, and finally the newly founded World Trade Organization (WTO), but the American position remained the same. Canada must either accept American tariffs or enforce its own export tax or a strictly limited quota (about a third) of the American market. As usual in trade and tariff disputes, the consumer's interest was largely forgotten, because consumers were so widely dispersed as to be ineffective; because the American tariff was an indirect and unseen tax; and because the U.S. lumber coalition could concentrate its lobbying and its influence in key states from the Atlantic (Georgia) to the Pacific (Washington). Canadians might huff and puff in response (as they did) and call down the wrath of the free trade gods on the Americans, but Canadians didn't vote in American elections. Free trade remained ... mostly free, and the American government's commitment to the FTA's dispute-resolution mechanism had a large exception—softwood.[18]

TOXIC FEDERALISM

Mulroney's second ambitious project was to reform Canadian federalism. If he had a notable skill, it was his ability to bring people together, and to cajole them into compromises that, left to their own devices, they would have ignored or rejected. Federal–provincial relations seemed made to order.

Canadian federalism couldn't function without a fair amount of compromise between the layers of government. Some federal powers couldn't be exercised without provincial consent and cooperation, and some provincial responsibilities couldn't function without contributions from the federal government. At the same time, there had always been competition between the provinces, or some of them, and the federal government. In the nineteenth century, federal–provincial disputes centred on Ontario, the largest and richest province, whose Liberal government battled with Sir John A. Macdonald's Conservatives over everything from water power to its interprovincial boundary with Manitoba. In the twentieth, Ottawa fought with the Prairie provinces over control of their natural resources, with Ontario over water power (again, and eternally), and with Quebec over the great issues of war and peace during the 1930s and over Ottawa's ability to spend in areas of provincial jurisdiction.

After 1960 Quebec became the focus of federal–provincial concerns. Trudeau's record with Quebec we have seen, but he did manage both an amendment formula for the constitution and a Charter of Rights and Freedoms that bound the provinces as well as the federal government. Politically, Trudeau so demoralized Premier René Lévesque that his government began to come apart as its members quarrelled over what they could do now, independence being no longer an option. Lévesque resigned in October 1985, and was succeeded briefly by one of his ministers, Pierre-Marc Johnson, the son of the Union Nationale premier of the 1960s, Daniel Johnson. Johnson in turn was swept out of office in December 1985 by a revived provincial Liberal party under Robert Bourassa, who had returned from the political wilderness and personal exile in Europe to lead his party. In Europe Bourassa had studied the European Economic Community and its institutions; he concluded that cooperative institutions and a cooperative policy with the rest of Canada would benefit his province, and that separatism would not. On the other hand, Bourassa had never accepted the Trudeau style of federalism and was determined that he would, if possible, alter Trudeau's legacy, which was widely understood in Quebec to be centralization.

Mulroney was attracted to Bourassa's vision. Like almost all other anglophone Quebeckers, he had supported the provincial Liberals in their struggle for federalism against separatism, but by 1984–85 he was no fan of Trudeau or Trudeau's approach to Quebec, which he argued weakened rather than strengthened federalism by driving away moderate nationalists who would be satisfied by a reasonable compromise. He could do better, given the right partner, and Bourassa was that partner.

Bourassa argued that Trudeau's constitutional package of 1982 was legal but not legitimate, because it hadn't been accepted by the Quebec government of the day or ratified by Quebec's legislature. He and his justice minister, Gil Rémillard, proposed that this gap could be made whole by trading Quebec's ratification for an amendment to the constitution embodying five conditions. These were recognition of Quebec as "a distinct society"; restoration of Quebec's veto over constitutional change, traded away by Lévesque back in 1981 as part of his failed constitutional negotiation; greater power for Quebec over immigration (meaning, notionally, more immigrants for Quebec to balance the English); reduction of the federal spending power (never again a Canada Pension Plan or medicare); and provincial participation in the naming of Supreme Court judges.

Mulroney and his ministers carefully canvassed the provinces. There was some concern in the West, especially in Alberta where Senate reform had become a panacea for redressing the balance between the populous East and the resource-rich West. Here the subtext was "no more NEP," which could have been prevented by a Senate that was Equal (the same number of senators for every province), Elected (free of the control of the prime minister of the day and presumably more responsive to local demands), and Effective (more like the American Senate). This added up to the slogan Triple-E, which one enthusiastic farmer plowed onto his wheat field so that it could be seen by aircraft far above. Mulroney persuaded Alberta's Progressive Conservative premier, Don Getty, to deal with Quebec's agenda first; then Alberta's turn would come.

The premiers convened at the government's rural retreat at Meech Lake, Quebec, in the Gatineau Hills north of Ottawa, in April 1987. Mulroney wanted consent to Quebec's five points, and he got it. This wasn't surprising, since Mulroney offered the provinces, collectively, a glittering bundle of concessions. The federal government's power to make appointments to the Supreme Court and the Senate was handed over to the provinces; henceforth the prime minister could appoint justices and senators only from lists handed in by the provincial premiers. Quebec would get a veto over constitutional amendments, as demanded, but so would every other province. And to ensure that this constitutional package wasn't the last, the premiers and prime minister—the "First Ministers"—would convene every year to discuss ... the constitution. All this suggested that Canada would have not so much a constitution as a kaleidoscope. Quebec specifically would be designated a "distinct society," and this phrase would be entered in the preamble of the amended constitution. Experts differed on whether this positioning would or would not give Quebec's distinctiveness a privileged position in the interpretation of the clauses that followed; but that was certainly a possibility.

The amendments took the name of Meech Lake, though they wouldn't be finally agreed upon until a later conference in Ottawa in June. Using his formidable negotiating skills, Mulroney brought the premiers, one after another, on side. The last to come over was Ontario's Liberal premier, David Peterson, but eventually Peterson too bought the argument that he should agree for the sake of national unity. (Peterson had some misgivings over what Quebec would do to assert its "distinct society.") At dawn on 3 June 1987, Mulroney announced to a bedazzled media the completion of the "Quebec Round" of constitution-making, while the premiers staggered back to their hotels to go to bed.

Meech Lake was an act of confidence and trust: trust in Quebec, trust in the provinces, trust in goodwill—blind trust in the eyes of its opponents, who were not slow to speak up. Pierre Trudeau was Meech Lake's most trenchant critic. In French and English he condemned the accord as an unacceptable weakening of the federal government's ability to speak for Canada. "In addition to surrendering to the provinces important parts of its jurisdiction (the spending power, immigration)," Trudeau wrote in a statement published in *La Presse* and the *Toronto Star*, "in addition to weakening the Canadian Charter of Rights, the Canadian state made subordinate to the provinces its legislative power (Senate) and its judicial power (Supreme Court); and it did this without hope of ever getting any of it back (a constitutional veto granted to each province). It even committed itself to a constitutional 'second round' at which the demands of the provinces will dominate the agenda."[19]

In testimony before a joint parliamentary committee, the former prime minister damned Meech Lake as incoherent and its supporters as weaklings. Committee members waxed indignant that Trudeau could so characterize Meech Lake's political parentage; but in the words of a journalistic critic, Peter Trueman, the current generation of Canada's political leaders were at best "merely ordinary ... and some of them we wouldn't allow in our own living rooms."[20]

At first the critics hardly mattered. Prime minister and premiers agreed that the agreement had to be swallowed whole, without amendments except of the most technical kind, where the drafting had been in error. All three federal parties, Progressive Conservatives, Liberals, and NDP, were agreed that Meech Lake was a good thing, and that its passage was essential for national unity. Their provincial counterparts—at least the provincial governing parties—took the same view. There would be committee hearings in Ottawa and the provinces, but the committee members were instructed only to hear, not listen.

Meech Lake had to be passed under the rules set down in the 1982 constitution. An amendment of this kind required unanimous consent, and thus had to be passed by the federal Parliament and every provincial legislature. It must be passed within three years of the first ratification by a province—and that ratification came on 23 June 1987, by Quebec.

With three years to go, the ticking of the constitutional clock wasn't audible at first. Yet it was only the governments that were in office in June 1987 that had agreed to pass Meech Lake. The first of those governments disappeared in October 1987 when the Progressive Conservatives of New Brunswick were erased at the polls (rather literally—the premier and all members of his party were defeated by the opposition Liberals). The new premier, Frank McKenna, wasn't a supporter of Meech, though as events would show he wasn't exactly opposed either. The government of Manitoba also went to the polls, and was replaced by a three-party house of minorities with one party, the Liberals, taking its cue from Pierre Trudeau and breathing defiance. The Manitoba government, like New Brunswick's, postponed the question.

The other provinces, one after another, fell into line and ratified Meech. It seemed that Manitoba and New Brunswick must eventually follow, but in April 1989 something quite different occurred. The Progressive Conservative government of Newfoundland was defeated at the polls by the Liberals under Clyde Wells. Wells was a constitutional lawyer, and a strong supporter of federal power; he believed that Meech Lake would not only reduce the federal government's ability to act on issues important to his province, but would reduce Newfoundland's influence on the national stage. He promised that he would rescind Newfoundland's ratification of Meech Lake, and he proved as good as his word. The Newfoundland legislature cancelled its earlier ratification of Meech on 5 April 1990.[21]

There were now three provinces that hadn't ratified Meech. As pressures mounted, Mulroney appeared insouciant. He thrived on pressure—especially the application of pressure to others. Rumblings began to be heard that refusal of Meech would insult Quebec, abandon Quebec federalists, and put the future of the country at risk. Only Meech would make the constitution legitimate in Quebec—an argument repeated in that province by Mulroney, Bourassa, and their supporters. As 23 June 1990, the deadline for the ratification of Meech, approached, the public mood, fed by an excited media, became alarmed.[22]

In New Brunswick, McKenna buckled and ratified Meech. That left two holdouts, Manitoba with its minority government, and Newfoundland. The premiers were convened to Ottawa, packs of journalists gathered, and as the crisis bubbled behind closed doors television mounted the portentous and endless coverage reserved for solemn occasions.

Finally, Wells and the Manitoba delegation (all three Manitoba parties were represented) appeared to give way. They would present Meech to their legislatures, and in the overheated atmosphere of the time, it was expected that the resulting votes would approve the deal.

Mulroney exulted. In an interview with two journalists after Meech's triumph seemed certain, he stated, "I told [my advisers] a month ago when we were going to [meet]. It's like an election campaign; you count backward. [I said], 'That's the day we're going to roll the dice.'"[23] It was an unwise remark. Public gloating is never well advised; premature gloating is definitely a poor strategy. "Rolling the dice" with the country's future reminded many Canadians that their prime minister was often unnecessarily self-congratulatory—and that he had a shallow understanding of how to direct the country.

Mulroney attempted to undo the damage, visiting St. John's to encourage Newfoundlanders to roll the dice with him, one more time. But it was too late there, and too late in Manitoba, where a Cree NDP member of the legislature refused the unanimous consent that was necessary to get Meech debated and passed. The agreement was dead.

Mulroney and Bourassa had sown the wind and summoned the storm clouds. No one was really surprised when the storm broke. In Quebec, where the political class—except for Trudeau and a few of his supporters—was virtually unanimous, the failure of Meech was taken to be the latest and worst humiliation served up by the English and their allies to the long-suffering Québécois.[24] Mass demonstrations took place, the separatist opposition, now led by the *"pur et dur"* separatist Jacques Parizeau, dominated the agenda, and Bourassa had nothing to put in Meech's place. In Ottawa, Mulroney's party split, as one of his most talented ministers, Lucien Bouchard, resigned and expressed his sympathies for separatism.

The Liberals were coincidentally holding their leadership convention in Calgary. One candidate, Paul Martin Jr., was pro-Meech; in the spirit of the times, his supporters accused his rival, Jean Chrétien, of being a *"vendu,"* a "sell-out," to the English, and when Chrétien won, some of Martin's Quebec supporters walked out and joined Bouchard. As a consequence, for the first time an organized separatist group, the Bloc Québécois, sat in the federal House of Commons.

THE END OF MULRONEY

The Mulroney government had three more painful years to live. While scrambling to catch his breath after Meech, the prime minister faced another crisis: a Mohawk rebellion on reserves strategically placed north and south of Montreal. The revolt began because of a property dispute over land the Mohawks considered improperly alienated and then improperly used. Developers proposed to place a golf course over a Native cemetery. Confrontation, police intervention, and violence followed, in which the Quebec provincial police, the Sûreté, were driven off and lost one man to gunfire. The Mohawks blockaded provincial roads passing through their reserves, including one that was a major access route from Montreal's southern suburbs to Montreal Island. Premier Bourassa appealed for the second time in his career for the intervention of the Canadian army, and the army was duly deployed. Mohawks and soldiers glared at one another, tempers rose, rock-throwing incidents followed. Fortunately, common sense and the passage of time eventually prevailed: the blockade was lifted, the golf course didn't happen, and life returned more or less to normal.

It was a changed normality. The Meech Lake agreement and the way in which it was handled, mainly by Mulroney, had produced the exact opposite of what had been intended. Quebec was in ferment, a condition that the cautious Bourassa did not favour. Bourassa too played for time, appointing commissions, holding hearings, issuing ultimatums with retractable deadlines, threatening to hold a referendum on separatism, allowing an excited and disappointed population to let off steam.

Mulroney too appointed a commission headed by Keith Spicer, which perambulated around the country allowing Canadians to "vent" at it.

Mulroney and the premiers tried yet another constitutional round in response to one of Bourassa's deadlines. This produced an agreement named the Charlottetown Accord, after its place of origin. Charlottetown was complicated, incomprehensible, and quite possibly unworkable, but it was an agreement, it did have Quebec in, and Canada's official political leaders recommended it. Put to a referendum in October 1992, it was rejected, both in Quebec and in Canada as a whole. The constitution would not be amended, and Mulroney and Bourassa would not be remembered, after all, as the re-founders of Canada—or Quebec.

Mulroney was responsible for one other major reform. For decades Canadian governments had employed a federal sales tax on manufactures. The tax was widely regarded as inefficient and harmful to Canadian manufacturing, which it handicapped. It didn't bring in enough revenue, but such as it was, the government needed it—Mulroney was running deficits, every year. Imitating New Zealand, which in the 1980s and 1990s was a beacon of fiscal and economic reform to the English-speaking world, the Mulroney government proposed a much more comprehensive federal sales tax, the Goods and Services Tax, or GST. New taxes were always politically volatile, and it did no good to argue that the GST was better than what it replaced. After a wild and woolly battle in Parliament, in which Mulroney took advantage of an obscure provision of the constitution (never before used) to appoint extra senators, the tax passed.

There is no doubt that the GST played a part in the political decline of the Mulroney government, and that it was especially unpopular in western Canada, including the Conservative heartland of Alberta, where, unique in Canada, there was no provincial sales tax and the idea of any sales tax was unspeakable. Though the Mulroney cabinet had a number of strong and prominent ministers from western Canada, western Canadians distrusted the prime minister's propensity to play to Quebec and favour that province in his policies. That was particularly the case with a lucrative maintenance contract for the air force's newly acquired fleet of F-18 fighters (bought by the Trudeau government). The air force, on the grounds of economy and efficiency, favoured a Winnipeg firm; the government in 1987 awarded the contract to a Montreal company in order to reinforce that city's aerospace industry. Critics suspected, reasonably, that Quebec was being paid off. Bourassa had used the slogan "profitable federalism," and this was certainly profitable federalism—for Quebec. (Given that Quebeckers believed that their province lost economically in remaining in the Canadian federation, Mulroney was addressing their perception.) Politics, in a particularly crass form, had trumped economics.

The decision had consequences far beyond what Mulroney had anticipated. Discontented Westerners gathered in Vancouver for an exploratory talk, which eventually resulted in a political movement that consisted mostly of ex-Conservatives, including Stephen Harper, the former political assistant to a sitting Conservative MP. The leader and focus of the discontent, however, was Preston Manning, the son of a former Social Credit premier of Alberta, Ernest Manning. In the 1988 federal election Manning fielded over seventy candidates under the banner of "Reform," and while they failed to win any seats—they weren't well enough known or organized for that—they promised trouble for the future.

Sniffing the political winds, Mulroney made a reasonable calculation. With his party's approval rating in opinion polls fixed firmly and irretrievably in the cellar (as low as 15 percent in 1991), he announced he would retire in the spring of 1993. A Progressive Conservative convention in Ottawa chose as his successor Kim Campbell, who had been national defence minister and then minister of justice, over Jean Charest, one of Mulroney's younger ministers.

Campbell's authority was brief. An election had to be held by the fall of 1993, when the 1988 Parliament's mandate expired. Campbell delayed to the last possible minute, and called the election for October. She had enjoyed a brief blip in the polls—she was brainy and fresh—but too fresh as it turned out, when she unwisely told the press that an election was no time to debate serious issues. Her advisers set to quarrelling among themselves, the media caught the smell of political death, and Canadians settled in to watch a foregone conclusion on election night, 25 October.

It was quite a night. The Progressive Conservatives lost, massively, reduced from 169 seats in 1988 to precisely two in 1993. (They had held 151 seats just before the dissolution of Parliament.) Campbell lost her own seat as Conservative voters fled in all directions, though her erstwhile rival, Jean Charest, did win his. In Quebec, they went to Lucien Bouchard's new Bloc Québécois, in the West to Reform, mostly, and where they did not, and in Ontario and the Maritimes, they went to the Liberals. The NDP collapsed, plunging from its greatest number of seats won in 1988 to its lowest, nine, in 1993.

The Liberals won by default. They picked up 41 percent of the popular vote and a majority of seats, 177. No other party had even 20 percent of the vote total. The separatist Bloc Québécois (BQ) came second, with 54 seats, and became Her Majesty's official opposition in the House of Commons. Reform, with Preston Manning, came third, with 52, though with a higher vote total than the BQ's. The NDP's miserable results were attributed not so much to the party's federal performance, though that was unmemorable, but to the record of the NDP governments in British Columbia and Ontario, where the party's ideology and policies were unsuited to coping with the economic recession which, to be sure, also helped undermine the federal Conservatives.

The election result showed a fractured country. Only one of Canada's traditional omnibus parties, the Liberals, emerged intact from the election, with seats in every province including, miraculously, four in Alberta, their best performance in that province in a generation. But Quebec, which for most of the twentieth century had been the Liberals' bastion, was lost to the BQ. The BQ was a purely regional party, and, in fact, a purely French-speaking party, though it claimed, without much plausibility, to welcome English speakers too. Reform also had pretensions to being a national party, and did manage to elect an MP in Ontario; even if it wasn't a purely regional creation, it was ideologically limited to areas and voters that favoured the right or the traditional in politics—and that was far from being a majority.

It was up to Jean Chrétien, a very traditional politician, to see whether the customary arts of compromise and balance could restore Canada after the wild ride of the eighties, the recession of the nineties, and the catastrophe of Meech Lake. It was a formidable challenge.

17

A NEW
MILLENNIUM
AND A NEW WORLD

Canada's energy future? A Caterpillar truck, the world's largest,
carries four hundred tons of oil sands at Fort McMurray, Alberta.

In December 1999 *Maclean's* magazine published a feature entitled "The Vanishing Border." The magazine had polled Canadians on Americans and Americans on Canadians, asking what they thought of themselves and of each other. On the American side, the general picture that emerged was positive. Americans thought Canadians friendly, if bland. Canada was the United States' best friend, edging out Great Britain.

Canadians, on the other hand, seemed rather confused. They applied a mixture of adjectives to Americans, mostly negative, but then emerged with the opinion that Canadians were becoming more like Americans. About a quarter of Canadians, overall, said they would accept American citizenship, but the figure rose markedly in Quebec, where about a third of respondents said they would take the opportunity, if offered, to become Americans. Quebeckers were also the readiest to contemplate political union with the United States, at 28 percent, compared with 19 percent for Canadians as a whole.[1] That winter, an American poll for the Pew Research Center reported that 71 percent of Canadians had a favourable opinion of the United States—behind the British and a few other countries, but higher than most.[2]

As far as Canadian–American relations went, this was standard fare. The citizens of both countries took each other largely for granted. In the tenth year of the free trade agreement with the United States (which for Canadians loomed much larger than NAFTA), Canadians saw the border as a bit of a nuisance, a formal barrier that prevented them from getting on with life. This view did not please the Canadian customs service, which pointed out that while the border delayed traffic it at least helped keep guns out of the country and allowed immigration to screen out unsavoury characters. Of course, it also kept thousands of customs and immigration agents employed.

The *Maclean's* polling data did not reflect an event that occurred on 14 December, when the regular ferry from Victoria, British Columbia, docked in Port Angeles, Washington. On board the ferry was a young man named Ahmed Ressam, who was travelling on a Canadian passport under the name "Benni Noris." Because "Noris" seemed nervous, customs agents began to search his car; when he tried to flee, he was arrested. His car was packed with explosives; his destination was Los Angeles international airport, which he proposed to blow up as the new millennium struck, at midnight on 31 December 1999.

Ressam's arrest was a new and significant factor in Canadian–American relations. Canada was or could be a source of insecurity in the United States. Like the U.S., Canada received immigrants by the hundreds of thousands every year. That year, 1999, more than 189,000 immigrants that we know of came to Canada; most years there were over 200,000. In 1999, 12.8 percent of immigrants were classified as "refugees," claiming the right to remain in Canada because of a fear of persecution in their country of origin or citizenship.[3] Ressam, Algerian by origin, claimed to be such a refugee, though his activities in Canada subsequent to his arrival placed him clearly outside the law.[4] As frequently happened, however, an under-funded and inadequately supported immigration service could not keep track of immigrants, legal and illegal, inside the country. Ressam, for example, had an outstanding arrest warrant against him. He'd even taken a trip to Afghanistan to be trained in the theory and practice of *jihad,* holy war, and returned to Canada tasked with a mission (and with $12,000) to attack the United States. But the police couldn't find him.

Ressam was extensively interrogated by American authorities while Canadian police investigated his activities in Canada. It appeared that he was a member of a mysterious terrorist organization called al-Qaeda, which some years before had declared war on the United States. Some of

Ressam's information was included in a briefing given to President George W. Bush in August 2001, entitled "Bin Laden Determined to Strike in U.S."

MULTICULTURALISM

The Canada that sat north of the United States was very different in 2000 from the Canada of 1960. There were, of course, more Canadians—up from fourteen million at mid-century to more than double that fifty years later—thirty million in the 2001 census. Much of the increase was the baby boom—the "natural increase" of births minus deaths. People lived longer—life expectancy for a child born in 2001 was eleven years more than for a child born in 1951.[5] The fastest growing "visible minority" in Canada was, in fact, grey, as the numbers of the elderly steadily increased.

It was, however, also true that the numbers of Canadian residents born in South Asia, East Asia, Africa, the Caribbean, and Latin America were steadily increasing. Immigration totals for the 1990s were the highest in the twentieth century at 2.2 million, although proportionately the immigration of 1901–10 was bigger. The religious balance was changing too. Roman Catholicism was the largest religious preference, at 43 percent, as it had been for many years. The next largest religious grouping was "no religion," at 16 percent, with the various Protestant sects further down the list, headed by the United Church of Canada (9.6 percent) and Anglicans (6.9 percent); 2 percent of the population were inscribed as Muslims, and 1.1 percent as Jews.[6]

The effects of immigration were most obvious in the largest cities, Toronto, Vancouver, and Montreal, though no Canadian community of any size went untouched. Indo-Canadian, Chinese-Canadian, and latterly Latino-Canadian politicians began to become prominent as the political system adapted to the new realities; Italian Canadians were already solidly entrenched. In 2000–01 an Indo-Canadian, the Sikh Ujjal Dosanjh, became British Columbia's first non-white premier, a striking commentary on changes in a province where anti-Asian racism had been, as late as the 1940s, embodied in law and where "orientals" were formerly denied the vote in provincial elections.

Not all migration was external. Canada's Native population grew markedly in the late twentieth century. This reflected, first, far lower infant mortality after 1950, and second, a higher-than-average birth rate, which peaked in 1967, about ten years after the baby boom peak in the rest of the country. (In the 1990s the Native birth rate was about 1.5 times the birth rate in the country as a whole, a considerable decline from the 1960s but still substantial.) Another important factor was a greater awareness of Native issues and identity, and a consequent inclination on many people's part to take pride in Aboriginal ancestry. In the 2001 census, this produced a self-identifying Native population (First Nations, Inuit, and Métis) of 3.3 percent. Of these, about half (49 percent) lived in cities—notably Winnipeg, Edmonton, Saskatoon, and Vancouver. The highest proportion of the total population was in Saskatoon, at 9 percent, with Winnipeg just behind (and with a higher absolute number) at 8 percent.

The federal government attempted to meet the influx of immigrants by instituting a program of multiculturalism in the 1970s. Multiculturalism was suspected to be yet another way for politicians (mainly Liberal) to pander to institutionalized ethnic communities.[7] More seriously, it was criticized as an impediment to the development of any true sense of place and country in Canada. One of the most prominent critics was Neil Bissoondath, who in his 1994 book *Selling Illusions: The Cult of Multiculturalism in Canada* condemned multiculturalism for herding immigrant groups into ethnic ghettoes, dividing Canadians rather than unifying them. Defenders of multiculturalism praised it as an avenue to equity among diverse groups, but especially between new arrivals and the European-descended "old Canadians"; by that token, multiculturalism promoted satisfaction, if not exactly unity.[8]

UNREST IN QUEBEC

Quebec was the focus of discontent in Canada in the early 1990s. This was nothing new; what was new was that support for separatism had tipped into the majority opinion among francophones in the province—the legacy of Meech Lake. It had been expressed in the election of a large separatist contingent (the Bloc Québécois) to the federal House of Commons in the October 1993 elections, and it was expected that the separatists would sweep the next Quebec provincial elections, due at the latest in 1994.

Liberal premier Robert Bourassa had skilfully manoeuvred his province past a number of political pitfalls after 1990. But by 1994 it was obvious, despite Bourassa's legendary talents at obfuscation, that he preferred Quebec to stay part of Canada. Major health problems forced him to resign as premier early in 1994, to be succeeded by Daniel Johnson Jr., one of his ministers and the son and namesake of a former premier.

It would be Johnson who led the Liberals to defeat in the 1994 Quebec election, though not by much, in terms of the popular vote.[9] The separatist Parti Québécois won massively in terms of seats, seventy-seven to forty-seven. (The spoiler in the election was the Action démocratique du Québec, or ADQ, whose leader, Mario Dumont, had once been president of the Liberal party's youth wing.) The PQ probably had a majority of the Quebec francophone vote, and the party leader and new premier, Jacques Parizeau, knew that very well.

Parizeau was committed intellectually and emotionally to Quebec independence. A prominent economist and political veteran (he'd been René Lévesque's finance minister after 1976), he had never liked the strategy of "sovereignty-association" that Lévesque had used to tempt an uncertain population toward separatism in the 1970s. As premier, Parizeau was determined to achieve independence, and planning for a referendum began as soon as the PQ took office.

The PQ used its ample resources as a government to promote unity of feeling around separatism, at least among the French-speaking population. Johnson, as leader of the opposition, and formally the province's chief federalist, was considered worthy but dull. Jean Chrétien, the Canadian prime minister, was unpopular in his home province. He had opposed Meech Lake, he had been Pierre Trudeau's political lieutenant (and Trudeau had been successfully demonized among most francophone Quebeckers), and, among the intellectuals ("intellos") he was despised as crude and uncultured, unlike Trudeau.

Parizeau had the opposite problem: many Quebeckers considered him to be pompous. Coming like Trudeau from a rich family, largely educated like Trudeau outside the province, Parizeau was definitely not a man of the people; unlike Trudeau, he looked rather like a British banker—not an image calculated to win affection.

Parizeau was not especially adapted to compromise either, and he would have preferred to fight the battle for independence—sovereignty—on clear and simple lines. But the polls showed that even after Meech Lake, and even with Chrétien in Ottawa and a weak opposition in Quebec, Quebeckers did not wish for a clean break with the rest of Canada. And so, unwillingly, Parizeau was forced into a political gavotte with the ADQ and its leader Mario Dumont, whose 6.5 percent of the votes in 1994 might make the difference between success and failure in a referendum. He was forced to invite Lucien Bouchard as well—though relations between the two men were not of the best. Despite hesitation and rivalry, and perhaps more fundamental differences, the three agreed in June 1995 that the "yes" side, their side, in the approaching referendum should promise to try to negotiate a new kind of "economic and political partnership" with Canada and only afterward proclaim Quebec's sovereignty.

With victory in the referendum the undisputed objective, the means to achieve it became negotiable. The result was a convoluted question that asked voters to approve the June agreement and vote for sovereignty. Parizeau, scenting victory, began serious preparations. As an economist, he knew that business and international finance preferred stability, and that a separatist victory would promise anything but. It would hardly be an advertisement for Quebec independence to face immediate economic convulsions as the result of a vote for sovereignty. Accordingly, he began laying by a reserve fund to stabilize the Canadian dollar in the immediate aftermath of a "yes" victory.

Then, in September, he launched the "yes" campaign by listening to a Quebec declaration of independence in a theatre in Quebec City. The vote was set for 30 October, and the electoral debate began. At first, it seemed that Parizeau had misjudged. Polls weren't especially encouraging, and the federalist "no" side took heart. One federalist spokesman talked of "crushing" separatism once and for all. It seemed sufficient to leave the campaign to the pedestrian Johnson, and to the federal Conservative leader Jean Charest, who, although not a political heavyweight, at least had a reputation as a good orator.

The voters hesitated, and began to move to "yes," but before that could happen Parizeau, recognizing the handicap his personality posed for the "yes" camp, turned the direction of the campaign over to the more charismatic Bouchard. Bouchard entered the lists with his characteristic fervour, assuring the hesitant that independence would act like a "magic wand" to dispel the glooms of federalism and bring Quebec into the land of opportunity and prosperity and sovereignty. Voters began to follow Bouchard and his beckoning wand.

Jean Chrétien in Ottawa was thunderstruck. He prided himself on his practical political judgment, and it had deserted him. Speaking to the Liberal caucus in Ottawa, he burst into tears. The best he could do was promise some last-minute concessions to Quebec—which were taken, reasonably enough, to be a deathbed repentance. More practically, the American ambassador, James Blanchard, offered and delivered a statement by the U.S. president, Bill Clinton, expressing his clear preference for a united Canada. One of Chrétien's ministers, Brian Tobin, organized a huge pro-Canada rally in Montreal the weekend before the referendum, and bussed and flew thousands of citizens from across Canada to come and express their patriotism and their love for Quebec—in Canada. It was an extraordinary gesture, and it had the effect of bucking up federalist morale; whether it actually accomplished its object, or whether it struck many francophone Quebeckers as one more example of outside manipulation, remains debatable. The American pronouncement was closer to the mark, and there the "yes" camp had no riposte but spluttering.[10]

The result on 30 October was hair-raisingly close. Parizeau began the evening believing that he'd won, but the vote gradually swung against him and his cause. Furious, the premier charged into the "yes" rally and proclaimed that the sovereignists had been cheated of their prize by only two things—money and the ethnics. He wasn't wrong, and Quebec premiers had said it before—most notably the nationalist premier Duplessis in 1944, when he explained that the fact that the Liberals had got more votes didn't matter—they were English votes. And indeed, had it been up to French-speaking voters alone, independence would have won.

Parizeau had planned to act decisively. He would have proclaimed Quebec's sovereignty even if he had only 50 percent plus one in the popular vote. He expected, and claimed he had assurances, that France would recognize a sovereign Quebec.[11] If that happened, France would probably not have been alone—there was talk of recognition from some Latin American countries, and possibly some from the francophone Africa.

All this was now moot, as was Parizeau. His emotional harangue on referendum night terminated his career. He was an embarrassment even to most separatists, who considered him a throwback to a distant and darker age. Parizeau announced his resignation, and in January 1996 was succeeded by the inevitable man, Lucien Bouchard.

Bouchard, as far as English Canadians were concerned, wasn't much of an improvement. He led off by explaining that proposals for part of Quebec to separate from the province by remaining in Canada were absurd, because, as he put it, "Canada is not a real country." Quebec was. But if Quebec was "real," why was it real? Presumably he meant that it was more than a geographical expression, but if it had any justification to be "real" it was as the homeland of the Québécois—the French Québécois. If it was just another multi-ethnic state—like Canada—with the majorities reversed, what was the point?

That question didn't have to be answered, at least for the next few years. Quebec would remain part of Canada, Canadian laws would apply there, and Quebeckers would pay their taxes and vote in Canadian elections. A Quebecker was prime minister of Canada, and Quebeckers were prominent in his cabinet. Jean Chrétien had received a considerable shock in the referendum. Canadians now looked to him to devise a strategy whereby there would be no more such shocks.

The response to separatism was usually described as "Plan A" or "Plan B." Plan A was compromise, concessions, attempts to adapt the constitution and federal institutions to accommodate more moderate Quebec nationalists. The problem with this option was that the constitution was, to all intents and purposes, beyond amendment, at least for the foreseeable future.[12] Meech and Charlottetown had demonstrated that. Chrétien got the House of Commons to pass a resolution in 1996 recognizing Quebec as a "distinct society," to no discernible effect inside the province. The provincial premiers, meeting in Calgary in September 1996, did their best, by issuing an anodyne declaration that proclaimed the right of Quebec to promote its "unique character ... within Canada." On the other hand, Canadians outside Quebec were showing fatigue at the prospect of an infinity of referendums, held whenever the separatists could manage them, unless or until the separatists won.

Plan B, on the other hand, was defined as "tough love." Its premise was that the rest of Canada had been entirely too accommodating to Quebec separatists, playing the referendum game according to rules that the separatists themselves had devised, including referendum questions that were designed to obfuscate the issue of independence.[13] What other sovereign state would tolerate a periodic ballot on whether it would continue to exist in its current territory?

Tough love took various forms. Its common theme was that concessions along the lines of Meech Lake, Charlottetown, or the Calgary declaration wouldn't work. The proponents of one version argued that if Canada was divisible, then so was Quebec. In any case, Canadians generally had an interest in an issue that could drastically and negatively affect the stability of their currency, not to mention trade, transportation, and communications, as well as the viability and continuing legitimacy of their existing political institutions. To take one example, if the separatists had won in 1995, who or what would have been empowered to negotiate with them?

To answer such questions, the Chrétien government referred the issue of separatism to the Canadian Supreme Court. Could a province secede from Canada and, if so, how? Would a unilateral declaration of independence by a province—what Parizeau had in mind in 1995[14]—be legal? The notion that Canadians outside the province might have an interest, and a say, in the question of Quebec sovereignty offended Quebec nationalists of all stripes, including the provincial Liberals, who joined the separatist PQ majority in the provincial legislature in condemning any such idea. Quebec's right to self-determination was absolute, it appeared, however Quebeckers chose to exercise it.[15] In the federal election of June 1997 Chrétien and his newly appointed minister for intergovernmental affairs, Stéphane Dion, defended the Supreme Court reference, and with it the idea that Canada as a whole must be involved in the issue of Quebec separation. In the election, Chrétien and the Liberals improved their standing in Quebec, as did the Progressive Conservatives under their new leader, Jean Charest. Evidently the Supreme Court reference hadn't made matters any worse for the Liberals in Quebec.

The Supreme Court, when it eventually delivered its opinion on the question in August 1998, agreed that Canadians in general had an interest in what happened to Quebec. Quebec by itself had no right either under domestic or international law to secede. On the other hand, if Quebec did vote for separation, the rest of Canada must negotiate its prospective departure. Chrétien took this as a victory, arguing that in future Quebeckers must have a straight question put to them in any referendum. But Lucien Bouchard, the Quebec premier, took it as vindication that the rest of Canada must eventually respect a decision by the majority of Quebeckers for separation.

Bouchard wouldn't ask the question any time soon. He wanted, as he said, "winning conditions," and they weren't there. In the opinion of the fervent supporters of separation, Bouchard was too supple, too prone to compromise, and had no sympathy for the more extreme and exclusionary forms of Quebec nationalism. Bouchard led the Parti Québécois to victory over the provincial Liberals in 1998, but he didn't take that to be a mandate for organizing another referendum. The premier's passivity on the issue of sovereignty caused discontent among PQ militants, and undoubtedly played a role in precipitating Bouchard's resignation as premier and departure from politics in 2001. His successor, Bernard Landry, was a separatist veteran, unimpeachably orthodox on the great question of independence; yet he, too, had his hesitations, and with Landry as premier it was clear that a third referendum wasn't imminent.

Bouchard and Landry may have been influenced by clear signs of fatigue in the Quebec electorate. When, following the Supreme Court opinion, Chrétien and Dion passed a Clarity Act through Parliament in June 2000, outlining the conditions under which Canada could accept a vote for separation, the premier tried to mobilize Quebec opinion against it. Instead, polls showed that Quebeckers didn't think Ottawa's position— that there should be a clear question, and that a majority of more than 50 percent plus one was necessary—to be unreasonable. When, in November 2000, Chrétien held another general election, he again improved his party's standing in Quebec, outpolling the separatist Bloc Québécois by 44.2 percent to 39.9 percent.[16]

Extreme Politics

The decade after 1993 was unusual if not unique in Canadian political history. In three elections, 1993, 1997, and 2000, the Liberal party won clear majorities in the House of Commons over an opposition that couldn't realistically hope to defeat them. The Parti Québécois did not aim for power on the national level. Its function, it claimed, was merely to represent Quebec pending the inevitable victory of separatism in a provincial referendum. But as the referendum faded into the distance, so did the rationale for the PQ, as the 2000 election showed.

The main opposition to the Liberals during the 1990s came from the Reform party, founded and led by Preston Manning of Alberta. Its appeal tended to be confined to the Western provinces, but even there it had to struggle for a foothold in the some of the larger cities like Vancouver and Winnipeg. In an attempt to transcend its regional identification, Reform renamed itself the Canadian Alliance in 2000.[17] Manning hoped to capture the Progressive Conservative vote, and with it some standing in the Atlantic provinces and in Quebec, but the Progressive Conservative leader, Joe Clark, who took on the job in 1998 after Jean Charest departed for provincial politics in Quebec, firmly opposed any such idea. In its quest, Manning sacrificed himself, losing the Alliance leadership to a provincial Progressive Conservative minister from Alberta, Stockwell Day. Day proved an inept leader for the Alliance, losing first the 2000 election to Jean Chrétien and then the Alliance leadership in the face of discontent in his own party.

Through the 1990s the NDP remained firmly in the cellar, managing only thirteen MPs in the 2000 election. (It was hobbled by the unpopularity of NDP governments in British Columbia and Ontario.) For many NDP voters, plainly, the Liberals were the party of choice, especially in the face of the openly right-wing Alliance. The Liberals understood this point very well, and centred their election campaigns on demonizing the opposition. They were helped in this strategy by the record of the very right-wing Progressive Conservative government in Ontario under Mike Harris (1995–2002).[18]

Fortunate in their opponents, the Liberals were lucky in their ability to manipulate political issues to their advantage. Quebec separatism aside, the politics of the 1990s were dominated by the Battle of the Deficit. Canada had, since the mid-1970s, run a steady succession of deficits, which steadily added to the national debt and drained the federal government's ability to spend money on anything more than debt service. Separatists in Quebec proclaimed that the Canadian debt was a drag on Quebec's prosperity—yet another argument, and a powerful one, in the run-up to the 1995 referendum. *The Wall Street Journal* bluntly nominated Canada as a third-world country because of the size of its debt; within Canada, public opinion decided that debt reduction was a priority.

The Liberals had taken power in 1993 with mildly reformist aspirations. They intended to spend more money, not less, and were shaken by the prospect that Canada could hit a "debt wall" and no longer raise cash on international markets. Chrétien and his finance minister, Paul Martin (son and namesake of Pearson's external affairs minister, Paul Martin Sr.), reluctantly switched their financial course. The government, with a very few reserved exceptions, would spend less. It drastically cut transfer payments to the provinces, meaning that they would have less money to spend on health, welfare, and education. Federal politicians had long complained that the provinces took the credit and got the political benefit of federal subsidies. Now the provinces took the blame for cuts in services. While cuts may have been philosophically congenial for right-wing governments like Harris's in Ontario, the decline in federal largesse undoubtedly exaggerated the impact of their policies, and probably over the longer term contributed to their political demise. (The same phenomenon didn't help left-wing governments either, like Glen Clark's NDP administration in British Columbia.)

Federal economizing hit military spending in particular. With the Cold War over, the size of the armed forces was already drifting downward, but the process accelerated under the Liberals. It wasn't just numbers of troops, but their equipment. Purchases were cancelled or postponed, and aging tanks, aging fighter planes, and aged helicopters came to symbolize the plight of the armed services in the later 1990s. Though under Chrétien Canada still had an active foreign policy, it was increasingly unsupported by military force. American observers darkly compared Canada's military contribution to Iceland's.

Chrétien and Martin were successful in their domestic battle. The federal deficit was slashed, and then, in 1997, abolished. Martin began to pay down the national debt, which moved from being the largest in relation to GDP among the G8 group of advanced industrialized nations to being the smallest. (More concretely, Canada's national debt was 68.4 percent of GDP in 1995–96, and 38.7 percent in 2004–05.)[19] Canada's deficit fight mirrored that in the United States, where Bill Clinton's Democratic administration also reversed the deficit. Not for the first time, or the last, Canadian and American politics moved along parallel lines.

A mere listing of issues and policies, and a roster of Chrétien's three successive election victories (1993, 1997, and 2000), do not do justice to the highly partisan character of politics during his decade as prime minister (1993–2003). That Chrétien managed to stay in power owed as much to the improving economic climate of the later 1990s as to his ruthless political instincts. Chrétien was no innovator in policy: he worked with what he had, and gave his government a largely managerial cast; and in truth, for most of his time in government there was no money for innovative policies.

That Chrétien and the Liberals led the country meant that it was governed from the political centre, while the right wing was consigned to the provinces, especially Ontario and Alberta.[20] But even NDP Saskatchewan swung to the right, as provincial ministers discovered the virtues of balanced budgets and pay-as-you-go politics.

Canada was also influenced by a spillover of American political issues and sometimes, it seemed, American political moods. American politics in the 1990s were viciously partisan and highly personal. Yet behind the personalities there was real change, as the Republican party and American society lurched to the right. The issue was mainly the legitimacy of the American welfare state (or any welfare state) against a conservative movement that had come to believe that the state was the problem, not the solution, for the country's woes.[21] The politics of entitlement were to be replaced by the politics of opportunity, the welfare state by the "market state." There was, as well, the rise of "the religious right," usually conservative Protestants who combined American nationalism with deep disapproval of the liberalization of public attitudes toward abortion and homosexuality.[22] Their failure to prevail in politics and legislation was a source of deep frustration, as indeed it was for their counterparts in Canada.

The welfare state was defended, rather half-heartedly, in the United States by the Democratic party and the Democratic president, Bill Clinton (1993–2001). Unable to defeat Clinton in the presidential elections of 1992 and 1996, the Republicans nevertheless won a majority in Congress and used it to launch endless investigations into the president's financial probity and sexual morality, and tried unsuccessfully to impeach him in 1999.

The welfare state had retreated further, and faster in the United States and Great Britain than in Canada. Canada was the odd man out among English-speaking countries. It was still equipped with a social safety net that the right was convinced it could and should not afford. Worse, the right had come to believe that the safety net hobbled the Canadian economy through high taxes and state interference. The measure of the country's failure, according to right-wing organs like Conrad Black's *National Post*, was the frustration of individual initiative and responsibility and the consequent departure of talented Canadians for the United States—"the brain drain" of headline writers in the late 1990s. Canada, it sometimes seemed, could do nothing right while the United States, despite the occupation of the White House by the Democrat Clinton, could do almost nothing wrong, and that little would be remedied by getting rid of Clinton and the Democrats.

What was good for the United States was also good for Canada. Like Bill Clinton, Chrétien was tarred with corruption by the right-wing press (again the *National Post*), but their choice of scandal, centring on a golf-course development in Chrétien's hometown in Quebec, was so complicated and so apparently trivial that it failed to convince the electorate to unseat the Liberals.

It is probable that Canadian conservatives were pursuing Chrétien more as a symbol of what they believed to be the corruption of Liberal politics on the grand scale than in a truly personal sense; it merely happened that personalization was the most efficacious means of undermining your opponent and thereby effecting political change. Their failure to do so only increased their rage, but it didn't diminish their belief that the

Liberal party must not only be removed from office but actually destroyed, as the bulwark of everything they believed to be wrong with Canada.

As so often happens, great issues moved by trivial means: on the surface, wild charges and personal attacks prevailed; beneath, issues like lower taxes, less state regulation and interference, and a return to more traditional values were what the right wing sought, in Canada as in Great Britain, New Zealand, Australia, and the United States. It meant that politics was being played for high stakes, and as a result Canadian politics at the end of the twentieth century was characterized by extreme bitterness and partisan division.

LIBERAL DIPLOMACY

Canada, the American secretary of state Henry Kissinger wrote, once had "an influence out of proportion to its military contribution" because of its "somewhat aloof position [and] the high quality of its leadership.... It conducted a global foreign policy; it participated in international peace-keeping efforts; it made a constructive contribution to the dialogue between developed and developing nations."[23]

Kissinger's admiring description of the Canadian role in foreign affairs was in doubt in the 1990s. The reason was largely structural or systemic. Canada was no longer as important a country as it had been in the 1970s, when Kissinger wrote. At that time, Canada qualified to be a member of the Group of Seven industrialized nations forum because it had, in fact, the world's sixth or seventh largest economy. By the mid-1990s that was no longer the case.

Canada remained, as it had always been, a strong supporter of the United Nations and peacekeeping.[24] At one time, it was unthinkable that a major peacekeeping exercise could occur without Canada but, by the 1990s, Canada was struggling to keep up. Reductions in the armed services, and penny-pinching policies that affected the foreign service as they affected every other branch of government, meant that the quality of the foreign service suffered.[25]

Chrétien was not especially or continuously interested in foreign affairs. He had a politician's normal sensitivity to high-profile events abroad, but he didn't ordinarily seek the international limelight. On the other hand, he believed deeply that trade was the key to restoring and increasing Canadian prosperity. He also saw it as a means of reinforcing national unity, for who could afford to stand up against trade, or seem indifferent to the economic welfare of the voters? As prime minister, therefore, Chrétien organized and led repeated "Team Canada" trade missions abroad. These were on the grand scale: all or most of the provincial premiers, high officials, and prominent businesspeople were loaded on board aircraft and flown to the country of choice—China, for example, where Chrétien hoped not only to increase exports but to sell Canadian-designed and -made CANDU nuclear reactors.

Chrétien's preoccupation with trade and economic benefit led to compromises in Canada's approach to foreign policy. Under Mulroney human rights had been a focus for Canadian policy, and Mulroney and his external affairs minister Joe Clark had stuck to the policy despite the risk of offending some of Canada's allies—the British, in the case of South Africa, and the United States, in the case of Central America.

Chrétien was less consistent. China's economic importance overshadowed its oppressive human-rights record. To be fair, the Mulroney government had already turned a blind eye to the domestic excesses of China's dictatorial government, as had most of Canada's allies, including and especially the United States. Team Canada was welcome in Beijing; the economic benefit, as opposed to the spectacle it occasioned, remains a matter of speculation.

Not even spectacles were entirely safe. Hosting a summit of Asia-Pacific powers in Vancouver in 1997, the Canadian government found itself on the wrong side of a public issue, using a very heavy hand to suppress demonstrations of public outrage at the presence of the Indonesian dictator, Suharto. Chrétien's office took the blame, and the prime minister's image suffered accordingly.

Nor did peacekeeping produce reliable results. When peace broke down in the Sinai in 1967, there was nothing the peacekeepers could do. They had a symbolic presence and, usually, not enough force in numbers or equipment to be able to impose peace where there was none. Canada was involved in a number of peacekeeping missions under the United Nations in the 1990s, in Bosnia, Croatia, Somalia, Rwanda, and Haiti, among other places. Of these, Bosnia, Croatia, and Somalia were already underway when Chrétien took office.

In Bosnia, an inadequate UN mandate and the inconsistent and evasive policies of Canada's principal allies prolonged a civil war among Bosnian Serbs, Muslims, and Croats. Canadian and other UN troops were caught in the middle, without the strength or the authority to enforce peace on the local combatants. At best, the presence of UN troops prevented a Serb victory—but it could do nothing about the Serbian bombardment of the Bosnian capital, Sarajevo, or prevent the massacre of Muslims at Srbenica in 1995. Canada gave troops to the UN force, but despite the size of its contribution, Canada was excluded from the "contact group" that attempted to guide the Western approach to ex-Yugoslavia after 1991.[26] The Bosnian war was solved militarily in 1995, by victory (of the Croats) and defeat (of the Bosnian Serbs) on the battlefield, and not by invoking the mantra of peace or peacekeeping. It was a lesson that peacekeeping, Canadian-style, didn't work when there was no peace to keep.

Somalia and Rwanda were, if possible, worse. In January 1993 the Mulroney government had sent the Canadian Airborne regiment into Somalia, where government and most aspects of organized society had collapsed. The Somalia mission may have been hopeless from the start, but it was not enhanced by the torture and murder of a Somali teenager by members of the Airborne, who recorded their deeds on film. Eventually the news got out and investigations began, first under the Conservatives and then under the new Liberal government.

The Somalia inquiry was an object lesson in what not to do. The Liberals hadn't set up the Somalia mission, and logically had nothing to lose, but the defence department proved to be evasive and obfuscating. Ministers were dragged in, and the Somalia affair became a lawyers' carnival, at public expense, deeply fascinating to the media because villains could be depicted in bright primary colours. Eventually, the affair proved to be as damaging to the politicians as it was to the military. As a precaution in the lead-up to the 1997 election, Chrétien closed down the inquiry. The inquiry commissioners predicted dire consequences for the government that dared to interfere with their desire for infinity, but the consequences never materialized and Somalia passed into history as a stain on the reputation of the Canadian army, and on peacekeeping.

Liberal foreign policies weren't much different from those of their Conservative predecessors, just as theirs hadn't been much different from those of the Liberals under Trudeau. As Kissinger said, Canada was noted for its support of international peacekeeping, usually under the aegis of the United Nations, another Canadian icon. Canadians took pride in the fact, without really understanding what the implications might be. But as the 1990s advanced, and one peacekeeping failure followed another, Canadians began to lose faith in peacekeeping as a practical policy.

Peacekeeping also received a black eye in the African country of Rwanda, where a Canadian-led UN force, commanded by General Roméo Dallaire, stood helplessly by in the face of a genocidal assault on that country's Tutsi minority in the spring of 1994. Dallaire had done his best to avert the catastrophe; in response the United Nations not only refused to take action but reduced the forces it had already deployed there. Close to a million souls perished in Rwanda, an indelible black mark against the United Nations. Canada by itself could do little, and even that little had gradually been drained by the diminution of Canada's armed forces since the end of the Cold War.

The Canadian government continued to act as if peacekeeping was a viable policy no matter what the circumstances. The Canadian public, spurred on by the media and by special-interest non-governmental organizations (NGOs in the universal jargon of international affairs), was prone to demand action as one crisis after another was perceived and adopted by journalists—sometimes for good reason, sometimes not. One such case occurred in the eastern Congo late in 1996 when it appeared that a repeat of the Rwanda disaster was impending. Encouraged by his nephew Raymond, a professional diplomat and at the time Canadian ambassador in Washington, Jean Chrétien advanced the idea of a Canadian-led UN force for the region, ironically dubbed "Operation Assurance." The operation lasted about six weeks, failed utterly to accomplish its mission of providing assurance to refugees in the Congo, and was hastily withdrawn when it became clear it could do little good. As one Canadian general, Maurice Baril, put it at the time, Canada was in over its head. "We are dealing with big players in a very complex situation," he wrote, "without the tools or knowledge necessary to control either specific events or the general situation."[27] Adapting the words of a song, "Operation Assurance" became better known as "The Bungle in the Jungle."[28]

Failure in Somalia and Rwanda and frustration in Bosnia suggested that classic peacekeeping, respecting the sovereignty of the nations whose peace was to be kept, was not the right formula for the 1990s. In all three countries, the danger was internal, not international. The threat to peace didn't come from organized, uniformed armies, but from irregulars and guerrillas, even gangsters. The appropriate international response must be to respect or preserve not so much national sovereignty, but the human rights of populations. This was an old liberal theme, though not one that had traditionally been identified with the Canadian Liberal party. Nevertheless, it became a signature of the Chrétien government as Canada sought to ban the use of land mines in warfare and promoted the establishment of an International Criminal Court.

Both issues—land mines and the court—differentiated Canada's policy from that of the United States, even under the Clinton administration. Clinton, on the advice of his generals, resisted the regulation of land mines, and signed the International Criminal Court agreement only at the very last minute in 2001, when it was already certain to be defeated in a Republican-dominated Congress. Yet the abolition of land mines was popular with many Americans, who rejoiced when a treaty was signed in

Ottawa in 1998 doing just that, under the approving eye of Chrétien's foreign minister of the day, Lloyd Axworthy.

In one area, however, there was no difference between the two countries. A single item of unfinished business lingered in ex-Yugoslavia—the Serbian government's attempt to "solve" the problem of the Albanian majority in its province of Kosovo. Well-publicized Serb brutality recalled the horrors of "ethnic cleansing" in Bosnia and elsewhere. Owing to a Russian veto the United Nations Security Council was unable to agree on remedial action, and so the Western powers decided to act alone, using NATO as their instrument. After an American-led bombing campaign in the skies over Serbia, and with the threat of a land invasion in the background, the Serbian government caved in, and evacuated Kosovo.

Canada was an early and effective participant in the NATO air attacks—one of the few allies with the necessary aircraft and equipment to do so. Kosovo illustrated the principle that "human security" transcended even national sovereignty. Its supporters argued that it also demonstrated the utility of concerted international action. But, as critics noted at the time, the NATO action bypassed the United Nations. If, as some claimed, international armed action required UN authorization, then the legality of the Kosovo campaign was dubious.

OLD LEADER, NEW ISSUES, NEW CENTURY

As the 1990s drew to a close the world marked the occasion by generating the wild rumour (called an "urban legend" in the jargon of the day) that its computer systems would collapse with the advent of two new digits—20** instead of 19**. It was a measure of how widespread computers had become, and how dependent individuals and institutions had become on the machines, in the office and at home. By 1997, 36 percent of households had personal computers, and they had become standard equipment in any business of any size. With computers came the internet, which transformed communications and the flow of information—so much so that society faced grave disruption if computers failed and the internet suddenly shut down. Governments immediately set up task forces, the task forces spent money, new computers arrived in home and office, and 31 December 1999 passed into 1 January 2000 largely without incident. It was not in fact *the* new millennium—that would be a year later.

Canada celebrated the new millennium with its old Liberal government, then entering its eighth year. Jean Chrétien returned briefly to Ottawa from his Florida vacation and, finding that everything was all right, left the snow and the pines for the sands and the palms. The government was ticking over, though slowly, political problems were few, the election was past, and the economy was going well. Chrétien could relax and take credit for a job well done.

If Canadians watched the New Year's celebrations, the odds were that they were watching on a colour television. A relative rarity as late as 1970, colour televisions were in 99 percent of Canadian households (65 percent of Canadians watched television on cable networks, another relatively recent innovation). Telephones, already 120 years old, had achieved 100 percent coverage, and during the 1990s cellphones had spread (59 percent household coverage by 2004). Refrigerators were nearly universal. The great exception for most of the twentieth century had been Native reserves, but even there, by the 1990s, over 90 percent of households had sewage disposal and connections to running water. Video recorders, CD players, and microwave ovens had all moved from luxuries in the early 1980s to ordinary (and much cheaper) household goods by 2000.

The houses that contained the households were different too—bigger. The size of Canadian dwellings shrank during the Second World War and after, but that trend had long since reversed.[29] Bigger houses had more rooms (up one room per house in the forty years after 1961) but fewer people—from an average 3.9 people per house in 1961 to 2.6 people per house in 2001.

Canadians in the mid-twentieth century aspired to "a job for life," and many actually had one, as far as the vicissitudes of the Depression and the war allowed. That had gone by the wayside in the 1990s: according to a government study, "Today's worker will have on average approximately 3 careers and 8 jobs over a lifetime."[30] A single full-time job was getting scarcer too, down from 67 percent of workers in 1989 to 63 percent in the first years of the twenty-first century. Part-time or temporary workers had fewer benefits, and thus cost less, and were easier to fire, allowing employers to adjust rapidly to changing economic conditions.

Those conditions were determined in large part by a decline in industrial capacity and a rise in the importance of the service sector. (The decline was indeed very marked, as the number of Canadians employed in manufacturing dropped while the numbers engaged in finance, or tourism, or other "soft" sectors of the economy grew.) Already apparent in the late 1970s, this change accelerated as trade barriers such as tariffs fell, not only as a consequence of NAFTA, but with a general liberalization of international rules and practices governing trade and investment. This was labelled "globalization," a term that had gradually become current since the 1960s.

The theory behind globalization was clear enough. "A rising tide raises all boats" was a convenient way of summarizing it. More precisely, it argued that true prosperity came about not through government direction but through the unfettered growth of markets, the abolition of barriers in the international economy, and the disestablishment of privileged special-interest groups.

It was a doctrine that fitted well with the neo-conservative reaction to liberal excess in the 1960s and 1970s. In a larger sense, it replayed the battles between mercantilists and protectionists and free traders in the early nineteenth century that had led to the abolition of the Corn Laws and the involuntary departure of Canada from British economic protection and direction.[31] In the fall of 1999 a meeting of the International Trade Organization (ITO), the successor to the old GATT, was disrupted in the "Battle of Seattle" by thousands of anti-globalization activists who'd been summoned to combat over the internet. Canada's trade minister, Pierre Pettigrew, was among the hundreds of delegates who had to scramble over walls and around barricades to escape. (The "battle" would be repeated in Quebec City in 2001, and around many other international meetings and especially summits, as demonstrators sought to show that national leaders could not transact their business undisturbed, or, ideally, at all.)[32] A Canadian writer, Naomi Klein, became a bestselling participant in the international debate in 2000 with her book *No Logo,* which denounced international corporations for their indifference to the interests of the people who worked for them, often in shocking conditions and for very low wages.[33]

Proof of the appropriateness of globalization was found in the rapid growth of the economies of East and Southeast Asia, where capitalism, not socialist planning, had led first Japan and then South Korea, Taiwan, Hong Kong, and Thailand from dire poverty to prosperity.[34] (The extent of free marketeering in these countries was sometimes exaggerated in the eye of the Western beholder, to be sure, but there was no doubt that they were capitalists all.) Then, in the late 1980s, China joined the parade and the world's largest country, after forty years of Maoist delusion, reformed its economy. Even India, for many years considered a hopeless basket case of regulation and protection, began to discover the joys of a large, well-trained, English-speaking elite workforce. (Canada had already discovered it through immigration from the subcontinent.) The full consequences wouldn't be seen for twenty years and more, but even partially revealed they were stunning, and important for Canada, among others.

As noted above, manufacturing was becoming less important in the Canadian economy. The manufacturing formerly done in Canada, or in the United States, or in other developed countries was beginning to move to the lower-wage Third World, or at least to that part of the Third World that was politically and economically stable enough ("free" enough of state interference) to guarantee investment. Scholars in Canada and elsewhere learnedly debated whether stability preceded democracy, or prosperity was a necessary precondition for membership in the democratic club. Bankers and international lending agencies struggled to impose something called the "Washington consensus," a doctrine devised in the World Bank and International Monetary Fund, which were located in Washington, whereby the first freedom, the one that preceded and underlay all others, was economic.[35] Without prosperity, the credo went, there could be no democracy, and without economic freedom, the freedom to invest, there could be no political freedom.

There was no effective opposition to globalization in Canada, though trade wasn't absent from the political agenda, especially as it became apparent that "free trade" with the United States was not absolute. Softwood, a problem since the 1980s, surfaced again and again. Canada repeatedly tried to secure free access for its softwood to the United States, and was repeatedly blocked by a powerful American lumber coalition operating through Congress and the byzantine American legal system. (All legal systems are to some extent byzantine, and this is not to suggest that the American one is necessarily worse than any other.) In what was only the most recent manifestation of the eternal softwood problem, the new Conservative government marked its accession to power in 2006 by agreeing to terms in the latest softwood lumber dispute.

THE ETERNAL BORDER

The morning of 11 September 2001 promised a classically beautiful day, sunny, warm, and cloudless all over eastern North America. Toward nine o'clock, late risers were alerted by their radios to turn to the various television news channels, where there was word of an aircraft crashing into one of the World Trade Center's towers in New York City. Horrified viewers then saw another airplane crash into the other tower. Shortly after there was another plane crash, this time into the Pentagon. Plainly this was a concerted attack, and it didn't take long for the probable culprits to be identified—an Islamist terrorist group, al-Qaeda, the same group to which Ahmed Ressam had belonged.

The American government promptly closed American airspace in case of another attack. Canada was asked to receive all trans-oceanic flights that could not be turned back to Europe or Asia; in the event, some thirty-three thousand air travellers landed in Canada, where they were hospitably entertained until they could get home. Canadian reaction to the attack, like that of most of the world, was overwhelmingly sympathetic, and unlike most of the world, Canada had actually been able to do something immediate and practical to help. A memorial service was held on Parliament Hill on 14 September, and 100,000 people attended.

The American president, George W. Bush, phoned Chrétien on 12 September to thank him for his efforts, but publicly Canada went unmentioned in a list of countries thanked by Bush in an address to Congress soon after. Canadians were surprised, and some were resentful.[36]

It was not a promising omen for Canadian–American relations in a time of crisis. Rumours circulated that Bush had no regard for Chrétien, or vice-versa. An urban legend took root—in Canada—that Chrétien had been lukewarm or unsupportive, to the United States or to Bush, and that Bush knew it and resented it.[37] In truth the two had little in common ideologically: Bush's right-wing philosophy did not attract the Canadian prime minister, and for right-wingers of the Bush stripe Canada's moderate welfare state was entirely passé, a hangover from the nightmarish 1970s. It didn't help that Chrétien's political adversaries at home ceaselessly praised the recent right-wing American model of society as a cure for the diseased liberalism that they believed infected Canada.

Bush decided that an immediate and forceful response was required to strike at al-Qaeda's base in Afghanistan. The United Nations authorized the use of force, and so there was no contradiction between Canada's desire to assist the Americans and the stipulations of the UN Charter, as there had been over Kosovo. Canada sent troops to Afghanistan, and maintained Canadian participation in a surveillance and interdiction naval patrol in the Persian Gulf. American victory in Afghanistan was unexpectedly swift, and a pro-American government was implanted in the Afghan capital, Kabul. But the victory was not complete, and the government the Americans installed was not stable.

Afghanistan immediately went on the back burner. Bush and his deputies became convinced that an assertion of American power was necessary to change the balance of power and politics in the Middle East once and for all. The object of their attention was Iraq, whose atrocious dictator, Saddam Hussein, had been straining for a decade to escape from the web of sanctions and restrictions placed on him at the end of the Gulf War in 1991. Saddam's strategy was to divide the allies of 1991, evade the sanctions, and ultimately reconstruct his power by such means as bacteriological or even nuclear weapons—the "weapons of mass destruction," or WMDs. Through a combination of luck and insistent UN arms inspections, Saddam, as we now know, was thwarted; but a reasonable case can be made that this wasn't entirely self-evident in 2001 or 2002. On the other hand, there was no positive proof. And despite American suspicions, there was no proof either of Iraqi collusion with al-Qaeda.

Nevertheless, by the middle of 2002 it was clear that Bush intended war on Iraq, and it was at this time that Chrétien met Bush in Detroit. Public reports of the meeting were accurate enough—that Bush had urged his case against Iraq, and that Chrétien had reiterated his known position that Iraq must pose a clear and present danger to the world before armed action was necessary.[38] In private, Chrétien told Bush that Canada's support for a war in Iraq would be greatly enhanced if the United States could secure the support of the United Nations.

UN support was not forthcoming, and neither was Chrétien's. The official American case for war—that Iraq had WMDs and was ready to use them—was weak, and widely doubted in the intelligence communities of the Western world. Diplomacy at the UN hadn't helped the American case; the American determination not to wait for the final reports of UN weapons inspectors counted heavily against the United States. France took the lead at the UN, but as a senior American diplomat later reflected, "The Mexicans, Canadians, and Chileans—our closest friends in the hemisphere—were not with us."[39]

Intelligence and diplomacy undermined the American case, but the ultimate consideration seems to have been public opinion, in Canada in general but particularly in Quebec. Nowhere in Canada did public opinion support going to war as part of an American-constructed "coalition of the willing," but that was especially the case in Quebec.

Quebec was important for two reasons: history and politics. Three times in forty years Canada had gone to wars for which Quebec either was or became unenthusiastic. In 1917 and again in 1942 the government had imposed conscription for overseas service in the teeth of opinion in Quebec, and these facts were lovingly recorded and dwelt upon in the Quebec nationalist version of history. The Korean War, it was true, hadn't created the same conflict, and certainly the UN peacekeeping operations of the later twentieth century hadn't awakened the old English–French demons.

But Iraq had. In some ways this was surprising, because in order to offset English-Canadian influence Quebec *nationalistes* and separatists had made much of their affinity for the United States from the 1970s through the 1990s. The United States was the real thing, they argued, and English Canada merely a pale copy. This view of the United States appears to have reversed strongly, and suddenly, between 2001 and 2003. Analysts disagree as to exactly why, but the most plausible explanation seems to be that Quebec's tradition of anti-militarism had confronted the recent war-making image of the United States, and it did not like what it saw.[40] A poll published in November 2004 compared opinions of the United States held among various countries—including Canada's, but also Quebec's: it found that 79 percent of English Canadians seemed to like Americans, but that only 52 percent of Quebeckers felt the same way—similar to the level of approval in Spain.

The surge in Quebec public opinion was indicated by a huge anti-war demonstration in Montreal in March 2003, when 150,000 to 250,000 took to the streets to manifest disapproval of American policy. In Toronto, the comparable demonstration gathered only 10,000 to 30,000. This doesn't mean that opinion in English Canada favoured the Iraq war; all polls concur that it did not, even in Alberta, considered the most pro-American and right-wing section of the country. In a poll taken in March 2003, over 50 percent of Quebeckers had an unfavourable view of the U.S. government compared with 21.1 percent in the rest of Canada. As for "the American people," 24.3 percent of Quebeckers were "not favourable at all" compared with 8.9 percent in the rest of the country (and 5.9 percent on the Prairies).[41]

On the particular issue of the war, only 7.6 percent of Quebeckers were willing to follow the United States into Iraq without UN authorization (which was what happened). The figure for the rest of Canada was 20 percent, which broken down regionally at 22.7 percent for on the Prairies, 16.5 percent for in British Columbia, 17.8 percent for in the Atlantic provinces, and 20.4 percent for in Ontario. Had the Iraq war been authorized by the UN, 59.6 percent of the rest of Canada would have favoured Canadian participation; but in Quebec that figure dipped to 42.4 percent, with 50 percent still opposed. It was this policy that the Chrétien government publicly favoured. Bush's decision to proceed without UN authorization therefore spared the Canadian government a great deal of domestic political turmoil in the face of Quebec's probable dissent.

What was interesting, and significant, to any politician with a sense of history was the convergence of two of the main currents of Canadian history—the two-language divide between English and French Canada, and the political divide with the United States. It was a powerful combination, and Jean Chrétien paid it due homage.

It is also possible that English- and French-Canadian opinions had a common root—one not unique to Canada. As the Pew Global Attitudes Survey expressed it in early 2005, "Simply put, the rest of the world both fears and resents the unrivalled power that the United States has amassed since the Cold War ended."[42] Opinion of the United States as a superpower slopped over onto opinions about Americans. To quote Pew again, in a different survey, "In most Western countries surveyed, majorities associate Americans with the positive characteristics 'honest,' 'inventive' and 'hardworking.' At the same time, substantial numbers also associate Americans with the negative traits 'greedy' and 'violent.' Canadians, who presumably have the greatest contact with Americans, agree with Europeans on the negatives, but are less likely to view Americans as honest. And Canada is the only Western nation in which a majority (53%) regards Americans as rude."[43]

Some commentators went further. The prominent sociologist and pollster Michael Adams argued that Canadians, including English Canadians, were becoming more distant from Americans and closer to Europeans in values. On subjects like religion, Adams certainly had the polls on his side.[44] It is also true, as the historian J.L. Granatstein has repeatedly argued, that Canadians have and have always had a streak of anti-Americanism in their character.[45] At its extreme, this shade of opinion seems to hold Canadians uniquely responsible for differences with Americans, and argues that if Canadians hold negative sentiments about the United States, they should keep them to themselves.

Such feelings appear to ebb and flow. If anti-Americanism is a constant in Canadian life, so is attraction to the United States; and the attraction occasionally works in reverse. Some Americans are closer to Canadians, culturally, than they are to others in their vast and exceedingly diverse land. When George W. Bush prevailed in the very divisive 2004 presidential election, a cartoon-map immediately circulated around the United States depicting "The United States of Canada" (the Northeast down to Washington plus most of the Midwest and Pacific states) as a separate country from "Jesus-Land," the South, Plains states, and Southwest.[46] Opinions about the United States or Canada and their respective cultures are not only regional, but generational, with the older generations—those who remember the American New Deal and the Second World War—most likely to feel similarity to Americans. When Bush went to war in 2003 and Chrétien did not, the official opposition and three provincial premiers, Ernie Eves of Ontario, Ralph Klein of Alberta, and Gordon Campbell of British Columbia, vociferously supported Bush.

Interestingly, it was traditional Canadians (presumably represented by the three premiers) to whom George W. Bush appealed when he made a speech in Halifax in December 2004. He recalled what Canada had done in the Second World War, agreed that it had been right to do so, and argued that the time for action in a common cause had come again. His host, the Liberal prime minister Paul Martin, applauded appropriately.

His government wouldn't send troops to Iraq: public opinion forbade that. But it would send them (again) to Afghanistan.

DIVIDED POLITICS

Afghanistan wasn't on the Canadian political horizon between 2003 and 2005. The Liberal succession was at first the main item, and it was closely followed by two years of scandal.

Jean Chrétien had overstayed his welcome with the Liberal party. Though Chrétien had an enviable record of success as Liberal leader, with three straight election victories, he hadn't managed to make himself loved by his party or his parliamentary caucus. Irascible, imperious, and distant from his MPs, he created a vacuum of loyalty into which an ambitious aspirant might step. As it happened, there was one to hand, the minister of finance, Paul Martin Jr. Chrétien had defeated Martin for the Liberal leadership in a bitter contest in 1990, and subsequently relations between the two men were never warm or trusting. Martin was prepared to wait awhile for Chrétien to depart, but with each passing election, and each passing year, he was growing older. Assisted by some very able political operatives, Martin set about securing the loyalty of constituency associations across the country. Chrétien might have won, but Martin, Liberals were persuaded, would win bigger. The future of the party was tied to displacing the old leader and making room for the new: Martin.

Chrétien responded by firing Martin as finance minister, which only allowed Martin extra time to pursue his goal of the leadership. (Martin thereby avoided participating in the cabinet debates of March 2003 around the Iraqi war, and didn't have to take sides.) Finally, under pressure, Chrétien agreed to step down. A convention was called for Toronto in November 2003. Martin was the inevitable winner, but Chrétien in his farewell address was the star of the show. He rang all the chimes—the Liberal tradition of social welfare, the Battle of the Deficit, the Clarity Act. He added, "And it was because of our deep belief as Canadians in the values of multilateralism and the United Nations that we did not go to war in Iraq." The convention rose and cheered the old leader to the echo. Martin, many believed, would have done things differently in foreign policy, including Iraq; Chrétien's speech was a warning not to try.

Martin's moment at the centre of the national stage was brief, from December 2003 to February 2006. At first, he seemed to concentrate more on removing opposing elements in the Liberal party rather than attacking the opposition, apparently assuming that a victory over the previously hapless Conservatives was a sure bet. Confronted with a classic scandal, the misspending of federal money on Liberal-friendly ad agencies in Quebec in return for piffling work ostensibly boosting federalism and Canada, Martin chose to be indignant and, repeating Chrétien's tactic over Somalia, appointed an investigatory commission into what was called "Adscam." Then, hoping that the electorate had been appeased, Martin called an election in June 2004, just over three years into the term of the existing Parliament, expecting to harvest his own majority instead of Chrétien's and to consolidate his authority over the party.

It was a poor gamble. Martin underestimated his enemy. The Conservatives had finally united, for the first time since Mulroney, under a new and talented leader, the Calgarian Stephen Harper. Harper had been a Progressive Conservative back in the 1980s, had quit Ottawa in disgust, and had been one of the first to call for a new right-wing party to replace the bumbling, compromise-prone Progressive Conservatives. He served for a term as a Reform MP before returning to the private sector to lead a right-wing interest group, the National Citizens' Coalition. Replacing Stockwell Day as leader of the Alliance party, Harper made it his object to swallow up the remnants of the old Progressive Conservatives, who had returned to minor-party status under their former leader, Joe Clark. Clark opposed any such deal, but after his resignation as leader there was little to prevent it, and the merger formally took place in October 2003. The merged party reverted to the title "Conservative Party," last used in 1942.

Harper's merger extended the Conservatives geographically to the Atlantic provinces, and into Ontario. Harper was a much more solid and impressive figure than his predecessor, Day, but he carried with him a few liabilities, including his subscription to a 2000 declaration calling on the Alberta government to "build a firewall" around the province to keep out iniquitous Liberal influences. He had supported Bush's war in Iraq in March 2003, and had denounced the government for not following its natural ally's lead.[47] In terms of Canadian politics, it would not have been unfair to label Harper a provincialist, or, perhaps, a strict constructionist, arguing that the federal government should stay within its enumerated powers under the 1867 constitution. It should, on the other hand, return its attention to neglected areas like national defence.

Harper was unsuccessful at putting his ideas across in the 2004 campaign. Canadians were disappointed in Martin and the Liberals, but not disappointed enough to want to take a chance on Harper and the Conservatives.[48] Martin's campaign, based on his presumed popularity (election signs bore the slogan "Paul Martin's Liberals," evidently to distinguish them from the bad old Liberals of Jean Chrétien),[49] stumbled badly at first. His handlers immediately switched from the positive to the negative, stressing Harper's extremism and rigidity—deficiencies for which the Conservative leader then provided some corroborating evidence. In a classic negative campaign, the Liberals pulled off a minority government, giving Martin a second chance at fulfilling his promise of a new, fresh face to Canadian politics. In one ominous development, the Liberals lost very badly in Quebec, signifying Quebec's irritation at the Adscam scandal. Regardless of the cause, Martin had hoped to do better than Chrétien in Quebec, with a softer and more accommodating approach—the incoherent doctrine of "asymmetric federalism"—to Quebec nationalists; instead he did considerably worse.

Martin's second chance dragged on for eighteen months. The government did score some successes, concluding a broad financial accord with Canada's Natives in November 2005 and reaching agreement with the provinces on funding affordable daycare centres across the country. There was movement on getting new equipment for Canada's hard-pressed armed forces. In foreign policy, it patched up relations with the Bush administration, sending Canadian troops to Afghanistan. (The Americans, facing an endless insurgency in Iraq, needed all the help they could get to relieve their own hard-pressed army, in this case by allowing them to reduce the U.S. forces in Afghanistan.) On the other hand, it failed to agree on one of Bush's policy preferences, cooperation in a continental system of missile defence.

It was probably not a bad record, but it was offset by the increasing perception of the prime minister as unable to make up his mind on large themes, which was reinforced by the sometimes breathtaking opportunism of Liberal tactics in maintaining a majority in the House of Commons. (Martin was dubbed "Mr. Dithers" by a newspaper columnist, and the name stuck.)[50] A prominent Conservative moved to the Liberals, and was promptly appointed a minister. Shortly after, the Liberals squeaked by in a tie vote in the House, rescued, according to parliamentary custom, by the Speaker's casting vote.

Martin wasn't so lucky in November 2005. Defeated in the House of Commons, he was propelled into an election in January 2006. He repeated his tactics of the 2004 campaign, but the second time out, these had less effect. He lost this election, more impressively in terms of popular vote than actual seat totals. Martin resigned as Liberal leader as well as prime minister. In February 2006 Stephen Harper became prime minister at the head of a Conservative minority government.

CONCLUSION

It's too early to speculate on the prospects or duration of a Harper government. It's possible that it represents a coda on the prolonged Liberal and liberal era in Canadian history—one that lasted seventy years from 1935, or possibly even a century from the era of Sir Wilfrid Laurier. The shape of Canadian history has always been related to ideas and politics that have crossed over Canada's political boundaries, and the ebb and flow of liberalism and conservatism during the twentieth century have been no exception.

The ideology that accompanied Harper's election win in 2006 was, in some respects, a return to the Canada of the 1930s, both in domestic policy and foreign affairs—a return, in fact, to the last decade before "liberalism" in its current welfare-state collectivist guise had taken hold. The Canadian government of the 1930s was a low-tax, low-risk affair, which avoided meddling in provincial priorities—not all that different from what Harper might wish to see. All that had changed in 1939, when Canada's external alliances dictated an active participation in overseas conflicts. What followed, of course, was the expansion of the Canadian state, and the diminution of provincial power, in order to support the Canadian war effort.

There were other reasons to remember the 1930s. Relations then with Canada's principal ally, Great Britain, were uncomfortable and contradictory as they were expressed in both domestic politics and foreign policy. There was good reason to lack confidence in the direction of British policy, and deep concern that English and French Canada were heading in different directions. That had also happened after 1911, when Sir Robert Borden's Conservative government had got itself elected on different platforms in French Quebec and English Canada, with lasting and detrimental results for the Conservative party. In the years after 2001 the possibility existed of another split over foreign policy, and running along linguistic lines.

Unlike Great Britain, which lost interest in Canada along with the disappearance of its empire in the 1960s, the withdrawal of the United States from Canadian shores was not exactly in prospect. Geography, economics, and culture made sure of that. The fact of the United States, of another larger and richer English-speaking society right next to Canada, was, along with English–French relations and Native relations, one of the great constants of Canadian history. Two Liberal governments, Chrétien and Martin, struggled with the contradiction between two of the central themes of Canadian history—English–French harmony versus good relations with Big Brother. Was this a question that only benign neglect would eventually solve, or would it require more forceful and immediate action? Only time and circumstance would tell.

Circumstance demanded an adjustment to Canadian realities, which had changed over the century of Liberal dominance, and especially in the years after 1945. Demographics had changed in Canada. Most obviously, Canada's Native population, including the Métis, hadn't disappeared but expanded over time, making Natives and Native issues, and Native opinions, a much more important part of Canada's reality than they had been since 1815. Canada was in some respects returning to its origins.

There were other signs of its origins in the first years of the twenty-first century. Climate, and climate change, had shaped Canada in the fifteenth and sixteenth centuries. Global warming was by 2006 taken to be more fact than theory, and its effects on Canada and North America, from melting glaciers to hurricanes, reminded Canadians that "national" boundaries couldn't protect them against international, in fact intercontinental, developments. Nor was climate change all. Disease was no respecter of boundaries, and the history of Canada and its Aboriginal inhabitants showed what could happen to whole peoples confronted by unknown and uncontrolled pestilence. Would the twenty-first century see a recurrence of the plagues that had decimated Canada's First Peoples? Many believed it would, or believed that if it were to be prevented, it would require a strong and unified commitment from Canada, and from all other nations.

At the same time, large-scale immigration was changing Canada, as it was changing the United States. The political system mirrored the change, as far as representation was concerned, as one minority group after another found its way into elected or appointed office. Whether that would have an effect on the policies of Canadian governments, or on the attitudes of Canadian society as a whole, remained to be seen. Canada's forms, its parliaments, its democratic culture, its monarchy, had proved surprisingly durable. But the monarch's representative, symbolizing the continuity and adaptability of Canadian institutions, was first a woman born in Hong Kong, Adrienne Clarkson, and then a woman born in Haiti, Michaëlle Jean. It was a case of new wine in old bottles—familiar, but symbolizing renewal.

Multiculturalism, the standard buzzword to describe (and also obscure) the nature of a multi-immigrant society, might not be enough; might even prove to be a temporary phenomenon preceding the amalgamation of immigrants into a larger, but different, whole. Nevertheless, it seemed a safe bet that the demography of the late twentieth century harboured within itself a recalibration of the nature of Canada, if not an outright modification of what it meant to be Canadian.

Endnotes

1: NATIVE LAND

1. For some time a site at Old Crow in Yukon Territory was regarded as harbouring proof of a very early arrival (twenty-seven thousand years ago) of human immigration to North America, but re-dating according to more advanced scientific methods has reduced that date to a mere thirteen hundred years ago: Alan D. McMillan, *Native Peoples and Cultures of Canada: An Anthropological Overview*, 2nd ed. (Vancouver: Douglas & McIntyre, 1995), 28.

2. See on these points Jared Diamond, *Guns, Germs, and Steel: The Fates of Human Societies* (New York: Norton, 1999), 362–63.

3. Dean R. Snow, "The First Americans and the Differentiation of Hunter-Gatherer Cultures," in Bruce Trigger and Wilcomb E. Washburn, eds., *The Cambridge History of the Native Peoples of the Americas*, vol. 1, part 1, *North America* (Cambridge: Cambridge University Press, 1996), 182.

4. Quoted in James V. Wright, *A History of the Native People of Canada*, vol. II, *1000 BC–AD 500* (Ottawa: Canadian Museum of Civilization, 1999), 896.

5. Bruce Trigger and William R. Swagerty, "Entertaining Strangers: North America in the Sixteenth Century," in Trigger and Washburn, *Cambridge History of the Native Peoples*, 362–63. See also Olive Dickason, *Canada's First Nations: A History of Founding Peoples from Earliest Times*, 2nd ed. (Don Mills: Oxford University Press, 1997), 8–9, which discusses the issue of population figures and links it to the decimation of North America's population following the arrival of the Europeans.

6. Dean Snow, *The Iroquois* (Oxford: Blackwell, 1996), 88–89.

7. J.R. Miller, *Skyscrapers Hide the Heavens: A History of Indian White Relations in Canada* (Toronto: University of Toronto Press, 1989), 18.

2: LAND FOR THE TAKING

1. Scurvy was hardly a novelty. Cartier had faced the problem first among French explorers, but each generation seems to have had to face the disease anew. An effective cure for scurvy, lemon juice, was established as early as 1617, but it took the next 150 years for the cure to take effect in the world's navies.

2. Gilles Havard and Cécile Vidal, *Histoire de l'Amérique Française* (Paris: Flammarion, 2003), 65.

3. Diarmuid MacCulloch, *Reformation: Europe's House Divided, 1490–1700* (London: Allen Lane, 2003), 440.

4. Miller, *Skyscrapers Hide the Heavens*, 55–57.

5. Laval had been appointed bishop of a defunct diocese, where no Christians had lived for centuries; but defunct or not, the title of bishop remained.

6. There is an amusing account of the affair, which occurred in 1694, in W.J. Eccles, *Frontenac: The Courtier Governor* (Toronto: McClelland & Stewart, 1959), 297ff.

7. See John Mack Faragher, *A Great and Noble Scheme: The Tragic Story of the Expulsion of the French Acadians from Their American Homeland* (New York: Norton, 2005), 58–59.

3: EXPANSION AND CONSOLIDATION

1. The actual presidency of the council was sometimes disputed: Havard and Vidal, *Histoire de l'Amérique Française*, 107.

2. W.J. Eccles, *Canada Under Louis XIV* (Toronto: McClelland & Stewart, 1964), 32–33.

3. Havard and Vidal, *Histoire de l'Amérique Française*, 106.

4. R. Cole Harris and John Warkentin, *Canada Before Confederation* (Toronto: Oxford University Press, 1974), 21.

5. Marcel Trudel, *Memoirs of a Less Travelled Road: A Historian's Life* (Montreal: Véhicule Press, 2002), 22.

6. Talon could import goods free of duty and freight on the king's ships. The goods so imported, for example 220 barrels of brandy, must have been re-sold: Eccles, *Canada Under Louis XIV*, 56.

7. Allan Greer, *Brève Histoire des Peuples de la Nouvelle France* (Quebec: Boréal, 1998), 32–37.

8. See the analysis of the St. Ours family in Allan Greer, *Peasant, Lord and Merchant: Rural Society in Three Quebec Parishes 1740–1840* (Toronto: University of Toronto Press, 1985), 105–12. From their officer-founder in the 1670s, the St. Ours enjoyed a succession of official (military) appointments, pensions, and donations from the state; this persisted even after the end of the French regime in 1760.

9. Harris and Warkentin, *Canada Before Confederation*, 57–58.

10. E.E. Rich, *The Fur Trade and the Northwest, to 1857* (Toronto: McClelland & Stewart, 1967), 36–37.

11. Richard White, *The Middle Ground: Indians, Empires and Republics in the Great Lakes Region, 1650–1815* (Cambridge: Cambridge University Press, 1991), 34.

4: THE WARS FOR AMERICA (1)

1. An emissary from Massachusetts spent the summer of 1705 moored off Quebec City, negotiating a proposal of neutrality with Governor Vaudreuil: Dale Miquelon, *New France, 1701–1744* (Toronto: McClelland & Stewart, 1987), 40–41.

2. Cotton Mather, in 1691, quoted in Linda Colley, *Captives: Britain, Empire and the World, 1600–1850* (London: Pimlico, 2003), 147.

3. In the most famous incident, the Deerfield massacre of 1704, 47 settlers were killed outright and 111 taken into captivity: Miquelon, *New France*, 40.

4. Faragher, *Great and Noble Scheme,* 135. The Indians were a combination of Abenakis, Maliseets, and Mi'kmaq.

5. Bruce P. Lenman, "Colonial Wars and Imperial Instability," in P.J. Marshall, ed., *The Oxford History of the British Empire,* vol. 2, *The Eighteenth Century* (Oxford: Oxford University Press, 1998), 156.

6. Faragher, *Great and Noble Scheme,* 136–45.

7. Harold Kalman, *A History of Canadian Architecture,* vol. 1 (Toronto: Oxford University Press, 1994), 48–50.

8. Peter Kalm, *Travels in North America,* vol. 2 (New York: Dover, 1964), 428.

9. Intendant Duchesneau, quoted in White, *Middle Ground,* 36.

10. See for example the description in White, *Middle Ground,* 70–75, of a complicated marriage entanglement in 1694.

11. Quoted in Havard and Vidal, *Histoire de l'Amérique Française,* 251.

12. Alan Taylor, *American Colonies* (New York: Viking, 2001), 389–90.

13. In some respects the religious wars of 1520–1648 "sickened" many Europeans, but religion nevertheless remained an important political force, and changes in the balance of religion in Europe were viewed with alarm. James II thought his Catholic religion important enough to risk—and lose—his crown in 1688. The War of the Spanish Succession was seen by many in Great Britain as a Protestant struggle against advancing and aggressive Catholic power. See MacCulloch, *Reformation,* 669–71, for the state of mind at the beginning of the eighteenth century.

14. David Landes points out the British advantages in efficient internal transport, availability of coal, and efficient agriculture, all of which contributed to British economic growth in the eighteenth and early nineteenth centuries: David Landes, *The Wealth and Poverty of Nations: Why Some Are So Rich and Some So Poor* (New York: Norton, 1998), chapter 15.

15. Fred Anderson, *Crucible of War: The Seven Years' War and the Fate of Empire in British North America* (New York: Knopf, 2000), 36.

16. Anderson, *Crucible of War,* 18–20.

17. Eccles, *Canadian Frontier,* 160; Anderson, *Crucible of War,* 32, estimates that the French spent four million livres on the expedition.

18. Ian K. Steele, *Betrayals: Fort William Henry and the "Massacre"* (New York: Oxford University Press, 1990), 117–22.

19. Linda Colley, *Captives,* 181–82, uses the massacre to suggest a change in British attitudes to Indians, from romantic glorification earlier in the century to a kind of negative realism in the 1750s and after. But her treatment is brief and, while suggestive, is hardly conclusive. It seems more reasonable that opinions of the Indians differed widely both before and after Fort William Henry.

20. The site had first been occupied by the farm of Abraham Martin, an early settler—hence "the plains of Abraham."

21. It takes a great deal to deflate Wolfe's reputation, and the task may well be fruitless. The eminent historian Paul Kennedy (*The Rise and Fall of British Naval Mastery* [London: Ashfield Press, 1983], 108) suggests that Wolfe had few if any equals in the British army, either in the Seven Years' War or later in the century. W.J. Eccles thought little of both Wolfe and Montcalm, especially the latter: *Canadian Frontier,* 181–82. Fred Anderson, in his *Crucible of War,* 351–55, argues that Wolfe was seeking death, "his grim muse," in September 1759, and I'm inclined to agree with his argument.

5: THE WARS FOR AMERICA (2)

1. Ian Buruma, *Anglomania: A European Love Affair* (New York: Random House, 1998), catches some of the varieties of anglomania in Europe from Voltaire to the age of Margaret Thatcher.

2. W.S. MacNutt, *The Atlantic Provinces: The Emergence of Colonial Society, 1712–1857* (Toronto: McClelland & Stewart, 1965), 72–75.

3. T.F. McIlwraith, "British North America, 1753–1967," in T.F. McIlwraith and E.K. Muller, eds., *North America: The Historical Geography of a Changing Continent,* 2nd ed. (Lanham, Md.: Rowman and Littlefield, 2001), 207.

4. Philip Lawson, *The Imperial Challenge: Quebec and Britain in the Age of the American Revolution* (Montreal and Kingston: McGill-Queen's University Press, 1989), 144–45.

5. Piers Mackesy, *The War for America, 1775–1783* (Cambridge, Mass.: Harvard University Press, 1964), 511.

6. David Hackett Fischer, *Paul Revere's Ride* (New York: Oxford University Press, 1994), 64.

7. Alan Taylor, *The Divided Ground: Indians, Settlers, and the Northern Borderland of the American Revolution* (New York: Knopf, 2006), chapter 3.

8. The theory accepted at Paris was that the British held America by right of conquest (from the French) and discovery, and that the Americans inherited from the British by right of conquest (from the British) too: Michael D. Green, "The Expansion of European Colonization to the Mississippi Valley, 1780–1880," in Trigger and Washburn, *Cambridge History of the Native Peoples,* 465–66. The argument went further: Congress maintained that because the Indians had supported the British, they had forfeited their lands and not merely their sovereignty.

9. See Simon Schama, *Rough Crossings: Britain, the Slaves, and the American Revolution* (Toronto: Viking Canada, 2006).

10. The term "mob" was used by John Adams to characterize rioters in Boston in his defence of the British soldiers charged with their murder in the "Boston Massacre" of 1770: quoted in Hiller Zobel, *The Boston Massacre* (New York: Norton, 1970), 292. The soldiers were acquitted.

11. Schama, *Rough Crossings,* 144–49.

12. On this point see Jane Errington, *The Lion, the Eagle, and Upper Canada* (Montreal and Kingston: McGill-Queen's University Press, 1987), 4–5, 28–30.

13. "I think we're all Anglophiles," commented the historian and Librarian of Congress Daniel Boorstin in 1961. "How can we fail to be Anglophiles? Unless we hate ourselves." Boorstin is quoted in Christopher Hitchens, *Blood, Class and Empire: The Enduring Anglo–American Relationship* (New York: Nation Books, 2004), 14.

6: THE WARS FOR AMERICA (3)

1. www.statcan.ca/english/freepub/98-187-XIE/pop.htm, Statistics Canada, Estimated Population of Canada, 1605 to present.

2. Taylor, *Divided Ground*, 17–18, notes how the material needs of late eighteenth-century Iroquois greatly exceeded those of their seventeenth-century ancestors.

3. Gerald Craig, *Upper Canada: The Formative Years, 1784–1841* (Toronto: McClelland & Stewart, 1963), 142–43.

4. Edward Ermatinger, *Life of Colonel Talbot and the Talbot Settlement*, reprinted with an introduction by J.J. Talman (Belleville: Mika Silk Screening, 1972), original edition 1859, 111–15. The colonel's double entendres over dinner so appalled the local Anglican parson that he never visited again.

5. This adherence to principle, or resignation in the face of political reality, cost money: in the late 1780s the British government paid £150,000 per annum to subsidize Quebec: John Ehrman, *The Younger Pitt: The Years of Acclaim* (London: Constable, 1969, paperback ed., 1984), 364.

6. Some time later there followed a highland unit, the Glengarry Fencibles, the first Catholic regiment in the British army, raised in 1794 by Alexander Macdonell, a Catholic priest, to serve in the war just beginning against revolutionary France; Macdonell served as the regiment's chaplain. When the war paused, in 1802, the regiment was disbanded, leaving its soldiers unemployed and stimulating Macdonell to apply to the British government for help in settling them in Upper Canada. Leave and land were granted, two hundred acres (eighty-one hectares) for each soldier.

7. See Taylor, *Divided Ground*, 119–36.

8. J.M. Bumsted, *Fur Trade Wars* (Winnipeg: Great Plains Publications, 1999), 39.

9. The transition to British (as opposed to French-Canadian) dominance was not immediate, but by the 1780s was clearly in place: see Kenneth Norrie and Douglas Owram, *A History of the Canadian Economy*, 1st ed. (Toronto: Harcourt Brace Jovanovich, 1991), 134–35.

10. The miniature St. John's Island colony in fact already had a lieutenant governor, in token of its small size and dependent status.

11. The notion of a single governor general was strongly supported by Sir Guy Carleton, the former governor of Quebec, who had carried off the unpleasant assignment of evacuating the British army from the new United States after peace was signed.

Carleton's presumed accomplishments and expertise made him the expert of the moment on Canada in London in the later 1780s.

12. There was also a lieutenant governor in Lower Canada, but with no authority except when the governor was absent.

13. Ehrman, *Pitt,* 363.

14. For the celebrations and toasts see Mason Wade, *The French Canadians, 1760–1945* (Toronto: Macmillan, 1955), 94. For one banquet, Prince Edward, son of George III and later father of Queen Victoria, then an army officer stationed in Quebec, lent his private band.

15. Quoted in Peter Marshall, "British North America, 1760–1815," in Marshall, *Oxford History of the British Empire,* vol. 2, 385.

16. Michael Smith, "Upper Canada During the War of 1812," in Gerald Craig, *Early Travellers in the Canadas, 1791–1867* (Toronto: Macmillan, 1955), 33. Smith, an American-born Baptist minister, published his analysis of the province in 1813.

17. Wade, *French Canadians,* 94.

18. John Richardson to Alexander Ellice, 16 February 1793, quoted in Wade, *French Canadians,* 97.

19. Circular letter by Bishop Hubert, quoted in Wade, *French Canadians,* 99.

20. Douglas Hay, "Tradition, Judges and Civil Liberties in Canada," *Osgoode Hall Law Journal,* XLI/2 & 3, 320–21. McLane was unlucky in the judge, Chief Justice Osgoode, who tried him, for Osgoode pushed the then current interpretation of treason to its limits and beyond. The witnesses against McLane were promised land grants in return for their testimony; one of McLane's counsel, as well as the judge, participated in the deal.

21. Wade, *French Canadians,* 100–01.

22. One unanticipated effect of the British conquest was the survival of the Jesuits in Lower Canada long after the suppression by the Pope of the Jesuit order in France, Spain, and Portugal and their colonies. Canada's Jesuits retained their property, which wasn't confiscated by the Protestant state—unlike their colleagues in the Catholic monarchies.

23. Michael D. Green, "The Expansion of European Colonization to the Mississippi Valley, 1780–1880," in Trigger and Washburn, *Cambridge History of the Native Peoples,* 492–93.

24. Smith, "Upper Canada During the War of 1812," 44.

25. Helen Taft Manning, *The Revolt of French Canada, 1800–1835* (Toronto: Macmillan, 1962), 102–03.

26. Proclamation of 3 July 1812, quoted in J. Mackay Hitsman, *Safeguarding Canada, 1763–1871* (Toronto: University of Toronto Press, 1968), 89.

27. Hitsman, *Safeguarding Canada,* 87. The local population was opposed to "Mr. Madison's War."

28. Wellington to Prime Minister Lord Liverpool, 9 November 1814, quoted in Hitsman, *Safeguarding Canada*, 109.

7: TRANSFORMATIONS AND CONNECTIONS, 1815-1840

1. Donald Akenson, *The Irish in Ontario: A Study in Rural History*, 2nd ed. (Montreal and Kingston: McGill-Queen's University Press, 1999), 11–12, tables 1 and 2, and 31, table 4.

2. Akenson, *The Irish in Ontario*, 25–26. Contrary to the usual impression, Irish Catholics did come to Canada in significant numbers before the Irish Potato Famine of the later 1840s—although, again, they were outnumbered by Irish Protestants.

3. Longer voyages were, however, the norm. Travellers' accounts of the transatlantic voyage centre on the sheer boredom of the experience, as well as seasickness: see Charlotte Gray, *Sisters in the Wilderness: The Lives of Susanna Moodie and Catharine Parr Traill* (Toronto: Viking, 1999), chapter 4. These were, however, the stories of the more literate and wealthier immigrants, who had the time and education to set down their stories. The usual transatlantic voyage was much nastier and, in times of epidemics, much more hazardous.

4. Quoted in Marcus Tanner, *The Last of the Celts* (New Haven: Yale University Press, 2004), 292. The source was a medical officer in Sydney, Nova Scotia, in 1827.

5. Kenneth Bourne, *Britain and the Balance of Power in North America, 1815–1908* (Berkeley: University of California Press, 1967), 40–41.

6. At one point the earl occupied the North West Company post at Fort William on Lake Superior, and arrested the North West partners he found there. As J.M. Bumsted points out, he was acting in response to the North Westers' violent and illegal behaviour: Bumsted, *Fur Trade Wars*, 157–61.

7. Quoted in Bumsted, *Fur Trade Wars*, 224.

8. Henry David Thoreau, *A Yankee in Canada* (originally published in 1853), chapter 3, www.walden.org/institute/thoreau/writings/canada/03_St_Anne.htm.

9. Anna Jameson, "An English Gentlewoman in Upper Canada, 1836 1837," in Craig, *Early Travellers*, 124. Jameson was referring back to the Loyalist roots of the province, but also describing social and political opinions as she found them in 1837.

10. Caleb Upham, quoted in Reginald C. Stuart, *United States Expansionism and British North America, 1775–1871* (Chapel Hill: University of North Carolina Press, 1988), 98. Haliburton's Yankee peddler was called "Sam Slick of Slickville."

11. Quoted in "George Ramsay, ninth Earl of Dalhousie," *Dictionary of Canadian Biography*.

12. Diary entry for 28 August, 1831: George W. Pierson, *Tocqueville in America* (Baltimore: Johns Hopkins University Press, 1996), 191. See also www.tocqueville.org/ca.htm.

13. It should not be forgotten that the provinces and the neighbouring states were in active competition for settlers during this period, and some books were written to further one side or another of the competition.

14. The question of the nature of the political and cultural differences between Canadians and Americans was lively in the 1820s and remains a hot item today. Essentially, one school of academics argues that profound differences separate Canadians and Americans, with Canadians more traditional and more Tory in their attitudes, and Americans less deferential, less bound by tradition and authority. Canadians are held to be more communitarian and more prone to rely on the state, while Americans are thought to be more individualistic and more personally enterprising. Most recently Seymour Martin Lipset, an American political scientist, has made the case for cultural differences, especially in his book *Continental Divide: The Values and Institutions of the United States and Canada* (New York: Routledge, 1990), and two Canadian sociologists, Edward Grabb and James Curtis, in their book *Regions Apart: The Four Societies of Canada and the United States* (Toronto: Oxford University Press, 2005) have strongly and convincingly argued the contrary. Naturally, it's doubtful that a firm conclusion will ever be reached. The subject of Canadian and American differences remains a staple of popular culture, and in the early 2000s was even the subject of a TV series, *Due South*, juxtaposing a Canadian Mountie and an American policeman.

15. £233,882 was spent on fortifying Halifax, including the completion of the Citadel: Bourne, *Britain and the Balance of Power*, 48.

16. Quoted in Tanner, *Last of the Celts*, 293.

17. Quoted in Tanner, *Last of the Celts*, 294.

18. Quoted in MacNutt, *The Atlantic Provinces*, 200.

19. Sir John Harvey to Christopher Hagerman, the Upper Canadian solicitor general, in 1837: "Sir John Harvey," *Dictionary of Canadian Biography*. Harvey, a former army officer but a conciliatory and generally liberal official, managed the feat of governing successively all four Atlantic provinces, Prince Edward Island, New Brunswick, Newfoundland, and Nova Scotia.

20. Craig, *Upper Canada*, 134.

21. Douglas McCalla, *Planting the Province: The Economic History of Upper Canada* (Toronto: University of Toronto Press, 1993), 163–66 and 298–99, table 9.2. The annual income from the Canada Company hovered around £22,000.

22. Galt was later associated with the British American Land Company, which settled much of the Eastern Townships in Lower Canada: "John Galt," *Dictionary of Canadian Biography*.

23. There is a useful summary of the dispute in Norrie and Owram, *History of the Canadian Economy*, 141–45.

24. Frank Mackey, *Steamboat Connections: Montreal to Upper Canada, 1816–1843* (Montreal and Kingston: McGill-Queen's University Press, 2000).

25. Montreal had been governed by a board of magistrates from 1796 to 1832, and would be again from 1836 to 1840. Silliman is quoted in Jean-Claude Marsan, *Montreal in Evolution* (Montreal and Kingston: McGill-Queen's University Press,

1981), 146. Montreal's population in 1825 was 26,154, divided roughly 55–45 between francophones and anglophones.

26. Quoted in "George Ramsay, ninth Earl of Dalhousie," *Dictionary of Canadian Biography.*

27. Manning, *Revolt,* 126–27. Dalhousie considered some of the Tory ministers at home to be dangerous radicals, and strongly disapproved of the idea of reforming the British, let alone the Canadian, constitution.

28. Quoted in Manning, *Revolt,* 137.

29. Fernand Ouellet, "Louis Joseph Papineau," *Dictionary of Canadian Biography.*

30. "Matthew Whitworth-Aylmer, fifth baron Aylmer," *Dictionary of Canadian Biography.*

31. "Archibald Acheson, second earl of Gosford," *Dictionary of Canadian Biography.* Ironically, as Phillip Buckner, Gosford's biographer, observes, Gosford had a better sense of the crisis than his military commander, Colborne, and brought in troops from Nova Scotia long before Colborne realized they were necessary.

32. Allan Greer, *The Patriots and the People: The Rebellion of 1837 in Rural Lower Canada* (Toronto: University of Toronto Press, 1993), 193–94.

33. Colborne was a veteran of the bloody war in Spain, 1808–13, which gave rise to the term "guerrilla" (little war), in which the distinction between civilian and soldier was effectively obliterated.

34. Greer, *Patriots and People,* 328–29.

35. The exiles were sent variously to Bermuda and to distant Australia.

36. Carol Wilton, *Popular Politics and Political Culture in Upper Canada, 1800–1850* (Montreal and Kingston: McGill-Queen's University Press, 2000), 11.

37. The Americans and their Canadian guerrilla adherents burned his uncle's mill.

38. Strachan, originally a schoolmaster, tried and failed to become minister at Montreal's St. Gabriel's Presbyterian Church, and only afterward became an Anglican, a detail his opponents periodically raised.

39. Elgin, a fellow Scot, is quoted in Gerald Craig's judicious *Dictionary of Canadian Biography* entry on Strachan.

40. S.J.R. Noel, *Patrons, Clients, Brokers: Ontario Society and Politics, 1791–1896* (Toronto: University of Toronto Press, 1990), 95–96.

41. Craig, *Upper Canada,* 247–51.

42. Stuart, *United States Expansionism,* 142.

43. He had at first refused the Canadian post in July 1837, and took the job only after news of the December 1837 uprisings arrived in London.

44. Craig, *Upper Canada,* 263.

45. Fernand Ouellet, "John George Lambton, First Earl of Durham," *Dictionary of Canadian Biography.*

46. Noel, *Patrons, Clients, Brokers,* 108.

47. Thomson was a politician of the first rank, unlike Durham. He had been president of the Board of Trade (trade minister) through most of the 1830s, and had been offered the

position of Chancellor of the Exchequer (finance minister) earlier in 1839. He'd refused the offer because he knew that most of his cabinet colleagues disagreed with him on what he considered to be necessary financial reforms: *Dictionary of Canadian Biography.*

8: COLONIES INTO PROVINCES

1. Though there was some suspicion in 1832 that water was at the basis of the epidemics, it was only in 1849 that an observant London doctor concluded that the disease was indeed waterborne, and only in 1883 that the bacillus causing cholera was isolated and identified.

2. Akenson, *The Irish in Ontario,* 241.

3. Quoted in J. David Wood, *Making Ontario: Agricultural Colonization and Landscape Re-Creation Before the Railway* (Montreal and Kingston: McGill-Queen's University Press, 2000), 139.

4. Letty Anderson, "Water Supply," in Norman Ball, ed., *Building Canada: A History of Public Works* (Toronto: University of Toronto Press, 1988), 200. Montreal had a "partial system" after 1801. Saint John's water company dated from 1837 and Toronto's from 1841.

5. Wood, *Making Ontario,* 158. About one-third of southern Ontario's forest cover was gone by 1850; by 1914 the figure would be 90 percent.

6. James Dixon, "The Canadian Temper at the Start of the Free Trade Era," originally published in 1849, in Craig, *Early Travellers,* 167.

7. MacNutt, *The Atlantic Provinces,* 228–29.

8. Beginning in the seventeenth century, Britain regulated, or attempted to regulate, who might trade what in colonial ports. The new United States was of course subject to the Navigation Acts, which were more honoured in the breach than the observance. In 1822 commerce across the Great Lakes was officially exempted from the laws, and none too soon, since enforcement was virtually impossible.

9. Bourne, *Britain and the Balance of Power,* 164–69.

10. Donald Akenson, "Irish Migration to North America, 1800–1920," in Andy Bielenberg, ed., *The Irish Diaspora* (Harlow, England: Longman, 2003), 120–21.

11. Akenson, "Irish Migration," 121.

12. The movie *Gangs of New York* (2002) presents a vision of Irish immigration and American reaction to it in a spectacularly unpleasant way. There is one Canadian reference, to the battle of Lundy's Lane in 1814, as a source of American patriotism.

13. According to his entry in the *Dictionary of Canadian Biography,* Cartier would later say with a smile that he had been a "rebel" in 1837; in a letter to Lord Durham in 1838, he claimed that he had opposed only the local oligarchy, not the British crown. Durham didn't believe him, and put Cartier's name on a list of fugitives wanted for treason. Cartier did, however, compose some memorable songs of a sentimental, nationalist kind.

14. Lord Elgin, the governor general, explained the issue to Lord Grey, the colonial secretary, in a letter of 23 May 1848: "The true policy in this matter according to

my judgment, is—to secure for Her Majesty's subjects in Canada, free access to the markets of the States and all the advantages with respect to reduction of freights which competition on the St. Lawrence & the Ocean will afford.... You must then trust to [the Canadian subject's] affection for his own Institutions ... to induce him to remain steady, and to resist the blandishments of the 'Stars & Stripes.'" See Elgin to Grey, 23 May 1848, in Sir Arthur Doughty, ed., *The Elgin–Grey Papers*, vol. 1 (Ottawa: King's Printer, 1937), 178.

15. Upper Canada had provided for the emancipation of slaves in 1793, though gradually. In 1833 the British Parliament legislated the end of slavery in the whole British Empire, effective in 1834.

16. Under the American constitution, each state was equally represented in the Senate. In 1850, after the admission of California, there were fourteen "free" states and fourteen "slave" states.

17. A letter from an experienced American showed what might be expected. "Not less than fifty thousand dollars has been expended for procuring the passage of a Bill for establishing a line of Steamboats," the Canadian government was informed in December 1850: confidential enclosure in Lord Elgin, governor general, to Lord Grey, colonial secretary, 4 December 1850, in Doughty, *Elgin–Grey Papers*, vol. 3, 752. See also Alfred Eckes, *Opening America's Market: US Foreign Trade Policy Since 1776* (Chapel Hill: University of North Carolina Press, 1995), 67.

18. Access to the fishery meant fishing and drying one's catch on the shore. The British fishery was covered under Article I, and the American under Article II.

19. Under the Webster-Ashburton Treaty of 1842, persons could be extradited for trial from one country to the other, as long as the offence with which they were charged was common to both countries. Slavery existed in only one country, the United States, and so the treaty could not be used to remove slaves from British territory back to their American owners.

20. Stuart, *United States Expansionism,* 175–76.

21. G.R. Stevens, *History of the Canadian National Railways* (New York: Macmillan, 1973), 46–47.

22. E.G. Hornby, quoted in Stevens, *Canadian National Railways*, 48.

23. Two Canadians won the newly created Victoria Cross, the empire's highest award for gallantry—one at Balaclava in 1854 (a battle best known for the Charge of the Light Brigade) and one at Lucknow in 1857.

24. Stuart, *United States Expansionism*, 177. One editorialist described British Americans as "hardy and thrifty and homogeneous with our own Anglo-Saxon and Anglo-Celtic population," ideal Americans, in fact.

25. Disraeli to Prime Minister Lord Derby, 30 September 1866, quoted in Bourne, *Britain and the Balance of Power*, 294.

9: EXPANSION AND DISAPPOINTMENT, 1867–1896

1. No figure for migration across the porous Canadian–American border can be completely accurate for this period; two million is an approximation derived from figures in David Corbett, *Canada's Immigration Policy: A Critique* (Toronto: University of Toronto Press, 1957), 121.

2. According to the *Dictionary of Canadian Biography*, Scott was an Ulsterman and was most definitely an Orangeman. The Orange Order called on Macdonald to "avenge his death," and Macdonald, not the most bloodthirsty of men, had little choice but to seem to comply. In the event, until 1885, Macdonald did what he could to control rather than exterminate Riel.

3. Walter Russell Mead, *Special Providence: American Foreign Policy and How It Changed the World* (New York: Routledge, 2002), 117, notes that "Canada served as a hostage for British behavior in North America."

4. Attitudes toward Great Britain in the United States were complex, and far from uniform, then and later.

5. Stevens, *Canadian National Railways*, 94.

6. Doug Owram, *Promise of Eden: The Canadian Expansionist Movement and the Idea of the West* (Toronto: University of Toronto Press, 1980), 176.

7. Miller, *Skyscrapers Hide the Heavens*, 187.

8. The best known and most influential historical treatment of Riel is George F.G. Stanley, *The Birth of Western Canada* (Toronto: University of Toronto Press, 1960; original edition, 1936), but there are many, many others, both scholarly and popular.

9. John Palliser had surveyed the Canadian southern plains in 1858–59; he also identified land suitable for stock raising.

10. Graeme Wynn, "Realizing the Idea of Canada," in McIlwraith and Muller, *North America: Historical Geography*, 363.

11. The Prince Edward Island section of the Intercolonial, incomplete when PEI joined Canada in 1873, also had to be finished. The historian of the later Canadian National Railway called it "a stupid project from the start," unnecessary, given the availability of sea transportation, expensive to construct, and ruinous to operate, costing $1.44 for every dollar of revenue: Stevens, *Canadian National Railways*, 98. On patronage and corruption in the operation of the Intercolonial, Stevens is especially colourful: ibid., 99–105.

12. This phenomenon is described by the French sociologist André Siegfried, in his *The Race Question in Canada*, originally published in French in 1906 and translated in 1907, republished in English in 1966 (Toronto: McClelland & Stewart, 1966). See especially chapter 20.

13. The military analogy is obvious, and indeed the military were the first large-scale organization to be located in Canada. But the qualities of large-scale organization were also inculcated by engineering training, and what the railways required for construction and maintenance was professional engineers. See Alfred Chandler, *The*

Visible Hand: The Managerial Revolution in American Business (Cambridge: Harvard University Press, 1977), 94–109.

14. See the excellent analysis in Ian Drummond, *Progress Without Planning: The Economic History of Ontario* (Toronto: University of Toronto Press, 1987), 114–15.

15. Eugene Forsey, *Trade Unions in Canada, 1812–1902* (Toronto: University of Toronto Press, 1982), 27.

16. Norrie and Owram, *History of the Canadian Economy*, 383, comment that "the continental integration that was taking place in business was thus paralleled, even exceeded, by that taking place in unionism."

17. Quoted in ibid, 47. The reference is to a Grand Trunk strike in 1876.

18. Drummond, *Progress Without Planning*, 242–43.

19. The process is described in Ben Forster, *A Conjunction of Interests: Business, Politics and Tariffs 1825–1879* (Toronto: University of Toronto Press, 1986), chapter 10. The most notable compromise on the tariff involved coal, which Ontario wished to import from the neighbouring United States and which coal-producing Cape Breton wished to exclude. The result placed a sizeable but not prohibitive tariff on coal, and therefore enriched the federal treasury.

20. Legally, the fisheries regime reverted to the Convention of 1818, which forbade American access to the Canadian inshore fishery; that is, within the recognized three-mile (4.8-kilometre) limit of national jurisdiction. It did not necessarily prevent American boats from calling at Canadian ports, clearing customs, and then purchasing Canadian supplies, including fish bait. On this point see C.C. Tansill, *Canadian–American Relations, 1875–1911* (Gloucester, Mass.: Peter Smith, 1964, a reprint of the original 1943 edition), 23–25.

21. Arthur Silver, *The French-Canadian Idea of Confederation, 1864–1900*, 2nd ed. (Toronto: University of Toronto Press, 1997), 228.

22. See Mark McGowan, *The Waning of the Green: Catholics, the Irish and Identity in Toronto, 1887–1922* (Montreal and Kingston: McGill-Queen's University Press, 1999), 132: "Between 1887 and 1922 Catholic schools in Toronto were committed to produce virtuous Christians and good citizens of Canada and the Empire."

10: BOOM AND BUST, 1896–1914

1. "Heaven is blue, Hell is red." The Canadian party colours are still Liberal red and Tory blue—the reverse of the left–right colours in the United States. The later New Democratic Party appropriated orange, and the defunct Social Credit party took green.

2. The total population in 1913 is estimated at 7.6 million.

3. Interestingly, the Canadian imperialist George Parkin made these observations, which are still plausible, in 1892: Carl Berger, *The Sense of Power: Studies in the Ideas of Canadian Imperialism* (Toronto: University of Toronto Press, 1970), 145.

4. Jean-Claude Robert, "Quebec," screens 25–26 and table, in Bob Hesketh and Chris Hackett, *Canada: Confederation to Present* CD-ROM.

5. Norrie and Owram, *History of the Canadian Economy,* 321: "In 1909 Winnipeg handled more wheat than any other centre in the world."

6. See the analysis in Robert Bothwell, Ian Drummond, and John English, *Canada 1900–1945* (Toronto: University of Toronto Press, 1989), 81–82.

7. Quoted in H.V. Nelles, *The Politics of Development: Forests, Mines and Hydro-Electric Power in Ontario, 1849–1941* (Toronto: Macmillan, 1974), 220 and 221.

8. Blair's biographer in the *Dictionary of Canadian Biography,* D.M. Young, quotes an appraisal of the Board as "the prototype federal administrative tribunal and the first significant domestic manifestation of the rise of the modern regulatory state."

9. See especially Duncan McDowall, *Quick to the Frontier: Canada's Royal Bank* (Toronto: McClelland & Stewart, 1993), 171–87.

10. In 1913, during the Mexican revolution, the British legation in Mexico City asked Ottawa what it should do to protect certain Canadian investments. Ottawa, of course, had no idea. Six years later, however, the Canadian cabinet was interested in getting the powers to intervene in Mexico before the establishment of the League of Nations prohibited such international policing.

11. Banks were not allowed to lend for mortgages.

12. Michael Hart, *A Trading Nation* (Vancouver: UBC Press, 2002), 74, 182.

13. It was officially known as the Hydro Electric Power Commission of Ontario, or HEPCO.

14. There were those in right-wing Catholic circles in Quebec who so feared contamination by the English and Protestants that they propagandized for a separate French and Catholic state. See the biography of Jules-Paul Tardivel in the *Dictionary of Canadian Biography.*

15. There is the quip about the (Catholic) Austro-Hungarian Empire, defended, it was said, by "a standing army of soldiers, a sitting army of bureaucrats, and a kneeling army of priests." See especially William J. Callahan, *The Catholic Church in Spain 1875–1998* (Washington, DC: Catholic University of America Press, 2000), 46.

16. See Lionel Groulx, *Mémoires,* vol. 1 (Montréal: Fides, 1970), 106–08.

17. Nancy Christie and Michael Gauvreau, *A Full-Orbed Christianity: The Protestant Churches and Social Welfare in Canada, 1900–1940* (Montreal and Kingston: McGill-Queen's University Press, 1998), xiii.

18. Booth had been a Methodist clergyman working in the slums of London in the 1860s, but in the face of the social problems he confronted in mid-century England he changed the emphasis of his preaching, founding the Salvation Army in 1878. The Salvationists began activities in Canada in 1882.

19. On this point see William F. Ryan, *The Clergy and Economic Growth in Quebec, 1896–1914* (Quebec: Presses de l'Université Laval, 1966).

20. She was invited by fawning Canadian politicians in the 1850s.

21. These were, respectively, the Duke of Kent; the Duke of Clarence (later William IV); the Prince of Wales (later Edward VII); Princess Louise, the marchioness of Lorne and

wife of the governor general; the Duke of York (later George V); and the Duke of Connaught, governor general from 1911 to 1916.

22. Lord Monck, the first governor general, and Lord Lisgar, the second, were distinctly second-class political and social figures at home, but by the 1880s and 1890s the position was occupied by better connected individuals, culminating in Prince Arthur of Connaught, Queen Victoria's youngest son, who made up in lineage and good intentions for what he lacked in brains.

23. There was a tiny permanent force made up of professionals, but they were heavily outnumbered by the summer soldiers of the militia.

24. Sir John Macdonald to Sir Charles Tupper, 12 March 1885, quoted in C.P. Stacey, *Canada and the Age of Conflict*, vol. 1, *1867–1921* (Toronto: Macmillan, 1977), 43–44.

25. J.L. Granatstein, *Canada's Army: Waging War and Keeping the Peace* (Toronto: University of Toronto Press, 2002), 27.

26. They were Newfoundland, the five Australian colonies, New Zealand, Cape Colony and Natal in South Africa, and Canada.

27. The jingo song and many others were performed in music halls of the period, and were "enormously popular" in Britain and, probably, in English Canada too: John M. Mackenzie, "Empire and Metropolitan Cultures," in Andrew Porter, ed., *The Oxford History of the British Empire*, vol. 4, *The Nineteenth Century* (Oxford: Oxford University Press, 1999), 278–79.

28. There were some French-Canadian imperialists. Sir Percy Girouard made his name carving out chunks of Africa for the empire, while Sir James LeMoine (granted, LeMoine was half-French and apparently an Anglican, but very much a fixture in Quebec society) could be relied on to wave the British flag from the battlements of Quebec City.

29. Carman Miller, *Canada's Little War: Fighting for the British Empire in Southern Africa, 1899–1902* (Toronto: Lorimer, 2003), 21–23.

30. *Montreal Star*, 5 October 1899.

31. Miller, *Canada's Little War*, 52.

32. The Australian colonies had been federated into a single dominion in 1901, reducing the numbers of premiers at the conference table.

33. As recently as 2003 Americans produced a prime example of folk memories: a francophobia that must surely recall the constant Anglo–French wars stretching from the twelfth century to the nineteenth. The best recent analysis of this phenomenon is David Hackett Fischer, *Albion's Seed: Four British Folkways in America* (New York: Oxford University Press, 1989).

34. See Walter Russell Mead, *Special Providence: American Foreign Policy and How It Changed the World* (New York: Routledge, 2002), 119.

35. To take one example, the British abandoned an old treaty providing for a joint interest in a Central American canal when the American government decided that a

uniquely American canal—American only—was in the United States' true national interest. The result gratified President Theodore Roosevelt, as it was meant to.

36. Roosevelt believed the Canadian claims to be bogus at best, and sharp practice at worst. Even conceding an arbitration of the Canadian claim was designed mainly to save face for the Canadians and by extension the British Empire.

37. The most judicious account of the boundary dispute is in Stacey, *Age of Conflict*, vol. 1, 86–103. Roosevelt's biographer, Edmund Morris, ignores the politics behind the award, and its pre-cooked nature: *Theodore Rex* (New York: Random House, 2001), 281. He does accurately describe it as "a near-total victory." Roosevelt would have settled for nothing less.

38. Sir Joseph Pope came from a prominent Prince Edward Island Conservative family, and had been Sir John A. Macdonald's secretary in an earlier incarnation.

39. It would also manage the division of water on certain rivers between Canadian and American interests, and govern diversions and obstructions such as dams or weirs. In its work, the principle of equality was to be applied between Canadian and American rights.

40. William R. Willoughby, *The Joint Organizations of Canada and the United States* (Toronto: University of Toronto Press, 1979), 22.

41. The events of 1908 are described in a splendid book by H.V. Nelles, *The Art of Nation-Building: Pageantry and Spectacle in Quebec's Tercentenary* (Toronto: University of Toronto Press, 1999).

42. To a later generation, Laurier's proposed navy of five cruisers and six destroyers appears lavish. Certainly the destroyers would have been more useful on convoy duty in the First World War than an extra dreadnought or two in the Grand Fleet.

43. In defence of the British ministers, it should be noted that they hadn't even told the whole British cabinet, far less the British Parliament; so why should they tell Borden?

11: BREAKING THE MOULD, 1914-1930

1. Eric Arthur, quoted in Kalman, *History of Canadian Architecture*, vol. 2, 738. Kalman notes that the Sun Life Building was "one of several Canadian claimants to the title of largest or tallest buildings in the British Empire."

2. *Historical Statistics of Canada*, 2nd ed., tables D 125, Y 235, and Y 241.

3. Informed readers will object with the case of John Diefenbaker, Baptist and abstainer. Nevertheless, Diefenbaker was known to quaff the odd beer.

4. The act was intended to give the government emergency powers. Laurier advised that it should be comprehensive and non-specific in its language. The resulting act permitted the federal government to legislate as it saw fit by order-in-council, during a declared war emergency.

5. Bourassa was at this point an odd mixture of religious fervour, Canadian nationalism, and "good government," meaning an end to the old patterns of corruption he correctly identified with Laurier's Liberals. In response, the Liberals called Bourassa's

journal and other similar papers "la bonne presse." In this context "bonne" translates as "goody-goody."

6. "The Allies" refers to Britain, France, Russia, Belgium, and Serbia in 1914, with the additions of Italy in 1915 and Romania in 1916. Their enemies were known as "the Central Powers": Germany and Austria-Hungary in August 1914, joined by Turkey in November 1914 and Bulgaria in 1915.

7. Granatstein, *Canada's Army*, 55.

8. One of the mistakes in Robert Holland's essay, "The British Empire and the Great War," in Judith M. Brown and Wm. Roger Louis, eds., *The Oxford History of the British Empire*, vol. 4, *The Twentieth Century* (Oxford: Oxford University Press, 1999), 130, is the assertion that General Sir Arthur Currie, the Canadian Corps commander, 1917–19, was "a professional officer before the war." In fact Currie had been a real estate agent and a militia officer. J.L. Granatstein, *Canada's Army*, 94–95, observes that by 1916 the usual understanding of Canada's army as a citizens' force "was effectively dead," and that soldiers and officers had become professionals through bitter experience.

9. 804,000 out of 7.2 million.

10. Granatstein, *Canada's Army*, 57.

11. McGowan, *The Waning of the Green*, 244–46, notes the Ontario English-speaking bishops' fear that Catholic education as a whole would be endangered by Ontarians' resentment of French-language education. There was in this period great concern over French-speaking immigration into northern and eastern Ontario, which, some argued, imperilled the English-speaking and Protestant character of the province. On this point see Susan M. Trofimenkoff, *The Dream of Nation: A Social and Intellectual History of Quebec* (Toronto: Gage, 1983), 203–05.

12. Bill Waiser, *Saskatchewan: A New History* (Calgary: Fifth House, 2005), 73–74, 231–32, traces the reception of non-British immigrants on the Prairies, noting that the Great War sharpened differences among ethnic groups and increased pressures for conformity and assimilation.

13. Silver, *French-Canadian Idea*, 263–66.

14. Holland, "The British Empire and the Great War," 126, makes the absurd assertion that Bourassa was a separatist.

15. The rabid editorials of an Ottawa paper, the *Journal*, had much to do with creating and exciting a mob of soldiers who rushed the stage. One of Bourassa's sponsors, A.C. Glennie, an English Canadian, was roughed up; his wife the next day horse-whipped the *Journal*'s editor. Glennie was, however, fired from his job. Wade, *French Canadians*, 659, gives a vivid description of the incident.

16. Quoted in Wade, *French Canadians*, 660.

17. Twelve thousand tons were fired in the prelude to the battle of the Somme in 1916.

18. David Stevenson, *Cataclysm: The First World War as Political Tragedy* (New York: Basic Books, 2004), 149: 58 percent of deaths in battle were caused by artillery.

19. www.junobeach.org/e/4/can-tac-med-org-ep.htm: "The Army Medical Organization."

20. A report to Borden by a Montreal Conservative pointedly and disapprovingly mentioned the sources of this sentiment as members of Britain's Liberal government: Stacey, *Age of Conflict*, 186.

21. Borden to Sir George Perley, Canadian High Commissioner in Great Britain, 4 January 1916, quoted in Stacey, *Age of Conflict*, 192–93.

22. The dominion representatives were the Canadian, Australian, New Zealand, and Newfoundland prime ministers, and the South African minister of defence, General Jan Smuts. Of these, Smuts was the most important in terms of the value the British placed on his participation and advice.

23. J.E. Rea, *T.A. Crerar: A Political Life* (Montreal and Kingston: McGill-Queen's University Press, 1997), 55–56.

24. Quoted in Waiser, *Saskatchewan*, 282.

25. Robert Holland claims that "Bourassa displaced Laurier as the acknowledged leader of Quebec," an argument that is simply erroneous. See Holland, "The British Empire and the Great War," 126.

26. Ontario and Quebec farmers were particularly angry, and vocal: Rea, *T.A. Crerar*, 55–56.

27. Called the Income War Tax, it represented not only an innovation in the kind of tax imposed, but also an incursion into "direct" taxation. This would eventually perturb the provinces, whose limited tax jurisdiction the federal government now proposed to share. At a dominion–provincial conference in 1918 the provinces urged that the federal government turn half the receipts of the income tax over to them: Christopher Armstrong, *The Politics of Federalism: Ontario's Relations with the Federal Government, 1867–1942* (Toronto: University of Toronto Press, 1981), 128–30.

28. There were a few small issues in 1915 and 1916: R.C. Brown and G.R. Cook, *Canada 1896–1921: A Nation Transformed* (Toronto: McClelland & Stewart, 1974), 230–31.

29. They withdrew Canadian troops from Siberia and Murmansk as soon as they practically could, thereby undermining British intervention in those two areas.

30. The "Progressives" covered the ideological spectrum. Some were markedly conservative in their attitudes toward government, taxation, and regulation, the hallmarks of "progressivism" elsewhere in the world. Some took a contrary view. To make matters worse, "progressive" with a small *p* was used in Canada in the usual international sense, which made for a great deal of muddle in political identities and definitions.

31. J.W. Pickersgill, *Seeing Canada Whole: A Memoir* (Markham, Ont.: Fitzhenry & Whiteside, 1994), 74–75.

32. W.A. Motherwell and Charles A. Dunning, both prominent Saskatchewan Liberals, joined the King cabinet in the 1920s, Motherwell as minister of agriculture, Dunning as minister of finance.

33. There was a further complication. Under centuries-old British practice, members of the House of Commons accepting a new office under the crown had to resign their

seats and seek to return in a by-election in their new, ministerial guise. In a house of minorities, Meighen could not afford to swear in a complete cabinet, and so he alone took office and consequently had to watch proceedings from the galleries. This usage was soon abolished, and MPs can now accept office without having to quit their seats.

34. Armstrong, *Politics of Federalism*, 140.

35. Ontario and Quebec also wanted control over waterpower from Canada's greatest navigable river system, the St. Lawrence and its tributaries. Navigation, however, fell under federal control even if "natural resources" were provincial.

12: UNFRIENDLY WORLDS, 1930–1945

1. There were at least thirteen RCMP movies in the 1930s. The best-known was probably *Rose Marie*, starring Jeanette MacDonald and Nelson Eddy, but others included *Susannah of the Mounties, Renfrew of the Royal Mounted,* and *Murder on the Yukon.* There was also a children's book series, beginning with *Dale of the Royal Canadian Mounted Police* in 1935.

2. What was left of the Progressives got twelve seats, mostly in Alberta, and there were as well a couple of Labour members.

3. Waiser, *Saskatchewan*, 261–63.

4. The port elevators were truly impressive in size and sweep: one, Saskatchewan Number 7 at Port Arthur, built by the C.D. Howe Company, was cited by the architect LeCorbusier as a model of modern design.

5. Social Credit eventually became a right-wing party, but at the time it was a reforming movement that hoped to revolutionize money and credit so as to solve the Depression.

6. Louisiana, the other great French-speaking enclave in the United States, was well on the way to assimilation, though the "Cajuns" of that state had a more secure position, legally, socially, and politically, than their New England "Canuck" counterparts.

7. It is this world that is depicted in the much later Claude Jutra film, *Mon Oncle Antoine.*

8. Quoted in Max and Monique Nemni, *Young Trudeau, 1919–1944: Son of Quebec, Father of Canada* (Toronto: McClelland & Stewart, 2006), 72–73.

9. "The crowd booed Taschereau and the Jews."

10. It is nevertheless true that some old-time English Conservatives stayed on in the new party, and equally true that some of the French Conservatives in the Union Nationale were more conservative than nationalist. Some of these left the UN in 1939 and some more later in the Second World War, but there was always an English remnant in the party.

11. Lapointe was especially worried by the apparent willingness of the head of the Catholic Church in Quebec, Rodrigue Cardinal Villeneuve, to cozy up to the nationalists. See Lita Rose Betcherman, *Ernest Lapointe: Mackenzie King's Great Quebec Lieutenant* (Toronto: University of Toronto Press, 2002), 233.

12. Betcherman, *Lapointe*, 269–70, discusses the minister's refusal to admit Jewish refugees from the ship *St. Louis* to Canada, and Mackenzie King's concurrence.

13. King was not alone in this: Sir John A. Macdonald carried the nickname "Old Tomorrow," which certainly didn't mean that Sir John was accounted to be a man of sudden, decisive action and clarity of purpose.

14. King's most effective critic, though posthumously, was the Montreal poet and law professor Frank Scott, in his poem "W.L.M.K.," which was published in his *The Eye of the Needle: Satires, Sorties, Sundries* (Montreal: Contact Press, 1957).

15. The question of anti-Semitism in Canada ranks with the Riel rebellion as a subject for bitter controversy among academics and other commentators, because like Riel it strikes at the heart of the English–French divide. That there was anti-Semitism is beyond dispute, but who were the anti-Semites, and where were they influential? There is also the implied question, Who was worse, the English or the French?

    Canadian society in general—English and French—displayed anti-Semitic characteristics. On the English side, Jews weren't admitted to rich men's clubs, there were real estate covenants in some places which restricted where Jews could live, and Canadian universities maintained quotas as to the number of Jews they would admit. There were anti-Semitic incidents in Toronto and other English-Canadian cities. On the other hand, society reacted adversely to these incidents, which did not have the effect of creating a general anti-Semitic movement in Canada. Nevertheless, it's quite clear that Quebec was not alone in the incidence of anti-Semitism in the 1930s.

    It's also true that some of the most virulent anti-Semitic manifestations were in Quebec, and true that it was the French-Canadian parliamentary delegation, almost entirely Liberal, that was most nervous of offending the Quebec right wing by admitting Jewish refugees to Canada in the 1930s. (Some of the "Liberals," to be sure, shared the right's anti-Jewish prejudices.) Disputes over French-Canadian anti-Semitism burst into a bitter public quarrel among historians in the 1990s. On one side, see Esther Delisle, *The Traitor and the Jew: Anti-Semitism and the Delirium of Extremist Right-wing Nationalism in French Canada from 1929 to 1939* (Montreal: Robert Davies, 1993), supported by Mordecai Richler, especially in his *O Canada, O Quebec: Requiem for a Divided Country* (Toronto: Viking, 1992). Richler made Quebec nationalism a laughingstock, or so its partisans believed, and they responded with great bitterness. Delisle's book appeared as the controversy over Richler raged, but her arguments were already familiar to him.

    On the other hand, see Gary Caldwell, "La controverse Delisle–Richler: Le discours sur l'antisémitisme au Québec, et l'orthodoxie néo-libérale au Canada," *L'Agora*, juin 1994, vol. 1, no. 9. The subject was politically explosive in the 1990s, because separatist nationalism in Quebec was considered by many to be anti-immigrant and fixated on the "pure laine" French-Canadian race, Quebec branch. Normand Lester, an amateur historian, strung together four volumes of abuse on the subject of English Canadians in a book aptly entitled *Le livre noir du Canada anglais* (Montreal: Les Intouchables, 2001 and subsequent years). *Le livre noir*, which lovingly listed English-Canadian deficiencies, some real and some fancied, resonated in Quebec, where it became a bestseller.

16. The key work on this subject is Irving Abella and Harold Troper, *None Is Too Many* (Toronto: Lester and Orpen Dennys, 1983).

17. King called on Hitler, and dictated some gaseous and notably obtuse comments in his diary on the peasant nature of the German dictator (King, after all, had a Ph.D., and Hitler did not).

18. Waiser, *Saskatchewan*, 324–26.

19. Conrad Black, Duplessis's biographer, argues that the Quebec premier "was, literally, roaring drunk": Black, *Duplessis* (Toronto: McClelland & Stewart, 1977), 208–09. This is a reasonable explanation, but drunk or sober Duplessis could seldom resist creating the maximum political effect through demagoguery. As one Liberal MP put it in the late 1930s, at the time of Stalin's murderous purges in the Soviet Union, "Staline tue, Duplessis salit." ("Stalin kills [you], but Duplessis makes you dirty.")

20. By 1944 1.1 million Canadians were working in war industries, and 37 percent of the total population over fourteen was working in "non-agricultural industry": Michael D. Stevenson, *Canada's Greatest Wartime Muddle: National Selective Service and the Mobilization of Human Resources During World War II* (Montreal and Kingston: McGill-Queen's University Press, 2001), 26. In addition, over a million Canadians, male and female, served at one time or another in the armed forces.

21. Winnipeg had sixty thousand war workers, Vancouver eighty-nine thousand.

22. Figures for 1944 were actually higher than for 1945, when war production was winding down and finally terminated in September 1945.

23. Bothwell, Drummond, and English, *Canada 1900–1945*, 375.

24. Paul-André Linteau, René Durocher, Jean-Claude Robert, et François Ricard, *Histoire du Québec contemporain*, vol. 2, rev. ed. (Montréal: Boréal, 1989), 149.

13: A TIME OF GIFTS, 1945-1963

1. Jeff Keshen, *Saints, Sinners and Soldiers: Canada's Second World War* (Vancouver: UBC Press, 2004), 262, quoting a straw poll.

2. Angus Maddison, *The World Economy: Historical Statistics* (Paris: OECD, 2003), 88, Table 2c, Per Capita GDP in Western Offshoots.

3. The best description of the often ingenious government regulations governing consumption is in James H. Gray, *Troublemaker: A Fighting Journalist's Record of the Two Booming Decades That Followed the Winter Years* (Toronto: Macmillan, 1978), 124–27.

4. W.J. Eccles interview in Robert Bothwell, *Canada and Quebec: One Country: Two Histories*, rev. ed. (Vancouver: UBC Press, 1998), 77–78.

5. *Canada Year Book, 1948–1949* (Ottawa: King's Printer, 1949), 822 and Table 24.

6. The actual phrase used by the government was "a high and stable level of employment"—what we might call not-quite-full employment.

7. On this point see Robert Bothwell and William Kilbourn, *C.D. Howe: A Biography* (Toronto: McClelland & Stewart, 1979), 194–96.

8. Keshen, *Saints, Sinners and Soldiers*, 146ff.

9. Doug Owram, *Born at the Right Time: A History of the Baby Boom Generation* (Toronto: University of Toronto Press, 1996), 12.

10. The first marriage took place six weeks after the arrival of Canadian troops in England in December 1939. Ninety-three percent of the war brides were British, and the remaining 7 percent French, Belgian, Dutch, and Italian—the countries the Canadian army traversed during the war. The figures refer to the period 1942 to 1948: they are derived from www.canadianwarbrides.com. Keshen, *Saints, Sinners and Soldiers*, 268, gives 47,783 as the total for war brides, and on page 233 quotes the figure of 30,000 for illegitimate children.

11. Keshen, *Saints, Sinners and Soldiers*, quotes a poll taken among soldiers in late 1944 that shows 54 percent believing that things would be better or at least no worse for them after the war, while only 15 percent were pessimistic.

12. A book by Tom Brokaw on the comparable group of American veterans calls them *The Greatest Generation* (New York: Random House, 1998); generally speaking, the characteristics I have mentioned are ascribed to that group, in William Strauss and Neil Howe, *Generations: The History of America's Future, 1584 to 2069* (New York: William Morrow, 1991), 261–78.

13. The first recorded usage is thought to be 1941, in the United States; the term "baby boomers" as descriptive of the generation appears to date from 1974.

14. The rate was 61 deaths in the first year per thousand population in 1940–45, and 31.3 in 1956–60. *Historical Statistics of Canada*, 2nd ed., table B24.

15. Polio increased in severity after 1945, reaching a rate of 60 cases per 100,000 population in 1953, and sinking, after Salk, to 1.6 in 1957, though with a sharp one-year spike in 1959 to 15: ibid., table B522.

16. Ibid., tables W340–438 and D8–85.

17. See Joy Parr, *Domestic Goods: The Material, the Moral, and the Economic in the Postwar Years* (Toronto: University of Toronto Press, 1999), 87, for an example of the government's rejection of micro controls.

18. Alvin Finkel in his *Our Lives: Canada After 1945* (Toronto: Lorimer, 1997), 15–21, takes a different view, accusing King of hypocrisy and painting the reconstruction conference exercise as a charade. I think the situation was a great deal more nuanced.

19. By way of comparison, 480,000 American troops served in Korea.

20. There was a moment in the fall of 1950 when it seemed that the UN (U.S.) forces were on the verge of defeat at the hands of an interventionist Chinese Communist army, and Truman made an incautious remark that seemed to indicate he would use atomic weapons. That was not his intention, but it did cause intense worry in Canada.

21. These would soon be called "the Third World," a term just being invented in the 1950s. By extension the Western industrialized democracies would be called "the First World," and the Communist bloc "the Second World." The original reference is to the three estates of pre-revolutionary France.

22. Escott Reid, memorandum of 30 August 1947, quoted in Escott Reid, *Radical Mandarin: The Memoirs of Escott Reid* (Toronto: University of Toronto Press, 1989), 270–71.

23. H.S. Ferns, *Reading from Left to Right: One Man's Political History* (Toronto: University of Toronto Press, 1983), 172–73.

24. His real opinion would slip out in November 1956 in a heedless remark to the House of Commons about "the supermen of Europe." As the reaction to his remarks would show, many Canadians felt quite comfortable with "the supermen."

25. As Matthew Connolly points out in *A Diplomatic Revolution: Algeria's Fight for Independence and the Origins of the Post–Cold War Era* (New York: Oxford University Press, 2002), 278–79, "international norms" in the 1950s were again beginning to" trump national sovereignty," and if a colonial power was unable to maintain its rule without resorting to barbarism, its control over a colonial territory lost its legitimacy. This was not an entirely unfamiliar idea—it had been applied to Italy in the 1860s, to the Balkans in the 1880s and after, and, of course, to Ireland.

26. Greg Donaghy, "'The Most Important Place in the World,' Escott Reid in India, 1953–1957," in Greg Donaghy and Stéphane Roussel, eds., *Escott Reid: Diplomat and Scholar* (Montreal and Kingston: McGill-Queen's University Press, 2004), 71–72.

27. Donaghy, "Escott Reid," 78–80.

28. *Historical Statistics*, series Q82. By 1976 thermal capacity would reach 23.3 million kilowatts.

29. Howe was an American by birth and, as he liked to remind his cabinet colleagues, a Canadian by choice. None of them, he pointed out, had actually had to choose.

30. Ontario actually had the distinction of having North America's first oil well.

31. NRX, designed by a British engineer, was exceptional at producing radioactive isotopes, which became a Canadian specialty.

32. Canada's reactor program is described in Robert Bothwell, *Nucleus* (Toronto: University of Toronto Press, 1988).

33. His experience was hardly unique, and indeed many years later it was repeated by David T. Jones, a former officer at the U.S. embassy in Ottawa, who became something of a specialist in reminding Canadians of their deficiencies, in articles published in the Canadian journal *Policy Options*.

34. The minister was Alvin Hamilton, Diefenbaker's last minister of agriculture and a star in his cabinet. Hamilton added that the Conservatives were surprised to find that the civil servants' advice was not always good.

35. George Perlin, *The Tory Syndrome: Leadership Politics in the Progressive Conservative Party* (Montreal and Kingston: McGill-Queen's University Press, 1980).

36. See Owram, *Born at the Right Time*, 154–55.

37. Naturally there were Canadian singers too, like the Crew-Cuts (an early group), Bobby Curtola, and Paul Anka.

38. Politically and socially it was the Second World War veterans who were dominating Canadian life at the end of the fifties; and of course it was they who were paying the bills for the teenagers.

39. Though very few knew it outside Washington, even Kennedy's defence secretary, Robert McNamara, was appalled when he learned what Western strategy would be in the event of war: Deborah Shapley, *Promise and Power: The Life and Times of Robert McNamara* (Boston: Little, Brown, 1993), 185, 187–201. McNamara would eventually push hard for the limitation of atomic weaponry, especially after his experience in the Cuban Missile Crisis, when he "felt vividly that the nuclear danger could not be controlled or fine-tuned."

40. The acronym stands for Boeing Michigan Aeronautical Research Center.

14: AFFLUENCE AND ITS DISCONTENTS, 1960–1980

1. In constant dollars, using 1981 as a base, the gross national product increased 4.6 times, from $74.1 billion in 1949 to $344.5 billion in 1982: Norrie and Owram, *History of the Canadian Economy*, 549.

2. "Gross Domestic Product per Capita: Purchasing Power per Capita: Purchasing Power Parity (EKS): Compared to United States," The Public Purpose, Labor Market Reporter, www.publicpurpose.copm/lm-ppp60+.htm.

3. www.publicpurpose.copm/lm-intlunem.htm. The statistics are derived from the U.S. Department of Labor, Bureau of Labor Statistics, and may vary slightly from their Canadian equivalents.

4. The Trans-Canada Highway was authorized in 1948; the final section, in Newfoundland, was completed in 1965. Quebec was a late and rather reluctant participant, but joined when it became clear how much of the province's new highway system could be paid for out of federal funds.

5. Rita Joe, "Skyscrapers Hide the Heavens," used as the title of J.R. Miller's book, *Skyscrapers Hide the Heavens: A History of Indian–White Relations in Canada.*

6. See Bruce McCall's memoir, *Thin Ice: Coming of Age in Canada* (Toronto: Random House of Canada, 1997), which captures aspects of small-town Ontario, and small-town Toronto, in the 1950s. See also the perceptive comment by Robert Fulford in the *National Post*, 26 September 2000.

7. Between 1976 and 1981 Alberta's population grew at the truly remarkable rate of 21.7 percent, compared with Ontario's 4.4 percent and Newfoundland's 1.8 percent.

8. Daniel Bell, *The End of Ideology: On the Exhaustion of Political Ideas in the Fifties* (New York: Collier, 1961), and subsequent editions. The notion of an "end of ideology" wasn't confined to North America; it appeared in Europe as well: see Tony Judt, *Postwar: A History of Europe Since 1945* (New York: Penguin, 2005), 384.

9. George Grant, *Lament for a Nation* (Toronto: McClelland & Stewart, 1965).

10. Owram, *Born at the Right Time*, 207.

11. Owram, *Born at the Right Time*, 207–08.

12. William Strauss and Neil Howe, *Generations: The History of America's Future, 1584 to 2069* (New York: Quill, 1991), 299ff.

13. The two went on into the later CCF.

14. The intellectual end of the NDP may be found in Michael Oliver's edited collection of essays, *Social Purpose for Canada* (Toronto: University of Toronto Press, 1961). It posed a challenge to the simultaneous intellectual renovation of the Liberal party.

15. The intellectual climate was exceptionally favourable. Much public discussion in Canada as well as in the United States focused on the notion that there was "poverty in the midst of plenty." On Galbraith's ideas, see Richard Parker, *John Kenneth Galbraith: His Life, His Politics, His Economics* (Toronto: HarperCollins, 2005), 282ff. See also Penny Bryden, *Planners and Politicians: Liberal Politics and Social Policy* (Montreal and Kingston: McGill-Queen's University Press, 1997); Tom Kent, *A Public Purpose* (Montreal and Kingston: McGill-Queen's University Press, 1988), 56, 81, 83.

16. Even the Saskatchewan Liberal party, originally strongly opposed to medicare, hastily recanted, and supported it in the 1964 provincial election: Bryden, *Planners and Politicians,* 130.

17. Ottawa would estimate the cost of doctors' services per capita across the country in any given year, and then give the provinces a fee based on the population of each province. If a given province wished to pay for more, it was free to do so, but it wouldn't get more than the national average in return: Kent, *Public Purpose,* 365–66.

18. Premier Manning objected at some length to the program in discussions with Pearson; according to Tom Kent, *Public Purpose,* 369, his objections "had little logic but much vehemence." On shared cost programs, see Mitchell Sharp, *Which Reminds Me … A Memoir* (Toronto: University of Toronto Press, 1994), 138–39.

19. Kent, *Public Purpose,* 365.

20. This is effectively described in Dimitri Anastakis, *Auto Pact: Creating a Borderless North American Auto Industry 1960–1971* (Toronto: University of Toronto Press, 2005), chapter 3.

21. The Créditiste leader, Réal Caouette, was however a very firm federalist—firmer than many of his followers.

22. He liked to call the NATO secretary general, the Dutch diplomat Josef Luns, simply "General" Luns, meaning somebody who echoed what the real generals told him.

23. There is the occasional contrary item, like Claude Julien, *Canada: Europe's Last Chance* (Toronto: Macmillan, 1968).

24. Flying over Canada in 1987, en route to a Commonwealth summit in Vancouver, Denis Thatcher, the husband of the British prime minister, turned to a group of British reporters and opined, "Y'know what Canada is? Canada is full of fuck all." Thatcher is quoted in Martin Kettle, "Let me tell you about Canada. No, really, it's very interesting," *Guardian,* 7 January 2006.

25. Miller, *Skyscrapers Hide the Heavens,* 227–29.

26. According to one estimate, there were four federal–provincial conferences from 1902 to 1927, eight from 1927 to 1944, ten from 1945 to 1959, and fifteen from 1960 to 1969. They were called "dominion–provincial conferences" down to 1960, and "federal–provincial" thereafter.

27. As in the classic study, Richard Simeon's *Federal–Provincial Diplomacy: The Making of Recent Policy in Canada* (Toronto: University of Toronto Press, 1972).

28. *Historical Statistics of Canada*, 2nd ed., tables E190–197.

29. Ibid., table E194.

30. It was in fact the Year of the Child, a UN promotion designed to draw attention to children and their plight.

15: TWO NATIONALISMS

1. A demographer, Richard Joy, wrote the aptly titled *Languages in Conflict: The Canadian Experience* (Toronto: McClelland & Stewart Canadian Library, 1972).

2. The best known revolutionary document is the offensively titled *Nègres blancs d'Amérique* by Pierre Vallières (Montréal: Parti Pris, 1968). It argues that the English ruled Quebec through "rois nègres" like Duplessis.

3. On this point testimony is abundant. Perhaps the most accessible glimpse of aspects of Westmount and the other sections of English Montreal is to be found in the irreverent and usually scathing works of Mordecai Richler: *The Apprenticeship of Duddy Kravitz* (London: Deutsch, 1959, but first published in *Maclean's* magazine some years earlier) and *St. Urbain's Horseman* (Toronto: McClelland & Stewart, 1971) are excellent examples.

4. Quoted by Tom Kent, *The Globe and Mail*, 11 October 2005.

5. Quoted in Robert Bothwell, Ian Drummond, and John English, *Canada Since 1945*, 2nd ed. (Toronto: University of Toronto Press, 1989), 269.

6. Albert Breton, an economist, argued at the time that Quebec's activity should be seen as self-interested benefits for the province's French-speaking middle class: Breton, "The Economics of Nationalism," *Journal of Political Economy*, LXXII (August 1964).

7. Marc Lalonde, quoted in Robert Bothwell, *Canada and Quebec: One Country, Two Histories* (Vancouver: UBC Press, 1995), 105–06.

8. As the automobile industry developed, location and delivery times became extremely important, and Ste. Thérèse's isolated location, far from the car factories of Ontario and the U.S. Midwest, didn't help.

9. As Allan Gotlieb, then a senior member of the Legal Division of the Department of External Affairs in Ottawa, has pointed out, Gérin-Lajoie was resurrecting an argument first put forward by Ontario in the Labour Conventions case before the Imperial Privy Council in 1937. The Privy Council ignored the assertion, though it did agree that the federal government couldn't use international agreements as a means of legislating in areas granted to the provinces under the British North America Act: *The Globe and Mail*, 5 October, 2005.

10. Gotlieb and Tom Kent, in *The Globe and Mail* on 5 and 11 October 2005, have clarified what was or was not agreed to by Pearson and Lesage. The meeting took place at the Queen Elizabeth Hotel. Pearson didn't concede any of Lesage's arguments, and Lesage didn't expect him to. This account differs from the one given in J.L. Granatstein and Robert Bothwell, *Pirouette: Pierre Trudeau and Canadian Foreign Policy* (Toronto: University of Toronto Press, 1989), 115.

11. Both terms were used by René Lévesque to describe his aspirations in an interview with Larry Zolf and Pierre Elliott Trudeau on the CBC TV program *This Hour Has Seven Days* on 6 December 1964: http://archives.cbc.ca/IDC-1-73-870-5014/politics_economy/rene_levesque.

12. Translated in Dale Thomson, *Vive le Québec Libre* (Toronto: Deneau, 1988), 199; see also Alain Peyrefitte, *C'était de Gaulle*, III. (Paris: Fayard, 1997), 307.

13. Thomson, *Vive le Québec Libre*, 203.

14. Quoted in Eric Roussel, *Charles de Gaulle* (Paris: Gallimard, 2002), 841. The politest translation for *connerie* is "rubbish."

15. The CBC news interviewed various demonstrators, who in good Canadian fashion almost choked on their desire to be fair and polite, and at the same time indignant. The result is presented in the CBC's internet archives: "Standing Up to de Gaulle," http://archives.cbc.ca/IDC-1-74-1265-7658/people/lester_b_pearson/clip7.

16. The best remembered incident during the election was a well-publicized cavalcade of Brinks security trucks carrying valuables out of the province to safety in Ontario. Effective at the time in stimulating pro-federalist votes, it would be remembered and exploited by separatists as an illegitimate political tactic of the kind only to be expected from federalists.

17. Cross's title was "trade commissioner," but his function was effectively that of consul. Laporte had been a prominent journalist, and had run unsuccessfully for the provincial Liberal leadership. He was thus both senior and well known.

18. See for example the film *Les Ordres*, by Michel Brault (1974), which won a prize at Cannes in 1975. Even twenty years on, the October Crisis served as subject matter for a dramatization by Pierre Falardeau, *Octobre*, of the kidnapping of Laporte, and for a National Film Board documentary by Jean-Daniel Lafond, *La liberté en colère*, in 1994.

19. Claude Morin, quoted in Ron Graham, *The One Eyed Kings: Promise and Illusion in Canadian Politics* (Toronto: Collins, 1986), 66.

20. English had to be either the child's maternal language, or the child had to take a test to prove knowledge of English. This latter provision panicked but also irritated immigrant parents. The administration of the test became a byword for heavy-handed government intervention.

21. On individual versus collective right in language, see Paul-André Linteau, René Durocher, Jean-Claude Robert, et François Ricard, *Histoire du Québec contemporain*, vol. 2, *Le Québec depuis 1930*, 2nd ed. (Montréal: Boréal, 1989), 603–04.

22. Garth Stevenson, *Community Besieged: The Anglophone Minority and the Politics of Quebec* (Montreal and Kingston: McGill-Queen's University Press, 1999), 124.

23. Graham Fraser, *Sorry, I Don't Speak French: Confronting the Canadian Crisis That Won't Go Away* (Toronto: McClelland & Stewart, 2006), 105–10; Keith Spicer, *Life Sentences: Memoirs of an Incorrigible Canadian* (Toronto: McClelland & Stewart, 2004), chapter 9.

24. As Garth Stevenson points out, *Community Besieged*, 258–59, the English in Quebec found federal aid lacking, for a variety of reasons.

25. The stadium was originally budgeted at $315 million, and eventually clocked in at $1.3 billion. It never worked exactly as advertised, and when the city's major-league baseball team, the Expos, finally decamped in 2004 it was said to be the worst venue in the sport.

26. The stadium architect, Roger Taillibert, long afterward claimed that Bourassa had bought off the construction unions. In an article in the *Montreal Gazette*, 14 September 2000, by Hubert Bauch, "Taillibert: blame Ottawa, Quebec," Taillibert is reported as complaining about "… petty politicians, incompetent local engineers, crooked contractors, quasi-Mafia construction unions and xenophobically parochial Quebecers, who treated him as a 'maudit Français.'"

27. In Canada as a whole, the mid-1970s was a period of almost constant strikes, or so it seemed. Over three million work days were lost in the third quarter of 1976, though only 175,000 workers were involved. Compare that with the million-plus workers involved in strikes or lockouts in the fourth quarter of the same year: figures from Statistics Canada, "Chronological Perspective on Work Stoppages in Canada," www110.hrdcdrhc.gc.ca/millieudetravail_workplace/chrono//index.cfm/doc/english.

28. The leader in question was the very Scottish Joe Davidson of the Canadian Union of Postal Workers.

29. Linteau et al., *Québec contemporain*, vol. 2, 573, comment on the adverse impression made on public opinion by repeated public service strikes.

30. Claude Forget, quoted in Bothwell, *Canada and Quebec*, 152.

31. Pierre Godin, *René Lévesque*, vol. 3, *L'espoir et le chagrin* (Montreal: Boréal, 2001), 157–58.

32. Jean-Claude Picard, *Camille Laurin: L'homme debout* (Montreal: Boréal, 2003), 247, writes of the "therapeutic" effects of Bill 101, in repairing the "trauma" caused to French Canadians by the Conquest of 1760.

33. Stevenson, *Community Besieged*, 144–51.

34. Picard, *Laurin*, 250, observes that the minister became convinced that there was no hope of compromise between his views and those of the anglophones, and that it was therefore better to proceed as if the minority "n'existait pas."

35. See the remarks by the author and commentator Ron Graham, in Bothwell, *Canada and Quebec*, 153. Laurin spoke for a substantial part of the PQ caucus, who were overjoyed at seeing Bill 101 pass, and who viewed it as an essential defence for the

French language on a continent where French speakers were outnumbered forty to one: Godin, *Lévesque*, vol. 3, 221–22.

36. There had actually been a confrontational meeting between Laurin and Thomas Galt, the president of Sun Life: Picard, *Laurin*, 251.

37. Stevenson, *Community Besieged*, 185.

38. "Net Loss Due to Inter-Provincial Migration, Anglophones from Quebec," www.pco-bcp.gc.ca/olo/docs/reference/demodata_e.pdf. The diminution slowed markedly after 1986.

39. There is a good description of the atmosphere of the time in Ron Graham, *The French Quarter: The Epic Struggle of a Family—and a Nation Divided* (Toronto: Macfarlane, Walter and Ross, 1992), 224–29.

40. Polls showed that 57 percent of Quebec voters believed that economic conditions would improve or remain the same in a sovereign Quebec.

41. Fifty-three percent of Quebeckers preferred Trudeau to Lévesque (22 percent). The figures are 46 percent and 27 percent if only French speakers are considered: Bothwell, Drummond, and English, *Canada Since 1945*, 386.

42. Kenneth McRoberts, *Misconceiving Canada: The Struggle for National Unity* (Toronto: Oxford University Press, 1997), 158, 174.

43. Quoted in Robert Sheppard and Michael Valpy, *The National Deal: The Fight for a Canadian Constitution* (Toronto: Fleet, 1982), 42.

44. The ultimate product of the 1970s constitutional negotiations, a draft agreement with the provinces, would have produced, in the words of some well-informed Saskatchewan observers, "a major redirection of Canadian federalism ... augmenting provincial powers at the expense of federal authority." See Roy Romanow, John Whyte, and Howard Leeson, *Canada ... Notwithstanding* (Toronto: Carswell-Methuen, 1984), 53.

45. An example of the usage may be found in Bob Plecas, *Bill Bennett: A Mandarin's View* (Vancouver: Douglas & McIntyre, 2006), 140ff.

46. A point made by the constitutional expert Peter Russell in his *Constitutional Odyssey: Can Canadians Be a Sovereign People?* (Toronto: University of Toronto Press, 1992), 111.

47. Lawrence Martin, *Chrétien*, vol. 1, *The Will to Win* (Toronto: Lester, 1995), 299: of 124 amendments, Martin observes, over half were adopted.

48. The issue that divided Lévesque from the rest was an offer by Trudeau of a referendum. Lévesque, true to his democratic principles and thinking he might win it, considered it a good idea. The other provincial premiers, fearful that they might lose, considered it political poison.

49. Stephen Clarkson and Christina McCall, *Trudeau and Our Times*, vol. 1, *The Magnificent Obsession* (Toronto: McClelland & Stewart, 1990), 9.

50. Daniel Schwanen, "Ranking Prime Ministers of the Last 50 Years: The Numbers Speak," *Policy Options/Options Politiques*, June–July 2003, 18–20.

51. Michael Valpy, "Trudeau: The Response," *The Globe and Mail*, 4 October 2000.

52. James Marsh, "Pierre Elliott Trudeau," in *The Canadian Encyclopedia*.

16: BUST AND BOOM IN THE EIGHTIES

1. Jeffrey A. Frieden, *Global Capitalism: Its Fall and Rise in the Twentieth Century* (New York: Norton, 2006), 372–74.

2. Brian L. Scarfe, "The Federal Budget and Energy Program, October 28th, 1980: A Review," *Canadian Public Policy*, VII: 1, Winter 1981, 1–14. The best study of the energy crisis in Canada is Bruce Doern and Glen Toner, *The Politics of Energy: The Development and Implementation of the National Energy Program* (Toronto: Methuen, 1985).

3. Editorial, "But a superb energy plan," *Toronto Star*, October 29, 1980, A4, quoted in Doug Owram, "The Perfect Storm: The National Energy Program and the Failure of Federal–Provincial Relations," in Richard Connors and John M. Law, eds., *Forging Alberta's Constitutional Framework* (Edmonton: University of Alberta Press, 2005).

4. Editorial, *Edmonton Journal*, 3 November 1980, A4, quoted in Owram, "The Perfect Storm."

5. See Bothwell, English, and Drummond, *Canada Since 1945*, 451–54.

6. Arthur Campeau, law partner, quoted in Peter C. Newman, *The Secret Mulroney Tapes: Unguarded Confessions of a Prime Minister* (Toronto: Random House Canada, 2005), 53.

7. Newman, *Mulroney Tapes*, 189–90.

8. The Turner Liberals did have the support of the Liberal government of Ontario, which bitterly opposed free trade.

9. Derek Burney, *Getting It Done: A Memoir* (Montreal and Kingston: McGill-Queen's University Press, 2005), 128.

10. The Conservatives swept Quebec, sixty-three members to twelve for the Liberals, and even edged the Liberals forty-six to forty-three in Ontario, although in the latter province the Liberals won more of the popular vote.

11. Maryse Robert, *Negotiating NAFTA: Explaining the Outcome in Culture, Textiles, Autos and Pharmaceuticals* (Toronto: University of Toronto Press, 2000), 29–31, 33–35.

12. Donald Barry, "The Road to NAFTA," in Donald Barry, Mark Dickerson, and James Glaisford, eds., *Toward a North American Community? Canada, the United States and Mexico* (Boulder: Westview Press, 1995), 10.

13. George Bush and Brent Scowcroft, *A World Transformed* (New York: Knopf, 1998), 62–63. Interestingly, however, neither NAFTA nor Mexico is discussed in Bush's memoir.

14. See Bruce Doern and Brian Tomlin, *Faith and Fear: The Free Trade Story* (Toronto: Stoddart, 1991), 121–25, and Michael Hart with Bill Dymond and Colin Robertson, *Decision at Midnight: Inside the Canada–US Free Trade Negotiations* (Vancouver: UBC Press, 1994), 377–78.

15. Charles Roh, interviewed on Bill Moyers's PBS series, *NOW*, 1 February 2002, www.pbs.org/now/transcript/transcript_tdfull.html. See also Stephen Clarkson, *Uncle Sam and Us: Globalization, Neoconservatism, and the Canadian State* (Toronto: University of Toronto Press, 2002), 227–28, 348–51.

16. Steven Pearlstein, "10 Years Later, Canada Sharply Split on Free Trade," *Washington Post*, 29 June 1999, E01; John McCallum, senior economist for the Royal Bank of Canada (and later Liberal cabinet minister), "Two Cheers for the FTA," Royal Bank of Canada Economics Department, June 1989.

17. Jimmy Carter, "A Flawed Timber Market," *The New York Times*, 24 March 2001.

18. In 2006 the new Harper government reached an agreement with the Bush administration on softwood exports; it imposed an export tax, sought to drop Canadian lawsuits, and returned $4 billion out of $5 billion that had been—possibly illegally—collected by the United States on Canadian softwood imports. Canadian lumber producers were not, on the whole, charmed.

19. Trudeau, "Say Good-bye to the Dream of One Canada," *La Presse, Toronto Star*, 27 May 1987.

20. Quoted in Bothwell, Drummond, and English, *Canada Since 1945*, 397.

21. Mulroney had wasted little time negotiating with Newfoundland premier Clyde Wells prior to the "rescission" of Newfoundland's approval of Meech Lake: Andrew Cohen, *A Deal Undone: The Making and Breaking of the Meech Lake Accord* (Vancouver: Douglas & McIntyre, 1990), 224.

22. James Winter, "The Media, the Meech Accord, and the Attempted Manufacture of Consent," *Electronic Journal of Communication/Revue électronique de communication*, vol. 1, no. 2, Winter 1991. One does not have to agree with Winter's evidently leftist politics to find his evidence of media bias toward the government and in favour of Meech Lake, especially in the CBC, very compelling.

23. Susan Delacourt and Graham Fraser, "Marathon Talks Were All Part of Plan," PM says, *The Globe and Mail*, 12 June 1990.

24. One ordinarily sober Quebec academic put it this way to the author: "We said 'We love you' and you [the English] said 'Fuck off.'"

17: A NEW MILLENNIUM AND A NEW WORLD

1. Chris Wood, "The Vanishing Border," *Maclean's*, 20 December 1999.

2. Pew Global Attitudes Project, 23 June 2005, table "Favorable Opinions of the U.S.," using Environics data reported by the Department of State for 1999–2000: http://pewglobal.org/reports/display.php?ReportID=247.

3. The U.S. State Department's 2005 "Country Reports on Terrorism" singled out Canada's "liberal immigration and asylum policies" as contributing to a terrorist presence: www.state.gov/documents/organization/65473.pdf.

4. Stewart Bell, *Cold Terror: How Canada Nurtures and Exports Terrorism Around the World* (Toronto: Wiley, 2004), 132–33, describes Ressam's life as a pickpocket in

Montreal. Even though Ressam's claim to merit refugee status was rejected, he wasn't deported because of Canada's lack of confidence in the treatment he'd receive back in Algeria.

5. A 1951 boy baby could expect to live sixty-six years, a girl, seventy-one years; their 2001 counterparts were expected to live seventy-seven and eighty-two years, respectively.

6. Given the apparent decline in religion in Quebec, one might have expected to see "no religion" appear more prominently in that province's census figures, but that's not the case: "no religion" was more frequent in Ontario by far, and even in Alberta the number of "no-religionists" is absolutely higher than in Quebec by a considerable margin.

7. Immigrant communities when they came to Canada had always been prone to support the party in power, and the Liberals were in power most of the time after 1896 and again after 1945, the periods of greatest immigration. There is striking evidence for this phenomenon in the 2000 election. That year, 72 percent of non-European immigrants voted Liberal: André Blais, Elizabeth Gidengil, Richard Nadeau, and Neil Nevitte, *Anatomy of a Liberal Victory: Making Sense of the Vote in the 2000 Canadian Election* (Peterborough: Broadview Press, 2002), 92, table 6.1.

8. See, for example, Pico Iyer, *The Global Soul: Jet Lag, Shopping Malls, and the Search for Home* (New York: Knopf, 2000), 117–71.

9. The English-speaking population of Quebec voted overwhelmingly for the Liberals and against separatism in 1994, but because the English were geographically concentrated in a few ridings their votes had no more than a marginal impact in seat totals.

10. The polls cited in footnote 1 suggest that pro-American sentiment was strong in Quebec, but not necessarily for the obvious reason of love and admiration for the U.S. per se; rather, expressing affection for the United States was a useful alternative for nationalist and separatist Quebeckers—they didn't have to depend on English Canada when they could depend on the stronger and richer United States.

11. Indeed, French president Jacques Chirac told an American interviewer during the referendum that France would recognize a sovereign Quebec in the event of a "yes" vote: Lawrence Martin, *Iron Man: The Defiant Reign of Jean Chrétien* (Toronto: Viking Canada, 2003), 128.

12. This was confirmed when Chrétien failed to get the necessary provincial support for some constitutional fiddling in the fall of 1995: Martin, *Iron Man*, 141.

13. William Johnson in *Stephen Harper and the Future of Canada* (Toronto: McClelland & Stewart, 2005), 170, points to a poll that showed that only a third of Canadians thought that recognizing Quebec as a "unique society" would discourage separatism. In Quebec, 49 percent thought that such recognition would actually encourage separatism.

14. Parizeau conveniently published a book, *Pour un Québec souverain*, in the spring of 1997, which detailed what he had done and would have done had he been successful in the referendum.

15. *Canadian Annual Review of Politics and Public Affairs, 1997* (Toronto: University of Toronto Press, 2003), 125.

16. The election also showed that federalists needed more than a five-point spread to win more seats in Quebec than the separatists, who in this case got thirty-eight seats to the Liberals' thirty-six.

17. There was some uncertainty over precisely which formulation would best capture its essence. One idea, briefly favoured, was the Canadian Reform Alliance Party, which produced the acronym CRAP. When this coincidence was realized, it became the Canadian Reform Conservative Alliance, or the Alliance party for short.

18. Harris had demons of his own: unions, teachers, Natives, welfare recipients, and the public sector generally. His confrontations with these elements produced a steady diet of strikes punctuated by the occasional riot. All this served to remind potential NDP supporters that the Liberals were, at least, better than Harris and his political cousins in the Canadian Alliance.

19. Canada, Department of Finance, *Canada's Fiscal Update*, chapter 3, "Canada's Fiscal Progress," www.fin.gc.ca/ec2005/ec/ecc3e.html.

20. In Ontario, a Liberal government under David Peterson (1985–90) was succeeded by an NDP administration (1990–95) under Bob Rae, and then by the Progressive Conservatives under Mike Harris (1995–2002) and Ernie Eves (2002–04). The disastrous experience of the Rae government, which governed in a time of economic recession and falling revenues, had an impact not only in Ontario but across the country.

21. See David Runciman, *The Politics of Good Intentions: History, Fear and Hypocrisy in the New World Order* (Princeton: Princeton University Press, 2006), 136–37.

22. The title of Kevin Phillips's book, *American Theocracy: The Peril and Politics of Radical Religion, Oil and Borrowed Money in the 21st Century* (New York: Viking, 2006), says it all.

23. Henry Kissinger, *White House Years* (Boston: Little, Brown, 1979), 383.

24. See Jocelyn Coulon, *Soldiers of Diplomacy: The United Nations, Peacekeeping and the New World Order* (Toronto: University of Toronto Press, 1998), x.

25. A survey in 2002 placed Canadian salaries and benefits behind many comparable countries, not to mention international agencies and private business: see Andrew Cohen, *While Canada Slept: How We Lost Our Place in the World* (Toronto: McClelland & Stewart, 2003), 138.

26. It appears to have been the British who did the running in persuading the Canadians under Mulroney not to insist on membership in the contact group.

27. Peter Kasurak, "Accountability for Intelligence in Peacekeeping Operations: Canada's Operation Assurance as a Case Study," www.carleton.ca/csds/pki/doc/Kasurak.doc.

28. The song was by Jethro Tull.

29. Natural Resources Canada, *Energy Use Data Handbook, 1990 and 1995–2001* (Ottawa: Natural Resources Canada, 2002), 26–27.

30. Federal Labour Standards review, Backgrounder, www.fls-ntf.gc.ca/en/bg_01.asp.

31. The debate was and remained very lively. See for example Jeff Faux, *The Global Class War: How America's Bipartisan Elite Lost Our Future—And What It Will Take to Win It Back* (New York: Wiley, 2006).

32. Governments responded by kitting out their police in bulletproof outfits not seen since the great days of armour in the sixteenth century. This reflected an apparently all-pervasive sense of insecurity that gave bulletproof vests to parking meter enforcers and caused otherwise sane city dwellers to buy all-terrain military-style vehicles like the Hummer, which they could then drive to the shopping centre.

33. Although *No Logo: Taking Aim at the Brand Bullies* (New York: HarperCollins, 2000) was part of print culture, it spawned an enthusiastic internet world, including a website under the same name.

34. See Jeffry A. Frieden, *Global Capitalism: Its Fall and Rise in the Twentieth Century* (New York: Norton, 2006), chapter 18.

35. A point usefully made by Faux, *Global Class War*, 98–99.

36. There are two muddled explanations for the omission, one by a Bush speechwriter, the right-wing pundit David Frum, which seems to argue that the omission was deliberate, and one from the American ambassador, Paul Celucci, who noted that "Canada should have been mentioned," but that there was "no deliberate snub." See "Canada was purposely cut from speech, Frum says," *The Globe and Mail,* 8 January 2003, A4, and Paul Celucci, *Unquiet Diplomacy* (Toronto: Key Porter, 2005), 85.

37. Celucci, *Unquiet Diplomacy,* 87–88, tries to refute such rumours.

38. The meeting was only half an hour, followed by a press conference: http://archives.cnn.com/2002/ALLPOLITICS/09/09/bush.iraq/index.html.

39. Martin Indyk, quoted in Philip H. Gordon and Jeremy Shapiro, *Allies at War: America, Europe and the Crisis Over Iraq* (New York: McGraw-Hill, 2004), 145. According to one insider, the American response at the time was to try to get the Canadian, Chilean, and Mexican ambassadors fired.

40. David Haglund, "Does Quebec Have an 'Obsession anti-américaine'?" Seagram Lecture, McGill University, 11 April 2005, www.misciecm.mcgill.ca/enpages/pdf/haglundseagramtext.pdf.

41. The most useful breakdown of opinion is by the Calgary polling firm, JMCK Polling, in its "Global Sunday: Attitudes Towards the US and War with Iraq (March 2003)," www.queensu.ca/cora/polls/2003/March-Support_for_USA_Iraq_Plan.pdf. I am obliged to Carrie Spear for this reference.

42. Pew Research Center Report, Trends 2005, 106: http://pewresearch.org/reports/?Report ID=6.

43. Pew Global Research Project, "U.S. Image Up Slightly, but Still Negative," 23 June 2005, http://pewglobal.org/reports/display.php?ReportID=247.

44. Michael Adams, *Fire and Ice: The United States, Canada and the Myth of Converging Values* (Toronto: Penguin, 2003), 50.

45. J.L. Granatstein, *Yankee Go Home? Canadians and Anti-Americanism* (Toronto: HarperCollins, 1996).

46. In his radio show *A Prairie Home Companion,* the humorist Garrison Keillor told his audience after the 2004 election that Canadians should have been allowed to vote too, since those who voted for Bush were already "citizens of another country," meaning some kind of religious rapture-state. A CBC documentary aired in the weeks following the outbreak of the Iraq war examined the feelings of Americans about Canada and discovered that most were not especially irritated at Canada for not participating in the war: Paul Rutherford, *Weapons of Mass Persuasion: Marketing the War Against Iraq* (Toronto: University of Toronto Press, 2004), 150–51.

47. William Johnson, *Stephen Harper and the Future of Canada* (Toronto: McClelland & Stewart, 2005), 319–22.

48. The most interesting example of the Conservatives' determination to rid Canada of its Liberal taint came after the 2006 election, in an article in the *Toronto Star* (Les Whittington, "Emerson Frustrated with Conservatives," 21 April 2006), from one of his ministers, an ex-Liberal named David Emerson in a conversation with his former Liberal aide, David Epworth: "Behind closed doors, the Conservatives are worse partisans than the Liberals ever were," Emerson said, according to notes Epworth wrote after his conversation with the minister. "They hate the f—ing Liberals and they're doing everything they can to screw them," he quoted Emerson as saying.

49. There was even some discussion of "rebranding" the Liberal party, giving it another name, to escape the presumed negative connotations of its immediate past. What the new name might have been is hard to imagine—Paulistas, perhaps, or Martinizers.

50. The reference is to the irascible boss in the comic strip "Blondie."

Illustration/Photo Credits

Acknowledgments

The writing of this book has been a complicated and laborious task, though mainly for those who had to witness the process. I owe a great debt of gratitude to my wife, Gail, whose tolerance and support helped keep the project on an even keel.

That there is a book at all is owing to an old friend, Roy MacLaren, at the time Canada's High Commissioner to Great Britain. Hearing that Penguin was in search of an author, Roy devised a way of bringing the publisher and this author together.

Bringing the author to completion was another task entirely. I am most grateful to my research assistants over time, especially Rutha Astravas, Maria Banda, Yasemin Akcakir, and Jen Hassum, to my students who sat through what must have seemed like endless droning on the eighteenth and nineteenth centuries, and to my assistant Marilyn Laville, who was an endless fount of good counsel and good cheer as this book lumbered toward a finish. I am also indebted to my friends Doug Owram and John English, who provided timely advice and ready facts when I was at my wits' end.

During the writing of this book I was privileged to hold the Gluskin chair in Canadian history at the University of Toronto. The Gluskin chair is generously funded by the Gluskin family to encourage research. Among other things, it relieves its lucky occupant of the pursuit of grants, effectively bypassing the agony and tedium of endless applications for small sums that are one of the most repellent parts of academic life in the twenty-first century. I am most grateful to the Gluskins for their practical and well-conceived help.

Robert Bothwell
Trinity College
University of Toronto

Index